OFFICIAL TOURIST BOARD GUIDE

New 39th edition

B&Bs and Hotels

England's star-rated guest accommodation

2014

...p within a unique destination: England. Described by William Shakespeare as "This other Eden, demi-paradise....This blessed plot, this earth, this realm...", this relatively small country continues to dazzle and delight its visitors with experiences that offer large rewards 450 years after the Bard's birth.

Shakespeare's words evoke the very special place England is, with its rich heritage and vibrant city culture; verdant countryside and spectacular coastline; a twenty-first century tapestry woven from unique and colourful threads; a culture deep and layered and exciting.

This year why not take the trip you've always promised yourself? Within a half day's drive of all our major towns and cities lies a landscape of rolling hills, wooded river valleys, patchwork fields and small stone villages. Forest trails and mountain walks; body-boarding and sailing courses. Literary trails and historic houses; landscaped gardens and local museums. Thriving country towns offering delicious local foods and coastal destinations to sample the catch of the day. Ancient pubs and pop-up restaurants; open-air theatres and world-renowned music festivals. During 2014 a range of anniversaries and commemorations will inspire a calendar of special events and exhibitions. The experience you've always said you'd try but never quite got round to organising is easier than ever to find. For inspiration and information I invite you to look at www.visitengland.com.

Whatever your reason for taking your trip or wherever you decide to stop for the night, in England you'll find a broad range of accommodation types to meet your needs and match your budget. As Chairman of VisitEngland I am proud to represent a destination and an industry that continues to raise its game. On-going investment in England's tourism means that there is always more for our visitors to enjoy.

This book, produced on our behalf by Hudson's Media and packed full of information and ideas, is designed to help you get the most from your stay. All the accommodation featured comes with the trusted VisitEngland Quality Assurance Rose Mark which indicates that our inspectors have checked it out so that you can check in with confidence.

Enjoy your stay!

Penelope, Viscounte
Chairman of VisitEng

2

Contents

How to use this guide

This official VisitEngland guide is packed with information from where to stay, to how to get there and what to see on arrival. In fact, this guide captures everything you need to know when exploring England.

Choose from a wide range of quality-assessed accommodation to suit all budgets and tastes. This guide contains a comprehensive listing of all bed and breakfast properties participating in the VisitEngland Quality Assessment Scheme, as well as hotels, guesthouses, farmhouses, inns, hostels and campus accommodation.

Each property has been visited annually by professional assessors, who apply nationally agreed standards, so that you can book with confidence knowing your accommodation has been checked and rated for quality.

Check out the places to visit in each region, from towns and cities to spectacular coast and countryside, plus historic homes, castles and great family attractions! Maps show accommodation locations, selected destinations and some of the National Cycle Networks. For even more ideas go online at www.visitengland.com.

Regional tourism contacts and tourist information centres are listed – contact them for further information. You'll also find events, travel information, maps and useful indexes.

Accommodation entries explained

Each accommodation entry contains detailed information to help you decide if it is right for you. This has been provided by proprietors and our aim is to ensure that it is as objective and factual as possible.

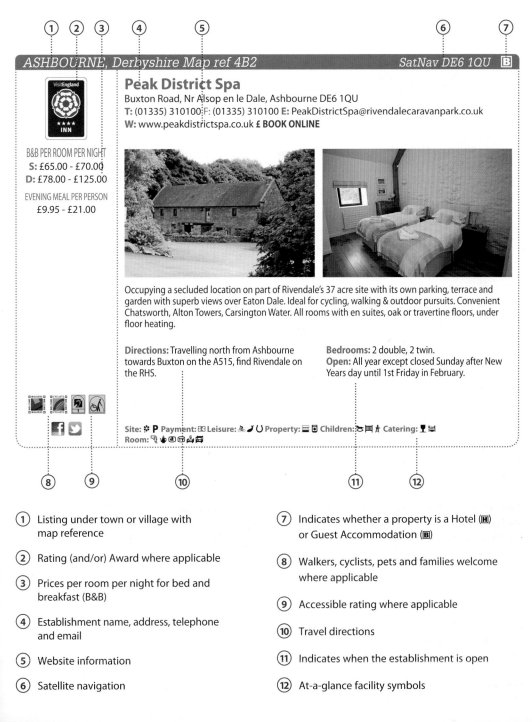

(1) (2) (3) (4) (5) (6) (7)

ASHBOURNE, *Derbyshire Map ref 4B2*   SatNav DE6 1QU [B]

VisitEngland ★★★★ INN

B&B PER ROOM PER NIGHT
S: £65.00 - £70.00
D: £78.00 - £125.00
EVENING MEAL PER PERSON
£9.95 - £21.00

Peak District Spa
Buxton Road, Nr Alsop en le Dale, Ashbourne DE6 1QU
T: (01335) 310100 **F:** (01335) 310100 **E:** PeakDistrictSpa@rivendalecaravanpark.co.uk
W: www.peakdistrictspa.co.uk **£ BOOK ONLINE**

Occupying a secluded location on part of Rivendale's 37 acre site with its own parking, terrace and garden with superb views over Eaton Dale. Ideal for cycling, walking & outdoor pursuits. Convenient Chatsworth, Alton Towers, Carsington Water. All rooms with en suites, oak or travertine floors, under floor heating.

Directions: Travelling north from Ashbourne towards Buxton on the A515, find Rivendale on the RHS.

Bedrooms: 2 double, 2 twin.
Open: All year except closed Sunday after New Years day until 1st Friday in February.

Site: ✿ **P Payment:** **Leisure:** **Property:** **Children:** **Catering:** **Room:**

(8) (9) (10) (11) (12)

(1) Listing under town or village with map reference

(2) Rating (and/or) Award where applicable

(3) Prices per room per night for bed and breakfast (B&B)

(4) Establishment name, address, telephone and email

(5) Website information

(6) Satellite navigation

(7) Indicates whether a property is a Hotel ([H]) or Guest Accommodation ([B])

(8) Walkers, cyclists, pets and families welcome where applicable

(9) Accessible rating where applicable

(10) Travel directions

(11) Indicates when the establishment is open

(12) At-a-glance facility symbols

5

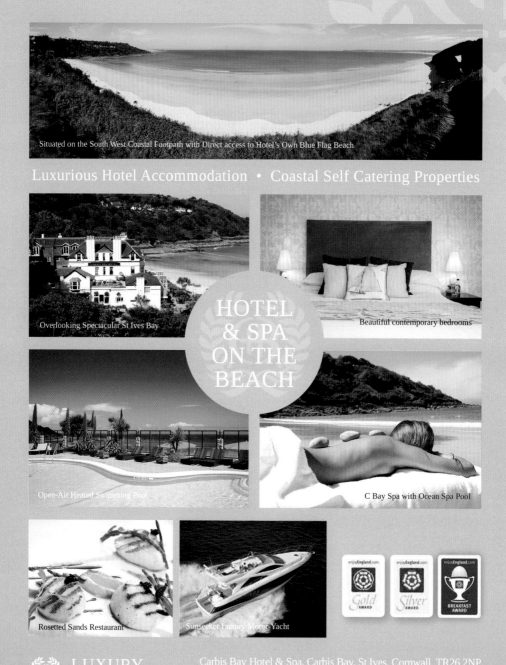

Key to symbols

Information about many of the accommodation services and facilities is given in the form of symbols.

Sits Features

P Private parking
✿ Garden

Site Features

€ Euros accepted
£ Visa/Mastercard/Switch accepted

Leisure Facilities

Q Tennis court(s)
⌇ Swimming pool – outdoor
⌇ Swimming pool – indoor
⌇ Sauna on site
⊗ Health/beauty facilities onsite
✶ Gym on site
● Games room
U Riding/pony-trekking nearby
▶ Golf available (on site or nearby)
♪ Fishing nearby
% Cycles for hire nearby

Property Facilities

∅ Real log/coal fires
⊞ Passenger lift
◑ Night porter
Я Lounge for residents' use
☐ Laundry facilities
⚏ WiFi or internet access
⋔ Dogs/pets accepted by arrangement
⊺ Conference facilities
⊛ Air conditioning

Children

⋏ High chairs available
▥ Cots available
⋈ Children welcome

Catering

⊌ Special diets available
♀ Licenced (table or bar)
(✗ Evening meals

Room Facilities

⊡ DVD player
☏ Television
◐ Satellite/cable/freeview TV
☎ Telephone
☕ Tea/coffee making in bedrooms
🗋 Hairdryer
🛌 Bedrooms on ground floor
🛏 Four-poster bed(s)
🚬 Smoking rooms available

Campus/Hostels

▦ Cooking facilities available

Visitor Attraction Quality Assurance

Participating attractions are visited annually by a professional assessor. High standards in welcome, hospitality, services, presentation; standards of the toilets, shop and café (where provided) must be achieved to receive this VisitEngland award.

Places of Interest Quality Assurance

The Places of Interest sign indicates that the site has a biennial visit from an independent assessor and meets the standard required to be awarded the Quality Rose Marque.

Pets Come Too - Accommodation displaying this symbol offer a special welcome to pets. Please check for any restrictions when booking.

Businesses displaying this logo have undergone a rigorous verification process to ensure that they are sustainable (green). See page 15 for further information.

VisitEngland's Breakfast Award recognises hotels and B&Bs that offer a high quality choice of breakfast, service and hospitality that exceeds what would be expected at their star rating. Look out for the following symbol in the entry ⊡.

National Accessible Scheme

The National Accessible Scheme includes standards for hearing and visual impairment as well as mobility impairment – see pages 10-11 for further information.

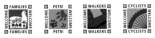

Welcome Schemes

Walkers, cyclists, families and pet owners are warmly welcomed where you see these signs – see page 9 for further information.

Motorway Service Area Assessment Scheme

The star ratings cover over 300 different aspects of each operation including cleanliness, the quality and range of catering and also the quality of the physical aspects as well as the service provided.

– See page 372 for further information.

A special welcome

To help make booking your accommodation easier VisitEngland has four special Welcome schemes which accommodation in England can be assessed against. Owners participating in these schemes go the extra mile to welcome walkers, cyclists, families or pet owners to their accommodation and provide additional facilities and services to make your stay even more comfortable.

For further information go online at www.qualityintourism.com/types-of-schemes/welcome-schemes

Families Welcome

 If you are searching for the perfect family holiday look out for the Families Welcome sign. The sign indicates that the proprietor offers additional facilities and services catering for a range of ages and family units. For families with young children, the accommodation will have special facilities such as cots and highchairs, storage for push-chairs and somewhere to heat baby food or milk. Where meals are provided, children's choices will be clearly indicated, with healthy options also available. They'll have information on local walks, attractions, activities or events suitable for children, as well as local child-friendly pubs and restaurants. However, not all accommodation is able to cater for all ages or combinations of family units, so do remember to check for any restrictions before confirming your booking.

Welcome Pets!

 Do you want to travel with your faithful companion? To do so with ease make sure you look out for accommodation displaying the Welcome Pets! sign. Participants in this scheme go out of their way to meet the needs of guests bringing dogs, cats and/or small birds. In addition to providing water and food bowls, torches or nightlights, spare leads and pet washing facilities, they'll buy in pet food on request, and offer toys, treats and bedding. They'll also have information on pet-friendly attractions, pubs, restaurants and recreation. Of course, not everyone is able to offer suitable facilities for every pet, so do check if there are any restrictions on the type, size and number of animals before you confirm your booking.

Walkers Welcome

 If walking is your passion, seek out accommodation participating in the Walkers Welcome scheme. Facilities include a place for drying clothes and boots, maps and books for reference and a first-aid kit. Packed breakfasts and lunches are available on request in hotels and guesthouses, and you have the option to pre-order basic groceries in self-catering accommodation. On top of this proprietors provide a wide range of information including public transport, weather forecasts, details of the nearest bank, all night chemists and local restaurants and nearby attractions.

Cyclists Welcome

 Are you an explorer on two wheels? If so seek out accommodation displaying the Cyclists Welcome symbol. Facilities at these properties include a lockable undercover area, a place to dry outdoor clothing and footwear, an evening meal if there are no eating facilities available within one mile, and a packed breakfast or lunch on request. Information is also available on cycle hire, cycle repair shops, maps and books for reference, weather forecasts, details of the nearest bank, all night chemists and much much more.

National Accessible Scheme

Finding suitable accommodation is not always easy, especially if you have to seek out rooms with level entry or large print menus. Use the National Accessible Scheme to help you make your choice.

Proprietors of accommodation taking part in the National Accessible Scheme have gone out of their way to ensure a comfortable stay for guests with special hearing, visual or mobility needs. These exceptional places are full of extra touches to make everyone's visit trouble-free, from handrails, ramps and step-free entrances (ideal for buggies too) to level-access showers and colour contrast in the bathrooms. Members of staff may have attended a disability awareness course and will know what assistance will really be appreciated.

Appropriate National Accessible Scheme symbols are included in the guide entries (shown opposite). If you have additional needs or special requirements, we strongly recommend that you

make sure these can be met by your chosen establishment before you confirm your reservation. The index at the back of the guide gives a list of accommodation that has received a National Accessible Scheme rating.

'Holiday in the British Isles' is an annual guidebook produced by Disability Rights UK. It lists NAS rated accommodation and offers extensive practical advice to help you plan your trip.

£12.99 (inc. P&P),
www.disabilityrights.org

England

Mobility Impairment Symbols

Older and less mobile guests
Typically suitable for a person with sufficient mobility to climb a flight of steps but who would benefit from fixtures and fittings to aid balance.

Part-time wheelchair users
Typically suitable for a person with restricted walking ability and for those who may need to use a wheelchair some of the time and can negotiate a maximum of three steps.

Independent wheelchair users
Typically suitable for a person who depends on the use of a wheelchair and transfers unaided to and from the wheelchair in a seated position. This person may be an independent traveller.

Assisted wheelchair users
Typically suitable for a person who depends on the use of a wheelchair and needs assistance when transferring to and from the wheelchair in a seated position.

Access Exceptional is awarded to establishments that meet the requirements of independent wheelchair users or assisted wheelchair users shown above and also fulfil more demanding requirements with reference to the British Standards BS8300.

The criteria VisitEngland has adopted does not necessarily conform to British Standards or to Building Regulations. They reflect what the organisation understands to be acceptable to meet the practical needs of guests with mobility or sensory impairments and encourage the industry to increase access to all.

Visual Impairment Symbols

Typically provides key additional services and facilities to meet the needs of visually impaired guests.

Typically provides a higher level of additional services and facilities to meet the needs of visually impaired guests.

Hearing Loss Symbols

Typically provides key additional services and facilities to meet the needs of guests with hearing loss.

Typically provides a higher level of additional services and facilities to meet the needs of guests with hearing loss.

For more information on the NAS and tips and ideas on holiday travel in England go to:
www.visitengland.com/accessforall

Additional help and guidance on accessible tourism can be obtained from the national charity Tourism for All:

Tourism for All

Tourism for All UK
7A Pixel Mill
44 Appleby Road
Kendal
Cumbria LA9 6ES

Information helpline 0845 124 9971
(lines open 9-5 Mon-Fri)
E info@tourismforall.org.uk
W www.tourismforall.org.uk
   www.openbritain.net

Peace of Mind with VisitEngland Star Ratings

Most hotels and bed and breakfast properties in England are star rated by VisitEngland. We annually check that our standards are comparable with other British tourist boards to ensure that wherever you visit you receive the same facilities and services at any star rated accommodation.

All the accommodation in this guide is annually checked by VisitEngland assessors and an on site assessment is made every year. This means that when you see the Quality Rose marque promoting the star rating of the property you can be confident that we've checked it out.

The national standards used to assess accommodation are based on VisitEngland research of consumer expectations. The independent assessors decide the type (classification) of accommodation, for example if it's a 'small hotel', 'country house hotel', 'bed and breakfast', 'guest accommodation' etc. and award star ratings based on the quality of the service and accommodation offered, as well as, where appropriate, a further special quality award.

Our assessors consider every aspect of your stay, such as the warmth of welcome, comfort of furnishings, including beds, food quality (breakfast and dinner for hotels, breakfast for guest accommodation), cleanliness and the level of care offered.

The Quality Rose marque helps you decide where to stay, giving you peace of mind that the accommodation has been thoroughly checked out before you check in.

Accommodation Types

Always look at or ask for the classification of accommodation, as each offers a very distinct experience.

The hotel designators you'll find in this guide are:

Hotel – minimum of 5 bedrooms, but more likely to have over 20.

Small Hotel – maximum of 20 bedrooms, usually more personally run.

Country House Hotel – set in ample grounds or gardens, in a rural or semi-rural location and an emphasis on peace and quiet.

Town House Hotel – maximum of 50 rooms in a city or town-centre location, high quality with distinctive and individual style, high ratio of staff to guests. Dinner may not be served but room service available. Might not have a dining room so breakfast may be served in bedroom.

Metro Hotel – can be any size and in a city or town centre location - offering full hotel services, but not dinner (although will be within easy walking distance of a range of places to eat).

Budget Hotel – part of a large, 'branded' hotel group offering clean and comfortable en suite facilities, 24-hour reservations. Budget hotels are not awarded individual star ratings.

Accredited Hotel – accredited hotels have been visited by VisitEngland assessors to check the standards of cleanliness and maintenance meet or exceed guests' expectations. This annual assessment does not include an overnight stay and no star ratings are awarded.

The bed and breakfast designators you'll find in this guide are:

Guest Accommodation – wide range of establishments from one-room bed and breakfast to larger properties, which may offer dinner and hold an alcohol licence.

Bed and Breakfast – accommodating generally no more than six people, the owners of these establishments welcome you into their home as a special guest.

Guest House – generally comprising more than three rooms. Dinner may be available (if it is, it will need to be booked in advance). May possibly be licensed.

Farmhouse – bed and breakfast, and sometimes dinner, but always on a farm.

Inn – pubs with rooms, and many with restaurants as well.

Room Only – accommodation that either does not offer breakfast or, if it does, it will not be served (ie self-service or breakfast pack)

Hostel – safe, budget-priced, short-term accommodation for individuals and groups. The Hostel classification includes Group Hostel, Backpacker and Activity Accommodation (all of which are awarded star ratings).

Campus – accommodation provided by educational establishments, including university halls of residence and student village complexes. May be offered on a bed and breakfast or sometimes on a self-catering basis.

Looking for something a little different?

Within this guide you'll find some interesting alternatives to hotels. **Restaurants with Rooms** are just that – the restaurant is the main business and they will be licensed. **Hotel Boats** are generally narrow boats and are worked by a crew. They can be booked by individuals or groups and provide all the services of a hotel, including meals and refreshments.

Star ratings you can trust

Hotels are awarded a rating from 1 to 5 stars. All star ratings assure you of certain services which are:

- All rooms have an en suite or private bathroom
- Designated reception and staff available during day and evening (24 hrs in case of emergency)
- Licence to serve alcohol
- Access to hotel at all times for registered guests
- Dinner available at least five days a week (except Town House or Metro Hotels)
- All statutory obligations will be met including Fire Safety

Star ratings you can trust

All bed and breakfast accommodation that is awarded a star rating (from 1 to 5 stars) will assure you of minimum standards, so you can be confident that you will find the basic services that you would expect, such as:

• A clear explanation of booking charges, services offered and cancellation terms.
• A full cooked breakfast or substantial continental breakfast.
• May offer ensuite facilities, but also shared bathroom facilities.
• For a stay of more than one night, rooms cleaned and beds made daily.
• Printed advice on how to summon emergency assistance at night.
• All statutory obligations will be met, including Fire Safety.

To achieve higher star ratings, an increasing level of facilities and services are offered. For example, at 3-star, bed and breakfast must offer a guest bathroom which cannot be shared with the owners and bedrooms must have a washbasin if not en suite. 4-star, 50% of bedrooms will be en suite or with private bathroom. At 5-star, all rooms must be en suite or with a private bathroom.

Star ratings are based on a combination of the range of facilities, the level of service offered and quality - if an establishment offers facilities required to achieve a certain star rating but does not achieve the quality score required for that rating, a lower star rating is awarded. Accommodation with limited facilities but high quality standards may be capped at a lower star rating, but may achieve a Silver or Gold award.

Gold and Silver Awards

How can you find those special places to stay – those that, regardless of the range of facilities and services, achieve top scores for quality (for hospitality and service, bedrooms and bathrooms, food and cleanliness)? Look for VisitEngland's Gold and Silver awards. These awards are given to establishments offering the highest level of quality within their particular star rating.

High star ratings mean top quality in all areas and all the services expected of that classification. Lower star ratings with a Silver or Gold award indicate more limited facilities or services but top quality. You may therefore find that a 2-star Gold Award hotel offering superior levels of quality may be more suited to your needs if, for example, enhanced services such as a concierge or 24-hour room service are not essential for your stay.

Sometimes a bed and breakfast establishment has exceptional bedrooms and bathrooms and offers guests a very special welcome, but cannot achieve a higher star rating because, for example, there are no en suite bedrooms. This is sometimes the case with period properties. Look out for accommodation with Gold or Silver Awards which recognise quality rather than specific facilities.

VisitEngland's unique Gold and Silver Awards are given in recognition of exceptional quality. A list of all Gold and Silver Award winning accommodation with a detailed entry in this guide is given on page 392.

The more stars, the higher the quality and the greater the range of facilities and level of service. The following refers to the Hotel scheme:

★ ★ Two-Star must provide

Dinner five nights a week (unless Metro hotel)

★ ★ ★ Three-Star must provide

All en suite bedrooms (i.e. no private bathrooms)

Telephones in all rooms

Room service during core hours

A permanently staffed reception

★ ★ ★ ★ Four-Star must provide

Enhanced guest services e.g. 24 hour room service, porterage, afternoon tea etc.

Superior bedrooms and bathrooms

★ ★ ★ ★ ★ Five-Star must provide

Some permanent suites

Enhanced services, such as concierge, valet parking etc.

Sustainable Tourism in England

More and more operators of accommodation, attractions and events in England are becoming aware of sustainable or "green" issues and are acting more responsibly in their businesses. But how can you be sure that businesses that 'say' they're green, really are?

Who certifies green businesses?

There are a number of green certification schemes that assess businesses for their green credentials. VisitEngland only promotes those that have been checked out to ensure they reach the high standards expected. The members of those schemes we have validated are truly sustainable (green) businesses and appear amongst the pages of this guide with our heart-flower logo on their entry.

Businesses displaying this logo have undergone a rigorous verification process to ensure that they are sustainable (green) and that a qualified assessor has visited the premises.

The number of participating green certification scheme organisations applying to be recognised by us is growing all the time. At the moment we promote the largest green scheme in the world - Green Tourism Business Scheme (GTBS) - and the Peak District Environmental Quality Mark.

Peak District Environmental Quality Mark

This certification mark can only be achieved by businesses that actively support good environmental practices in the Peak District National Park. When you buy a product or service that has been awarded the Environmental Quality Mark, you can be confident that your purchase directly supports the high-quality management of the special environment of the Peak District National Park.

Green Tourism Business Scheme

GTBS recognises places to stay and attractions that are taking action to support the local area and the wider environment. With over 2000 members in the UK it's the largest sustainable (green) scheme to operate globally and assesses hundreds of fantastic places to stay and visit in Britain. From small bed and breakfasts to large visitor attractions and activity holiday providers.

Businesses that meet the standard for a GTBS award receive a Bronze, Silver, or Gold award based on their level of achievement. Businesses are assessed in areas that include Management and Marketing, Social Involvement and Communication, Energy, Water, Purchasing, Waste, Transport, Natural and Cultural Heritage and Innovation.

How are these businesses being green?

Any business that has been certified 'green' will have implemented initiatives that contribute to reducing their negative environmental and social impacts whilst trying to enhance the economic and community benefits to their local area.

Many of these things may be behind the scenes such as energy efficient boilers, insulated lofts or grey water recycling, but there are many fun activities that you can expect to find too. For example, your green business should be able to advise you about traditional activities nearby, the best places to sample local food and buy craft products, or even help you to enjoy a 'car-free' day out.

Gold and Silver Awards

VisitEngland's unique Gold and Silver Awards are given in recognition of exceptional quality in hotel and bed and breakfast accommodation.

VisitEngland professional assessors make recommendations for Gold and Silver Awards during assessments. They look for aspects of exceptional quality in all areas, in particular, housekeeping, hospitality, bedrooms and bathrooms.

While star ratings are based on a combination of quality, range of facilities and level of service offered, Gold and Silver Awards are based solely on quality. Therefore a 2 star property with limited facilities but exceptional quality could still achieve the gold award status.

Hotels and Bed & Breakfast establishments with a Gold Award are featured below. Detailed entries for these properties are also included in the regional pages and can be found using the property index on page 392.

An index of Gold and Silver Award-winning properties with a detailed entry in this guide can be found at the back of this guide.

Gold Award Hotels *with entries in the regional pages*

Brudenell Hotel
Aldeburgh, Suffolk

Barnsley House
Barnsley, Gloucestershire

**Lucknam Park
Hotel and Spa**
Bath (6 miles), Somerset

Swan Hotel
Bibury, Gloucestershire

Northcote
Blackburn, Lancashire

**Stanley House
Hotel & Spa**
Blackburn, Lancashire

The Broadway Hotel
Broadway, Worcestershire

Bay Tree Hotel
Burford, Oxfordshire

The Lamb Inn
Burford, Oxfordshire

Millstream Hotel
Chichester, Sussex

Clare House
Grange-over-Sands,
Cumbria

Rudding Park
Harrogate, North
Yorkshire

Langley Castle Hotel
Hexham, Northumberland

Combe House Devon
Honiton, Devon

Manor House Hotel
Moreton-in-Marsh,
Gloucestershire

Chewton Glen
New Milton, New Forest,
Hampshire

Scafell Hotel
Rosthwaite, Cumbria

Rye Lodge Hotel
Rye, East Sussex

Tides Reach Hotel
Salcombe, Devon

Hotel Riviera
Sidmouth, Devon

**The Bear of
Rodborough Hotel**
Stroud, Gloucestershire

Calcot Manor Hotel & Spa
Tetbury, Gloucestershire

**Hanbury Manor, A
Marriott Hotel &
Country Club**
Ware, Hertfordshire

Gilpin Hotel & Lake House
Windermere, Cumbria

Abbey Guest House
Abingdon-on-Thames, Oxfordshire

Greycroft
Alnwick, Northumberland

The Barn at Penfolds
Arundel, Sussex

Manor Farm Barn B&B
Bampton, Oxfordshire

Marlborough House Guest House
Bath, Somerset

The Walls
Berwick-upon-Tweed, Northumberland

Kerscott Farm
Bishops Nympton, Devon

Number One St Luke's
Blackpool, Lancashire

Pendragon Country House
Camelford, Cornwall

Magnolia House
Canterbury, Kent

Ashburton Country House
Chorleywood, Hertfordshire

Druid House
Christchurch, Dorset

Beacon Hall House
Cranbrook, Kent

Hubert House Guesthouse and Bistro
Dover, Kent

The Victorian Town House
Durham, Co Durham

Burton Row Farmhouse
East Brent, Somerset

Broom House and Whites Guest House & Restaurant
Egton Bridge, North Yorkshire

The Hill on the Wall
Gilsland, Cumbria

Double-Gate Farm
Godney, Somerset

Glebe House Muston
Grantham, Lincolnshire

Grassington House Hotel & Restaurant
Grassington, North Yorkshire

Tosson Tower Farm B&B
Great Tosson, Northumberland

Cold Cotes Guest Accommodation, Gardens & Nursery
Harrogate, North Yorkshire

Colliers Farm
Haslemere, Surrey

Primrose Cottage
Launceston, Cornwall

Hazelmere House
Lostwithiel, Cornwall

Highcliffe House
Lynton, Devon

Ash Cottage
Maidstone, Kent

Higher Bodley Farm
Parracombe, Devon

Lowe Farm B&B
Pembridge, Herefordshire

Powe House
Portinscale, Cumbria

Low Hedgeley Farm
Powburn, Northumberland

Colton House
Rugeley, Staffordshire

Jeake's House
Rye, Sussex

Lantallack Getaways
Saltash, Cornwall

White Rose Lodge
Sandwich, Kent

St Cuthbert's House
Seahouses, Northumberland

The Barn & Pinn Cottage Guest House
Sidmouth, Devon

Pentillie Castle & Estate
St. Mellion, Cornwall

1 Woodchester Lodge
Stroud, Gloucestershire

The Old Coach House
Stroud, Gloucestershire

Carricks at Castle Farm
Swanton Morley, Norfolk

Tor Cottage
Tavistock, Devon

The Somerville
Torquay, Devon

Uplands House
Upton, Warwickshire

Bradle Farmhouse
Wareham, Dorset

Machrimore
Wells-Next-The-Sea, Norfolk

Meadow View Guest House
Wighton, Norfolk

Looking for something else?

The official and most comprehensive guide to independently inspected, star rated accommodation.

B&Bs and Hotels - B&Bs, Hotels, farmhouses, inns, serviced apartments, campus and hostel accommodation in England.

Self Catering - Self-catering holiday homes, approved caravan holiday homes, boat accommodation and holiday cottage agencies in England.

Camping, Touring and Holiday Parks - Touring parks, camping holidays and holiday parks and villages in Britain.

Now available in all good bookshops and online at **www.hudsons.co.uk/shop**

VisitEngland Awards for Excellence

VisitEngland awards for Excellence recognise the best of the best in the tourism industry. Whether it's for a day trip, a weekend break or a fortnight's holiday.

Celebrating its Silver Jubilee in 2014, the VisitEngland Awards for Excellence celebrate the best of English tourism. They promote healthy industry competition and help drive high standards in the industry, ensuring England's place as a world-class destination.

Competition is fierce and entries are submitted to regional tourism organisations across England, before being short-listed for the national finals, culminating in an Awards ceremony in May each year.

The 15 award categories are fiercely contested and the 2013 self-catering category winners include an elegant Tudor-Style house with a two star Michelin starred restaurant and a 5 star bed and breakfast nestled in the heart of Cheshire commended for it home cooked wholesome food.

Seek them out and experience them for yourself – you won't be disappointed.

The complete list of winners can be found online at **www.visitengland.com/awards**

Large Hotel of the Year 2013

GOLD WINNER

The Swan Hotel, Suffolk ★ ★ ★ ★

SILVER WINNER

Bedruthan Hotel & Spa, Cornwall ★ ★ ★ ★

BRONZE WINNER

The Lowry Hotel, Manchester ★ ★ ★ ★ ★

Small Hotel of the Year 2013

GOLD WINNER

Gidleigh Park, Devon ★ ★ ★ ★ ★

SILVER WINNER

Holbeck Ghyll, Cumbria ★ ★ ★ ★

BRONZE WINNER

Northcote, Lancashire ★ ★ ★ ★

Hotels

This year's gold Hotel winners are The Swan Hotel in Lavenham, Suffolk (Large Hotel of the Year) and Gidleigh Park in Chagford, Devon (Small Hotel of the Year).

With its picture perfect exterior, luxurious surroundings, oak beamed interiors and open fires the hotel brings together a deep sense of history and occasion with the very best in contemporary styling. Combined with the professionalism and efficiency of the friendly and approachable staff, you are guaranteed a wam and welcoming visit to The Swan Hotel.

This Tudor-style house in Devon was built in 1928 for shipping magnate Charles McIlwraith.

The mansion was transformed into a country house hotel in 1977, with Andrew and Christina Brownsword becoming its 'custodians' in 2005. In 2006 Gidleigh Park underwent a substantial transformation, when the number of bedrooms increased from 14 to 24, all with modern comforts and decor reflecting the Arts and Crafts period.

The restaurant, home to Executive Chef Michael Caines MBE, has held two Michelin stars since 1999.

Guest Accommodation

This years Gold winner of the Bed & Breakfast of the Year award is Alkham Court Farmhouse Bed and Breakfast. Alkham Court's stunning location overlooks the beautiful Kent countryside. During breakfast in the Oak Room guests enjoy a 'taste of Kent' breakfast and panoramic views. Also the country garden, hot tub and sauna allow guests the perfect opportunity to unwind to glorious sunsets over the valley.

Owners Wendy and Neil show true dedication in running an excellent business, with the commitment to exceed every guest's expectations so they will leave feeling relaxed and with great memories of their stay at Alkham Court.

The Silver winner of the Bed & Breakfast of the year award is Pendragon Country House in Camelford, Cornwall. This enchanting and elegant residence was originally constructed in 1870 by the church and was used as the rectory for the Parish of Davidstow. It is believed that it was intended for the Rev. Edward Benson, but in the mean time the Reverend became the first Bishop of Truro and subsequently the Archbishop of Canterbury. The house therefore, has an exciting and interesting history with many respected individuals as well as many wonderful guests having stayed here over the years.

B&B of the Year 2013

GOLD WINNERS

Alkham Court Farmhouse Bed and Breakfast, Kent ★ ★ ★ ★ ★

SILVER WINNER

Pendragon Country House, Cornwall ★ ★ ★ ★

BRONZE WINNER

The Salty Monk Restaurant with Rooms, Devon ★ ★ ★ ★ ★

Award-winning B&B/ Guest Accommodation

Pendragon Country House

When Sharon and Nigel Reed arrived at Pendragon Country House in Cornwall in 2008 it was their mission to create high quality and truly guest centric accommodation in relaxed yet sumptuous surroundings.

The house was a private residence and looked out-dated after modernisation in the 70s and 80s, so the couple set about refitting the building from top to bottom while keeping to a strong Victorian/ Edwardian style.

Today, the converted 1871 vicarage is an elegant, yet informal, warm and welcoming space, offering seven individually appointed luxurious rooms with fine antiques, rich luscious fabrics and just the right amount of modern convenience to make the visitor experience special.

But it is the personal attention that each guest receives from the genuinely friendly and attentive hosts that continually lifts this multi-award winning country house towards excellence. Pendragon oozes luxury and Sharon and Nigel make sure that every aspect, every detail and every ingredient they use is the best it can be, from the comfiest beds, to the most delicious breakfast to the nicest environment to relax in. And all this is achieved with sustainability and respect for the environment in mind. To keep to their high standards, Sharon and Nigel lead busy lives. They spend a lot of time making sure their guests have everything they need, and because they have many roles within the business every day is different.

During busy times they employ three local part-time staff members to help with the kitchen duties and running to tables, but guests will always receive the full attention of the owners. But it's evident the couple love what they do and where we live, and take a tremendous amount of satisfaction from knowing they've contributed towards visitors having great holidays.

"We get so much joy from running Pendragon Country House," adds Nigel. *"It involves hard work and long days but we're in it for the love of the area, the house and its surroundings, and for the feedback and gratitude of those who choose us for a visit to Cornwall."*

Contact details: Pendragon Country House, Davidstow, Camelford, Cornwall PL32 9XR. Tel: 01840 261131, website: www.pendragoncountryhouse.com

"We have many hats to wear and you never know what will happen on any given day. You could say our life is like a box of chocolates,"
Nigel

South West

Cornwall & Isles of Scilly, Devon, Dorset,
Gloucestershire, Somerset, Wiltshire

This is the home of Stonehenge, magnificent Bath Spa and quaint honey-coloured Cotswolds villages. Beautiful Cornish beaches, gently rolling Devon hills and miles of lush English countryside make this landscape heaven for anyone who loves the great outdoors. Exciting cities mix fascinating history with vibrant culture and you'll find superb festivals, and events all year round. The South West can rightly claim to be one of the most beautiful areas of the UK.

Bodmin Moor

Bodmin Moor is of one the last great unspoilt areas in the South West and much of its prehistoric and medieval past remains untouched by the passing of the centuries. The Moor is dominated by dramatic granite tors which tower over the sweeping expanses of open moorland.

City of Bath

Founded by the Romans as a thermal spa, Bath became an important centre of the wool industry in the Middle Ages. In the 18th century it developed into an elegant town with neo-classical Palladian buildings.

Cornwall and West Devon Mining Landscape

Tin and copper mining in Devon and Cornwall boomed in the 18th and 19th centuries, and at its peak the area produced two-thirds of the world's copper.

Dartmoor

Purple, heather clad moorland, wide open landscapes, rushing rivers and obscure stone tors shape the landscape of Dartmoor.

Dorset and East Devon Coast

The cliffs that make up the Dorset and Devon coast are an important site for fossils and provide a continuous record of life on land and in the sea since 185 million years ago.

Dorset

Dorset's countryside is almost entirely designated as an Area of Outstanding Natural Beauty. It includes iconic landmarks such as the Gold Hill in Shaftesbury (famous for the 1973 Hovis Advert).

English Riviera

Incorporating Torquay, Paignton and Brixham, this area is one of the UK's most popular holiday destinations. Famous for its award winning beaches and exotic palm trees, it is also a Global Geopark.

Exmoor

Exmoor National Park contains a variety of landscapes within its 267 square miles, including moorland, woodland, valleys and farmland.

Land's End

The most westerly point of mainland Cornwall and England. The headland has been designated as an Important Plant Area, by the organisation Plantlife, for rare species of flora.

Stonehenge

The Neolithic sites of Avebury and Stonehenge in Wiltshire are two of the most famous megalithic monuments in the world, and relate to man's interaction with his environment.

Editor's Picks

Defy gravity in a canal boat

At Caen Hill, near Devizes, canal boats defy gravity and take to hill climbing in one of the most spectacular stretches of waterway thanks to 29 locks in just two miles.

Walk the South West Coast Path

Trek all 630 stunning miles of unbroken coastline or maybe just a section. The path takes you from Minehead, round Devon and Cornwall, to Poole Harbour in Dorset.

Travel through time

Take a boat trip from Poole and witness the dramatic geology of the Jurassic Coast. Switch to the Swanage Steam Railway and be transported on a magical journey to Corfe castle.

Beat the tides

The tidal causeway linking the Devon coast with Burgh Island can catch out the casual visitor. But fear not as the unique Sea Tractor – an amphibious 'bus-on-stilts' – will carry you safely to shore.

See Land's End from the sky

Take off from a Cornish cliff and fly past the spectacular Longships Lighthouse before getting a spectacular bird's eye view of the Isles of Scilly archipelago.

Things to do

 Attractions with this sign participate in the Places of Interest Quality Assurance Scheme.

 Attractions with this sign participate in the Visitor Attraction Quality Assurance Scheme.

Both schemes recognise high standards in all aspects of the visitor experience (see page 7)

Entertainment & Culture

Castle Combe Museum
Castle Combe,
Wiltshire SN14 7HU
(01249) 782250
www.castle-combe.com
*Displays of life in Castle Combe
over the years.*

City Sightseeing - The Bristol Tour
Central Bristol, BS1 4AH
(03333) 210101
www.citysightseeingbristol.co.uk
*Open-top bus tours, with guides and headphones,
around the city of Bristol, a service that runs daily
throughout the summer months.*

Corinium Museum
Cirencester, Gloucestershire GL7 2BX
(01285) 655611
www.cotswold.gov.uk/go/museum
*Discover the treasures of the Cotswolds as you explore
its history at this award winning museum.*

Dean Heritage Centre
Cinderford, Gloucestershire GL14 2UB
(01594) 822170
www.deanheritagemuseum.com
*The Centre is open again after the fire. On display is an
exhibition showing the damage caused by the fire so
that visitors can come along and see what plans the
Museum has in place to clean and refurbish.*

Gloucester Waterways Museum
Gloucester GL1 2EH
(01452) 318200
www.nwm.org.uk
*Three floors of a Victorian warehouse house, interactive
displays and galleries, which chart the story of Britain's
waterways.*

Haynes International Motor Museum
Yeovil, Somerset BA22 7LH
(01963) 440804
www.haynesmotormuseum.co.uk
*An excellent day out for everyone. With more than 400
vehicles displayed in stunning style, dating from 1886
to the present day, it is the largest international motor
museum in Britain.*

National Maritime Museum Cornwall
Falmouth, Cornwall TR11 3QY
(01326) 313388
www.nmmc.co.uk
Voted SW Attraction of the Year, this Museum delivers something for everyone.

Plymouth City Museum and Art Gallery
Devon PL4 8AJ
(01752) 304774
www.plymouth.gov.uk/museumpcmag.htm
The museum presents a diverse range of contemporary exhibitions, from photography to textiles, modern art to natural history.

Roman Baths
Bath, Somerset BA1 1LZ
(01225) 477785
www.romanbaths.co.uk
The Romans built a magnificent temple and bathing complex that still flows with natural hot water.

Tate St Ives
St. Ives, Cornwall TR26 1TG
(01736) 796226
www.tate.org.uk/stives
Tate St Ives offers an introduction to international Modern and contemporary art, including works from the Tate Collection.

The Jane Austen Centre
Bath, Somerset BA1 2NT
(01225) 443000
www.janeausten.co.uk
Celebrating Bath's most famous resident.

Family Fun

At-Bristol
Bristol BS1 5DB
0845 345 1235
www.at-bristol.org.uk
21st century science and technology centre, with hands-on activities, interactive exhibits.

Corfe Castle Model Village and Gardens
Corfe Castle, Dorset BH20 5EZ
(01929) 481234
www.corfecastlemodelvillage.co.uk
Detailed 1/20th scale model of Corfe Castle and village before its destruction by Cromwell.

Cornwall's Crealy Great Adventure Park
Wadebridge, Cornwall PL27 7RA
(01841) 540276
www.crealy.co.uk/cornwall/index.aspx.
Enter the magical land of Cornwall's Crealy and hold on tight for Morgawr, the exciting NEW roller coaster.

Flambards
Helston, Cornwall TR13 0QA
(01326) 573404
www.flambards.co.uk
"Do not forget to visit the award-winning and unique exhibitions including the Victorian Village and the Britain in the Blitz."

Food & Drink

Wadworth Visitor Centre
Devizes, Wiltshire SN10 1JW
(01380) 732277
www.wadworthvisitorcentre.co.uk
Sample the delights and discover the history & heritage of Wadworth brewing. Featuring an exhibition of Wadworth brewing memorabilia, and products created by our Master Cooper.

Heritage

Avon Valley Railway
Bristol, Gloucestershire BS30 6HD
(0117) 932 5538
www.avonvalleyrailway.org *Railway that's much more than your average steam train ride, offering a whole new experience for some or a nostalgic memory for others.*

Brunel's SS Great Britain
Bristol BS1 6TY
(0117) 926 0680
www.ssgreatbritain.org
Award-winning attraction showing the world's first great ocean liner and National Brunel Archive.

Dartmouth Castle
Dartmouth, Devon TQ6 0JN
(01803) 833588
www.english-heritage.org.uk/dartmouthcastle
For over six hundred years Dartmouth Castle has guarded the narrow entrance to the Dart Estuary and the busy, vibrant port of Dartmouth.

Forde Abbey & Gardens
Chard, Dorset TA20 4LU
(01460) 221290
www.fordeabbey.co.uk
Founded 850 years ago, Forde Abbey was converted into a private house in c.1649.

Glastonbury Abbey

Somerset BA6 9EL
(01458) 832267
www.glastonburyabbey.com
Glastonbury Abbey – Somewhere for all seasons ! From snowdrops and daffodils in the Spring, to family trails and quizzes during the school holidays and Autumn colour on hundreds of trees.

Gloucester Cathedral
Gloucestershire GL1 2LR
(01452) 528095
www.gloucestercathedral.org.uk
A place of worship and an architectural gem with crypt, cloisters and Chapter House set in its precincts.

Lulworth Castle & Park

Wareham, Dorset BH20 5QS
0845 450 1054
www.lulworth.com
Walk in the footsteps of Kings & Queens as you enjoy wide open spaces, historic buildings & stunning landscapes. Enjoy the tranquillity of the nearby 18th century Chapel, wander through the park & woodland & bring a picnic.

Number One Royal Crescent
Bath, Somerset BA1 2LR
(01225) 428126
www.bath-preservation-trust.org.uk
The magnificently restored and authentically furnished town house creates a wonderful picture of fashionable life in 18th century Bath.

Old Sarum
Salisbury, Wiltshire SP1 3SD
(01722) 335398
www.english-heritage.org.uk/oldsarum
Discover the story of the original Salisbury and take the family for a day out to Old Sarum, two miles north of where the city stands now. The mighty Iron Age hill fort was where the first cathedral once stood and the Romans, Normans and Saxons have all left their mark.

Quay House Visitor Centre
Exeter, Devon EX2 4AN
(01392) 271611
www.exeter.gov.uk/quayhouse
Discover the history of Exeter in 15 minutes at the Quay House Visitor Centre on Exeter's Historic Quayside.

Portland Castle
Portland, Dorset DT5 1AZ
(01305) 820539
www.english-heritage.org.uk/portland
A well preserved coastal fort built by Henry VIII to defend Weymouth harbour against possible French and Spanish attack.

Salisbury Cathedral
Salisbury, Wiltshire SP1 2EJ
(01722) 555120
www.salisburycathedral.org.uk
Britain's finest 13th century cathedral with the tallest spire in Britain. Discover nearly 800 years of history, the world's best preserved Magna Carta (AD 1215) and Europe's oldest working clock (AD 1386).

Stonehenge
Amesbury, Wiltshire SP4 7DE
0870 333 1181
www.english-heritage.org.uk/stonehenge
Stonehenge stands impressively as a prehistoric monument of unique importance, a World Heritage Site, surrounded by remains of ceremonial and domestic structures - some older than the monument itself.

Sudeley Castle Gardens and Exhibition
Winchcombe, Gloucestershire GL54 5JD
(01242) 602308
www.sudeleycastle.co.uk
Award-winning gardens surrounding Castle and medieval ruins.

Swanage Railway
Swanage, Dorset BH19 1HB
(01929) 425800
www.swanagerailway.co.uk
Enjoy a nostalgic steam-train ride on the Purbeck line.

West Somerset Railway
Minehead, Somerset TA24 5BG
(01643) 704996
www.west-somerset-railway.co.uk
Longest independent steam railway in Britain, (20 miles).

Nature & Wildlife

Blue Reef Aquarium
Newquay, Cornwall TR7 1DU
(01637) 878134
www.bluereefaquarium.co.uk
A dazzling undersea safari through the oceans of the world.

Bristol Zoo Gardens
Bristol BS8 3HA
(0117) 974 7300
www.bristolzoo.org.uk
A visit to this city zoo is your passport for a day trip into an amazing world of animals, exhibits and other attractions.

Eden Project
St. Austell, Cornwall PL24 2SG
(01726) 811911
www.edenproject.com
With a worldwide reputation this epic destination definitely deserves a day of your undivided attention.

Escot Gardens, Maze & Forest Adventure
Ottery St. Mary, Devon EX11 1LU
(01404) 822188
www.escot-devon.co.uk
Historical gardens and fantasy woodland surrounding the ancestral home of the Kennaway family.

Fistral Beach
Newquay, Cornwall TR7 1HY
(01637) 850584
www.fistralbeach.co.uk
Excellent surfing conditions, a large beach, west facing with fine golden sand. International surfing events regularly take place here.

Hidcote Manor Garden
Chipping Campden,
Gloucestershire GL55 6LR
(01386) 438333
www.nationaltrust.org.uk/hidcote
Famous for its rare trees and shrubs, outstanding herbaceous borders and unusual plants from all over the world.

HorseWorld
Bristol, Somerset BS14 0QJ
(01275) 540173
www.horseworld.org.uk
Meet and help feed the rescued horses, ponies, donkeys in order to support this charity's animal welfare work.

Ilfracombe Aquarium
Ilfracombe, Devon EX34 9EQ
(01271) 864533
www.ilfracombeaquarium.co.uk
A fascinating journey of discovery into the aquatic life of North Devon.

Longleat
Warminster, Wiltshire BA12 7NW
(01985) 844400
www.longleat.co.uk
Widely regarded as one of the best loved tourist destinations in the UK, Longleat has a wealth of exciting attractions and events to tantalise your palate.

Lost Gardens of Heligan
St. Austell, Cornwall PL26 6EN
(01726) 845100
www.heligan.com
An exploration through Victorian Productive Gardens & Pleasure Grounds, a sub-tropical Jungle, pioneering Wildlife Project and beyond.

National Seal Sanctuary
Helston, Cornwall TR12 6UG
(01326) 221361
www.sealsanctuary.co.uk
The National Seal Sanctuary rescues, rehabilitates and releases over 40 seal pups a year, providing a home for those that can't be released back to the wild.

Newquay Zoo
Newquay, Cornwall TR7 2LZ
(01637) 873342
www.newquayzoo.org.uk
Multi-award winning Newquay Zoo set in sub-tropical lakeside gardens and home to over 130 species of animals.

Painswick Rococo Garden
Painswick, Gloucestershire GL6 6TH
(01452) 813204
www.rococogarden.org.uk
A unique Garden restoration, situated in a hidden valley.

Stourhead House and Garden
Warminster, Wiltshire BA12 6QD
(01747) 841152
www.nationaltrust.org.uk/stourhead
A breathtaking 18th century landscape garden with lakeside walks, grottoes and classical temples is only the beginning.

Westonbirt, The National Arboretum
Tetbury, Gloucestershire GL8 8QS
(01666) 880220
www.forestry.gov.uk/westonbirt
600 acres with one of the finest collections of trees in the world.

Events 2014

Swanage and Purbeck Walking Festival
April-May, Swanage
An exciting blend of special and general interest walks in this stunning area of Dorset.
www.walkswanage.com

Sherborne Abbey Music Festival
May, Sherborne
Five days of music performed by both nationally acclaimed artists and gifted young musicians.
www.sherborneabbey.org

Lyme Regis Fossil Festival
May 2-4, Lyme Regis
A natural science and arts cultural extravaganza on the UNESCO World Heritage Jurassic Coast.
www.fossilfestival.com

BMAD Bike Festival
May 2-5, Paignton
A festival of motorbikes on Paignton seafront, including live music and acrobatic displays.
www.bmad.co.uk/festival

Brixham Pirate Festival
May 4-5, Brixham
Brixham turns pirate with live music, games, re-enactments, skirmishes on the Golden Hind.
www.brixhampiratefestival.co.uk

Dorset Knob Throwing Festival
May, Cattistock, nr Dorchester
World famous quirky festival.
www.dorsetknobthrowing.com

Baby swans hatching at Abbotsbury Swannery
Mid May-late June, Abbotsbury, nr Dorchester
Hundreds of fluffy cygnets hatch from eggs in nests on or near the pathways.
www.abbotsbury-tourism.co.uk

Christchurch Food and Wine Festival
May 10-11, Christchurch
Celebrity chefs, over 100 trade stands, culinary treats, cookery theatres and some eminent food critics.
www.christchurchfoodfest.co.uk

The Super Weekend
June, Torquay
A celebration of all things super on England's Riviera coast – super cars, super bikes and super yachts.
www.thesuperweekend.co.uk

Glastonbury Festival
June 25-29, Shepton Mallet
Best known for its contemporary music, but also features dance, comedy, theatre, circus, cabaret and other arts.
www.glastonburyfestivals.co.uk

Spirit of the Sea Festival
June-July, Weymouth
Celebrating the area's close relationship with the sea, the festival brings together a range of sporting activities, cultural events and entertainment.
www.spiritofthesea.org.uk

Larmer Tree Festival
July 16-20, Cranborne Chase, North Dorset
Boutique festival featuring over 70 diverse artists across six stages, a comedy club, 150 free workshops, street theatre, carnival procession, all in front of an intimate crowd of 4,000.
www.larmertreefestival.co.uk

Tolpuddle Martyrs Festival
July 18-20, Tolpuddle, nr Dorchester
An annual festival to commemorate the bravery of the martyrs' struggle featuring music, speakers and family entertainment.
www.tolpuddlemartyrs.org.uk

Camp Bestival
July 31- August 3, Lulworth Castle, nr Wareham
Camp Bestival is a fairytale jamboree with a great mix of music, comedy and performing arts, suitable for all ages.
www.campbestival.net

Swanage Regatta
July 26-August 2, Swanage
The South's premier carnival.
www.swanagecarnival.com

Boardmasters
August 6-10, Newquay
Europe's largest surf and music festival on Fistral Beach and Watergate Bay.
www.boardmasters.co.uk

Buckham Fair
August 17, Beaminster
Martin Clunes' country show with funfair, dog show, dressage, entertainment, beer tent and food stalls.
www.buckhamfair.co.uk

Great Dorset Steam Fair
August 27-31, Tarrant Hinton, nr Blandford Forum
Dorset's biggest festival – five days of nostalgia and steam, widely recognised as the leading event of its kind in the world with over 2,000 exhibits and 500 trade stands, and traditional working demonstrations.
www.gdsf.co.uk

Dorset County Show
TBC, Dorchester
The South West's biggest two-day show featuring over 450 trade stands and a fantastic array of attractions.
www.dorsetcountyshow.co.uk

Bournemouth Air Festival
August 28-31, Bournemouth
Free four-day seafront air show.
www.bournemouthair.co.uk

Sturminster Newton Cheese Festival
September 13-14, Sturminster
A celebration of the region's dairy heritage with quality local food and crafts.
www.cheesefestival.co.uk

The Agatha Christie Festival
September, Torquay
Celebrate the life and works of the world's most famous crime writer, Dame Agatha Christie, who was born in Torquay in 1890. A literary festival with a murder mystery twist!
www.agathachristiefestival.co.uk

Bridport Hat Festival
September, Bridport
A three-day celebration of hats with live music, stalls and competitions.
www.bridporthatfest.org

Fishstock
September, Brixham
A one-day festival of seafood and entertainment held in Brixham.
www.fishstockbrixham.co.uk

Newquay Fish Festival
September, Newquay
Three days celebrating Newquay harbour and delightful fresh local produce.
www.newquayfishfestival.co.uk

Crantock Bale Push
September, Crantock, nr Newquay
Over 100 teams pushing giant hay bale around the village September 2013.
www.balepush.co.uk

Forest Food Showcase
October, Forest of Dean
A celebration of the foods and fruits of the forest. Held annually at Speech House on the first Sunday in October. With many food stalls and demonstrations it's a great opportunity to try what the area has to offer.
www.forestshowcase.org

Cornwall Film Festival
November, Newquay
3 days of iconic films in the Lighthouse Cinema -
www.cornwallfilmfestival.com

Tourist Information Centres

When you arrive at your destination, visit an Official Partner Tourist Information Centre for quality assured help with accommodation and information about local attractions and events, or email your request before you go. To find a Tourist Information Centre visit www.visitengland.com

Bath	Abbey Chambers	0906 711 2000	tourism@bathtourism.co.uk
Bodmin	Shire Hall	01208 76616	bodmintic@visit.org.uk
Bourton-on-the-Water	Victoria Street	01451 820211	bourtonvic@btconnect.com
Bridport	Bridport Town Hall	01308 424901	bridport.tic@westdorset-weymouth.gov.uk
Bristol : Harbourside	E Shed	0906 711 2191	ticharbourside@destinationbristol.co.uk
Brixham	18-20 The Quay	01803 211 211	holiday@englishriviera.co.uk
Bude	Bude Visitor Centre	01288 354240	budetic@visitbude.info
Cartgate	South Somerset TIC	01935 829333	cartgate.tic@southsomerset.gov.uk
Chard	The Guildhall	01460 260051	chard.tic@chard.gov.uk
Cheltenham	Municipal Offices	01242 522878	info@cheltenham.gov.uk
Chippenham	High Street	01249 665970	info@chippenham.gov.uk
Chipping Campden	The Old Police Station	01386 841206	info@campdenonline.org
Christchurch	49 High Street	01202 471780	enquiries@christchurchtourism.info
Cirencester	Corinium Museum	01285 654180	cirencestervic@cotswold.gov.uk
Corsham	31 High Street	01249 714660	enquiries@corshamheritage.org.uk
Dorchester	11 Antelope Walk	01305 267992	dorchester.tic@westdorset-weymouth.gov.uk
Fowey	5 South Street	01726 833616	info@fowey.co.uk
Frome	The Library	01373 465757	touristinfo@frome-tc.gov.uk
Glastonbury	The Tribunal	01458 832954	info@glastonburytic.co.uk
Gloucester	28 Southgate Street	01452 396572	tourism@gloucester.gov.uk

Looe	The Guildhall	01503 262072	looetic@btconnect.com
Lyme Regis	Guildhall Cottage	01297 442138	lymeregis.tic@westdorset-weymouth.gov.uk
Malmesbury	Town Hall	01666 823748	tic@malmesbury.gov.uk
Moreton-in-Marsh	High Street	01608 650881	moreton@cotswold.gov.uk
Padstow	Red Brick Building	01841 533449	padstowtic@btconnect.com
Penzance	Station Approach	01736 335530	beth.rose@nationaltrust.org.uk
Plymouth: Mayflower	Plymouth Mayflower Centre	01752 306330	barbicantic@plymouth.gov.uk
Salisbury	Fish Row	01722 342860	visitorinfo@salisburycitycouncil.gov.uk
Shepton Mallet	70 High Street	01749 345258	enquiries@visitsheptonmallet.co.uk
Sherborne	3 Tilton Court	01935 815341	sherborne.tic@westdorset-weymouth.gov.uk
Somerset Visitor Centre	Sedgemoor Services	01934 750833	somersetvisitorcentre@somerset.gov.uk
St Austell	Southbourne Road	01726 879 500	staustelltic@gmail.com
St Ives	The Guildhall	01736 796297	ivtic@stivestic.co.uk
Street	Clarks Village	01458 447384	info@streettic.co.uk
Stroud	Subscription Rooms	01453 760960	tic@stroud.gov.uk
Swanage	The White House	01929 422885	mail@swanage.gov.uk
Swindon	Central Library	01793 466454	infocentre@swindon.gov.uk
Taunton	The Library	01823 336344	tauntontic@tauntondeane.gov.uk
Tetbury	33 Church Street	01666 503552	tourism@tetbury.org
Tewkesbury	100 Church Street	01684 855040	tewkesburytic@tewkesbury.gov.uk
Torquay	The Tourist Centre	01803 211 211	holiday@englishriviera.co.uk
Truro	Municipal Building	01872 274555	tic@truro.gov.uk
Wareham	Discover Purbeck	01929 552740	tic@purbeck-dc.gov.uk
Warminster	Central Car Park	01985 218548	visitwarminster@btconnect.com
Wells	Wells Museum	01749 671770	visitwellsinfo@gmail.com
Weston-Super-Mare	The Winter Gardens	01934 417117	westontic@parkwood-leisure.co.uk
Weymouth	The Pavilion	01305 785747	tic@weymouth.gov.uk
Winchcombe	Town Hall	01242 602925	winchcombetic@tewkesbury.gov.uk
Yeovil	Petters House	01935 462781	yeoviltic@southsomerset.gov.uk

Regional Contacts and Information

For more information on accommodation, attractions, activities, events and holidays in South West England, contact one of the following regional or local tourism organisations. Their websites have a wealth of information and many produce free publications to help you get the most out of your visit.

Visit the following websites for further information on South West England:

- visitsouthwest.co.uk
- swcp.org.uk
- accessiblesouthwest.co.uk

Or call 01392 360050
Email: post@swtourism.co.uk

Publications available from South West Tourism:

- The Trencherman's Guide to Top Restaurants in South West England
- Adventure South West
  Your ultimate activity and adventure guide.
- World Heritage Map
  Discover our World Heritage.

South West

Where to Stay

Entries appear alphabetically by town name in each county. A key to symbols appears on page 7

★★★
HOTEL

B&B PER ROOM PER NIGHT
S: £45.00 - £55.00
D: £75.00 - £155.00
HB PER PERSON PER NIGHT
£77.50 - £110.00

Wellington Hotel

The Harbour, Boscastle, Cornwall PL35 0AQ   **T:** (01840) 250202
E: info@wellingtonhotelboscastle.com
W: wellingtonhotelboscastle.com   **£ BOOK ONLINE**

Overlooking the harbour in the village of Boscastle and surrounded by the beautiful North Cornwall coastline, the Wellington Hotel has been providing a warm welcome to its guests for many years. The Hotel has 14 bedrooms, a traditional pub serving Cornish ales and home-cooked food and an award winning restaurant.

Directions: From Exeter, A30 to Launceston. At Kennards House junction, A395 to Camelford. At Davidstow, B3262 to A39. Turn left, then right onto B3266.

Bedrooms: 3 single, 8 dble, 2 twin, 1 family
Open: All year

Site: ✿ **Payment:** 🖃 **Leisure:** 🎣 ⚓ ⛳ ♻ **Property:** 🍴 🐾 🖥 📱 **Children:** 🚼 🛏 ⚲ **Catering:** 🍴 🍽
Room: 📶 🚿 ☎ 📷 📺 🔌 💨

Looking for something else?

The official and most comprehensive guide to independently inspected, star rated accommodation.

B&Bs and Hotels - B&Bs, Hotels, farmhouses, inns, serviced apartments, campus and hostel accommodation in England.

Self Catering - Self-catering holiday homes, approved caravan holiday homes, boat accommodation and holiday cottage agencies in England.

Camping, Touring and Holiday Parks - Touring parks, camping holidays and holiday parks and villages in Britain.

Now available in all good bookshops and online at **www.hudsons.co.uk/shop**

OFFICIAL TOURIST BOARD GUIDE
New 39th edition
Self Cateri
England's star-rated holiday h
2014
www.visitor-guides.co.uk

OFFICIAL TOURIST BOARD GUIDE
New 39th edition
B&Bs and Hotels
England's star-rated guest accommodation
2014
www.visitor-guides.co.uk

New 39th edition
Camping, Touring & Holiday Parks
Britain's star-rated holiday parks
2014
www.visitor-guides.co.uk

CAMELFORD, Cornwall Map ref 1B2 SatNav PL32 9XR B

Pendragon Country House

Old Vicarage Hill, Davidstow, Camelford, Cornwall PL32 9XR **T:** (01840) 261131
E: enquiries@pendragoncountryhouse.com
W: www.pendragoncountryhouse.com **£ BOOK ONLINE**

B&B PER ROOM PER NIGHT
S: £60.00 - £65.00
D: £90.00 - £130.00
EVENING MEAL PER PERSON
£25.00 - £50.00

Beautifully presented family run luxury country guest house set in mature grounds offering bed & breakfast at its best. 7 en suite rooms offer a wide range of accommodation, from a spacious single to a grand superior king with a 4 poster bed. **Directions:** From the east, entering Davidstow continue past the church. Signposted Pendragon Country House will be on the right hand side 1/4 mile from A39 **Bedrooms:** All en suite, TV+DVD, Tea Tray & Luxury Furnishings **Open:** All Year except 24th 25th 26th 27th Dec.

Site: P Payment: £ € Leisure: Property: Children: Catering: Room:

CHARLESTOWN, Cornwall Map ref 1B3 SatNav PL25 3NJ H

Pier House Hotel

Harbour Front, Charlestown Road, St Austell PL25 3NJ **T:** (01726) 67955 **F:** (01726) 69246
E: pierhouse@btconnect.com
W: pierhousehotel.com

B&B PER ROOM PER NIGHT
S: £60.00 - £70.00
D: £112.00 - £146.00

Small, family-run hotel situated in a lovely 18th century harbour. We have a superb a la carte restaurant serving many exciting dishes and a selection of fish and seafood. **Directions:** Please see our website for full directions. **Bedrooms:** 7 single, 17 dble, 3 twin, 3 family **Open:** All year except Christmas

Site: P Payment: £ Leisure: Property: Children: Catering: Room:

CONSTANTINE BAY, Cornwall Map ref 1B2 SatNav PL28 8JH H

Treglos Hotel

Constantine Bay, Padstow PL28 8JH **T:** (01841) 520727 **F:** (01841) 521163
E: stay@tregloshotel.com
W: www.tregloshotel.com **£ BOOK ONLINE**

B&B PER ROOM PER NIGHT
S: £64.00 - £110.00
D: £128.00 - £220.00
HB PER PERSON PER NIGHT
£104.50 - £155.50

SPECIAL PROMOTIONS
Prices vary throughout the seasons - please contact or visit website for further details.

This luxurious hotel on the North Cornish coast has 42 rooms and suites, many with dramatic views over Constantine Bay. Facilities include indoor pool, whirlpool, treatment rooms and award-winning restaurant. Treglos has its own golf course and self-catering apartments. Beaches and coastal paths are within a short stroll. Please contact for evening meal prices.

Directions: Please contact us for directions.

Bedrooms: 3 single, 23 double/twin, 10 family, 6 suite
Open: February - November

Site: P Payment: £ Leisure: Property: Children: Catering: Room:

FALMOUTH, Cornwall Map ref 1B3 SatNav TR11 4EL B

The Beach House

1 Boscawen Road, Falmouth TR11 4EL **T:** (01326) 210407
E: beachhousefalmouth@hotmail.com
W: beachhousefalmouth.co.uk

enjoyEngland.com ★★★★ GUEST ACCOMMODATION · enjoyEngland.com Silver AWARD

B&B PER ROOM PER NIGHT
D: £40.00 - £47.00

Stunning sea views, gorgeous sub-tropical gardens and total relaxation. The Beach House offers stylish accommodation in a unique setting overlooking Falmouth Bay. Britain in Bloom - Judges Award 2009. **Bedrooms:** 2 double or 1 twin **Open:** All year

Site: P **Leisure:** **Property:** **Catering:** **Room:**

FALMOUTH, Cornwall Map ref 1B3 SatNav TR11 5LG H

Budock Vean Hotel on the River

Helford Passage, Mawnan Smith, Falmouth, Cornwall TR11 5LG **T:** (01326) 250288
F: (01326) 250892 **E:** relax@budockvean.co.uk
W: www.budockvean.co.uk **£ BOOK ONLINE**

enjoyEngland.com ★★★★ COUNTRY HOUSE HOTEL · enjoyEngland.com Silver AWARD

B&B PER ROOM PER NIGHT
S: £71.00 - £128.00
D: £142.00 - £256.00
EVENING MEAL PER PERSON
£39.95

Budock Vean is a family-owned hotel nestled in 65 acres of organic subtropical gardens and parkland with private foreshore on the tranquil Helford river. Outstanding leisure facilities include golf, indoor swimming, sauna, outdoor hot tub, health spa, and award-winning restaurant.

Directions: Please contact us for directions.

Bedrooms: 7 single, 24 double, 23 twin, 2 family, 1 suite.
Open: 24th January 2014 to 2nd January 2015.

Site: **Payment:** **Leisure:** **Property:** **Children:**
Catering: **Room:**

HELSTON, Cornwall Map ref 1B3 SatNav TR130RZ B

Tregathenan House

The Old Farmhouse, Tregathenan, nr Helston TR13 0RZ **T:** (01326) 569840
E: tregathenan@hotmail.com
W: www.tregathenan.co.uk

enjoyEngland.com ★★★★ BED & BREAKFAST · enjoyEngland.com Silver AWARD

B&B PER ROOM PER NIGHT
S: £35.00 - £47.00
D: £57.00 - £80.00

Cornish Country House B&B dating from 1640, set in 5 acres of gardens and meadows 3 miles from Helston. Liz, Ian and the alpacas offer you a warm welcome to their tranquil home to relax and enjoy high standards of comfort and service. **Directions:** 3 miles north of Helston, between Coverack Bridges and Crowntown. See website for detailed directions. **Bedrooms:** All en suite/private bathroom; TV/DVD, tea, coffee **Open:** All Year

Site: P **Payment:** **Leisure:** **Property:** **Catering:** **Room:**

LANDS END, Cornwall Map ref 1A3
SatNav TR19 7RD **B**

Bosavern House
Bosavern, St. Just, Lands End TR19 7RD **T:** (01736) 788301 **E:** info@bosavern.com
W: bosavern.com

B&B PER ROOM PER NIGHT
S: £40.00 - £48.00
D: £80.00 - £96.00

C17th country house in attractive grounds. Centrally heated, comfortable accommodation. Most rooms have sea or moorland views. Home cooking using local produce. Ideally situated for exploring West Cornwall. Ample parking. **Directions:** Take A3071 from Penzance towards St Just, turn left onto B3306 signed Lands End. Bosavern House is 0.5 mile on left. **Bedrooms:** 1 single, 3 double, 2 twin, 2 family **Open:** All year except Christmas

Site: ✿ **P Payment:** 💷 € **Leisure:** 🏊 🦯 🎣 **Property:** 🖥 📺 **Children:** 🧸 🛏 ⛹ **Catering:** 🍷 🍴 **Room:** 🍵 ♨ 📺 🔌 🔌

LAUNCESTON, Cornwall Map ref 1C2
SatNav PL15 9PE **B**

Primrose Cottage
Primrose Cottage, Lawhitton, Launceston PL15 9PE **T:** (01566) 773645
E: enquiry@primrosecottagesuites.co.uk
W: primrosecottagesuites.co.uk

B&B PER ROOM PER NIGHT
S: £70.00 - £90.00
D: £90.00 - £130.00

EVENING MEAL PER PERSON
£13.00 - £17.00

SPECIAL PROMOTIONS
Discounts on stays of 2 or 3 days. Please see website for details.

Primrose Cottage is set in gardens and woodland leading to the River Tamar. Each luxury suite has its own sitting room, entrance and en suite facilities with beautiful views across the Tamar Valley. Five minutes from the A30 with easy access to both north and south coasts and the moors.

Directions: Leave Launceston on the A388 Plymouth road. After 1 mile turn left on B3362 signposted Tavistock. Primrose Cottage is on the left after 2.5 miles.

Bedrooms: 2 double, 1 twin
Open: All year except Christmas

Site: ✿ **P Payment:** 💷 **Leisure:** 🦯 **Property:** 🖥 **Catering:** 🍴 **Room:** 🍵 ♨ 📺 🔌

LOOE, Cornwall Map ref 1C2
SatNav PL13 1LP **B**

Barclay House
St Martins Road, Looe PL13 1LP **T:** (01503) 262929 **F:** (01503) 262632
E: info@barclayhouse.co.uk
W: www.barclayhouse.co.uk **£ BOOK ONLINE**

B&B PER ROOM PER NIGHT
S: £65.00 - £105.00
D: £115.00 - £195.00

EVENING MEAL PER PERSON
£8.00 - £45.00

Located high on the hill offering spectacular river views just minutes away from the historic fishing port of Looe. Smart contemporary rooms, 2AA Rosette, Taste of the West Gold Award Restaurant. We offer a 4 course meal at £32.00 pp, a 6 course taster meal at £45 or Brasserie menu from £8 - £28. Amazing staff, luxury 5 star cottages, outdoor pool, gym, sauna, hair salon, 6 acres of beautiful gardens. **Bedrooms:** 1 single, 8 double, 2 twin, 1 suite **Open:** All year

Site: ✿ **P Payment:** 💷 € **Leisure:** 🏊 🦯 ▶ ♿ 🎣 **Property:** 🖥 📺 **Children:** 🧸 🛏 ⛹ **Catering:** 🍷 🍴 **Room:** 🍵 ♨ 📞 🔌 📺 🔌 🔌

South West - Cornwall

LOOE, Cornwall Map ref 1C2 — SatNav PL13 2DG [H]

Hannafore Point Hotel and Spa

Marine Drive, West Looe, Looe PL13 2DG **T:** (01503) 263273
E: stay@hannaforepointhotel.com
W: hannaforepointhotel.com

B&B PER ROOM PER NIGHT
S: £50.00 - £72.00
D: £100.00 - £154.00
HB PER PERSON PER NIGHT
£52.00 - £92.00

SPECIAL PROMOTIONS
Special-event packages. Extensive range of conference and business facilities. Weddings and special occasions. Christmas and New Year celebrations.

A warm welcome awaits you. Set in picturesque Cornish village with spectacular, panoramic sea views. Indulge in superb home-cooked food. Dining options include quality local produce and fresh fish. The terrace is a popular rendezvous for cream teas or cocktails. Spa pool, gym, sauna, Steam and Beauty Therapies.

Directions: A38 from Plymouth, then A387 to Looe. Cross over stone bridge, turn 1st left (sign 'Hannafore') and uphill until overlooking bay.

Bedrooms: 4 single, 33 dble
Open: All year

Site: ✿ Payment: 🔲 Leisure: 🏊 ♒ ▶ ♨ 🎯 🎣 ✎ Property: ⚓ 🐴 🖥 🖨 ◑ Children: 🍼 🎠 🎋
Catering: 🍷 🍴 Room: 🔌 🛁 📞 📺 ☕ 🔥 🧺

LOSTWITHIEL, Cornwall Map ref 1B2 — SatNav PL22 0RA [B]

Hazelmere House

58 Grenville Road, Lostwithiel, Cornwall PL22 0RA **T:** (01208) 873315
E: Hazelmerehouse@aol.com
W: hazelmerehouse.co.uk

B&B PER ROOM PER NIGHT
S: £50.00 - £55.00
D: £85.00 - £90.00

Situated in the beautiful Fowey Valley with rural views overlooking the Historic town of Lostwithiel, Hazelmere House offers exceptional bed and breakfast. Centrally situated, close to the Eden Project, Heligan Gardens and many National Trust properties, join us for a comfortable and informal base to explore all the joys of Southern Cornwall. **Directions:** On A390, North of Lostwithiel
Bedrooms: All rooms en suite, 1 kingsize, 1 super kingsize, 1 single.
Open: All year

Site: ✿ P Payment: € Leisure: 🏊 ♒ ▶ ♨ Property: 🐴 🖥 🖨 ✎ Children: 🍼 🎠 🎋
Catering: 🍴 Room: 🔌 🛁 📞 📺

MEVAGISSEY, Cornwall Map ref 1B3 — SatNav PL26 6ND [B]

Tregilgas Farm

Gorran, St Austell PL26 6ND **T:** (01726) 842342 / 07789 113620 **E:** dclemes88@aol.com
W: tregilgasfarmbedandbreakfast.co.uk

B&B PER ROOM PER NIGHT
S: £35.00 - £40.00
D: £55.00 - £60.00
EVENING MEAL PER PERSON
£20.00 - £25.00

Lovely 5-bedroomed detached farmhouse on working farm. Tastefully decorated. Very central for touring Cornwall. Lovely food for breakfast. Friendly welcome awaits you. **Directions:** Follow signs to Heligan Gardens. Go past gardens, take 4th turning on right, go to crossroads, go straight across. Tregilgas is 1st farm on right. **Bedrooms:** 2 double, 1 twin **Open:** March - September

Site: ✿ P Payment: € Leisure: 🏊 ♒ ▶ ♨ Property: 🐴 🖥 🖨 Children: 🍼 🎠 🎋 Catering: 🍴 Room: 🔌 🛁 📺 ☕

The Official Tourist Board Guide to **B&Bs and Hotels 2014**

NEWQUAY, Cornwall   Map ref 1B2
SatNav TR7 2NQ **B**

★★★
GUEST HOUSE

B&B PER ROOM PER NIGHT
S: £25.00 - £29.00
D: £40.00 - £58.00

Harrington Guest House
25 Tolcarne Road, Newquay TR7 2NQ **T:** (01637) 873581
E: harringtonguesthouse@yahoo.com
W: harringtonguesthouse.com

Harrington Guest House, newly furnished and decorated, less than 200 metres from the beach. Offers excellent value accommodation, en suite facilities, price reductions for children, LCD TVs, Wi-Fi. **Bedrooms:** 2 double, 2 twin, 2 family **Open:** All year except Christmas

Site: P Payment: £Ξ **Leisure:** ♪ ▶ ∪ **Property:** 🖥 ♘ **Children:** ⛺ ⚲ **Catering:** 🍴 **Room:** ⚷ ♨ 📺

PADSTOW, Cornwall   Map ref 1B2
SatNav PL28 8SB **B**

★★★
GUEST
ACCOMMODATION

B&B PER ROOM PER NIGHT
S: £50.00 - £70.00
D: £55.00 - £120.00

EVENING MEAL PER PERSON
£6.00 - £30.00

The Harlyn Inn
Harlyn Bay, Padstow PL28 8SB **T:** (01841) 520207 **E:** mail@harlyn-inn.com
W: harlyn-inn.com **£ BOOK ONLINE**

The Harlyn Inn is situated adjoining the beautiful sandy beach of Harlyn Bay. Just a couple of miles outside Padstow it is the ideal place for an enjoyable Cornish holiday. The Inn has two bars and two restaurants, catering for the whole family. All of our accommodation is finished to a high standard and ranges from bed and breakfast rooms to fully equipped three-bedroom self-catering cottages. Our adjoining beach shop provides all your beach essentials, snacks and clothing as well as surf hire & surf school facilities.

Directions: Please contact us for directions.

Bedrooms: 11 single, 8 double, 4 twin, 3 family
Open: All year

Site: P Payment: £Ξ **Leisure:** 🚲 ♪ ▶ ∪ **Property:** 🐾 🖥 **Children:** ⛺ 🏊 ⚲ **Catering:** ⟨✗ 🍷 🍴
Room: ⚷ ♨ 🅐 📺

PENZANCE, Cornwall   Map ref 1A3
SatNav TR18 2HA **B**

★★★
GUEST HOUSE

B&B PER ROOM PER NIGHT
S: £35.00 - £38.00
D: £76.00 - £79.00

EVENING MEAL PER PERSON
£19.50

Cornerways Guest House
5 Leskinnick Street, Penzance TR18 2HA **T:** (01736) 364645 / 800110
E: enquiries@cornerways-penzance.co.uk
W: www.cornerways-penzance.co.uk

Cornerways is an attractively decorated townhouse, 3 minutes away from car parks, bus/railway stations. Freshly cooked breakfast to order including vegetarian, using local & organic produce where possible. Ideal touring base, rooms en suite. **Directions:** Walk up from the rail or bus station towards the main street and cross the road using the pedestrian crossing. Leskinnick Street is facing you. **Bedrooms:** All rooms en suite, free wi-fi, TV, tea & coffee **Open:** All year

Site: ❀ **Payment:** £Ξ € **Leisure:** 🚲 ♪ ∪ **Property:** 🖥 **Children:** ⛺ **Catering:** 🍴 **Room:** ⚷ ♨ 📺

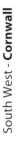

South West - Cornwall

Hotel Penzance

Britons Hill, Penzance TR18 3AE **T:** (01736) 363117 **F:** (01736) 361127
E: reception@hotelpenzance.com
W: www.hotelpenzance.com **£ BOOK ONLINE**

B&B PER ROOM PER NIGHT
S: £85.00 - £95.00
D: £145.00 - £210.00
EVENING MEAL PER PERSON
£25.50

SPECIAL PROMOTIONS
Various special offers available thoughout Oct-Mar period in addition to Walking Breaks and Romantic packages at anytime. Please phone or visit hotel website.

Be assured of consistently high levels of comfort and friendly service at this award winning Cornish hotel. The Bay restaurant presents fine food served all day with evening a la carte and tasting menus. Traditional or contemporary-style rooms with sea views across Penzance Harbour and towards St Michael's Mount. The ideal base for a weekend break or holiday in West Cornwall.

Directions: Enter Penzance on A30 Dual carriageway. At roundabout keep left signed towards Town Centre. Third turn right onto Britons Hill. Hotel 70m on right.

Bedrooms: 4 single, 12 doubles, 9 twin. All Superior and most Classic rooms have sea views.
Open: All year

Site: ❋ **Payment:** 🆑 **Leisure:** ♿ ♪ ♈ ✻ **Property:** 🏋 🐕 🖥 📺 🌙 **Children:** 🧸 ♿ 🎿 **Catering:** 🍷 🍴
Room: 🦺 🌢 📞 📺 🛗

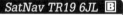

Ardensawah Farm

St Levan, Penzance, Cornwall TR19 6JL **T:** (01736) 871520 / 07877 124550
E: ardensawah@btinternet.com
W: porthcurnofarmholidays.com

B&B PER ROOM PER NIGHT
D: £85.00 - £90.00

SPECIAL PROMOTIONS
Special Promotions available - Please contact for details.

Discover our delightful Cornish farmhouse in this wonderful area of outstanding natural beauty. A warm welcome, magnificent sea views and our delicious award winning breakfasts await you. Relax, unwind and enjoy the peace and tranquility of both the countryside and stunning beaches around us. The perfect holiday choice.

Directions: 2 miles from Lands End. Situated between Porthcurno and Porthgwarra. On migratory path for birdwatching. Surfing, rock climbing, coastal path, fabulous beaches nearby.

Bedrooms: 2 double, 1 family
Open: All year except Christmas

Site: ❋ **P** **Payment:** 🆑 € **Leisure:** ♿ ♪ ♈ ♈ **Property:** 🖥 **Children:** 🧸 **Catering:** 🍴
Room: 🦺 🌢 📞 📺

SALTASH, Cornwall Map ref 1C2

Lantallack Getaways

Landrake, Saltash, Cornwall PL12 5AE **T:** (01752) 851281 **E:** enquiries@lantallack.co.uk
W: www.lantallackgetaways.co.uk

B&B PER ROOM PER NIGHT
D: £100.00 - £120.00

Lantallack offers luxury accommodation with beautiful views across undulating countryside and wooded valleys, big open skies and unforgettable sunsets. Its peaceful situation makes it an ideal retreat for a truly relaxing holiday. **Directions:** A38 thro' Saltash, continue 3 miles. At Landrake 2nd right at West Lane. After 1 mile left at white cottage for Tideford. House 150 yds on, on right. **Bedrooms:** Comfortable beds, en suite, tea/coffee, tv & wifi **Open:** All Year

Site: ✿ P Leisure: ✦ ⚷ Property: ▤ ▣ ⌂ ∅ Catering: ▼ ⌗ Room: ℞ ♿ TV ▦

ST. AGNES, Cornwall Map ref 1B3

Little Trevellas Farm

Trevellas, St Agnes TR5 0XX **T:** (01872) 552945 **F:** (01872) 552945
E: velvet-crystal@xlninternet.co.uk
W: stagnesbandb.co.uk **£ BOOK ONLINE**

B&B PER ROOM PER NIGHT
S: £27.50 - £30.00
D: £50.00 - £60.00

A 250-year-old house on a working farm on the B3285 provides a peaceful, comfortable base for a holiday that will appeal to lovers of both coast and countryside. Wi-Fi now available. **Directions:** Please contact us for directions. **Bedrooms:** 1 single, 1 double, 1 twin **Open:** All year

Site: P Property: ♞ ▤ Catering: ⌗ Room: ♿ TV

ST. AGNES, Cornwall Map ref 1B3

Penkerris

Penwinnick Road, St. Agnes TR5 0PA **T:** (01872) 552262 **F:** (01872) 552262
E: penkerris@gmail.com
W: penkerris.co.uk

B&B PER ROOM PER NIGHT
S: £20.00 - £45.00
D: £40.00 - £70.00
EVENING MEAL PER PERSON
£15.00 - £25.00

Edwardian House with parking, lawned garden for relaxation & games, cosy lounge & delightful dining room serving real food. Close to dramatic cliff walks & iconic surfing beaches (nearest 1km). Ideal location, central for all of Cornwall. **Directions:** From A30, big roundabout at Chiverton, 3 miles to village on B3277. Penkerris is just inside St Agnes and 30mph sign and before the Museum. **Bedrooms:** 2 Double 2 Twin 2 Family 2 Singles. **Open:** All year

Site: ✿ P Payment: £ € Leisure: ⚐ ▸ ∪ Property: ♞ ▤ ▣ Children: ⛐ ▥ ⚲ Catering: ⌗ Room: ♿ TV

ST. AUSTELL, Cornwall Map ref 1B3

The Chapel Guest House

The Old Chapel, Carthew, St. Austell, Cornwall PL26 8XG **T:** (01726) 851602
E: bookings@thechapelguesthouse.co.uk
W: www.thechapelguesthouse.co.uk

B&B PER ROOM PER NIGHT
S: £40.00 - £50.00
D: £70.00 - £80.00

Comfortable accommodation in a converted Bible Christian Chapel, north of St Austell, convenient for the Eden Project, Wheal Martyn Museum & many other local attractions. Family, Double and Twin en suites incl.wheelchair accessible room. **Directions:** From A30 take A381 (St Austell) through Bugle and Stenalees. At roundabout take second exit onto B3274 (Carthew) and Chapel is 3/4 mile on the right. **Bedrooms:** Flat screen tv, tea/coffee, hairdryer, clock. **Open:** All year except Christmas

Site: ✿ P Payment: £ Property: ▤ Children: ⛐ ▥ ⚲ Catering: ⌗ Room: ℞ ♿ TV ♿

ST. MELLION, Cornwall Map ref 1C2
SatNav PL12 6QD B

Pentillie Castle & Estate
Paynters Cross, Saint Mellion, Saltash PL12 6QD **T:** (01579) 350044 **F:** (01579) 212002
E: contact@pentillie.co.uk
W: pentillie.co.uk **£ BOOK ONLINE**

B&B PER ROOM PER NIGHT
S: £120.00 - £210.00
D: £120.00 - £210.00
EVENING MEAL PER PERSON
£30.00 - £40.00

17th century Pentillie Castle boasts a riverside location with views over the Tamar Valley. With luxuriously appointed bedrooms, Pentillie is available for exclusive hire, weddings or corporate events. Dinner subject to availability. **Directions:** 10 miles from Plymouth on the River Tamar, off the A388 between Saltash and Callington. **Bedrooms:** 9 double (some can be twin), all are en suite **Open:** All year

Site: ✿ P Payment: 💷 € Leisure: ॐ 🎵 ♪ ∪ ♣ ⤢ Property: 🐾 ⬛ 🖥 ♨ Children: 🚼 🎮 🎎 Catering: 🍽 🍴 Room: 🔌 ♨ ▣ 📺 🔥 🧺

ST. MINVER, Cornwall Map ref 1B2
SatNav PL27 6RG B

Tredower Barton
St Minver, Wadebridge, Cornwall PL27 6RG **T:** (01208) 813501
E: dally.123@btinternet.com

B&B PER ROOM PER NIGHT
D: £60.00 - £75.00

Tredower Barton is a farm bed and breakfast set in beautiful countryside near the North Cornish coast. New for 2014, a lovely garden/sun room with beautiful panoramic views available for guests use. Delicious breakfast and relaxing stay guaranteed. Near to local attractions, Padstow and Port Isaac. Wi-Fi available. **Directions:** 3 miles from Wadebridge on road B3314 to Port Issac. **Bedrooms:** 1 twin, 1 family (Can be used as family or double) **Open:** Easter to October

Site: ✿ P Leisure: ॐ ♪ ⤢ ⤢ Property: ⬛ ♨ Children: 🚼 🎮 🎎 Room: 🔌 ♨ 📺 🔥 🧺

TRURO, Cornwall Map ref 1B3
SatNav TR1 3SY B

Tor Vean Bed & Breakfast
Kenwyn Road, Truro TR1 3SY **T:** (01872) 271766 **E:** heather591@hotmail.com
W: www.torveanbedandbreakfast.co.uk

B&B PER ROOM PER NIGHT
S: £55.00
D: £75.00

Tor Vean is a Victorian House offering refurbished comfortable and spacious accommodation in the conveniently located and favoured Conservation Area of Kenwyn. Truro City centre, bus stop (opposite Tor Vean and providing hourly service), Railway Station, Kenwyn Church and Victoria Gardens are within close proximity, as is Truro Bowling Club. **Directions:** On B3284 directly opposite Hendra Hill turning. Car parking: turn into Cyril Road, just before Mountford House entrance take left lane, first carpark on left. **Bedrooms:** 2 King Size, 1 twin **Open:** All year

Site: ✿ P Payment: 💷 € Leisure: ▶ Property: 🐾 ⬛ Catering: 🍽 Room: 🔌 ♨ ▣ 📺 🔥

TRURO, Cornwall Map ref 1B3
SatNav TR1 2HX B

Townhouse Rooms
City Centre, 20 Falmouth Road, Truro TR1 2HX **T:** (01872) 277374 **F:** (01872) 241666
E: info@trurotownhouse.com
W: www.trurotownhouse.com **£ BOOK ONLINE**

B&B PER ROOM PER NIGHT
D: £59.00 - £79.00

The Townhouse is different, relaxed, friendly, flexible, our guests say so! Lovely rooms, fully equipped. Rates include Buffet continental breakfast & vat. Walking distance to all amenities. **Directions:** Please see website for detailed directions. **Bedrooms:** 10 en suite double rooms. Single or double guests **Open:** All year except Christmas and New Year

Site: ✿ P Payment: 💷 Property: ⬛ 🖥 Catering: 🍽 Room: 🔌 ♨ ▣ 📺 🔥 🧺

SatNav PL27 6LA H

St Enodoc Hotel Rock

Rock, Wadebridge PL27 6LA **T:** (01208) 863394 **F:** (01208) 863970 **E:** info@enodoc-hotel.co.uk
W: www.enodoc-hotel.co.uk

B&B PER ROOM PER NIGHT
S: £150.00 - £220.00
D: £180.00 - £285.00

SPECIAL PROMOTIONS
3 nights for the price of 2 available, please call us for details.

Distinctive style and a relaxed atmosphere. Ideally located for relaxing breaks, golf or visiting Cornwall's stunning gardens. The two restaurants are run by Nathan Outlaw and his team. 2 Michelin Star Restaurant Nathan Outlaw and the more casual dining room Outlaws A la Carte Restaurant.

Directions: M4 West to Exeter, M5 Southbound, A30 to Bodmin, A389 to Wadebridge and B3314 to Rock.

Bedrooms: 8 double, 8 twin, 3 family, 1 suite.
Open: February to December

Site: ✿ **Payment:** 💳 **Leisure:** 🎿 🎵 ⛳ ♘ ☂ **Property:** 🍴 📺 📶 🌙 **Children:** 🍼 🛏 🎠 **Catering:** 🍽 🍴
Room: 📶 🛁 📞 💻 📺 🚪

SatNav TR23 0PR H

Hell Bay Hotel

Bryher, Isles of Scilly TR23 0PR **T:** (01720) 422947 **F:** (01720) 423004
E: contactus@hellbay.co.uk
W: hellbay.co.uk **£ BOOK ONLINE**

B&B PER ROOM PER NIGHT
S: £125.00 - £356.25
D: £200.00 - £570.00
EVENING MEAL PER PERSON
£39.00

SPECIAL PROMOTIONS
Please see our website for all special rates and breaks.

Bryher's only hotel and England's last boasts a spectacular, natural location that blends with the contemporary style of the hotel to produce a unique venue. All accommodation is beautifully appointed, and most bedrooms have direct sea views. The award-winning food and informal service combine to complete the experience.

Directions: Flights from Exeter, Newquay or Land's End or ferry from Penzance all to the neighbouring island of St Mary's. A local boat transfer will take you to Bryher, a 15 minute journey.

Bedrooms: 4 family, 21 suite
Open: March to November

Site: ✿ **Payment:** 💳 **Leisure:** 🎵 ⛳ ♘ ❄ 🎾 🎿 🏊 ☂ 🎯 **Property:** 🐾 📺 📶 🍴 **Children:** 🍼 🛏 🎠
Catering: 🍴 🍽 **Room:** 📶 🛁 📞 💻 📺 📀 🚪 🔌 🖨 🏺

ST. MARY'S, Isles of Scilly Map ref 1A3
SatNav TR21 0NW **B**

GUEST HOUSE

B&B PER ROOM PER NIGHT
S: £37.00 - £49.00
D: £78.00 - £112.00

Isles of Scilly Country Guest House
Sage House, High Lanes, St. Mary's TR21 0NW **T:** (01720) 422440
E: scillyguesthouse@hotmail.co.uk
W: www.scillyguesthouse.co.uk **£ BOOK ONLINE**

The Guesthouse offers a wide choice of en suite rooms to suit your personal needs. You will find this an ideal location for those seeking a peaceful and tranquil environment. Please contact us for prices. **Directions:** Isles of Scilly on Saint Marys near Telegraph hill **Bedrooms:** 8 single, 5 double, 2 twin, 1 family **Open:** All year

Site: ✿ **Payment:** 🔢 € **Leisure:** 🚣 🎣 ➤ **Property:** 🐾 🚭 **Children:** 🐾 🎮 🏇
Catering: 🍽 🍴 **Room:** 🔌 ♨ 📺 🛁

ST. MARY'S, Isles of Scilly Map ref 1A3
SatNav TR21 0HX **B**

GUEST ACCOMMODATION

B&B PER ROOM PER NIGHT
S: £32.00 - £38.00
D: £64.00 - £76.00

Treboeth Guest House
Buzza Street, Porth Cressa, St Mary's, Isles of Scilly TR21 0HX **T:** (01720) 422548

Very close to Porth Cressa beach, within walking distance of town centre and Quay for Off Islands. Peaceful and tranquil area next to coastal walks. **Directions:** Please contact us for directions **Bedrooms:** 1 single, 3 double, 1 family **Open:** March-November

Site: **P** **Leisure:** 🚣 🎣 ➤ ∪ **Property:** 🐾 🚭 **Children:** 🐾5 **Catering:** ✖ **Room:** 🔌 ♨ 📺

BISHOPS NYMPTON, Devon Map ref 1C1
SatNav EX36 4QG **B**

FARMHOUSE **Gold AWARD**

B&B PER ROOM PER NIGHT
D: £70.00 - £76.00
EVENING MEAL PER PERSON
£20.00

Kerscott Farm
Ash Mill, Bishops Nympton, South Molton, Devon EX36 4QG
T: (01769) 550262 / 07793 526260 **E:** kerscott.farm@btinternet.com
W: www.devon-bandb.co.uk

Peacefully quiet Medieval Farmhouse (mentioned Domesday Book 1086) Real working farm. Beautiful all round views onto Exmoor and surrounding farmland. Wonderful character antique interior. Own spring water. Traditional wholesome English Farmhouse cooking using much of own produce. Smart/Sky TVs, Wi-Fi. Full central heating, log fires. Warm and comforting welcome - an absolute rare find. **Bedrooms:** 2 doubles and 1 double/twin room **Open:** All year except Christmas Day & New Years Day

Site: ✿ **P** **Leisure:** 🚣 🎣 ➤ ∪ **Property:** 🚭 🎮 ∅ **Children:** 🐾13 **Catering:** ✖ 🍴 **Room:** 🔌 ♨ 📶 📺

BLACKAWTON, Devon Map ref 1D3
SatNav TQ9 7BG **B**

INN

B&B PER ROOM PER NIGHT
S: £63.00 - £76.00
D: £78.00 - £90.00
EVENING MEAL PER PERSON
£7.00 - £13.00

The George Inn
Main Street, Blackawton, Devon TQ9 7BG **T:** (01803) 712342
E: tgiblackawton@yahoo.co.uk
W: blackawton.com

Traditional village inn at the heart of Blackawton village, offering well kept cask ales, good food, excellent service, real value & choice and comfortable en suite accommodation. **Directions:** Between Totnes & Kingsbridge take A3122 towards Dartmouth, turn right to Blackawton at Forces Cross, right into the village centre.
Bedrooms: 3 double, 1 twin, 1 family **Open:** All year

Site: ✿ **P** **Payment:** 🔢 **Property:** 🐾 🚭 📻 ∅ **Children:** 🐾 🏇 **Catering:** ✖ 🍽 🍴 **Room:** 🔌 ♨ 📺 📀

BRIXHAM, Devon   Map ref 1D2   SatNav TQ5 9AJ 🄷

HOTEL ★★★

B&B PER ROOM PER NIGHT
S: £55.00 - £78.00
D: £96.00 - £168.00
HB PER PERSON PER NIGHT
£58.00 - £94.00

SPECIAL PROMOTIONS
Special-event
packages. Extensive
range of conference
and business facilities.
Weddings and special
occasions. Christmas
and New Year
celebrations.

Berry Head Hotel
Berry Head Road, Brixham TQ5 9AJ **T:** (01803) 853225 **F:** (01803) 882084
E: stay@berryheadhotel.com
W: berryheadhotel.com

Steeped in history, nestling on the water's edge in acres of outstanding natural beauty. Traditional hospitality, excellent, friendly and personal service with attention to detail. Comfortable accommodation, thoughtfully equipped. Imaginative menus, varied dining options, featuring quality local produce and fresh fish. Lounge, bars and terrace, popular with locals and residents.

Directions: Enter Brixham, continue to harbour and around, up King Street for 1 mile to Berry Head.

Bedrooms: 3 single, 12 dble, 10 twin, 7 family
Open: All year

Site: ❀ **Payment:** 💳 € **Leisure:** 🚵 ♪ ▶ ∪ ☂ **Property:** ⛵ 🛏 🗑 ◑ **Children:** 🍼 🛏 ♿ **Catering:** ⛵ 🍴
Room: 🔌 ♨ 📞 🅰 📺 🍴 🎵

DARTMOUTH, Devon   Map ref 1D3   SatNav TQ6 9PS 🄷

HOTEL ★★★   *Silver* AWARD

B&B PER ROOM PER NIGHT
S: £100.00
D: £230.00
EVENING MEAL PER PERSON
£9.00 - £23.00

Royal Castle Hotel
11 The Quay, Dartmouth TQ6 9PS **T:** (01803) 833033 **E:** enquiry@royalcastle.co.uk
W: royalcastle.co.uk **£ BOOK ONLINE**

Historic 17th century quayside coaching inn set in the heart of Dartmouth. Two busy bars, a restaurant overlooking the river and 25 luxurious bedrooms. Please contact us for prices and special offers. **Directions:** See website, and full route details sent on booking. **Bedrooms:** 2 single, 14 dble, 6 twin, 3 family
Open: All year

Payment: 💳 **Leisure:** 🚵 ♪ ▶ ∪ 🎿 **Property:** ⛵ 🐴 🛏 🗑 ◑ **Children:** 🍼 🛏 ♿ **Catering:** ⛵ 🍴 **Room:** 🔌 ♨ 📞 🅰 📺 🍴

Book your accommodation online

Visit our new 2014 guide websites for detailed information, up-to-date availability and to book your accommodation online. Includes over 20,000 places to stay, all of them star rated.
www.visitor-guides.co.uk

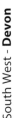

Langstone Cliff Hotel

Mount Pleasant Road, Dawlish Warren, Dawlish, Devon EX7 0NA   **T:** (01626) 868000
F: (01626) 868006   **E:** info@langstone-hotel.co.uk
W: langstone-hotel.co.uk   **£ BOOK ONLINE**

B&B PER ROOM PER NIGHT
S: £81.00 - £95.00
D: £126.00 - £212.00
EVENING MEAL PER PERSON
£12.50 - £35.00

SPECIAL PROMOTIONS
Children under 10 free
when sharing with 2
adults. Special cabaret
weekend breaks
throughout the year.

Set in 19 acres of Devon woodland overlooking the sea close to Exeter & Torquay. Extensive leisure facilities include 2 swimming pools, snooker, tennis, table tennis, fitness room, hairdressing Salon. Regular entertainment, children welcome, dinner dance and cabaret weekends, Dance Holidays, extensive Christmas and New Year Programme.

Directions: From M5 jct 31 follow A379 for Dawlish. Turn left at harbour after Starcross. Follow road approx 1.5 miles, hotel is on left.

Bedrooms: 1 single, 19 dble, 8 twin, 30 family, 6 suite
Open: All year

Site: ❈ **P** Payment: 💳 Leisure: 🏊 ⏰ ♨ 🎱 🎾 🏓 🎯 🔭 🏹 Property: 📇 🐾 💻 📠 🅿 ◗ Children: 🐾 🛏 🚼
Catering: (✗ 🍽 🍴 Room: 🛎 🍵 📞 📺 📻

Visit our 2014 guide websites...

- Detailed information
- Up-to-date availability
- Book your accommodation online

Includes over 20,000
places to stay,
all of them star rated.

Win amazing prizes,
every month...

Enter our monthly competition at
www.visitor-guides.co.uk/prizes

EXETER, Devon Map ref 1D2 SatNav EX4 4HD B

Raffles Hotel

11 Blackall Road EX4 4HD **T:** (01392) 270200 **E:** raffleshtl@btinternet.com
W: www.raffles-exeter.co.uk

Raffles is a large Victorian townhouse 5 minutes walk from city centre and close to the university. Car park available. Wildlife garden for guests use. Spacious accommodation. Vegetarian, organic breakfast on request. 24 hours notice for Haddock or Kippers. First choice for The Lonely Planet Exeter. Enjoy your stay. Trip Advisor certificate of excellence. Family Room £86-96. **Bedrooms:** All single, twin, double or family rooms have en suite, Wi-Fi, Television and tea/coffee making facilities. **Open:** All Year

B&B PER ROOM PER NIGHT
S: £48.00 - £55.00
D: £78.00

Site: **P** Payment: Property: Children: Room:

FROGMORE, Devon Map ref 1C3 SatNav TQ7 2NR B

Globe Inn

Frogmore, Nr Kingsbridge TQ7 2NR **T:** (01548) 531351 **E:** info@theglobeinn.co.uk
W: www.theglobeinn.co.uk

The inn is situated in the pretty village of Frogmore, between Kingsbridge and Dartmouth, in glorious unspoilt South Hams countryside. The pub has undergone tasteful renovation and now boasts 8 well appointed en suite bedrooms. Downstairs the pub has a cosy bar restaurant frequented be friendly locals. **Directions:** Via Kingsbridge take the A379 to Dartmouth and Torcross. After 2 miles look out for the Inn on the left as you enter Frogmore. **Bedrooms:** 5 double, 2 twin, 1 family **Open:** All year

B&B PER ROOM PER NIGHT
S: £60.00
D: £85.00
EVENING MEAL PER PERSON
£10.00 - £20.00

Site: **P** Payment: Leisure: Property: Children: Catering: Room:

HOLSWORTHY, Devon Map ref 1C2 SatNav EX22 6SJ B

Leworthy Farmhouse B&B

Lower Leworthy, Holsworthy, Devon EX22 6SJ **T:** (01409) 254484
E: leworthyfarmhouse@btconnect.com
W: www.leworthyfarmhouse.co.uk **£ BOOK ONLINE**

B&B PER ROOM PER NIGHT
S: £60.00 - £65.00
D: £72.00 - £85.00
EVENING MEAL PER PERSON
£15.00 - £25.00

SPECIAL PROMOTIONS
Please see our website for regular seasonal offers.

If it's the 'good life' you're seeking, look no further than Leworthy Farmhouse, tucked away in the peace and tranquility of a small hamlet, close to the North Devon/Cornwall border. This stunning Georgian farmhouse provides a relaxed base to explore the 'Ruby Country', the seaside town of Bude or spend a peaceful afternoon being entertained by the smallholdings rare breed livestock.

Directions: From Holsworthy take the North Tamerton Road, after 3 miles turn left signed Leworthy/Southdown. Follow tarmac lane to island, stay left, B&B straight ahead. Enter via wooden gates to reception.

Bedrooms: Fresh towels, freeview flatscreen TV/DVD player, Free Wi-Fi Available. Hairdryer, radio/alarm, complimentary toiletries and tea/coffee making with fresh milk. **Open:** Closed between 22 December and 9 February

Site: **P** Payment: Leisure: Property: Catering: Room:

HONITON, Devon   Map ref 1D2
SatNav EX14 3AD **H**

HOTEL   *Gold* AWARD

B&B PER ROOM PER NIGHT
S: £190.00 - £399.00
D: £215.00 - £450.00
HB PER PERSON PER NIGHT
£159.00 - £277.00

Combe House Devon
Gittisham, Honiton, Nr Exeter, Devon EX14 3AD **T:** (01404) 540 400
E: stay@combehousedevon.com
W: combehousedevon.com **£ BOOK ONLINE**

In top Best Foodie Hotels in South West England, 2013. Romantic, privately owned 450yr old Elizabethan Manor in 3,500 acres of some of England's finest countryside, with the South Devon coast nearby, Lyme Regis to Sidmouth. **Directions:** Only 15 minutes from M5/J29 & A30/London-Honiton. 'Halfway to Cornwall'.
Bedrooms: 4 double, 9 twin, 2 suite **Open:** All year

Site: ✿ **Payment:** ⌹ **Leisure:** ♿ ♪ ▶ ∪ **Property:** ♟ 🐎 ⛳ ⊡ **Children:** 🛏 🎠 ⚺ **Catering:** 🍽 🍴 **Room:** 🕾 ☎ 📺 ♨ 📠

ILFRACOMBE, Devon   Map ref 1C1
SatNav EX34 8NA **B**

GUEST ACCOMMODATION

B&B PER ROOM PER NIGHT
S: £45.00 - £50.00
D: £60.00 - £70.00

Mullacott Farm
Mullacott Farm, Ilfracombe, Devon EX34 8NA **T:** (01271) 866877
E: relax@mullacottfarm.co.uk
W: mullacottfarm.co.uk **£ BOOK ONLINE**

Family run working farm, with many animals. Ideal base for beach, walking and riding, near Woolacombe, Ilfracombe, Exmoor. En suite, colour TV, hospitality tray. Access 24/7. Children welcome. No smoking. Scrumptious farm produced, award winning breakfast, (own sausages, bacon, free range eggs) complements the high standards of cleanliness and comfort.

Directions: Follow A361 Ilfracombe. At Mullacott Cross, 400m from roundabout turn left, through two pillars, with horses heads, take first turning right. Follow signs, to farmhouse.

Bedrooms: 2 double, 2 twin, 2 family
Open: All year except Christmas and New Year

Site: ✿ **P** **Payment:** ⌹ € **Leisure:** ♿ ♪ ▶ ∪ **Property:** ⛳ **Children:** 🛏 🎠 ⚺ **Catering:** 🍴
Room: 🕾 ♨ 📺 ♨

LYNTON, Devon   Map ref 1C1
SatNav EX35 6AR **B**

GUEST ACCOMMODATION   *Gold* AWARD

B&B PER ROOM PER NIGHT
S: £75.00 - £112.00
D: £100.00 - £150.00

Highcliffe House
Sinai Hill, Lynton, Devon EX35 6AR **T:** (01598) 752235 **E:** info@highcliffehouse.co.uk
W: www.highcliffehouse.co.uk

Exclusively for adults, Highcliffe House is situated on the Exmoor coast with stunning sea views across the Bristol Channel to Wales. Six beautifully appointed bedrooms and an award winning breakfast makes this a special place to stay. **Bedrooms:** All rooms en suite, tea & coffee, flat screen TV's **Open:** Mid March to the end of October

Site: ✿ **P** **Payment:** ⌹ € **Leisure:** ♿ ♪ ▶ ∪ **Property:** ⛳ ♙ **Catering:** 🍴 **Room:** 🕾 ♨ 📺 📀

MORETONHAMPSTEAD, Devon   Map ref 1C2   SatNav TQ13 8QF B

FARMHOUSE

B&B PER ROOM PER NIGHT
S: £45.00 - £50.00
D: £75.00 - £85.00

Great Sloncombe Farm

Great Sloncombe Farm, Moretonhampstead, Dartmoor, Devon TQ13 8QF
T: (01647) 440595 **F:** (01647) 440595 **E:** hmerchant@sloncombe.freeserve.co.uk
W: greatsloncombefarm.co.uk

13th century farmhouse in a magical Dartmoor valley. Meadows, woodland, wild flowers and animals. Farmhouse breakfast with freshly baked bread. Everything provided for an enjoyable break. **Directions:** From Moretonhampstead take A382 towards Chagford. Take left turn (farm signed) up lane, through hamlet, farm is on right. **Bedrooms:** 2 double, 1 twin **Open:** All year

Site: ❊ Payment: ▦ Leisure: ♿ ♪ ▶ ☾ Property: 🐾 ☷ Children: ☝⁸ Catering: 🍴 Room: ♨ ♠ 📺 ♿ 🛏 ☕

NORTHAM, Devon   Map ref 1C1   SatNav EX39 3QB H

HOTEL

B&B PER ROOM PER NIGHT
S: £40.00 - £55.00
D: £70.00 - £100.00

EVENING MEAL PER PERSON
£7.50 - £25.00

SPECIAL PROMOTIONS
Please contact us for prices

Durrant House Hotel

Heywood Road, Northam, Bideford EX39 3QB **T:** (01237) 472361 **F:** 01237 421709
E: info@durranthousehotel.com
W: www.durranthousehotel.com **£ BOOK ONLINE**

Dating back to the 1800's this is the largest hotel in North Devon with 125 refurbished, comfortable guest rooms and suites, fully equipped to high standards. Some of our rooms come with Jacuzzi, four poster beds and fire places. Relax and enjoy the varied cuisine in the luxurious Olive Tree Restaurant and Appledore Bar. New! R&R Spa is now open featuring Elemis treatments. Open 7 days a week.

Directions: Take J27 On M5 towards A39 North Devon, follow to Bideford, after the bridge turn right at the roundabout the hotel is on the right.

Bedrooms: 4 single, 40 dble, 60 twin, 21 family, 3 suite
Open: All year

Site: ❊ P Payment: ▦ Leisure: ▶ ✗ ♨ ☷ ⚘ Property: 🍽 🐾 ☷ 🗗 📵 ◑ Children: ☝ 🛏 ♿ Catering: ⟨✗ 🍷 🍴 Room: ♨ ♠ ☎ 📺 ♿ 🛏

OKEHAMPTON, Devon   Map ref 1C2   SatNav EX20 1HD H

HOTEL

B&B PER ROOM PER NIGHT
S: £60.00 - £70.00
D: £70.00 - £95.00

HB PER PERSON PER NIGHT
£60.00 - £67.50

White Hart Hotel

Fore Street, Okehampton EX20 1HD **T:** (01837) 52730 **F:** (01837) 53979
E: enquiry@thewhitehart-hotel.com
W: thewhitehart-hotel.com **£ BOOK ONLINE**

Historic coaching inn. An ideal centre for walking and cycling. Good food menu sourced from local suppliers. HB's restaurant & Vines Pizzeria. Leisure centre nearby. Conference facilities. Free car park. **Directions:** Okehampton town centre on the edge of the Dartmoor National Park. Easy access to and from the A30. **Bedrooms:** 2 single, 9 double, 5 twin, 2 family, 1 suite **Open:** All year

Payment: ▦ Leisure: ♿ ♪ ▶ ☾ Property: 🍽 🐾 ☷ 🗗 Children: ☝ 🛏 ♿ Catering: 🍷 🍴 Room: ♨ ♠ ☎ 📺 ♿ 🛏 ☕

PAIGNTON, Devon   Map ref 1D2

SatNav TQ3 2NJ

HOTEL

Redcliffe Lodge Hotel

Marine Drive, Paignton TQ3 2NJ **T:** (01803) 551394 **F:** (01803) 551394
E: davies.valleyview@tiscali.co.uk
W: redcliffelodge.co.uk **£ BOOK ONLINE**

B&B PER ROOM PER NIGHT
S: £20.00 - £35.00
D: £40.00 - £70.00

HB PER PERSON PER NIGHT
£35.00 - £50.00

SPECIAL PROMOTIONS
2-4 year olds half-price
when sharing with
adults. Winter 2-night
breaks, B&B and 3
course evening meal
from £30pppn.

Redcliffe Lodge occupies one of Paignton's finest seafront positions, in its own grounds with large free car park. All rooms are en suite and comfortably furnished with modern facilities. Licensed bar. Panoramic views from both our sun lounge and dining room, where you will enjoy our high standard of cuisine.

Directions: Follow A3022 to Paignton seafront. The hotel is situated at the end of Marine Drive, on the right adjacent to Paignton Green.

Bedrooms: 2 single, 10 dble, 3 twin, 2 family
Open: All year

Site: ❀ Payment: 🖃 Leisure: ♨ ♪ ♭ ⵁ Property: ♈ 🛏 🖳 🗐 ◑ Children: 🛏 🎒 Catering: ♇ 🍴
Room: ☎ ♨ 🎧 📺

PAIGNTON, Devon   Map ref 1D2

SatNav TQ4 6BU 🅱

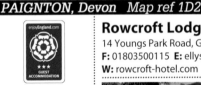

★★★
GUEST ACCOMMODATION

Rowcroft Lodge

14 Youngs Park Road, Goodrington Sands, Paignton, Devon TQ4 6BU **T:** (01803) 559420
F: 01803500115 **E:** ellys14@btconnect.com
W: rowcroft-hotel.com **£ BOOK ONLINE**

B&B PER ROOM PER NIGHT
S: £35.00 - £40.00
D: £50.00 - £60.00

A double fronted Victorian licensed guest house overlooking a beautiful park, lakes and sea. A short level walk to 2 sandy beaches, new children's play area, crazy golf, aquatic park and Leisure Centre. All rooms en suite with television. **Directions:** Along Paignton seafront to mini-roundabout at south end. Left past harbour to top of Roundham Road. Bear right into Alta Vista Road. Youngs Park Road 1st left. **Bedrooms:** En suite rooms, either overlooking garden or park **Open:** All year

Site: P Payment: 🖃 Leisure: ♨ ♪ Property: 🛏 🖳 ⵗ Children: 🛏 🎒 Catering: ♇ 🍴 Room: ☎ ♨
📺

Need more information?

Visit our new 2014 guide websites for detailed information, up-to-date availability and to book your accommodation online. Includes over 20,000 places to stay, all of them star rated.

www.visitor-guides.co.uk

2014 Official Tourist Board Guides

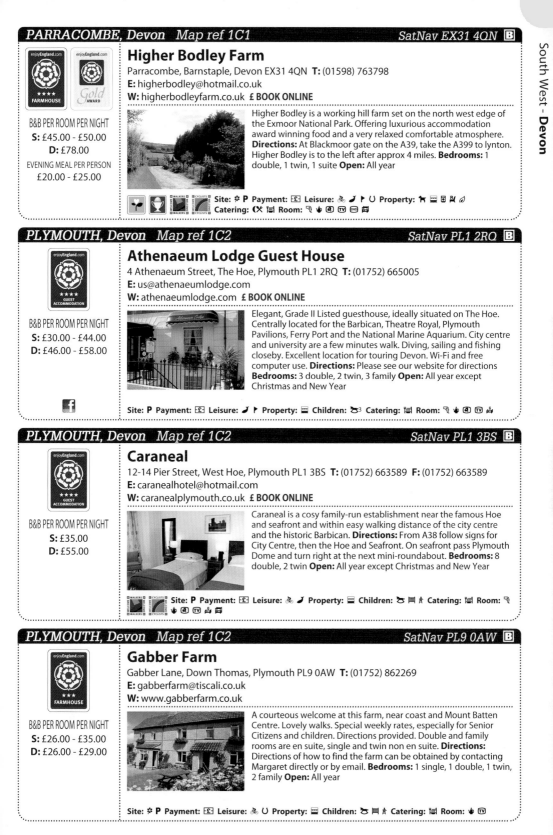

PARRACOMBE, Devon   Map ref 1C1   SatNav EX31 4QN B

FARMHOUSE ★★★★   **Gold AWARD**

B&B PER ROOM PER NIGHT
S: £45.00 - £50.00
D: £78.00
EVENING MEAL PER PERSON
£20.00 - £25.00

Higher Bodley Farm

Parracombe, Barnstaple, Devon EX31 4QN **T:** (01598) 763798
E: higherbodley@hotmail.co.uk
W: higherbodleyfarm.co.uk **£ BOOK ONLINE**

Higher Bodley is a working hill farm set on the north west edge of the Exmoor National Park. Offering luxurious accommodation award winning food and a very relaxed comfortable atmosphere. **Directions:** At Blackmoor gate on the A39, take the A399 to lynton. Higher Bodley is to the left after approx 4 miles. **Bedrooms:** 1 double, 1 twin, 1 suite **Open:** All year

Site: ❀ P Payment: 🖃 Leisure: 🚴 ♪ ▶ ♒ Property: 🔥 ☎ ▣ ☒ ∅
Catering: (✗ 🍴 Room: 🔌 🖐 ⬛ 📺 📀 🛏

PLYMOUTH, Devon   Map ref 1C2   SatNav PL1 2RQ B

GUEST ACCOMMODATION ★★★★

B&B PER ROOM PER NIGHT
S: £30.00 - £44.00
D: £46.00 - £58.00

🅵

Athenaeum Lodge Guest House

4 Athenaeum Street, The Hoe, Plymouth PL1 2RQ **T:** (01752) 665005
E: us@athenaeumlodge.com
W: athenaeumlodge.com **£ BOOK ONLINE**

Elegant, Grade II Listed guesthouse, ideally situated on The Hoe. Centrally located for the Barbican, Theatre Royal, Plymouth Pavilions, Ferry Port and the National Marine Aquarium. City centre and university are a few minutes walk. Diving, sailing and fishing closeby. Excellent location for touring Devon. Wi-Fi and free computer use. **Directions:** Please see our website for directions **Bedrooms:** 3 double, 2 twin, 3 family **Open:** All year except Christmas and New Year

Site: P Payment: 🖃 Leisure: ♪ ▶ Property: ☎ Children: ☒3 Catering: 🍴 Room: 🔌 🖐 ⬛ 📺 🛏

PLYMOUTH, Devon   Map ref 1C2   SatNav PL1 3BS B

GUEST ACCOMMODATION ★★★★

B&B PER ROOM PER NIGHT
S: £35.00
D: £55.00

Caraneal

12-14 Pier Street, West Hoe, Plymouth PL1 3BS **T:** (01752) 663589 **F:** (01752) 663589
E: caranealhotel@hotmail.com
W: caranealplymouth.co.uk **£ BOOK ONLINE**

Caraneal is a cosy family-run establishment near the famous Hoe and seafront and within easy walking distance of the city centre and the historic Barbican. **Directions:** From A38 follow signs for City Centre, then the Hoe and Seafront. On seafront pass Plymouth Dome and turn right at the next mini-roundabout. **Bedrooms:** 8 double, 2 twin **Open:** All year except Christmas and New Year

Site: P Payment: 🖃 Leisure: 🚴 ♪ Property: ☎ Children: ☒ 🏚 ⚲ Catering: 🍴 Room: 🔌 🖐 ⬛ 📺 🛏 🍴

PLYMOUTH, Devon   Map ref 1C2   SatNav PL9 0AW B

FARMHOUSE ★★★

B&B PER ROOM PER NIGHT
S: £26.00 - £35.00
D: £26.00 - £29.00

Gabber Farm

Gabber Lane, Down Thomas, Plymouth PL9 0AW **T:** (01752) 862269
E: gabberfarm@tiscali.co.uk
W: www.gabberfarm.co.uk

A courteous welcome at this farm, near coast and Mount Batten Centre. Lovely walks. Special weekly rates, especially for Senior Citizens and children. Directions provided. Double and family rooms are en suite, single and twin non en suite. **Directions:** Directions of how to find the farm can be obtained by contacting Margaret directly or by email. **Bedrooms:** 1 single, 1 double, 1 twin, 2 family **Open:** All year

Site: ❀ P Payment: 🖃 Leisure: 🚴 ♒ Property: ☎ Children: ☒ 🏚 ⚲ Catering: 🍴 Room: 🖐 📺

South West - Devon

Tides Reach Hotel
South Sands, Salcombe TQ8 8LJ **T:** (01548) 843466 **F:** (01548) 843954
E: enquire@tidesreach.com
W: tidesreach.com **£ BOOK ONLINE**

B&B PER ROOM PER NIGHT
S: £76.00 - £114.00
D: £134.00 - £320.00
HB PER PERSON PER NIGHT
£86.00 - £185.00

SPECIAL PROMOTIONS
Winter, Spring and Autumn Bargain Breaks. Pampered Spa Breaks, Indulgent Breaks, Romantic Breaks.

Elegant and well-appointed hotel with superb estuary/sea views in area of outstanding natural beauty on edge of a sandy cove. Well-equipped indoor pool and leisure complex with tropical atmosphere. Award-winning cuisine and friendly, caring staff. All combine to produce an ideal location for a short break or holiday.

Directions: Leave A38 at Buckfastleigh to Totnes, then take A381 to Salcombe, then follow signs to South Sands.

Bedrooms: 2 single, 15 dble, 10 twin, 3 family, 2 suite
Open: Open February to December

Site: ❀ **P** Payment: 🖃 Leisure: ♪ ▶ ♜ ⚔ ⚲ ⚘ ≷ Property: ⋔ 🖾 🗔 ♨ ◐ Children: ⛱8
Catering: (✕ 🍽 ⛾ Room: ▽ ♨ ☎ 📺

The Barn & Pinn Cottage Guest House
Bowd, Sidmouth, Devon EX10 0ND **T:** (01395) 513613
E: barnpinncottage@btinternet.com
W: www.thebarnandpinncottage.co.uk

B&B PER ROOM PER NIGHT
S: £42.00 - £48.50
D: £78.00 - £118.00
EVENING MEAL PER PERSON
£19.00 - £22.50

SPECIAL PROMOTIONS
3 nights for price of 2 offers. 3 day Christmas break. 2 night Valentines. Special occasions & functions by arrangement. Please enquire for details.

This beautiful 15th Century thatched cottage nestles within two acres of award winning gardens 5 minutes drive from Sidmouth. All en suite rooms have full central heating, Digital TV, and tea/coffee making facilities. Dinner available Thur-Sun. Good home cooking, varied menu, well stocked bar. Comfortable guest lounge, large private car park.

Directions: Located on A3052 12 Miles from Exeter, 15 miles from Lyme Regis. Between Newton Poppleford and Sidford. 5 mins from beach at Sidmouth using B3176.

Bedrooms: 1 single, 3 double, 1 Kingsize, 2 Luxury Four Posters with private garden, 2 twin, 1 Holiday let as B&B or Self catering. Family rooms possible
Open: All year

Site: ❀ **P** Payment: 🖃 Leisure: ⚘ ♪ ▶ ♈ Property: ⋔ Children: ⛱ Catering: ⛾ 🍽
Room: ▽ ♨ 📷 📺 ♨ ⟐

SIDMOUTH, Devon   Map ref 1D2   SatNav EX10 8AY 🄷

Hotel Riviera

The Esplanade, Sidmouth, Devon EX10 8AY **T:** (01395) 515201 **F:** (01395) 577775
E: enquiries@hotelriviera.co.uk
W: hotelriviera.co.uk **£ BOOK ONLINE**

B&B PER ROOM PER NIGHT
S: £109.00 - £179.00
D: £218.00 - £338.00
HB PER PERSON PER NIGHT
£99.00 - £220.00

SPECIAL PROMOTIONS
Seasonal breaks available throughout the year. Christmas and New Year programme also available.

The Hotel Riviera is splendidly positioned at the centre of Sidmouth's esplanade, overlooking Lyme Bay. With its mild climate and the beach just on the doorstep, the setting echoes the south of France and is the choice of the discerning visitor in search of relaxation and quieter pleasures. Glorious sea views can be enjoyed from the recently re-designed en suite bedrooms, all of which are fully appointed and have many thoughtful extras. In the elegant bay-view dining room guests are offered a fine choice of dishes from extensive menus, prepared by English trained chefs with local seafood being a particular speciality. The hotel has a long tradition of hospitality and is perfect for unforgettable holidays, long weekends, unwinding breaks and all the spirit of the glorious Festive Season… you will be treated to the kind of friendly personal attention that can only be found in a private hotel of this quality.

Directions: Sidmouth is 165 miles from London and 13 miles from M5 exit 30 then follow A3052.   **Bedrooms:** 7 Single, 10 Doubles, 7 Twin, 2 Suite **Open:** All year

Site: ❋ Payment: 💷 Leisure: 🎣 ♪ ⏲ ⏱ Property: ⚓ 🐎 🖥 🖧 ◐ Children: ⛵ ♨ 🎠 Catering: 🍴 🍽 Room: 📶 💧 🎄 📺

SIDMOUTH, Devon   Map ref 1D2   SatNav EX10 8AZ 🄷

Royal York & Faulkner Hotel

The Esplanade, Sidmouth EX10 8AZ **T:** (01395) 513043 **F:** (01395) 577472
E: stay@royalyorkhotel.co.uk
W: royalyorkhotel.co.uk **£ BOOK ONLINE**

B&B PER ROOM PER NIGHT
S: £45.00 - £80.00
D: £90.00 - £160.00
HB PER PERSON PER NIGHT
£60.00 - £105.00

Magnificent Regency hotel on centre of Esplanade & adjacent picturesque town. Personally run by the Hook family with a long standing reputation for hospitality and service. Beautifully appointed throughout, with all amenities & superb spa. **Directions:** Exit M5 at junction 30. Follow A3052 signposted Sidmouth. All approach routes lead to Esplanade. **Bedrooms:** 22 single, 10 double, 30 twin, 8 family, 2 suites **Open:** Closed January

Site: P Payment: 💷 Leisure: ⏲ ♨ ♬ ⚲ Property: 🐎 🖧 🖥 ◐ Children: ⛵ ♨ 🎠 Catering: ✗ 🍴 🍽 Room: 📶 💧 🎄 📺 ♿

SOURTON, Devon   Map ref 1C2   SatNav EX20 4HH 🄷

Collaven Manor Hotel

Sourton, Okehampton EX20 4HH **T:** (01837) 861522 **F:** (01837) 861614
E: collavenmanor@supanet.com
W: collavenmanor.co.uk **£ BOOK ONLINE**

B&B PER ROOM PER NIGHT
D: £98.00 - £146.00
HB PER PERSON PER NIGHT
£67.00 - £84.00

Historic 15th century manor on edge of Dartmoor. Character bedrooms, log fires, four-posters and charming beamed lounges. Home-cooked food including vegetarian specialities. Three minutes from A30 yet located in four-acre grounds and surrounded by open countryside. Riding, fishing and golf nearby. **Directions:** Two miles south of the A30 along A386 on right-hand side, 0.5 miles past Sourton village. **Bedrooms:** 4 double, 2 twin, 1 family. **Open:** February to December

Site: ❋ Payment: 💷 € Leisure: 🎣 ♪ ⏲ ⏱ Property: ⚓ 🐎 🖧 🖥 Children: ⛵ ♨ 🎠 Catering: 🍴 🍽 Room: 📶 💧 🎄 🕤 📺 ♿ 🍳

TAVISTOCK, Devon   Map ref 1C2
SatNav PL16 0JE **B**

GUEST ACCOMMODATION ★★★★★

Gold AWARD

B&B PER ROOM PER NIGHT
S: £98.00
D: £150.00 – £155.00

Tor Cottage
Tor Cottage, Chillaton, Lifton, Devon PL16 0JE **T:** (01822) 860248 **F:** (01822) 860126
E: info@torcottage.co.uk
W: www.torcottage.co.uk **£ BOOK ONLINE**

Peace & tranquility in beautiful en suite bedsitting rooms each with logfire, fridge, terrace & private garden. Nestling in private valley adjacent to Dartmoor. 10 minute drive from Tavistock & Cornwall. Lovely garden, heated pool. **Directions:** In Chillaton drive up hill towards Tavistock. 300m on right you will see a Lane with a "Bridlepath" sign. Drive all the way to end of Lane to find us!
Bedrooms: En suite, flat screen TV, tea & coffee, Microwave
Open: All Year except Christmas and New Year

Site: ✿ P Payment: 💳 Leisure: ⚷ Property: 🛏 ⊘ Catering: 🍴 Room: ☎ ♨ 📺 📀

TORQUAY, Devon   Map ref 1D2
SatNav TQ2 5BA **B**

GUEST HOUSE ★★★

B&B PER ROOM PER NIGHT
S: £24.00 – £35.00
D: £48.00 – £60.00

Acorn Lodge
28 Bridge Road, Torquay TQ2 5BA **T:** (01803) 296939 **F:** (01803) 295984
E: enquiries@bnbtorquay.co.uk
W: http://www.bnbtorquay.co.uk **£ BOOK ONLINE**

Welcome to Acorn Lodge. Relax after your journey with a cup of tea/coffee and home baked biscuits or cake either in your room or on the sun terrace. We hope you have a wonderful stay.
Bedrooms: Single, double, triple & family rooms, all en suite
Open: All year

Site: ✿ P Payment: 💳 € Property: 🛏 Children: ⛹ 🛏 ☂ Catering: 🍴 Room: ☎ ♨ 📺 📀

TORQUAY, Devon   Map ref 1D2
SatNav TQ1 3LP **B**

GUEST ACCOMMODATION ★★★★

B&B PER ROOM PER NIGHT
S: £36.00 – £39.00
D: £72.00 – £78.00
EVENING MEAL PER PERSON
£17.00 – £24.00

Coombe Court
67 Babbacombe Downs Road, Torquay TQ1 3LP **T:** (01803) 327097 **F:** (01803) 327097
E: enquiries@coombecourthotel.co.uk
W: www.coombecourthotel.co.uk

Coombe Court is a family run establishment, situated in a level location just 50 yards from Babbacombe Downs, Babbacombe Theatre and the famous Cliff Railway. Within easy walking distance to St Marychurch and Wellswood. All bedrooms have en suite facilities, digital freeview TV, complimentary tea & coffee tray & free Wi-Fi. There is private off road parking, licensed bar, guests TV lounge and guest lounge with views over the garden, nearby woodland and Babbacombe Bay. Traditional cooking and optional evening meal available. We look forward to offering you a warm and friendly welcome at Coombe Court Guest House.

Directions: Please contact us for directions.

Bedrooms: 1 single, 10 double, 3 twin, 1 family
Open: All year except Christmas and New Year

Site: ✿ P Payment: 💳 Leisure: 🎱 ♪ ⚑ ♞ Property: 🛏 ⋈ Children: ⛹10 Catering: (✗ 🍷 🍴
Room: ☎ ♨ 📺 📀

TORQUAY, Devon Map ref 1D2

SatNav TQ2 6RH **H**

Corbyn Head Hotel

Sea Front, Torquay, Devon TQ2 6RH **T:** (01803) 213611 **F:** (01803) 296152
E: info@corbynhead.com
W: corbynhead.com **£ BOOK ONLINE**

B&B PER ROOM PER NIGHT
S: £35.00 - £110.00
D: £60.00 - £230.00
EVENING MEAL PER PERSON
£15.00 - £29.50

The Corbyn Head Hotel is one of Torquay's leading hotels with its seafront location. Many of the bedrooms boast sea views and have private balconies. Award-winning Restaurant with outstanding service, free WI-FI and free onsite parking. **Directions:** Torquay Seafront, turn right and follow signs for Cockington Village. Hotel on right. **Bedrooms:** 3 single, 29 dble, 10 twin, 3 family
Open: All year

Site: ✿ P Payment: 🖭 Leisure: ⚒ ✗ ⚯ ⚘ Property: ♟ ⚒ 🖵 🖫 ⛊ ◕ Children: ⚐ 🛏 ⚐ Catering: (✗ 🍷 🍽 Room: ⚒ ⚒ ⚒ 📺 ⚒

TORQUAY, Devon Map ref 1D2

SatNav TQ1 3LN **B**

The Downs, Babbacombe

Seafront, 41-43 Babbacombe Downs Road, Babbacombe, Torquay TQ1 3LN
T: (01803) 328543 **F:** (01803) 670557 **E:** enquiries@downshotel.co.uk
W: www.downshotel.co.uk **£ BOOK ONLINE**

B&B PER ROOM PER NIGHT
S: £57.00 - £69.00
D: £72.00 - £84.00
EVENING MEAL PER PERSON
£16.95 - £18.95

SPECIAL PROMOTIONS
Stay 3 or more nights & get 1 extra night free - available Jan, Feb & November. Stay 7 nights & get 5% off - accom only. Upgrade to ½ Board for 6 consecutive nights and get dinner free for 1 night.

The Downs, Babbacombe in Torquay is family run with 12 en suite rooms, 8 with balconies & uninterrupted sea views over Lyme Bay. We have a Lounge Bar & Restaurant serving optional evening meals and are fully licensed. We have an elegant feel whilst maintaining a comfortable and relaxed atmosphere. Dogs & children welcome.

WINNERS OF SOUTH DEVON TOURISM AND HOSPITALITY AWARDS 2013 - B&B, GUEST HOUSE AND INN OF THE YEAR.

Directions: M5 South to Torquay A380, at Torquay Harbour take left at r/a to Babbacombe. On entering Babbacombe take right turn into Princes Street, left onto Babbacombe Downs Rd, we are on the left.

Bedrooms: All bedrooms are fully en suite with simple yet stylish oak furniture & pocket sprung beds, luxurious toiletries & towels, in keeping with a 4*hotel.
Open: All year, Christmas breaks available

Site: P Payment: 🖭 Leisure: ▸ Property: ⚒ 🖵 🖫 Children: ⚐ 🛏 ⚐ Catering: (✗ 🍷 🍽
Room: ⚒ ⚒ ⚒ 📺

TORQUAY, Devon Map ref 1D2

SatNav TQ2 6QJ **H**

Livermead House Hotel

Torbay Road, Seafront, Torquay TQ2 6QJ **T:** (01803) 294361 **F:** (01803) 200758
E: info@livermead.com
W: www.livermead.com **£ BOOK ONLINE**

B&B PER ROOM PER NIGHT
S: £35.00 - £110.00
D: £60.00 - £230.00
HB PER PERSON PER NIGHT
£40.00 - £140.00

The Livermead House Hotel in Torquay, situated on the edge of the Cockington Valley was built in 1820 & is positioned on Torquay's sea front. The Hotel offers breathtaking sea views, beautifully manicured lawns and exceptionally high standards of service and cuisine from Award Winning Chef, Tony Hetherington.
Directions: Full directions and map available on our website.
Bedrooms: 7 single, 34 dble, 25 twin, 1 family, all en suite
Open: All year

Site: ✿ Payment: 🖭 Leisure: ⚒ ♪ ▸ ∪ ✗ ⚘ Property: ♟ ⚒ 🖵 🖫 ◕ Children: ⚐ 🛏 ⚐ Catering: 🍷
🍽 Room: ⚒ ⚒ ⚒ ⚒ 📺 ⚒ ⚒

The Osborne Hotel

Hesketh Crescent, Meadfoot Beach, Torquay TQ1 2LL **T:** (01803) 213311
F: (01803) 296788 **E:** enq@osborne-torquay.co.uk
W: osborne-torquay.co.uk **£ BOOK ONLINE**

B&B PER ROOM PER NIGHT
S: £65.00 - £105.00
D: £79.00 - £180.00
EVENING MEAL PER PERSON
£15.00 - £40.00

SPECIAL PROMOTIONS
Year round offers available, see website for details, or ring our friendly reception team.

The Osborne Hotel, known by the discerning as 'The Country House Hotel by the Sea', is the centrepiece of an elegant Regency crescent. Most Rooms provide panoramic views of the broad sweep of Torbay. There are 2 hotel restaurants, the gourmet Langtry's offering regional specialities, and the more informal Brasserie.

Directions: From Torquay harbour, turn left at clocktower signposted Meadfoot Beach, turn right at traffic lights. Follow road straight ahead to the bottom of the hill.

Bedrooms: 1 single, 16 dble, 5 twin, 2 family, 8 suite
Open: All year

Site: ✿ P Payment: 💳 Leisure: ♪ ▶ 🎿 ✕ 🏊 ⚕ ⛱ ⤢ ⚲ Property: ⚷ 🖥 📠 ◑ Children: 🧸 🛏 🪑
Catering: 🍴 🍽 Room: 🍵 ☕ 📞 📺 💻

The Somerville

515 Babbacombe Road, Torquay TQ1 1HJ **T:** (01803) 294755 **F:** (01803) 215810
E: stay@somervillehotel.co.uk
W: www.somervillehotel.co.uk **£ BOOK ONLINE**

B&B PER ROOM PER NIGHT
S: £55.00 - £110.00
D: £75.00 - £155.00

SPECIAL PROMOTIONS
Throughout the autumn and winter: Book 3 nights and get 50% of 3rd night. Book 4 nights and get 75% off 4th night.

The multi award winning Somerville is located in the centre of Torquay close to the harbour with its restaurants bars and cafes. Offering boutique style accommodation ranging from standard doubles to sumptuous sutes, The Somerville is ideal for visitors celebrating special occasions, The award winning breakfast has extended times at weekends for a more relaxed start to the day.

Directions: Follow signs to Torquay harbour.

Bedrooms: Hairdryers, irons and ironing boards, iPod docking stations, flat screen TVs.
Open: All year

Site: ✿ P Payment: 💳 Property: ⚷ 🖥 🅿 Children: 🧸 🛏 🪑 Catering: 🍴 🍽 Room: 🍵 ☕ 📺 💻

TORQUAY, Devon *Map ref 1D2*

Whitburn Guest House

Saint Lukes Road North, Torquay, Devon TQ2 5PD **T:** (01803) 296719
E: lazenby1210@btinternet.com
W: whitburnguesthouse.co.uk **£ BOOK ONLINE**

B&B PER ROOM PER NIGHT
S: £30.00 - £65.00
D: £45.00 - £65.00

Anne and Joe warmly welcome you to our clean comfortable guest house, 5 mins walk or local bus to harbour, beach, seafront, town centre shops, clubs, resturaunts. Lovely residential area, parking. Full cooked breakfast included in price. **Directions:** At Seafront go up Shedden Hill, take 2nd right into St Lukes Road, then 1st left into St Lukes Road North. Whitburn Guest House 150 metres on left. **Bedrooms:** 1 double, 1 twin, 3 family, en suite or private fac **Open:** All year

Site: **P** Payment: Leisure: Property: Children: Room:

TOTNES, Devon *Map ref 1D2*

Royal Seven Stars Hotel

The Plains, Totnes, Devon TQ9 5DD **T:** (01803) 862125 **F:** 01803 867925
E: enquiry@royalsevenstars.co.uk
W: www.royalsevenstars.co.uk

B&B PER ROOM PER NIGHT
S: £90.00 - £122.00
D: £125.00 - £156.00

Situated in the centre of beautiful Totnes, the Royal Seven Stars Hotel, a former coaching inn dating back to 1660, is ideally located close to the beautiful river Dart and is perfectly placed to enjoy everything South Devon has to offer. **Directions:** Please contact us for directions **Bedrooms:** 6 doubles, 2 twins, 1 single, 2 family, 10 double/twin **Open:** All Year

Site: **P** Payment: Leisure: Property: Children: Catering: Room:

WOOLACOMBE, Devon *Map ref 1C1*

Trimstone Manor Country House Hotel

Trimstone, Nr Woolacombe, Ilfracombe, North Devon EX34 8NR **T:** (01271) 862841
F: (01271) 863808 **E:** info@trimstone.co.uk
W: trimstone.co.uk **£ BOOK ONLINE**

B&B PER ROOM PER NIGHT
S: £42.00 - £75.00
D: £96.00 - £149.00
EVENING MEAL PER PERSON
£23.50 - £28.50

Trimstone Hotel is a beautiful Manor House in North Devon in 44 acres of gardens and countryside, within minutes of beaches such as Woolacombe, Saunton, Croyde. The Hotel boasts facilities including en suite bedrooms, Bar, Restaurant and indoor heated swimming pool. **Directions:** From Barnstaple drive north on A361 through Braunton. 3 miles after Knowle, beyond layby, turn left into Trimstone Lane. Hotel is 300 yards on left **Bedrooms:** 2 single, 12 double **Open:** All year

Site: Payment: Leisure: Property: Children: Catering: Room:

YELVERTON, Devon *Map ref 1C2*

Barnabas House B&B

Harrowbeer Lane, Yelverton PL20 6DY **T:** (01822) 853268
E: enquiries@barnabas-house.co.uk
W: barnabas-house.co.uk **£ BOOK ONLINE**

B&B PER ROOM PER NIGHT
S: £48.00 - £65.00
D: £70.00 - £90.00

A peaceful Edwardian residence, most rooms with views over Dartmoor. Clean spacious rooms with all modern amenities, and a delicious locally sourced breakfast. Ideal for walking, cycling or just relaxing. Free wi-fi and off-road parking **Directions:** A386 from Plymouth towards Tavistock. At the Yelverton roundabout, take the Princetown Road, then left into Harrowbeer Lane. Car park 100m down on the right. **Bedrooms:** 1 single, 4 double, 1 twin, 1 family **Open:** All year

Site: **P** Payment: Leisure: Property: Children: Catering: Room:

YELVERTON, Devon   Map ref 1C2 SatNav PL20 7RA **B**

GUEST ACCOMMODATION

B&B PER ROOM PER NIGHT
S: £65.00 - £75.00
D: £80.00 - £90.00

Overcombe House

Old Station Road, Horrabridge, Yelverton PL20 7RA **T:** (01822) 853501
E: enquiries@overcombehotel.co.uk
W: overcombehotel.co.uk **£ BOOK ONLINE**

Offering a warm, friendly welcome in relaxed, comfortable surroundings with a substantial breakfast using local & home-made produce. The dining room & some bedrooms enjoy stunning views of Dartmoor. Conveniently located for exploring the varied attractions of Devon & Cornwall, in particular Dartmoor National Park & the adjacent Tamar Valley. **Directions:** Located on edge of Horrabridge village just off A386 1 mile from Yelverton heading towards Tavistock. **Bedrooms:** 5 dble, 3 twin **Open:** All year

Site: ❀ P **Payment:** 💳 **Leisure:** 🎣 ♪ ⛵ ♢ **Property:** 🏠 **Catering:** 🍷 🍽
Room: 🖎 🕯 📺 ⚷

BRIDPORT, Dorset   Map ref 2A3 SatNav DT6 3LB **H**

HOTEL

B&B PER ROOM PER NIGHT
S: £82.00 - £122.00
D: £130.00 - £170.00

SPECIAL PROMOTIONS
Please check our website or call for our current offers.

Bridge House Hotel

115 East Street, Bridport, Dorset DT6 3LB **T:** (01308) 423371 **F:** (01308) 459573
E: info@bridgehousebridport.co.uk
W: bridgehousebridport.co.uk **£ BOOK ONLINE**

18th Century Georgian character town house, next to the river and its gardens. Offers quiet elegance, traditional ambience and friendly service. Elegant lounge, ten en suite bedrooms and a fully licensed wine bar, offering the ideal venue for functions, from parties to funerals, buffets to full bespoke menus, using fresh local quality produce. Free parking, near the town centre.

Directions: Located at the eastern end of Bridport's main street; 400m from the town centre and 200m before the roundabout on the right-hand side.

Bedrooms: 3 single, 3 double, 1 twin, 3 family
Open: All year

Site: ❀ P **Payment:** 💳 € **Leisure:** 🎣 ♪ ⛵ ♢ **Property:** 🍷 🐾 🖥 ♨ **Children:** 🚼 🛏 🎨
Catering: 🍷 🍽 **Room:** 🖎 🕯 ☎ 📶 📺

The Official Tourist Board Guide to **B&Bs and Hotels 2014**

BRIDPORT, Dorset   Map ref 2A3
SatNav DT6 4PE **B**

Dippers
42 Uploders, Bridport DT6 4PE **T:** (01308) 485504 / 07855 344121
E: liz@dipperswestdorset.co.uk
W: dipperswestdorset.co.uk **£ BOOK ONLINE**

B&B PER ROOM PER NIGHT
S: £30.00 - £35.00
D: £60.00 - £70.00
EVENING MEAL PER PERSON
£12.50

Dippers sits on the banks of the River Asker in the beautiful West Dorset village of Uploders. 2mls from Bridport: a wonderful location for exploring Jurassic Coast and Hardy Country.
Directions: Uploders is ½ mile north of the A35, 2 miles east of Bridport. Turn right at Crown Inn and Dippers is 200m on the left.
Bedrooms: 1 single, 1 double, 1 twin **Open:** All year

Site: ✿ P Property: 🐕 🚃 Children: 🛏 Catering: 🍴 Room: 🍷 ♨ ⊚ 📺

BRIDPORT, Dorset   Map ref 2A3
SatNav DT6 4EL **H**

Haddon House Hotel
West Bay, Bridport DT6 4EL **T:** (01308) 423626 / (01308) 425323 **F:** (01308) 427348
E: info@haddonhousehotel.co.uk
W: www.haddonhousehotel.co.uk

B&B PER ROOM PER NIGHT
S: £73.00 - £92.50
D: £82.50 - £130.00

Country house hotel, 300 yards from picturesque harbour, Jurassic Coast and 18 hole golf course at Westbay. Lounge bar and restaurant offering excellent cuisine. Ideally situated for Dorset, Devon and Somerset. **Directions:** At Bridport Crown Inn roundabout take the B3157 to Westbay. On entering Westbay, the Hotel can be found on the right hand side. **Bedrooms:** 2 single, 6 double, 4 twin, 2 family **Open:** All year

Site: ✿ Payment: 💷 Leisure: ♿ ♪ ⏸ ↻ Property: 🍴 🐕 🚃 🖥 Children: 🛏 🛏 🛁 Catering: 🍷 🍴 Room: 🍷 ♨ 📞 ⊚ 📺 🛁 🔌

BRIDPORT, Dorset   Map ref 2A3
SatNav DT6 3LY **B**

The Tiger Inn
14-16 Barrack Street, Bridport DT6 3LY **T:** (01308) 427543
E: jacquie@tigerinnbridport.co.uk
W: www.tigerinnbridport.co.uk

B&B PER ROOM PER NIGHT
D: £70.00 - £140.00

Traditional town centre freehouse inn, serving a selection of west country ales and ciders. Luxury en suite rooms with free Wi-Fi, flat-screen TV's, hairdryers, etc. Delicious locally sourced breakfast.
Directions: Please contact us for directions **Bedrooms:** 3 King, 2 family. **Open:** All year

Site: ✿ Payment: 💷 Leisure: ♿ ♪ ⏸ ↻ Property: 🚃 Children: 🛏 🛁 Catering: 🍷 🍴 Room: 🍷 ♨ ⊚ 📺

CHARMINSTER, Dorset   Map ref 2B3
SatNav DT2 9QT **B**

The Three Compasses
The Square, Charminster, Dorchester DT2 9QT **T:** (01305) 263618

Traditional village inn with skittle alley set in village square. Lunch and evening meals provided. Please contact us for prices.
Directions: Please contact us for directions **Bedrooms:** 1 single, 1 double, 1 twin, 1 en suite **Open:** All year except Christmas

Site: P Leisure: ⏸ Property: 🐕 Children: 🛏 Catering: (✗ 🍷 Room: ♨ 📺

Druid House

26 Sopers Lane, Christchurch BH23 1JE **T:** (01202) 485615 **F:** (01202) 473484
E: reservations@druid-house.co.uk
W: druid-house.co.uk

B&B PER ROOM PER NIGHT
S: £50.00 - £90.00
D: £80.00 - £135.00

SPECIAL PROMOTIONS
Weekend 3 day breaks
£119-£130 pp
3 night stay. Weekday
breaks available upon
request. November -
March inc. Prices based
on 2 people sharing

Overlooking park, this delightful family-run establishment is just a stroll from the High Street, Priory and Quay. Bedrooms, some with balconies, are modern and very comfortably furnished, with many welcome extras, iPod docking, flat screen tv with dvd/cd, Wi-Fi access. Beautiful rear garden, patio and relaxing lounge and bar areas.

Directions: A35 exit Christchurch main round about onto Sopers Lane, establishment on the left. Christchurch train station 10 min walk and Bournemouth International Airport 3 miles.

Bedrooms: 1 single, 4 double, 2 twin, 2 family
Open: All year

Site: ✿ **P Payment:** 📇 **Leisure:** ♨ ♪ ▶ ♉ **Property:** 🛏 **Children:** ⏳ 🎮 ⚒ **Catering:** 🍷 🍽
Room: 🔌 ✆ ⓦ 📺 📀 ⛓

Looking for something else?

The official and most comprehensive guide to independently inspected, star rated accommodation.

B&Bs and Hotels - B&Bs, Hotels, farmhouses, inns, serviced apartments, campus and hostel accommodation in England.

Self Catering - Self-catering holiday homes, approved caravan holiday homes, boat accommodation and holiday cottage agencies in England.

Camping, Touring and Holiday Parks - Touring parks, camping holidays and holiday parks and villages in Britain.

Now available in all good bookshops and online at **www.hudsons.co.uk/shop**

CRANBORNE, Dorset   Map ref 2B3
SatNav BH21 5PR **B**

La Fosse at Cranborne
London House, The Square, Cranborne, Wimborne BH21 5PR **T:** (01725) 517604
E: lafossemail@gmail.com
W: www.la-fosse.com **£ BOOK ONLINE**

B&B PER ROOM PER NIGHT
S: £65.00
D: £115.00
EVENING MEAL PER PERSON
£22.00 - £27.50

SPECIAL PROMOTIONS
Dinner, Bed and
Breakfast rate
Short Break
Long term stay

Mark and Emmanuelle would like to extend a very warm welcome to you and invite you to experience our homely Restaurant with Rooms in this beautiful countryside of Dorset. Providing six quality accommodations, as well as delicious home cooked dinners with friendly and efficient service, in comfortable idyllic rural surroundings. The perfect base for exploring Dorset, Wiltshire and Hampshire, as we are located in Cranborne village centre, on the boundary of these historic counties. We are also open for dinner Monday to Saturday and lunch for private larger parties.

Directions: M27 towards Bournemouth, Ringwood. Exit to Verwood. Through Verwood, signs for Cranborne. In Cranborne, pass Fleur de Lys pub, left into Square. We are on right in the Square. Park in Square. No parking restrictions.

Bedrooms: 2 double, 2 twin, 1 family, 1 suite
Open: All Year

Site: ✿ **Payment:** 💳 **Leisure:** ⚓ ♪ ⚑ ♺ **Property:** 🖥 **Children:** ♿ ≬ **Catering:** ♟ 🍽
Room: 🗝 💧 📞 📻 📺

DORCHESTER, Dorset   Map ref 2B3
SatNav DT1 2ES **B**

Aquila Heights Guest House
44 Maiden Castle Road, Dorchester, Dorset DT1 2ES **T:** (01305) 267145
E: enquiries@aquilaheights.co.uk
W: www.aquilaheights.co.uk **£ BOOK ONLINE**

B&B PER ROOM PER NIGHT
S: £38.00 - £45.00
D: £69.00 - £84.00

Superb en suite accommodation. Happy to welcome both tourists and business guests for short or longer stays and offer competitive room rates for all visitors. Comfortable and relaxed atmosphere. Excellent breakfast menu. Local produce. **Directions:** From town centre follow Weymouth signs then 3rd right after the lights by Maumbury Rings. From A35 turn on to the B3147 then first left. 600m on right **Bedrooms:** LCD TV + Freeview. Hospitality tray. Free Wi-Fi **Open:** All Year but Room Only over Christmas

Site: ✿ P **Payment:** 💳 **Leisure:** ⚑ **Property:** 🖥 🏠 ♺ **Children:** ♿ 🛏 ≬ **Catering:** 🍽
Room: 🗝 💧 📺 ♿

DORCHESTER, Dorset   Map ref 2B3
SatNav DT1 1UP **H**

Wessex Royale Hotel
32 High West Street, Dorchester DT1 1UP **T:** (01305) 262660 **F:** (01305) 251941
E: info@wessexroyalehotel.co.uk
W: wessexroyalehotel.co.uk **£ BOOK ONLINE**

B&B PER ROOM PER NIGHT
S: £85.00 - £109.00
D: £99.00 - £185.00
HB PER PERSON PER NIGHT
£74.50 - £104.50

A delightful Georgian building with 27 comfortable en suite rooms. Guests can relax in the cosy lounge area and our Ã la carte restaurant is open from 6pm each evening. **Directions:** Please see our website for map & full directions. **Bedrooms:** 2 single, 15 dble, 5 twin, 2 family, 3 suite **Open:** All year except Christmas and New Year

Site: ✿ **Payment:** 💳 **Leisure:** ⚓ ♪ ⚑ ♺ **Property:** ♟ 🖥 ◐ **Children:** ♿ 🛏 ≬ **Catering:** ♟ 🍽
Room: 🗝 💧 📞 📻 📺 ♿ 🍽

EYPE, Dorset   Map ref 1D2   SatNav DT6 6AL   H

Eype's Mouth Country Hotel
Eype, Bridport DT6 6AL **T:** (01308) 423300 **F:** (01308) 420033
E: info@eypesmouthhotel.co.uk
W: eypesmouthhotel.co.uk **£ BOOK ONLINE**

B&B PER ROOM PER NIGHT
S: £75.00 - £100.00
D: £105.00 - £125.00
EVENING MEAL PER PERSON
£26.00 - £28.00

Picturesque village of Eype, Bridport amidst downland and cliff tops of Heritage Coastline. Stunning sea views, lovely walking nearby, excellent hospitality, food and drink, in peaceful surroundings of family-run hotel. Perfect for relaxing. **Directions:** A35, Bridport bypass, take turning to Eype, also signed to service area, then 3rd right to beach. Hotel 0.5 miles down lane. **Bedrooms:** 1 single, 12 dble, 3 twin, 1 family **Open:** All year

Site: ❀ Payment: 📇 € Leisure: 🚲 ♪ ♪ ♾ Property: ⚡ 🐾 ☰ Children: 🍼 ♨ 🎠 Catering: ♟ 🍴
Room: 🛏 ✋ ☎ 📺 🖥

SHAFTESBURY, Dorset   Map ref 2B3   SatNav SP7 8AE   B

The Retreat
47 Bell Street, Shaftesbury, Dorset SP7 8AE **T:** (01747) 850372 **E:** info@the-retreat.co.uk
W: the-retreat.co.uk

B&B PER ROOM PER NIGHT
S: £52.00 - £55.00
D: £80.00 - £88.00

SPECIAL PROMOTIONS
Special promotions available upon request.

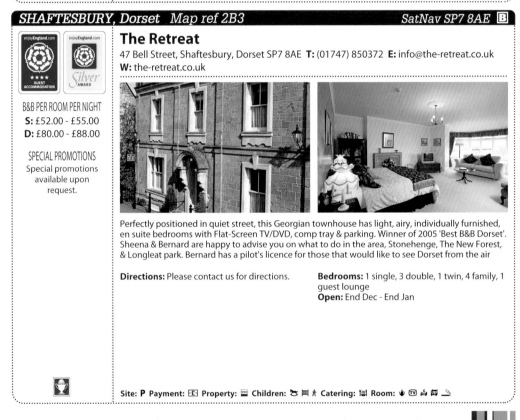

Perfectly positioned in quiet street, this Georgian townhouse has light, airy, individually furnished, en suite bedrooms with Flat-Screen TV/DVD, comp tray & parking. Winner of 2005 'Best B&B Dorset'. Sheena & Bernard are happy to advise you on what to do in the area, Stonehenge, The New Forest, & Longleat park. Bernard has a pilot's licence for those that would like to see Dorset from the air

Directions: Please contact us for directions.

Bedrooms: 1 single, 3 double, 1 twin, 4 family, 1 guest lounge
Open: End Dec - End Jan

Site: P Payment: 📇 Property: ☰ Children: 🍼 ♨ 🎠 Catering: 🍴 Room: ♨ 📺 🖥 🖥 ✎

Book your accommodation online

Visit our new 2014 guide websites for detailed information, up-to-date availability and to book your accommodation online. Includes over 20,000 places to stay, all of them star rated.
www.visitor-guides.co.uk

Corner Meadow

24 Victoria Avenue, Swanage BH19 1AP **T:** (01929) 423493 **E:** geogios@hotmail.co.uk
W: www.cornermeadow.co.uk

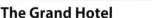

BED & BREAKFAST

B&B PER ROOM PER NIGHT
S: £54.00 - £64.00
D: £68.00 - £86.00

Family run bed and breakfast in Swanage. All you should expect from a Visit Britain four star establishment. High quality rooms, facilities and breakfast. Everyone welcome. 4* AA approved. **Directions:** We are situated in Victoria Avenue Swanage opposite the main beach car park, five minutes level walk from blue flag beach, town and steam railway. **Bedrooms:** 2 double, 1 twin, 1 family **Open:** All year except 31 Oct to 1 Mar

Site: ❀ **P** **Leisure:** ⚑ ♪ ⚐ ∪ **Property:** ⊟ **Children:** ⚑ ⊞ ⚐ **Catering:** ⚑ **Room:** ⚐ ⚐ ⚐ ⚐

The Grand Hotel

Burlington Road, Swanage BH19 1LU **T:** (01929) 423353 **F:** (01929) 427068
E: reservations@grandhotelswanage.co.uk
W: www.grandhotelswanage.co.uk

HOTEL

B&B PER ROOM PER NIGHT
S: £55.00 - £80.00
D: £75.00 - £160.00
HB PER PERSON PER NIGHT
£73.00 - £98.00

The Grand Hotel, Swanage is a classic Victorian seaside hotel that nestles in the heart of the beautiful Isle of Purbeck and dates back to 1898. The Hotel, The Coast restaurant and Lounge Bar command spectacular views across Swanage Bay and Peveril Point and many of the bedrooms and public areas take advantage of these delightful views. Direct access from the gardens to our private beach. Available for weddings, conferences and exclusive use. Health spa including indoor pool, spa bath, sauna and a large gymnasium. Group accommodation available. Free Wi-Fi available. Prices are based on a standard room. Sea view rooms will incur a supplement.

Directions: Please see the 'Getting Here' page on our website for directions.

Bedrooms: 3 Single, 17 Double, 8 Twin and 2 Family - All en suite.
Open: All year

Site: ❀ **Payment:** 🔲 **Leisure:** ♪ ⚐ ∪ ☀ ⚑ **Property:** ⚑ ⚑ ⊟ ⚐ ● **Children:** ⚑ ⊞ ⚐ **Catering:** ⚑ ⚑ **Room:** ⚐ ⚐ ⚐ ⚐ ⚐

The Pines Hotel

Burlington Road, Swanage BH19 1LT **T:** (01929) 425211 **F:** (01929) 422075
E: reservations@pineshotel.co.uk
W: www.pineshotel.co.uk **£ BOOK ONLINE**

HOTEL

B&B PER ROOM PER NIGHT
S: £70.00
D: £140.00 - £190.00
EVENING MEAL PER PERSON
£6.00 - £30.00

Family-run hotel in Purbeck countryside at quiet end of Swanage Bay. Access to beach for walks encompassing coastal views. Friendly staff, refurbished sea-facing lounges and highly acclaimed seaview restaurant. **Directions:** A351 to seafront. Turn left then 2nd or 3rd turn on your right (either Victoria road or Burlington road).We are at the end of these roads. **Bedrooms:** 2 single, 15 dbl, 8 twin, 8 family, 8 suite **Open:** All year

Site: ❀ **P** **Payment:** 🔲 **Leisure:** ⚑ ♪ ⚐ ∪ **Property:** ⚑ ⚑ ⊟ ⚐ ⚑ ● **Children:** ⚑ ⊞ ⚐ **Catering:** (✗ ⚑ ⚑ **Room:** ⚐ ⚐ ⚐ ⚐ ⚐

WAREHAM, Dorset   *Map ref 2B3*   SatNav BH20 5NU **B**

★★★★ FARMHOUSE • *Gold* AWARD

B&B PER ROOM PER NIGHT
S: £65.00 - £70.00
D: £80.00 - £85.00

Bradle Farmhouse

Bradle Farm, Church Knowle, Wareham, Dorset BH20 5NU **T:** (01929) 480712
F: (01929) 481144 **E:** info@bradlefarmhouse.co.uk
W: www.bradlefarmhouse.co.uk

Picturesque farmhouse set in the heart of Purbeck. Fine views of Corfe Castle and surrounding countryside, with many spectacular walks. Large spacious rooms, delicious breakfast with home produce and a warm welcome assured. Local pub 1 mile. **Directions:** A351 from Wareham to Corfe Castle. At Corfe take a right turn at the foot of the castle signed Church Knowle. After Church Knowle turn left 1 mile **Bedrooms:** Spacious rooms all en suite, TVs, Tea & coffee facilities. **Open:** All Year except Christmas

Site: ❀ **P** Property: ▦ ⌀ Room: ☜ ♨ TV

BARNSLEY, Gloucestershire   *Map ref 2B1*   SatNav GL7 5EE **H**

★★★★ COUNTRY HOUSE HOTEL • *Gold* AWARD

B&B PER ROOM PER NIGHT
S: £262.00 - £582.00
D: £280.00 - £600.00

Barnsley House

Barnsley, Cirencester, Barnsley GL7 5EE **T:** (01285) 740000
E: reception@barnsleyhouse.com
W: barnsleyhouse.com

Luxury 18 bedroom hotel, once the home of the late famous garden designer Rosemary Verey. Beautiful Cotswold house built in 1697 set in stunning gardens, with contemporary bedrooms. We now have a hydrotherapy pool. Weekend prices vary. **Directions:** Centre of Barnsley, on the B4425 (Cirencester to Bibury and Burford road), 4m NE of Cirencester. **Open:** All year

Site: ❀ **P** Payment: 💷 Leisure: ♿ ♪ ♂ ∪ ⋈ ✂ Property: ♜ ⌐ ▦ 🗄 ♬ ◐ ⌀ Children: ☖¹⁴ ▥ ⚹ Catering: (✗ 🍷 🍴 Room: ☜ ♨ ✆ 📻 TV 📀 📠 🛏

BIBURY, Gloucestershire   *Map ref 2B1*   SatNav GL7 5NW **H**

★★★★ HOTEL • *Gold* AWARD

B&B PER ROOM PER NIGHT
D: £160.00 - £325.00
HB PER PERSON PER NIGHT
£120.00 - £220.00

Swan Hotel

Bibury, Near Cirencester, Gloucestershire GL7 5NW **T:** (01285) 740695 **F:** (01285) 740473
E: info@swanhotel.co.uk
W: cotswold-inns-hotels.co.uk/swan **£ BOOK ONLINE**

The Swan Hotel is an enchanting 17th century former coaching inn sitting in the heart of Bibury on the banks of the River Coln. Friendly atmosphere, wonderful food and wine. **Directions:** M5 jct 11, A40 (signposted Cheltenham) for 23 miles. Right onto B4425 (signposted Bibury). Once in Bibury, The Swan is on the right. **Bedrooms:** 12 dble, 5 twin, 1 family, 4 suite **Open:** All year

Site: ❀ Payment: 💷 Leisure: ♪ Property: ♜ ⌐ ▦ 🗄 ◐ Children: ☖ ▥ ⚹ Catering: 🍷 🍴 Room: ☜ ♨ ✆ TV 📠 🛏

Need more information?

Visit our new 2014 guide websites for detailed information, up-to-date availability and to book your accommodation online. Includes over 20,000 places to stay, all of them star rated.

www.visitor-guides.co.uk

BOURTON-ON-THE-WATER, Gloucestershire Map ref 2B1 SatNav GL54 2AZ B

BED & BREAKFAST ★★★

B&B PER ROOM PER NIGHT
S: £45.00
D: £60.00

Trevone Bed & Breakfast
Moore Road, Bourton-on-the-Water GL54 2AZ **T:** 07740 805250
E: trevonebandb@gmail.com
W: trevonebb.co.uk **£ BOOK ONLINE**

Cotswold stone house ideally situated for exploring the picturesque and historic delights of the Cotswolds. Within one minute walk from the village centre. **Directions:** Please contact us for directions. **Bedrooms:** 2 double **Open:** All year

Site: P Payment: 🖭 Leisure: 🛠 ♪ ▶ ∪ Property: 🚗 Children: 🐾10 Catering: 🍴 Room: 🔌 ♨ 📺

BRISTOL, Gloucestershire Map ref 2A2 SatNav BS13 8AG B

GUEST ACCOMMODATION ★★★

B&B PER ROOM PER NIGHT
S: £65.00 - £75.00
D: £75.00 - £85.00

EVENING MEAL PER PERSON
£9.50 - £19.50

SPECIAL PROMOTIONS
Stay Fri and Sat night and get Sunday night free (incl Bank Holiday weekends).

The Town & Country Lodge
A38 Bridgwater Road, Bristol BS13 8AG **T:** (01275) 392441 **F:** (01275) 393362
E: reservations@tclodge.co.uk
W: www.tclodge.co.uk

Highly comfortable lodge offering genuine value for money. Splendid, rural location on the A38 only three miles from central Bristol and handy for airport, Bath, Weston and all major, local attractions. Excellent restaurant offering bar menus. Ideal for functions, wedding receptions and conferences.

Directions: Situated on A38 halfway between Airport and city centre. From North M5 exit J18 Avonmouth. A4 Bristol Airport. From South exit M5 J22. A38 Bristol.

Bedrooms: 4 single, 11 double, 14 twin, 7 family
Open: All year except Christmas

Site: ❀ P Payment: 🖭 Leisure: ♪ ▶ Property: 🚗 Children: 🐾 ⚘ Catering: 🍷 🍴
Room: 🔌 ♨ 📞 📻 📺 🛁

CIRENCESTER, Gloucestershire Map ref 2B1 SatNav GL7 2DG H

HOTEL ★★★

B&B PER ROOM PER NIGHT
S: £55.00 - £80.00
D: £65.00 - £120.00

HB PER PERSON PER NIGHT
£55.00 - £85.00

Corinium Hotel & Restaurant
Gloucester Street, Cirencester GL7 2DG **T:** (01285) 659711 **F:** (01285) 885807
E: info@coriniumhotel.co.uk
W: www.coriniumhotel.co.uk **£ BOOK ONLINE**

Delightful 16th century hotel quietly situated, though 5 mins walk from town. Offers character bedrooms, locally renowned restaurant and cosy bar full of Cotswold charm. Free parking and attractive garden. **Directions:** Follow ring road round town, signs to Cheltenham (A435). At traffic lights turn left, Spitalgate Lane then 1st right. Car park 50 metres on left.
Bedrooms: 1 single, 10 dble, 2 twin, 2 family **Open:** All year

Site: ❀ Payment: 🖭 € Leisure: ♪ ▶ ∪ Property: 🐾 🚗 Children: 🐾 🍴 ⚘ Catering: 🍷 🍴 Room: 🔌 ♨ 📞 📻 📺 🛁 🎮

CIRENCESTER, Gloucestershire   Map ref 2B1
SatNav GL7 1LF **B**

B&B PER ROOM PER NIGHT
S: £55.50 - £65.50
D: £71.00 - £81.00
EVENING MEAL PER PERSON
£10.00 - £21.00

SPECIAL PROMOTIONS
Special group discounts are available at weekends. Ideal for clubs and societies.

Riverside House
Watermoor, Cirencester GL7 1LF **T:** (01285) 647642 **F:** (01285) 647615
E: riversidehouse@mitsubishi-cars.co.uk
W: riversidehouse.org.uk **£ BOOK ONLINE**

Located 15 minutes walk from the centre of the historic market town of Cirencester with easy access to and from M4/M5 and the Cotswolds. Riverside House is fully licensed and provides superb bed and breakfast for private and corporate guests. Built in the grounds of Mitsubishi UK headquarters.

Directions: Located just off A419 opposite the Tesco superstore.

Bedrooms: 15 double, 9 twin
Open: All year

Site: ✿ P Payment: 💳 Leisure: 🏊 ♪ ▶ ♨ Property: 🖥 Children: ⚓ Catering: ♟ 🍴
Room: 📞 ♨ ☎ 🕻 📺

DOWN HATHERLEY, Gloucestershire   Map ref 2B1
SatNav GL2 9QB **B**

B&B PER ROOM PER NIGHT
S: £50.00 - £55.00
D: £90.00 - £120.00

Newbridge House Bed & Breakfast
Down Hatherley Lane, Down Hatherley, Gloucester GL2 9QB **T:** (01452) 730404
E: info@newbridgehouse.co.uk
W: www.newbridgehouse.co.uk **£ BOOK ONLINE**

Hidden from the beaten track Newbridge House nestles within five acres of beautiful private gardens. Despite its sense of privacy we are just ten minutes away from Gloucester and Cheltenham.

Directions: M5 Junction 11 left to Cheltenham, follow B4063, right into Down Hatherley Lane, follow lane to Z bend, church on left, next right, follow drive.

Bedrooms: 3 double, 1 suite
Open: Open from March to Mid December

Site: ✿ P Payment: 💳 Leisure: ▶ Property: 🖥 Children: ⚓12 Catering: ♟ 🍴
Room: 📞 ♨ ☎ 📺 🍴 🖥 ⬚

FRAMPTON-ON-SEVERN, Gloucestershire   Map ref 2B1   SatNav GL2 7EP B

Bell Inn

The Green, Frampton-on-Severn GL2 7EP **T:** (01452) 740346
E: relax@thebellatframpton.co.uk
W: thebellatframpton.co.uk

INN ★★★★

B&B PER ROOM PER NIGHT
S: £50.00 - £60.00
D: £70.00 - £90.00
EVENING MEAL PER PERSON
£8.95 - £16.95

Lying at the top of the largest green in England in the centre of the beautiful village of Frampton. The Bell has undergone major refurbishment and transformation and is now a contemporary-designed, welcoming pub and restaurant with gastro food. The rooms are large and well equipped, overlooking the village green. **Directions:** Exit jct 13 M5 onto A38 towards Bristol. Two miles to Frampton-on-Severn. **Bedrooms:** 2 double, 2 suite **Open:** All year except Christmas

Site: ✿ P Payment: 💷 Leisure: ♿ 🍴 ☾ Property: 🖥 🅰 Children: 🛏 ♿ Catering: ☕ 🍴 Room: 📺 🛁 ☕

GUITING POWER, Gloucestershire   Map ref 2B1   SatNav GL54 5TZ B

Guiting Guest House

Post Office Lane (formerly Cow Pat Lane), Guiting Power, Gloucestershire GL54 5TZ
T: (01451) 850470 **E:** guiting.guesthouse@virgin.net
W: guitingguesthouse.com **£ BOOK ONLINE**

GUEST HOUSE ★★★★
Silver AWARD

B&B PER ROOM PER NIGHT
S: £67.00 - £90.00
D: £80.00 - £90.00
EVENING MEAL PER PERSON
£18.00 - £34.00

Converted 16thC Cotswold-stone farmhouse in centre of delightful village. Dining room with polished elm floor and inglenook fireplace. Some rooms have four-poster beds, all have colour TV, and touches of luxury. **Directions:** See our website for map/directions. **Bedrooms:** 4 double, 1 twin **Open:** All year

Site: ✿ P Payment: 💷 Leisure: ♿ 🍴 ☾ Property: 🐾 🖥 🅰 Children: 🛏 ♿ Catering: 🍴
Room: 📺 🛁 📺 🛁 ☕

MORETON-IN-MARSH, Gloucestershire   Map ref 2B1   SatNav GL56 0LJ H

Manor House Hotel

High Street, Moreton-in-Marsh GL56 0LJ **T:** (01608) 650501 **F:** (01608) 651481
E: info@manorhousehotel.info
W: cotswold-inns-hotels.co.uk/manor **£ BOOK ONLINE**

HOTEL ★★★★
Gold AWARD

B&B PER ROOM PER NIGHT
S: £138.00 - £178.00
D: £178.00 - £198.00
HB PER PERSON PER NIGHT
£118.00 - £214.00

Historic Manor House Hotel, tastefully furnished in country house style, formerly a 16th Century manor. Award winning Mulberry Restaurant overlooks sun terrace and garden. Unwind with afternoon tea in the traditional gardens. **Directions:** M40 junction 15, follow A429 for approx. 22 miles. The hotel is on the left-hand side. **Bedrooms:** 1 single, 24 dble, 8 twin, 2 suite **Open:** All year

Site: ✿ Payment: 💷 Leisure: ♿ 🍴 ☾ Property: ☕ 🐾 🖥 🅰 ◐ Children: 🛏 ♿ Catering: ☕ 🍴
Room: 📺 🛁 ☕ 📺 🛁 ☕

Win amazing prizes, every month...

Visit our new 2014 guide websites for detailed information, up-to-date availability and to book your accommodation online. Includes over 20,000 places to stay, all of them star rated.

**Enter our monthly competition at
www.visitor-guides.co.uk/prizes**

For **key to symbols** see page 7

STOW-ON-THE-WOLD, Gloucestershire   Map ref 2B1   SatNav GL54 1AF H

SMALL HOTEL

Old Stocks Hotel, Restaurant & Bar

The Square, Stow on the Wold GL54 1AF **T:** (01451) 830666 **F:** (01451) 870014
E: welcome@oldstockshotel.co.uk
W: oldstockshotel.co.uk

17th century family run 18 (en suite) bedroom hotel. Modern-day comforts combined with the hotel's original charm, large patio garden (including 3 en suite 'garden' rooms), mouth-watering menus and friendly staff make this an ideal base for touring the Cotswolds. Budget Breaks; Christmas and New Year Breaks are available. Please contact us for prices. **Directions:** Centrally located in Stow-on-the-Wold, 18 miles from Cheltenham. **Bedrooms:** 1 single, 12 dble, 2 twin, 3 family **Open:** All year

Site: ✿ P Payment: ⛌ Leisure: ⚓ ► ʊ Property: ⛾ ⛛ 🖥 ♨ ⌀ Children: ⛱ ⛳ ⚐ Catering: ⟨✗ ⚈ ⛾
Room: ⛾ ♨ ℂ ⛿ TV ⛾

STROUD, Gloucestershire   Map ref 2B1   SatNav GL5 5PA B

BED & BREAKFAST **Gold AWARD**

1 Woodchester Lodge

Southfield Road, Woodchester, Stroud GL5 5PA **T:** (01453) 872586
E: anne@woodchesterlodge.co.uk
W: woodchesterlodge.co.uk

B&B PER ROOM PER NIGHT
S: £50.00 - £55.00
D: £75.00 - £80.00
EVENING MEAL PER PERSON
£7.00 - £20.00

Historic, Victorian timber merchant's property; peaceful village setting near Cotswold Way. Attractive gardens, parking, spacious and comfortable rooms, separate TV lounge/dining room. Meals cooked by qualified chef using our own produce and eggs. **Directions:** From Stroud/M5, take A46 towards Bath. Pass the Old Fleece pub. Right into Selsley Road. 2nd left, Southfield Road. 200yds on left-hand side. **Bedrooms:** 2 double, 1 family. **Open:** All year except Christmas, New Year and Easter.

 Site: ✿ P Payment: ⛌ Leisure: ► ʊ Property: 🖥 🖫 Children: ⛱ Catering: ⛾ Room: ⛾ ♨ TV

STROUD, Gloucestershire   Map ref 2B1   SatNav GL5 5AF B

INN

The Amberley Inn

Culver Hill, Amberley, Stroud, Gloucestershire GL5 5AF **T:** (01453) 872565
E: trevor@theamberleyinn.co.uk
W: www.theamberleyinn.co.uk

B&B PER ROOM PER NIGHT
S: £65.00 - £85.00
D: £85.00 - £125.00
EVENING MEAL PER PERSON
£12.95 - £30.00

A fine example of a traditional Country Inn situated in the heart of the Cotswolds. Only ten minutes drive from J13 of M5, The Amberley Inn sits proudly overlooking the famous Woodchester Valley in an area of outstanding natural beauty. **Bedrooms:** En suite, Wi-Fi, Tea & Coffee, flat screen TV. **Open:** All Year

WALKERS CYCLISTS
WALKERS CYCLISTS

Site: ✿ P Payment: ⛌ Leisure: ► Property: ⚐ ⛛ 🖥 🖫 ♨ ⌀ Children: ⛱ ⛳ ⚐
Catering: ⟨✗ ⚈ ⛾ Room: ⛾ ♨ ℂ ⛿ TV

STROUD, Gloucestershire   Map ref 2B1   SatNav GL5 5DE H

HOTEL **Gold AWARD**

The Bear of Rodborough Hotel

Rodborough Common, Stroud GL5 5DE **T:** (01453) 878522 **F:** (01453) 872523
E: info@bearofrodborough.info
W: cotswold-inns-hotels.co.uk/bear **£ BOOK ONLINE**

B&B PER ROOM PER NIGHT
S: £85.00 - £95.00
D: £140.00 - £250.00
HB PER PERSON PER NIGHT
£102.00 - £157.00

Former 17th century coaching inn offering comfortable accommodation in an area of outstanding beauty. Many original features and the en suite bedrooms are exquisite, blending traditional architecture with luxurious interiors. **Directions:** From M5 junction 13, take A419 to Stroud. Turn onto A46, follow Bear Hill. At crossroads Bear is on the right. **Bedrooms:** 8 single, 19 dble, 18 twin, 1 suite **Open:** All year

Site: ✿ Payment: ⛌ Leisure: ⚓ ► ʊ Property: ⚐ ⛛ 🖥 🖫 ● Children: ⛱ ⛳ ⚐ Catering: ⚈ ⛾
Room: ⛾ ♨ ℂ TV ⛾ ⛾

The Old Coach House

Dr. Crouch's Road, Eastcombe, Stroud GL6 7EA **T:** (01452) 771196
E: admin@oldcoachhousebandb.co.uk
W: oldcoachhousebandb.co.uk/

B&B PER ROOM PER NIGHT
S: £60.00
D: £80.00
EVENING MEAL PER PERSON
£15.00 - £20.00

The Old Coach House, was originally built as the stabling and coach house for the local doctor. Only four miles from the busy market town of Stroud with its award winning weekly Farmers Market, and the delightful Market Town of Nailsworth. Also within easy reach of the historic Roman Cirencester. All major credit and debit cards accepted.

Directions: From the London direction, take the M4 to junction 15 Swindon, and then the A417 to Cirencester. Pick up the A419 for Stroud and follow for about 8 miles. From the South west or Midlands, take Junction 13 off the M5 for Stroud. Once on the very outskirts of the Town Centre, pick up the A419 for Cirencester.

Bedrooms: Two en suite, one on ground floor, suitable for guests with mobility issues.
Open: All year

Site: ❄ P Payment: 💷 Leisure: ▶ Property: 🏠 Children: 🛏 ♿ Catering: 🍴 Room: 📺

Pretoria Villa

Wells Road, Eastcombe, Stroud GL6 7EE **T:** (01452) 770435
E: pretoriavilla@btinternet.com
W: bedandbreakfast-cotswold.co.uk **£ BOOK ONLINE**

B&B PER ROOM PER NIGHT
S: £40.00
D: £60.00 - £70.00

Enjoy luxurious bed and breakfast in a relaxed family country house, set in peaceful secluded gardens. Spacious bedrooms with many home comforts. Guest lounge with TV. Superb breakfast served at your leisure. An excellent base from which to explore the Cotswolds. Personal service and your comfort guaranteed.
Directions: At bottom of village green in Eastcombe take the lane with the red telephone box, at first crossroad very sharp right. 400yds on right. **Bedrooms:** 1 double, 2 twin. All bedrooms are en suite **Open:** All year except Christmas

Site: ❄ P Leisure: ▶ U Property: 🏠 Children: 🛏 ♿ Catering: 🍴 Room: 📺

Star Inn

Main Road, Whiteshill, Stroud GL6 6AE **T:** (01453) 765321
E: whiteshillstarinn@btconnect.com
W: www.the-star-inn-whiteshill.co.uk

B&B PER ROOM PER NIGHT
D: £60.00 - £100.00

17th Century Village Inn, Stroud. CAMRA 2012 Pub of Year. 4 real ales served straight from the barrel. Great views, glorious walks on the doorstep. Annual beer festival. Featured in Good Beer Guide 3rd Successive year. **Directions:** 4 Star accommodation close to the Cotswold Way. Between Stroud and Gloucester. Easy reach of Cheltenham. 3 miles M5 Junction, 13.1 mile Stroud rail station. **Bedrooms:** 1 double, 1 twin, 2 x 2 room suite. **Open:** All year

Site: ❄ P Payment: 💷 € Property: 🏠 Children: 🛏 Catering: 🍴 Room: 📺

TETBURY, Gloucestershire Map ref 2B2 SatNav GL8 8YJ Ⓗ

Calcot Manor Hotel & Spa
Tetbury, Gloucestershire GL8 8YJ **T:** (01666) 890391 **F:** (01666) 890394
E: reception@calcotmanor.co.uk
W: www.calcotmanor.co.uk **£ BOOK ONLINE**

B&B PER ROOM PER NIGHT
S: £280.00 - £490.00
D: £280.00 - £490.00

A 17thC manor house quietly situated in south Cotswolds with relaxing atmosphere amidst elegant surroundings. **Directions:** 3 miles West of Tetbury on A4135 **Bedrooms:** 7 dble, 15 twin, 12 family, 1 suite **Open:** All year

Site: Payment: Leisure: Property: Children: Catering: Room:

WESTONBIRT, Gloucestershire Map ref 2B2 SatNav GL8 8QL Ⓗ

Hare & Hounds Hotel
Westonbirt, Tetbury GL8 8QL **T:** (01666) 881000 **F:** (01666) 880241
E: reception@hareandhoundshotel.com
W: hareandhoundshotel.com **£ BOOK ONLINE**

B&B PER ROOM PER NIGHT
S: £99.00 - £109.00
D: £158.00 - £350.00
HB PER PERSON PER NIGHT
£118.00 - £214.00

Charming Cotswold country hotel 21 miles from Bath and adjoining Westonbirt Arboretum. Beautiful grounds, excellent food and accommodation, fine wines, real ale and friendly locals. Tennis, squash and nearby golf. **Directions:** 10 miles from M4 jct 17, A433. 15 miles from M5 jct 13, Stroud then A46. **Bedrooms:** 23 dble, 12 twin, 4 family, 3 suite **Open:** All year

Site: Payment: Leisure: Property: Children: Catering: Room:

BATH, Somerset Map ref 2B2 SatNav BA2 4HG Ⓑ

Apple Tree Guest House
7 Pulteney Gardens, Bath BA2 4HG **T:** (01225) 337642
E: enquiries@appletreeguesthouse.co.uk
W: appletreeguesthouse.co.uk **£ BOOK ONLINE**

B&B PER ROOM PER NIGHT
S: £60.00 - £66.00
D: £90.00 - £110.00

Bath central guest house. Newly renovated, 5 minutes level walk to the city centre attractions. Parking included. Family owned and operated. Spotlessly clean and comfortable. **Directions:** Please check our website for exact directions, with journey description and mapping details available. **Bedrooms:** 2 single, 3 double, 1 family **Open:** All year

Site: P Payment: Leisure: Property: Children: Catering: Room:

Book your accommodation online

Visit our new 2014 guide websites for detailed information, up-to-date availability and to book your accommodation online. Includes over 20,000 places to stay, all of them star rated.

www.visitor-guides.co.uk

Bath YMCA

International House, Broad Street Place, Bath BA1 5LH **T:** (01225) 325900
F: (01225) 462065 **E:** stay@bathymca.co.uk
W: http://bathymca.co.uk

HOSTEL ★★★

B&B PER ROOM PER NIGHT
S: £32.00 - £36.00
D: £28.00 - £65.00

The YMCA is centrally located, just a minute away from all the major tourist attractions, we have over 200 beds in the form of dormitories, singles, twins, triples and quad rooms. **Directions:** From the bus or train station walk north up Manvers Street. Go past Bath Abbey on your left and, keeping the river Avon on you right, continue via Orange Grove (on left) and High Street to Walcot Street or Broad Street. **Open:** All year

Site: ✿ **Payment:** 💳 **Leisure:** 🚴 ▶ ◀ 🎋 ✄ **Property:** ® ♈ 🖥 📺 🔲 **Children:** ᴤ 🛏 🏃 **Catering:** 🍴 **Bedroom:** ✎ 🖥

Church Farm Monkton Farleigh

Monkton Farleigh, Bradford-on-Avon BA15 2QJ **T:** (01225) 858583 / 07599 998213
F: 0871 714 5859 **E:** reservations@churchfarmmonktonfarleigh.co.uk
W: www.churchfarmmonktonfarleigh.co.uk

FARMHOUSE ★★★

B&B PER ROOM PER NIGHT
S: £55.00
D: £70.00 - £100.00

Converted barn, Spectacular views. 5 miles from Bath, easy access to all Visit Bath attractions and pleasures. Expensive lounge, conservatory, gardens and pool. Excellent pub in village. Ideal base for touring South West England. Families & Dogs are Welcome. **Directions:** On A363 between Bath and Bradford on Avon, 1 mile off main road. Centre of village, On T junction, turn right downhill. Located bottom of hill on the right. **Bedrooms:** 2 double, 1 family **Open:** All year

Site: ✿ **P Leisure:** 🚴 ▶ ∪ ⚘ **Property:** 🐎 🖥 **Children:** ᴤ 🛏 🏃 **Catering:** 🍴 **Room:** ✎ ♨ 🍵 📺

Griffin Inn

Beauford Square, Bath BA1 2AP **T:** (01225) 420919 **F:** (01225) 789572
E: bookings@griffinbath.co.uk
W: www.griffinbath.co.uk **£ BOOK ONLINE**

INN ★★★★

SPECIAL PROMOTIONS
Please contact us for prices

The Griffin Inn boasts four star en suite accommodation above the traditional bar. The location is central and peaceful by the Theatre Royal and the elegant Queen Square. It is a quaint Georgian Grade II listed inn, refurbished in 2009. There are 5 double/twin rooms and 2 single rooms.

Directions: Just off the South West corner of Queen Square via Princes Street and to the rear of the Theatre Royal.

Bedrooms: 3 single, 5 double (2 of which can be made into twin rooms)
Open: All year except Christmas

Site: ✿ **Payment:** 💳 **Property:** 🖥 **Children:** 🛏 🏃 **Catering:** ♈ 🍴 **Room:** ✎ ♨ 🍵 📺

Marlborough House Guest House

1 Marlborough Lane, Bath BA1 2NQ **T:** (01225) 318175 **F:** (01225) 466127
E: mars@manque.dircon.co.uk
W: marlborough-house.net

B&B PER ROOM PER NIGHT
S: £85.00 - £135.00
D: £85.00 - £145.00

Enchanting Victorian town house in Bath's Georgian centre, exquisitely furnished. Beautiful en suite rooms with four poster or king size beds. Generous and organic breakfast choices. Free parking. **Directions:** M4 take exit 18 to Bath. Head for Bath city centre and follow the road through Queen Square and Monmouth Street to Marlborough Lane. **Bedrooms:** 2 double, 2 twin, 2 family **Open:** All year except Christmas

Site: ☿ **P** **Payment:** 💷 € **Leisure:** **Property:** 🛏 **Children:** 🛏 🚼 **Catering:** 🍽 **Room:** 🖊 ♨ 📞 📺

Membland Guest House

7 Pulteney Terrace, Pulteney Road, Bath BA2 4HJ **T:** (01225) 839847 (07958) 599572
E: memblandguesthouse@sky.com
W: www.memblandguesthouse.co.uk

B&B PER ROOM PER NIGHT
D: £75.00 - £90.00

Warm and friendly accommodation with delicious freshly cooked breakfasts. Great location, only 5 minutes level stroll to the stunning attractions of the City, Thermae Spa, Roman Baths and the magnificent Bath Abbey. Situated below the Kennet & Avon canal with beautiful walks, perfect for exploring the picturesque villages surrounding Bath.

Directions: Membland Guest House is on the corner of Pulteney Terrace and Pulteney Avenue. Under the Railway Bridge of Pulteney Road, opposite the Royal Oak Pub.

Bedrooms: 4 doubles
Open: All year

Site: P Payment: € **Property:** 🛏 **Catering:** 🍽 **Room:** 🖊 ♨ 📺 💿 🛁 🚿

Lucknam Park Hotel and Spa

Lucknam Park, Colerne, Chippenham SN14 8AZ **T:** (01225) 742777 **F:** (01225) 743536
E: reservations@lucknampark.co.uk
W: lucknampark.co.uk **£ BOOK ONLINE**

B&B PER ROOM PER NIGHT
D: £410.00 - £1280.00

Luxury hotel within private estate of 500 acres, Bath 6mls. Extensive leisure facilities including The Spa, Well-being House, equestrian and Fine dining in The Park, informal dining in The Brasserie. A fabulous new cookery school. **Directions:** Located 6 miles from Bath and 15 minutes from junction 17 of the M4. Please see website for directions. **Bedrooms:** 29 dble, 13 suite **Open:** All year

Site: P Payment: 💷 € **Leisure:** 🏊 ♪ ⛳ ♻ 🎾 ⚹ 🚲 🎣 ♨ **Property:** 🍷 🛏 💿 🌙 **Children:** 🛏 🚼 **Catering:** 🍽 **Room:** 🖊 📞 📺

BREAN, Somerset Map ref 1D1 SatNav TA8 2QT B

GUEST ACCOMMODATION
★★★★

B&B PER ROOM PER NIGHT
S: £39.50 - £50.00
D: £57.50 - £80.00

Yew Tree House Bed and Breakfast

Hurn Lane, Berrow Nr Brean, Burnham on Sea TA8 2QT **T:** (01278) 751382
E: yewtree@yewtree-house.co.uk
W: yewtree-house.co.uk **£ BOOK ONLINE**

We warmly welcome visitors to our charming old house. We are easy to reach from the motorway and in the perfect location for a short break or holiday. The house is on a quiet lane just 10 minutes walk from Berrow Beach. **Directions:** M5 jct 22. B3140 to Burnham and Berrow. From Berrow follow signs to Brean. 0.5miles after church turn right, we are 300yds on left. **Bedrooms:** 2 double, 2 twin, 1 family, 2 family suite. **Open:** All year except Christmas

Site: ❀ **P Payment:** 💷 **Leisure:** 🚴 🎣 🏌 ∪ **Property:** 🖥 **Children:** 🐾 🛏 ⚲ **Catering:** 🍴 **Room:** 🕯 🌢 📷 📺 ♨

CHEDDAR, Somerset Map ref 1D1 SatNav BS28 4SN B

BED & BREAKFAST
★★★

B&B PER ROOM PER NIGHT
S: £38.00 - £40.00
D: £68.00
EVENING MEAL PER PERSON
£8.95 - £18.50

Yew Tree Farm

Wells Road, Theale, Nr Wedmore, Somerset BS28 4SN **T:** (01934) 712475
F: (01934) 712475 **E:** enquiries@yewtreefarmbandb.co.uk
W: yewtreefarmbandb.co.uk **£ BOOK ONLINE**

17th century farmhouse Nr Cheddar, Wells and Wookey. Idyllic walks fishing/golf/cycling. 1, 2, 3 course home cooked and freshly prepared evening meals available, as well as snacks and cream teas. Large secure off street parking area available and free Wi-Fi. **Directions:** From Wells, take B3139 towards Burnham-on-Sea. Drive through Wookey, Henton, Panborough. **Bedrooms:** 1 double, 1 twin, 1 family **Open:** All year

Site: ❀ **P Payment:** € **Leisure:** 🎣 🏌 ∪ **Property:** 🐾 🖥 🖸 **Children:** 🐾 🛏 ⚲ **Catering:** ⟨✗ 🍴 **Room:** 🕯 🌢 📷 📺 💿

DUNSTER, Somerset Map ref 1D1 SatNav TA24 6SF H

HOTEL
★★★

B&B PER ROOM PER NIGHT
S: £65.00 - £90.00
D: £90.00 - £140.00
EVENING MEAL PER PERSON
£17.00 - £27.00

SPECIAL PROMOTIONS
Discounted rates for longer stays and midweek bookings. Ring for newsletter with information on special events. Group bookings welcome.

Yarn Market Hotel

25-33 High Street, Dunster TA24 6SF **T:** (01643) 821425 **F:** (01643) 821475
E: hotel@yarnmarkethotel.co.uk
W: www.yarnmarkethotel.co.uk **£ BOOK ONLINE**

Within Exmoor National Park, our hotel is ideal for walking, riding, fishing. Family-run with a friendly, relaxed atmosphere. All rooms en suite with colour TV. Four-poster and superior rooms available. Non-smoking. Home-cooked dishes to cater for all tastes. Group bookings welcomed. Conference facilities. Special Christmas and New Year breaks.

Directions: From M5 jct 25 follow signs for Exmoor/Minehead A358/A39. Dunster signed approx 0.5 miles from A39 on left. Hotel in village centre beside Yarn Market.

Bedrooms: 2 single, 12 dble, 7 twin, 2 family **Open:** All year

Payment: 💷 € **Leisure:** 🚴 🎣 🏌 ∪ **Property:** 🍴 🐾 🖥 🖸 **Children:** 🐾 🛏 ⚲ **Catering:** 🍷 🍴 **Room:** 🕯 🌢 📷 📺 ♨ 🖨 🛎

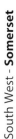

South West - Somerset

Burton Row Farmhouse

Burton Row, East Brent TA9 4DA **T:** (01278) 769252 **F:** (01278) 769252
E: lindaisgrove@btinternet.com
W: www.somersetbandb.co.uk

B&B PER ROOM PER NIGHT
D: £70.00 - £110.00

SPECIAL PROMOTIONS
Discounts for longer stays.

A wisteria clad 16th Century Somerset longhouse on the Somerset Levels, rural but central to all the delights of Somerset and beyond, beautifully renovated to a high standard. We offer a high quality bed and breakfast experience. Enjoy tea or coffee with homemade cake to refresh you after your journey.

Directions: From M5 Junction 22, at the roundabout A38 north. Next roundabout 1st exit. Traffic lights East Brent turn left. House on the right.

Bedrooms: 2 double, 1 suite
Open: All year except December, January and February

Site: ✿ **P** Payment: 💷 Leisure: 🏊 🏌 ▶ ♻ Property: 🏠 Catering: 🍽 Room: 🍵 👟 🎲 📺 ⚓ 🍴

The Lighthouse

Tytherington, Frome, Somerset BA11 5BW **T:** (01373) 453585 **E:** reception@lighthouse-uk.com
W: www.lighthouse-uk.com

B&B PER ROOM PER NIGHT
S: £40.00 - £50.00
D: £70.00 - £80.00
EVENING MEAL PER PERSON
£6.00 - £12.00

SPECIAL PROMOTIONS
We are able to offer 1 day tickets for Longleat Safari & Adventure Park at a discounted rate if ordered 48 hours before your arrival

The Lighthouse offers beautiful 4 star Bed & Breakfast Accommodation in the rolling Somerset countryside. Guests are welcome to come and enjoy our wide range of facilities - the stunning 30 acre setting with lake and woodland walks, gluten & dairy free nutritional teahouse, brand new conference facilities and access to indoor Pool in adjacent building - or simply take some time to unwind in the tranquil environment and experience some of our relaxing Healing Treatments.

Directions: As you come off the A361 and enter the village of Tytherington, The Lighthouse is the first property on the right

Bedrooms: Modern and tastefully renovated en suite rooms in the courtyard of a C17th Country House, set within 30 acres of stunning parkland.
Open: All Year except between Christmas and New Year

Site: ✿ **P** Payment: 💷 Leisure: 🏌 ⚲ Property: 🎣 🐾 🖥 🅱 🏵 🖊 Children: 🚼 🎠 Catering: (✗ 🍽 Room: 🍵 👟 📺 🍴

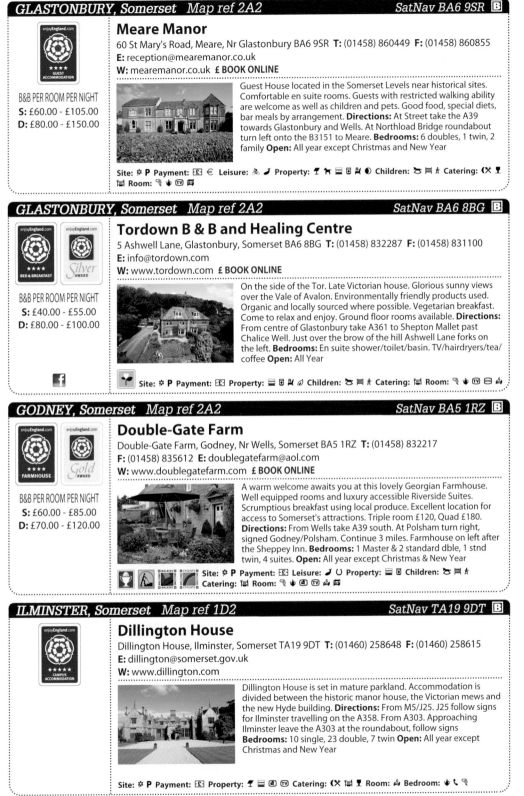

GLASTONBURY, Somerset Map ref 2A2 — SatNav BA6 9SR B

Meare Manor

60 St Mary's Road, Meare, Nr Glastonbury BA6 9SR **T:** (01458) 860449 **F:** (01458) 860855
E: reception@mearemanor.co.uk
W: mearemanor.co.uk **£ BOOK ONLINE**

GUEST ACCOMMODATION

B&B PER ROOM PER NIGHT
S: £60.00 - £105.00
D: £80.00 - £150.00

Guest House located in the Somerset Levels near historical sites. Comfortable en suite rooms. Guests with restricted walking ability are welcome as well as children and pets. Good food, special diets, bar meals by arrangement. **Directions:** At Street take the A39 towards Glastonbury and Wells. At Northload Bridge roundabout turn left onto the B3151 to Meare. **Bedrooms:** 6 doubles, 1 twin, 2 family **Open:** All year except Christmas and New Year

Site: P Payment: € Leisure: Property: Children: Catering: Room:

GLASTONBURY, Somerset Map ref 2A2 — SatNav BA6 8BG B

Tordown B & B and Healing Centre

5 Ashwell Lane, Glastonbury, Somerset BA6 8BG **T:** (01458) 832287 **F:** (01458) 831100
E: info@tordown.com
W: www.tordown.com **£ BOOK ONLINE**

BED & BREAKFAST **Silver AWARD**

B&B PER ROOM PER NIGHT
S: £40.00 - £55.00
D: £80.00 - £100.00

On the side of the Tor. Late Victorian house. Glorious sunny views over the Vale of Avalon. Environmentally friendly products used. Organic and locally sourced where possible. Vegetarian breakfast. Come to relax and enjoy. Ground floor rooms available. **Directions:** From centre of Glastonbury take A361 to Shepton Mallet past Chalice Well. Just over the brow of the hill Ashwell Lane forks on the left. **Bedrooms:** En suite shower/toilet/basin. TV/hairdryers/tea/coffee **Open:** All Year

Site: P Payment: Property: Children: Catering: Room:

GODNEY, Somerset Map ref 2A2 — SatNav BA5 1RZ B

Double-Gate Farm

Double-Gate Farm, Godney, Nr Wells, Somerset BA5 1RZ **T:** (01458) 832217
F: (01458) 835612 **E:** doublegatefarm@aol.com
W: www.doublegatefarm.com **£ BOOK ONLINE**

FARMHOUSE **Gold AWARD**

B&B PER ROOM PER NIGHT
S: £60.00 - £85.00
D: £70.00 - £120.00

A warm welcome awaits you at this lovely Georgian Farmhouse. Well equipped rooms and luxury accessible Riverside Suites. Scrumptious breakfast using local produce. Excellent location for access to Somerset's attractions. Triple room £120, Quad £180. **Directions:** From Wells take A39 south. At Polsham turn right, signed Godney/Polsham. Continue 3 miles. Farmhouse on left after the Sheppey Inn. **Bedrooms:** 1 Master & 2 standard dble, 1 stnd twin, 4 suites. **Open:** All year except Christmas & New Year

Site: P Payment: Leisure: Property: Children: Catering: Room:

ILMINSTER, Somerset Map ref 1D2 — SatNav TA19 9DT B

Dillington House

Dillington House, Ilminster, Somerset TA19 9DT **T:** (01460) 258648 **F:** (01460) 258615
E: dillington@somerset.gov.uk
W: www.dillington.com

CAMPUS ACCOMMODATION

Dillington House is set in mature parkland. Accommodation is divided between the historic manor house, the Victorian mews and the new Hyde building. **Directions:** From M5/J25. J25 follow signs for Ilminster travelling on the A358. From A303. Approaching Ilminster leave the A303 at the roundabout, follow signs **Bedrooms:** 10 single, 23 double, 7 twin **Open:** All year except Christmas and New Year

Site: P Payment: Property: Catering: Room: Bedroom:

SOUTH PETHERTON, Somerset   Map ref 1D2   SatNav TA13 5DB B

Rock House B&B

5 Palmer Street, South Petherton, Somerset TA13 5DB **T:** (01460) 240324
E: enquiries@unwindatrockhouse.co.uk
W: unwindatrockhouse.co.uk

B&B PER ROOM PER NIGHT
S: £65.00
D: £90.00

Rock House, an unexpected discovery in the heart of South Petherton; an unspoilt Somerset village - a place to unwind. Garden for guests' sole use, secure parking. National Trust nearby. **Directions:** See website for accurate directions **Bedrooms:** 2 suite **Open:** All year

Site: ✿ **P Payment:** 💷 **Property:** 🖳 🖥 **Catering:** 🍴 🍳 **Room:** 🔌 🖐 📺 📀 ♨

TAUNTON, Somerset   Map ref 1D1   SatNav TA1 4AF H

The Castle at Taunton

Castle Green, Taunton TA1 1NF **T:** (01823) 272671 **F:** (01823) 336066
E: reception@the-castle-hotel.com
W: the-castle-hotel.com **£ BOOK ONLINE**

B&B PER ROOM PER NIGHT
S: £99.00 - £162.00
D: £180.00 - £230.00
EVENING MEAL PER PERSON
£25.00 - £34.00

The Castle has won a host of awards for the excellence of its kitchens and the warmth of its hospitality. Both of its restaurants offer the best local produce and Castle Bow Bar & Grill has Somerset's highest rating in the Good Food Guide. **Directions:** From M5 take junction 25 or 26 and follow signs to the town centre. Pick up "Castle Hotel" tourist signs **Bedrooms:** 12 single, 18 dble, 9 twin, 2 family, 3 suite. **Open:** All year

Site: ✿ **Payment:** 💷 **Leisure:** 🚵 ✈ **Property:** 🍴 🐾 🖳 🖥 ◐ **Children:** 🛏 🍼 🎎 **Catering:** 🍴 🍳 **Room:** 🔌 🖐 📞 📀 📺

Visit our 2014 guide websites...

- Detailed information
- Up-to-date availability
- Book your accommodation online

Includes over 20,000 places to stay, all of them star rated.

Win amazing prizes, every month...

Enter our monthly competition at
www.visitor-guides.co.uk/prizes

South West - **Somerset**

Burcott Mill Guesthouse

Wells Road, Wookey, Nr Wells, Somerset BA5 1NJ **T:** (01749) 673118
E: enquiries@burcottmill.com
W: www.burcottmill.com

B&B PER ROOM PER NIGHT
S: £35.00 - £45.00
D: £65.00 - £90.00

SPECIAL PROMOTIONS
Enjoy a tour of the historic mill during your stay. Taste the homemade bread made from Burcott Mill flour as part of the wide range of locally sourced breakfast options

Grade II listed Miller's House adjoining a working Victorian watermill. Ideal location for Wells, Cheddar and Wookey Hole. A warm welcome and a great breakfast at this family run guesthouse.

Directions: From Wells take the Cheddar road, and then the B3139 left fork to Burnham on Sea. Burcott Mill is about 1 mile along this road, opposite the Burcott Inn pub.

Bedrooms: A wide range of accommodation, including a taste of luxury in a suite, a cosy single and spacious family rooms. All rooms with flatscreen TV and free Wi-Fi.
Open: All Year

Site: ✿ P **Payment:** 💷 **Property:** 🐾 🖥 ♨ **Children:** 🛏 🍴 ⚇ **Catering:** 🍽 **Room:** 🍵 🖐 📺 📀 🚿

Beachlands Hotel

Uphill Road North, Weston-super-Mare BS23 4NG **T:** (01934) 621401 **F:** (01934) 621966
E: info@beachlandshotel.com
W: www.beachlandshotel.com **£ BOOK ONLINE**

SPECIAL PROMOTIONS
Please contact us for prices

On the level, overlooking Weston Golf Course and 300yds from beach. Extensive refurbishment of public areas and bedrooms completed in June 2011 have transformed the Hotel in to a contempory, elegant Haven for all your leisure and business needs.

Directions: M5 jct 21, follow signs for Weston-Super-Mare, beach car parks and hospital. Beachlands is past the hospital 300yds before the beach, 6.5 miles from motorway.

Bedrooms: 1 single, 10 double, 4 twin, 5 family
Open: All year except Christmas

Site: ✿ **Payment:** 💷 € **Leisure:** 🎵 🏇 ∪ 🎣 🎿 Property: 🐕 🖥 🔲 **Children:** 🛏 🍴 ⚇ **Catering:** 🍷 🍽
Room: 🍵 🖐 📞 🔌 📺 🚿

The Red Lion

74 High Street, Cricklade SN6 6DD **T:** (01793) 750776 **E:** info@theredlioncricklade.co.uk
W: www.theredlioncricklade.co.uk **£ BOOK ONLINE**

B&B PER ROOM PER NIGHT
D: £80.00

Situated on the Thames path, The Red Lion Inn dates back to the 1600s. Roaring log fires, 9 traditional ales and 53 bottled beers combine with a contemporary restaurant serving homemade and seasonal food, a traditional bar area serving pub classics, a garden and 5 recently built en suite bedrooms.

Directions: Located just off the A419 between Swindon and Cirencester, which is minutes from junction 15 of the M4.

Bedrooms: 3 double, 2 twin
Open: All year

Site: ❄ Payment: 🔄 Leisure: ♨ ♪ ⚑ ♻ Property: ⚓ 🖥 Children: 👶 ♿ Catering: ⚔ ⚑ 🍴
Room: ✎ ♨ 📶 📺 🍴

Marshwood Farm B&B

Dinton, Salisbury SP3 5ET **T:** (01722) 716334 **E:** marshwood1@btconnect.com
W: marshwoodfarm.co.uk

B&B PER ROOM PER NIGHT
S: £45.00 - £60.00
D: £60.00 - £75.00

SPECIAL PROMOTIONS
Discount for stays of 2 consecutive nights or more.

Come and enjoy the peace and tranquility of the Wiltshire countryside in one of our spacious rooms. We look forward to welcoming you in our farmhouse dating from 17th century. Within easy reach to explore Stonehenge, Salisbury, Bath, Longleat, English Heritage and National Trust Properties. Walkers and cyclists welcome.

Directions: At A303/A36 intersection turn into Wylye, follow the Dinton signs. Marshwood Farm is approx 4 miles.

Bedrooms: 1 twin, 1 family
Open: All year

Site: ❄ P Payment: 🔄 € Leisure: ✂ Property: ⚓ Children: 👶 🛏 ♿ Catering: 🍴 Room: ✎ ♨ 📺

MANNINGFORD ABBOTS, Wiltshire   Map ref 2B2   SatNav SN9 6HZ [B]

★★★★
BED & BREAKFAST

Huntly's Farmhouse
Manningford Abbots, Pewsey SN9 6HZ **T:** (01672) 563663 / 07900211789
E: gimspike@esend.co.uk
W: www.huntlys.co.uk

B&B PER ROOM PER NIGHT
S: £30.00 - £40.00
D: £55.00 - £80.00
EVENING MEAL PER PERSON
£15.00 - £17.00

Peaceful thatched 17th century farmhouse including horse-stabling/grazing. Good walking country. Heated outdoor swimming pool. Free range and organic food. Family room comprises 1 twin adjoining separate single room. **Directions:** Turn off A345 SW of Pewsey signed Manningford Abbotts. Huntlys is 0.5 mile on RHS just past turn to Sharcott. Opposite post box in wall. **Bedrooms:** 1 double, 1 family **Open:** All year

Site: ✿ P Leisure: 🎿 ♪ ▶ ♻ ↻ Property: 🐴 🖃 🗑 Children: 👶⁵ Catering: (✗ 🍴 Room: 🍳 🚿 🔌 📺

MELKSHAM, Wiltshire   Map ref 2B2   SatNav SN12 8EF [H]

★★
SMALL HOTEL

Shaw Country Hotel
Bath Road, Shaw, Nr Melksham, Wiltshire SN12 8EF **T:** (01225) 702836 **F:** (01225) 790275
E: shawcountryhotel@hotmail.co.uk
W: shawcountryhotel.com **£ BOOK ONLINE**

B&B PER ROOM PER NIGHT
S: £65.00 - £90.00
D: £90.00 - £110.00
HB PER PERSON PER NIGHT
£85.00 - £110.00

Four hundred year old farmhouse in own grounds, nine miles from Bath. Licensed bar and restaurant, with table d'hote and a la carte menus. All rooms en suite. **Bedrooms:** 3 single, 7 dble, 3 twin **Open:** All year

Site: ✿ Payment: 💳 Property: 🍴 🐴 🖃 🗑 Children: 👶 🍴 🚶 Catering: 🍷 🍴 Room: 🍳 🚿 🔌 📺 🍽

Looking for something else?

The official and most comprehensive guide to independently inspected, star rated accommodation.

B&Bs and Hotels - B&Bs, Hotels, farmhouses, inns, serviced apartments, campus and hostel accommodation in England.

Self Catering - Self-catering holiday homes, approved caravan holiday homes, boat accommodation and holiday cottage agencies in England.

Camping, Touring and Holiday Parks - Touring parks, camping holidays and holiday parks and villages in Britain.

Now available in all good bookshops and online at **www.hudsons.co.uk/shop**

South West - Wiltshire

MONKTON FARLEIGH, Wiltshire Map ref 2B2

SatNav BA15 2QH B

Muddy Duck

42 Monkton Farleigh, Monkton Farleigh BA15 2QH **T:** (01225) 858705
E: dishitup@themuddyduckbath.co.uk
W: www.themuddyduckbath.co.uk

Individually styled boutique rooms above a stunning 17th century country pub. Situated in the picturesque village of Monkton Farleigh just 5 miles from Bath. Friendly service, local seasonal food. Please contact us for prices. **Directions:** Junction 18 M4 towards Bath. Just off the A36 Bath to Bradford on Avon road follow signs to Monkton Farleigh Bath Spa Train Station 5m. **Bedrooms:** 3 double **Open:** All year

Site: ❉ P Payment: 🖃 Leisure: 🚲 ♪ ∪ Property: 🖳 Children: 🚼 🛏 🎿 Catering: 🍷 🍴 Room: 🕿 📺

SALISBURY, Wiltshire Map ref 2B3

SatNav SP1 2JA B

Alabare House

15 Tollgate Road, Salisbury SP1 2JA **T:** (07802) 631968 **F:** (01722) 501586
E: info@alabare.org
W: alabare.org **£ BOOK ONLINE**

B&B PER ROOM PER NIGHT
S: £45.00 - £55.00
D: £60.00 - £80.00

SPECIAL PROMOTIONS
Special rates for extended stays of 3 weeks or more out of season.

This is a small oasis in the heart of Salisbury with ample off-road parking. A family-run B&B, the venue is a good choice for a holiday break. There are many local places of interest, and Salisbury offers a wide variety of restaurants and shops. Online booking available.

Directions: From A36 (Southampton), off Salisbury ringroad take first left into Tollgate Road. After 200 yards Alabare House is opposite you on the lefthand bend.

Bedrooms: 1 single, 2 double, 6 twin, 1 family
Open: All year except Christmas

Site: ❉ P Payment: 🖃 Leisure: 🚲 ∪ Property: 🖳 Children: 🚼 🛏 🎿 Room: 🚿 📺

SALISBURY, Wiltshire Map ref 2B3

SatNav SP2 0EJ B

Burcombe Manor

Burcombe Lane, Burcombe, Salisbury SP2 0EJ **T:** (01722) 744288 **F:** (01722) 744600
E: enquires@burcombemanor.co.uk
W: www.burcombemanor.co.uk

B&B PER ROOM PER NIGHT
S: £60.00 - £65.00
D: £75.00 - £80.00

Burcombe Manor is set in the Nadder Valley, four miles west of Salisbury. The Victorian house, with central heated rooms and a sitting room for guests to plan their day trips or relax in. Local base to explore Wilton, Salisbury and the surrounding area. **Directions:** Come out of Wilton 1 mile on A30. Left to Burcombe. At T-junction, turn right. Burcombe Manor drive is on the left. **Bedrooms:** 1 double, 1 twin both en suite & 1 double with a private bathroom. **Open:** All year

Site: P Payment: 🖃 Leisure: ♪ ∪ Property: 🖳 Children: 🚼 🛏 Catering: 🍴 Room: 🕿 🚿 📺

The Official Tourist Board Guide to **B&Bs and Hotels 2014**

HOTEL

Cathedral Hotel

7-9 Milford Street, Salisbury, Wiltshire SP1 2AJ **T:** (01722) 343700 **F:** (01722) 343701
E: info@cathedralhotelsalisbury.co.uk
W: cathedralhotelsalisbury.co.uk **£ BOOK ONLINE**

B&B PER ROOM PER NIGHT
S: £75.00
D: £65.00 - £85.00
EVENING MEAL PER PERSON
£7.95 - £20.00

SPECIAL PROMOTIONS
Check our website for
great Christmas and
New Year Packages
and for best online
rates. All rates include
breakfast.

Free WIFI, Weekdays we offer a quiet, relaxed environment which is a great base for touring or
business. Weekends we are a vibrant, lively environment where locals and tourists enjoy, watching
sport or chatting in friendly surroundings. Weekend evenings the bar is open until 2am, with D.J.
entertainment. Great menu that includes lots of home dishes, traditional fish and chips, pastas and
more.

Directions: M3/J8 (A303) onto A343 to
Salisbury. A36 Roundabout, 2nd exit. A338
Roundabout, 2nd exit. Next Roundabout, 3rd
exit Exeter Street. Right turn Milford Street.

Bedrooms: En suite, flat screen tv, ceiling fans,
free wifi, tea and coffee in rooms. Modern
contemporary rooms in an old building. Small
lift to all floors
Open: All year

Site: ✿ Payment: 💳 Property: 🍸 📺 🔵 Children: 🛋 🏛 🏃 Catering: 🍽 🍴 Room: 🔌 ♨ 🔟 📺

BED & BREAKFAST

Evening Hill

Blandford Road, Coombe Bissett, Salisbury, Wiltshire SP5 4LH **T:** (01722) 718561
E: info@eveninghill.com
W: eveninghill.com

B&B PER ROOM PER NIGHT
S: £36.00 - £40.00
D: £46.00 - £50.00

A quiet village location 10 mins from the city of Salisbury. Ideal for
visiting Salisbury city and Cathedral, Stonehenge, New Forest, Bath,
Southampton, Portsmouth, Winchester. **Directions:** 2 miles south
of Salisbury on the A354. Drive through the village of Coombe
Bissett 500 meters past the church on right hand side. **Bedrooms:** 1
double, 1 family **Open:** All year

Site: ✿ P Leisure: 🚲 Property: 🐾 📺 Children: 🛋 🏛 🏃 Catering: 🍴 Room: 🔌 ♨ 🔟 📺 ☕

Book your accommodation online

Visit our new 2014 guide websites
for detailed information, up-to-
date availability and to book your
accommodation online. Includes
over 20,000 places to stay, all of
them star rated.
www.visitor-guides.co.uk

Lodge Farmhouse Bed & Breakfast

Lodge Farmhouse, Broad Chalke, Salisbury SP5 5LU **T:** (01725) 519242
E: info@lodge-farmhouse.co.uk
W: lodge-farmhouse.co.uk **£ BOOK ONLINE**

B&B PER ROOM PER NIGHT
S: £40.00
D: £70.00 - £80.00

SPECIAL PROMOTIONS
For bookings of 3 nights, or more, discount of £5 per person per night.

Peaceful brick-and-flint farmhouse with Wiltshire's most stunning views overlooking 1,000 square miles of Southern England. Comfortable and welcoming, the perfect tour base for Wessex. Lying on the Ox Drove 'green lane', a paradise for walkers. For nature reserves and archaeological sites.

Directions: A354 from Salisbury (8mls) or Blandford (14mls). Turn to Broad Chalke at crossroads on only stretch of dual carriageway on the A354. One mile signposted.

Bedrooms: 2 double, 1 twin
Open: All year except Christmas to New Year

Site: ✿ P Payment: 💷 Leisure: 🏌 Property: 📶 Children: 👶12 Room: 📶 ♿ 📺

The Wheatsheaf

1 King Street, Wilton, Salisbury SP2 0AX **T:** (01722) 742267
E: mail@thewheatsheafwilton.co.uk
W: www.thewheatsheafwilton.co.uk

B&B PER ROOM PER NIGHT
S: £50.00 - £65.00
D: £70.00 - £90.00

Grade II listed country pub with en suite B&B accommodation. Tasty home-cooked evening meals and lunches. Riverside garden and private car park. Free wireless internet access. Open all day. **Directions:** Wilton is three miles west of Salisbury on the A36 heading towards Bath. The nearest railway station is Salisbury (5-10 minutes by taxi). **Bedrooms:** 3 double, 1 family **Open:** All year

Site: ✿ P Payment: 💷 Leisure: 🏊 🏌 ⚲ ♻ Property: 📶 ✂ Children: 👶 🍴 Catering: ⤬ 🍽 🍴
Room: 📶 ♿ 🍵 📺

Newhouse Farm

Littleton, Semington, Trowbridge, Wiltshire BA14 6LF **T:** (01380) 870349
E: stay@newhousefarmwilts.co.uk
W: www.newhousefarmwilts.co.uk

B&B PER ROOM PER NIGHT
S: £44.00 - £60.00
D: £70.00 - £80.00

Former Victorian farmhouse, lovely gardens and grounds with wildflower meadow. Warm welcome, comfortable spacious rooms. Ideal touring centre for Longleat, Bowood, Lacock and Bath. Perfect for walking and cycling along the Kennet and Avon Canal. Great pubs nearby. **Directions:** On A361 between Trowbridge and Devizes. No.49 bus stops outside. **Bedrooms:** 2 double and 1 twin room, all en suite with tea/coffee making facilities. **Open:** All year

Site: ✿ P Property: 📶 🍴 🐾 Children: 👶 🍴 🍴 Catering: 🍽 Room: 📶 ♿ 📺 🍴

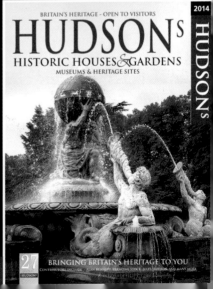

South East

Berkshire, Buckinghamshire, Hampshire,
Isle of Wight, Kent, Oxfordshire, Surrey, Sussex

Miles of delightful coastline and
countryside, the historic cities of
Oxford and Winchester, and the naval
centres of Portsmouth and Southampton
make the South East one of the country's
most popular areas to visit. The region
boasts a plethora of some of the best
attractions and outdoor pursuits
anywhere in the country. Come rain or
shine, there are endless options when
you're looking for things to do. And once
you've toured the mainland you can take a
ferry trip to the Isle of Wight and explore.

Highlights

Blenheim Palace

Standing in a romantic park created by 'Capability' Brown, Blenheim Palace was presented to John Churchill, first Duke of Marlborough, in recognition of his victory in 1704 over French and Bavarian troops.

Canterbury Cathedral

The cathedral exhibits Romanesque and Gothic architecture, and is the seat of the Church of England. St Martin's Church and St Augustine's Abbey were founded during the early stages of Christianity among Anglo-Saxons.

Chilterns

The Chiltern Hills stretch from the River Thames in Oxfordshire to Hitchin in Hertfordshire and are nationally-protected as some of the finest countryside in the UK. They're a fantastic place to explore all year round.

New Forest

The New Forest was England's first official visitor destination, named by William the Conqueror way back in 1079AD. Over 3000 ponies, 3000 cattle and 2500 deer wander freely around this National Park.

Oxford

The world famous city of Oxford, with its university, colleges, and library, has always been at the forefront of achievement – shaping so many national leaders, scientists, writers and philosophers.

South Downs

Combining a biodiverse landscape with bustling towns and villages, the South Downs National Park is recognised as an area of outstanding beauty.

White Cliffs of Dover

Known as the Garden of England, Kent has an extensive and varied coastline, encompassing some stunning landscapes, including the White Cliffs of Dover.

Winchester

Winchester is a historic city and former capital city of England. Its major landmark is Winchester Cathedral, one of the largest in Europe, with the distinction of having the longest nave and overall length of all Gothic cathedrals in Europe.

Windsor

Windsor is home to two of the UK's Top 20 visitor attractions – Windsor Castle and Legoland Windsor. It also feature boat trips on the River Thames and romantic horse-drawn carriage rides through Windsor Great Park.

SHOE REPAIRS

SHOE
REPAIRS

KEY
CUTTING

WATCH
REPAIRS

Café Mauresque

GAP

Coffee
Shop
&
Take
Away

Coffee
Shop

THE
CITY ARMS
INN

CASEY'S

Designs

GUY

TO LET

Blacks

CITY ARMS
FOOD SERVED
12-8

Take a guide with you

By booking a guided city tour you will discover things about places like Oxford or Windsor that you will never discover if you go it alone.

Climb aboard a boat trip

South East England is blessed with a multitude of picturesque waterways, and there's no better way to explore and relax than on an organised boat trip.

Raise a glass

As this region is one of the main hop-growing counties in the country, take a tour of the 300-year-old Shepherd Neame Brewery in Kent and sample their ales.

High speed action

If you want to experience the thrills of high speed action then head for Buckmore Park International Kart Circuit near Chatham in Kent where Lewis Hamilton learned his trade.

Step back in time

Discover the fascinating world of animals and plants from millions of years ago to the present day at Paradise Park in East Sussex.

Things to do

Attractions with this sign participate in the Places of Interest Quality Assurance Scheme.

Attractions with this sign participate in the Visitor Attraction Quality Assurance Scheme.

Both schemes recognise high standards in all aspects of the visitor experience (see page 7)

Entertainment & Culture

Beaulieu National Motor Museum
Hampshire SO42 7ZN
(01590) 612123
www.beaulieu.co.uk
Beaulieu featuring the world famous National Motor Museum, Palace House home of the Montagu family and Abbey Ruins containing an exhibition of monastic life.

City Sightseeing Windsor and Eton
Berkshire SL4 1NJ
(01708) 866000
www.city-sightseeing.com
Enjoy the dignified tranquillity of Windsor, including Windsor Castle, home of the British monarchy for centuries, and Eton College.

Dinosaur Isle
Sandown,
Isle of Wight PO36 8QA
(01983) 404344
www.dinosaurisle.com
In a spectacular pterosaur shaped building on Sandown's blue flag beach walk back through fossilised time and meet life sized replica dinosaurs.

Museum of English Rural Life
Reading, Berkshire RG1 5EX
(0118) 378 8660
www.merl.org.uk
MERL houses one of England's most fascinating collections relating to life and work in the countryside over the last 200 years.

REME Museum of Technology
Reading, Berkshire RG2 9NJ
(0118) 976 3375
www.rememuseum.org.uk
The museum shows the developing technology used by the Royal Electrical and Mechanical Engineers in maintaining and repairing the army's equipment since 1942.

Roald Dahl Museum and Story Centre
Great Missenden,
Buckinghamshire HP16 0AL
(01494) 892192
www.roalddahlmuseum.org
Where Roald Dahl (1916-1990) lived and wrote many of his well-loved books.

Family Fun

Aerial Extreme Milton Keynes
Buckinghamshire MK15 0DS
0845 652 1736
www.aerialextreme.co.uk/courses/willen-lake
Amaze yourself as you take each of the challenges head on.

Bekonscot Model Village and Railway
Beaconsfield,
Buckinghamshire HP9 2PL
(01494) 672919
www.bekonscot.com
Use your imagination in this unique world of make-believe that has delighted generations of visitors.

Blackgang Chine
Chale, Isle of Wight PO38 2HN
(01983) 730330
www.blackgangchine.com
Set in over 40 acres of spectacular cliff-top gardens.

Gulliver's Land
Milton Keynes,
Buckinghamshire MK15 0DT
(01908) 609001
www.gulliversfun.co.uk
Family theme park with 40 rides aimed at children between 2 and 12 years.

Go Ape! High Wire Forest Adventure - Bracknell
Berkshire RG12 7QW
0845 643 9215
www.goape.co.uk
Go Ape! and tackle a high-wire forest adventure course of rope bridges, Tarzan swings and zip slides up to 35 feet above the forest floor.

LEGOLAND® Windsor
Berkshire SL4 4AY
0870 504 0404
www.legoland.co.uk
With over 55 interactive rides and attractions, there's just too much to experience in one day!

The Look Out Discovery Centre
Bracknell, Berkshire RG12 7QW
(01344) 354400
www.bracknell-forest.gov.uk/be
A hands-on, interactive science exhibition with over 80 exhibits, set in 1,000 hectares of Crown woodland.

Thorpe Park
Chertsey, Surrey KT16 8PN
0871 663 1673
www.thorpepark.com
New in 2010, prepare for SAW Alive, the world's most extreme live action horror maze.

Food & Drink

Denbies Wine Estate
Dorking, Surrey RH5 6AA
(01306) 876616
www.denbiesvineyard.co.uk
Established in 1986, Denbies Wine Estate is England's largest single estate vineyard with 265 acres of vines.

Heritage

1066 Battle Abbey and Battlefield
East Sussex TN33 0AD
(01424) 775705
www.english-heritage.org.uk/daysout/properties/1066-
battle-of-hastings-abbey-and-battlefield/
*An abbey founded by William the Conqueror on the site
of the Battle of Hastings.*

Bateman's
Etchingham,
East Sussex TN19 7DS
(01435) 882302
www.nationaltrust.org.uk/batemans/
*A 17th century Ironmaster's house which was the home
of Rudyard Kipling between 1902-35. His study and Rolls
Royce can be seen. Garden with working watermill.*

Blenheim Palace
Woodstock,
Oxfordshire OX20 1PX
(01993) 811091
www.blenheimpalace.com
*Birthplace of Sir Winston Churchill and home to the
Duke of Marlborough, Blenheim Palace, one of the finest
baroque houses in England, is set in over 2,000 acres of
landscaped gardens.*

Brighton Pier
East Sussex BN2 1TW
(01273) 609361
www.brightonpier.co.uk
*A Victorian pier with various food and drink outlets,
fairground attractions and Palace of Fun arcade.*

Chichester Cathedral
West Sussex PO19 1RP
(01243) 782595
www.chichestercathedral.org.uk
*A magnificent Cathedral with treasures ranging from
medieval stone carvings to world famous 20th century
artworks.*

Didcot Railway Centre
Oxfordshire OX11 7NJ
(01235) 817200
www.didcotrailwaycentre.org.uk
*Living museum recreating the golden age of the Great
Western Railway. Steam locomotives and trains, Brunel's
broad gauge railway, engine shed and small relics
museum.*

Frogmore House
Windsor, Berkshire SL4 1NJ
(020) 7766 7305
www.royalcollection.org.uk
*Late 17th century royal residence, particularly associated
with Queen Charlotte and Queen Victoria.*

Guildford Cathedral
Surrey GU2 7UP
(01483) 547860
www.guildford-cathedral.org
*New Anglican Cathedral, the foundation stone of which
was laid in 1936. Notable sandstone interior and marble
floors. Restaurant and shops.*

Hever Castle and Gardens
Edenbridge, Kent TN8 7NG
(01732) 865224
www.hevercastle.co.uk
*Romantic 13th century moated castle, once Anne
Boleyn's childhood home. Magnificently furnished
interiors, spectacular award winning gardens. Miniature
Model House Exhibition, Yew Maze, unique Splashing
Water Maze.*

Kent & East Sussex Railway
Tenterden, Kent TN30 6HE
(01580) 765155
www.kesr.org.uk
*England's finest rural light railway enables visitors to
experience travel and service from a bygone age aboard
beautifully restored Victorian coaches and locomotives.*

Loseley Park
Guildford, Surrey GU3 1HS
(01483) 405112
www.loseley-park.com
*A beautiful Elizabethan mansion, is set in stunning
gardens and parkland. Built in 1562 it has a fascinating
history and contains a wealth of treasures.*

Osborne House
East Cowes,
Isle of Wight PO32 6JX
(01983) 200022
www.english-heritage.org.uk/daysout/properties/
osborne-house
*Step into Queen Victoria's favourite country home and
experience a world unchanged since the country's longest
reigning monarch died here just over 100 years ago.*

Oxford Castle Unlocked
Oxfordshire OX1 1AY
(01865) 260666
www.oxfordcastleunlocked.co.uk
*For the first time in 1000 years, the secrets of Oxford Castle
have been 'unlocked', revealing episodes of violence,
executions, great escapes, betrayal and even romance.
Visit Oxford Castle and uncover the secrets for yourself.*

Petworth House and Park
West Sussex GU28 0AE
(01798) 342207
www.nationaltrust.org.uk/petworth
Discover the National Trust's finest art collection displayed in a magnificent 17th century mansion within a beautiful 700-acre park. Petworth House contains works by artists such as Van Dyck, Reynolds and Turner.

Portsmouth Historic Dockyard
Hampshire PO1 3LJ
(023) 9272 8060
www.historicdockyard.co.uk
Be a part of your history at Portsmouth Historic Dockyard.

Rochester Castle
Kent ME1 1SW
(01634) 335882
www.visitmedway.org/site/attractions/rochester-castle-p44583
One of the finest keeps in England. Also the tallest, partly built on the Roman city wall. Good views from the battlements over the River Medway.

Shanklin Chine
Shanklin Isle of Wight PO37 6BW
(01983) 866432
www.shanklinchine.co.uk
Historic gorge with dramatic waterfalls and nature trail.

Spinnaker Tower
Portsmouth, Hampshire PO1 3TT
(023) 9285 7520
www.spinnakertower.co.uk
The Spinnaker Tower is a national icon. It is a striking viewing tower on the south coast offering the public spectacular views from three platforms.

The Historic Dockyard Chatham
Kent ME4 4TZ
(01634) 823807
www.thedockyard.co.uk
A unique, award-winning maritime heritage destination with a fantastic range of attractions, iconic buildings and historic ships to explore, plus a fabulous programme of touring exhibitions at No.1 Smithery.

Waddesdon Manor
Aylesbury,
Buckinghamshire HP18 0JH
(01296) 653226
www.waddesdon.org.uk
This National Trust property houses the Rothschild Collection of art treasures and wine cellars. It also features spectacular grounds with an aviary, parterre and woodland playground, licensed restaurants, gift and wine shops.

Windsor Castle
Berkshire SL4 1NJ
(020) 7766 7304
www.royalcollection.org.uk
The oldest and largest inhabited castle in the world and The Queen's favourite weekend home.

Nature & Wildlife

Arundel Wetland Centre
West Sussex BN18 9PB
(01903) 883355
www.wwt.org.uk/visit/arundel
WWT Arundel Wetland Centre is a 65-acre reserve in an idyllic setting, nestled at the base of the South Downs National Park.

Bedgebury National Pinetum & Forest
Cranbrook, Kent TN17 2SL
(01580) 879820
www.forestry.gov.uk/bedgebury
Visit the world's finest conifer collection at Bedgebury National Pinetum.

British Wildlife Centre
Lingfield, Surrey RH7 6LF
(01342) 834658
www.britishwildlifecentre.co.uk
The best place to see and learn about Britain's own wonderful wildlife, with over 40 different species including deer, foxes, otters, badgers, pine martens and red squirrels.

Chiltern Sculpture Trail
Watlington, Oxfordshire
(01865) 778918
www.chilternsculpturetrail.co.uk
Woodland trail with sculpture sited around the forest. Artists work at the site during some months of the year.

Denmans Garden
Fontwell, West Sussex BN18 0SU
(01243) 542808
www.denmans-garden.co.uk
Beautiful 4 acre garden designed for year round interest through use of form, colour and texture. Beautiful plant centre, award-winning and fully licensed Garden Cafe.

Drusillas Park
Alfriston, East Sussex BN26 5QS
(01323) 874100
www.drusillas.co.uk
Widely regarded as the best small zoo in the country Drusillas Park offers an opportunity to get nose to nose with nature with hundreds of exotic animals from monkeys and crocodiles to penguins and meerkats.

Exbury Gardens and Steam Railway

Beaulieu, Hampshire SO45 1AZ
(023) 8089 1203
www.exbury.co.uk
World famous woodland garden, home to the Rothschild Collection of rhododendrons, azaleas, camellias, rare trees and srubs, with its own steam railway.

Fishers Adventure Farm Park

Billingshurst, West Sussex RH14 0EG
(01403) 700063
www.fishersfarmpark.co.uk
Award-winning Adventure Farm Park and open all year. Ideally suited for ages 2-11 years. Huge variety of animals, rides and attractions from the skating rink, to pony rides, toboggan run, bumper boats, theatre shows and much much more!

Marwell Wildlife

Winchester, Hampshire SO21 1JH
(01962) 777407
www.marwell.org.uk
A visit to Marwell Wildlife is a chance to get close to the wonders of the natural world – and play a big part in helping to save them.

Great Dixter House and Gardens

Rye, East Sussex TN31 6PH
(01797) 252878
www.greatdixter.co.uk
An example of a 15th century manor house with antique furniture and needlework. The house is restored and the gardens were designed by Lutyens.

Pashley Manor Gardens

Wadhurst, East Sussex TN5 7HE
(01580) 200888
www.pashleymanorgardens.com
Pashley Manor Gardens offer a blend of romantic landscaping, imaginative plantings and fine old trees, fountains, springs and large ponds with an exciting programme of special events for garden and art lovers.

Paultons Family Theme Park

Romsey, Hampshire SO51 6AL
(023) 8081 4455
www.paultonspark.co.uk
A great family day out with over 60 different attractions and rides included in the price!

RHS Garden Wisley

Woking, Surrey GU23 6QB
0845 260 9000
www.rhs.org.uk/wisley
Stretching over 240 acres of glorious garden.

RSPB Pulborough Brooks

West Sussex RH20 2EL
(01798) 875851
www.rspb.org.uk/pulboroughbrooks
Set in the scenic Arun Valley with views to the South Downs, the two mile circular nature trail leads around this beautiful reserve.

Stowe Landscape Gardens

Buckinghamshire MK18 5DQ
(01280) 822850
www.nationaltrust.org.uk/stowegardens
Over 40 temples and monuments, laid out against an inspiring backdrop of lakes and valleys.

Ventnor Botanic Gardens

St. Lawrence, Isle of Wight PO38 1UL
(01983) 855397
www.botanic.co.uk
The Botanic Garden on the Isle of Wight is a place where the pleasure of plants can be enjoyed to the fullest.

Outdoor Activities

French Brothers Ltd

Windsor, Berkshire SL4 5JH
(01753) 851900
www.boat-trips.co.uk
Large range of public trips on weather-proof vessels from Windsor, Runnymede and Maidenhead.

Guildford Boat House

Surrey GU1 3XJ
(01483) 504494
www.guildfordboats.co.uk
Regular trips operate from Guildford along this tranquil stretch of the River Wey.

Xscape

Milton Keynes, Buckinghamshire MK9 3XS
0871 200 3220
www.xscape.co.uk
Xscape, Milton Keynes offers a unique combination of extreme sports and leisure activities for all ages.

Events 2014

Brighton & Hove Food & Drink Festival
April 17-April 21, Brighton
This spring event celebrates local producers, growers, restaurants, bars and food retailers and showcases fantastic food, drink and hospitality, with events across the city.
www.brightonfoodfestival.com

Eastbourne Festival
April 19-May 11, Eastbourne
Eastbourne Festival is an Open Access Arts Festival which takes place annually for three weeks from Easter Saturday each year. Now in its fifth year it has become recognised as an annual showcase for local professional and amateur talent.
www.eastbournefestival.co.uk

End of the Pier Film Festival
April-May, Worthing
The festival is a short and feature film competition for independent, low-budget and new film makers.
www.eotpfilmfestival.co.uk

Tulip Festival at Pashley Manor
April-May, Wadhurst
Now in its 18th year, the festival gives visitors the chance to lose themselves among the 25,000 blooms gracing this quintessential English garden.
www.pashleymanorgardens.com

Brighton Marathon
April 6, Brighton
Having grown enormously in just two years, the Brighton Marathon is now one of the top 12 running events in the UK.
www.brightonmarathon.co.uk

Brighton Fringe
May-June, Brighton
One of the largest fringe festivals in the world, offering cabaret, comedy, classical concerts, club nights, theatre and exhibitions, as well as street performances.
www.brightonfestivalfringe.org.uk

Isle of Wight Walking Festival
May
The festival boasts 16 days of unbeatable, informative and healthy walks.
www.isleofwightwalkingfestival.co.uk

Artists' Open Houses
Weekends throughout May, Brighton
The biggest free arts event in Britain with over 1,000 artists exhibiting in 200 houses and studios across the city.
www.aoh.org.uk

Brighton Festival
May 3-25, Brighton
The Brighton Festival continues to grow each year, with its sensational programme of art, theatre, dance, music, literature and family shows. The festival is started with a Children's Parade, which winds its way through the city.
www.brightonfestival.org

The Great Escape
May 8-10, Brighton
This city-wide music festival showcases over 350 new local, national and international bands in various venues throughout the city taking place over three days.
www.escapegreat.com

Glyndebourne Festival
May 1-August 31, Lewes
An English opera festival held at Glyndebourne, an English country house near Lewes.
www.glyndebourne.com

Surrey County Show
May 26, Stoke Park
Surrey County Show attracts up to 40,000 visitors and features hundreds of top quality animals from giant beef bulls to bantam hens.
www.surreycountyshow.co.uk

Alton Summer Beer Festival
May 30-May 31, Alton
Celebrating the cultural heritage of Alton as a traditional area for brewing, based on the clear waters rising from the source of the River Wey, and locally grown hops.
www.altonbeerfestival.co.uk

Investec Derby
June 7, Epsom Racecourse
The biggest horse race in the flat-racing calendar.
www.epsomderby.co.uk

South of England Show
June 5-7, Haywards Heath
The South of England Agricultural Society's flagship event.
www.seas.org.uk

Folkestone Airshow
June 7, Folkestone
The airshow will include ground displays, exhibitions, entertainment, family fun and children's activities.
www.folkestoneairshow.com

Isle of Wight Festival
June 12-15, Newport
A music festival featuring some of the UK's top acts and bands.
www.isleofwightfestival.com

Marlow Regatta
June 21, Eton Dorney
Marlow Regatta is one of the multi-lane regattas in the British Rowing calendar.
www.themarlowregatta.com

London to Brighton Bike Ride
June 15, Ends on Madeira Drive, Brighton
The annual bike ride from the capital to the coast in aid of the British Heart Foundation. The UK's largest charity bike ride with 27,000 riders.
www.bhf.org.uk/london-brighton

Reading Real Ale and Jazz Festival
June 26-29, Reading
This year's festival is going to be the biggest and best yet, featuring some of the best jazz acts on the circuit.
www.raaj.info

Deal Festival of Music and the Arts
June 27-Jul 6, Deal
Experience great classical and contemporary music from some of the world's finest music-makers, as well as theatre, opera, cinema and dance – in the beautiful and historic surroundings of Deal and Dover on England's south coast.
www.dealfestival.co.uk

Henley Royal Regatta
July 2-6, Henley
Attracting thousands of visitors over a five-day period and spectators will be thrilled by over 200 races of international standard.
www.hrr.co.uk

Winchester Hat Fair
July, Winchester
Named after the tradition of throwing donations into performance hats, it's Britain's longest running festival of street theatre and outdoor arts.
www.hatfair.co.uk

Roald Dahl Festival
July, Aylesbury Town Centre
An annual celebration of the famous author, including a 500-strong parade of pupils, teachers and musicians with puppets and artwork based on the Roald Dahl stories.
www.aylesburyvaledc.gov.uk/dahl

Paddle Round the Pier
July, Brighton & Hove seafront
A weekend of beach events which gets bigger every year, Paddle Round the Pier invites all kinds of vessels to take to the sea and spectators to enjoy the festivities on land.
www.paddleroundthepier.com

Hampton Court Palace Flower Show
July 8-13, Hampton Court
One of the biggest events in the horticulture calendar.
www.rhs.org.uk

Swan Upping
Starts third week of July
This is the annual census of the swan population on stretches of the Thames in the counties of Middlesex, Surrey, Buckinghamshire, Berkshire and Oxfordshire. This historic ceremony dates from the 12th century, when the Crown claimed ownership of all mute swans.
www.royalswan.co.uk

Lammas Festival
July-26-27, Eastbourne
A friendly family-oriented free festival of music, dance and entertainment.
www.lammasfest.org

Glorious Goodwood
July 29-Aug 2, Chichester
Bursting with fabulous fashions, succulent strawberries, chilled Champagne and top horse racing stars, as well as music and dancing.
www.goodwood.com

New Forest and Hampshire Show
July 29-31, New Park, Brockenhurst
The show attracts, on average, 95,000 visitors every year and brings together a celebration of traditional country pursuits, crafts, produce and entertainment.
www.newforestshow.co.uk

Cowes Week
August 2-8, Cowes
Cowes Week is one of the longest-running regular regattas in the world.
www.aamcowesweek.co.uk

Isle of Wight Garlic Festival
August 16-17, Newchurch
Garlic is of course, at the heart of this event – coming in all shapes and forms, some of them traditional, some surprising.
www.garlic-festival.co.uk

Arundel Festival
August 16-25, Arundel
Ten days of the best music, theatre, art and comedy.
www.arundelfestival.co.uk

England's Medieval Festival
**August 23-25,
Herstmonceux Castle**
A celebration of the Middle Ages.
www.mgel.com

Wings & Wheels
**August 23-24,
Dunsfold Aerodrome**
Outstanding variety of dynamic aviation, motoring displays and iconic cars.
www.wingsandwheels.net

Reading Festival
August 22-24, Reading
The Reading and Leeds Festivals are a pair of annual music festivals that take place simultaneously.
www.readingfestival.com

Shoreham Airshow 2014
August 30-31, Shoreham-by-Sea
One of the UK's finest airshows with a fantastic air display and excting attractions.
www.shorehamairshow.co.uk

Brighton Digital Festival
September, Brighton
With a month of exhibitions, performances, workshops and outdoor events, Brighton & Hove is certainly a leading digital destination. There will be workshops, interactive demonstrations and displays throughout the city.
www.brightondigitalfestival.co.uk

Southampton Boat Show
September 12-21, Southampton
See the best boats and marine brands gathered together in one fantastic water-based show.
www.southamptonboatshow.com

Kop Hill Climb
**September 20-21,
Princes Risborough**
In the 1900s Kop Hill Climb was one of the most popular hill climbs in the country for cars and motorcycles. Now the spirit of the climb is being revived.
www.kophillclimb.org.uk

Brighton Comedy Festival
October, Brighton Dome
The land of one-liners, whimsical thoughts, innuendo, ridiculous characters, clever puns and hand over mouth dirty jokes descends on Brighton for three weeks of laughter, mirth and merriment.
www.brightoncomedyfestival.com

Eastbourne Beer Festival
**October 9-11,
Winter Gardens, Eastbourne**
Eastbourne's annual beer festival features over 120 cask ales, plus wines, international bottled beers, ciders and perries. Each session features live music.
www.visiteastbourne.com/beer-festival

Burning the Clocks
**December,
Brighton Winter Solstice Parade**
Started in 1993, Burning the Clocks represents an alternative to the commercial Christmas. Thousands of people gather to make paper and willow lanterns to carry through the city before burning them on the beach as a token for the end of the year and to greet the lengthening days.
www.burningtheclocks.co.uk

Tourist Information Centres

When you arrive at your destination, visit an Official Partner Tourist Information Centre for quality assured help with accommodation and information about local attractions and events, or email your request before you go. To find a Tourist Information Centre visit www.visitengland.com

Ashford	Ashford Gateway Plus	01233 330316	tourism@ashford.gov.uk
Aylesbury	The Kings Head	01296 330559	tic@aylesburyvaledc.gov.uk
Banbury	Castle Quay Shopping Centre	01295 753752	banbury.tic@cherwell-dc.gov.uk
Bicester	Bicester Village	01869 369055	bicestervisitorcentre@valueretail.com
Brighton	Royal Pavilion Shop	01273 290337	visitorinfo@visitbrighton.com
Burford	33a High Street	01993 823558	burford.vic@westoxon.gov.uk
Canterbury	Canterbury Heritage Museum	01227 378100	canterburyinformation@canterbury.gov.uk
Chichester	The Novium	01243 775888	chitic@chichester.gov.uk
Dover	Market Square	01304 201066	tic@doveruk.com
Gravesend	Towncentric	01474 337600	info@towncentric.co.uk
Guildford	155 High Street	01483 444333	tic@guildford.gov.uk
Hastings	Queens Square	01424 451111	hic@hastings.gov.uk
Lewes	187 High Street	01273 483448	lewes.tic@lewes.gov.uk
Maidstone	Maidstone Museum	01622 602169	tourism@maidstone.gov.uk
Marlow	55a High Street	01628 483597	tourism_enquiries@wycombe.gov.uk
Newbury	The Wharf	01635 30267	tourism@westberks.gov.uk
Oxford	15/16 Broad Street	01865 252200	info@visitoxfordshire.org
Portsmouth	Clarence Esplanade	023 9282 6722	vis@portsmouthcc.gov.uk
Rochester	95 High Street	01634 338141	visitor.centre@medway.gov.uk
Romsey	13 Church Street	01794 512987	romseytic@testvalley.gov.uk
Royal Tunbridge Wells	The Old Fish Market	01892 515675	touristinformationcentre@tunbridgewells.gov.uk
Rye	4/5 Lion Street	01797 229049	ryetic@tourismse.com
Swanley	Library & Information Centre	01322 614660	touristinfo@swanley.org.uk
Thanet	The Droit House	01843 577577	visitorinformation@thanet.gov.uk
Winchester	Guildhall	01962 840500	tourism@winchester.gov.uk
Windsor	Old Booking Hall	01753 743900	windsor.tic@rbwm.gov.uk
Witney	3 Welsh Way	01993 775802	witney.vic@westoxon.gov.uk
Worthing	22a Marine Parade	01903 239868	tic@dur-worthing.gov.uk

Regional Contacts and Information

For more information on accommodation, attractions, activities, events and holidays in South East England, contact the regional or local tourism organisations. Their websites have a wealth of information and many produce free publications to help you get the most out of your visit.

The following publications are available from Tourism South East by logging on to www.visitsoutheastengland.com, emailing enquiries@tourismse.com or by calling (023) 8062 5400.

- E-Brochures
- Family Fun
- Time for Us

South East England – We know just the place...

Visit our 2014 guide websites...

- Detailed information
- Up-to-date availability
- Book your accommodation online

Includes over 20,000 places to stay, all of them star rated.

Win amazing prizes, every month...

Enter our monthly competition at
www.visitor-guides.co.uk/prizes

Entries appear alphabetically by town name in each county. A key to symbols appears on page 7

South East - Berkshire

Holly House

Goughs Lane, Bracknell RG12 2JR **T:** (01344) 411750 **F:** (01344) 411750
E: reservations@hollyhousebracknell.co.uk
W: hollyhousebracknell.co.uk

B&B PER ROOM PER NIGHT
S: £65.00 - £80.00
D: £80.00 - £150.00

SPECIAL PROMOTIONS
Complimentary drink
of choice on arrival.

An elegant charming house with a beautiful garden in a quiet leafy lane offering exceptional yet affordable bed and breakfast in a warm and relaxing atmosphere. Comfort and cleanliness are our bywords. Close to Windsor, Ascot, Henley, Marlow and Reading with London and Gatwick airport an hour away.

Directions: Once along Warfield Road (A3095) turn right by pedestrian traffic lights into Holly Spring Lane then left into Goughs Lane. 350 yards on left entrance.

Bedrooms: 1 single, 2 double, 1 twin
Open: All year except Christmas and New Year

Site: ✿ P **Payment:** 🔲 **Leisure:** 🎿 🎣 ▶ ♻ **Property:** 🚪 📖 ♨ ⌀ **Children:** 🐾10 **Catering:** 🍴
Room: 🥤 🖐 📶 📺 🍵 🔌 🛏 🔽

The Black Boys Inn

Henley Road, Hurley near Henley on Thames, Maidenhead SL6 5NQ **T:** (01628) 824212
E: info@blackboysinn.co.uk
W: www.blackboysinn.co.uk **£ BOOK ONLINE**

B&B PER ROOM PER NIGHT
S: £75.00 - £87.50
D: £80.00 - £120.00
EVENING MEAL PER PERSON
£14.95 - £22.50

Situated on the outskirts of Henley-on-Thames and Maidenhead overlooking the beautiful Chiltern Valley - the Black Boys Inn is a stylish and comfortable retreat from today's hustle and bustle. **Directions:** Via M4: Leave the M4 at Junction 8/9 and follows signs for the A404. After 2 miles exit for Henley on the A4130. Follow the signs for Hurley and Henley. **Bedrooms:** Our 8 en suite bedrooms, converted from the original stables and carriage rooms of the Inn, offer simple elegance and style. **Open:** All year

Site: ✿ P **Payment:** 🔲 **Leisure:** 🎿 ▶ ♻ **Property:** ⚡ 🐴 ♨ ⌀ **Children:** 🐾 🏠 🍴 **Catering:** ❌ 🍷 🍴
Room: 🥤 🖐 📶 📺 🔌

Thatched House B&B

High Street, Chieveley, Newbury, Berks RG20 8TE **T:** (01635) 248295
E: s.malty@btinternet.com
W: mychieveley.co.uk/info/thatchedhousebandb

B&B PER ROOM PER NIGHT
S: £55.00 - £70.00
D: £75.00 - £90.00

Our B&B offers all the things we like when we stay away - lovely, spacious, self-contained accommodation. Suitable for families (sleeps 5 people). Several good restaurants and pubs close by! **Directions:** From South, at M4 J13 take A34 north to Oxford. Exit Chieveley. From North, exit A34 at Beedon. Thatched House between shop and Village Hall. **Bedrooms:** 1 suite - double rm, bathrm + living rm + sofabed **Open:** All year

Site: ✿ P **Payment:** € **Property:** 🛏 **Children:** 🐾 🏠 🍴 **Catering:** 🍴 **Room:** 🥤 🖐 📶 📺 🔌

South East - Berkshire

WINDSOR, Berkshire Map ref 2C2 — SatNav SL4 2DG **B**

★★★★ ROOM ONLY / **Silver AWARD**

B&B PER ROOM PER NIGHT
S: £65.00 - £85.00
D: £75.00 - £95.00

Bluebell House

Lovel Lane, Woodside, Windsor, Berkshire SL4 2DG T: (01344) 886828
E: info@bluebellhouse-windsor.co.uk
W: www.bluebellhouse-windsor.co.uk **£ BOOK ONLINE**

Bluebell House is an ex coaching Inn located on the outskirts of Windsor and Ascot. We are close to Legoland, Ascot and Windsor racecourses and golf and polo are close by. You will be sure of a pleasant welcome and stay at Bluebell House. **Directions:** M4 jct 6 to Windsor. Take A332 to Ascot through Windsor Great Park. Take 2nd exit off roundabout and we are behind Loch Fyne.
Bedrooms: 3 double, 1 twin **Open:** All year except Christmas

Site: ☼ P Payment: 💷 Leisure: & ⚑ Property: 🖦 Children: 🐾 🏚 Catering: 🍴 Room: 🔌 👄 🖫 TV 🍵

WINDSOR, Berkshire Map ref 2D2 — SatNav SL4 1RU **B**

★★★★ GUEST ACCOMMODATION

B&B PER ROOM PER NIGHT
S: £70.00 - £90.00
D: £75.00 - £100.00

Charles House

89 Arthur Road, Windsor SL4 1RU T: (01753) 831433
E: info@accommodationinwindsor.co.uk
W: www.accommodationinwindsor.co.uk **£ BOOK ONLINE**

Charles House, built circa 1898, is situated just a 5 minute walk from Windsor Town centre. We use PIN entry code system, so no need to worry about keys or fobs. For either business or pleasure, Charles House is the place to stay. **Directions:** Take exit 6 off the M4 and follow signs to Windsor. Take the first exit towards Windsor. We are on the corner at the 3rd set of trafic lights. **Bedrooms:** En suite, flat screen tv, tea/coffee, hair dryer **Open:** All year except Christmas and New Year

Payment: 💷 Property: 🖦 Room: 🔌 👄 TV 🍵

WINDSOR, Berkshire Map ref 2D2 — SatNav SL4 5AE **B**

★★★ GUEST HOUSE

B&B PER ROOM PER NIGHT
S: £45.00 - £84.00
D: £55.00 - £94.00

Clarence Hotel

9 Clarence Road, Windsor SL4 5AE T: (01753) 864436 F: (01753) 857060
E: clarence.hotel@btconnect.com
W: clarencehotelwindsor.co.uk

Recently upgraded, located in town centre close to restaurants, Windsor Castle & Eton. Licensed bar, steam sauna. All rooms en suite, TV, beverage trays, hairdryer, radio alarm. Free WiFi Internet. **Directions:** Exit M4 at jct 6 to Windsor. Stay on dual carriageway and turn left at the roundabout onto Clarence Road. **Bedrooms:** 4 single, 4 double, 6 twin, 6 family **Open:** All year except Christmas

Site: ☼ P Payment: 💷 Property: 🐾 🖦 Children: 🐾 Catering: 🍷 Room: 🔌 👄 🖫 TV 🍵

WINDSOR, Berkshire Map ref 2D2 — SatNav RG42 6LD **H**

★★★ HOTEL

Stirrups Country House Hotel

Maidens Green, Bracknell RG42 6LD T: (01344) 882284 F: (01344) 882300
E: reception@stirrupshotel.co.uk
W: stirrupshotel.co.uk

Stirrups, with its Tudor origins, is located between Bracknell, Ascot and Windsor and is the perfect venue for visits to Legoland Windsor (three miles). Round off your day by relaxing in the oak-beamed bar, by the inglenook fire, prior to dinner. Please contact for prices. **Directions:** Stirrups lies on the B3022, 200 metres south of the crossroads in Maidens Green Village.
Bedrooms: 19 dble, 4 twin, 7 family, 4 suite - all en suite
Open: All year

Site: ☼ P Payment: 💷 Property: 🍴 🖦 🖥 🏚 ◐ Children: 🐾 🏚 🏃 Catering: (✗ 🍷 🍴 Room: 🔌 👄 ☎ 📺 TV 🍵

f **t**

For **key to symbols** see page 7

107

BUCKINGHAM, Buckinghamshire   Map ref 2C1   SatNav MK18 5ND   B

★★★★
BED & BREAKFAST

B&B PER ROOM PER NIGHT
S: £45.00
D: £70.00

Huntsmill Farm B&B

Huntsmill Farm, Shalstone, Nr. Buckingham MK18 5ND **T:** (01280) 704852 / 07970 871104
E: fiona@huntsmill.com
W: huntsmill.com

Home-made bread and preserves welcome you at Huntsmill Farm. Comfortable, en suite rooms adjacent to farmhouse. Quiet location, views over open countryside. Close to National Trust properties and Silverstone. **Directions:** Midway between Buckingham and Brackley on A422. South side, signposted 'Finmere & Mixbury', 1/3mile on the left. **Bedrooms:** 1 double, 2 twin **Open:** All year except Christmas

Site: ❀ **P** **Payment:** 🖭 € **Leisure:** ♪ ▶ ♪ 🔍 **Property:** 🖥 🗎 🍴 **Children:** ➶5 🛏 🎿 **Catering:** 🍽
Room: 🍵 ✆ 📷 📺 🎽

DENHAM, Buckinghamshire   Map ref 2D2   SatNav UB9 5BE   B

★★★★
INN

B&B PER ROOM PER NIGHT
S: £65.00 - £100.00
D: £65.00 - £100.00

SPECIAL PROMOTIONS
Check our website for latest offers.

The Falcon Inn

Village Road, Denham Village UB9 5BE **T:** (01895) 832125 **E:** mail@falcondenham.com
W: www.falcondenham.com **£ BOOK ONLINE**

Situated in a delightful conservation village with many local walks including Denham Country park and a stroll along the canal. With a stay at the Falcon you will be close to both Denham & The Buckinghamshire Golf Club. Easy access into London Marylebone (25mins train) or drive A40 into London. We are also 20 minutes from London Heathrow Airport.

Directions: M25 J16, M40 J1

Bedrooms: All rooms are en suite with power showers. Complimentary toiletries, towels, hairdryer, tea/coffee, refrigerator/flat screen tv. Iron/board. Free wi-fi
Open: All year

Site: ❀ **Payment:** 🖭 **Leisure:** ♪ ▶ ♪ **Property:** 🖥 **Catering:** (✗ 🍷 🍽 **Room:** 🍵 ✆ 📺 📀

GREAT MISSENDEN, Buckinghamshire   Map ref 2C1   SatNav HP16 0AX   B

★★★
BED & BREAKFAST

B&B PER ROOM PER NIGHT
S: £33.00 - £35.00

Forge House

Forge House, 10 Church Street, Great Missenden, Buckinghamshire HP16 0AX
T: (01494) 867347

Set in the wooded Chiltern Hills, quiet village location - a charming 18th century beamed house traditionally refurbished with three en suite double bedrooms. Set in the home town of Roald Dahl, and a regular film site for Midsummer Murders, Forge House welcomes walkers and cyclists alike and is only a 35 minute trip from Marlborough train station. Prices are based on per person per night with English/continental breakfast included. **Bedrooms:** 2 double rooms and 1 twin, all en suite. **Open:** All Year

Site: ❀ **P** **Leisure:** ♪ **Property:** 🍴 ∅ **Children:** ➶5 **Catering:** 🍽 **Room:** 🍵 ✆ 📷 📺 📀

Rye Lodge Hotel

Hilders Cliff, Rye, East Sussex TN31 7LD **T:** (01797) 223838 **F:** (01797) 223585
E: info@ryelodge.co.uk
W: www.ryelodge.co.uk **£ BOOK ONLINE**

B&B PER ROOM PER NIGHT
D: £130.00 - £220.00

SPECIAL PROMOTIONS
Champagne
Celebreak! One night
stay in the Champagne
room with fruit,
flowers, chocolates
and Champagne in
your room, and travel
to the Mermaid Inn for
dinner in our Rolls
Royce! The cost is
£295.00.

Staying at Rye Lodge is always an enjoyable experience at any time of the year. The surroundings are elegant, the atmosphere relaxed - and the service second to none! Luxurious rooms and suites furnished to the highest standards with all the little extras that make such a difference. Room Service. Champagne Bar and Terrace, Leisure Centre with swimming pool and Sauna. Private Car Park.

Bedrooms: All rooms en suite with shower or bath.
Open: All year

Site: P **Payment:** 🏛 **Leisure:** 🏊 **Property:** 🐾 ⬜ **Children:** 🐴 ♨ **Catering:** ▼
Room: 🍵 🚽 📞 📺 ♿

May Cottage

Thruxton, Andover SP11 8LZ **T:** (01264) 771241 / 07768 242166
E: maycottagethruxton@gmail.com
W: maycottage-thruxton.co.uk

B&B PER ROOM PER NIGHT
S: £40.00 - £65.00
D: £70.00 - £90.00

Dating back to 1740, May Cottage is situated in the heart of this picturesque village. All rooms en suite/private bathroom. Guests own sitting/dining room. Secluded garden. Historic attractions nearby. Non-smoking. **Directions:** From Andover take A303 towards Exeter, then take turning for Thruxton (village only). Left at T-junction. May Cottage is on right opposite The George Inn.
Bedrooms: 2 double, 1 twin **Open:** All year

Site: ❁ P **Leisure:** ♪ ▶ **Property:** ⬜ **Children:** 🐴 ♨ **Catering:** 🍴 **Room:** 🍵 🚽 📞 📺 ♿

Spring Cottage

Main Road, Kingsley, Bordon GU35 9NA **T:** (01420) 472703 **F:** (01420) 472703
E: paulineansell@aol.com
W: springcottagekingsley.co.uk

B&B PER ROOM PER NIGHT
S: £22.50 - £25.00
D: £50.00

A warm welcome awaits you in an 18th Century family home, in a village and close to pub serving food. Shared guest bathroom, hence two stars. Easy reach Alton, Farnham, Petersfield. Largegarden, views of woods and fields. Free WIFI. **Directions:** Enter village of Kingsley. On each side of road are bus shelters. 50yds past these on right is a track leading to our house.
Bedrooms: 1 single, 1 double **Open:** All year except Christmas

Site: ❁ P **Leisure:** ♪ ▶ **Property:** ⬜ 🅿 **Children:** 🐴⁹ **Catering:** 🍴 **Room:** 🍵 🚽 📞 📺 ♿ 🛏 ⬛

CADNAM, Hampshire   Map ref 2C3   SatNav SO40 2NQ B

GUEST HOUSE ★★★★
Silver AWARD

Twin Oaks Guest House

Southampton Road, Cadnam SO40 2NQ T: (02380) 812305
E: enquiries@twinoaks-guesthouse.co.uk
W: www.accommodationinthenewforest.com **£ BOOK ONLINE**

B&B PER ROOM PER NIGHT
S: £46.00 - £48.00
D: £80.00 - £86.00

A warm welcome awaits at Twin Oaks. The New Forest and National Park, a perfect base to explore the area. Two excellent restaurants minutes walk away. Plenty of off road parking. **Directions:** M27 westbound junction 1: take sign for Cadnam, then follow brown directional signs for Twin Oaks Guest House. **Bedrooms:** 1 single, 3 double, 1 twin, 1 family **Open:** All year except Christmas and New Year

Site: ❀ P Payment: 🖃 € Leisure: 🎣 ♪ ▶ ♿ ⚲ ⚲ Property: 🖿 🖥 Children: 🪀 ⛵ 🕮 ♿
Catering: 🍴 Room: 🔌 📺 🖥 🖨

EASTLEIGH, Hampshire   Map ref 2C3   SatNav SO50 9HQ H

HOTEL ★★★

Concorde Club & Ellington Lodge Hotel

Stoneham Lane, Eastleigh SO50 9HQ T: (023) 8065 1478 F: (023) 8065 1479
E: hotel@theconcordeclub.com
W: www.theconcordeclub.com **£ BOOK ONLINE**

SPECIAL PROMOTIONS
Special jazz/entertainment breaks at the award winning Concorde Club. Short term airport and cruise parking available to residents.

Comfortable air-conditioned bedrooms, just two minutes from Southampton International Airport/ Parkway railway station. In quiet woodland setting with ample free parking. The atmospheric Moldy Fig Wine Bar is open all day and offers excellent food and fine wines. Please contact for prices.

Directions: Situated on the outskirts of Southampton in Eastleigh, near Southampton International Airport. Exit M27 junction 5, follow signs to Concorde Club & Hotel.

Bedrooms: 29 double, 6 twin
Open: All year

Site: ❀ Payment: 🖃 Leisure: ♪ Property: ⊛ 🍴 🪀 🖿 🖥 ◐ Catering: 🍴 🍴 Room: 🔌 ☎ 📺

Need more information?

Visit our new 2014 guide websites for detailed information, up-to-date availability and to book your accommodation online. Includes over 20,000 places to stay, all of them star rated.

www.visitor-guides.co.uk

FORDINGBRIDGE, Hampshire   Map ref 2B3   SatNav SP6 2HF   H

The Three Lions

Stuckton, Fordingbridge SP6 2HF   T: (01425) 652489   F: (01425) 656144
E: the3lions@btinternet.com
W: thethreelionsrestaurant.co.uk

B&B PER ROOM PER NIGHT
S: £69.00 - £79.00
D: £79.00 - £125.00
HB PER PERSON PER NIGHT
£70.00 - £85.00

SPECIAL PROMOTIONS

Weekend Two Day
Break £200 incl
continental breakfast
£315 with 3 course
dinners Mid Week
£180 to £295
respectively

A restaurant with rooms in the New Forest. Come and stay, relax and enjoy English/French cuisine cooked by Mike a constantly hands on Michelin starred chef. Cosy informal bar, log fire, conservatory and gardens with sauna & hot tub. Three times Hampshire Restaurant of the Year, Good Food Guide. National Newcomer of the Year, Good Hotel Guide. We are family, cyclist & walker friendly & accept pets.

Directions: 15 mins M27 jct 1. 15 mins Salisbury. Locate Total garage east of Fordingbridge, follow brown tourist signs to the Three Lions.

Bedrooms: 2 dble, 2 twin, 3 family
Open: All year

Site: ✤ Payment: 💷 € Leisure: ⚓ ♪ ▶ ☋ Property: ♟ 🐕 🖼 ▣ Children: ⛵ ⚏ ♣ Catering: ♟ 🍴
Room: ☏ ♨ TV 🛁 🖨

NEW MILTON, NEW FOREST, Hampshire   Map ref 2B3   SatNav BH23 5QL   H

Chewton Glen

New Milton, New Forest, Hampshire BH25 6QS   T: (01425) 282212   F: (01425) 272310
E: reservations@chewtonglen.com
W: chewtonglen.com

B&B PER ROOM PER NIGHT
D: £377.00 -
£1652.00

SPECIAL PROMOTIONS
Two night minimum
stay at weekends

An English Original. Chewton Glen is a luxury countryhouse hotel and spa set in 130 acres of Hampshire countryside on the edge of the New Forest National Park, and just a few minutes walk from the sea. A very special place, Chewton Glen is a proud member of Relais & Châteaux, is one of the finest luxury hotels in the UK and has been voted 'Best Hotel for Service in the UK' and listed as one of the 'World's Best Hotels' by Conde Nast Traveller readers. The unsurpassed heritage of effortlessly gracious English hospitality and the balance between heritage and evolution is what makes Chewton Glen a 5 star, luxury country house hotel and spa that constantly surprises.

Directions: Please contact us for directions.

Bedrooms: 35 Double, 23 Suites, 12 Treehouse Suites
Open: All year

Site: ✤ Payment: 💷 € Leisure: ⚓ ♪ ▶ ☋ ✦ ⅏ ⚲ ⚲ Property: ⊚ ♟ 🖼 ▣ ◐ Children: ⛵ ⚏ ♣
Catering: ♟ 🍴 Room: ☏ ☏ 🖥 TV 🛁 🖨

PORTSMOUTH, Hampshire   Map ref 2C3
SatNav PO4 0RW   H

Ocean Hotel

★★ HOTEL

8-10 St. Helens Parade, Portsmouth PO4 0RW   T: (023) 9273 4233   F: (023) 9229 7046
E: enquiries@portsmouth-apartments.co.uk
W: portsmouth-apartments.co.uk/ocean-hotel-suites.html

B&B PER ROOM PER NIGHT
S: £45.00 - £55.00
D: £70.00 - £90.00
EVENING MEAL PER PERSON
£8.00 - £15.00

The Ocean Hotel has many recently refurbished rooms, many with sea-views all are en suite. All rooms have tea/coffee facilities and wireless internet. The Ocean Suites offer the facilities & services of a hotel bedroom with full facilities. **Directions:** Portsmouth & Southsea or The Hard train station is approximately 5 minutes by taxi or bus. Fratton train station is approximately 4 minutes. Also there is a bus stop directly opposite. **Bedrooms:** All rooms en suite tea and coffee and free wi-fi **Open:** All year

Site: P Payment: 🖃 Property: ⊛ 🍷 🐾 🖥 🖥 🎇 ◐ Children: 🌣 🛏 ⚱ Catering: 🕻 🍷 🍽 Room: 🕾 🕯 ℃ 📶 📺

PORTSMOUTH, Hampshire   Map ref 2C3
SatNav PO1 3HS   H

Royal Maritime Club

★★ HOTEL

75-80 Queen Street, Portsmouth PO1 3HS   T: (023) 9282 4231   F: (023) 9229 3496
E: info@royalmaritimeclub.co.uk
W: www.royalmaritimeclub.co.uk   £ BOOK ONLINE

B&B PER ROOM PER NIGHT
S: £51.00 - £55.00
D: £90.00 - £130.00
EVENING MEAL PER PERSON
£14.75 - £18.50

Situated at the heart of Portsmouth's unique naval heritage area. Within walking distance of HMS Victory, HMS Warrior, the Mary Rose, Gunwharf Quays shopping complex. Rail, coach, ferry links nearby. **Directions:** Take the M275 Portsmouth(W) and then follow signs to Historic Waterfront/Historic Dockyard. **Bedrooms:** 20 single, 33 dble, 19 twin, 8 family, 20 superior **Open:** All year except Christmas and New Year

Payment: 🖃 Leisure: 🐾 Property: 🍷 🖥 🖥 ◐ Children: 🌣 🛏 ⚱ Catering: 🍷 🍽 Room: 🕾 🕯 ℃ 📺 📶

SOUTHAMPTON, Hampshire   Map ref 2C3
SatNav SO19 6AJ   B

Eversley Guest House

★★★★ BED & BREAKFAST

Kanes Hill, Southampton, Hampshire SO19 6AJ   T: (023) 8046 4546
E: eversleyguesthouse@yahoo.co.uk
W: www.eversleyguesthouse.org.uk   £ BOOK ONLINE

B&B PER ROOM PER NIGHT
S: £45.00 - £60.00
D: £65.00 - £75.00

Four star rated, this friendly, family run B&B is conveniently located in the eastern suburbs of Southampton, close to the M27, junctions 7 & 8. Finished to a high standard throughout, we cater for holiday and business visitors alike. **Bedrooms:** All rooms en suite, flat screen tv, tea and coffee making facilities. **Open:** All year

Site: P Payment: 🖃 Property: 🖥 Catering: 🍽 Room: 🕾 🕯 📺 📀

SOUTHAMPTON, Hampshire   Map ref 2C3
SatNav SO31 5DQ   B

The Prince Consort

★★★ INN

Victoria Road, Netley Abbey, Southampton, Hampshire SO31 5DQ   T: (023) 8045 2676
E: info@theprinceconsortpub.co.uk
W: www.theprinceconsortpub.co.uk

B&B PER ROOM PER NIGHT
S: £50.00
D: £65.00 - £80.00

Grade 2 listed Victorian Pub with seperate annexe B&B in the Heart of Netley Abbey. Close to Hamble, Southampton, Winchester and Portsmouth. Rates include breakfast. **Directions:** Situated near A27 & M27 and mainline train links to and from Southampton and Portsmouth. Within easy walking distance of Hamble. **Bedrooms:** 4 double, 3 twin **Open:** All year

Site: ✿ P Payment: 🖃 Leisure: 🎵 ▶ ∪ Property: 🐾 🖥 Children: 🌣 🛏 ⚱ Catering: 🕻 🍷 🍽 Room: 🕯 ℃ 📺 📀

SWAY, Hampshire   Map ref 2C3   SatNav SO41 6DJ B

The Mill At Gordleton

Silver Street, Hordle, Lymington SO41 6DJ T: (01590) 682219
E: info@themillatgordleton.co.uk
W: themillatgordleton.co.uk

B&B PER ROOM PER NIGHT
S: £115.00 - £245.00
D: £150.00 - £275.00
EVENING MEAL PER PERSON
£22.95 - £47.00

A beautiful individual privately owned small restaurant with rooms, wonderful river, gardens. Homemade, local and organic food. We care passionately about the environment which is reflected in everything we do. **Directions:** A337 Lyndhurst to Brockenhurst to Lymington. Over two mini roundabouts first right Sway Road. The Mill at Gordleton Hotel 2m. **Bedrooms:** 3 kings, 3 twins, 2 suite **Open:** All year except Christmas day

Site: Payment: Leisure: Property: Children: Catering: Room:

WINCHESTER, Hampshire   Map ref 2C3   SatNav SO23 9SR B

12 Christchurch Road

12 Christchurch Road, Winchester SO23 9SR T: (01962) 854272 / 07879 850076
E: pjspatton@yahoo.co.uk

B&B PER ROOM PER NIGHT
S: £55.00 - £60.00
D: £65.00 - £70.00

Elegant Victorian house furnished with style. Easy, pleasant walk to city centre, cathedral, museums, shops and water meadows. Breakfast in conservatory, overlooking beautiful gardens (NGS), with home-made bread, preserves and local produce **Directions:** Please contact us for directions. **Bedrooms:** 1 double, 1 twin comfortable and well furnished **Open:** All year except Christmas and New Year

Property: Children: Catering: Room:

COWES, Isle Of Wight   Map ref 2C3   SatNav PO31 7EG B

Endeavour House

47 Mill Hill Road, West Cowes PO31 7EG T: (01983) 297406 F: (01983) 297406
E: enquiries@endeavourhousecowes.co.uk
W: www.endeavourhousecowes.co.uk

B&B PER ROOM PER NIGHT
D: £72.00 - £90.00

Luxury small, friendly, comfortable bed and breakfast conveniently situated near the ferrys, marinas, High Street and access to the island. We will help you make the most from your stay. Single occupancy rate available. **Directions:** Short walk from the Red Jet fast passenger service from Southampton. Car Ferrys to East Cowes and Fishbourne details on Redfunnel & Wightlink websites **Bedrooms:** En suites, Wi-Fi, flat screen tv, tea & coffee etc. **Open:** All year except Christmas & Boxing Day

Site: P Payment: Leisure: Property: Children: Catering: Room:

For **key to symbols** see page 7

EAST COWES, Isle of Wight   Map ref 2C3   SatNav PO32 6BD   H

Albert Cottage Hotel

York Avenue, East Cowes, Isle of Wight PO32 6BD   T: (01983) 299309   F: (01983) 296046
E: enquiries@albertcottagehotel.com
W: albertcottagehotel.com

B&B PER ROOM PER NIGHT
D: £99.00 - £159.00

SPECIAL PROMOTIONS
Promotions available
via the website.

Once owned by Queen Victoria, and used by her youngest daughter Princess Beatrice, historic
Albert Cottage in East Cowes, was originally part of the Royal Osborne Estate. Now a delightful
boutique hotel with fine dining and superb function facilities, Albert Cottage Hotel offers quality in
a sophisticated and relaxing setting.

Directions: Located next door to Osborne
House and within easy access of ferries.
Directions availabe on the website.

Bedrooms: 8 double, 1 twin, 1 family
Open: All year

Site: ✿ Payment: 💷 Property: ⚍ 🖥 📶 ◗ Children: ⛼ 🛏 🔥 Catering: 🏆 🍴
Room: 📺 🖐 🕯 ☎ 📺 🍴 🛁 🛌

FRESHWATER, Isle of Wight   Map ref 2C3   SatNav PO40 9ED   B

The Orchards

Princes Road, Freshwater PO40 9ED   T: (01983) 753795 / 07765 250614
E: paulaattheorchards@googlemail.com
W: www.theorchardsbandb.co.uk

B&B PER ROOM PER NIGHT
S: £35.00 - £45.00
D: £70.00 - £90.00
EVENING MEAL PER PERSON
£15.00 - £20.00

Enjoy a warm welcome, comfortable stay, located in Freshwater
village. Near Yarmouth ferry, local walks, beaches and amenities.
Locally-sourced food when available. Off-road parking and secure
bicycle storage. **Directions:** Please contact us for directions.
Bedrooms: 2 single, 1 double, 1 family **Open:** All year

Site: ✿ P Leisure: 🚲 🎣 ⛷ ♨ ⚓ Property: ⚍ Children: ⛼ 🛏 🔥 Catering: 🍴 Room: 📺 🖐 ☎ 📺 🛁

FRESHWATER, Isle of Wight   Map ref 2C3   SatNav PO40 9PP   🐾   B

Seahorses

Victoria Road, Freshwater, Isle of Wight PO40 9PP   T: (01983) 752574   F: (01983) 752574
E: seahorses-iow@tiscali.co.uk
W: seahorsesisleofwight.com   £ BOOK ONLINE

B&B PER ROOM PER NIGHT
S: £37.00 - £39.00
D: £74.00 - £78.00

A charming early 19th century rectory, standing in 2.5 acres of
lovely gardens with direct footpath access to Yarmouth and
Freshwater Bay. Art courses available in our studio. Pets welcome.
Directions: From the Freshwater Co-op (large), go up Stroud Road
becoming Victoria Road, just past St. Andrews Village Hall, turn left
into our driveway. Ample off-road parking. **Bedrooms:** 1 double, 2
twin, 2 family **Open:** All year

Site: ✿ P Leisure: 🚲 🎣 ⛷ ♨ Property: 🐕 ⚍ 📶 Children: ⛼ 🔥 Catering: 🍴 Room: 📺 🖐 📺 🛁

Cliff Lodge Guest House

13 Cliff Path, Lake PO36 8PL   T: (01983) 402963   E: clifflodge@uwclub.net
W: www.cliff-lodge-isle-of-wight.co.uk

B&B PER ROOM PER NIGHT
S: £26.00
D: £51.00 - £61.00
EVENING MEAL PER PERSON
£10.00 - £12.50

SPECIAL PROMOTIONS
Stay 6 nights get the
7th night half price
at all times.
Single night
supplement
included in above
prices.

Midway between Shanklin and Sandown near Lake station. Evening meals Sunday to Wednesday, licensed, local produce used, own car park, use of garden access always available to rooms. Any day bookings. Family rooms have TV's with DVD's all others have TV's. Guest Lounge with TV also books, games and puzzles.

Directions: Off Lake Hill, turn down Brownlow Road and keep going, past station we are first big house on left. use Sat Nav postcode PO36 8PA.

Bedrooms: 2 single, 4 double, 1 twin, 2 family
Open: All year except Christmas and New Year

Site: ❋ P Leisure: ♿ ♪ Children: ⛱ ♨ ⚲ Catering: ♟ ♨ Room: ⚓ ♨ ◉ TV ♨ ♨

Visit our 2014 guide websites...

- Detailed information
- Up-to-date availability
- Book your accommodation online

Includes over 20,000
places to stay,
all of them star rated.

Win amazing prizes,
every month...

Enter our monthly competition at
www.visitor-guides.co.uk/prizes

South East - Isle of Wight

★★★★
GUEST
ACCOMMODATION
enjoyEngland.com

B&B PER ROOM PER NIGHT
S: £28.00 - £35.00
D: £60.00 - £70.00

Sea View B&B

8 Dover Street, Ryde PO33 2AQ **T:** (01983) 810976 **E:** seaviewbandbinryde@hotmail.com

There is a warm welcome for all guests at this comfortable, no smoking, B&B located near beach, shops, restaurants and public transport links. **Directions:** A3054 to Ryde. 5 minutes walk from Ryde Esplanade Station, Bus Station and Hovercraft terminal. **Bedrooms:** 1 double room, 1 twin room, both en suite **Open:** All year except Christmas

Payment: € **Children:** ⛛¹⁰ **Catering:** 🍴 **Room:** 🥤 🖥 📻 📺

★★★★
GUEST HOUSE
enjoyEngland.com

Silver AWARD

The Belmore

101 Station Avenue, Sandown PO36 8HD **T:** (01983) 404189 **E:** belmorebandb@aol.com
W: thebelmore.co.uk

The Belmore is an eight bedroom, family run Guest House, all rooms are en suite and are situated within two minutes walk from the beach and town centre. Please contact for prices. **Bedrooms:** 1 single, 4 double, 2 twin, 1 family. Ironing facilities and safe in rooms **Open:** All year

Payment: 💳 € **Leisure:** 🐾 🎵 ▶ **Property:** 🖥 **Children:** ⛛ 🍴 🏊 **Catering:** 🍴 **Room:** 🥤 🖥 📺

★★★
GUEST
ACCOMMODATION
enjoyEngland.com

B&B PER ROOM PER NIGHT
S: £28.00 - £34.00
D: £56.00 - £68.00

f

The Montpelier

5 Pier Street, Sandown PO36 8JR **T:** (01983) 403964 / 07092 212734
E: steve@themontpelier.co.uk
W: www.themontpelier.co.uk

The Montpelier is situated opposite the pier and beaches with the High St just around the corner. We offer B&B, room-only and ferry-inclusive from Southampton. Rooms are en suite most with sea views and all have a fridge. Room only £4pn less. **Directions:** Make your way to Sandown Pier and Esplanade and as you come into Pier Street we are the blue building 15 metres down on your left. **Bedrooms:** 1 single, 3 double, 2 twin, 2 family **Open:** All year

Payment: 💳 € **Leisure:** 🎵 ▶ **Property:** 🖥 **Children:** ⛛ 🍴 **Catering:** 🍴 **Room:** 🥤 🖥 📺

★★★
GUEST
ACCOMMODATION
enjoyEngland.com

B&B PER ROOM PER NIGHT
S: £30.00 - £40.00
D: £60.00 - £80.00
EVENING MEAL PER PERSON
£6.00 - £18.00

f t

The Sandhill

6 Hill Street, Sandown, Isle of Wight PO36 9DB **T:** (01983) 403635 **F:** (01983) 403695
E: sandhillsandown@aol.com
W: sandhill-hotel.co.uk

Situated in quiet residential area, close to railway and bus services. The beautiful sandy beach and town centre are less than 10 minutes walk. Very family oriented. With 5 star food hygiene rating the restaurant is open every evening as is the well stocked bar. **Directions:** Located in quiet residential area, just of the main Broadway at the top of Leed Street, 100 yds from Railway Station. **Bedrooms:** 16 rooms, single, double, twin and family rooms. **Open:** All year

WALKERS CYCLISTS WELCOME
WALKERS CYCLISTS
Site: ✿ P **Payment:** 💳 € **Leisure:** 🐾 🎵 ▶ ∪ **Property:** 🐕 🖥 📺 🍴 🌀 **Children:** ⛛ 🍴 🏊 **Catering:** (✗ 🍷 🍴 **Room:** 🥤 🖥 🕯 📺 ♨

Bulltown Farmhouse Bed & Breakfast

Bulltown Lane, West Brabourne, Ashford TN25 5NB T: (01233) 813505
E: lily.wilton@bulltown.co.uk
W: bulltown.co.uk £ BOOK ONLINE

B&B PER ROOM PER NIGHT
S: £45.00 - £50.00
D: £70.00 - £90.00

Stunning 15th Century timber framed farmhouse with wealth of beams surrounded by cottage garden in Area of Outstanding Natural Beauty. Rooms have unspoilt views. All en suite. Guest lounge with large inglenook fireplace. Local produce used.
Directions: See website for directions but under 4 miles from Junction 10 M20. **Bedrooms:** 1 double, 1 twin, 1 family
Open: All year

Site: ❀ P Payment: € Leisure: ஃ ♩ ♪ ♫ Property: ▦ ▣ Children: ♨ ▦ ♣ Catering: ▦ Room: ♞ ♨

Downsview Guest House

Willesborough Road, Kennington, Ashford, Kent TN24 9QP T: (01233) 621391
F: (01233) 620364 E: downsviewguesthouse@msn.com
W: ashforddownsview.co.uk

B&B PER ROOM PER NIGHT
S: £51.00 - £61.00
D: £61.00 - £71.00

SPECIAL PROMOTIONS
Luxury 2 double bedroom apartment. Self contained. From £121.00 - £151.00

Downsview Guest House is situated in a semi rural setting located 3 minutes by car from Ashford town centre, offering comfortable, friendly service. Large private car park + long term, suitable for coaches. M20, J10 exit. Canterbury a short drive away. We have a licensed bar. William Harvey Hospital a short drive, neighbour with Olympic size Julie Rose Stadium. Good panoramic views of the Downs.

Directions: If you are travelling to us via the M20, leave at Junction 10 and take the road north to Canterbury (A28). After about a mile, pass by The Julie Rose Stadium, we are a further 600m on right hand side.

Bedrooms: 2 single, 3 double, 3 twin, 4 family
Open: All year

Site: ❀ P Payment: ▦ € Leisure: ஃ ♩ ♪ ♫ Property: ▦ ⚑ Children: ♨ ▦ ♣ Catering: ♟ ▦ Room: ♞ ♨ ▣ 📺 ⚰

Book your accommodation online

Visit our new 2014 guide websites for detailed information, up-to-date availability and to book your accommodation online. Includes over 20,000 places to stay, all of them star rated.
www.visitor-guides.co.uk

BROADSTAIRS, Kent Map ref 3C3
SatNav CT10 1DR **B**

★★★★
GUEST
ACCOMMODATION

B&B PER ROOM PER NIGHT
S: £48.00 - £72.00
D: £94.00 - £106.00

Bay Tree Broadstairs
12 Eastern Esplanade, Broadstairs CT10 1DR T: (01843) 862502 F: (01843) 860589
E: enquiries@baytreebroadstairs.co.uk
W: www.baytreebroadstairs.co.uk

The Eastern Esplanade overlooking Stone Bay, with panoramic sea views across the Channel. Close to the town centre and sandy beaches. A warm welcome awaits at this family-run establishment. **Directions:** By Road: M2 - A2 - A299, via Birchington and Margate or via Ramsgate. By Rail: London to Broadstairs then taxi or half mile walk. **Bedrooms:** 1 single, 7 double, 2 twin **Open:** All year except Christmas and New Year

Site: ✿ P Payment: 💳 € Leisure: 🏊 ► ♻ Property: 🔌 Children: 🍼10 Catering: 🍽 🍴 Room: 🔌 🖐 🛁
📺 🍳

CANTERBURY, Kent Map ref 3B3
SatNav CT4 6NY **B**

★★★★
INN

B&B PER ROOM PER NIGHT
S: £45.00
D: £70.00 - £80.00

The Duke of Cumberland
The Street, Barham, Canterbury CT4 6NY T: (01227) 831396
E: info@dukeofcumberland.co.uk
W: www.dukeofcumberland.co.uk **£ BOOK ONLINE**

The Duke of Cumberland is first and foremost, a traditional English Country Inn built in 1749. All our rooms are well presented. Newly refurbished and sensitively designed to echo a bygone age they provide warm, comfortable and pleasant accommodation. Each room has an en suite shower room and WC facilities. In addition each room has an LCD TV with freeview, Wi-Fi internet access, tea and coffee making facilities, hairdryer and alarm clock.

Directions: Please contact us for directions or visit our website for map.

Bedrooms: 2 double, 1 family
Open: All year

Site: ✿ P Payment: 💳 Leisure: 🎵 ► ♻ Property: 🔌 ⌀ Children: 🍼 🖼 🧍 Catering: 🍽 🍴
Room: 🔌 🖐 📺

CANTERBURY, Kent Map ref 3B3
SatNav CT1 3JT **B**

★★★
BACKPACKERS

B&B PER ROOM PER NIGHT
S: £25.00 - £35.00
D: £20.00 - £30.00
BED ONLY PER NIGHT
£10.00 - £24.50

Kipps Independent Hostel
40 Nunnery Fields, Canterbury CT1 3JT T: (01227) 786121 E: kippshostel@gmail.com
W: www.kipps-hostel.com **£ BOOK ONLINE**

Self-catering backpackers hostel only a short walk from the Cathedral and City Centre. We offer accommodation for individuals and Groups . Excellent facilities including kitchen, garden, lounge free Wifi, and nightly events. **Directions:** Please go to our website www.kipps-hostel.com for directions **Bedrooms:** Private/family and dormitory rooms **Open:** All year

WALKERS CYCLISTS
WALKERS CYCLISTS

Site: ✿ Payment: 💳 € Leisure: 🔍 Property: 🔌 📀 📺 Catering: 🍴 Bedroom: 🖐 ☎

Magnolia House

36 St Dunstans Terrace, Canterbury CT2 8AX **T:** (01227) 765121 **F:** (08721) 117681
E: info@magnoliahousecanterbury.co.uk
W: www.magnoliahousecanterbury.co.uk **£ BOOK ONLINE**

B&B PER ROOM PER NIGHT
S: £55.00
D: £95.00 - £125.00
EVENING MEAL PER PERSON
£35.00 - £45.00

Charming, late Georgian house, quiet residential street, ten minutes from city centre. Every facility for enjoyable stay. Breakfast served overlooking attractive walled garden. Evening meals served Nov-Feb by arrangement.

Directions: M2/A2 to Canterbury. First roundabout left-hand fork to university (London Road). St Dunstan's Terrace third right off London Road. Magnolia House is 100yds on left.

Bedrooms: 1 single, 5 double, 1 twin
Open: All year, except Christmas.

Site: ✿ **P** **Payment:** 💷 **Leisure:** 🚴 ♪ **Property:** 🖼 **Children:** 🔒12 **Catering:** 🍴 **Room:** 🔌 ♨ 🎧 📺

Looking for something else?

The official and most comprehensive guide to independently inspected, star rated accommodation.

B&Bs and Hotels - B&Bs, Hotels, farmhouses, inns, serviced apartments, campus and hostel accommodation in England.

Self Catering - Self-catering holiday homes, approved caravan holiday homes, boat accommodation and holiday cottage agencies in England.

Camping, Touring and Holiday Parks - Touring parks, camping holidays and holiday parks and villages in Britain.

Now available in all good bookshops and online at **www.hudsons.co.uk/shop**

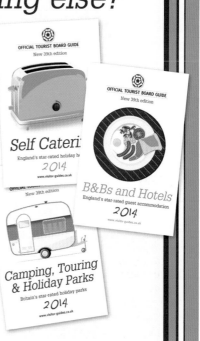

CRANBROOK, Kent   Map ref 3B4
SatNav TN17 4NH **B**

1 Maytham Cottages

Frogs Lane, Rolvenden Layne, Cranbrook TN17 4NH **T:** (01580) 241484
E: jobeddows@aol.com
W: rolvendenbedandbreakfast.co.uk

B&B PER ROOM PER NIGHT
S: £50.00 - £60.00
D: £70.00 - £80.00

SPECIAL PROMOTIONS
Short break prices on request only

A pretty grade II Lutyens cottage situated in the peaceful hamlet of Rolvenden Layne. Ideal for numerous National Trust sites/gardens/coast. Just 200 yards from excellent pub. We are the proud owners of a breakfast award that is accompanied by a five star food hygiene certificate. Always a warm welcome.

Directions: A28 Tenterden to Rolvenden village, turn left into Maytham Road, proceed 1 mile then turn right into Frogs Lane, we are 100yds on the left.

Bedrooms: Room 1: King size bed + single, en suite bathroom. Room 2: Double fourposter bed and shower en suite, Room 3: Double bed & shower en suite. All rooms have flat screen TV and Tea/Coffee making facilities.
Open: All year

Site: ❖ P **Leisure:** ⚓ ♪ ▶ ♄ **Property:** ⊨ ⊟ ♨ **Children:** ⊃ ⊪ ♣ **Catering:** ♨
Room: ♞ ♨ ⓐ TV DVD ♨ ⊞

CRANBROOK, Kent   Map ref 3B4
SatNav TN17 4BU **B**

Beacon Hall House

Rolvenden Road, Benenden, Cranbrook, Kent TN17 4BU **T:** (01580) 240434
E: julie.jex@btconnect.com
W: beaconhallhouse.co.uk

B&B PER ROOM PER NIGHT
S: £75.00 - £85.00
D: £95.00 - £110.00

EVENING MEAL PER PERSON
£15.00 - £30.00

A delightful country home - delicious award winning breakfast, locally sourced produce, supper by arrangement. Spacious light rooms with beautiful views over valley beyond. Hard tennis court. Tea/coffee facilities, TV, wireless broadband. **Directions:** Please see our website for detailed directions. **Bedrooms:** 1 double, 1 twin, 1 family. **Open:** All year except Christmas.

Site: ❖ P **Payment:** ⊞ € **Leisure:** ♪ ▶ ♄ ⚲ **Property:** ⊨ ⊟ ⊡ **Children:** ⊃ ⊪ ♣ **Catering:** (✕ ♨ **Room:** ♞ ♨ ⓐ TV DVD

Need more information?

Visit our new 2014 guide websites for detailed information, up-to-date availability and to book your accommodation online. Includes over 20,000 places to stay, all of them star rated.

www.visitor-guides.co.uk

CRANBROOK, Kent Map ref 3B4 SatNav TN17 2BP B

enjoyEngland.com
★★★★ GUEST ACCOMMODATION

B&B PER ROOM PER NIGHT
S: £45.00
D: £60.00 - £70.00

Tolehurst Barn

Cranbrook Road, Frittenden, Cranbrook, Kent TN17 2BP **T:** (01580) 714385
E: info@tolehurstbarn.co.uk
W: www.tolehurstbarn.co.uk

Quietly situated, set in 1 acre of garden, near Sissinghurst, Leeds, and Scotney Castles. Good walking area, TV, tea and coffee making facilities in all rooms and ample parking. For more info visit our website. **Directions:** A229 between staplehurst and Cranbrook, behind bumbles Garden centre **Bedrooms:** 2 doubles en suite, 1 family room with bathroom **Open:** All year

Site: P Payment: € Leisure: ♩ ↑ Property: ⋈ Children: 🐴1 Room: 🕯 🛉 🗐 📺

DOVER, Kent Map ref 3C4 SatNav CT16 1QW B

enjoyEngland.com
★★★★ GUEST HOUSE

B&B PER ROOM PER NIGHT
S: £36.00 - £40.00
D: £60.00 - £75.00

Castle House Guest House

10 Castle Hill Road, Dover CT16 1QW **T:** (01304) 201656 **E:** info@castle-guesthouse.com
W: castle-guesthouse.co.uk **£ BOOK ONLINE**

Situated in a conservation area just below Dover Castle, ideally located for the many local historic attractions, the beautiful surrounding Kent countryside and all cross channel connections. **Directions:** Approaching from A20, pass 4 roundabouts, turn left at lights past petrol station, then 1st right into Castle Hill Road. From A2, right onto A258. **Bedrooms:** 2 single, 1 double, 1 twin, 2 family **Open:** All year except Christmas

WALKERS FAMILIES CYCLISTS PETS
WALKERS FAMILIES CYCLISTS PETS
Site: ✿ Payment: 💷 Property: 🐴 🚃 Children: 🐴 🛏 🛉 Room: 🕯 🛉 🗐 📺

DOVER, Kent Map ref 3C4 SatNav CT15 4LQ B

enjoyEngland.com
★★★★ BED & BREAKFAST

B&B PER ROOM PER NIGHT
S: £65.00
D: £75.00 - £85.00

SPECIAL PROMOTIONS
Local pub 5 minutes walk away offers discounted meals to Farthingales guests

Farthingales Bed and Breakfast

Old Court Hill, Nonington, Dover, Kent CT15 4LQ **T:** 07599 303494
E: farthingalesbandb@yahoo.co.uk
W: www.farthingales.co.uk

Truly a rural retreat. Farthingales offers a unique blend of history and the comforts of 21st Century living in a beautiful Victorian building which was once the village shop. For those who enjoy living through medieval times, we offer rooms in our 15th century Kentish hall house. A secluded venue for those travelling alone, as couples, families or groups.

Directions: Via A2 towards Dover, turn off at Wingham/Aylesham exit and follow signs for Nonington. Left at The Royal Oak pub into Vicarage Lane under the tunnel of trees. We're opposite St Mary's Church.

Bedrooms: Twin and double in coverted village shop. Lounge and en suites, plus a 15th century suite with lounge, dining room and large en suite. £95 per night.
Open: All year

Site: ✿ P Payment: 💷 Leisure: 🧴 Property: 🚃 ⋈ ⌀ Room: 🛉 🗐 📺 evo

DOVER, Kent   Map ref 3C4

Hubert House Guesthouse and Bistro

9 Castle Hill Road, Dover CT16 1QW T: (01304) 202253 F: (01304) 210142
E: stay@huberthouse.co.uk
W: www.huberthouse.co.uk

B&B PER ROOM PER NIGHT
S: £40.00 - £50.00
D: £65.00 - £100.00

Hubert house is a georgian grade 2 listed building, our rooms are decorated a bit to suit the age of the building. Our continental buffet breakfast is included in our price, cooked breakfast is an optional extra (porridge and full monty etc) **Directions:** Easy walking distance to town centre, castle, bus stop, ferry port (3-5 min walk), a bit further to train station & cruise liner terminal (15-20 min walk). **Bedrooms:** 6 bedrooms all en suite, parking available on site **Open:** All year except Christmas and New Year

Site: ✿ P **Payment:** 💷 **Leisure:** 🎣 🎵 ▶ ∪ **Property:** 🐾 🖥 **Children:** 🚼 🛏 🧍 **Catering:** 🍴 **Room:** 🍵 ☕ 🛁 📺 🔌

DOVER, Kent   Map ref 3C4

Longfield Guest House

203 Folkestone Road, Dover, Kent CT17 9SL T: (01304) 204716
E: res@longfieldguesthouse.co.uk
W: www.longfieldguesthouse.co.uk **£ BOOK ONLINE**

B&B PER ROOM PER NIGHT
S: £25.00 - £30.00
D: £47.00 - £60.00

The Longfield is a family run Guest House in Dover, Kent. Our rooms are clean and comfortable with en suite or standard rooms. We have a security lit car park (locked overnight) for your cars, vans, motorbikes and cycles. Also a lock-up garage. We are 5 minutes drive to the Ferry Port and Cruise Terminal. We have single, double, and family rooms, and a family ground floor room.

Directions: M20 to Dover at 4th roundabout turn left into York St. At next roundabout turn left into Folkestone road. From M2 at York St roundabout turn right. At next roundabout turn left into Folkestone road.

Bedrooms: We have en suite and standard rooms. All our rooms have television, tea/coffee facilities, wash basin and free WIFI. All rooms are centrally heated.
Open: All year

Site: P **Payment:** 💷 **Property:** 🖥 **Children:** 🚼1 🛏 🧍 **Catering:** 🍴 **Room:** ☕ 📺 🔌

★★★
HOTEL

King Charles Hotel

Brompton Road, Gillingham ME7 5QT   **T:** (01634) 830303   **F:** (01634) 829430
E: reservations@kingcharleshotel.co.uk
W: kingcharleshotel.co.uk   **£ BOOK ONLINE**

A privately owned, modern hotel, situated in the heart of Medway. All bedrooms have en suite bathroom, tea/coffee facilities, hairdryer, telephone, TV and wireless internet. We offer extremely competitive group rates.

Directions: M2 jct 4 to Gillingham/Medway Tunnel. Turn left to Brompton before tunnel. We are on left.

Bedrooms: 4 single, 33 dble, 33 twin, 26 family, 2 suite
Open: All year

B&B PER ROOM PER NIGHT
S: £49.00
D: £59.00

SPECIAL PROMOTIONS
Special Sunday night rates. Please see website for details.

Site: ✿ **Payment:** £3 € **Leisure:** ♿ ♪ ▶ ∪ **Property:** ¶ ✝ ⊟ 🗃 ◑ **Children:** ⊃ ⊨ ⚥ **Catering:** ♟ ⊌
Room: ⌨ ✆ 🗇 📺 🎧 🗃 ⏋

★★★★★
BED & BREAKFAST

Gold
AWARD

Ash Cottage

Penfold Hill, Leeds Village, Nr Maidstone, Kent ME17 1RQ   **T:** (01622) 863142
E: rayne@ashcottagekent.co.uk
W: ashcottagekent.co.uk

Hot tea, fresh cake, a good nights sleep, hearty breakfast, candlelight and home made jam. Welcome to Ash Cottage. Grade II listed building and formerly part of the Leeds Castle estate. Fine country pubs in comfortable walking distance, we have a lovely country cottage garden for your enjoyment, secure parking.

Directions: At M20 Junction 8 follow sign for Leeds Castle. Pass castle entrance, Ash Cottage on right after bridge and 30 mph sign before bend.

Bedrooms: 2 double, 1 twin
Open: All year

B&B PER ROOM PER NIGHT
S: £65.00 - £75.00
D: £80.00 - £95.00

SPECIAL PROMOTIONS
Seasonal special offers available, please see website.

Site: ✿ **P** **Leisure:** ▶ **Property:** ⊟ **Children:** ⊃¹⁰ **Catering:** 🎜 **Room:** ⌨ ✆ 🗇 📺

MAIDSTONE, Kent   Map ref 3B3
SatNav ME14 2BD **B**

The Limes

118 Boxley Road, Maidstone ME14 2BD **T:** (01622) 750629 / 07889 594700
F: (01622) 750629 **E:** info@thelimesmaidstone.co.uk
W: thelimesmaidstone.co.uk **£ BOOK ONLINE**

B&B PER ROOM PER NIGHT
S: £38.00 - £45.00
D: £72.00 - £78.00

Large Georgian house, 2 Star guest accommodation. Close to town centre, motorways, railway stations and shopping centres. Good location for walkers and cyclists. Off-road parking. Silver award for breakfast. **Directions:** From M2 Junction 3 take A229 to Maidstone. From M20 Junction 6 A229 Signposted Penenden Heath. Turn right at roundabout for town centre. **Bedrooms:** 3 single, 1 twin **Open:** All year

Site: ✿ P **Leisure:** 🎣 ♪ ► ∪ ⚲ ✎ **Property:** 🛏 **Children:** ⚲12 **Catering:** 🍴 **Room:** 🕯 ♨ ☎ 🖭 📺

MAIDSTONE, Kent   Map ref 3B3
SatNav ME14 1BH **H**

The Townhouse Hotel

74 King Street, Maidstone, Kent ME14 1BH **T:** (01622) 663266 **E:** reservations@tthh.co.uk
W: www.tthh.co.uk **£ BOOK ONLINE**

B&B PER ROOM PER NIGHT
S: £65.00 - £85.00
D: £75.00 - £99.00
EVENING MEAL PER PERSON
£15.95 - £55.00

Located in the heart of Maidstone, the hotel was built as a vicarage in 1802, retaining may original features. On site restaurant and bar. All rooms en suite. Wireless internet connection. English breakfast cooked to order. **Bedrooms:** All rooms are en suite **Open:** All year

Payment: 💳 **Property:** 🛏 **Children:** ⚲ 🛏 ♿ **Catering:** (✕ ♀ 🍴 **Room:** 🕯 ♨ ☎ 🖭 📺

RAMSGATE, Kent   Map ref 3C3
SatNav CT11 8DT **H**

Comfort Inn Ramsgate

Victoria Parade, Ramsgate, Kent CT11 8DT **T:** (01843) 592345 **F:** (01843) 580157
E: reservations@comfortinnramsgate.co.uk
W: www.comfortinnramsgate.co.uk **£ BOOK ONLINE**

B&B PER ROOM PER NIGHT
S: £35.00 - £50.00
D: £40.00 - £120.00

SPECIAL PROMOTIONS
Promotional rate available mid week and weekends, ring 01843 592345 for details.

Victorian Grade 2 Listed building with modern facilities situated on the cliff top with panoramic views of English Channel. Free Wi-Fi, well stocked bar selling local ale, restaurant offering wide variety of dishes, Beauty Salon. Sea view rooms, some with enclosed balcony, Garden. Free parking. Live Entertainment fortnightly.

Directions: From M2 take the A299 then A253 to Ramsgate. Follow signs for East Cliff. From Victoria Road turn left, hotel is on the left.
Bedrooms: 7 single, 14 double, 9 twin, 7 family, 7 suite
Open: All year

Site: ✿ **Payment:** 💳 € **Leisure:** 🎣 ♪ ∪ **Property:** ⊛ ♀ 🛏 🖥 ◑ **Children:** ⚲ 🛏 ♿ **Catering:** ♀ 🍴
Room: 🕯 ♨ ☎ 🖭 📺 ♨ ▦

RAMSGATE, Kent   Map ref 3C3
SatNav CT11 8DB **B**

★★★★ GUEST HOUSE
Silver AWARD

Glendevon Guest House
8 Truro Road, Ramsgate CT11 8DB **T:** 0800 035 2110 **F:** (01843) 570909
E: info@glendevonguesthouse.co.uk
W: www.glendevonguesthouse.co.uk

B&B PER ROOM PER NIGHT
S: £50.00 - £60.00
D: £70.00 - £85.00

Victorian house near beach, harbour and town. All rooms have en suite, modern kitchen/dining area. Some rooms with sea views. Free Wi-Fi TV/VCR/Freeview, Fairtrade tea, coffee & hot chocolate. Excellent full English breakfast. **Directions:** We are situated on the East Cliff, directly behind The Granville Building (the large building with a castle turret that overlooks The Granville Cinema). **Bedrooms:** 3 double, 1 twin, 2 family **Open:** All year

Payment: £ **Leisure:** **Property:** **Children:** **Catering:** **Room:**

ROYAL TUNBRIDGE WELLS, Kent   Map ref 2D2
SatNav TN4 9SS **B**

★★ BED & BREAKFAST

Badgers End Bed & Breakfast
47 Thirlmere Road, Royal Tunbridge Wells, Kent TN4 9SS **T:** (01892) 533176

B&B PER ROOM PER NIGHT
S: £30.00 - £35.00
D: £50.00

Modern house in quiet cul-de-sac with large garden backing onto woodland. Close to A26. Full English breakfast. Freeview TV plus broadband. Tea and coffee making facilities. Non smoking establishment throughout. **Directions:** 1.5 miles from Tunbridge Wells station. 1 mile from shopping centre. Varying directions, given upon request. **Bedrooms:** 1 single, 1 double. **Open:** All year except Christmas and New Year

Leisure: **Property:** **Catering:** **Room:**

ROYAL TUNBRIDGE WELLS, Kent   Map ref 2D2
SatNav TN3 9TB **B**

★★★ FARMHOUSE
Silver AWARD

Manor Court Farm Bed & Breakfast
Ashurst Road, Ashurst, Tunbridge Wells, Kent TN3 9TB **T:** (01892) 740279
F: (01892) 740919 **E:** jsoyke@jsoyke.freeserve.co.uk
W: manorcourtfarm.co.uk

B&B PER ROOM PER NIGHT
S: £30.00 - £45.00
D: £60.00 - £72.00

SPECIAL PROMOTIONS
Reductions for longer stays. Reductions for children.

Georgian farmhouse with friendly atmosphere, spacious rooms and lovely views of Medway Valley. Mixed 350-acre farm, many animals. Good base for walking. Penshurst Place, Hever Castle, Chartwell, Sissinghurst etc all within easy reach by car. Excellent camping facilities. Good train service to London from Ashurst station (two minutes away).

Directions: On A264 road 5 miles west of Tunbridge Wells, towards East Grinstead/Gatwick etc. ½ mile east of Ashurst village, in hamlet of Stone Cross.

Bedrooms: 2 twin, 1 double
Open: All year except Christmas

Site: P **Payment:** € **Leisure:** **Property:** **Children:** **Catering:** **Room:**

South East - Kent

SANDWICH, Kent *Map ref 3C3* SatNav CT139LE B

White Rose Lodge

88 St George's Road, Sandwich, 88 St George's Rd CT13 9LE **T:** (01304) 620406
E: gillhardy54@gmail.com
W: www.whiteroselodge.co.uk **£ BOOK ONLINE**

B&B PER ROOM PER NIGHT
S: £80.00 – £90.00
D: £95.00 – £110.00

Our award winning bed and breakfast accommodation is situated in the beautiful medieval cinque port town of Sandwich, Kent. You will find White Rose Lodge a peaceful and tranquil experience, whilst enjoying the large garden and orchard. **Bedrooms:** Two double & one twin bedroom, private facilities **Open:** All year

Site: ❀ **Leisure:** ♿ ♪ ► ♻ ⅄ **Property:** 🖳 ▣ 🎄

SHORNE, Kent *Map ref 3B3* SatNav DA12 3HB H

The Inn on the Lake Hotel

Watling Street, Shorne, Gravesend DA12 3HB **T:** (01474) 823333 **F:** (01474) 823175
E: reservations@innonlake.co.uk
W: innonlake.co.uk **£ BOOK ONLINE**

B&B PER ROOM PER NIGHT
S: £59.50 – £69.50
D: £69.50 – £79.50

Set in 12 acres of woodland, the Inn on the Lake offers a friendly and comfortable stay in a modern, family run establishment. We have 80 bedrooms, many of them with direct access to the 2 beautiful lakes, offering en suite bathrooms, television, telephone, tea & coffee making facilities and hairdryer.

Directions: The hotel is situated on the A2 midway between Rochester and Dartford, just past Gravesend.

Bedrooms: 35 dble, 35 twin, 8 family
Open: All year

Site: ❀ **Payment:** 🆔 € **Leisure:** ♪ ► **Property:** 🎿 🐾 🖳 ◑ **Children:** 🐎 🍴 🛝 **Catering:** 🍷 🍽
Room: 🖥 ♨ 📞 📺 🎧 🛁

STELLING MINNIS, Kent *Map ref 3B4* SatNav CT4 6DE B

Great Field Farm B&B

Misling Lane, Stelling Minnis, Canterbury CT4 6DE **T:** (01227) 709223 **F:** (01227) 709223
E: greatfieldfarm@aol.com
W: great-field-farm.co.uk

B&B PER ROOM PER NIGHT
S: £35.00 – £75.00
D: £70.00 – £90.00

Delightful farmhouse set amidst lovely gardens and countryside. Spacious, private suites; B&B or self-catering. Hearty breakfasts with home-grown fruits and eggs. Ten minutes to Canterbury/Channel Tunnel. **Directions:** From M20 exit J11 onto B2068 to Canterbury. Look out for brown B & B signs after about 6 miles. **Bedrooms:** 3 double, 2 twin **Open:** All year

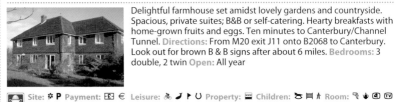

Site: ❀ **P Payment:** 🆔 € **Leisure:** ♿ ♪ ► ♻ **Property:** 🖳 **Children:** 🐎 🍴 🛝 **Room:** 🖥 ♨ 📞 📺

126 The Official Tourist Board Guide to **B&Bs and Hotels 2014**

ST-MARGARETS-AT-CLIFFE, Kent Map ref 3C4 SatNav CT15 6AT H

The White Cliffs Hotel

High Street, Saint Margarets-at-Cliffe, Dover, Kent CT15 6AT T: (01304) 852229
F: 0800 7569964 E: mail@thewhitecliffs.com
W: thewhitecliffs.com £ BOOK ONLINE

★★★ HOTEL

B&B PER ROOM PER NIGHT
S: £79.00 - £89.00
D: £99.00 - £149.00
HB PER PERSON PER NIGHT
£79.50 - £99.50

Set in the heart of a picturesque village just 3 miles from Dover ideal for a cross channel stopover. A perfect base from which to explore White Cliffs Country. **Directions:** From Dover, A258 for Deal, right turn for St. Margaret's-at-Cliffe then right at T-junction, hotel is opposite the church on the left. **Bedrooms:** 2 single, 10 dble, 2 twin, 2 family, 1 suite **Open:** All year

Site: ❀ Payment: £3 € Leisure: 🎣 ♪ ▶ ♻ Property: ❡ 🐕 🖳 📠 Children: ➰
🍴 🏃 Catering: ♟ 🍴 Room: 🖤 ⬆ ☎ 📺 📠 ⚒

TENTERDEN, Kent Map ref 3B4 SatNav TN30 6RL B

Collina House

5 East Hill, Tenterden TN30 6RL T: (01580) 764852 E: enquiries@collinahousehotel.co.uk
W: www.collinahousehotel.co.uk

★★★★ GUEST ACCOMMODATION

B&B PER ROOM PER NIGHT
S: £45.00 - £65.00
D: £75.00 - £99.00
EVENING MEAL PER PERSON
£22.50 - £25.00

Attractive Edwardian house set in peaceful location only a few minutes walk from town centre. Spacious, well equipped en suite bedrooms. Restaurant offering imaginative homemade dishes with local wines. **Directions:** Off High Street east onto B2067 Oaks Road, leads into East Hill and the property is on the left opposite an orchard. **Bedrooms:** 2 single, 7 double, 4 twin, 2 family **Open:** All year except Christmas and New Year

Site: ❀ P Payment: £3 Property: 🖳 Children: ➰ 🍴 🏃 Catering: ♟ 🍴 Room: 🖤 ⬆ ☎ 📺 ⚒

ABINGDON, Oxfordshire Map ref 2C1 SatNav OX14 3BT B

The Railway Inn

Station Road, Culham, Abingdon, Oxon OX14 3BT T: (01235) 528046 F: (01235) 525183
E: info@railwayinnculham.co.uk
W: www.railwayinnculham.co.uk

★★★ INN

B&B PER ROOM PER NIGHT
S: £50.00
D: £70.00
EVENING MEAL PER PERSON
£5.50 - £16.00

Bed and breakfast. Evening meals range from home made pies to steaks. Free house. Cask ales. Free parking. Friendly staff. Pets welcome with prior arrangement. **Directions:** A415 2miles East of Abingdon. Adjacent to main London Paddington railway at Culham Station. Close to A34, M40 and M4. 1 mile from Thames Path. **Bedrooms:** 4 double, 3 twin, 2 family **Open:** All year

Site: ❀ P Payment: £3 Leisure: ♪ ▶ Property: 🐕 🖳 Children: ➰ 🏃 Catering: ♟ 🍴 Room: ⬆ ☎ 📺

ABINGDON-ON-THAMES, Oxfordshire Map ref 2C1 SatNav OX14 2BE B

Abbey Guest House

136 Oxford Road, Abingdon-on-Thames OX14 2AG T: (01235) 537020 / 07976 627252
F: (01235) 537020 E: info@abbeyguest.com
W: www.abbeyguest.com £ BOOK ONLINE

★★★★ GUEST HOUSE Gold AWARD

B&B PER ROOM PER NIGHT
S: £50.00 - £66.00
D: £90.00 - £99.00

We are a quiet, 'Home from Home', non smoking, multi-award winning, highly accessible B&B, in the historic town of Abingdon-on-Thames. Guests enjoy private parking, excellent bus services and local amenities, Fair Trade items + Free Wi-Fi. **Directions:** Oxford Road is the A4183. Detailed walking & driving directions, and information if travelling by bus, train or plane is available on website. **Bedrooms:** 7 en suite rooms inc Easy Access, Allergy Friendly. **Open:** All Year - Add. Chge for Xmas & New Year.

Site: ❀ P Payment: £3 Property: 🖳 ♨ Children: ➰ 🍴 🏃
Catering: 🍴 Room: 🖤 ⬆ 📺 📀 ⚒

BAMPTON, Oxfordshire Map ref 2C1 SatNav OX18 2DN [B]

Manor Farm Barn B&B

Bull Street, Aston, Bampton OX18 2DN T: (01993) 852907
E: enquiries@manorfarmbarn.net
W: manorfarmbarn.net £ BOOK ONLINE

B&B PER ROOM PER NIGHT
S: £85.00 - £75.00
D: £95.00 - £105.00
EVENING MEAL PER PERSON
£18.00 - £28.00

Located in the village of Aston, Manor Farm Barn is close to the River Thames and conveniently placed for visits to Burford, the Cotswolds, Oxford and Stratford upon Avon. Directions: Turn into Bull Street from the centre of the village and Manor Farm Barn is 400 metres on the left hand side. Bedrooms: 3 double
Open: All year

Site: ✿ P Payment: £ € Leisure: Property: Children: Catering: Room:

BICESTER, Oxfordshire Map ref 2C1 SatNav OX26 1TE [H]

Bicester Hotel Golf and Spa

Bicester Hotel Golf and Spa, Akerman Street, Chesterton, Bicester, Oxfordshire OX26 1TE
T: (01869) 241204 F: (01869) 240754 E: carol.barford@bicesterhgs.com
W: bicesterhotelgolfandspa.com £ BOOK ONLINE

B&B PER ROOM PER NIGHT
S: £80.00 - £169.00
D: £90.00 - £189.00

A unique, independently run 52 bedroomed hotel with extensive leisure and spa facilities andan 18 hole golf course, set in 134 acres. Close to Bicester Village and other local attractions. Directions: Just minutes from J9 of M40 motorway. Direct rail links into London and Birmingham from Bicester North. Bedrooms: 24 double, 25 twin, 3 suite Open: All year except Christmas day and boxing day

Site: ✿ P Payment: £ Leisure: Property: Children: Catering: Room:

BLACK BOURTON, Oxfordshire Map ref 2C1 SatNav OX18 2PF [B]

The Vines

Burford Road, Black Bourton, Bampton OX18 2PF T: (01993) 843559
E: info@vineshotel.com
W: vineshotel.com

B&B PER ROOM PER NIGHT
S: £65.00 - £70.00
D: £95.00 - £120.00
EVENING MEAL PER PERSON
£15.00 - £28.00

Renowned for fine dining in elegant surroundings and with eighteen en suite bedrooms. Rooms are well furnished. Most have king sized beds and wet rooms. All have internet access. Directions: Signposted from A4095 Faringdon to Witney. Also be reached from A40 Cheltenham to Witney road. Telephone or see website for map. Bedrooms: 2 single, 8 double, 4 twin, 4 family
Open: All year

Site: ✿ P Payment: £ Leisure: Property: Children: Catering: Room:

Book your accommodation online

Visit our new 2014 guide websites for detailed information, up-to-date availability and to book your accommodation online. Includes over 20,000 places to stay, all of them star rated.
www.visitor-guides.co.uk

Bay Tree Hotel

Sheep Street, Burford OX18 4LW T: (01993) 822791 F: (01993) 823008
E: info@baytreehotel.info
W: www.cotswold-inns-hotels.co.uk/baytree £ BOOK ONLINE

B&B PER ROOM PER NIGHT
S: £160.00 - £170.00
D: £180.00 - £270.00
HB PER PERSON PER NIGHT
£123.00 - £168.00

Wooden staircases, stone fireplaces, woven tapestries and flagstone floors lend a warm, traditional country feel. The award-winning restaurant serves local seasonal produce. Secluded walled gardens are a place to unwind, take tea and relax. **Directions:** From A40 at Burford turn onto A361. Take 2nd left into Sheep Street. The Bay Tree is found on the right. **Bedrooms:** 10 dble, 4 twin, 7 suite **Open:** All year

The Lamb Inn

Sheep Street, Burford OX18 4LR T: (01993) 823155 F: (01993) 822228
E: info@lambinn-burford.co.uk
W: www.cotswold-inns-hotels.co.uk/lamb £ BOOK ONLINE

B&B PER ROOM PER NIGHT
S: £150.00 - £170.00
D: £160.00 - £310.00
HB PER PERSON PER NIGHT
£119.00 - £194.00

This traditional country Inn offers old-world charm with stylish interiors, stone flagged floors, cosy armchairs, log fires and friendly atmosphere. Award winning restaurant, bar, courtyard and walled garden...the perfect place to unwind. **Directions:** From A40 at Burford, turn onto A361, take 2nd left onto Sheep Street. The Lamb Inn will be found on the right. **Bedrooms:** 13 dble, 4 twin **Open:** All year

Badgemore Park Golf Club

Badgemore Park Golf Club, Badgemore, Henley-on-Thames, Oxfordshire RG9 4NR
T: (01491) 637300 F: (01491) 637301 E: info@badgemorepark.com
W: www.badgemorepark.com £ BOOK ONLINE

SPECIAL PROMOTIONS
Please contact us for prices.

Located only 5 minutes from Henley town centre, Badgemore Park offers unique accommodation within the grounds of our Parkland Golf Course. Bedrooms 1 to 5 are situated on the first floor, with 2 new luxury rooms, 6 & 7 on the ground floor. Accommodation has use of a kitchenette, with fridge, microwave and tea/coffee making facilities, adjacent to a large lounge area with flat screen TV & dining area. There is ample parking, a large secluded and private walled garden with outdoor decking/seating area. Ideal base for a weekend away.

Directions: Less than 1 mile from the River Thames and Henley town centre, easily accessible from the M4 & M40.

Bedrooms: 3 double, 2 family, 2 kingsize.
Open: All year

HENLEY-ON-THAMES, Oxfordshire Map ref 2C2   SatNav RG9 3NY B

The Baskerville

Station Road, Lower Shiplake, Henley-on-Thames RG9 3NY T: (01189) 403332
E: enquiries@thebaskerville.com
W: thebaskerville.com £ BOOK ONLINE

B&B PER ROOM PER NIGHT
S: £89.00
D: £99.00

Quality village pub close to the River Thames and minutes from Henley-on-Thames. Outstanding food with menus that change frequently using fresh local produce. Excellent wine list, cosy, comfortable bar with a good choice of cask-conditioned ales. 50 cover restaurant and a garden with seating for 100.

Directions: From Henley-on-Thames, take Reading road for 2 miles, turn left down Station Road for 0.5 mile. Baskerville is on right after cross roads before station.

Bedrooms: 2 double, 1 twin, 1 family.
Open: All year except Christmas and New Year.

Site: ✿ P Payment: 💳 Leisure: 🏊 🎣 🚶 ∪ Property: 🍽 🐕 🖥 ◑ ⌂ Children: 🏫 🛏 🎠
Catering: ✕ 🍷 🍽 Room: 🛎 🍵 📶 📺 📀

MILTON-UNDER-WYCHWOOD, Oxfordshire Map ref 2B1   SatNav OX7 6JH B

Hillborough House

The Green, Shipton Road, Burford OX7 6JH T: (01993) 832352 F: (01993) 832352
E: hillboroughhouse@btinternet.com
W: www.hillboroughhouse.co.uk £ BOOK ONLINE

B&B PER ROOM PER NIGHT
S: £50.00 - £55.00
D: £70.00 - £80.00

A Victorian village house with spacious en suite rooms overlooking the green with views to distant hills. You will be assured of a warm welcome and a great breakfast. **Directions:** Please contact us for directions. **Bedrooms:** 1 double, 1 twin, 1 family, all en suite **Open:** All year

Site: P Leisure: 🏊 🎣 🚶 ∪ Property: 🐕 🖥 🖱 Children: 🏫 🛏 🎠 Catering: 🍽 Room: 🛎 🍵 📶 📺 📀 🔌

MOULSFORD, Oxfordshire Map ref 2C2   SatNav OX10 9JF H

Beetle & Wedge Boathouse

Ferry Lane, Moulsford, Wallingford OX10 9JF T: (01491) 651381 F: (01491) 651376
E: boathouse@beetleandwedge.co.uk
W: www.beetleandwedge.co.uk

B&B PER ROOM PER NIGHT
S: £75.00
D: £90.00 - £100.00

Riverside restaurant with rooms offering charming accommodation, delicious food & great wines. Boat hire & picnics also available. **Directions:** Located on the River Thames between Reading & Oxford, 15 minutes from the M4 & M40, convenient for Heathrow. **Bedrooms:** 3 Double/Twin rooms. **Open:** All Year

Site: ✿ Payment: 💳 Leisure: 🏊 🎣 ∪ Property: 🍽 🖥 Children: 🏫 🛏 🎠 Catering: 🍷 🍽 Room: 🛎 🍵 📶 📺 🔌 📻

★★★
GUEST
ACCOMMODATION

B&B PER ROOM PER NIGHT
S: £40.00 - £50.00
D: £60.00 - £70.00

Arden Lodge

34 Sunderland Avenue, Oxford OX2 8DX   **T:** (01865) 552076   **F:** (01865) 512265
E: ardenlodge34@googlemail.com
W: www.ardenlodgeoxford.co.uk

Arden Lodge is a modern, detached house set in a tree-lined avenue, in one of Oxford's most select areas. It offers 3 attractively furnished bedrooms, with private facilities, colour TV and beverage tray. An excellent base for touring: within easy reach of the Cotswolds, London, Stratford and Warwick. The position is convenient for Oxford City Centre, parks, river, meadows, golf course and country inns, including the world famous Trout Inn as featured in 'Inspector Morse'. Ample parking is available, and there is an excellent bus service, with Oxford City Centre about 10 minutes away.

Directions: Please contact us for directions.

Bedrooms: 1 single, 1 double, 1 twin
Open: All year except Christmas

Site: **P** Leisure: ▶ Catering: 🍴 Room: ♿ 📺

★★★★
GUEST
ACCOMMODATION

B&B PER ROOM PER NIGHT
S: £69.00 - £115.00
D: £99.00 - £149.00

The Buttery

11 Broad Street, Oxford OX1 3AP   **T:** (01865) 811950   **F:** (01865) 811951
E: enquiries@thebutteryhotel.co.uk
W: www.thebutteryhotel.co.uk   **£ BOOK ONLINE**

Set on Broad Street, surrounded by historic Oxford colleges and museums, The Buttery welcomes you to explore the wonders of Oxford from its central location. Spacious well-furnished en suite rooms. **Directions:** Please contact us for directions. **Bedrooms:** 1 single, 9 double, 3 twin, 3 family **Open:** All year

Payment: 💷 Property: 🔲 ◐ Children: 🍼 🛏 ♿ Catering: 🍴 Room: 📶 ♿ 📞 📟 📺

★★★★
GUEST
ACCOMMODATION

B&B PER ROOM PER NIGHT
S: £69.00 - £85.00
D: £110.00 - £150.00

Cotswold House

363 Banbury Road, Oxford OX2 7PL   **T:** (01865) 310558   **F:** 08721107068
E: d.r.walker@talk21.com
W: cotswoldhouse.co.uk   **£ BOOK ONLINE**

A well-situated and elegant property, offering excellent accommodation and service. Cotswold House is in a most desirable part of Oxford. Free parking and Wi-Fi. **Directions:** Exit Oxford ring road on North side, following sign to Summertown. We are half a mile on right as you head towards city centre. **Bedrooms:** 2 single, 2 double, 1 twin, 2 family, 1 deluxe suite **Open:** All year

Site: **P** Payment: 💷 Property: 🔲 Children: 🍼³ Room: 📶 ♿ 📺 ⛳

For **key to symbols** see page 7

Cotswold Lodge Hotel

66A Banbury Road, Oxford OX2 6JP **T:** (01865) 512121 **F:** (01865) 512490
E: info@cotswoldlodgehotel.co.uk
W: cotswoldlodgehotel.co.uk **£ BOOK ONLINE**

B&B PER ROOM PER NIGHT
S: £75.00 - £165.00
D: £115.00 - £220.00
EVENING MEAL PER PERSON
£25.00 - £45.00

SPECIAL PROMOTIONS
Dinner, Bed and
Breakfast offers from
£60.00 - £130.00 pp
based on 2 people
sharing.

An elegant 4 Star retreat set in a peaceful conservation area 0.5 miles from Oxford's city centre. The hotel is known for its individuality and excellent levels of service. The Restaurant 66A welcomes non-residents for breakfast, lunch and dinner daily. Please contact us for prices.

Directions: Located in North Oxford. 2 minutes drive from A34.

Bedrooms: 6 single, 27 dble, 6 twin, 10 feature room. All rooms en suite, flat screen tv, tea and coffee facilities, toiletries
Open: All year

Site: ✿ P **Payment:** 💷 **Leisure:** 🚲 🎵 ▶ ♻ **Property:** 🍽 🖥 🗄 🅿 ◐ ⌀ **Children:** 🍼 🛏 🧍
Catering: (✕ 🍷 🍴 **Room:** 🍵 ♨ 📞 🔌 📺 🧺 🖤

Newton House Guest House B&B Oxford

82-84 Abingdon Road, Oxford OX1 4PL **T:** (01865) 240561 **F:** (01865) 244647
E: newton.house@btinternet.com
W: oxfordcity.co.uk/accom/newton **£ BOOK ONLINE**

B&B PER ROOM PER NIGHT
S: £62.00 - £98.00
D: £75.00 - £130.00

SPECIAL PROMOTIONS
Ask about special
offers

Close to Oxford's city centre, on foot, bus, coach, train or car. A perfect opportunity to visit Oxford's university central city attractions, research facilities, museums, hospitals. Family run with a personal touch, free Wi-Fi, car park, English traditional breakfast, vegetarian and continental special diets catered for.

Directions: Situated on A4144 (OX1 4PL) Postal code 1/2 mile (800 mtrs) from the city centre 10 to 15 min walk see us on google maps.

Bedrooms: 8 double, 4 twin, 2 family
Open: All year

Site: P **Payment:** 💷 € **Leisure:** 🚲 🎵 **Property:** 🖥 ◐ **Children:** 🍼 🛏 🧍 **Catering:** 🍴
Room: 🍵 ♨ 📞 🔌 📺 🖤

OXFORD, Oxfordshire   Map ref 2C1   SatNav OX2 6EH B

★★ BED & BREAKFAST

Park House
7 St Bernards Road, Oxford OX2 6EH **T:** (01865) 310824 **E:** krynpark@hotmail.com

Traditional Victorian terraced house in north Oxford, five minutes walk from city centre and within easy reach of all amenities. Friendly and relaxed atmosphere. Please contact us for prices. **Directions:** Please contact us for directions. **Bedrooms:** 1 single, 1 double **Open:** All year except Christmas

B&B PER ROOM PER NIGHT
S: £40.00 - £45.00
D: £60.00 - £70.00

Site: ✿ P Payment: € Leisure: ♿ Property: ♞ ☎ ⊟ Children: ⚲ ♨ ♣ Catering: ⊯ Room: ☏ ♨ ◉ ▣

WOODSTOCK, Oxfordshire   Map ref 2C1   SatNav OX20 1SY B

★★★★ INN   Silver AWARD

The Blenheim Buttery
7 Market Place, Woodstock OX20 1SY **T:** (01993) 813660 **F:** (01993) 811212
E: contact@theblenheimbuttery.co.uk
W: http://theblenheimbuttery.co.uk

Comprising of 6 en suite rooms and a ground floor restaurant, The Blenheim Buttery offers clean and comfortable accommodation refurbished to reflect the traditional charm and warmth of this 17th century building. Latest check-in is at 8pm **Directions:** Please see our website for directions. **Bedrooms:** 6 en suite- 4 double, 2 twin **Open:** All year

B&B PER ROOM PER NIGHT
S: £59.00 - £125.00
D: £69.00 - £135.00

Site: ✿ Property: ☎ Children: ⚲ ♨ ♣ Catering: ♟ ⊯ Room: ☏ ♨ ☏ ◉ ▣

WOODSTOCK, Oxfordshire   Map ref 2C1   SatNav OX20 1HT B

★★★★ INN

The Duke of Marlborough
A44 Woodleys, Woodstock, Oxford OX20 1HT **T:** (01993) 811460 **F:** (01993) 810165
E: sales@dukeofmarlborough.co.uk
W: dukeofmarlborough.co.uk

Family run and friendly and well known locally for its good food. Situated close to Woodstock. Nearby Blenheim Palace and Oxford. Ideally situated for exploring the surrounding countryside. **Directions:** We are positioned on the A44 Oxford to Stratford road just 2 mile north of Woodstock at the junction with the B4437. **Bedrooms:** 4 double, 2 twin, 5 family, 2 suites **Open:** All year

B&B PER ROOM PER NIGHT
S: £59.50 - £90.00
D: £77.00 - £120.00
EVENING MEAL PER PERSON
£8.95 - £25.00

Site: ✿ P Leisure: ♪ ⊦ ♺ Property: ☎ Children: ♨ Catering: (✗ ♟ ⊯ Room: ☏ ♨ ☏ ▣

Need more information?

Visit our new 2014 guide websites for detailed information, up-to-date availability and to book your accommodation online. Includes over 20,000 places to stay, all of them star rated.
www.visitor-guides.co.uk

★★★
GUEST HOUSE

Shepherds Hall

Witney Road, Freeland, Witney OX29 8HQ T: (01993) 881256 F: (01993) 883455
W: shepherdshall.co.uk

B&B PER ROOM PER NIGHT
S: £35.00
D: £50.00

SPECIAL PROMOTIONS
Please add £5 on top
of above prices for
breakfast.

Well-appointed licensed guest house offering excellent Bed and Breakfast accommodation. All
rooms en suite. Ideally situated for Oxford, Woodstock, Blenheim Palace and the Cotswolds.

Directions: About 18 miles north west of Oxford
on the A4095 Woodstock to Witney road, just
outside the village of Long Hanborough.

Bedrooms: 1 single, 2 double, 2 twin
Open: All year except Christmas

Site: P Payment: ⊞ Property: ♟ ⊞ 🐕 Children: ⚲ ⊞ ⚡ Catering: ♟ Room: ⚲ ⚡ ☎ TV

Visit our 2014 guide websites...

- Detailed information
- Up-to-date availability
- Book your accommodation online

Includes over 20,000
places to stay,
all of them star rated.

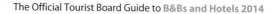

Win amazing prizes,
every month...

Enter our monthly competition at
www.visitor-guides.co.uk/prizes

DORKING, Surrey Map ref 2D2
SatNav RH5 5JA **B**

GUEST ACCOMMODATION ★★★★ **Silver AWARD**

B&B PER ROOM PER NIGHT
S: £50.00 - £60.00
D: £80.00 - £95.00

Stylehurst Farm
Weare Street, Capel, Dorking RH5 5JA T: (01306) 711259 / 07866 399231
E: rosemary.goddard@virgin.net
W: stylehurstfarm.com

Stylehurst Farm set in the beautiful Surrey countryside. The house, recently converted from old farm buildings, provides comfortable accommodation. There is an attractive garden and many places of interest nearby. **Directions:** Five miles south of Dorking on A24. At Clarks Green roundabout take 4th exit. 200yds left to Ockley Station. After station, left into Weare Street. **Bedrooms:** 1 double, 2 twin. **Open:** All year except Christmas and New Year.

Site: ✿ P Property: 🚗 Children: 🎠³ Catering: 🍴 Room: 📺 ♨ 📺

EGHAM, Surrey Map ref 2D2
SatNav TW20 0AG **H**

HOTEL ★★★★ **Silver AWARD**

SPECIAL PROMOTIONS
Please call us or check our website for details of our spa breaks, family packages and other special seasonal offers.

the runnymede-on-thames
Windsor Road, Egham TW20 0AG T: (01784) 220600 F: (01784) 436340
E: info@therunnymede.co.uk
W: therunnymede.co.uk **£ BOOK ONLINE**

Set right on the banks of the river Thames we are the perfect location for a short break. Our family friendly hotel is near attractions, theme parks and fantastic sights. There's so much to do right here too with riverside walks, our award-winning spa, gorgeous riverside dining and much more.

Directions: Located on the banks of the Thames on the A308 to Windsor, just off junction 13 of the M25.

Bedrooms: 11 single, 132 double, 35 twin, 3 family
Open: All year

Site: ✿ P Payment: 💷 € Leisure: 🏊 ♪ ▶ ♿ 🎾 ⛳ 🚴 🎣 🎾 Property: ⊕ 🚆 📺 📶 🎱 ●
Children: 🍼 🛏 🎠 Catering: (✗ 🍷 🍴 Room: 📺 ♨ ☎ 📺

HASLEMERE, Surrey Map ref 2C2
SatNav GU27 3EX **B**

FARMHOUSE ★★★★★ **Gold AWARD**

B&B PER ROOM PER NIGHT
S: £75.00 - £100.00
D: £100.00 - £150.00

Colliers Farm
Midhurst Road, Fernhurst, Haslemere, Surrey GU27 3EX T: (01428) 652265
E: info@colliersfarm.co.uk
W: www.colliersfarm.co.uk

A beautifully renovated Grade II Listed 17th century farmhouse within South Downs National Park. Friendly and comfortable home with excellent facilities and stunning views. **Directions:** Colliers Farm is ½ mile south of the village centre of Fernhurst off the A286 approx midway between Haslemere and Midhurst. **Bedrooms:** En suite, king size beds, tea & coffee, Wi-Fi & TV.

Site: ✿ P Payment: 💷 Leisure: ▶ ♿ Property: 🚗 ⊘ Catering: 🍴 Room: 📺 ♨ ☎ 📺 📀

ARUNDEL, Sussex Map ref 2D3
SatNav RH20 1PA **B**

B&B PER ROOM PER NIGHT
S: £50.00 - £55.00
D: £70.00 - £85.00

SPECIAL PROMOTIONS
We are very happy to discuss discounted rates for longer stays and low season. Please call us for more details.

The Barn at Penfolds

The Street, Bury, West Sussex RH20 1PA **T:** (01798) 831496
W: thebarnatpenfolds.co.uk

The accommodation comprises two double rooms in the main house, a double and a single in the thatched-roof barn as well as a double in the Shepherds Hut. All rooms en suite. Use of the garden room for breakfast and relaxation. Our own chickens provide the eggs for breakfast.

Directions: Just off the A29. From Arundel turn right past the Squire & Horse, 300 yards, turn left. From Pulborough turn left after Turners garage.

Bedrooms: 1 single, 4 double
Open: All year

Site: ✿ P Payment: € Property: ⋈ Children: ⛛12 Catering: 🍴 Room: 🖊 ☕ 📺 ⚅

BEXHILL-ON-SEA, Sussex Map ref 3B4
SatNav TN40 1JN **H**

B&B PER ROOM PER NIGHT
S: £49.00 - £59.00
D: £89.00 - £109.00
EVENING MEAL PER PERSON
£19.95

SPECIAL PROMOTIONS
3 & 4 day Christmas breaks. Reduced rates for 3+ nights & 10+ nights. Winter rate reductions & breaks.

The Northern Hotel

72-78 Sea Road, Bexhill-on-Sea TN40 1JN **T:** (01424) 212836
E: reception@northernhotel.co.uk
W: northernhotel.co.uk

The Sims Family have developed and improved this fine Edwardian Hotel over 55 years. Modern features blend well with classic period furniture to create an ambiance of a time gone by. Our family atmosphere & friendly staff help create a warm, homely environment within elegant surroundings. Adjacent: Seafront, town centre, train station. Restaurants, bar, short breaks, holiday, Christmas, functions.

Directions: By Road: One mile from A259. Follow signs for Bexhill Seafront. We are in Sea Road, 70 metres from seafront, 200 metres from Rail Station. Train: Hours from London (2), Brighton (1), Eastbourne (1/2)

Bedrooms: 7 Single, 8 Double, 3 Twin, 2 Family
Open: All year

Payment: 💳 Property: ♟ 🖥 ∅ Children: ⛛ 🏨 ♿ Catering: 🍳 🍷 🍴 Room: 🖊 ☕ 📞 📺

BOGNOR REGIS, Sussex   Map ref 2C3   SatNav PO22 7AH H

Best Western Beachcroft Hotel

Clyde Road, Felpham, Bognor Regis PO22 7AH T: (01243) 827142
F: (01243) 863500 E: reservations@beachcroft-hotel.co.uk
W: beachcroft-hotel.co.uk £ BOOK ONLINE

B&B PER ROOM PER NIGHT
S: £54.50 - £92.50
D: £74.50 - £116.50

HB PER PERSON PER NIGHT
£62.50 - £80.50

Situated on seafront in Felpham village, within 0.5 miles of restaurants, shops, pubs, tennis, putting. En suite bedrooms with telephone, TV, hospitality tray. Renowned restaurant, indoor heated pool. Within ten miles Chichester Cathedral and theatre, Arundel Castle and Goodwood horse-racing. Seven golf courses. **Directions:** Signposted from A29 in both directions, follow signs to Felpham Village & brown bed signs until Beachcroft hotel sign. **Bedrooms:** 2 single, 16 dble, 12 twin, 4 family **Open:** All year

Site: ❀ Payment: 💷 Leisure: 🏊 ↑ ⚬ Property: 🍴 🖥 🔲 Children: 🚼 🛏 🎠 Catering: 🍽 🍴
Room: 🍵 💧 📞 📷 📺 🎧 🌡 🏊

BRIGHTON, Sussex   Map ref 2D3   SatNav BN2 1TL H

Amsterdam Hotel

11-12 Marine Parade, Brighton BN2 1TL T: (01273) 688825 F: (01273) 688828
E: info@amsterdam.uk.com
W: amsterdam.uk.com £ BOOK ONLINE

B&B PER ROOM PER NIGHT
D: £85.00 - £295.00

Hotel with modern, fully equipped rooms, bar, restaurant and sun terrace. The hotel is in a prime location on Brighton's seafront and everyone is welcome. **Directions:** Hotel is situated on Brighton Sea front opposite The Palace Pier. **Bedrooms:** 21 dble, 3 twin, 1 suite **Open:** All year

Site: ❀ Payment: 💷 Leisure: 🚲 🏊 ↑ Property: 🍴 🐕 🖥 ◐ Catering: 🍽 🍴 Room: 🍵 💧 📞 📷 📺 🎧

BRIGHTON, Sussex   Map ref 2D3   SatNav BN2 9JA B

Kipps Brighton

76 Grand Parade, Brighton BN2 9JA T: (01273) 604182 E: kippshostelbrighton@gmail.com
W: www.kipps-brighton.com £ BOOK ONLINE

BED ONLY PER NIGHT
£15.00 - £80.00

Award winning hostel situated in the heart of Brighton. We offer private rooms as well as dormitory rooms. Excellent facilities, including a self catering kitchen, lounge & outside patio. Views overlooking the historic Royal Pavillion. **Directions:** We are situated in the centre of Brighton. Visit our website to print off a map. **Bedrooms:** 1 single, 6 Doubles, 4 Twins, & Dormitory Rooms **Open:** All year

Site: ❀ Payment: 💷 € Leisure: 🚲 🏊 ↑ ⚬ Property: 🖥 📷 📺 🔲 Catering: 🍴 🍽 🍽 Room: 📠
Bedroom: ⚲

Chichester & Bognor Regis Campuses

College Lane, Chichester PO19 6PE T: (01243) 812120 E: conference@chi.ac.uk
W: http://www.chi.ac.uk/conference

B&B PER ROOM PER NIGHT
S: £33.00 - £48.00

The University of Chichester is able to offer a variety of venues for all types of events/conferences and meetings all year round. During the summer vacation months we let our accommodation facilities to external clients such as bed and breakfast guests, conferences and summer schools. Both campuses offer a range of different facilities which include; dance, performance and music studios, a theatre-style showroom, chapel, assembly hall, sports hall, lecture and meeting rooms, dining halls and bars.

Directions: Chichester Campus is a short walk from the city centre and railway/bus station. Bognor Campus is within walking distance of the town centre, railway station and seafront.

Bedrooms: 250 single
Open: All year except Christmas and New Year

Site: P Payment: [icons] Leisure: [icon] Property: [icons] Children: [icon]10 Catering: [icons] Room: [icons]
Bedroom: [icon]

George Bell House

4 Canon Lane, Chichester, West Sussex PO19 1PX T: (01243) 813586
E: bookings@chichestercathedral.org.uk
W: www.chichestercathedral.org.uk / www.cathedralenterprises.co.uk

B&B PER ROOM PER NIGHT
S: £79.00
D: £117.00 - £138.00

SPECIAL PROMOTIONS
Winter Break Offer-
40% discount on room
rate in January,
February and March
2014 (not including
breakfast)

George Bell House is a beautifully restored eight bedroom house situated in the historic precincts of Chichester Cathedral. All bedrooms are en-suite and offer stunning views of the Cathedral or gardens. Breakfast is available in the dining room of the house which looks out over the private, walled garden. Free Wi-Fi and parking are available. Rooms are to be booked in advance.

Directions: Turn though the archway into Canon Lane off South Street and George Bell House is the last house on the left before the next archway.

Bedrooms: 4 x double / twin, 3 x standard double, 1 x single room with disabled access
Open: All Year *Christmas and New Year on application*

Site: [icon] P Payment: [icon] Property: [icons] Children: [icons] Catering: [icon] Room: [icons]

138

CHICHESTER, Sussex   Map ref 2C3
SatNav PO21 3QB [H]

Inglenook Hotel
253-255 Pagham Road, Pagham, Bognor Regis PO21 3QB T: (01243) 262495
F: (01243) 262668 E: reception@the-inglenook.com
W: www.the-inglenook.com

B&B PER ROOM PER NIGHT
S: £55.00 - £75.00
D: £80.00 - £175.00
HB PER PERSON PER NIGHT
£70.00 - £110.00

Family-owned 16th century hotel. Cosy bars, inglenook fireplaces, attractive restaurant opening on to gardens and patio. Seafood specialities. Rooms individually furnished, some four-posters and jacuzzis. Weddings, conferences & parties. Car Parking. Directions: Gatwick 1hr away. 3 miles from Bognor. 4 miles from Chichester. Bedrooms: 1 single, 14 dble, 2 twin, 1 family Open: All year

Site: ✿ Payment: 🖃 € Leisure: ♪ ► Property: ♟ ♞ 🖳 ▤ Children: ⛹ ▦ ♿ Catering: ♨ ⛏
Room: ⌨ ♨ ☏ 📺 ♨ ⛵ 🛏

CHICHESTER, Sussex   Map ref 2C3
SatNav PO18 8HL [H]

Millstream Hotel
Bosham Lane, Bosham, Bosham Nr Chichester, West Sussex PO18 8HL T: (01243) 573234
F: (01243) 573459 E: info@millstream-hotel.co.uk
W: www.millstreamhotel.com £ BOOK ONLINE

B&B PER ROOM PER NIGHT
S: £99.00 - £139.00
D: £159.00 - £229.00
EVENING MEAL PER PERSON
£34.00

This charming English country hotel is situated in picturesque Bosham, just 4 miles west of Chichester.The bright and airy en suite bedrooms are all individually decorated. The Millstream Restaurant serves modern British cuisine and has 2 AA Rosettes. Alternatively, Marwick's Brasserie provides a contemporary and relaxed eating environment. Guests can enjoy afternoon tea in the gardens or lounge.

Bedrooms: Bedrooms are individually decorated, en suite, with fresh milk and water in the fridge, tea & coffee making facilities and dressing gowns.
Open: All Year

Site: ✿ P Payment: 🖃 Property: ♟ 🖳 ⛵ ◐ Catering: (✗ ♨ Room: ⌨ ♨ ⛵ 📺 ♨ 🛏

COCKING CAUSEWAY, Sussex   Map ref 2C3
SatNav GU29 9QH [B]

Sunnyside
Cocking Causeway, Midhurst GU29 9QH T: (01730) 814370

B&B PER ROOM PER NIGHT
S: £38.00 - £70.00
D: £40.00 - £100.00

A private home where you are welcome to stay. The two rooms in the house and the annexe in the garden are light and comfortable with en suite facilities. Twin Room priced from £75. Bedrooms: 2 double, 1 twin Open: All year except Christmas and New Year.

Site: ✿ P Payment: € Property: ♞ ▤ ⊘ Children: ⛹ ▦ ♿ Catering: 🍴 Room: ⌨ ♨ 📺 ♨

CROWBOROUGH, Sussex   Map ref 2D3
SatNav TN6 2BF **B**

GUEST ACCOMMODATION

B&B PER ROOM PER NIGHT
S: £40.00 - £45.00
D: £60.00 - £100.00

EVENING MEAL PER PERSON
£15.00

Yew House Bed & Breakfast
11 Pellings Farm Close, Crowborough, East Sussex TN6 2BF
T: (01892) 610522 / 07789 993982 E: yewhouse@yewhouse.com
W: www.yewhouse.com

One Double en suite room and one single room, use of bathroom. Close to shops, station, parking. Quiet location. Silver award for green. Free Wi-Fi Available. Garden room with comfortable seating and PC open to guests use. **Directions:** Please contact us for directions. **Bedrooms:** 1 double en suite, 1 single **Open:** All year except Christmas Day

Site: ✿ P Payment: 💷 Leisure: 🏊 ♪ Property: 🖥 ⬚ Children: 🧸 🛏 ☂ Catering: 🍴 Room: ✏ ♨
📞 📷 📺 🖨

EASTBOURNE, Sussex   Map ref 2D3
SatNav BN21 4EE **H**

HOTEL

B&B PER ROOM PER NIGHT
S: £59.00 - £80.00
D: £109.00 - £189.00

HB PER PERSON PER NIGHT
£75.00 - £109.00

SPECIAL PROMOTIONS
Golf breaks, Christmas, New Year and Easter programme also available.

Best Western Lansdowne Hotel
King Edwards Parade, Eastbourne BN21 4EE T: (01323) 725174
F: (01323) 739721 E: sales@lansdowne-hotel.co.uk
W: bw-lansdownehotel.co.uk £ BOOK ONLINE

Best Western

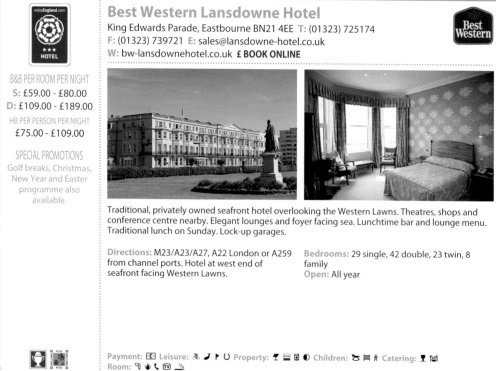

Traditional, privately owned seafront hotel overlooking the Western Lawns. Theatres, shops and conference centre nearby. Elegant lounges and foyer facing sea. Lunchtime bar and lounge menu. Traditional lunch on Sunday. Lock-up garages.

Directions: M23/A23/A27, A22 London or A259 from channel ports. Hotel at west end of seafront facing Western Lawns.

Bedrooms: 29 single, 42 double, 23 twin, 8 family
Open: All year

Payment: 💷 Leisure: 🏊 ♪ ♭ ∪ Property: 🎓 🖥 ⬚ ◐ Children: 🧸 🛏 ☂ Catering: 🍴 🍴
Room: ✏ ♨ 📞 📺 🖨

Book your accommodation online

Visit our new 2014 guide websites for detailed information, up-to-date availability and to book your accommodation online. Includes over 20,000 places to stay, all of them star rated.

www.visitor-guides.co.uk

EASTBOURNE, Sussex   Map ref 3B4
SatNav BN21 4DH **H**

Cavendish Hotel
Grand Parade, Eastbourne, East Sussex BN21 4DH T: (01323) 410222 F: (01323) 410941
E: info@cavendishhotel.co.uk
W: www.cavendishhotel.co.uk

B&B PER ROOM PER NIGHT
S: £51.00 - £92.00
D: £92.00 - £143.00

HB PER PERSON PER NIGHT
£133.00 - £288.00

A large 4* hotel on the English South Coast, stylish and unpretentious, elegant but relaxed. En suite bedrooms and fine dining complemented by the welcoming friendly and professional service. **Directions:** Located in Eastbourne on the South Coast, regular trains from London Victoria, Gatwick Airport is 43 miles away and good road links from M25. **Bedrooms:** 23 single, 27 dble, 64 twin, 5 suite **Open:** All year

Payment: ⊞ Leisure: 🏋 🎿 Property: 🍷 💺 🅱 ◑ Children: 👶 🛏 🚶 Catering: 🍷 🍽 Room: 🔌 🖥 📞 📺

FOREST ROW (3 MILES), Sussex   Map ref 2D2
SatNav RH19 4JF **B**

Courtlands Nurseries
Chilling Street, Forest Row, East Grinstead, West Sussex RH19 4JF T: (01342) 810780
E: lindsay.shurvell@virgin.net
W: courtlandsnurseries.co.uk

B&B PER ROOM PER NIGHT
S: £30.00 - £50.00
D: £55.00 - £80.00

Courtlands Nurseries is a walled kitchen garden and nursery within in a peaceful old Sussex country estate, ideally located for visiting Ashdown Forest, numerous National Trust properties, and the Bluebell Steam Railway. Spacious rooms. **Directions:** 20 minutes Gatwick, 6 miles from M23, 5 miles East Grinstead (trains to London),1 mile Ashdown Forest. Sharpthorne village 0.7 mile (shop and pub) **Bedrooms:** 2 twin, 1 family **Open:** All year

Site: ❀ P Property: 🖥 Children: 👶 Catering: 🍽 Room: 🔌 🖥 📺 🚿

GATWICK, Sussex   Map ref 2D2
SatNav RH6 7DS **B**

Southbourne Guest House Gatwick
34 Massetts Road, Horley RH6 7DS T: (01293) 771991 F: (01293) 820112
E: reservations@southbournegatwick.com
W: southbournegatwick.com **£ BOOK ONLINE**

B&B PER ROOM PER NIGHT
S: £49.00 - £60.00
D: £69.00 - £80.00

A warm welcome awaits you in our family-run guesthouse. Ideally located for Gatwick Airport, and exploring Surrey, Sussex and London. Five minutes walk from Horley train station, restaurants, shops and pubs and 30 minutes by train from London. Five minutes drive from Gatwick with free courtesy transport from 0930-2130.

Directions: M23 jct 9, follow the A23 through 3 roundabouts. At 3rd roundabout take 3rd exit and continue to the 2nd right-hand turn into Massetts Road.

Bedrooms: 2 single, 3 double, 3 twin, 4 family
Open: All year

Site: ❀ P Payment: ⊞ Property: 🖥 Children: 👶 🛏 🚶 Catering: 🍽 Room: 🔌 🔟 📺 🚿 🛋

HAILSHAM, Sussex   Map ref 2D3   SatNav BN27 1RN B

B&B PER ROOM PER NIGHT
S: £22.00 - £49.00
D: £73.00 - £90.00

Bader International Study Centre

Herstmonceux Castle, Hailsham, East Sussex BN27 1RN   T: (01323) 834400
F: (01323) 834499   E: accom@bisc.queensu.ac.uk
W: www.herstmonceux-castle.com

Herstmonceux is renowned for its magnificent moated castle, set in beautiful parkland and superb Elizabethan gardens. Built originally as a country home in the mid 15th Century. An ideal base for exploring Sussex. **Directions:** See website **Bedrooms:** Double rooms, single rooms and twin rooms available. **Open:** All year except Christmas and New Year.

Site: ✿ P Payment: 💷 Leisure: ⚡ Property: ⊤ ⊟ 🔲 📺 ⊟ Children: 🏇 🛏 🅰 Catering: 🍴 ⬥
Bedroom: ⬥ 📞 🖵 🖨

HASTINGS, Sussex   Map ref 3B4   SatNav TN37 6DB B

B&B PER ROOM PER NIGHT
S: £30.00 - £45.00
D: £60.00 - £75.00

Seaspray Bed and Breakfast

54 Eversfield Place, St. Leonards-on-Sea, Hastings TN37 6DB   T: (01424) 436583
E: jo@seaspraybb.co.uk
W: seaspraybb.co.uk **£ BOOK ONLINE**

Seafront extra special home from home. High standard refurbishment. Quiet location 5mins to amenities. Superking, Wi-Fi, plasma Freeview, fridge. Complimentary parking. Extensive breakfast menu, all diets catered. Silver award. **Directions:** M25 jct 5 onto A21 Hastings. Follow signs to seafront to A259. Located on promenade 100m west of pier. **Bedrooms:** 3 single, 3 double, 3 twin, 1 family **Open:** All year except Christmas

♿ 🐾 🅿 Site: P Leisure: ⚖ 🧦 🏃 Property: ⊟ ⊟ Children: 🏇 🛏 🅰 Catering: 🍴 Room: 🖵 ⬥ 📺
📺 🖨

HAYWARDS HEATH, Sussex   Map ref 2D3   SatNav RH16 1JH B

B&B PER ROOM PER NIGHT
S: £40.00 - £50.00
D: £65.00 - £75.00

The Old Forge

16 Lucastes Avenue, Haywards Heath RH16 1JH   T: (01444) 451905 / 07884 408618
F: (01444) 451905   E: rowlandandhelen@hotmail.com

The Old Forge is a charming, late-Victorian home set in delightful conservation area within easy reach of the mainline station. Friendly owners, warm welcome. Delicious cooked breakfast. Centrally heated rooms with TV. Wi-fi access. **Directions:** Please contact us for directions. **Bedrooms:** 2 double en suite rooms, plus attic room for children **Open:** All year except Christmas

Site: P Property: 🐕 ⊟ Children: 🏇 🛏 🅰 Room: 🖵 ⬥ 📺 🖨 ♿

HENFIELD, Sussex   Map ref 2D3   SatNav BN5 9RQ B

No1 The Laurels B&B

1 The Laurels, Martyn Close, Henfield, West Sussex BN5 9RQ   T: (01273) 493518
E: malc.harrington@lineone.net
W: no1thelaurels.co.uk

A detached house faced with traditional knapped Sussex flint stones. Comfortable rooms, a warm welcome, easy access to Brighton. Many places of interest nearby. Please contact us for prices. **Directions:** Please refer to website. **Bedrooms:** 1 single, 2 double and 1 twin. **Open:** All year.

Site: ✿ P Payment: 💷 Property: ⊟ Children: 🏇 Catering: 🍴 Room: 🖵 ⬥ 📺

LEWES, Sussex Map ref 2D3 — SatNav BN7 3QD B

The Blacksmiths Arms
Offham, Lewes BN7 3QD T: (01273) 472971 E: blacksmithsarms@shineadsl.co.uk
W: theblacksmithsarms-offham.co.uk

18th century village inn close to South Downs Way on main A275. Close to historic town of Lewes. Convenient for Sussex University and Glyndebourne. Mentioned in Good Pub Guide. **Directions:** Please contact us for directions. **Bedrooms:** 4 double **Open:** All year

B&B PER ROOM PER NIGHT
D: £65.00 - £95.00
EVENING MEAL PER PERSON
£10.00 - £25.00

Site: P Payment: Leisure: Property: Children: Catering: Room:

LEWES, Sussex Map ref 2D3 — SatNav BN7 1EQ B

Lill Stugan
33 Houndean Rise, Lewes BN7 1EQ T: (01273) 483580 E: lillstugan@hotmail.com / alanaghraikes1@gmail.com
W: www.lillstuganlewes.com

Modern self-contained garden flat in Swedish house backing on to National Park. Own access to flat and patio area. Kitchen/diner, breakfast foods and newspapers supplied. Parking. Use of beach hut. **Directions:** Coming from Brighton direction on the A27 turn left at the roundabout as you approach Lewes. Buses and taxis from Lewes Station. **Bedrooms:** 1 single, 1 double **Open:** All year

ROOM ONLY
B&B PER ROOM PER NIGHT
S: £65.00
D: £95.00

Site: P Leisure: Property: Children: Catering: Room:

MIDHURST, Sussex Map ref 2C3 — SatNav GU29 9PP B

18 Pretoria Avenue
18 Pretoria Avenue, Midhurst, West Sussex GU29 9PP T: (01730) 814868
F: (01730) 814868 E: ericstratford@uwclub.net

Family house with one double room for guests. Private bathroom with power shower. Coffee/tea making facilities, hair dryer, colour TV, clothes press. **Bedrooms:** Double bed, flat screen tv, tea & coffee facilities available. **Open:** All year except December & January.

BED & BREAKFAST
B&B PER ROOM PER NIGHT
S: £30.00 - £40.00
D: £60.00 - £70.00

Property: Catering: Room:

RINGMER, Sussex Map ref 2D3 — SatNav BN8 5RU B

Bryn Clai
Uckfield Road (A26), Ringmer, Lewes BN8 5RU T: (01273) 814042
E: daphne@brynclai.co.uk
W: brynclai.co.uk £ BOOK ONLINE

Set in seven acres with beautiful garden. Parking. Comfortable interior. Large bedrooms (ground-floor rooms), views over farmland. Walking distance country pub with excellent food. Glyndebourne, South Downs and Brighton nearby. **Directions:** From A26, 2 miles north of Lewes, 5 miles south of Uckfield. **Bedrooms:** 1 double, 1 twin, 2 family **Open:** All year

B&B PER ROOM PER NIGHT
S: £65.00 - £75.00
D: £75.00 - £85.00

Site: P Payment: Leisure: Property: Children: Catering: Room:

Jeake's House

Jeake's House, Mermaid Street, Rye TN31 7ET T: (01797) 222828
E: stay@jeakeshouse.com
W: jeakeshouse.com

B&B PER ROOM PER NIGHT
S: £70.00 - £79.00
D: £90.00 - £140.00

SPECIAL PROMOTIONS
20% Mid-week Winter Special.
Jan-March offer available.

Ideally located historic house on winding, cobbled street in the heart of ancient medieval town. Individually restored rooms provide traditional luxury combined with all modern facilities. Book-lined bar, cosy parlours, extensive breakfast menu to suit all tastes. Easy walking distance to restaurants and shops. Private car park nearby.

Directions: Within the cobbled medieval town centre, approached either from the High Street via West Street or from The Strand Quay, A259.

Bedrooms: 7 double, 3 twin, 1 suite
Open: All year

Payment: Leisure: Property: Children: Catering: Room:

Old Borough Arms

The Strand, Rye, East Sussex TN31 7DB T: (01797) 222128 E: info@oldborougharms.co.uk
W: oldborougharms.co.uk

B&B PER ROOM PER NIGHT
S: £60.00 - £79.00
D: £79.00 - £115.00

There are nine tastefully decorated en suite rooms at The Old Borough Arms which is located in the heart of Rye. Clean and comfortable rooms and an excellent breakfast are guaranteed. Free Wi-Fi throughout the building. **Directions:** We are located at the foot of the famous Mermaid Street in the centre of the historic town of Rye. **Bedrooms:** 1 single, 6 double, 1 twin, 1 family
Open: All year

Site: Payment: Leisure: Property: Children: Catering: Room:

The Silverdale

21 Sutton Park Road, Seaford, East Sussex BN25 1RH T: (01323) 491849
E: info@silverdaleseaford.co.uk
W: www.silverdaleseaford.co.uk £ BOOK ONLINE

B&B PER ROOM PER NIGHT
S: £45.00 - £65.00
D: £60.00 - £90.00

Beautiful Edwardian guest house in the centre of Seaford. A few minutes walk to beach, Seven Sisters country park and many friendly pubs and restaurants in Seaford. **Directions:** On A259 in centre of Seaford. **Bedrooms:** 2 double, 1 family, 1 suite **Open:** All year except Christmas and New Year

Payment: Leisure: Property: Children: Catering: Room:

SELSEY, Sussex Map ref 2C3
SatNav PO20 0LX B

St Andrews Lodge
Chichester Road, Selsey PO20 0LX **T:** (01243) 606899 **F:** (01243) 607826
E: info@standrewslodge.co.uk
W: www.standrewslodge.co.uk **£ BOOK ONLINE**

B&B PER ROOM PER NIGHT
S: £50.00 - £80.00
D: £72.00 - £140.00

SPECIAL PROMOTIONS
Special Winter Offer.
Stay 3 nights or more
and get a 25%
discount.

St Andrews Lodge is licensed Guest Accommodation in the old Seaside town of Selsey. Close to unspoilt beaches and countryside. Afternoon tea available in beautiful suntrap garden. Superb breakfast. 15 minute stroll to the beach and 5 minute drive to Pagham Harbour Nature Reserve. Ideally situated for visiting Chichester, Arundel, Portsmouth and Goodwood. Large car park and pet friendly.

Directions: Take the B2145 from the A27 at Chichester for approx 7 miles. St Andrews Lodge is on the right hand side of the road just before St Peters Church.

Bedrooms: 11 individually decorated rooms. 6 rooms are on the ground floor, 5 with direct access to the garden. One wheelchair accessible room.
Open: All year

Site: ✿ P **Payment:** 🔳 **Leisure:** ♩ ▸ **Property:** ⚲ 🛏 ♨ ⌀ **Children:** 🐴 🛏 🛝 **Catering:** ♟ 🍴
Room: ☎ ✋ TV ♿

ST. LEONARDS-ON-SEA, Sussex Map ref 3B4
SatNav TN38 0RJ B

Sea Spirit Guest House
17 Tower Road West, Saint. Leonards on Sea TN38 0RJ **T:** (01424) 729518
E: lorraineedwards@btinternet.com
W: sea-spirit-guesthouse.co.uk

B&B PER ROOM PER NIGHT
S: £50.00 - £60.00
D: £79.00 - £89.00
EVENING MEAL PER PERSON
£6.95 - £25.00

The Sea Spirit Guest House is a 4 star silver award winning family run guest house in a quiet residential road with free non restricted parking in St Leonards on sea. **Directions:** A21 signposted Hastings, at the silverhill lights turn left, follow road to the next lights take right hand lights then 100yards turn right **Bedrooms:** 4 double rooms 1 twin room 1 family room **Open:** All year

Site: ✿ P **Payment:** 🔳 **Leisure:** ♿ ♩ ▸ **Property:** 🛏 ♨ ⌀ **Children:** 🐴 🛏 🛝 **Catering:** (✗ 🍴
Room: ☎ ✋ ⓒ TV 📀

STEYNING, Sussex Map ref 2D3
SatNav BN44 3GG B

Springwells
9 High Street, Steyning, West Sussex BN44 3GG **T:** (01903) 812446 **F:** (01903) 879823
E: contact@springwells.co.uk
W: www.springwells.co.uk

B&B PER ROOM PER NIGHT
S: £43.00 - £65.00
D: £72.00 - £120.00

Once a Georgian merchant's town house now an elegant 11 bedroom bed and breakfast hotel. Lovely walled gardens. Victorian style conservatory. Outdoor heated swimming pool. Two four poster beds. **Directions:** Please contact us for directions.
Bedrooms: 2 single, 6 double, 2 twin, 1 suite **Open:** All year

Site: ✿ P **Payment:** 🔳 **Leisure:** ♿ ♩ ▸ ∪ ⚘ **Property:** ⚲ 🛏 📱 **Children:** 🐴 🛏 🛝 **Catering:** ♟
Room: ☎ ✋ ☎ ⓒ TV 📀

London

Historical landmarks, museums, theatres, sporting venues...the list goes on. The capital of the UK has everything a tourist could ever want. Whether it's a visit to the Tower of London or a ride on the London Eye, this city will not disappoint. You can spend a day sightseeing and then sample one of the world-famous West End shows in the evening. A single trip to London will not be enough to take in the most popular attractions – you'll leave with the intention of returning quickly to see what else the capital has in store.

Highlights

Art galleries

Don't miss out on the best London art exhibitions, from sculpture and installations to painting and photography.

Buckingham Palace

The official London residence and principal workplace of the British monarch, the palace is a setting for state occasions and royal hospitality. The changing of the guard is a popular visitor attraction.

Hampton Court Palace

Discover the magnificence of Henry VIII's favourite royal residence. Immerse yourself in the sights and sounds of the bustling Base Court and marvel at the breath taking grandeur of Henry's State Rooms.

London Eye

Get a fantastic view of the capital from the London Eye, a giant Ferris wheel on the South Bank of the River Thames. The entire structure is 135 metres tall and the wheel has a diameter of 120 metres.

London Zoo

Set in leafy Regent's Park amid iconic architecture and beautiful gardens, London Zoo is an oasis in the heart of the city. With over 760 animal species, exciting and innovative new exhibits and heritage-listed building almost as famous as their inhabitants, a visit to the zoo is a great day out.

Maritime Greenwich

The area is significant for the Royal Observatory where the understanding of astronomy and navigation were developed. The complex was until recently the Royal Naval College.

Museums

Visitors to London are able to enjoy access to some of the greatest museums in the world, including the Natural History Museum, Victoria & Albert Museum and the National Maritime Museum.

Royal Botanic Gardens, Kew

The gardens house botanic collections that have been considerably enriched through the centuries.

Tower of London

Started in 1066 by William the Conqueror during the Norman conquest of England, the Tower of London is a symbol of power and an example of Norman military architecture that spread across England.

Westminster

Westminster Palace is an example of neo-Gothic architecture. The site comprises the Church of Saint Margaret and Westminster Abbey, where all the sovereigns since the 11th century have been crowned.

Editor's Picks

Take in the view

For unrivalled views of the capital, hop on the London Eye. The UK's top paid-for visitor attraction provides a magical and entertaining way to experience the city.

Discover another angle

The view from the top of Primrose Hill is one of London's best, affording a fantastic panorama across the city.

Fit for a princess

Explore Kate Middleton's London haunts including the National Portrait Gallery, Kensington Palace and Bluebird restaurant.

Step back in time

Leave modern London behind with a visit to one of the city's historic houses. Learn about the people who lived there, find out about historic interiors and design, or get inspiration from their exquisite gardens.

Explore London's maritime history

Venture aboard the Cutty Sark, one of the world's most famous ships and last surviving tea clipper. Visits to the Golden Hinde and HMS Belfast are also worthwhile.

Things to do

Entertainment & Culture

Apsley House
Westminster W1J 7NT
(020) 7499 5676
www.english-heritage.org.uk/daysout/properties/apsley-house/
This great 18th century town house pays homage to the Duke's dazzling military career, which culminated in his victory at Waterloo in 1815.

British Museum
Camden WC1B 3DG
(020) 7323 8299
www.thebritishmuseum.ac.uk
Founded in 1753, the British Museum's remarkable collections span over two million years of human history and culture, all under one roof.

Down House - Home of Charles Darwin
Bromley BR6 7JT
(01689) 859119
www.english-heritage.org.uk/daysout/properties/home-of-charles-darwin-down-house/
The family home and workplace of Charles Darwin.

Estorick Collection of Modern Italian Art
Islington N1 2AN
(020) 7704 9522
www.estorickcollection.com
World-famous collection of Italian Futurists, Modigliani, Morandi and others in a beautiful Georgian house. Also temporary exhibitions, events, library and shop.

Greenwich Heritage Centre
Greenwich SE18 4DX
(020) 8854 2452
www.greenwich.gov.uk
Local history museum with displays of archaeology, natural history and geology. Also temporary exhibitions, schools service, sales point and Saturday club.

London Transport Museum
Westminster WC2E 7BB
(020) 7379 6344
www.ltmuseum.co.uk
The history of transport for everyone, from spectacular vehicles, special exhibitions, actors and guided tours to film shows, gallery talks and children's craft workshops

Lord's Tour
Westminster NW8 8QN
(020) 7616 8595
www.lords.org/history/tours-of-lords/
Guided tour of Lord's Cricket Ground including the Long Room, MCC Museum, Real Tennis Court, Mound Stand and Indoor School.

Imperial War Museum

Southwark SE1 6HZ
(020) 7416 5320
www.iwm.org.uk
This award-winning museum tells the story of conflict involving Britain and the Commonwealth since 1914. See thousands of imaginatively displayed exhibits, from art to aircraft, utility clothes to U-boats.

Museum of London
City of London EC2Y 5HN
(020) 7001 9844
www.museumoflondon.org.uk
Step inside Museum of London for an unforgettable journey through the capital's turbulent past.

National Gallery
Westminster WC2N 5DN
(020) 7747 2888
www.nationalgallery.org.uk
The National Gallery houses one of the greatest collections of Western European painting in the world. Discover inspiring art by Botticelli, Caravaggio, Leonardo da Vinci, Monet, Raphael, Rembrandt, Titian, Vermeer and Van Gogh.

Natural History Museum
Kensington and Chelsea SW7 5BD
(020) 7942 5000
www.nhm.ac.uk
The Natural History Museum reveals how the jigsaw of life fits together. Animal, vegetable or mineral, the best of our planet's most amazing treasures are here for you to see - for free.

National Maritime Museum
Greenwich SE10 9NF
(020) 8858 4422
www.nmm.ac.uk
Britain's seafaring history housed in an impressive modern museum. Themes include exploration, Nelson, trade and empire, passenger shipping, luxury liners, maritime London, costume, art and the sea, the future and environmental issues.

National Portrait Gallery
Westminster WC2H 0HE
(020) 7306 0055
www.npg.org.uk
The National Portrait Gallery houses the world's largest collection of portraits. Visitors come face to face with the people who have shaped British history from Elizabeth I to David Beckham. Entrance is free.

Royal Air Force Museum Hendon
Barnet NW9 5LL
(020) 8205 2266
www.rafmuseum.org
Take off to the Royal Air Force Museum and flypast the history of aviation with an exciting display of suspended aircraft, touch screen technology, simulator rides, hands-on section, film shows, licensed restaurant.

Science Museum
Kensington and Chelsea SW7 2DD
0870 870 4868
www.sciencemuseum.org.uk
The Science Museum is world-renowned for its historic collections, awe-inspiring galleries, family activities and exhibitions - and it's free!

Southbank Centre
Lambeth SE1 8XX
0871 663 2501
www.southbankcentre.co.uk
A unique arts centre with 21 acres of creative space, including the Royal Festival Hall, Queen Elizabeth Hall and The Hayward.

St Bartholomew's Hospital Archives and Museum
City of London EC1A 7BE
(020) 7601 8152
www.bartsandthelondon.nhs.uk/aboutus/st_bartholomews_hospital.asp
The museum tells the inspiring story of Bart's Hospital. Founded nearly 9 centuries ago, it is one of the oldest hospitals in Britain.

Tate Britain
Westminster SW1P 4RG
(020) 7887 8888
www.tate.org.uk
Tate Britain presents the world's greatest collection of British art in a dynamic series of new displays and exhibitions.

Tate Modern
Southwark SE1 9TG
(020) 7887 8888
www.tate.org.uk/modern
The national gallery of international modern art and is one of London's top free attractions. Packed with challenging modern art and housed within a disused power station on the south bank of the River Thames.

Tower Bridge Exhibition

Southwark SE1 2UP
(020) 7403 3761
www.towerbridge.org.uk
Inside Tower Bridge Exhibition you will travel up to the high-level walkways, located 140 feet above the Thames and witness stunning panoramic views of London before visiting the Victorian Engine Rooms.

Victoria and Albert Museum

Kensington and Chelsea SW7 2RL
(020) 7942 2000
www.vam.ac.uk
The V&A is the world's greatest museum of art and design, with collections unrivalled in their scope and diversity.

Wallace Collection

Westminster W1U 3BN
(020) 7563 9551
www.wallacecollection.org
The Wallace Collection is a national museum, displaying superb works of art in an historic London town house.

Wembley Stadium Tours

Brent HA9 0WS
0844 800 2755
www.wembleystadium.com/wembleystadiumtour/default.aspx
Until your dream comes true, there's only one way to experience what it's like winning at Wembley - take the tour.

Wimbledon Lawn Tennis Museum

Merton SW19 5AG
(020) 8944 1066
www.wimbledon.org
A fantastic collection of memorabilia dating from 1555, including Championship Trophies, Art Gallery, and special exhibitions, reflecting the game and championships of today.

Family Fun

Chessington World of Adventures

Kingston upon Thames KT9 2NE
0870 444 7777
www.chessington.com
Explore Chessington - it's a whole world of adventures! Soar on the Vampire rollercoaster or discover the mystery of Tomb Blaster. Take a walk on the wild side in the Trails of the Kings or visit the park's own SEA LIFE Centre.

London Eye

Lambeth SE1 7PB
0870 500 0600
www.londoneye.com
Get the best view of London when you visit The London Eye, a top London attraction and the world's largest observation wheel.

Royal Observatory Greenwich

Greenwich SE10 9NF
(020) 8858 4422
www.nmm.ac.uk/places/royal-observatory/
Stand on the Greenwich Meridian Line, Longitude Zero, which divides East and West. Watch the time-ball fall at 1 o'clock. Giant refracting telescope.

Heritage

Chiswick House

Hounslow W4 2RP
(020) 8995 0508
www.english-heritage.org.uk/daysout/properties/chiswick-house/
The celebrated villa of Lord Burlington with impressive grounds featuring Italianate garden with statues, temples, obelisks and urns.

Churchill Museum and Cabinet War Rooms

Westminster SW1A 2AQ
(020) 7930 6961
www.iwm.org.uk
Learn more about the man who inspired Britain's finest hour at the highly interactive and innovative Churchill Museum, the world's first major museum dedicated to life of the 'greatest Briton'. Step back in time and discover the secret.

Eltham Palace

Greenwich SE9 5QE
(020) 8294 2548
www.elthampalace.org.uk
A spectacular fusion of 1930s Art Deco villa and magnificent 15th century Great Hall. Surrounded by period gardens.

Hampton Court Palace

Richmond upon Thames KT8 9AU
0870 752 7777
www.hrp.org.uk
This magnificent palace set in delightful gardens was famously one of Henry VIII's favourite palaces.

HMS Belfast

Southwark SE1 2JH
(020) 7940 6300
www.iwm.org.uk
HMS Belfast, launched 1938, served throughout WWII, playing a leading part in the destruction of the German battle cruiser Scharnhorst and in the Normandy Landings.

Kensington Palace State Apartments
Kensington and Chelsea W8 4PX
0870 751 5170
www.hrp.org.uk
Home to the Royal Ceremonial Dress Collection, which includes some of Queen Elizabeth II's dresses worn throughout her reign, as well as 14 of Diana, Princess of Wales' evening dresses.

Kenwood House
Camden NW3 7JR
(020) 8348 1286
www.english-heritage.org.uk/daysout/properties/kenwood-house/
Beautiful 18th century villa with fine interiors, and a world class collection of paintings. Also fabulous landscaped gardens and an award-winning restaurant.

Queen Elizabeth's Hunting Lodge
Waltham Forest E4 7QH
(020) 8529 6681
www.cityoflondon.gov.uk
Timber-framed hunting grandstand built in 1543 for Henry VIII. It still stands in a beautiful part of Epping Forest overlooking the old hunting field for which it was designed.

Southwark Cathedral
Southwark SE1 9DA
(020) 7367 6700
www.southwark.anglican.org/cathedral
Oldest Gothic church in London (c.1220) with interesting memorials connected with the Elizabethan theatres of Bankside.

Somerset House
Westminster WC2R 1LA
(020) 7845 4670
www.somerset-house.org.uk
This magnificent 18th century building houses the celebrated collections of the Courtauld Institute of Art Gallery, Gilbert Collection and Hermitage Rooms.

Tower of London
Tower Hamlets EC3N 4AB
0870 756 6060
www.hrp.org.uk
The Tower of London spans over 900 years of British history. Fortress, palace, prison, arsenal and garrison, it is one of the most famous fortified buildings in the world, and houses the Crown Jewels, armouries, Yeoman Warders and ravens.

Nature & Wildlife

London Wetland Centre
Richmond upon Thames SW13 9WT
(020) 8409 4400
www.wwt.org.uk
The London Wetland Centre is a unique wildlife visitor attraction just 25 minutes from central London. Run by the Wildfowl and Wetlands Trust (WWT), it is acclaimed as the best urban site in Europe to watch wildlife.

ZSL London Zoo
Westminster NW1 4RY(020) 7722 3333
www.londonzoo.co.uk
Come face to face with some of the hairiest, scariest, tallest and smallest animals on the planet - right in the heart of the capital.

Outdoor Activities

Bateaux London Restaurant Cruisers
Westminster WC2N 6NU
(020) 7695 1800
www.bateauxlondon.com
Bateaux London offers lunch and dinner cruises, combining luxury dining, world-class live entertainment and five-star customer care.

London Eye River Cruise Experience
Lambeth E1 7PB
0870 500 0600
www.londoneye.com
See London from a different perspective and enjoy a unique 40 minute circular sightseeing cruise on the river Thames.

London Ice Sculpting Festival at Canary Wharf
January, date TBC
At this super-cool, free annual event, talented sculptors from around the world compete against the clock to create chilly artworks from two-metre glistening blocks of ice in a nail-biting competition.

Burns Night in London
January 25, Various venues
Celebrate Scotland's favourite son on Burns Night in London. Burns Night is the anniversary of the Scottish poet Robert Burns' birthday. Many London restaurants and bars hold special Burns Night events.

Chinese New Year
February, date TBC Various venues
London's Chinese New Year celebrations are the largest outside Asia, with parades, performances and fireworks.
www.visitlondon.com

Vodafone London Fashion Weekend
February, dates TBC, Somerset House
London's largest and most exclusive designer shopping event.
www.londonfashionweekend.co.uk

The Boat Race
April 6, Putney Bridge
Boat crews from the universities of Oxford and Cambridge battle it out on the Thames.
www.theboatrace.org

Virgin London Marathon
April 13, Various venues
Whether you run, walk or cheer from the sidelines, this is a London sporting institution you won't want to miss.
www.virginlondonmarathon.com

Covent Garden May Fayre and Puppet Festival
May 11, The Actors' Church, St Paul's Covent Garden
Enjoy a day of traditional British entertainment at the Actor's Church in Covent Garden.

Museums At Night 2014
May 15-17, Various venues
Explore arts and heritage after dark at museums across London. Packed with special events, from treasure trails to pyjama parties, Museums at Night is a great opportunity to explore culture in a new light.

RHS Chelsea Flower Show
May 20-24, Royal Hospital Chelsea
Experience the greatest flower show in the world at London's Royal Hospital Chelsea.
www.rhs.org.uk/Chelsea-Flower-Show

Taste of London
June 19-22, Regent's Park and Primrose Hill
Taste of London is the capital's largest open-air food and drink festival, bringing together big-name chefs, popular restaurants and top-notch food.
www.tastefestivals.com/london

Greenwick+Docklands International Festival

June, dates TBC, Various venues

The Greenwick+Docklands International Festival returns with a ten-day rollercoaster of theatre, dance and spectacle. The best of UK and international street arts brings extraordinary sights and sounds to Greenwich and East London.
www.festival.org

London Festival of Architecture

June 13-July 26

See London's buildings in a new light during the Festival of Architecture.
www.visitlondon.com

City of London Festival

June-July, Various venues

The City of London Festival is an annual extravaganza of music, dance, art, film, poetry, family and participation events that takes place in the city's Square Mile.
www.visitlondon.com

Wimbledon Lawn Tennis Championships

June 23-July 6, Wimbledon

The world of tennis descends on Wimbledon in South West London every summer for two weeks of tennis, strawberries and cream, and good-natured queuing.
www.wimbledon.com

RideLondon

August 9-10, Various venues

A world class festival of cycling in London, it includes four main cycling events. Even if you can't ride as fast as Bradley Wiggins, you can still take part riding in the Freecycle and the 100 races through central London. As a spectator, you'll love cheering on the expert riders in the Classic race and Grand Prix.
www.ridelondon.co.uk

Notting Hill Carnival

August 24-25, Various venues

The streets of West London come alive every August Bank Holiday weekend as London celebrates Europe's biggest street festival.
www.thenottinghillcarnival.com

The Mayor's Thames Festival

September

A spectacular weekend of free events celebrating London and its river.
www.visitlondon.com

London Design Festival

September, Various venues

A celebration of international design, with talks, seminars, exhibitions, parties and private views.
www.visitlondon.com

Tour of Britain

September, Various venues

Celebrating its 10th anniversary this year, the Tour of Britain is a multi-stage cycling race that takes place across the UK.
www.tourofbritain.com

London Film Festival

October, Various venues

A two-week showcase of the world's best new films, the BFI London Film Festival is one of the most anticipated events in London's cultural calendar.
www.bfi.org.uk/lff

ATP World Tour Finals

November, O2 Arena

See the world's top eight singles players and doubles teams in London for the prestigious season-ending tennis tournament.
www.atpworldtour.com

Tourist Information Centres

When you arrive at your destination, visit an Official Partner Tourist Information Centre for quality assured help with accommodation and information about local attractions and events, or email your request before you go. To find a Tourist Information Centre visit www.visitengland.com

| City of London | St Paul's Churchyard | 020 7606 3030 | stpauls.informationcentre@cityoflondon.gov.uk |
| Greenwich | 2 Cutty Sark Gardens | 0870 608 2000 | tic@greenwich.gov.uk |

Regional Contacts and Information

For more information on accommodation, attractions, activities, events and holidays in London, contact Visit London.

The publications listed are available from the following organisations:

Go to visitlondon.com for all you need to know about London. Look for inspirational itineraries with great ideas for weekends and short breaks.

Or call 0870 1 LONDON (0870 1 566 366) for:

• A London visitor information pack
• Visitor information on London
• Accommodation reservations

Speak to an expert for information and advice on museums, galleries, attractions, riverboat trips, sightseeing tours, theatre, shopping, eating out and much more! Or simply go to visitlondon.com

Entries appear alphabetically by town name in each county. A key to symbols appears on page 7

The Railway Tavern

131 Angel Lane, Stratford, London E15 1DB **T:** (020) 8534 3123 **F:** (020) 8519 0864
E: therailwaytavern@btconnect.com
W: railwaytavernhotel.co.uk

B&B PER ROOM PER NIGHT
S: £80.00 - £90.00
D: £89.00 - £99.00
EVENING MEAL PER PERSON
£6.95 - £9.95

Family run inn, providing quality accommodation within easy access of Stratford regional &
International stations, DLR, Central & Jubilee Lines. Conveniently placed for London, Canary Wharf,
Stratford Westfield and Stratford Town Centre shopping. Directly opposite the QEII Olympic Park,
ideal for tourists visiting the area and well placed for London attractions. East End Hospitality, West
End Style.

Directions: By road A112. National Coaches
from Stansted. Central, Jubilee, DLR lines to
Stratford regional station. Five minute walk from
Stratford station.

Bedrooms: 3 double, 6 twin, all en suite with flat
screen TV and Tea/Coffee making facilities in
each room.
Open: All year

Site: ❀ P Payment: 💳 Property: 🖵 Children: 🐾 🛏 Catering: 🍽 🍴 Room: ✋ 🕘 📺 🔌

Barry House Hyde Park

12 Sussex Place, Hyde Park, London W2 2TP **T:** (020) 7723 7340 **F:** (020) 7723 9775
E: hotel@barryhouse.co.uk
W: www.barryhouse.co.uk **£ BOOK ONLINE**

B&B PER ROOM PER NIGHT
S: £48.00 - £90.00
D: £89.00 - £120.00

Family-friendly, Barry House offers warm hospitality in a central
location. Comfortable en suite rooms, English breakfast served.
Located close to West End. Paddington Station, Hyde Park just
three minutes walk. **Directions:** Near Paddington Station: From the
station walk down London Street. At the traffic lights, cross over on
to Sussex Place. **Bedrooms:** 3 single, 4 double, 4 twin, 6 family
Open: All year

Payment: 💳 Leisure: 🎿 ⛵ Property: 🖵 Children: 🐾 🛏 🧍 Room: 📶 ✋ 📞 🕘 📺 🔌

Need more information?

Visit our new 2014 guide websites for
detailed information, up-to-date availability
and to book your accommodation online.
Includes over 20,000 places to stay, all of
them star rated.

www.visitor-guides.co.uk

HOTEL ★★★★   *Silver* AWARD

The Caesar Hotel

26-33 Queen's Gardens, Hyde Park, London W2 3BE   **T:** (020) 7262 0022   **F:** (020) 7402 5099
E: thecaesar@derbyhotels.com
W: www.thecaesarhotel.com   **£ BOOK ONLINE**

B&B PER ROOM PER NIGHT
S: £320.00
D: £350.00

SPECIAL PROMOTIONS
Please see our website.

The Caesar is an oasis of tranquillity combining contemporary style with modern thinking. The 140 rooms are designed to ensure maximum comfort. The XO restaurant offers international cuisine and the XO bar Spanish Tapas. The hotel is a few minutes walk from Notting Hill, Hyde Park and Oxford Street.

Directions: Heathrow Express Train (15 min) Paddington Station (10min walk). Underground stations: Paddington - Bakerloo/Circle/District; Lancaster Gate - Central 5min walk.

Bedrooms: 32 single, 66 double / twins, 6 family, 12 suite Deluxe.
Open: All year

Site: ✿ **Payment:** 💳 € **Leisure:** 🚲 🏃 **Property:** ⊛ 🍴 🐾 🖥 🗄 ◑ **Children:** 🍼 🛏 🚸 **Catering:** 🍷 🍽
Room: 🍴 🕯 📞 💿 📺 ♨

★★★ **GUEST ACCOMMODATION**

Temple Lodge Club Ltd

Temple Lodge, 51 Queen Caroline Street, Hammersmith, London W6 9QL
T: (020) 8748 8388   **E:** templelodgeclub@btconnect.com
W: www.templelodgeclub.com

B&B PER ROOM PER NIGHT
S: £55.00 - £90.00
D: £72.00 - £120.00

SPECIAL PROMOTIONS
Please see website for special promotions.

Hidden away from the hustle and bustle of central Hammersmith, yet a surprisingly short walk from its main transport hub, this listed building provides a quiet and relaxing haven after the exertions of a busy day or night out. Breakfast is hearty, vegetarian and mainly organic. Bedrooms are comfortably furnished, light and airy. Most rooms, including library, look out onto our secluded garden.

Directions: Exit Hammersmith tube towards the Apollo Theatre, turn left towards the river and Hammersmith Bridge, next door but one is Temple Lodge. Enter small courtyard, come to red front door and ring doorbell!

Bedrooms: 5 single with companion bed if needed, 4 double (1 en suite, 1 private bathroom, 1 shower only in room, 1 facilities on corridor) 2 twin-bedded.
Open: All year

Site: ✿ **Payment:** 💳 **Property:** 🖥 📺 **Children:** 🍼 **Catering:** 🍽 **Room:** 🍴 ♿

Goodenough Club

23 Mecklenburgh Square, London WC1N 2AB T: (02077) 694727
E: reservations@goodenough.ac.uk
W: www.club.goodenough.ac.uk £ BOOK ONLINE

B&B PER ROOM PER NIGHT
S: £108.00 - £135.00
D: £160.00 - £175.00

Occupies 5 Georgian town houses in the heart of Bloomsbury overlooking Mecklenburgh Square, walking distance to West End, Covent Garden and the Eurostar. Luxurious Garden Suites are available and guests may attend events at the adjacent Goodenough College. Health club day passes can be purchased. **Bedrooms:** TV, Wi-Fi, Hairdryer & Hospitality tray. **Open:** All year

Site: ✿ Payment: 🖭 Leisure: ☌ Property: 🖼 🅗 ● Children: 🪀 🛏 Room: 🖳 🕯 📞 📺 🖨

Woodstock Guest House

30 Woodstock Road, Croydon CR0 1JR T: (020) 8680 1489 F: (020) 8680 1489
E: guesthouse.woodstock@gmail.com
W: www.woodstockhotel.co.uk

B&B PER ROOM PER NIGHT
S: £40.00 - £45.00
D: £60.00

SPECIAL PROMOTIONS
For stays longer than four nights, discounts will be given.

Victorian house located in a quiet residential area, only a five minute walk to the town centre, local amenities and East Croydon Railway Station. Well-appointed and spacious rooms. High standard of housekeeping and homely atmosphere. Single rooms from £40 to £45 pn, twin/double rooms £60 pn and family rooms £75 pn. Continental breakfast optional extra: £3.00 per person.

Directions: From East Croydon Station via George Street turn left into Park Lane. After roundabout exit A212. Woodstock Road is 2nd left off Park Lane.

Bedrooms: 4 single, 2 twin/double, 2 family.
Open: All year except Christmas and New Year

Site: ✿ P Payment: 🖭 Leisure: 🚲 ▶ Property: 🅗 Children: 🪀³ Catering: 🍴 Room: 🖳 🕯 🔌 📺 📀 🖨

The Red Cow

59 Sheen Road, Richmond TW9 1YJ T: (020) 8940 2511 F: (020) 8940 2581
E: tom@redcowpub.com
W: www.redcowpub.com

B&B PER ROOM PER NIGHT
S: £90.00
D: £125.00 - £140.00
EVENING MEAL PER PERSON
£8.00 - £14.95

Traditional Victorian inn retaining lovely original features. Short walk from Richmond town centre, river, royal parks, rail links to London. Nearby, Heathrow Airport, Twickenham RFU, Hampton Court, Windsor. **Directions:** Five-minute walk from Richmond town centre and train station. Easily accessed from M25, M4 and M3. **Bedrooms:** 4 double/twin, option for family room. **Open:** All year

Site: ✿ Payment: 🖭 Leisure: 🚲 ▶ ♻ Property: 🐾 🖼 Children: 🪀 🛏 Catering: 🝖 🍷 🍴 Room: 🖳 🕯 🔌 📺 📀

f

★★
METRO HOTEL

Richmond Park Hotel

3 Petersham Road, Richmond TW10 6UH **T:** (020) 8948 4666 **F:** (020) 8940 7376
E: richmdpk@globalnet.co.uk
W: therichmondparkhotel.com

B&B PER ROOM PER NIGHT
S: £72.00 - £87.00
D: £82.00 - £99.00

Privately owned hotel in the heart of Richmond. All rooms en suite with direct-dial telephone, colour TV, radio and tea/coffee making facilities with Wi-fi. **Directions:** The Richmond Park Hotel is on Petersham Road in the centre of town, where the Petersham Road forks with Hill Rise (leading to the Park). **Bedrooms:** 2 single, 17 double, 3 twin. **Open:** All year except Christmas and New Year

Payment: 🖃 **Leisure:** ♪ ▶ ♂ **Property:** 🐾 🖥 🗑 🏚 **Children:** 🧸 🛏 🎒 **Catering:** 🍽 **Room:** 🔌 🕭 📞 📺

enjoyEngland.com
★★★★
HOTEL

Lensbury

Broom Road, Teddington TW11 9NU **T:** (020) 8614 6400 **F:** (020) 8614 6445
E: accommodation@lensbury.com
W: lensbury.com **£ BOOK ONLINE**

B&B PER ROOM PER NIGHT
S: £90.00 - £190.00
D: £105.00 - £210.00

HB PER PERSON PER NIGHT
£110.00 - £230.00

SPECIAL PROMOTIONS
Weekend offer if you stay two or three nights. Best rate available. Prices include Breakfast, Car Parking, Wi-Fi internet and use of extensive leisure facilities including a 25m pool.

The Lensbury is a 4 Star hotel, situated in 25 acres of grounds on the banks of the River Thames. Located just 35 minutes by train from London Waterloo and within easy reach of London's airports and the M3, M4 and M25 motorways. The Lensbury has 169 en suite bedrooms, each designed to offer maximum comfort and relaxation. Accommodation rates also include use of the extensive leisure facilities.

Directions: Near Heathrow & Gatwick Airports. Motorways: 15 minutes from the M25. 10 minutes from the M3. Rail: 35 minutes to London Waterloo. Complementary shuttle bus to local station Mon to Fri peak times.

Bedrooms: Standard Rooms, Superior, Executive, Deluxe, Disabled room and a Family room. Rooms can take upto a maximum of 4 people.
Open: All year

Site: ✿ P **Payment:** 🖃 € **Leisure:** 🏊 ♪ ▶ ♂ 🍸 🎿 🏹 🌀 🎏 ❓ **Property:** 🏨 🛎 🖥 🗑 🏚 🌐
Children: 🧸 🛏 🎒 **Catering:** (X 🍽 🍴 **Room:** 🔌 🕭 📞 📺

East of England

Bedfordshire, Cambridgeshire, Essex,
Hertfordshire, Norfolk, Suffolk

Explore East Anglia and you'll discover a diverse mixture of vibrant cities, individual towns and villages, beautiful countryside and idyllic seaside – and all attractions are within easy reach. Based around the ancient kingdom of East Anglia, the area is made up of the six counties of Norfolk, Suffolk, Bedfordshire, Cambridgeshire, Essex and Hertfordshire to form the well-known 'hump' on England's eastern side. Directly to the north of London, the region has preserved much of its unspoiled character, rural landscape, architecture and traditions.

Highlights

Cambridge

An elegant yet compact city, Cambridge boasts a blend of history, scientific discovery, hi-tech innovation, culture and beauty. Try some punting along the River Cam, passing age-old colleges.

Ely Cathedral

A magnificent Norman Cathedral, which attracts visitors from all over the world. It dominates the Cambridgeshire skyline and can be seen for miles.

Fenland

A naturally marshy region, most of the fens were drained several centuries ago, resulting in a flat, damp, low-lying agricultural region. It is home to a wide range of wildlife.

Huntingdon

This Cambridgeshire market town was chartered by King John in 1205 and was the birthplace in 1599 of Oliver Cromwell. Huntingdon is an important bridge-head where the Great North Road, crosses the River Great Ouse near to Hinchingbrooke House, once home to Cromwell.

Ipswich

Ipswich enjoys a wonderful position on the meandering River Orwell and is known as East Anglia's premier waterfront town. For centuries, the river has been the lifeblood of the town – even today it acts as the social focal point for both residents and visitors.

Knebworth House

One of England's most beloved stately homes, Knebworth House is famous worldwide for its rock concerts and as the home of Victorian novelist Edward Bulwer Lytton – author of the words "The pen is mightier than the sword".

Norfolk Broads

The Broads is Britain's largest protected wetland and third largest inland waterway, and is home to some of the rarest plants and animals in the UK.

Norwich

This medieval city, on the banks of the River Wensum is bursting with cultural vibrancy and heritage buildings, plus stunning 1000 year old architecture. From the medieval period until the start of the Industrial Revolution, Norwich was England's second city, enormously prosperous and culturally active.

Norfolk and Suffolk Coast

Mile upon mile of stunning beaches and unspoiled coastline can be found in these two counties. One of the best beaches is at Holkham near Wells-on-Sea, and there are numerous nature reserves along the coastal path.

Woburn Abbey

Set in a beautiful 3000 acre deer park, Woburn Abbey is home to The Duke of Bedford. It is also well-known for its safari park. to man's interaction with his environment.

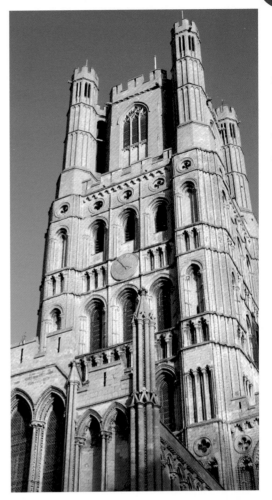

Editor's Picks

Take a punt

The best way to soak up the heritage and culture of Cambridge is to take a punt on the River Cam.

Binoculars at the ready

Take in the fresh air, see stunning views and set your eyes on some of the region's rare wildlife.

Enjoy a festival

Suffolk is the UK's festival county with an event for all tastes – music, comedy, theatre and dance are all covered.

Jump on your bicycle

Explore the countryside, with some of the best cycle routes in the country…and they're suitable for everyone.

Learn about our aviation heritage

From the very beginnings of flight with balloons and airships, to the present day airfields of the RAF, this region is steeped in aviation history.

Things to do

Attractions with this sign participate in the Places of Interest Quality Assurance Scheme.

Attractions with this sign participate in the Visitor Attraction Quality Assurance Scheme.

Both schemes recognise high standards in all aspects of the visitor experience (see page 7)

Entertainment & Culture

Central Museum and Planetarium
Southend-on-Sea, Essex SS2 6ES
(01702) 434449
www.southendmuseums.co.uk
An Edwardian building housing displays of archaeology, natural history, social and local history.

Gainsborough's House
Sudbury, Suffolk CO10 2EU
(01787) 372958
www.gainsborough.org
Gainsborough's House is the only museum situated in the birthplace of a great British artist. The permanent collection is built around the works of Thomas Gainsborough.

Hitchin Museum and Art Gallery
Hertfordshire SG5 1EH
(01462) 434476
www.north-herts.gov.uk/art_museums_and_heritage.htm
Local history museum and art gallery which tells the story of Hitchin. Two art galleries. Victorian pharmacy, costume gallery, and more.

Imperial War Museum Duxford
Cambridge CB22 4QR
(01223) 835000
www.iwm.org.uk/duxford
With its air shows, unique history and atmosphere, nowhere else combines the sights, sounds and power of aircraft quite like Duxford.

National Horseracing Museum and Tours
Newmarket, Suffolk CB8 8JH
(01638) 667333
www.nhrm.co.uk
Discover the stories of racing from its early origins at Newmarket to its modern-day heroes

Norwich Castle Museum and Art Gallery
Norfolk NR1 3JU
(01603) 493625
www.museums.norfolk.gov.uk
Ancient Norman keep of Norwich Castle dominates the city and is one of the most important buildings of its kind in Europe.

Peterborough Museum and Art Gallery
Cambridgeshire PE1 1LF
(01733) 864663
www.peterborough.gov.uk/leisure_and_culture/museum_and_galleries.aspx
Discover the rich & varied history of the Peterborough area -from Jurassic Sea Monsters to Napoleonic Prisoners of War to the haunted Museum building.

Royal Gunpowder Mills
Waltham Abbey, Essex EN9 1JY
(01992) 707370
www.royalgunpowdermills.com
A spectacular 170-acre location for a day of family fun. Special events including Spitfire flypast, award winning Secret History exhibition, tranquil wildlife walks, guided land train tours and rocket science gallery.

Family Fun

Adventure Island
Southend-on-Sea, Essex SS1 1EE
(01702) 443400
www.adventureisland.co.uk
One of the best value 'theme parks' in the South East with over 60 great rides and attractions for all ages. No admission charge you only 'pay if you play'.

Bodyflight Bedford
Clapham, MK41 6AE
0845 200 2960
www.bodyflight.co.uk
Indoor Skydiving! Learn to fly like a skydiver on a vertical column of air! Offering lessons for all abilities.

Go Ape! High Wire Forest Adventure - Thetford
Santon Downham, Suffolk IP27 0AF
0845 643 9215
www.goape.co.uk
Take to the trees and experience an exhilarating course of rope bridges, tarzan swings and zip slides... all set high above the forest floor.

Go Ape! High Wire Forest Adventure - Woburn Safari Park
Milton Keynes, Bedfordshire MK17 9QN
0845 643 9215
www.goape.co.uk
Take to the trees and experience an exhilarating course of rope bridges, tarzan swings and zip slides...all set high above the forest floor.

Sea-Life Adventure
Southend-on-Sea, Essex SS1 2ER
(01702) 442200
www.sealifeadventure.co.uk
With more than 30 display tanks and tunnels to explore, there are loads of fishy residents to discover at Sea-Life Adventure.

The National Stud
Newmarket, Cambridgeshire CB8 0XE
(01638) 663464
www.nationalstud.co.uk
The beautiful grounds & facilities are a recognised tourist attraction in the eastern region.

Heritage

Audley End House and Gardens
Saffron Walden, Essex CB11 4JF
(01799) 522842
www.english-heritage.org.uk/audleyend
Audley End is one of England's most magnificent stately homes.

Blickling Hall, Gardens and Park
Norwich, Norfolk NR11 6NF
(01263) 738030
www.nationaltrust.org.uk/blickling
A Jacobean redbrick mansion with a garden, orangery, parkland and lake. Spectacular long gallery, plasterwork ceilings and fine collections of furniture, pictures and books. Walks.

Bressingham Steam and Gardens
Diss, Norfolk IP22 2AA
(01379) 686900
www.bressingham.co.uk
World-renowned gardener and horticulturalist Alan Bloom combined his passion for plants and gardens with his love of steam, to create a truly unique attraction at Bressingham.

Cathedral and Abbey Church of St Alban
St. Albans, Hertfordshire AL1 1BY
(01727) 860780
www.stalbanscathedral.org
St Alban is Britain's first Christian martyr and the Cathedral, with its shrine, is its oldest place of continuous worship.

Holkham Hall
Wells-next-the-Sea, Norfolk NR23 1AB
(01328) 710227
www.holkham.co.uk
Magnificent Palladian hall. Rolling parkland. A wealth of wildlife. The best beach in England.

Ickworth House, Park and Gardens
Bury St. Edmunds, Suffolk
IP29 5QE
(01284) 735270
www.nationaltrust.org.uk/ickworth
Fine paintings, a beautiful collection of Georgian silver, an Italianate garden and stunning parkland.

Kings College Chapel
Cambridge CB2 1ST
(01223) 331212
www.kings.cam.ac.uk
It's part of one of the oldest Cambridge colleges sharing a wonderful sense of history and tradition with the rest of the University.

Knebworth House
Hertfordshire SG1 2AX
(01438) 812661
www.knebworthhouse.com
Historic house, home to the Lytton family since 1490.

Oliver Cromwell's House
Ely, Cambridgeshire CB7 4HF
(01353) 662062
www.olivercromwellshouse.co.uk
Visit the former Lord Protector's family's home and experience an exhibition on 17th Century life.

Sandringham
King's Lynn, Norfolk PE35 6EN
(01485) 545408
www.sandringhamestate.co.uk
H.M. The Queen. A fascinating house, an intriguing museum and the best of the Royal gardens.

Somerleyton Hall and Gardens
Lowestoft, Suffolk NR32 5QQ
(01502) 734901
www.somerleyton.co.uk
12 acres of landscaped gardens to explore including our famous 1864 Yew hedge maze. Guided tours of the Hall.

Nature & Wildlife

Banham Zoo
Norwich, Norfolk NR16 2HE
(01953) 887771
www.banhamzoo.co.uk
Wildlife spectacular which will take you on a journey to experience tigers, leopards and zebra plus some of the world's most exotic, rare and endangered animals.

Colchester Zoo
Essex CO3 0SL
(01206) 331292
www.colchester-zoo.com
Enjoy daily displays, feed elephants and giraffes and see over 260 species in over 60 acres of parkland!

Fritton Lake Country World
Great Yarmouth,
Norfolk NR31 9HA
(01493) 488288
A woodland and lakeside haven with a children's assault course, putting, an adventure playground, golf, fishing, boating, wildfowl, heavy horses, cart rides, falconry and flying displays.

The Raptor Foundation
Huntingdon, Cambridgeshire PE28 3BT
(01487) 741140
www.raptorfoundation.org.uk
Bird of prey centre, offering 3 daily flying displays with audience participation, gift shop, Silent Wings tearoom, Raptor crafts shop.

RHS Garden Hyde Hall
Chelmsford, Essex CM3 8AT
(01245) 400256
www.rhs.org.uk/hydehall
A garden of inspirational beauty with an eclectic range of horticultural styles from traditional to modern providing year round interest.

RSPB Minsmere Nature Reserve
Saxmundham, Suffolk IP17 3BY
(01728) 648281
www.rspb.org.uk/minsmere
One of the UK's premier nature reserves, offering excellent facilities for people of all ages and abilities.

WWT Welney Wetland Centre
Wisbech, Norfolk PE14 9TN
(01353) 860711
www.wwt.org.uk/welney
A wetland nature reserve of 1,000 acres attracting large numbers of ducks and swans in winter and waders in spring and summer plus a range of wild plants and butterflies.

ZSL Whipsnade Zoo
Dunstable, Bedfordshire LU6 2LF
(01582) 872171
www.zsl.org/zsl-whipsnade-zoo
ZSL Whipsnade Zoo is one of Europe's largest wildlife conservation parks.

Woburn Safari Park
Bedfordshire MK17 9QN
(01525) 290407
www.woburn.co.uk
Drive through the safari park with 30 species of animals in natural groups just a windscreen's width away.

Events 2014

Essex Book Festival
March 1-31, Various locations throughout Essex
Venues throughout the county fill with people eager to listen to some of their favourite authors.
www.essexbookfestival.org.uk

Maldon Mud Race
May 25, Maldon
The annual Maldon Mud Race is a wacky fun competition in which participants race to become the first to finish a 400m dash over the bed of the River Blackwater.
www.maldonmudrace.com

Hertfordshire County Show
May 24-25, Redbourn
County show with all the usual attractions.
www.hertsshow.com

Suffolk Show
May 28-29, Ipswich
Animals, food and drink, shopping…there's lots to see and do at this popular county show.
www.suffolkshow.co.uk

King's Lynn
May Garland Procession
May, King's Lynn
The King's Morris dancers carry the May Garland around the town.
www.thekingsmorris.co.uk

Luton International Carnival
May, Luton
The highlight is the spectacular carnival parade – an eye-catching, breathtaking procession through the town centre, superbly reflecting the diverse mix of cultures in Luton.
www.luton.gov.uk

Colchester Medieval Fayre
June 7-8, Lower Castle Park, Colchester
This medieval style fair remembers a time when folk from the countryside and neighbouring villages would travel to the 'Big Fair' in the town.
www.oysterfayre.flyer.co.uk

Cambridgeshire County Show
June 1, Royston
Featuring traditional crafts, livestock, food hall, rural crafts and displays, vintage tractors, fairground, children's corner and ring events.
www.cambscountyshow.co.uk

Peterborough Dragon Boat Festival
June 14, Peterborough Rowing Lake, Thorpe Meadows
Teams of up to 11 people, dragon boats and all equipment provided, no previous experience required. Family entertainment and catering stalls
www.dragonboatfestivals.co.uk/peterborough

Royal Norfolk Show
June 25-26, Norwich
The Royal Norfolk Show celebrates everything that's Norfolk. It offers 10 hours of entertainment each day from spectacular grand ring displays, traditional livestock and equine classes, to a live music stage, celebrity guests and over 650 stands.
www.royalnorfolkshow.co.uk

Bedfordshire County Show
July, Biggleswade
Held in the beautiful grounds of Shuttleworth the Bedfordshire County Show is a showcase of town meets country.
www.bedfordshirecountyshow.co.uk

Rhythms of the World
July, dates TBC, Hitchin
This is a festival of world music.
www.rotw.org.uk

Latitude Festival
July, dates TBC, Southwold
Primarily a music festival but also has a full spectrum of art including film, comedy, theatre, cabaret, dance and poetry.
www.latitudefestival.com

Cambridge Folk Festival
July 31- August 3, Cherry Hinton
Top acts make this a must-visit event for folk fans.
www.cambridgefolkfestival.co.uk

Dunstable Downs Kite Festival
July, Dunstable
Kite enthusiasts from around the UK converge on Dunstable.
www.dunstablekitefestival.co.uk

Southend Carnival
August, Southend-on-Sea
A wide range of events held over eight days. www.southend-on-seacarnival.org.uk

Clacton Airshow
August 21-22, Clacton Seafront
Impressive aerobatic displays take to the skies while a whole host of exhibition, trade stands, food court and on-site entertainment are available at ground level.
www.clactonairshow.com

Chilli Festival
August 24-25, Benington Lordship Gardens, Stevenage
A popular family event attracting thousands of visitors over two days, offering a chance to buy Chilli plants, products and sample foods from around the world.
www.beningtonlordship.co.uk

Duxford Air Show
September 6-7, Duxford, nr Cambridge
Set within the spacious grounds of the famous former First and Second World War airfield, the Duxford Air Show features an amazing array of aerial displays.
www.iwm.org.uk/duxford

Great Yarmouth Maritime Festival
September 6-7, Great Yarmouth
A mix of traditional and modern maritime vessels will be moored on South Quay for visitors to admire and go aboard.
www.maritime-festival.co.uk

Essex Country Show
September 13-14, Barleylands, Billericay
The show, with an emphasis on agricultural history and rural crafts, is now in its 27th year.
www.barleylands.co.uk/essex-country-show

Aldeburgh Food & Drink Festival
September 27-28, Aldeburgh
A two-week celebration of the abundance of good local food and drink to be found in East Suffolk.
www.aldeburghfoodanddrink.co.uk

World Conker Championship
October, Oundle
A picturesque corner of Northamptonshire hosts the World Conker Championships on the second Sunday in October every year. Thousands flock to the venue to watch this great spectacle as modern day gladiators fight for glory armed only with a nut and 12 inches of string.
www.worldconkerchampionships.com

Britten Centenary
November, Snape Maltings
Benjamin Britten was the most celebrated British composer of the 20th century. The centenary of Benjamin Britten (1913-1976), born in Lowestoft, Suffolk, will be marked by special events.
www.aldeburgh.co.uk

Tourist Information Centres

When you arrive at your destination, visit an Official Partner Tourist Information Centre for quality assured help with accommodation and information about local attractions and events, or email your request before you go. To find a Tourist Information Centre visit www.visitengland.com

Aldeburgh	48 High Street	01728 453637	atic@suffolkcoastal.gov.uk
Bedford	St Pauls Square	01234 718112	TouristInfo@bedford.gov.uk
Bishop's Stortford	2 Market Square	01279 655831	tic@bishopsstortford.org
Bury St Edmunds	6 Angel Hill	01284 764667	tic@stedsbc.gov.uk
Cambridge	Peas Hill	0871 226 8006	info@visitcambridge.org
Colchester	1 Queen Street	01206 282920	vic@colchester.gov.uk
Diss	Meres Mouth	01379 650523	dtic@s-norfolk.gov.uk
Ely	Oliver Cromwell's House	01353 662062	tic@eastcambs.gov.uk
Felixstowe	91 Undercliff Road West	01394 276770	ftic@suffolkcoastal.gov.uk
Great Yarmouth	25 Marine Parade	01493 846346	gab@great-yarmouth.gov.uk
Hunstanton	Town Hall	01485 532610	info@visithunstanton.info
Ipswich	St Stephens Church	01473 258070	tourist@ipswich.gov.uk
King's Lynn	The Custom House	01553 763044	kings-lynn.tic@west-norfolk.gov.uk
Lavenham	Lady Street	01787 248207	lavenhamtic@babergh.gov.uk
Letchworth Garden City	33-35 Station Road	01462 487868	tic@letchworth.com
Lowestoft	East Point Pavilion	01502 533600	touristinfo@waveney.gov.uk
Luton	Luton Central Library	01582 401579	tourist.information@lutonculture.com
Maldon District	Wenlock Way	01621 856503	tic@maldon.gov.uk

Newmarket	63 The Guineas	01638 719749	tic.newmarket@forest-heath.gov.uk
Norwich	The Forum	01603 213999	tourism@norwich.gov.uk
Peterborough	9 Bridge Street	01733 452336	tic@peterborough.gov.uk
Saffron Walden	1 Market Place	01799 524002	tourism@saffronwalden.gov.uk
Southend-on-Sea	Pier Entrance	01702 215620	vic@southend.gov.uk
Southwold	69 High Street	01502 724729	southwold.tic@waveney.gov.uk
St Albans	Old Town Hall	01727 864511	tic@stalbans.gov.uk
Stowmarket	The Museum of East Anglian Life	01449 676800	tic@midsuffolk.gov.uk
Sudbury	Sudbury Library	01787 881320	sudburytic@sudburytowncouncil.co.uk
Witham	61 Newland Street	01376 502674	tic@witham.gov.uk
Woodbridge	New Street	01394 446510	felixstowetic@suffolkcoastal.gov.uk

Regional Contacts and Information

For more information on accommodation, attractions, activities, events and holidays in East of England, contact the regional or local tourism organisations. Their websites have a wealth of information and many produce free publications to help you get the most out of your visit.

East of England Tourism
Tel: (01284) 727470
Email: info@eet.org.uk
Web: www.visiteastofengland.com

The comprehensive website is updated daily. Online brochures and information sheets can be downloaded including Whats's New; Major Events; Stars and Stripes (connections with the USA) and a range of Discovery Tours around the region.

Where to Stay

Entries appear alphabetically by town name in each county. A key to symbols appears on page 7

BARTLOW, Cambridgeshire   Map ref 2D1   SatNav CB21 4PW   **B**

★★★
INN

Three Hills

Ashdon Road, Bartlow, Cambridge CB21 4PW **T:** (01223) 891259
E: threehills@rhubarb-inns.co.uk
W: rhubarb-inns.co.uk **£ BOOK ONLINE**

B&B PER ROOM PER NIGHT
S: £70.00
D: £70.00
EVENING MEAL PER PERSON
£9.95 - £10.95

In beautiful & historical countryside, ideal for walking, 12 miles from Cambridge & 6 miles from Saffron Walden. Delightful 17th Century Freehouse Inn with clean, modern en suite rooms, home-cooked food, real ales, inglenook fireplaces & warm welcome. **Directions:** From A1307 Cambridge to Haverhill, take turning to Bartlow. Turn right at cross roads, Three Hills is on left. Easy access from M11, A11 & A14. **Bedrooms:** 2 double, 2 twin **Open:** All year

Site: ❀ P Payment: 💳 Leisure: 🏊 ♪ ▶ ☾ Children: 🐾 ⍟ Catering: ♟ 🍴 Room: ♨ 🕪 📺 ⚲

CAMBRIDGE, Cambridgeshire   Map ref 2D1   SatNav CB4 1DE   **B**

★★★
GUEST HOUSE

Southampton Guest House

7 Elizabeth Way, Cambridge CB4 1DE **T:** (01223) 357780 **F:** (01223) 314297
E: southamptonhouse@btinternet.com
W: southamptonguesthouse.com

B&B PER ROOM PER NIGHT
S: £35.00 - £45.00
D: £48.00 - £58.00

Victorian property with friendly atmosphere, only 15 minutes walk along riverside to city centre, colleges and shopping mall. **Directions:** Please contact us for directions. **Bedrooms:** 1 single, 1 double, 3 family **Open:** All year

Site: P Payment: € Property: 🖵 Children: 🐾 ⍟ Room: 🖳 ♨ 🕻 📺 ⚲

CAMBRIDGE, Cambridgeshire   Map ref 2D1   SatNav CB2 1TP   **B**

★★★★
CAMPUS
ACCOMMODATION

St John's College

St Johns College, Cambridge, Cambridgeshire CB2 1TP **T:** (01223) 338615
F: 01223 338766 **E:** catering@joh.cam.ac.uk
W: www.joh.cam.ac.uk

B&B PER ROOM PER NIGHT
S: £72.00
D: £105.00

The College is one of the largest in Cambridge with beautiful grounds that span the River Cam, via the Bridge of Sighs. The College is just over 500 years old. The Rooms are very spacious. **Directions:** The College is centred in the middle of Cambridge with easy access to Major road routes, A14/ M11, Stansted airport and Cambridge Rail Station **Bedrooms:** All rooms en suite **Open:** In summer vacation, July to Sep.

Site: ❀ Payment: 💳 Property: ♟ 🖵 Catering: 🍴 ♟ Bedroom: ♨ 🕪 🖳

Need more information?

Visit our new 2014 guide websites for detailed information, up-to-date availability and to book your accommodation online. Includes over 20,000 places to stay, all of them star rated.

www.visitor-guides.co.uk

CAMBRIDGE, Cambridgeshire   Map ref 2D1   SatNav CB4 3HS   B

Tudor Cottage

292 Histon Road, Cambridge CB4 3HS **T:** (01223) 565212 **F:** (01954) 251117
E: email@tudor-cottage.net
W: tudorcottageguesthouse.co.uk

B&B PER ROOM PER NIGHT
S: £40.00 - £50.00
D: £60.00 - £70.00

Comfortable, friendly, Tudor-style cottage conveniently situated within 30 minutes walking distance of Cambridge city centre. En suite or shared facilities, Digital TV/DVD, Wi-Fi, tea/coffee-making facilities. Excellent food over looking our picturesque garden. A warm and personal service. Off-street parking. Easy access to bus stop and A14/M11. 5* Health and Hygiene rating.

Directions: Close to A14 and M11. For further details please refer to website.

Bedrooms: 2 single, 2 double, 1 twin
Open: All year

Site: ✿ P Payment: € Property: 🖥 Children: 🛏 🎏 🏃 Catering: 🍴 Room: 📻 📶 🖥 📺 ☕

CAMBRIDGE, Cambridgeshire   Map ref 2D1   SatNav CB4 1DA   B

Worth House

152 Chesterton Road, Cambridge CB4 1DA **T:** (01223) 316074 **F:** (01223) 360903
E: enquiry@worth-house.co.uk
W: worth-house.co.uk

B&B PER ROOM PER NIGHT
S: £55.00 - £75.00
D: £69.00 - £105.00

Worth House offers quiet, comfortable and spacious accommodation in this beautiful Victorian villa. Easy walk to city centre. 'Which?' recommended. Telegraph recommended. As featured on the Guardian 1000 Best B&Bs. **Directions:** Please contact us for directions. **Bedrooms:** 4 suite **Open:** All year

🏆 Site: ✿ P Payment: 💳 € Leisure: 🎿 🎵 Property: 🖥 Children: 🛏 🎏 🏃 Room: 📻 📶 🖥 📺 ☕

PETERBOROUGH, Cambridgeshire   Map ref 3A1   SatNav PE8 6XB   B

19 West Street

King's Cliffe, Peterborough PE8 6XB **T:** (01780) 470365 **E:** kjhl.dixon@gmail.com
W: www.kingjohnhuntinglodge.co.uk

B&B PER ROOM PER NIGHT
S: £45.00
D: £65.00 - £130.00

500 year old Grade II Listed rambling stone house clothed with wisteria and roses and a lovely walled garden. Located near Oundle, Stamford, Rutland Water, Rockingham Speedway and Tolethorpe. Many stately homes are located within a 30 minute drive. **Directions:** 4 miles to the west of the A1, at the junction of the A47 **Bedrooms:** 1 Single, 1 Double, 1 Twin and 1 Family **Open:** All Year

Site: ✿ P Payment: € Property: 🖥 Children: 🛏 🎏 Catering: 🍴 Room: 📻 📶 📞 🖥 📺

BURNHAM-ON-CROUCH, Essex Map ref 3B3   SatNav CM0 8BQ **B**

INN ★★★★

B&B PER ROOM PER NIGHT
S: £58.50 - £69.50
D: £77.00
EVENING MEAL PER PERSON
£5.00

The Railway
12 Station Road, Burnham-on-Crouch, Essex CM0 8BQ T: (01621) 786868
F: (01621) 783002 E: info@therailwayhotelburnham.co.uk
W: http://www.therailwayhotelburnham.co.uk

Originally built in the late 1800s lovingly restored by Jenny & Colin Newcombe to incorporate 21st century luxuries with Victorian charm. **Bedrooms:** All rooms en suite, dd phone. Tea/coffee facilities, colour tv. **Open:** All year

Site: P Payment: £ Property: ▫ ⌂ ◐ Children: ⤶ ⚹ Catering: ⟨✗ ⛾ ▦ Room: ⌕ ✆ ✆ 📺

CHELMSFORD, Essex Map ref 3B3   SatNav CM2 9AJ **H**

HOTEL ★★★

Miami Hotel
Princes Road, Chelmsford CM2 9AJ T: (01245) 269603 F: (01245) 259860
E: sales@miamihotel.co.uk
W: www.miamihotel.co.uk

Family-run hotel, one mile from town centre. All rooms have tea-making facilities, trouser press, direct-dial telephone with voice mail and PC access, cable TV and hairdryer. Five conference rooms available. Please contact for prices. **Bedrooms:** 23 dble, 32 twin **Open:** All year except Christmas

Payment: £ Property: ◉ ⛾ ▫ ▫ ◐ Children: ⤶ ▦ ⚹ Catering: ⟨✗ ⛾ ▦ Room: ⌕ ✆ ✆ 📺

CLACTON-ON-SEA, Essex Map ref 3B3   SatNav CO15 1RA **B**

GUEST ACCOMMODATION ★★★★   Silver AWARD

B&B PER ROOM PER NIGHT
S: £50.00 - £55.00
D: £80.00 - £85.00

Chudleigh
Agate Road, Marine Parade West, Clacton-on-Sea, Essex CO15 1RA T: (01255) 425407
F: (01255) 470280 E: chudleighhotel@btconnect.com
W: chudleighhotel.com

An oasis in a town centre location, 200m from seafront gardens, near pier and main shops. Ideal for the business visitor and for overnight stays. Free parking. Free Wi-Fi. VAT registered. TripAdvisor - Travellers choice 2013 winner. **Directions:** From A12 follow sign to Clacton. At seafront turn right. After pier traffic lights, with sea on your left, turn right into Agate Road. **Bedrooms:** 2 single, 4 double, 2 twin, 2 family **Open:** All year

Site: P Payment: £ € Leisure: ▶ Property: ⛾ ▫ Children: ⤶ ▦ ⚹ Catering: ▦ Room: ⌕ ✆ ✆ 📺 ⛾

Win amazing prizes, every month...

Visit our new 2014 guide websites for detailed information, up-to-date availability and to book your accommodation online. Includes over 20,000 places to stay, all of them star rated.

Enter our monthly competition at www.visitor-guides.co.uk/prizes

The Cricketers

Wicken Road, Clavering, Saffron Walden CB11 4QT **T:** (01799) 550442 **F:** (01799) 550882
E: info@thecricketers.co.uk
W: thecricketers.co.uk

SPECIAL PROMOTIONS
Please contact us for prices and special offers.

A delightful 16th century country Inn with award winning food and accommodation. Very popular for business and pleasure alike, good food being a core ingredient of a stay at The Cricketers. Owners' son, Jamie Oliver, grew up here and supplies vegetables, leaves and herbs from his nearby certifed organic garden. Six new double bedrooms have been added this year, now offering twenty double accommodation rooms to guests. Accommodation special offers and menus are shown on the website.

Directions: M11 jct 8. A120 west and B1383 to Newport. B1038 to Clavering.

Bedrooms: 17 double, 3 twin.
Open: All year except Christmas Day and Boxing Day

Site: ✿ P Payment: 💳 Leisure: ♪ ▶ ◡ Property: 🖥 ⌀ Children: 🛝 🛏 ♿ Catering: (✗ ▼ 🍴
Room: 🗝 🖐 🔟 📺 💇 🧺

Stoke by Nayland Hotel, Golf and Spa

Keepers Lane, Leavenheath, Colchester, Essex CO6 4PZ **T:** (01206) 265835
F: (01206) 265840 **E:** sales@stokebynayland.com
W: www.stokebynayland.com **£ BOOK ONLINE**

SPECIAL PROMOTIONS
Please contact us for prices.
For current special offers please see our website www.stokeby nayland.com
or call 01206 265835

In secluded tranquility yet only 10 minutes from Colchester, this multi award-winning, family-owned hotel is situated in 300 acres of stunning "Constable Country". Two championship golf courses, 2 AA Rosette Lakes Restaurant, extensive spa facilities, indoor pool, gym, free car parking and free hi-speed WiFi.

Directions: Situated north of Colchester on the Essex/Suffolk border just off the A134, only an hour from London via the A12.

Bedrooms: 80 en suite bedrooms including luxury honeymoon, executive and family rooms. Flat screen TVs, in-room safes, air conditioning and free hi-speed WiFi.
Open: All Year

Site: P Payment: 💳 Leisure: 🎣 ♪ ▶ ⚲ ✗ ⛳ 💇 ⚑ Property: ⊛ ▼ 🖥 🖥 🅿 🌙 ◑ ⌀ Children: 🛝 🛏 ♿
Catering: (✗ ▼ 🍴 Room: 🗝 🖐 🔟 📺 💇

FRINTON-ON-SEA, Essex   Map ref 3C2 — SatNav CO13 9EQ [H]

★★ SMALL HOTEL

B&B PER ROOM PER NIGHT
S: £57.00 - £79.50
D: £80.00 - £110.00
EVENING MEAL PER PERSON
£23.50

The Rock Hotel

The Esplanade, Frinton-on-Sea CO13 9EQ **T:** (01255) 677194 **F:** (01255) 675173
E: rockhotel@btconnect.com
W: www.therockhotel.co.uk

A warm welcome and Frinton's only hotel, this small luxury hotel is situated on the Esplanade at Frinton-on-Sea, facing the greensward with uninterrupted views of the sea/sands of Essex coastline. Free Wi-Fi & Free Parking. Please contact us for details. **Directions:** Please contact for directions **Bedrooms:** 1 single, 3 double, 1 twin, 2 family. **Open:** All year

Payment: 💷 **Leisure:** ⚓ 🎵 ▶ ↻ **Property:** 🐾 🖥 **Children:** 🐴10 🏇 **Catering:** 🍽 🍴 **Room:** 🔌 ♨ 📺 🖨

ORSETT, Essex   Map ref 3B3 — SatNav RM16 3LJ [B]

★★★★ ROOM ONLY

B&B PER ROOM PER NIGHT
S: £35.00 - £40.00
D: £50.00

Jays Lodge

Chapel Farm, Baker Street, Orsett, Grays RM16 3LJ **T:** (01375) 891663
E: info@jayslodge.co.uk
W: www.jayslodge.co.uk

Barn conversion to provide twelve rooms all with en suite, mini kitchen facility, colour television with Freeview and free WiFi access. Ample, free and secure car parking available. **Directions:** Please contact us for directions. **Bedrooms:** 2 single, 2 double, 8 twin **Open:** All year

Site: ❀ P **Payment:** 💷 **Leisure:** ▶ ↻ **Property:** 🖥 📋 **Catering:** 🍴 **Room:** 🔌 ♨ 📶 📺 🖨

WEST MERSEA, Essex   Map ref 3B3 — SatNav CO5 8LS [B]

★★★★ INN

B&B PER ROOM PER NIGHT
S: £60.00 - £90.00
D: £70.00 - £110.00
EVENING MEAL PER PERSON
£11.00 - £20.00

Victory at Mersea

Coast Road, Mersea Island, Colchester CO5 8LS **T:** (01206) 382907
E: info@victoryatmersea.com
W: victoryatmersea.com **£ BOOK ONLINE**

The Victory is situated on the Mersea waterfront. We have 7 really comfortable, superior quality rooms, individually decorated with a personal touch, some with fantastic estuary views. **Directions:** Mersea is clearly signposted from the A12 and you'll find us on the outskirts of the village centre, right on the waterfront. **Bedrooms:** 5 double, 1 twin, 1 family **Open:** All year

Site: ❀ P **Payment:** 💷 **Leisure:** ⚓ 🎵 ▶ ↻ **Property:** 🐾 🖥 **Children:** 🐴 🏇 **Catering:** (✗ 🍴 🍽 **Room:** 🔌 ♨ 📶 📺 🖨

WOODHAM MORTIMER, Essex   Map ref 3B3 — SatNav CM9 6TN [B]

★★★ BED & BREAKFAST

B&B PER ROOM PER NIGHT
S: £40.00 - £50.00
D: £60.00 - £65.00

Chase Farm Bed & Breakfast

Hyde Chase, Woodham Mortimer, Maldon CM9 6TN **T:** (01245) 223268
E: info@chasefarmbnb.uk
W: chasefarmbnb.co.uk

Chase Farm is set in peaceful country location ideal for an overnight or longer stay. 10 minutes from the A12 and 35 miles north of central London. Warm welcome assured. Wi-Fi available. **Directions:** From A12 onto A414 towards Maldon for 4 miles, at roundabout onto B1010 Burnham Road. First right into Marlpits Road. First right into Hyde Chase. **Bedrooms:** 1 double, 1 family **Open:** All year

Site: ❀ P **Leisure:** 🎵 ▶ ↻ **Property:** 🖥 **Children:** 🐴2 **Catering:** 🍴 **Room:** 🔌 ♨ 📶 📺

CHORLEYWOOD, Hertfordshire Map ref 2D2   SatNav WD3 5AH B

Ashburton Country House

48 Berks Hill, Chorleywood, Rickmansworth, Hertfordshire WD3 5AH **T:** (01923) 2855102
E: info@ashburtonhouse.co.uk
W: ashburtonhouse.co.uk

B&B PER ROOM PER NIGHT
S: £80.00 - £95.00
D: £95.00

An up to date Tudor style house, set in Green Belt Countryside, within walking distance to the London Underground. Chorleywood has a Village atmosphere, with a traditional parish church, horse riding, restaurants, pubs and shops, as well as having the added privilege of being named The Happiest Place in Britian. Free WIFI, off street parking, quiet location. **Bedrooms:** 2 double, 1 twin **Open:** All year

Site: ✿ P Payment: 💷 € Leisure: ♪ ► ♒ Property: 🖥 🔘 Catering: 🍴 Room: 🦮 👆 📶 📺 🛁 🧷

ST. ALBANS, Hertfordshire Map ref 2D1   SatNav AL3 4RY H

St Michael's Manor

St Michael's Village, Fishpool Street, St Albans, Hertfordshire AL3 4RY **T:** (01727) 864444
F: (01727) 848909 **E:** reservations@stmichaelsmanor.com
W: www.stmichaelsmanor.com

B&B PER ROOM PER NIGHT
D: £125.00 - £305.00

EVENING MEAL PER PERSON
£17.00 - £21.00

SPECIAL PROMOTIONS
Please check website for details.

Close to the city centre of St Alban's Hertfordshire, formerly the ancient Roman city of Verulanium, and near the famous Abbey Cathedral you will find this lovely manor house hotel. Set in five acres of beautiful private English country gardens with its own one acre lake this country-style venue is, surprisingly, only 20 minutes by train from London. The original house dates back over 500 years and was converted into a hotel in the early 1960s by the Newling Ward family. They still remain as private owners and managers, which gives the hotel its unique flavour. Bedroom prices start from £125, including breakfast. Evening meal prices based on The Lake Menu. Please see website for A la Carte, Sunday Lunch and Afternoon Tea menus.

Directions: Please contact us for directions

Bedrooms: Bedrooms, Suites, Luxury, Luxury Garden, Premier, Delux and Accessible rooms. Rooms include tea and coffee making facilities, biscuits and sweets, bottled water, irons and ironing boards, hair dryers and room service.

Site: ✿ P Payment: 💷 Leisure: ⚔ Property: 🅿 🍴 ☰ 🚪 ♨ Children: 🧒 🛏 ♿ Catering: ⊙✕ 🍷
Room: 🦮 👆 📺 💿 🛁 🧷

WARE, Hertfordshire Map ref 2D1   SatNav SG12 0SD H

Hanbury Manor, A Marriott Hotel & Country Club

Ware SG12 0SD **T:** (01920) 487722 **F:** (01920) 487692
W: marriotthanburymanor.co.uk

B&B PER ROOM PER NIGHT
S: £175.00
D: £160.00 - £220.00

Hanbury Manor provides the perfect venue for both business and pleasure. Relax in the 200 acres of Hertfordshire countryside, challenge yourself on the world championship golf course or luxuriate in the Romanesque Spa. **Directions:** Only 10 miles north of junction 25 of the M25, Hanbury Manor is located off the A10. For further directions please visit www.MarriottHanburyManor.co.uk **Bedrooms:** 74 dble, 38 twin, 37 family, 12 suite **Open:** All year

Site: ✿ P Payment: 💷 Leisure: ► ⛳ ⚔ ♨ 🏊 🎾 Property: 🍴 🐾 ☰ ♨ Children: 🧒 🛏 ♿
Catering: 🍷 🍴 Room: 🦮 👆 🛁 📺 🛁 🧷 〰

AYLMERTON, Norfolk   Map ref 3B1   SatNav NR11 8QD B

Roman Camp Inn

Holt Road, Aylmerton, Sheringham NR11 8QD **T:** (01263) 838291 **F:** (01263) 837071
E: enquiries@romancampinn.co.uk
W: www.romancampinn.co.uk

enjoyEngland.com
★★★★
INN

B&B PER ROOM PER NIGHT
S: £65.00 - £90.00
D: £50.00 - £140.00

An attractive inn with en suite accommodation (two rooms adapted for our disabled guests) with bars open all day and conservatory dining. Our garden and patio at the rear of the hotel have glorious views of open countryside leading to private access to fields and the grounds of Felbrigg Hall. **Directions:** On the A418 between Cromer and Sheringham. **Bedrooms:** 1 single, 10 dble, 4 twin - 2 accessible rooms **Open:** All year except Christmas and Boxing Day

Site: ✿ Payment: 💷 Leisure: ▶ ☺ Property: ☂ 🖼 Children: 🛏 🎠 ⚲ Catering: ☕ Room: 🗐 ✆ ☎ 📶 📺 ♨

CROMER, Norfolk   Map ref 3C1   SatNav NR27 0AB B

Cliff Cottage

18 High Street, Overstrand, Cromer, Norfolk NR27 0AB **T:** (01263) 578179
E: roymin@btinternet.com
W: www.cliffcottagebandb.com

enjoyEngland.com
★★★★
BED & BREAKFAST

B&B PER ROOM PER NIGHT
D: £34.00 - £42.00

A quiet, friendly atmosphere invites you to Cliff Cottage. Built in the 18th century, just 2 minutes walk from the sandy beach. We offer use of our secluded garden and private parking to make your stay relaxing and comfortable. Good food. **Directions:** Please contact us for directions. **Bedrooms:** 1 double, 1 twin **Open:** All Year

Site: ✿ P Leisure: 🎵 Property: 🖼 🖥 Catering: 🍳 Room: 🗐 ♨ ✆ 📶 📺

CROMER, Norfolk   Map ref 3C1   SatNav NR27 0JN H

Northrepps Cottage Country Hotel

Nut Lane, Northrepps, Cromer, Norfolk NR27 0JN **T:** (01263) 579202
E: enquiries@northreppscottage.co.uk
W: northreppscottagehotel.co.uk

enjoyEngland.com
★★★
COUNTRY HOUSE HOTEL

Silver
AWARD

B&B PER ROOM PER NIGHT
D: £130.00
EVENING MEAL PER PERSON
£50.00

SPECIAL PROMOTIONS
Special offers available, also events packages - please see our website for details.

One of East Anglia's finest bijou hotels from which you'll enjoy beautiful North Norfolk. The atmosphere inside is one of luxurious warmth. Our suites combine classic, stylish decor reflecting their elegant history, the height of modern comfort and luxurious features. Contemporary Humphrys bar and fine-dining in Reptons restaurant.

Directions: Cromer Coast Road, turn left at Overstrand Church.

Bedrooms: 6 dble, 1 twin, 1 family
Open: All year

Site: ✿ P Payment: 💷 Leisure: 🏊 🎵 ▶ ☺ Property: ☂ 🖼 🖥 🎱 Children: 🛏 ⚲ Catering: (✗ ☕ 🍴 Room: 🗐 ♨ ✆ 📶 📺

DEREHAM, Norfolk   Map ref 3B1   SatNav NR20 4JU [B]

Hunters Hall

Park Farm, Swanton Morley, Dereham, Norfolk NR20 4JU **T:** (01362) 637457
F: 01362 637987 **E:** office@huntershall.com
W: www.huntershall.com

B&B PER ROOM PER NIGHT
D: £45.00 - £65.00

Hunter's Hall offers a truly romantic setting for the most perfect wedding celebrations as well as for parties, dances, concerts, lectures, seminars, training and team-building events. By choosing Hunter's Hall you are assured of an exclusive and unique experience second to none. **Directions:** From the A47 take the B1147 to Swanton Morley. At Darby's Free House, take Elsing Road. Take third turning on the right to Hunters Hall. **Bedrooms:** Double, Twin and Family room available. **Open:** All Year

Payment: [£] Property: 🛏 Children: 🧒 🛏 Room: ♿ ☎ 📺 ♨

DOWNHAM MARKET, Norfolk   Map ref 3B1   SatNav PE38 9EB [B]

Chestnut Villa

44 Railway Road, Downham Market, Norfolk PE38 9EB **T:** (01366) 384099
E: chestnutvilla@talk21.com
W: www.chestnutvilla-downham.co.uk

B&B PER ROOM PER NIGHT
D: £35.00 - £60.00

Chestnut Villa is a family run guest house established over 20 years ago. We pride ourselves on our warm and friendly service. All our rooms are warm, spacious, bright and double glazed with little extras to make your stay as relaxing and enjoyable as possible. **Directions:** Please see website. **Bedrooms:** 2 double, 2 twin **Open:** All year

Site: P Leisure: 🎵 ▶ Property: 🐾 🖬 🗒 Children: 🧒 🛏 Catering: 🍴 Room: 🍵 ♿ 🗗 📺 📀

FAKENHAM, Norfolk   Map ref 3B1   SatNav NR21 0AW [B]

Abbott Farm B&B

Walsingham Road, Binham, Fakenham NR21 0AW **T:** (01328) 830519
E: abbot.farm@btinternet.com
W: abbottfarm.co.uk

B&B PER ROOM PER NIGHT
S: £30.00 - £35.00
D: £60.00 - £70.00

A 190-acre arable farm. Rural views of North Norfolk including the historic Binham Priory. Liz and Alan offer a warm welcome to their guest house. **Directions:** Please refer to website. **Bedrooms:** 1 single, 1 double (en suite), 1 twin (en suite) **Open:** All year except Christmas

Site: ✿ P Payment: € Leisure: 🚲 ♨ Property: 🐾 Children: 🧒 🛏 ☀ Catering: 🍴 Room: 🍵 ♿ 📺 ♨ ▤

Book your accommodation online

Visit our new 2014 guide websites for detailed information, up-to-date availability and to book your accommodation online. Includes over 20,000 places to stay, all of them star rated.

www.visitor-guides.co.uk

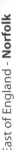

GREAT YARMOUTH, Norfolk   Map ref 3C1   SatNav NR30 1EG   H

Burlington Palm Hotel

North Drive, Great Yarmouth NR30 1EG **T:** (01493) 844568 **F:** (01493) 331848
E: enquiries@burlington-hotel.co.uk
W: burlington-hotel.co.uk **£ BOOK ONLINE**

B&B PER ROOM PER NIGHT
S: £55.00 - £120.00
D: £45.00 - £160.00

EVENING MEAL PER PERSON
£12.95 - £30.50

SPECIAL PROMOTIONS
Nightly discounts for
extended stays. Check
website for special
offers.

Seafront Hotel overlooking Great Yarmouth's Golden Sands. We are a short walk from all the main attractions and 1.5 miles from the train station. We are also the only Hotel in Great Yarmouth with a heated indoor swimming pool.

Directions: From the A12 or A47 follow signs for Seafront turn left, we are on North Drive about 600 Yards north of the Britannia Pier.

Bedrooms: 7 single, 23 double, 21 twin, 18 family
Open: All year except 28th December - 2nd January

Site: P Payment: 🔲 **Leisure:** ♪ ▶ ♒ ✧ **Property:** ✦ 🛏 🗄 🏛 **Children:** 🛝 🛏 🎎 **Catering:** ⟨✗ 🍷 🍽
Room: 🖥 🔌 📞 📺 🛏 ✍

NORWICH, Norfolk   Map ref 3C1   SatNav NR10 3AB   B

Becklands

105 Holt Road, Horsford, Norwich NR10 3AB **T:** (01603) 898582 **F:** (01603) 755010
E: becklands@aol.com
W: becklands.com

Quietly located modern house overlooking open countryside five miles north of Norwich. Central for the Broads and coastal areas. Please contact us for prices. **Directions:** Follow directions to Norwich Airport - follow signs to A140 roundabout - follow signs to B1449 to Horsford. **Bedrooms:** 2 single, 3 double, 2 twin, 1 family **Open:** All year

Site: ❀ **P Payment:** 🔲 **Leisure:** ♿ ♪ ▶ ♒ **Property:** 🗄 **Children:** 🛝 🛏 🎎 **Catering:** 🍽
Room: 🖥 🔌 📞 📺 🛏 ✍

NORWICH, Norfolk   Map ref 3C1   SatNav NR10 5NP   B

Marsham Arms Coaching Inn

40 Holt Road, Hevingham, Norwich, Norfolk NR10 5NP **T:** (01603) 754268
F: (01603) 754839 **E:** info@marshamarms.co.uk
W: marshamarms.co.uk **£ BOOK ONLINE**

B&B PER ROOM PER NIGHT
S: £65.00 - £75.00
D: £75.00 - £150.00

EVENING MEAL PER PERSON
£9.95 - £25.00

Welcome to one of Norfolk's best loved inns noted for its quiet rooms, country setting, wines & ales and freshly prepared food. **Directions:** 2 miles north of Horsford on B1149. 4 miles from Norwich International Airport. 7 miles from Norwich city centre. **Bedrooms:** 10 double, 4 twin, 2 family **Open:** All year

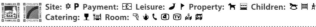

Site: ❀ **P Payment:** 🔲 **Leisure:** ♪ ▶ **Property:** 🐾 🖼 **Children:** 🛝 🛏 🎎
Catering: 🍷 🍽 **Room:** 🖥 🔌 📞 📺 🛏 ✍

NORWICH, Norfolk   Map ref 3C1
SatNav NR3 1BN **B**

★★★★
GUEST HOUSE

B&B PER ROOM PER NIGHT
S: £55.00
D: £85.00

Number 17

17 Colegate, Norwich NR3 1BN **T:** (01603) 764486 **E:** enquiries@number17.co.uk
W: www.number17norwich.co.uk **£ BOOK ONLINE**

This contemporary styled, family run bed and breakfast is close to Norwich city centre making it an ideal location whether your stay is for business or pleasure. Family suite prices £125 per night.
Directions: Number 17 is located about a 15 minute walk from both Norwich railway station or the bus station and about 10 miles from Norwich airport. **Bedrooms:** 1 single, 2 double, 3 twin, 2 family **Open:** All year except Christmas and New Year

Site: ✿ **Payment:** 💷 **Property:** 🖵 **Children:** 🧸2 🍴 **Catering:** 🍴 **Room:** 🍵 ☕ 📻 📺 🔌

NORWICH, Norfolk   Map ref 3C1
SatNav NR12 7BG **H**

★★★
HOTEL

B&B PER ROOM PER NIGHT
S: £57.00 - £60.00
D: £74.00 - £89.00

EVENING MEAL PER PERSON
£17.50

SPECIAL PROMOTIONS
Discounted mid week breaks from £37.00 pppn B&B or £54.50 pppn Dinner B&B. min 2 night stay between Mon/Fri. Excluding bank holidays.

Old Rectory Hotel

North Walsham Road, Crostwick, Norwich NR12 7BG **T:** (01603) 738513 **F:** (01603) 738712
E: info@oldrectorycrostwick.com
W: oldrectorycrostwick.com **£ BOOK ONLINE**

Ideal location for Norwich and Broads. This family run hotel offers excellent facilities and service in a beautiful setting in rural Norfolk. All rooms are ground floor, en suite and very well equipped. It also boasts 3.5 acres of gardens, patio seating, bar, restaurant, heated outdoor pool and ample free parking.

Directions: B1150 North Walsham Rd out of Norwich off the outer ring-road travel 4-miles. The Old Rectory is situated 200m past the Spixworth turning.

Bedrooms: 6 dble, 8 twin, 1 family, 1 suite
Open: All year

Site: ✿ **Payment:** 💷 **Leisure:** 🎣 ♪ ▶ ↻ ⚲ **Property:** 🐾 🐴 🖵 🔲 **Children:** 🧸 🍴 🧍 **Catering:** 🍷 🍴
Room: 🍵 ☕ 📞 📻 📺 🔌   **f**

RACKHEATH, Norfolk   Map ref 3C1
SatNav NR13 6NN **B**

★★★★
GUEST
ACCOMMODATION

B&B PER ROOM PER NIGHT
S: £30.00 - £35.00
D: £55.00 - £65.00

Barn Court

6 Back Lane, Rackheath, Norwich NR13 6NN **T:** (01603) 782536
E: barncourtbb@hotmail.com

Barn Court is a spacious, friendly and comfortable B&B 5 miles from the centre of Norwich, in a traditional barn conversion built around a courtyard. Good variety of breakfasts provided. **Directions:** From Norwich, take A1151 towards Wroxham, Back Lane is 3.5 miles from ring road on left, and Barn Court is first driveway on right. **Bedrooms:** 2 double, 1 twin **Open:** All year except Christmas and New Year

Site: ✿ **P** **Leisure:** 🎣 ♪ ▶ ↻ **Property:** 🐴 🖵 **Children:** 🧸1 🍴 🧍 **Catering:** 🍴
Room: ☕ 📻 📺 🔌

SAHAM TONEY, Norfolk   Map ref 3B1
SatNav IP25 7EX   **H**

Broom Hall Country Hotel

Richmond Road, Saham Toney, Thetford IP25 7EX **T:** (01953) 882125 **F:** (01953) 885325
E: enquiries@broomhallhotel.co.uk
W: broomhallhotel.co.uk **£ BOOK ONLINE**

B&B PER ROOM PER NIGHT
S: £75.00 - £110.00
D: £85.00 - £185.00
HB PER PERSON PER NIGHT
£119.00 - £150.00

SPECIAL PROMOTIONS
Two night breaks,
dinner B&B, priced per
couple for two nights.
Winter from £238.00,
summer from £272.00.

Family-run, Victorian country house offering peace and tranquillity in 15 acres of garden and parkland. Open fire warms winter evenings. After a swim in heated indoor pool, enjoy a cream tea on the terrace or in the conservatory or relax in the Rose Room Bar. Purpose-built, ground-floor, disabled rooms.

Directions: From A11, take A1075 to Watton. left at lights, 0.5m right at roundabout. From A47, take A1065 Newmarket, left onto B1108, left at roundabout.

Bedrooms: 9 double, 4 twin, 2 family all en suite, ground floor disabled access rooms.
Open: All year except Christmas and New Year

Site: ✿ P Payment: 🔳 Leisure: ♿ ♪ ♪ ☾ ♨ ✈ Property: 🦮 🐕 🖥 🗄 🚪 ∅ Children: 🐴 🛏 🚼
Catering: 🍽 🍴 Room: 🔌 🛁 ☎ 📺 🔥 📻

SHERINGHAM, Norfolk   Map ref 3B1
SatNav NR26 8LL   **H**

The Beaumaris Hotel & Restaurant

15 South Street, Sheringham NR26 8LL **T:** (01263) 822370 **F:** (01263) 821421
E: enquires@thebeaumarishotel.co.uk
W: www.thebeaumarishotel.co.uk **£ BOOK ONLINE**

B&B PER ROOM PER NIGHT
S: £60.00 - £65.00
D: £120.00 - £130.00
EVENING MEAL PER PERSON
£19.50 - £24.50

Family-run hotel established in 1947, with a reputation for personal service and English cuisine. Quietly located close to beach, shops and golf club, National Trust properties, bird-watching, coastal footpath and North Norfolk Railway. **Directions:** From the A149 turn towards Sheringham. At the roundabout turn left. Take the next right, then the next left by the church and then left again into South St. **Bedrooms:** 5 single, 8 dble, 8 twin **Open:** March to mid-December

Site: ✿ P Payment: 🔳 € Leisure: ♿ ♪ ♪ ☾ Property: 🦮 🖥 🗄 🚪 Children: 🐴 🛏 🚼 Catering: 🍽 🍴
Room: 🔌 🛁 ☎ 📺 🔥

SOUTH CREAKE, Norfolk   Map ref 3B1
SatNav NR21 9PG   **B**

Valentine Studio

62 Back Street, South Creake, Walsingham NR21 9PG **T:** (01328) 823413
E: ros@valentinehouse.fsnet.co.uk
W: valentinehouse.co.uk

B&B PER ROOM PER NIGHT
S: £65.00 - £80.00
D: £35.00 - £80.00

Charming 18th century former inn set in attractive, cottage-style garden. Ideal for families with connecting bedrooms, travel cot, high chair, fridge, microwave and black-out blinds. Will accept two well behaved dogs. **Directions:** From Fakenham, B1355 Burnham Market. At South Creake, left past village green. Studio entrance will be found on left-hand side past the old brewery building. **Bedrooms:** 1 suite **Open:** All year except Christmas

Site: ✿ P Property: 🦮 🖥 Children: 🐴 🛏 🚼 Catering: 🍴 Room: 🔌 🛁 📺 🔥

SWANTON MORLEY, Norfolk   Map ref 3B1   SatNav NR20 4JT B

Carricks at Castle Farm

Castle Farm, Elsing Road, Swanton Morley, Dereham NR20 4JT T: (01362) 638302
E: enquiries@carricksatcastlefarm.co.uk
W: carricksatcastlefarm.co.uk

B&B PER ROOM PER NIGHT
S: £65.00
D: £95.00
EVENING MEAL PER PERSON
£25.00

Located on the banks of the River Wensum in the parish of Swanton Morley. There are many farm walks, wild life abounds, fishing on banks of the River Wensum. **Directions:** Please refer to website. **Bedrooms:** 3 double, 1 twin **Open:** All year

Site: ❂ P Payment: ⊞ € Leisure: ⚇ ♪ ▶ ∪ Property: ▭ ▣ Catering: ♨ Room: ❜ ✿ ☎ ◉ TV

THETFORD, Norfolk   Map ref 3B2   SatNav IP26 5HU B

Colveston Manor

Mundford, Thetford, Norfolk IP26 5HU T: (01842) 878218 E: mail@colveston-manor.co.uk
W: colveston-manor.co.uk

B&B PER ROOM PER NIGHT
S: £35.00 - £37.50
D: £60.00 - £75.00
EVENING MEAL PER PERSON
£20.00

Colveston Manor set in the heart of Breckland birdwatcher's paradise, quiet and peaceful. Delicious Norfolk breakfasts. National Trust properties, cathedrals, gardens and coast within easy reach a true countryside experience. **Directions:** Please refer to website or phone. Sat navs do not know where we live and take you into the forest! **Bedrooms:** 1 single, 2 double, 1 twin **Open:** All year except Christmas and New Year

Site: ❂ P Payment: € Leisure: ⚇ ♪ ▶ ∪ Property: ▭ ▣ Children: ☞8 Catering: ♨ Room: ✿ ◉ TV ⚑ ⊞

THOMPSON, Norfolk   Map ref 3B1   SatNav IP24 1PX B

Chequers Inn

Griston Road, Thompson IP24 1PX T: (01953) 483360 F: (01953) 488092
E: richard@thompsonchequers.co.uk
W: thompsonchequers.co.uk

SPECIAL PROMOTIONS
Please contact us for prices

The Chequers is a 16th century village inn with a thatched roof, still retaining all of its original character. A true country retreat in the heart of Breckland. Local produce and fresh fish a speciality. Local real ales include Wolf, Wherry, Adnams and Greene King IPA to name a few.

Directions: Twelve miles north east of Thetford, just off the A1075. Snetterton Race Track just a short drive away.

Bedrooms: 2 double, 1 twin
Open: All year

Site: ❂ P Payment: ⊞ Leisure: ♪ ▶ Property: ♞ ▭ Children: ☞ ☂ Catering: ♟ ♨
Room: ❜ ✿ ☎ ◉ TV ⚑

WELLS-NEXT-THE-SEA, Norfolk   Map ref 3B1 — SatNav NR23 1HS **B**

B&B PER ROOM PER NIGHT
S: £65.00
D: £42.00 - £44.00

Machrimore

Burnt Street, Wells-next-the-Sea NR23 1HS **T:** (01328) 711653
E: enquiries@machrimore.co.uk
W: www.machrimore.co.uk **£ BOOK ONLINE**

A warm welcome awaits you at this attractive barn conversion, set in a quiet location close to the shops & picturesque Wells harbour. Ground floor bedrooms overlook own private garden & patio. Ample off street parking. Free wireless Internet. We pride ourselves in our Aga cooked breakfasts using fresh local produce. For the third time we were finalists in the Norfolk Tourism Awards 2012. **Directions:** Please contact us for directions. **Bedrooms:** One double en suite and two twin en suites **Open:** All year

Site: ✿ P Payment: € Leisure: ⚓ ♪ ⌂ ☋ Property: ☐ Children: ☺ ✿ Catering: ▥ Room: ✎ 💧 ☐ 📺 ⚗

WIGHTON, Norfolk   Map ref 3B1 — SatNav NR23 1PF **B**

B&B PER ROOM PER NIGHT
S: £80.00
D: £95.00

SPECIAL PROMOTIONS
Oct/Nov stay for 3 nights pay for 2 nights

Meadow View Guest House

53 High Street, Wighton, Wells-next-the-Sea, Norfolk NR23 1PF **T:** (01328) 821527
F: (01328) 821527 **E:** booking@meadow-view.net
W: meadow-view.net **£ BOOK ONLINE**

Guest house just 3 miles from the coast, 1 double, 1 twin, 3 suites all with seating area. Bath robes, slippers. Flat screen TV and iPod docking stations. Breakfast in or outside, hot tub in the garden. Beautiful house. Licensed. Wi-fi, ironing board and irons in each room. Mini bars, fresh milk in all rooms.

Directions: From B1105 Wighton is situated just off the B1105, accessible from the A149 coast road.

Bedrooms: 1 double, 1 twin, 3 suite
Open: All year

Site: ✿ P Payment: 💳 Leisure: ⚓ ♪ Property: ☐ Children: ☺ ▥ ✿ Catering: ♟ ▥
Room: ✎ 💧 ☐ 📺 ⚗

Need more information?

Visit our new 2014 guide websites for detailed information, up-to-date availability and to book your accommodation online. Includes over 20,000 places to stay, all of them star rated.

www.visitor-guides.co.uk

2014 Official Tourist Board Guides

ALDEBURGH, Suffolk Map ref 3C2

SatNav IP15 5BU **H**

HOTEL ★★★★ | *Gold* AWARD

B&B PER ROOM PER NIGHT
S: £80.00 - £120.00
D: £130.00 - £335.00

HB PER PERSON PER NIGHT
£85.00 - £120.00

Brudenell Hotel

The Parade, Aldeburgh IP15 5BU **T:** (01728) 452071 **F:** (01728) 454082
E: info@brudenellhotel.co.uk
W: brudenellhotel.co.uk **£ BOOK ONLINE**

Modern and contemporary hotel with a stunning location right on the beach. Bedrooms have unrivalled views over the sea, river and surrounding area. Superior and deluxe rooms (which include a king-size bed) available. Fresh, seasonally inspired menus served in our panoramic restaurant or al fresco in the Summer.

Directions: From A12 take A1094 to Aldeburgh. Turn right at crossroads in Aldeburgh (past church). Brudenell is on seafront, south end of town.

Bedrooms: 2 single, 22 double, 3 twin, 9 family, 8 suite
Open: All year

Site: ✿ **Payment:** ⊞ **Leisure:** ♿ ♪ ▸ ☋ **Property:** ⌂ ☰ ▣ ◗ **Children:** ⛱ ▦ ★ **Catering:** ♟ ▦
Room: ↺ ♨ ☏ TV

BUNGAY, Suffolk Map ref 3C1

SatNav NR35 2HL **B**

BED & BREAKFAST ★★★★ | *Silver* AWARD

B&B PER ROOM PER NIGHT
S: £50.00 - £55.00
D: £70.00 - £75.00

EVENING MEAL PER PERSON
£20.00

Rose Cottage Bed and Breakfast

School Road, Kirby Cane, Bungay, Suffolk NR35 2HL **T:** (01508) 518534
E: jenny@rosecottagebnb.co.uk
W: www.rosecottagebnb.co.uk

Luxury bed and breakfast between Beccles and Bungay. On a quiet country lane in South Norfolk. On the Norfolk / Suffolk border and close to the southern end of the Norfolk Broads. Rose Cottage overlooks the picturesque Waveney Valley. **Directions:** A143 from Bungay towards Beccles approx 4 miles - junction left into Church Road - at Xroads right into School Rd - approx 400 yds 1st house on left **Bedrooms:** En suite, twin or kingsize double available. **Open:** All year, except Christmas and New Year.

Site: ✿ **P** **Property:** ☰ **Catering:** ⟨✗ ▦ **Room:** ↺ ♨ TV DVD

BURY ST. EDMUNDS, Suffolk Map ref 3B2

SatNav IP33 1SZ **B**

GUEST ACCOMMODATION ★★★★ | *Silver* AWARD

B&B PER ROOM PER NIGHT
S: £42.00 - £50.00
D: £68.00

St Edmunds Guesthouse

35 St Andrews Street North, Bury St. Edmunds IP33 1SZ **T:** (01284) 700144
E: info@stedmundsguesthouse.net
W: stedmundsguesthouse.net **£ BOOK ONLINE**

Beautifully restored Victorian town house with 9 luxurious en suite rooms. Central to bus & rail stations. Tea/coffee, power shower, iron, free Wi-Fi & digital freeview TV. From £42 per room per night. **Directions:** Please contact us for directions. **Bedrooms:** 1 single, 3 double, 5 twin **Open:** All year except Christmas and New Year

Site: ✿ **P** **Payment:** ⊞ **Leisure:** ▸ **Property:** ☰ ⋈ **Children:** ⛱ ▦ ★ **Catering:** ▦
Room: ↺ ♨ ▣ TV

West Stow Hall

Icklingham Road, West Stow, Bury St. Edmunds IP28 6EY **T:** (01284) 728127
E: eileengilbert54@aol.com
W: www.weststowhall.com

B&B PER ROOM PER NIGHT
S: £60.00 - £75.00
D: £90.00 - £110.00
EVENING MEAL PER PERSON
£15.00 - £30.00

SPECIAL PROMOTIONS
Please see website for
details.

Enjoy the tranquility and beauty of this historic hall set in six acres of lovely grounds. Large comfortable bedrooms, great breakfasts and a warm welcome are guaranteed. The Garden Room, with ground floor access, is ideally suited for less mobile guests.

Directions: M11 to A11 direction Mildenhall. Before Mildenhall take A1101 to Bury St Edmunds, left turn West Stow. The hall is clearly signposted on the left.

Bedrooms: 2 double, 1 twin, 1 family
Open: All year except Christmas

Site: ❀ P Payment: 🏧 € Leisure: 🚴 ⛵ ⛳ ∪ Property: 🐎 🖼 🖊 Children: 🚲 🎋 Catering: 🍴
Room: 🍵 ♨ 💆 📻 🛏

Looking for something else?

The official and most comprehensive guide to independently inspected, star rated accommodation.

B&Bs and Hotels - B&Bs, Hotels, farmhouses, inns, serviced apartments, campus and hostel accommodation in England.

Self Catering - Self-catering holiday homes, approved caravan holiday homes, boat accommodation and holiday cottage agencies in England.

Camping, Touring and Holiday Parks - Touring parks, camping holidays and holiday parks and villages in Britain.

Now available in all good bookshops and online at **www.hudsons.co.uk/shop**

ELMSWELL, Suffolk   Map ref 3B2
SatNav IP30 9QR **B**

★★★★ GUEST HOUSE · *Silver* AWARD

B&B PER ROOM PER NIGHT
S: £40.00 - £50.00
D: £80.00 - £100.00
EVENING MEAL PER PERSON
£12.50

Kiln Farm Guest House
Kiln Lane, Elmswell, Bury St Edmunds, Suffolk IP30 9QR **T:** (01359) 240442
E: davejankilnfarm@btinternet.com

Welcoming Victorian farmhouse with courtyard of converted barns in secluded location just off A14. Licensed bar with conservatory for breakfasts and pre-booked evening meals. Ideal for exploring Suffolk. Businessmen welcome. **Directions:** A14 jct47. Travelling east Kiln Lane is right off exit slip road. From west, turn right over to roundabout, third exit. 50yds on left. **Bedrooms:** 5 double, 1 twin, 2 family **Open:** All year

Site: ✿ P Payment: 💷 € Property: ⛺ 🖿 Children: 🛏 🎮 🎏 Catering: 🍷 🍴 Room: 🍵 ♨ 📺 📶

FRAMLINGHAM, Suffolk   Map ref 3C2
SatNav IP13 9PD **B**

★★★★ FARMHOUSE

B&B PER ROOM PER NIGHT
S: £46.00 - £60.00
D: £70.00 - £95.00

High House Farm
Cransford, Woodbridge, Suffolk IP13 9PD **T:** (01728) 663461 **E:** info@highhousefarm.co.uk
W: highhousefarm.co.uk

A warm welcome awaits you in our beautifully restored 15th century farmhouse, featuring exposed beams, inglenook fireplaces and attractive gardens. Situated midway between Framlingham and Saxmundham. **Directions:** Please refer to website address. **Bedrooms:** 1 double, 1 family **Open:** All year

Site: ✿ P Leisure: ⚲ ♪ ♭ � Property: ⛺ 🖿 ⌂ ⌀ Children: 🛏 🎮 🎏 Catering: 🍴 Room: 🍵 ♨ 🎮 📺

HALESWORTH, Suffolk   Map ref 3C2
SatNav IP19 8BW **B**

★★★★ BED & BREAKFAST

B&B PER ROOM PER NIGHT
S: £35.00 - £40.00
D: £60.00 - £70.00

Fen-Way Guest House
School Lane, Halesworth IP19 8BW **T:** (01986) 873574
W: www.tiscover.co.uk

Spacious bungalow in seven acres of peaceful meadowland. Pets include sheep and lambs. Five minutes walk from town centre. Convenient for many places, including Southwold (9 miles). **Bedrooms:** 2 double, 1 twin all with en suite or private facilities **Open:** All year

Site: ✿ P Leisure: ♭ � Children: 🛏 Catering: 🍴 Room: 🍵 ♨ 📺 📶 🖥

HINTLESHAM, Suffolk   Map ref 3B2
SatNav IP8 3NT **B**

FARMHOUSE *Silver* AWARD

B&B PER ROOM PER NIGHT
S: £46.00 - £60.00
D: £70.00 - £80.00

College Farm Bed & Breakfast
College Farm, Hintlesham, Ipswich, Suffolk IP8 3NT **T:** (01473) 652253
E: bandb@collegefarm.plus.com
W: www.collegefarm.net

Peaceful 500-year-old Grade II Listed farmhouse on an arable farm 6 miles west of Ipswich on A1071 Hadleigh road. 3 well-appointed comfortable bedrooms with added luxuries. Convenient for Constable Country, Sutton Hoo (NT) and the coast. **Directions:** From Ipswich take A1071 towards Hadleigh. Go through Hintlesham, the farm is half a mile on towards Hadleigh. On left on z-bend, well signposted. **Bedrooms:** 3 double or twin rooms (2 ensuite), TV, tea trays **Open:** Mid-January to mid-December

Site: ✿ P Payment: 💳 Leisure: ♪ ► ♺ Property: 🖥 🏰 ⌀ Catering: 🍴 Room: 📶 ♨ 📺 ⚙

HITCHAM, Suffolk   Map ref 3B2
SatNav IP7 7NY **B**

FARMHOUSE

B&B PER ROOM PER NIGHT
S: £40.00
D: £70.00

Stanstead Hall
Buxhall Road, Hitcham, Ipswich IP7 7NY **T:** (01449) 740270 **E:** stanstead@btinternet.com
W: stansteadcamping.co.uk

Very friendly Moated Farmhouse standing off the road in the quiet open countryside. Large garden to relax in under a glass verandah. In easy reach of Lavenham, Long Melford, Bury St Edmunds and central to many of Suffolk's beauty spots. **Directions:** Directions on website. **Bedrooms:** Large rooms, with shower, tv and tea/coffee. **Open:** All year

f

Site: ✿ P Leisure: ⛷ ♪ ♺ Property: 🐴 🖥 Room: 📶 ♨ 📻 📺

KETTLEBURGH, Suffolk   Map ref 3C2
SatNav IP13 7JT **B**

GUEST ACCOMMODATION

B&B PER ROOM PER NIGHT
S: £40.00 - £50.00
D: £60.00 - £75.00
EVENING MEAL PER PERSON
£7.00 - £14.00

The Chequers Inn
The Street, Kettleburgh, Framlingham IP13 7JT **T:** (01728) 723760
E: debbie@thechequers.net
W: thechequers.net

A welcoming traditional country pub, serving real ales and wholesome, hearty food located in the beautiful Deben Valley. Single storey purpose built holiday accommodation, set in peaceful riverside gardens. **Directions:** Please contact us for directions. **Bedrooms:** 1 double, 1 twin, 1 suite **Open:** All year

Site: ✿ P Payment: 💳 Property: 🖥 ⌀ Children: 🧸 ⚲ Catering: ◖✗ ▼ 🍴 Room: 📶 ♨ ☎ 📺 ⚙

KETTLEBURGH, Suffolk   Map ref 3C2
SatNav IP13 7LF **B**

FARMHOUSE

B&B PER ROOM PER NIGHT
S: £35.00
D: £70.00
EVENING MEAL PER PERSON
£20.00

Church Farm
Church Road, Kettleburgh, Woodbridge IP13 7LF **T:** (01728) 723532
E: jbater@suffolkonline.net
W: churchfarmkettleburgh.co.uk **£ BOOK ONLINE**

Oak-beamed, 500-year-old farmhouse on a working farm. Bedrooms with lovely views and every comfort. Excellent food from home-grown produce. **Directions:** A12 North to Wickham Market, Easton, Kettleburgh. A14, A1120 to Earl Soham, Brandeston, Kettleburgh. **Bedrooms:** 2 double, 2 twin **Open:** All year

Site: ✿ P Leisure: ⛷ ♪ ► ♺ Property: 🐴 🖥 Children: 🧸 ▥ ⚲ Catering: 🍴 Room: 📶 ♨ ⚙

STOWMARKET, Suffolk   Map ref 3B2
SatNav IP14 5EU **B**

Three Bears Cottage
Mulberry Tree Farm, Middlewood Green, Stowmarket IP14 5EU **T:** (01449) 711707
F: (01449) 711707 **E:** gbeckett01@aol.com
W: www.3bearscottagesuffolk.co.uk **£ BOOK ONLINE**

B&B PER ROOM PER NIGHT
S: £30.00
D: £60.00

Self-contained converted barn offering comfort, privacy & country views. Lounge with TV, kitchenette, a substantial continental breakfast available. Ground floor bedroom, shower/bathroom sleeps 6. Well behaved dogs accepted, many bridalway walks at the back of the cottage. Within easy reach of Bury St Edmunds, Ipswich Cambridge & Suffolk coast. **Directions:** A14, A1120 through Stowupland turn into Saxham St, 1st right 1m, right into Blacksmiths Lane **Bedrooms:** 1 King size, 1 family **Open:** All year

Site: P Leisure: Property: Children: Catering: Room:

WRENTHAM, Suffolk   Map ref 3C2
SatNav NR34 7JF **B**

Five Bells
Southwold Road, Wrentham NR34 7JF **T:** (01502) 675249 **E:** debby669@msn.com

B&B PER ROOM PER NIGHT
D: £65.00 - £100.00
EVENING MEAL PER PERSON
£10.00 - £15.00

Traditional country inn set in a rural location. Close to Southwold. We are open all day for drinks and have a large beer garden. To the rear of the property you will find a caravan park available. Caravans are £20 per night. **Directions:** Leaving the A12 at Wrentham, head towards Southwold on the B1127. **Bedrooms:** 1 double, 1 twin, 1 family **Open:** All year

Site: P Payment: Leisure: Property: Children: Catering: Room:

YOXFORD, Suffolk   Map ref 3C2
SatNav IP17 3EX **B**

Sans Souci B&B
Yoxford, Saxmundham IP17 3EX **T:** (01728) 668827 **E:** sue.norris3@btinternet.com
W: www.sanssoucibandb.co.uk

B&B PER ROOM PER NIGHT
S: £50.00 - £60.00
D: £85.00 - £135.00

4 Star B&B in Yoxford, close to Minsmere Bird Sanctuary. Good local pub and bistro. Locally sourced breakfast ingredients, locally produced sausages. Free wifi. Great location for cycling holidays. **Directions:** Set back from main road, A12. Rail station is 10min walk. Local bus service. **Bedrooms:** 4 en suite doubles **Open:** All year

Site: P Payment: Leisure: Property: Children: Catering: Room:

Need more information?
Visit our new 2014 guide websites for detailed information, up-to-date availability and to book your accommodation online. Includes over 20,000 places to stay, all of them star rated.
www.visitor-guides.co.uk

2014 Official Tourist Board Guides

East Midlands

Derbyshire, Leicestershire, Lincolnshire, Northamptonshire, Nottinghamshire, Rutland

The East Midlands offer an exciting and varied landscape. From the Lincolnshire Wolds to the majestic Robin Hood country of Sherwood Forest, and from the honeycomb villages of Rutland and Northamptonshire to the famous hunting county of Leicestershire, there is much to be seen and admired. The region is a treasure trove of magnificent castles and historic houses, thriving cities and market towns.

Highlights

Chatsworth House

Chatsworth is home to the Duke and Duchess of Devonshire, and has been passed down through 16 generations of the Cavendish family. The house architecture has been evolving for five centuries, and it has one of Europe's most significant art collections.

Derwent Valley Mills

The cotton mills provide an industrial landscape of high historical and technological interest. The modern factory owes its origins to the mills where Richard Arkwright's inventions were first put into production.

Lincolnshire Wolds

The Lincolnshire Wolds is a range of hills designated an Area of Outstanding Natural Beauty, and is the highest area of land in Eastern England between Yorkshire and Kent.

National Forest

The National Forest is a forest in the making, an inspiring example for the country in the face of climate change and other environmental pressures. From one of the country's least wooded regions, the ambitious goal is to increase tree cover to about a third of all the land within its boundary.

Nottingham

Renowned around the world as the home of Robin Hood, Nottingham today is a destination for culture, heritage, shopping, sport and the arts.

Peak District

The stunning scenery may be the area's biggest free attraction, but there are plenty of other places to visit, including caves, ancient druidic stone circles and hilltop forts.

RAF Scampton

Lincolnshire has a proud history of aviation, having been an important base during World War Two. RAF Scampton was the home of the Dambusters and is the current base for the Red Arrows.

Rutland Water

This internationally famous nature reserve is managed by the Leicestershire & Rutland Wildlife Trust in partnership with Anglian Water, and provides one of the most important wildfowl sanctuaries in the UK, regularly holding in excess of 20,000 waterfowl. It is a Site of Special Scientific Interest.

Editor's Picks

Enjoy a bike ride

Cycling around Rutland Water is a favourite activity among locals and visitors – the off-road circular route is 23 miles.

Discover aviation history

During the Second World War Lincolnshire was known as 'Bomber County' because of the number of bomber bases dotted around the flatter countryside. Bring those days to life at the Lincolnshire Aviation Heritage Centre.

Enter the caves

Nottingham has a network of over 400 caves running beneath its streets. Many of are hidden below private homes but there are a few places where you can get a glimpse of what lies beneath.

Take the cable car

The Heights of Abraham has become one of the Peak District's most popular destinations. The observation cars transport you to the hilltop and stunning views of the Derwent Valley.

Things to do

 Attractions with this sign participate in the Places of Interest Quality Assurance Scheme.

 Attractions with this sign participate in the Visitor Attraction Quality Assurance Scheme.

Both schemes recognise high standards in all aspects of the visitor experience (see page 7)

Entertainment & Culture

Derby Museum and Art Gallery
Derby DE1 1BS
(01332) 716659
www.derby.gov.uk/museums
Derby Museum and Art Gallery holds collections and displays relating to the history, culture and natural environment of Derby and its region.

Galleries of Justice Museum
Nottingham NG1 1HN
(0115) 952 0555
www.galleriesofjustice.org.uk
You will be delving in to the dark and disturbing past of crime and punishment.

Mansfield Museum
Mansfield, Nottinghamshire NG18 1NG
(01623) 463088
www.mansfield.gov.uk/museum
Our dynamic museum and art gallerys permanent displays house a fascinating mix of local art and artefacts. Come and explore Mansfields social history or investigate 21st Century challenges facing our planet.

Newark Castle and Conflict
Newark, Nottinghamshire NG24 1BG
(01636) 655765
www.newark-sherwood.gov.uk
Newark Castle has been at the heart of the town for many centuries and has played an important role in historical events.

National Waterways Museum - Stoke Bruerne
Towcester, Northamptonshire NN12 7SE
(01604) 862229
www.stokebruernecanalmuseum.org.uk
Stoke Bruerne is an ideal place to explore the story of our waterways.

Newark Air Museum
Nottinghamshire NG24 2NY
(01636) 707170
www.newarkairmuseum.org
The museum is open to the public every day except December 24th, 25th, 26th and January 1st.

Northampton Museum & Art Gallery
Northampton NN1 1DP
(01604) 838111
www.northampton.gov.uk/museums
Displays include footwear and related items, paintings, ceramics and glass and the history of Northampton.

Silk Mill - Derby's Museum of Industry and History
Derby DE1 3AF
(01332) 255308
www.derby.gov.uk/museums
The Silk Mill was completed around 1723 and the re-built Mill now contains displays on local history and industry.

204

Family Fun

Foxton Locks
Market Harborough LE16 7RA
(01908) 302500
www.foxtonlocks.com
A great day out for all the family.

Gulliver's Theme Park
Matlock Bath, Derbyshire DE4 3PG
(01629) 580540
www.gulliversfun.co.uk
*With more than 40 rides &
attractions, Gulliver's provides the complete family
entertainment experience. Fun & adventure with Gully
Mouse, Dora the explorer, Diego and "The Lost World".*

National Space Centre
Leicester LE4 5NS
0845 605 2001
www.spacecentre.co.uk
*The award winning National Space Centre is the UK's
largest attraction dedicated to space. From the moment
you catch sight of the Space Centre's futuristic Rocket
Tower, you'll be treated to hours of breathtaking discovery
& interactive fun.*

Sherwood Pines Forest Park
Edwinstowe, Nottinghamshire NG21 9JL
(01623) 822447
www.forestry.gov.uk
*The largest forest open to the public in the
East Midlands and centre for a wide variety
of outdoor activities.*

Wicksteed Park
Kettering, Northamptonshire NN15 6NJ
(01536) 512475
www.wicksteedpark.co.uk
*Wicksteed Park remains Northamptonshire's most
popular attraction and entertainment venue*

Heritage

78 Derngate
Northampton NN1 1UH
(01604) 603407
www.78derngate.org.uk
*Charles Rennie Mackintosh transformed a typical
terraced house into a startlingly modern house for
local model maker W.J. Bassett-Lowke. It was his last major
commission and his only work in England.*

Althorp
Northampton NN7 4HQ
(01604) 770107
www.althorp.com
*Come and visit one of England's finest country houses,
home of the Spencer family for over 500 years and
ancestral home of Diana, Princess of Wales.*

Ashby-de-le-Zouch Castle
Leicestershire LE65 1BR
(01530) 413343
www.english-heritage.org.uk/daysout/properties/
ashby-de-la-zouch-castle
*Visit Ashby-de-la-Zouch Castle where you will
see the ruins of this historical castle, the original
setting for many of the scenes of Sir Walter Scott's
classic tale 'Ivanhoe'.*

Belton House
Belton, Lincolnshire NG32 2LS
(01476) 566116
www.nationaltrust.org.uk/main/w-beltonhouse
Belton, is a perfect example of an English Country House.

Belvoir Castle
Melton Mowbray, Leicestershire NG32 1PE
(01476) 871002
www.belvoircastle.com
*Home to the Duke and Duchess of Rutland, Belvoir
Castle offers stunning views of the Vale of Belvoir.*

Bosworth Battlefield Heritage Centre

Market Bosworth, Leicestershire CV13 0AD
(01455) 290429
www.bosworthbattlefield.com
Delve into Leicestershire's fascinating history at Bosworth Battlefield Country Park - the site of the 1485 Battle of Bosworth.

Chatsworth

Bakewell, Derbyshire DE45 1PP
(01246) 582204
www.chatsworth.org
One of Britain's best loved historic houses and estates.

Creswell Crags
Chesterfield, Derbyshire S80 3LH
(01909) 720378
www.creswell-crags.org.uk
A world famous archaeological site, home to Britain's only known Ice Age cave art.

Doddington Hall
Lincoln LN6 4RU
(01522) 694308
www.doddingtonhall.com
A superb Elizabethan mansion by the renowned architect Robert Smythson. The hall stands today as it was completed in 1600 with walled courtyards, turrets and gatehouse.

Great Central Railway
Leicester LE11 1RW
(01509) 230726
www.gcrailway.co.uk
The Great Central Railway is Britain's only double track main line steam railway. Enjoy an exciting calendar of events, a footplate ride or dine in style on board one of the steam trains.

Haddon Hall
Bakewell, Derbyshire DE45 1LA
(01629) 812855
www.haddonhall.co.uk
Haddon Hall is conveniently situated on the A6 between Bakewell and Matlock, Derbyshire.

Hardwick Hall
Chesterfield, Derbyshire S44 5QJ
(01246) 850430
www.nationaltrust.org.uk/hardwick
Owned by the National Trust the Estate includes Hardwick Hall, Stainsby Mill and a Park. The Hall is one of Britain's greatest Elizabethan houses, the water-powered Mill is fully functioning, the Park has a fishing lake and circular walks.

Kedleston Hall
Derby DE22 5JH
(01332) 842191
www.nationaltrust.org.uk/main/w-kedlestonhall
A fine example of a neo-classical mansion built between 1759-65 by the architecht Robert Adam and set in over 800 acres of parkland and landscaped pleasure grounds. Administered by The National Trust.

Lamport Hall and Gardens
Northamptonshire NN6 9HD
(01604) 686272
www.lamporthall.co.uk
Grade 1 listed building that was home to the Isham family and their collections for over four centuries.

Normanby Hall Museum and Country Park
Scunthorpe, Lincolnshire DN15 9HU
(01724) 720588
www.northlincs.gov.uk/normanby
Set in 300 acres of gardens, parkland, deer park, woods, ornamental and wild birds, well-stocked gift shop.

Nottingham Castle
Nottingham NG1 6EL
(0115) 915 3700
www.nottinghamcity.gov.uk/museums
Situated on a high rock, Nottingham Castle commands spectacular views over the city and once rivalled the great castles of Windsor and the Tower of London.

Papplewick Hall & Gardens
Nottinghamshire NG15 8FE
(0115) 963 3491
www.papplewickhall.co.uk
A fine Adam house, built in 1787 and Grade I listed building with a park and woodland garden.

Prebendal Manor Medieval Centre
Nassington, Northamptonshire PE8 6QG
(01780) 782575
www.prebendal-manor.co.uk
Visit a unique medieval manor and enjoy the largest recreated medieval gardens in Europe.

Rockingham Castle
Market Harborough, Northamptonshire LE16 8TH
(01536) 770240
www.rockinghamcastle.com
Rockingham Castle stands on the edge of an escarpment giving dramatic views over five counties and the Welland Valley below.

Sudbury Hall
Ashbourne, Derbyshire DE6 5HT
(01283) 585305
www.nationaltrust.org.uk/sudburyhall/
Explore the grand 17th Century hall with its richly decorated interior and see life below stairs.

Sulgrave Manor
Northamptonshire OX17 2SD
(01295) 760205
www.sulgravemanor.org.uk
A Tudor manor house and garden, the ancestral home of George Washington's family with authentic furniture shown by friendly guides

Tattershall Castle
Lincolnshire LN4 4LR
(01526) 342543
www.nationaltrust.org.uk/tattershall
Tattershall Castle was built in the 15th Century to impress and dominate by Ralph Cromwell, one of the most powerful men in England. The castle is a dramatic red brick tower.

Nature & Wildlife

Ayscoughfee Hall Museum and Gardens
Spalding, Lincolnshire PE11 2RA
(01775) 764555
www.ayscoughfee.org
Ayscoughfee Hall Museum is housed in a beautiful wool merchant's house built in 1451 on the banks of the River Welland.

Castle Ashby Gardens
Northamptonshire NN7 1LQ
(01604) 695200
www.castleashbygardens.co.uk
A haven of tranquility and beauty in the heart of Northamptonshire. Take your time to explore these beautiful gardens and enjoy the fascinating attractions from the rare breed farmyard to the historic orangery.

Conkers Discovery Centre
Ashby-de-la-Zouch, Leicestershire DE12 6GA
(01283) 216633
www.visitconkers.com/thingstodo/discoverycentre
Enjoy the great outdoors and explore over 120 acres of the award winning parkland.

Hardys Animal Farm
Ingoldmells, Lincolnshire PE25 1LZ
(01754) 872267
www.hardysanimalfarm.co.uk
An enjoyable way to learn about the countryside and how a farm works. There are animals for the children to enjoy as well as learning about the history and traditions of the countryside.

Renishaw Hall and Gardens
Dronfield, Derbyshire S21 3WB
(01246) 432310
www.renishaw-hall.co.uk
The Gardens are Italian in design and were laid out over 100 years ago by Sir George Sitwell. The garden is divided into 'rooms' with yew hedges, flanked with classical statues.

Salcey Forest
Hartwell, Northamptonshire NN17 3BB
(01780) 444920
www.forestry.gov.uk/salceyforest
Get a birds eye view of this wonderful woodland on the tremendous Tree Top Way.

Sherwood Forest Farm Park
Nottinghamshire NG21 9HL
(01623) 823558
www.sherwoodforestfarmpark.co.uk
Meet over 30 different rare farm breeds, plus other unusual species!

Sherwood Forest Country Park
Nottinghamshire NG21 9HN
(01623) 823202
www.nottinghamshire.gov.uk/sherwoodforestcp
Sherwood Forest Country Park covers 450 acres and incorporates some truly ancient areas of native woodland.

Twycross Zoo
Hinckley, Leicestershire CV9 3PX
(01827) 880250
www.twycrosszoo.com
Meet Twyford's famous orangutans, gorillas and chimpanzees plus many other mammals, birds and reptiles.

Events 2014

Dave's Comedy Festival
February 7-23, various venues
Confirmed acts are Alan Davies, Milton Jones, Russell Kane, Carl Donnelly, Doc Brown, Terry Alderton, Jenny Éclair, Seann Walsh, Al Murray and An Ideal Night Out hosted by Johnny Vegas.
www.comedy-festival.co.uk

Festival of Words
February date TBC, Nottingham
Celebrating Nottingham's Love of Words. This inaugural Festival of Words takes its inspiration from Nottingham's lace industry, an important thread in the city's heritage. nottwords.org.uk

Space Fiction
**February,
National Space Centre, Leicester**
Meet your favourite authors, discover new stories, champion a book and help us discover the greatest space fiction story ever written.
www.spacecentre.co.uk

Lincoln Music and Drama Festival
March (first two weeks), Lincoln
A competitive festival for children and adults of all ages, groups or individuals from schools or private entries. www.lincolnmdfest.org.uk

International Antiques & Collectors Fair
April, Newark Showground
The Newark International Antiques and Collectors Fair is the largest event of its kind in Europe – a world-wide phenomenon, this is one IACF event that needs to be experienced to be believed.
www.iacf.co.uk/newark

Easter Vintage Festival
April 18-21, Great Central Railway
A real treat for all this Easter with traction engines, classic cars and buses, fairground rides, trade stands, a beer tent as well as lots of action on the double track. www.gcrailway.co.uk

Brigstock International Horse Trials
May 2-4, Rockingham Castle
The Brigstock International Horse Trials is relocating to Rockingham Castle with a brand new course designed by International acclaimed designer Philip Herbert.
www.rockinghamcastle.com

Artisan Cheese Fair
May 3-4, Melton Mowbray
A chance to taste the huge range of cheeses that are made locally and further afield.
www.artisancheesefair.co.uk

Nottinghamshire County Show
May 10-11, Newark Showground
A fantastic traditional county show promoting farming, food, rural life and heritage in Nottinghamshire and beyond.
www.newarkshowground.com

Derbyshire Food & Drink Festival
May 17-18, Derby
Over 150 stalls will showcase the best local produce from Derbyshire and the Peak District region, as well as unique and exotic foods from further afield.
www.derbyshirefoodfestival.co.uk

Lincolnshire Wolds Walking Festival
May 17- June 1, Louth
Over 90 walks, taking place in an Area of Outstanding Natural Beauty and surrounding countryside.
www.woldswalkingfestival.co.uk

Lincolnshire Show
June 18-19, Lincolnshire Showground
Agriculture remains at the heart of the Lincolnshire Show with livestock and equine competitions, machinery displays and the opportunity not only to find out where your food comes from but to taste a lot of it too!
www.lincolnshireshow.co.uk

Earth & Fire International Ceramics Fair
June 20-22, Rufford Abbey Country Park
Earth and Fire is one of the country's premier ceramic events, and takes place in the historic grounds of Rufford Abbey.
www.nottinghamshire.gov.uk/earthandfire

Armed Forces Weekend
June 28, Wollaton Park, Nottingham
Nottingham welcomes the annual national event celebrating our Armed Forces past and present.
www.mynottingham.gov.uk/armedforces

British Grand Prix
June 30, Silverstone
Chance to see the world's best Formula One drivers in action.
www.silverstone.co.uk

RAF Waddington Air Show
July 5-6, Waddington, Lincoln
The largest of all RAF air shows, regularly attended by over 125,000 visitors.
www.waddingtonairshow.co.uk

Buxton Festival
July, Buxton
A summer celebration of the best opera, music and literature, at the heart of the beautiful Peak District.
www.buxtonfestival.co.uk

Robin Hood Festival
August 4-10, Sherwood Forest
Celebrate our most legendary outlaw in Sherwood Forest's medieval village.
www.nottinghamshire.gov.uk/robinhoodfestival/

Burghley Horse Trials
September, date TBC, Burghley House, Lincs
One of the most popular events in the equestrian calendar.
www.burghley-horse.co.uk

Robin Hood Beer Festival
October, Nottingham Castle
Set in the stunning grounds of Nottingham Castle, the Robin Hood Beer Festival offers the world's largest selection of real ales and ciders.
www.beerfestival.nottinghamcamra.org

Robin Hood Pageant
October, Nottingham Castle
Nottingham Castle transforms into a medieval village for a weekend of celebrations in honour of Robin Hood and his merry men.
www.nottinghamcity.gov.uk

GameCity
October, Nottingham
Now in its 8th year, GameCity is the largest festival dedicated to the videogame culture in Europe.
festival.gamecity.org

Tourist Information Centres

When you arrive at your destination, visit an Official Partner Tourist Information Centre for quality assured help with accommodation and information about local attractions and events, or email your request before you go. To find a Tourist Information Centre visit www.visitengland.com

Ashbourne	13 Market Place	01335 343666	ashbourneinfo@derbyshiredales.gov.uk
Ashby-de-la-Zouch	North Street	01530 411767	ashby.tic@nwleicestershire.gov.uk
Bakewell	Old Market Hall	01629 813227	bakewell@peakdistrict.gov.uk
Buxton	The Pavillion Gardens	01298 25106	tourism@highpeak.gov.uk
Castleton	Buxton Road	01433 620679	castleton@peakdistrict.gov.uk
Chesterfield	Rykneld Square	01246 345777	tourism@chesterfield.gov.uk
Derby	Assembly Rooms	01332 255802	tourism@derby.gov.uk
Leicester	51 Gallowtree Gate	0844 888 5181	info@goleicestershire.com
Lincoln Castle Hill	9 Castle Hill	01522 545458	visitorinformation@lincolnbig.co.uk
Newark	Keepers Cottage, Riverside Park	01636 655765	newarktic@nsdc.info
Northampton	Sessions House, County Hall	01604 367997/8	tic@northamptonshire.gov.uk
Nottingham City	1-4 Smithy Row	08444 775 678	tourist.information@nottinghamcity.gov.uk
Sherwood	Sherwood Heath	01623 824545	sherwoodheath@nsdc.info
Silverstone	Silverstone Circuit	0844 3728 200	Elicia.Bonamy@silverstone.co.uk
Swadlincote	Sharpe's Pottery Museum	01283 222848	gail.archer@sharpespotterymuseum.org.uk

Regional Contacts and Information

The publications listed are available from the following organisations:

East Midlands Tourism
Web: www.eastmidlandstourism.com
- Discover East Midlands

Experience Nottinghamshire
Tel: 0844 477 5678
Web: www.experiencenottinghamshire.com
- Nottinghamshire Essential Guide
- Where to Stay Guide, City Breaks
- The City Guide
- Robin Hood Breaks

Peak District and Derbyshire
Web: www.visitpeakdistrict.com
- Peak District and Derbyshire Visitor Guide
- Well Dressing
- Camping and Caravanning Guide
- Walking Festivals Guide and Visitor Guide

Discover Rutland
Tel: (01572) 722577
Web: www.discover-rutland.co.uk
- Discover Rutland
- Eat drink Rutland
- Attractions
- Uppingham
- Oakham
- Oakham Heritage Trail

Lincolnshire
Tel: (01522) 545458
Web: www.visitlincolnshire.com
- Visit Lincolnshire – Destination Guide
- Great Days Out
- Good Taste
- Keep up with the flow

Explore Northamptonshire
Tel: (01604) 838800
Web: www.britainonshow.co.uk
- Northamptonshire Visitor Guide
- Northamptonshire presents Britain on show
- County Map

Leicestershire
Tel: 0844 888 5181
Web: www.goleicestershire.com
- Leicestershire City Guide
- Stay, Play, Explore
- Great Days Out in Leicestershire

Where to Stay

Entries appear alphabetically by
town name in each county. A key
to symbols appears on page 7

ASHBOURNE, Derbyshire   Map ref 4B2 — SatNav DE6 1QU **B**

Peak District Spa

Buxton Road, Nr Alsop en le Dale, Ashbourne DE6 1QU **T:** (01335) 310100
F: (01335) 310100 **E:** PeakDistrictSpa@rivendalecaravanpark.co.uk
W: http://www.peakdistrictspa.co.uk **£ BOOK ONLINE**

B&B PER ROOM PER NIGHT
S: £49.00 - £83.00
D: £54.00 - £88.00

Occupying a secluded location on part of Rivendale's 37 acre site with its own parking, terrace and garden with superb views over Eaton Dale. Ideal for cycling, walking & outdoor pursuits. Convenient Chatsworth, Alton Towers, Carsington Water. All rooms with en suites, oak or travertine floors, under floor heating.

Directions: Travelling north from Ashbourne towards Buxton on the A515, find Rivendale on the RHS.

Bedrooms: 2 double, 2 twin
Open: All year except closed Sunday after New Years day until 1st Friday in February.

Site: ✿ P **Payment:** 💷 **Leisure:** ⚕ ♫ ♨ **Property:** 🖥 🕭 **Children:** ✗ 🛏 ⚲ **Catering:** 🍽 🍴
Room: 🕾 ♨ 🕮 📺 ♨ 📠

BAKEWELL, Derbyshire   Map ref 4B2 — SatNav DE45 1QN **B**

Chy-an-Dour

Vicarage Lane, Ashford-in-the-Water, Bakewell, Derbyshire DE45 1QN **T:** (01629) 813162
E: stuartandann@hotmail.com
W: www.chyandourashford.co.uk

B&B PER ROOM PER NIGHT
S: £60.00 - £70.00
D: £70.00 - £85.00

First class accommodation in a quiet position overlooking picturesque village. Our aim is the satisfaction and enjoyment of our guests. We look forward to welcoming you to our home. **Directions:** Please see website for map. **Bedrooms:** Room offers flat screen TV, a selection of complimentary beverages and biscuits, thermostatic controlled heating. **Open:** All Year

Site: ✿ P **Property:** 🖥 **Room:** 🕾 ♨ 📺

Win amazing prizes, every month...

Visit our new 2014 guide websites for detailed information, up-to-date availability and to book your accommodation online. Includes over 20,000 places to stay, all of them star rated.

**Enter our monthly competition at
www.visitor-guides.co.uk/prizes**

BAMFORD, Derbyshire   Map ref 4B2   SatNav S33 0AZ B

★★★★ INN

Silver AWARD

B&B PER ROOM PER NIGHT
S: £65.00 - £70.00
D: £78.00 - £120.00

EVENING MEAL PER PERSON
£9.95 - £19.95

SPECIAL PROMOTIONS
Go to our website to see the latest offers available. Discounts for 3 or more nights. For those that would like to stay longer we also have 5* self catering apartments.
www.ladybowerapartments.co.uk

Yorkshire Bridge Inn

Ashopton Road, Bamford in the High Peak, Hope Valley S33 0AZ **T:** (01433) 651361
F: (01433) 651361 **E:** info@yorkshire-bridge.co.uk
W: yorkshire-bridge.co.uk **£ BOOK ONLINE**

This famous inn enjoys an idyllic setting near the beautiful reservoirs of Ladybower, Derwent and Howden in the Peak District, and was voted one of the top six freehouses of the year for all-year-round excellence. Superb, en suite rooms, lovely bar and dining areas offering excellent cuisine. Brochure available.

Directions: M1 jct 29, Chesterfield - Baslow - Calver - Hathersage - Bamford. A6013 through Bamford. After 0.5 miles on left-hand side.

Bedrooms: 10 double, 2 twin, 2 family
Open: All year except Christmas

Site: ✿ P Payment: 💷 Leisure: ♪ ▶ ♒ Property: 🐾 🖼 Children: 🧸 🛏 🅰 Catering: ⟨✕ ♟ 🍴
Room: 🍵 🛆 📞 🍳 📺 🧺 🚗

BIGGIN-BY-HARTINGTON, Derbyshire   Map ref 4B2   SatNav SK17 0DH H

★★ COUNTRY HOUSE HOTEL

B&B PER ROOM PER NIGHT
S: £80.00 - £132.00
D: £90.00 - £142.00

EVENING MEAL PER PERSON
£25.00

SPECIAL PROMOTIONS
Available throughout the year. See website www.bigginhall.co.uk

Biggin Hall Hotel

Biggin by Hartington, Buxton SK17 0DH **T:** (01298) 84451 **E:** enquiries@bigginhall.co.uk
W: www.bigginhall.co.uk

Biggin Hall in the Peak District National Park is the ideal base for cycling and walking and for exploring stunning landscapes and glimpses of past grandeurs – including Chatsworth, Haddon Hall, Kedleston etc - and bold enterprises now preserved as industrial archaeology. The 17th century Grade II* listed main house oozes character and charm. 21st century comforts and Classical English cuisine.

Directions: Half a mile off the A515, midway between Ashbourne and Buxton.

Bedrooms: 1 single, 8 double, 9 twin, 2 family, 1 suite
Open: All year

Site: ✿ Payment: 💷 € Leisure: 🎿 ♪ ♒ Property: 🌳 🐾 🖼 Children: 🧸¹² Catering: ♟ 🍴
Room: 🍵 🛆 📞 🍳 📺 🧺 🚗

BUXTON, Derbyshire   Map ref 4B2   SatNav SK17 9BA [H]

Alison Park Hotel

3 Temple Road, Buxton, Derbyshire SK17 9BA   **T:** (01298) 22473   **F:** (01298) 72709
E: reservations@alison-park-hotel.co.uk
W: alison-park-hotel.co.uk   **£ BOOK ONLINE**

SMALL HOTEL ★★

B&B PER ROOM PER NIGHT
S: £54.00 - £60.00
D: £108.00 - £120.00
EVENING MEAL PER PERSON
£16.00 - £18.50

An Edwardian arts and crafts house, set within its own grounds in quiet location, just out of the town centre. The family management of the hotel ensures a warm welcome. **Bedrooms:** 3 single, 7 double, 3 twin, 2 family **Open:** All year

Site: Payment: Leisure: Property: Children: Catering: Room:

BUXTON, Derbyshire   Map ref 4B2   SatNav SK17 6JE [B]

Grosvenor House

1 Broad Walk, Buxton SK17 6JE   **T:** (01298) 72439   **E:** grosvenor.buxton@btopenworld.com
W: grosvenorbuxton.co.uk

GUEST HOUSE ★★★★   **Silver AWARD**

B&B PER ROOM PER NIGHT
S: £52.00 - £70.00
D: £65.00 - £90.00

Grade II listed Victorian residence, fully refurbished with en suite rooms and many extras. Noted for outstanding breakfast. Close to all Buxton attractions, shopping, railway and bus stations. **Directions:** In the centre of town, opposite the Old Hall Hotel overlooking the Pavilion Gardens and Opera House. **Bedrooms:** 1 single, 5 double, 1 twin, 1 family **Open:** All year

Site: **P** Payment: Leisure: Property: Children: Catering: Room:

BUXTON, Derbyshire   Map ref 4B2   SatNav SK17 9DP [B]

Kingscroft Guest House

10 Green Lane, Buxton, Derbyshire SK17 9DP   **T:** (01298) 22757   **F:** (01298) 27858
E: kingscroftbuxton1@btinternet.com
W: www.kingscroftguesthouse.co.uk

GUEST HOUSE ★★★★   **Silver AWARD**

B&B PER ROOM PER NIGHT
S: £40.00 - £55.00
D: £80.00 - £90.00

Late Victorian luxury guesthouse, in central yet quiet position in heart of Peak District. Comfortable surroundings with period decor. Enjoy our hearty, delicious, home cooked full English or continental breakfasts. **Directions:** Kingscroft is situated only 5 minutes walk from the town's shopping centre, pubs and restaurants, and easy reach at both railway and bus stations. **Bedrooms:** 1 single, 6 double, 1 twin **Open:** All year

Site: **P** Payment: Leisure: Property: Catering: Room:

Book your accommodation online

Visit our new 2014 guide websites for detailed information, up-to-date availability and to book your accommodation online. Includes over 20,000 places to stay, all of them star rated.

www.visitor-guides.co.uk

BUXTON, Derbyshire   Map ref 4B2 — SatNav SK17 6BD **H**

★★★ HOTEL

B&B PER ROOM PER NIGHT
S: £70.00
D: £79.00 - £165.00
EVENING MEAL PER PERSON
£18.00 - £35.00

SPECIAL PROMOTIONS
Chatsworth House Breaks, Theatre Breaks and Special promotions available throughout the year.

Old Hall Hotel

The Square, Buxton SK17 6BD **T:** (01298) 22841 **F:** (01298) 72437
E: reception@oldhallhotelbuxton.co.uk
W: www.oldhallhotelbuxton.co.uk **£ BOOK ONLINE**

This historic hotel, reputedly the oldest in England, offers a warm and friendly service. Ideally located opposite Pavillion Gardens and Edwardian opera house, we serve pre and post theatre dinner in our restaurant and wine bar. Rooms available on B&B and half-board basis. The perfect Peak District base.

Directions: Map available, please see our website for full directions.

Bedrooms: 14 classic double and twin bedrooms, 11 standard doubles, 6 executive doubles and twins, 4 four poster beds, 2 singles and a flat
Open: All year

CASTLETON, Derbyshire   Map ref 4B2 — SatNav S33 8WE **B**

★★★ BED & BREAKFAST

B&B PER ROOM PER NIGHT
S: £35.00
D: £70.00 - £85.00

Causeway House B&B

Back Street, Castleton, Hope Valley S33 8WE **T:** (01433) 623291
E: info@causewayhouse.co.uk
W: causewayhouse.co.uk **£ BOOK ONLINE**

A Former Cruck cottage from the 14th century with oak beams and low ceilings. Heart of the Peak district Castleton is renowned for its Hiking and Cycling trails. **Directions:** Castleton, Hope Valley Derbyshire. Nearest station Hope Derbyshire. Bus depot in the village. **Bedrooms:** 2 single, 1 double, 2 family **Open:** All year

CHESTERFIELD, Derbyshire   Map ref 4B2 — SatNav S40 4EE **B**

★★★ GUEST HOUSE

B&B PER ROOM PER NIGHT
S: £38.00
D: £56.00

Abigails Guest House

62 Brockwell Lane, Chesterfield S40 4EE **T:** (01246) 279391 **F:** (01246) 854468
E: gail@abigails.fsnet.co.uk
W: abigailsguesthouse.co.uk

Relax taking breakfast in the conservatory overlooking Chesterfield and surrounding moorlands. Garden with pond, private car park. Best B&B winners 2000. Free Wi-Fi. **Directions:** Please contact us for directions. **Bedrooms:** 2 single, 3 double, 2 twin **Open:** All year

Need more information?

Visit our new 2014 guide websites for detailed information, up-to-date availability and to book your accommodation online. Includes over 20,000 places to stay, all of them star rated.

www.visitor-guides.co.uk

CRESSBROOK, Derbyshire *Map ref 4B2*   *SatNav SK17 8SY* **B**

B&B PER ROOM PER NIGHT
S: £50.00 - £75.00
D: £100.00 - £120.00

Cressbrook Hall

Cressbrook, Buxton SK17 8SY **T:** (01298) 871289 **F:** (01298) 871845
E: stay@cressbrookhall.co.uk
W: cressbrookhall.co.uk

Accommodation with a difference. Enjoy this magnificent home built in 1835, set in 23 acres. Spectacular views around the compass. Elegance, simplicity, peace and quiet. Formal gardens by Edward Kemp. **Directions:** Please contact us for directions. **Bedrooms:** 2 double, 1 suite **Open:** All year except Christmas and New Year

Site: ❀ P Payment: 💷 Leisure: ♪ Property: 🖥 Children: 🐾 🖾 🔥 Room: 🍴 🐾 📺 🍴 🛏 🏊

HIGH PEAK, Derbyshire *Map ref 4B2*   *SatNav SK23 6EJ* **B**

B&B PER ROOM PER NIGHT
S: £69.00 - £75.00
D: £79.00 - £95.00
EVENING MEAL PER PERSON
£8.00 - £19.00

The Old Hall Inn

Whitehough, Chinley, High Peak SK23 6EJ **T:** (01663) 750529 **E:** info@old-hall-inn.co.uk
W: www.old-hall-inn.co.uk **£ BOOK ONLINE**

The Old Hall Inn is the quintessential country inn offering a famously warm welcome, excellent local produce menu & with a strong local trade all year round making for a great lively atmosphere any time of the year. The Old Hall has been voted Derbyshire Pub of the Year and have won the Great British Pub Awards for 'Best Cask Pub in the East Midlands' for the last four years running.

Directions: Please contact us for directions.

Bedrooms: With eight en suites including a large room with balcony overlooking the garden, we have accommodation choices to suit everyone!
Open: All year

Site: ❀ P Payment: 💷 Property: 🖥 ⌀ Children: 🖾 🔥 Catering: 🍴 ♟ 🍴 Room: 🍴 🐾 📺

Pear Tree Farm Guest House

Pear Tree Farm, Lea Main Road, Lea Bridge, Cromford, Matlock, Derbyshire DE4 5JN
T: (01629) 534215 **E:** sue@derbyshirearts.co.uk
W: derbyshirearts.co.uk **£ BOOK ONLINE**

B&B PER ROOM PER NIGHT
S: £50.00 - £60.00
D: £75.00 - £85.00

EVENING MEAL PER PERSON
£15.00 - £25.00

SPECIAL PROMOTIONS
Special discount for groups (hire of studio available) please telephone 01629 534215 for bespoke quotation.

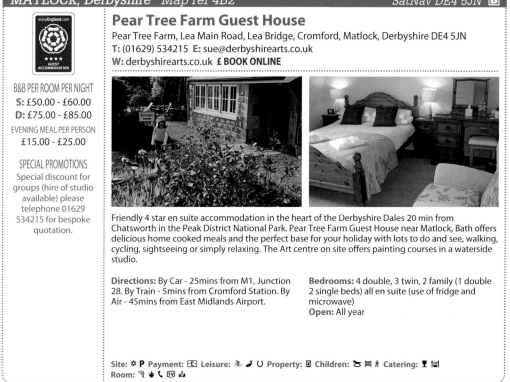

Friendly 4 star en suite accommodation in the heart of the Derbyshire Dales 20 min from Chatsworth in the Peak District National Park. Pear Tree Farm Guest House near Matlock, Bath offers delicious home cooked meals and the perfect base for your holiday with lots to do and see, walking, cycling, sightseeing or simply relaxing. The Art centre on site offers painting courses in a waterside studio.

Directions: By Car - 25mins from M1, Junction 28. By Train - 5mins from Cromford Station. By Air - 45mins from East Midlands Airport.

Bedrooms: 4 double, 3 twin, 2 family (1 double 2 single beds) all en suite (use of fridge and microwave)
Open: All year

Site: ✿ P **Payment:** 💷 **Leisure:** 🏊 ⚓ ☂ **Property:** 🏠 **Children:** 🛝 🛏 🚸 **Catering:** 🍷 🍴
Room: 🗝 🛁 ☎ 📺 📶

Looking for something else?

The official and most comprehensive guide to independently inspected, star rated accommodation.

B&Bs and Hotels - B&Bs, Hotels, farmhouses, inns, serviced apartments, campus and hostel accommodation in England.

Self Catering - Self-catering holiday homes, approved caravan holiday homes, boat accommodation and holiday cottage agencies in England.

Camping, Touring and Holiday Parks - Touring parks, camping holidays and holiday parks and villages in Britain.

Now available in all good bookshops and online at **www.hudsons.co.uk/shop**

OFFICIAL TOURIST BOARD GUIDE
New 39th edition

Self Cateri...
England's star-rated holiday h...
2014
www.visitor-guides.co.uk

OFFICIAL TOURIST BOARD GUIDE
New 39th edition

B&Bs and Hotels
England's star-rated guest accommodation
2014
www.visitor-guides.co.uk

OFFICIAL...
New 39th edition

Camping, Touring & Holiday Parks
Britain's star-rated holiday parks
2014
www.visitor-guides.co.uk

MATLOCK BATH, Derbyshire Map ref 4B2 SatNav DE4 3NS **B**

Ashdale Guest House

92 North Parade, Matlock Bath, Matlock DE4 3NS **T:** (01629) 57826
E: ashdale@matlockbath.fsnet.co.uk
W: www.ashdaleguesthouse.co.uk

B&B PER ROOM PER NIGHT
S: £40.00 - £50.00
D: £65.00 - £80.00

A Grade II Listed Victorian villa situated in the centre of Matlock Bath. Large, comfortable rooms, level walking to restaurants, pubs, museums and station. Home-made bread and marmalade. **Directions:** Centre of Matlock Bath, opposite The Jubilee Bridge. **Bedrooms:** 1 double, 3 family (2-5 persons) **Open:** All year

Site: ✿ **P** Payment: 💷 € Leisure: 🚴 ♪ ⏸ ∪ Property: 🐕 🖥 Children: 🌝 🎮 🏕 Catering: 🍴 Room: 🍵 💧 📺 ♨

LOUGHBOROUGH, Leicestershire Map ref 4C3 SatNav LE11 3GR **H**

Burleigh Court Conference Centre & Hotel

Loughborough University, Loughborough, Leicestershire LE11 3GR **T:** (01509) 211515
F: (01509) 211569 **E:** info@welcometoimago.com
W: www.welcometoimago.com **£ BOOK ONLINE**

B&B PER ROOM PER NIGHT
S: £65.00 - £110.00
D: £75.00 - £115.00
EVENING MEAL PER PERSON
£22.50

Burleigh Court offers 4 star accommodation ranging from the last word in luxury to unmatched quality and value, award winning cuisine and an on-site spa and leisure complex. **Directions:** Situated in the Midlands off junction 23 of the M1 motorway, 3 miles from Loughborough's mainline railway station and 8 miles from East Midlands Airport. **Bedrooms:** 40 single, 159 dble, 19 twin, 4 family, 4 suite. **Open:** All year, except for Christmas.

Payment: 💷 Leisure: 🎯 ⛳ 🏊 ‍ Property: ⚓ 🚆 🖥 🅿 ⏻ Children: 🌝 🎮 🏕 Catering: 🍴 🍷 🍴 Room: 🍵 💧 📞 📷 📺 ♨

BARKSTON, Lincolnshire Map ref 3A1 SatNav NG32 2NL **B**

Kelling House

17 West Street, Barkston, Nr Grantham NG32 2NL **T:** (01400) 251440
E: sue@kellinghouse.co.uk
W: www.kellinghouse.co.uk

B&B PER ROOM PER NIGHT
S: £45.00 - £55.00
D: £80.00 - £95.00
EVENING MEAL PER PERSON
£18.00 - £25.00

In quiet conservation village. C18th cottage with large South facing garden & serving locally sourced food. Perfectly placed to explore Belton House, Belvoir Castle, Burghley House, Lincoln Cathedral, etc **Directions:** A1/Grantham train station 4 miles. **Bedrooms:** 1 single, 1 double, 1 twin **Open:** All year

Site: ✿ **P** Payment: € Leisure: ♪ ⏸ ∪ Property: 🐕 🖥 🅿 🆔 ⌀ Children: 🌝 Catering: 🍴 🍴 Room: 🍵 💧 📺

BICKER, Lincolnshire   Map ref 3A1

SatNav PE20 3AN   **H**

★★★
HOTEL

B&B PER ROOM PER NIGHT
S: £59.50 - £69.50
D: £59.50 - £78.00
EVENING MEAL PER PERSON
£12.00 - £25.00

Supreme Inns
Bicker Bar, Bicker, Boston PE20 3AN   **T:** (01205) 822804   **E:** enquiries@supremeinns.co.uk
W: www.supremeinns.co.uk   **£ BOOK ONLINE**

Situated in Bicker Bar near Boston in Lincolnshire, the Boston Supreme Inn hotel has 55 large and
well equipped bedrooms all with en suite facilities. All rooms have internet access, telephone
points, flat screen televisions. We have a modern, relaxing bar area, serving homemade bar meals
all day, every day.

Directions: Located on the junction between
the A17/A52.

Bedrooms: 32 dble, 21 twin, 2 suite
Open: All year

Site: ❀ Payment: 🔳 Leisure: ♪ ► Property: ♥ 🖥 🅱 ◐ Children: 🛏 ♿ ♣ Catering: 🍽 🍴
Room: 📶 👄 📞 🎧 📺 🔌

CRANWELL, Lincolnshire   Map ref 3A1

SatNav NG34 8EY   **B**

★★★
BED & BREAKFAST

B&B PER ROOM PER NIGHT
S: £30.00
D: £60.00
EVENING MEAL PER PERSON
£6.50 - £15.00

Byards Leap Bed & Breakfast
Byards Leap Cottage, Cranwell, Lincolnshire NG34 8EY   **T:** (01400) 261537
E: byardsleapcottage@gmail.com
W: byardsleapcottage.co.uk

Comfortable cottage in beautiful gardens, on Viking Way long
distance footpath. Good home cooking using local and home
grown produce. Convenient for Lincoln, Grantham, Sleaford and
RAF Cranwell. **Directions:** Situated off A17 opposite junction with
B6403. If using SAT navigation please phone for final advice.
Bedrooms: 1 double, 1 twin **Open:** All year except Christmas

Site: ❀ P Leisure: ♪ Property: 🖥 Children: 🛏 ♿ ♣ Catering: 🍴 Room: 📶 👄 📺

CRANWELL, Lincolnshire   Map ref 3A1

SatNav NG34 8EY   **B**

★★★★
GUEST
ACCOMMODATION

Silver
AWARD

B&B PER ROOM PER NIGHT
S: £60.00 - £69.50
D: £65.00 - £69.50

Byards Leap Lodge and Country Kitchen
Byards Leap, Cranwell, Sleaford, Lincs NG34 8EY   **T:** (01400) 261375 / 07957885913
F: (01400) 262738   **E:** byards.leap@virgin.net
W: byards-leap-lodge.co.uk

Whether on leisure or business, you will find the hospitality of our
Country Kitchen and Lodge just as warm as it was in the times of
Bayard and Old Meg. RAF Cranwell just 1 minute away by car. For
Apartments, please contact us for prices. **Directions:** Situated on
the Viking long distance footpath, 2 minutes from RAF Cranwell.
Twenty minutes to city of Lincoln and central for many locations.
Bedrooms: 3 double, 2 twin, Apartments in Sleaford also available
Open: All year except Christmas

Site: ❀ P Payment: 🔳 Leisure: ♪ ► ♺ Property: 🐕 🖥 Catering: 🍽 🍴 Room: 📶 👄 📞 🎧
📺 🔌

GRANTHAM, Lincolnshire Map ref 3A1 SatNav NG32 1DL B

The Cedars

Low Road, Barrowby, Grantham, Lincolnshire NG32 1DL **T:** (01476) 563400
E: pbcbennett@mac.com

enjoyEngland.com ★★★★ BED & BREAKFAST

B&B PER ROOM PER NIGHT
S: £35.00 - £45.00
D: £70.00 - £80.00
EVENING MEAL PER PERSON
£12.50 - £15.00

Enjoy the relaxed atmosphere of this Grade II Listed farmhouse and gardens. Delicious breakfasts, and evening meals if required, using our own, and local fresh produce. Italian cuisine a speciality. Five minute drive from A1 motorway, two miles from Grantham mainline station. French and Italian spoken.

Directions: A1 North Sign says Nottingham A52 Barrowby. A1 South sign Grantham A52 Barrowby take Low Road Cedars on right free standing Farm House Gravelled Yard

Bedrooms: 1 double, 1 twin
Open: All year except Christmas and New Year

Site: **P** **Payment:** € **Leisure:** **Property:** **Children:** **Catering:** **Room:**

GRANTHAM, Lincolnshire Map ref 3A1 SatNav NG13 0FD B

Glebe House Muston

Glebe House, 26 Church Lane, Muston, Nottingham NG13 0FD **T:** (01949) 842993
E: glebehouse@glebehousemuston.co.uk
W: www.glebehousemuston.co.uk **£ BOOK ONLINE**

enjoyEngland.com ★★★★ BED & BREAKFAST
enjoyEngland.com Gold AWARD

B&B PER ROOM PER NIGHT
S: £60.00 - £75.00
D: £90.00 - £120.00
EVENING MEAL PER PERSON
£20.00 - £30.00

This fine Georgian house, a former rectory, lies in 16 acres of parkland in the tranquil Vale of Belvoir. Glebe House is a spacious, comfortable home with every modern convenience, wi-fi etc, yet it retains all its original 18C architectural details along with period furniture, four-poster beds, log fires and grand reception rooms.

Directions: From Al near Grantham take A52 towards Nottingham for 4 miles. After Leicestershire sign turn left at The Gap Inn (sign post Muston). Glebe House is 300 yds down the road on the left by the lamp post.

Bedrooms: Two en suite double bedrooms, and option of either a twin or further four-poster with private bathroom. Wi-fi, TVs, hairdryer and Tea/coffee facilities.
Open: Open All Year

Site: **P** **Payment:** € **Property:** **Children:** **Catering:**
Room:

LINCOLN, Lincolnshire   Map ref 4C2   SatNav LN5 9EF   B

Wheelwrights Cottage B&B

Wheelwrights Cottage, Haddington, Nr Aubourn, Lincoln LN5 9EF   **T:** (01522) 788154
E: dawn.dunning2@btopenworld.com
W: www.wheelwrightsbnb.co.uk

B&B PER ROOM PER NIGHT
S: £43.00 - £45.00
D: £56.00 - £58.00

Delightful country cottage in a small hamlet just south of Lincoln. Ideally situated to visit Lincoln & Newark. Approx. 2 miles off A46. A warm welcome with tea/coffee and homemade cake on arrival. **Directions:** Off A46, follow signs to Haddington. Over brow of hill, take 1st left. Enter village, round double bend. We are 1st on right past turn to Baileys Lane. **Bedrooms:** Double with en suite shower. Twin with bathroom **Open:** All year except Christmas and New Year.

Site: ✿ **P** Property: ▦ ♛ Children: ✿6 Catering: ⛽ Room: ☜ 🖊 📺 🍴

RUSKINGTON, Lincolnshire   Map ref 3A1   SatNav NG34 9AH   B

Sunnyside Farm Bed & Breakfast

Leasingham Lane, Ruskington NG34 9AH   **T:** (01526) 833010
E: sunnyside_farm@btinternet.com
W: sunnysidefarm.co.uk

B&B PER ROOM PER NIGHT
S: £30.00
D: £60.00

A family-run farmhouse with en suite guest bedrooms. Warm, friendly welcome. Local golf courses. Coast 40 miles. Boston, Grantham, Lincoln, Newark all within easy reach. **Directions:** From A17, take A153 towards Ruskington, B1188 into village. Left at mini roundabout, 400m turn left into Leasingham Lane, follow road 500m to Sunnyside Farm **Bedrooms:** 1 double, 1 twin **Open:** All year

Site: ✿ **P** Payment: € Leisure: ♪ ▶ Property: 🐾 ▦ ☐ ♛ Children: ✿ ▦ ♿ Catering: ⛽ Room: ☜ 🖊 📺 🚳

Looking for something else?

The official and most comprehensive guide to independently inspected, star rated accommodation.

B&Bs and Hotels - B&Bs, Hotels, farmhouses, inns, serviced apartments, campus and hostel accommodation in England.

Self Catering - Self-catering holiday homes, approved caravan holiday homes, boat accommodation and holiday cottage agencies in England.

Camping, Touring and Holiday Parks - Touring parks, camping holidays and holiday parks and villages in Britain.

Now available in all good bookshops and online at **www.hudsons.co.uk/shop**

SKEGNESS, Lincolnshire Map ref 4D2
SatNav PE25 2LA H

B&B PER ROOM PER NIGHT
D: £49.00 - £149.00

Southview Park Hotel
Burgh Road, Skegness PE25 2LA **T:** (01754) 896060 **F:** (01754) 896061
E: reception.southviewparkhotel@park-resorts.com
W: www.southviewparkhotel.co.uk **£ BOOK ONLINE**

A hotel where the emphasis is on style, comfort and, above all, relaxation. The hotel offers superior-quality accommodation, food and facilities. All bedrooms are en suite and have TV, internet access, telephone, ironing centre, safe and tea/coffee facilities. One restaurant, two bars, and much, much more. Visit our website to see all the tribute nights at the hotel.

Directions: On the A158, 2 miles from Skegness town centre.

Bedrooms: 24 double, 10 twin, 10 king, 2 family suites, 4 disabled twins, 4 superior doubles, 8 suite.
Open: All year

Site: ✿ Payment: 🖃 Leisure: ♪ ► ✕ ♜ Property: ♟ 🚲 ● Children: 🛏 🗮 ★ Catering: ♟ 🍴
Room: ℺ ♨ ☎ 📺 🛁 🖨

SKEGNESS, Lincolnshire Map ref 4D2
SatNav PE25 2TY B

B&B PER ROOM PER NIGHT
D: £48.00 - £54.00

EVENING MEAL PER PERSON
£7.00 - £11.00

Stepping Stones
4 Castleton Boulevard, Skegness PE25 2TY **T:** (01754) 765092
E: info@stepping-stones-hotel.co.uk
W: stepping-stones-hotel.co.uk **£ BOOK ONLINE**

Small and friendly we are 50yards from the prom and all its attractions, including Natureland, bowling greens and the theatre. Within walking distance of town centre. Breakfast menu. **Directions:** A158 head straight through all lights towards sea. A52 south turn L. at Ship Inn. A52 north, 2nd right (Scarborough Ave.) until pier, left, left. **Bedrooms:** 3 double, 1 twin, 2 family **Open:** All year except Christmas

Site: **P** Payment: 🖃 Children: 🛏 🗮 ★ Catering: ♟ 🍴 Room: ℺ ♨ 📺 🛁

TOFT, Lincolnshire Map ref 3A1
SatNav PE10 0JU H

B&B PER ROOM PER NIGHT
S: £65.00
D: £90.00

Toft Country House Hotel
Toft, Bourne, Lincolnshire PE10 0JT **T:** (01778) 590614 **E:** tofthouse@btconnect.com
W: www.tofthotelgolf.co.uk **£ BOOK ONLINE**

A lovely restored hotel from an original stone farmhouse retaining original features, stone walls & beams; 20 en suite bedrooms, with flat screen TVs, tea/coffee making facilities & telephones; 12 bedrooms on ground floor courtyard, for easy access; 18 hole golf course/driving range. On site hairdresser/beauty therapist. **Directions:** On the A6121 between Stamford & Bourne, in the village of Toft. Nearest airport East Midlands. **Bedrooms:** 2 single, 6 double, 7 twin, 4 family, 1 suite **Open:** All year

Site: ✿ **P** Payment: 🖃 Leisure: ► ✗ Property: ♟ 🐕 🚲 🖥 📮 ⊘ Children: 🛏 🗮 ★ Catering: (✗ ♟ 🍴
Room: ℺ ♨ ☎ 📺 🛁

Petwood Hotel

Stixwould Road, Woodhall Spa LN10 6QG **T:** (01526) 352411 **F:** (01526) 353473
E: reception@petwood.co.uk
W: www.petwood.co.uk **£ BOOK ONLINE**

HOTEL

B&B PER ROOM PER NIGHT
S: £70.00
D: £100.00 - £135.00

SPECIAL PROMOTIONS
Book 2 nights Dinner, B&B and get the third night B&B free valid Sunday to Thursday.

Friendly service, excellent food and a perfect location for exploring Lincolnshire. Enjoy stunning gardens, cosy log fires and a historical setting linked to the 'Dambusters'. Mid-week special offers available.

Directions: From Lincoln take the A15 south to Metheringham (from Sleaford take the A15 north to Metheringham) then take the B1191 to Woodhall Spa. Upon entering Woodhall Spa, continue to the roundabout and turn left (Petwood Hotel is signposted). The hotel is situated 500m on the right.

Bedrooms: 6 singles, 21 doubles, 13 twins, 10 executives, 3 four posters. Half board prices (per room per night) singles £95, doubles £150-£185
Open: All year

Site: ✿ **P** **Payment:** 🖃 **Leisure:** 🎿 ♩ ▶ ∪ ⋈ ⚲ **Property:** ⊛ ☂ 🐾 🖵 🗄 ♫ ❶ ⌀ **Children:** ⛱ 🏠 ☗
Catering: (✗ ☂ 🍴 **Room:** 🖳 ♨ ☎ ▣ TV 🖴 🖃

Village Limits Country Pub, Restaurant & Motel

Stixwould Road, Woodhall Spa, Lincolnshire LN10 6UJ **T:** (01526) 353312
E: info@villagelimits.co.uk
W: villagelimits.co.uk **£ BOOK ONLINE**

GUEST ACCOMMODATION

Silver AWARD

B&B PER ROOM PER NIGHT
S: £46.00 - £55.00
D: £70.00 - £85.00
EVENING MEAL PER PERSON
£8.50 - £22.00

Select Lincolnshire Food & Accommodation Winners 2006-2013. Free WiFi throughout. All rooms en suite with hairdryers & Sealy mattresses. Peaceful location. Air-conditioning in bar. Delicious, home-cooked pub food available. Ample parking. **Directions:** On Stixwould Road, next to Woodhall Country Park. 500m past Petwood Hotel. 1 mile to Woodhall Spa centre. 1.5 miles to Woodhall Spa Golf Club. **Bedrooms:** 8 twin **Open:** Open all year except New Year

Site: ✿ **P** **Payment:** 🖃 **Property:** 🖵 **Children:** ⛱ 🏠 **Catering:** (✗ ☂ 🍴 **Room:** 🖳 ♨ TV 🖴

Crockwell Farm

Crockwell Farm, Eydon, Daventry NN11 3QA **T:** (01327) 361358 **F:** (01327) 361573
E: info@crockwellfarm.co.uk
W: www.crockwellfarm.co.uk

FARMHOUSE

B&B PER ROOM PER NIGHT
S: £50.00 - £60.00
D: £90.00 - £100.00

Beautiful 18th century ironstone farmhouse and self-contained cottages in idyllic rural setting. Delicious breakfasts served in the farmhouse. Ideal for local attractions & walking. Great pub approximately one mile away. **Directions:** South Northamptonshire halfway between villages of Canons Ashby & Eydon. See website for detailed directions. **Bedrooms:** 3 twin, 4 family **Open:** All year

Site: ✿ **P** **Payment:** 🖃 **Leisure:** ♩ ▶ ∪ **Property:** 🖵 🗄 **Children:** ⛱ 🏠 ☗ **Room:** 🖳 ♨ ① ▣ TV 🖴 🖃 ⏻

NEWARK, Nottinghamshire Map ref 4C2 SatNav NG24 1RZ [H]

The Grange Hotel

73 London Road, Newark NG24 1RZ **T:** (01636) 703399 **F:** (01636) 702328
E: info@thegrangenewark.co.uk
W: grangenewark.co.uk **£ BOOK ONLINE**

B&B PER ROOM PER NIGHT
S: £85.00 - £120.00
D: £120.00 - £165.00
HB PER PERSON PER NIGHT
£85.00 - £115.00

SPECIAL PROMOTIONS
Weekend breaks: DB&B
£85-£115pppn,
minimum 2 nights,
based on sharing twin/
double bedroom.
Subject to availability.

Stylish Victorian hotel with tranquil landscaped gardens, sympathetically refurbished, retaining many of its original features. Located in a quiet residential area less than one mile from the town centre, it is owned and personally managed by Tom and Sandra Carr who will offer you a warm welcome and attentive service.

Directions: Hotel approx 2 miles from A1 (follow Newark signs, through village of Balderton). Hotel approximately 1 mile from town centre (follow signs for Balderton/Grantham).

Bedrooms: 3 single, 13 dble, 3 twin. All rooms en suite
Open: All year except Christmas and New Year

Site: ✿ Leisure: ♪ Property: 🖨 🅐 Children: 🛏 🍴 ☂ Catering: 🍷 🍽 Room: 🗝 🔌 ☎ 📺 🍳

BARNSDALE, Rutland Map ref 3A1 SatNav LE15 8AB [H]

Barnsdale Hall Hotel

Stamford Road, Barnsdale, Oakham LE15 8AB **T:** (01572) 757901 **F:** (01572) 756235
E: reception@barnsdalehotel.co.uk
W: http://www.barnsdalehotel.co.uk **£ BOOK ONLINE**

B&B PER ROOM PER NIGHT
S: £65.00 - £180.00
D: £65.00 - £550.00
EVENING MEAL PER PERSON
£12.00 - £40.00

SPECIAL PROMOTIONS
Lunch Menu 2 courses
for £12.50. Sunday
Carvery £15.95 per
person

With this unique setting, personal charm, character, and friendly but attentive personnel, Barnsdale Hall Hotel is the perfect venue whatever your occasion may be. Extensive spa and leisure facilities makes it a haven in which to retreat, relax and unwind. With its breathtaking views of Rutland Water where better to hold your wedding reception, corporate event, or a romantic getaway for two.

Directions: Please contact us for directions.

Bedrooms: All rooms have Tea/Coffee making facilities. Free Wifi, Iron, Ironing board and hairdryer. Some rooms can be made as twins please contact reception
Open: All year

Barnsdale Lodge Hotel

The Avenue, Rutland Water, Oakham LE15 8AH **T:** (01572) 724678 **F:** (01572) 724961
E: reception@barnsdalelodge.co.uk
W: www.barnsdalelodge.co.uk

SPECIAL PROMOTIONS
Special promotions
always available,
please see our website
for full details.

Enjoy a relaxing break on the beautiful north shore of Rutland Water. We offer you anything from a wedding to an intimate dinner for two. Our informal dining areas are reflected in our seasonal bistro menu. Our bedrooms are all comfortably and individually decorated and have garden or countryside views.

Directions: Please see our website for map and full directions.

Bedrooms: 7 single, 27 double, 9 twin, 1 family
Open: All year

Site: ✿ Payment: 📧 Leisure: ♿ ✈ ♪ ⋔ ⋃ ⽳ Property: ♟ 🐕 🚪 📼 ⏣ ◑ Children: 🛏 🏛 ⚲ Catering: ♟ 🍽
Room: 🧰 🛁 📞 📷 📺 🎛 🗄

Visit our 2014 guide websites...

- Detailed information
- Up-to-date availability
- Book your accommodation online

Includes over 20,000
places to stay,
all of them star rated.

Win amazing prizes,
every month...

Enter our monthly competition at
www.visitor-guides.co.uk/prizes

Heart of England

Herefordshire, Shropshire, Staffordshire, Warwickshire, West Midlands, Worcestershire

Take time to visit the Cotswolds – beautiful countryside dotted with honey-coloured villages with limestone cottages – or soak up the stunning landscape of the Malvern hills. Discover places that inspired the likes of Tolkien, George Eliot and William Shakespeare. There's also a wide selection of ancient and modern cathedrals and historic houses to visit. Birmingham has recently undergone substantial regeneration and offers a world-class cultural scene as well as superb shopping - an ideal location to explore the region… and don't forget the Jewellery Quarter and Cadbury's Bournville.

Highlights

Birmingham

With a fantastic network of transport links to the rest of the country, Birmingham is a cosmopolitan, bustling city. The city played a central role in the West Midlands' transport manufacturing heritage.

Cotswolds

The Cotswolds area is one of England's favourite destinations – famous for hundreds of honey-colour limestone villages in a beautiful rural setting.

Ironbridge Gorge

From mines to railway lines, Ironbridge is a symbol of the Industrial Revolution. The blast furnace of Coalbrookdale is a reminder of the discovery of coke while the bridge was the first to be built from iron.

Malvern Hills

The Malvern Hills have been described as a mountain range in miniature; the eight mile ridge contains some of the oldest rocks in Britain and their craggy outline is reminiscent of the uplands further west into Wales.

Potteries

At the Potteries Museum and Art Gallery, Stoke-on-Trent, you can travel back in time and discover the area's history and view the world's greatest collection of Staffordshire ceramics.

Stratford-upon-Avon

Stratford-upon-Avon is world famous as the birthplace of William Shakespeare and one of the country's leading heritage places to visit. It is home to the Royal Shakespeare Company and Theatre.

Worcester Cathedral

Before the English Reformation it was known as Worcester Priory. Today it's an Anglican cathedral situated on a bank overlooking the River Severn.

Editor's Picks

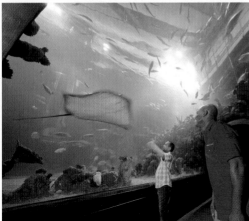

Go back in time

Immerse yourself in a thousand years of jaw-dropping history at Warwick Castle. The castle promises an experience where ancient myths and spell-binding tales will set your imagination.

Have an undersea experience

At Birmingham's National Sea Life Centre, you can walk through a glass tunnel surrounded by an enormous ocean tank where giant turtles, sharks and tropical reef fish swim inches from your head.

Discover the history of iron

It was at Ironbridge in Shropshire that first large scale production of cast iron was developed using a process pioneered by Abraham Darby. Find out more by visiting one of the many museums.

Taste the chocolate

Experience the magic, making and history of confectionery at Cadbury World in Birmingham.

Put on your walking boots

The Cotswolds Area of Outstanding Natural Beauty spans nearly 800 square miles and contains many outstanding walking trails and footpaths.

Things to do

Entertainment & Culture

Barber Institute of Fine Arts
Edgbaston, West Midlands B15 2TS
(0121) 414 7333
www.barber.org.uk
British and European paintings, drawings and sculpture from the 13th century to mid 20th century.

Black Country Living Museum
Dudley, West Midlands DY1 4SQ
(0121) 557 9643
www.bclm.co.uk
A warm welcome awaits you at Britain's friendliest open-air museum. Wander around original shops and houses, ride on fair attractions, take a look down the underground coalmine.

Cadbury World
Bournville, West Midlands B30 2LU
0845 450 3599
www.cadburyworld.co.uk
Story of Cadbury's chocolate includes chocolate-making demonstration and attractions for all ages, with free samples, free parking, shop and restaurant. Phone to check availability and reserve admission.

Compton Verney
Stratford-upon-Avon CV35 9HZ
(01926) 645500
www.comptonverney.org.uk
Award-winning art gallery housed in a grade I listed Robert Adam mansion.

Etruria Industrial Museum
Staffordshire ST4 7AF
(01782) 233144
www.stoke.gov.uk/museum
Discover how they put the 'bone' in bone china at the last working steam-powered potters mill in Britain. Includes a Bone and Flint Mill and family-friendly interactive exhibition.

Hereford Museum and Art Gallery
Herefordshire HR4 9AU
(01432) 260692
www.herefordshire.gov.uk/leisure/museums_
galleries/2869.asp
In the museum, aspects of Herefordshire history and life - in the Gallery, regularly changing exhibitions of paintings, photography and crafts.

Ledbury Heritage Centre
Herefordshire, HR8 1DN
(01432) 260692
www.herefordshire.gov.uk/leisure/museums_
galleries/2861.asp
The story of Ledbury's past displayed in a timber-framed building in the picturesque lane leading to the church.

Royal Air Force Museum Cosford
Shifnal, Shropshire TF11 8UP
(01902) 376200
www.rafmuseum.org
FREE Admission. The award winning museum houses one of the largest aviation collections in the United Kingdom.

Rugby Art Gallery and Museum
Warwickshire CV21 3BZ
(01788) 533201
www.ragm.org.uk
Contemporary art & craft exhibitions; museum showcasing the Tripontium Collection of Roman artefacts & Rugby's Social History; the Rugby Collection of 20th century & contemporary British art (annually); fun activities for children/families.

Thinktank-Birmingham Science Museum
West Midlands B4 7XG
(0121) 202 2222
www.thinktank.ac
Thinktank is Birmingham's science museum where the emphasis is firmly on hands on exhibits and interactive fun.

Wolverhampton Art Gallery
West Midlands WV1 1DU
(01902) 552055
www.wolverhamptonart.org.uk
Explore 300 years of art in this newly refurbished city centre gallery.

Worcester City Art Gallery & Museum
Worcestershire WR1 1DT
(01905) 25371
www.worcestercitymuseums.org.uk
The art gallery & museum runs a programme of exhibitions/events for all the family. Explore the fascinating displays, exhibitions, cafe, shop and Worcestershire Soldier Galleries.

Family Fun

Aerial Extreme Trentham
Staffordshire ST4 8AX
0845 652 1736
www.aerialextreme.co.uk/index.php/courses/
trentham-estate
Our tree based adventure ropes course, set within the tranquil grounds of Trentham Estate is a truly spectacular journey.

Enginuity
Telford, Shropshire TF8 7DG
(01952) 433424
www.ironbridge.org.uk
At Enginuity you can turn the wheels of your imagination, test your horse power and discover how good ideas are turned in to real things.

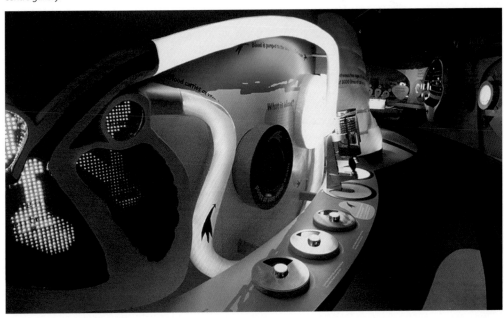

Heritage

Coventry Cathedral - St Michael's
West Midlands CV1 5AB
(024) 7652 1257
www.coventrycathedral.org.uk
Glorious 20th century Cathedral, with stunning 1950's art & architecture, rising above the stark ruins of the medieval Cathedral destroyed by German air raids in 1940.

Darby Houses (Ironbridge)
Telford, Shropshire TF8 7EW
(01952) 433424
www.ironbridge.org.uk
In the Darby houses, Dale House and Rosehill House, you can delve in to the everyday life of Quaker families.

Eastnor Castle
Ledbury, Herefordshire HR8 1RL
(01531) 633160
www.eastnorcastle.com
Fairytale Georgian Castle dramatically situated in the Malvern Hills.

Goodrich Castle
Ross-on-Wye, Herefordshire HR9 6HY
(01600) 890538
www.english-heritage.org.uk/goodrich
Come and relive the turbulent history of Goodrich Castle with our free audio and then climb to the battlements for breathtaking views over the Wye Valley.

Hanbury Hall
Droitwich Spa, Worcestershire WR9 7EA
(01527) 821214
www.nationaltrust.org.uk/hanburyhall
Early 18th century house, garden & park owned by the Vernon family for nearly 300 years.

Hereford Cathedral
Herefordshire HR1 2NG
(01432) 374202
www.herefordcathedral.org
Hereford Cathedral contains some of the finest examples of architecture from Norman times to the present day.

Iron Bridge and Toll House
Telford, Shropshire TF8 7DG
(01952) 433424
www.ironbridge.org.uk
You can peer through its railings and conjure a vision of sailing vessels heading downstream towards Bristol and the markets of the world.

Kenilworth Castle and Elizabethan Garden
Warwickshire CV8 1NE
(01926) 852078
www.english-heritage.org.uk/kenilworth
One of the most spectacular castle ruins in England.

Lichfield Cathedral
Staffordshire WS13 7LD
(01543) 306100
www.lichfield-cathedral.org
A medieval Cathedral with 3 spires in the heart of an historic City set in its own serene Close.

Much Wenlock Priory
Shropshire TF13 6HS
(01952) 727466
www.english-heritage.org.uk/wenlockpriory
Wenlock Priory, with it's stunning clipped topiary, has a pastoral setting on the edge of lovely Much Wenlock

National Memorial Arboretum
Lichfield, Staffordshire DE13 7AR
(01283) 792333
www.thenma.org.uk
150 acres of trees and memorials, planted as a living tribute to those who have served, died or suffered in the service of their Country.

Packwood House
Solihull, Warwickshire B94 6AT
0844 800 1895
www.nationaltrust.org.uk/main/w-packwoodhouse
Restored tudor house, park and garden with notable topiary.

Ragley Hall
Stratford-upon-Avon, Warwickshire B49 5NJ
(01789) 762090
www.ragleyhall.com
Ragley Hall is set in 27 acres of beautiful formal gardens

Severn Valley Railway
Bewdley, Worcestershire DY12 1BG
(01299) 403816
www.svr.co.uk
Steam-hauled trains running along the beautiful Severn Valley from Kidderminster - Bridgnorth.

Stokesay Castle
Craven Arms, Shropshire SY7 9AH
(01588) 672544
www.english-heritage.org.uk/stokesaycastle
Stokesay Castle, nestles in peaceful South Shropshire countryside near the Welsh Border. It is one of more than a dozen English Heritage properties in the county.

Tamworth Castle
Staffordshire B79 7NA
(01827) 709629
www.tamworthcastle.co.uk
The number one Heritage attraction located in the town. Explore over 900 years of history in the magnificent Motte and Bailey Castle.

The Almonry Museum and Heritage Centre
Evesham, Worcestershire WR11 4BG
(01386) 446944
www.almonryevesham.org
The 14th century house has 12 rooms of exhibits from 2000 years of Evesham history and pleasant gardens to the rear.

Warwick Castle
Warwickshire CV34 4QU
0871 265 2000
www.warwick-castle.co.uk
Imagine a totally electrifying, full day out at Britain's ultimate castle.

Wedgwood Visitor Centre
Stoke-on-Trent, Staffordshire ST12 9ER
(01782) 282986
www.wedgwoodvisitorcentre.com
Enjoy the past, buy the present and treasure the experience. The Wedgwood Visitor Centre offers a unique chance to immerse yourself in the heritage of Britain's greatest ceramics company.

Worcester Cathedral
Worcestershire WR1 2LA
(01905) 732900
www.worcestercathedral.co.uk
Worcester Cathedral is one of England's most magnificent and inspiring buildings, a place of prayer and worship for 14 centuries.

Wroxeter Roman City
Shrewsbury, Shropshire SY5 6PH
(01743) 761330
www.english-heritage.org.uk/wroxeter
Wroxeter Roman City, or Viroconium, to give it its Roman title, is thought to have been one of the largest Roman cities in the UK with over 200 acres of land, 2 miles of walls and a population of approximately 5,000.

Nature & Wildlife

Birmingham Botanical Gardens and Glasshouses
Edgbaston, West Midlands B15 3TR
(0121) 454 1860
www.birminghambotanicalgardens.org.uk
15 acres of ornamental gardens and glasshouses.

Cannock Chase
Staffordshire WS15 2UQ
(01543) 877666
www.visitcannockchase.co.uk
Central England's woodland jewel, packed with things to see and do.

Dudley Zoological Gardens
West Midlands DY1 4QB
(01384) 215313
www.dudleyzoo.org.uk
From lions and tigers to snakes and spiders there's something for all ages. Animal feeding, encounters, face painting, land train and fair rides.

Heart Park
Fillongley, Warwickshire CV7 8DX
(01676) 540333
www.heartpark.co.uk
"We believe that the heart of our Park is the beach and lake. But for those of you who'd like to try out a few 'different' activities - we've got a great assortment for you to try."

Hergest Croft Gardens
Kington, Herefordshire HR5 3EG
(01544) 230160
www.hergest.co.uk
The gardens extend over 50 acres, with more than 4000 rare shrubs and trees. With over 60 champion trees and shrubs it is one of the finest collections in the British Isles.

Park Hall - The Countryside Experience
Oswestry, Shropshire SY11 4AS
(01691) 671123
www.parkhallfarm.co.uk
With 40,000 square feet of indoor attractions, regular hands-on animal activities, lots of outdoor play and driving activities there is never a dull moment.

Ryton Pools Country Parks
Coventry, Warwickshire CV8 3BH
(024) 7630 5592
www.warwickshire.gov.uk/parks
The 100 acres of Ryton Pools Country Park are just waiting to be explored. The many different habitats are home to a wide range of birds and other wildlife.

West Midland Safari and Leisure Park
Bewdley, Worcestershire DY12 1LF
(01299) 402114
www.wmsp.co.uk
Fantastic family entertainment for the summer season.

Events 2014

John Smith's Midlands
Grand National
March 15, Uttoxeter Racecourse
Biggest fixture in Uttoxeter's
calendar.
www.uttoxeter-racecourse.co.uk

Shakespeare Birthday
Celebrations
April 26-27, Stratford
In 2014, the birthday celebrations
will mark the 450th anniversary
of Shakespeare's birth. The town's
streets overflow with pageantry,
music and drama and over the three
day birthday period you can enjoy
a packed programme of special
celebratory activities - great days
out at Shakespeare's historic houses,
literary and music events and
amazing theatre.
www.shakespearesbirthday.org.uk

Stratford Literary Festival
April 26-May 4, Stratford
A selection of events and workshops
running throughout the week
featuring an array of writers and
performers, so there is plenty to
keep everyone entertained, whether
you are a budding writer or poet, are
keen to meet favourite authors and
celebrities, or want to be involved
in workshops and creating original
pieces of work.
www.stratfordliteraryfestival.co.uk

The Telegraph Hay Festival
May 22-June 1, Hay-onWye
An annual literature festival held
in Hay-on -Wye
www.hayfestival.com

Staffordshire County Show
May 28-29, Stafford
Agricultural show with all the usual
country show attractions.
www.staffscountyshowground.co.uk

English Haydn Festival
June, Bridgnorth
An array of the music of Joseph
Haydn and his contemporaries,
performed in St. Leonards Church,
Bridgnorth.
www.englishhaydn.com

RAF Cosford Air Show
June 8, Shifnal
The main focus will be the 75th
Anniversary of RAF Cosford and this
will be celebrated both in the air
and on the ground. Other themes
include 75 years since the Spitfire
entered RAF Service and 40 years of
service from the Jaguar aircraft.
www.cosfordairshow.co.uk

Three Counties Show
June 13-15, Malvern
Three jam-packed days of family
entertainment and fun, all in
celebration of the great British
farming world and countryside.
www.threecounties.co.uk

Ludlow Festival
June, dates TBC, Ludlow
Annual Festival of the Arts. The Shakespeare production and Last Night Finale are both staged at Ludlow Castle.
www.ludlowfestival.co.uk

Lichfield Festival
July, dates TBC, Lichfield
Acclaimed arts festival with national and international artists and performers.
www.lichfieldfestival.org

Stratford River Festival
July, dates TBC, Stratford
The highly successful Stratford-upon-Avon River Festival brings the waterways of Stratford alive, with boatloads of family fun, on the first weekend of July.
www.stratfordriverfestival.co.uk

Godiva Festival
July, Coventry
The Godiva Festival is the UK's biggest free family festival held over a weekend in the War Memorial Park, Coventry. The event showcases some of the finest local, national and International artists, live comedy, family entertainment, Godiva Carnival, and lots more.
www.godivafestival.com

Wenlock Olympian Games
July, dates TBC, Much Wenlock
The games that inspired the modern Olympic Movement.
www.wenlock-olympian-society.org.uk

Birmingham International Jazz and Blues Festival
July 18-27, Birmingham
Musicians and fans come to the city from every corner of the UK as well as from further afield and significantly, almost all of the events are free to the public.
www.visitbirmingham.com

Shrewsbury Flower Show
August (mid), Shrewsbury
The world's longest running horticultural whow in Shrewsbury's beautiful 29-acre Quarry Park.
www.shrewsburyflowershow.org.uk

V Festival
August 16-17, Weston Park
Legendary rock and pop festival.
www.vfestival.com

Shrewsbury Folk Festival
August 22-25, Shrewsbury
Shrewsbury Folk Festival has a reputation for delivering the very finest acts from the UK and around the world.
www.shrewsburyfolkfestival.co.uk

Festival of Motoring
August, Stoneleigh
This major event takes place at Stoneleigh Park in Warwickshire. In addition to hundreds of fantastic cars to look at, there will be the traditional historic vehicle 'run' through delightful Warwickshire countryside, car gymkhanas and auto tests.
www.festival-of-motoring.co.uk

Abbots Bromley Horn Dance
September, Abbots Bromley
Ancient ritual dating back to 1226. Six deer-men, a fool, hobby horse, bowman and Maid Marian perform to music provided by a melodian player.
www.abbotsbromley.com

Ludlow Food Festival
September, Ludlow
Featuring more than 160 top quality independent food and drink producers inside Ludlow Castle.
www.foodfestival.co.uk

Artsfest
September, Birmingham
Artsfest is one of the UK's biggest free arts festival and showcases work across the performing arts, visual arts and digital arts genres to promote emerging and established talent.
visitbirmingham.com

Heritage Open Days
September, Coventry
Heritage Open Days celebrate England's architecture and culture by allowing visitors free access to interesting properties that are either not usually open or would normally charge an entrance fee. Heritage Open Days also include tours, events and activities that focus on local architecture and culture.
www.coventry.gov.uk/hod

Moseley Folk Festival
September, Birmingham
The Moseley Folk Festival offers an inner city Shangri-la bringing together people from all ages and backgrounds to witness folk legends playing alongside their contemporaries.
www.visitbirmingham.com

Stone Food & Drink Festival
October, Stone
Staffordshire's biggest celebration of all things gastronomic.
www.stonefooddrink.org.uk

Birmingham Book Festival
October, Birmingham
Celebrating the city's literature scene, the Birmingham Book Festival takes places every year with its trademark mix of literature events, talks and workshops.
www.visitbirmingham.com

Supersonic
October, Birmingham
The Festival is a combination of art, music and film along with other crafts.
www.visitbirmingham.com

Frankfurt Christmas Market & Craft Fair
November-December, Birmingham
The largest authentic German market outside Germany and Austria and the centrepiece of the city's festive event calendar.
www.visitbirmingham.com

Tourist Information Centres

When you arrive at your destination, visit an Official Partner Tourist Information Centre for quality assured help with accommodation and information about local attractions and events, or email your request before you go. To find a Tourist Information Centre visit www.visitengland.com

Bewdley	Load Street	0845 6077819	bewdleytic@wyreforestdc.gov.uk
Birmingham Central Library	Chamberlain Square	0844 888 3883/ 0121 202 5115	visit@marketingbirmingham.com
Bridgnorth	The Library	01746 763257	bridgnorth.tourism@shropshire.gov.uk
Church Stretton	Church Street	01694 723133	churchstretton.scf@shropshire.gov.uk
Coventry Cathedral	St Michael's Tower	024 7622 5616	tic@coventry.gov.uk
Hereford	1 King Street	01432 268430	reception@visitherefordshire.co.uk
Ironbridge	Museum of The Gorge	01952 433424/ 01952 435900	tic@ironbridge.org.uk
Leek	1 Market Place	01538 483741	tourism.services@staffsmoorlands.gov.uk
Lichfield	Lichfield Garrick	01543 412112	info@visitlichfield.com
Ludlow	Castle Street	01584 875053	ludlow.tourism@shropshire.gov.uk
Malvern	21 Church Street	01684 892289	info@visitthemalverns.org
Oswestry (Mile End)	Mile End	01691 662488	oswestrytourism@shropshire.gov.uk
Ross-on-Wye	Market House	01989 562768/ 01432 260675	visitorcentreross@herefordshire.gov.uk
Rugby	Rugby Art Gallery Museum & Library	01788 533217	visitor.centre@rugby.gov.uk
Shrewsbury	Barker Street	01743 281200	visitorinformation@shropshire.gov.uk
Solihull	Central Library	0121 704 6130	artscomplex@solihull.gov.uk
Stafford	Stafford Gatehouse Theatre	01785 619619	tic@staffordbc.gov.uk
Stoke-on-Trent	Victoria Hall, Bagnall Street	01782 236000	stoke.tic@stoke.gov.uk
Stratford-upon-Avon	Bridge Foot	01789 264293	tic@discover-stratford.com
Tamworth	Philip Dix Centre	01827 709581	tic@tamworth.gov.uk
Warwick	The Court House	01926 492212	info@visitwarwick.co.uk
Worcester	The Guildhall	01905 726311/ 01905 722561	touristinfo@visitworcester.com

Regional Contacts and Information

Marketing Birmingham
Tel: 0844 888 3883
Web: www.visitbirmingham.com

Visit Coventy & Warwickshire
Tel: (024) 7622 5616
Web: www.visitcoventryandwarwickshire.co.uk

Visit Herefordshire
Tel: (01432) 268430
Web: www.visitherefordshire.co.uk

Shakespeare Country
Tel: 0871 978 0800
Web: www.shakespeare-country.co.uk

Shropshire Tourism
Tel: (01743) 261919
Web: www.shropshiretourism.co.uk

Destination Staffordshire
Tel: (01785) 277397
Web: www.enjoystaffordshire.com

Stoke-on-Trent
Tel: (01782) 236000
Web: www.visitstoke.co.uk

Destination Worcestershire
Tel: 0845 641 1540
Web: www.visitworcestershire.org

Heart of England
Where to Stay

Entries appear alphabetically by town name in each county. A key to symbols appears on page 7

HEREFORD, Herefordshire   Map ref 2A1   SatNav HR2 7BP   H

Three Counties Hotel

Belmont Road, Hereford HR2 7BP **T:** (01432) 299955 **F:** (01432) 275114
E: enquiries@threecountieshotel.co.uk
W: threecountieshotel.co.uk **£ BOOK ONLINE**

B&B PER ROOM PER NIGHT
S: £69.00 - £85.00
D: £84.00 - £100.00
EVENING MEAL PER PERSON
£14.95 - £35.00

Excellently appointed hotel set in 3.5 acres. Emphasis on traditional, friendly service. Tasteful bedrooms, restaurant and bar offer today's guests all modern comforts. Free Wi-Fi in all public areas and selected bedrooms. Town centre 1.5 miles. **Directions:** Please see website. **Bedrooms:** 18 dble, 42 twin. **Open:** All year

Site: ✿ Payment: 💳 Property: ♟ 🐾 🚗 ◐ Children: ⛱ ♨ 🎿 Catering: 🍷 🍴 Room: 🔌 ☕ ☎ 📺 ⌂

PEMBRIDGE, Herefordshire   Map ref 2A1   SatNav HR6 9JD   B

Lowe Farm B&B

Lowe Farm, Pembridge, Leominster, Herefordshire HR6 9JD **T:** (01544) 388395
E: Juliet@lowe-farm.co.uk
W: www.lowe-farm.co.uk

B&B PER ROOM PER NIGHT
S: £43.00 - £55.00
D: £77.00 - £110.00
EVENING MEAL PER PERSON
£26.00

Juliet & Clive offer stress-free living, relaxation and late breakfasts (8-10am) and a free Hot Tub. Fantastic fresh farm produce and a healthy countryside for the perfect holiday. The farm has been in the Williams family since 1939 and has always offered high standards to meet everyones needs, whilst still keeping a personal and friendly touch. Herefordshire provides a nice place to walk, cycle and relax. **Directions:** Please see website **Bedrooms:** 1 single, 2 double, 2 twin. **Open:** All year except Christmas & New Year

Site: ✿ P Payment: 💳 Leisure: ▶ Property: 🚗 🖥 Catering: 🍴 Room: 🔌 ☕ 📺

ROSS-ON-WYE, Herefordshire   Map ref 2A1   SatNav HR9 5LH   H

The Chase Hotel

Gloucester Road, Ross-on-Wye, Herefordshire HR9 5LH **T:** (01989) 763161
F: (01989) 768330 **E:** res@chasehotel.co.uk
W: chasehotel.co.uk **£ BOOK ONLINE**

B&B PER ROOM PER NIGHT
S: £55.00 - £205.00
D: £75.00 - £205.00
EVENING MEAL PER PERSON
£11.00 - £35.00

SPECIAL PROMOTIONS
Check website for
regular special offers.

Whether on business or pleasure the Chase is the perfect rural location. Concessionary golf arrangements are available. Award-winning cuisine within our fine-dining restaurant and conference and events facility, catering for up to 300 guests, provide good quality of service and product within a country-house venue.

Directions: M50 jct 4, take the A449. Turn left onto the A40 for Gloucester. Turn right at roundabout, the Chase is 0.5 miles on your left.

Bedrooms: 28 dble, 9 twin, 1 single
Open: All year except Christmas

Site: ✿ Payment: 💳 Leisure: ♨ 🎵 ▶ ♺ Property: ♟ 🚗 🖥 ◐ Children: ⛱ ♨ 🎿 Catering: 🍷 🍴
Room: 🔌 ☕ ☎ 📺 🛏

BROSELEY, Shropshire Map ref 4A3
SatNav TF12 5EW B

Broseley House
1 The Square, Broseley, Ironbridge TF12 5EW **T:** (01952) 882043
E: info@broseleyhouse.co.uk
W: broseleyhouse.co.uk

B&B PER ROOM PER NIGHT
S: £45.00 - £55.00
D: £75.00 - £90.00

Period townhouse, one mile Ironbridge. Unique, comfortable bedrooms with Wi-Fi, freeview, plus many thoughtful extras and close good local amenities. Walkers, cyclists welcome. Self catering also available. **Directions:** Refer to the website or call for directions. **Bedrooms:** 3 double, 1 twin, 2 family **Open:** All year

Site: ✿ Payment: 💷 Leisure: 👟 ♩ ▶ ↺ Property: 🐾 🖾 🅳 Children: 🚲5 Catering: 🍴 Room: 🔌 ♨ 🅳 📺 ♨ 🍳

BUCKNELL, Shropshire Map ref 4A3
SatNav SY7 0AH B

Baron at Bucknell
Chapel Lawn Road, Bucknell SY7 0AH **T:** (01547) 530549 **F:** (01547) 530445
E: info@baronatbucknell.co.uk
W: baronatbucknell.co.uk **£ BOOK ONLINE**

B&B PER ROOM PER NIGHT
S: £80.00 - £100.00
D: £80.00 - £120.00

EVENING MEAL PER PERSON
£9.95 - £16.50

With stunning Shropshire views and only 20 minutes from Ludlow. Offering luxurious rooms with original wooden beams, succulent food, real ales, a log fire, charming restaurant and the warmest welcome in Shropshire. This inn is very special. **Directions:** Bucknell is just off the A4113 Ludlow to Knighton Road. 5 miles east of Knighton. 12 miles west of Ludlow. **Bedrooms:** 3 double, 2 twin/ double. **Open:** All year

Site: ✿ P Payment: 💷 Property: 🖾 ⌀ Children: ♫ Catering: (✗ 🍷 🍴 Room: 🔌 ♨ ☎ 🅳 📺

CLUN, Shropshire Map ref 4A3
SatNav SY7 8JA B

The White Horse Inn
The Square, Clun, Shropshire SY7 8JA **T:** (01588) 640305 **E:** room@whi-clun.co.uk
W: www.whi-clun.co.uk **£ BOOK ONLINE**

B&B PER ROOM PER NIGHT
S: £35.00 - £37.50
D: £60.00 - £65.00

EVENING MEAL PER PERSON
£5.95 - £16.95

Small, friendly, 'Good Pub Guide' listed pub with well-appointed, en suite family bedrooms in traditional style. Wide-ranging menu available in dining room. Specialising in Real Ales with own micro-brewery **Directions:** In the centre of Clun **Bedrooms:** 2 twin, 2 double **Open:** All year except Christmas

Site: ✿ Payment: 💷 Leisure: ♩ Property: 🖾 🅳 Children: 🚲 🛏 ♫ Catering: 🍷 🍴 Room: 🔌 ♨ 🅳 📺

Book your accommodation online

Visit our new 2014 guide websites for detailed information, up-to-date availability and to book your accommodation online. Includes over 20,000 places to stay, all of them star rated.

www.visitor-guides.co.uk

LUDLOW, Shropshire   Map ref 4A3   SatNav SY8 1NG **B**

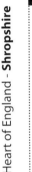

De Grey's

5-6 Broad Street, Ludlow, Shropshire SY8 1NG **T:** (01584) 872764
E: enquiries@degreys.co.uk
W: www.degreys.co.uk **£ BOOK ONLINE**

B&B PER ROOM PER NIGHT
S: £95.00 - £135.00
D: £110.00 - £165.00

SPECIAL PROMOTIONS
For last-minute offers
please visit our website
or twitter page
@degreysofludlow.
10% discount for
bookings of 3 nights or
more.

Elegant, comfortable and homely, De Grey's Townhouse rooms and suites offer the perfect luxury retreat in the heart of Ludlow. Our traditional Bed and Breakfast offers the highest standard of accommodation, with delicious, locally-sourced breakfasts served in our tearooms. Each room has beautifully hand-crafted oak furniture, rich fabrics, crisp white cotton sheets and luxurious bathrooms.

Directions: From the A49 drive into the town centre - De Grey's is located in a beautiful Elizabethan property on Broad Street, 50yds beyond the clock tower.

Bedrooms: 3 Deluxe doubles (2 of which can be converted into twin beds) 1 Deluxe twin room, 3 Superior rooms, 2 Suites
Open: Closed Christmas Day, Boxing Day & New Year's Day

Site: ✿ **Payment:** 💷 **Property:** 🖥 **Children:** 🧸 ⚤ **Catering:** 🍴 **Room:** 🔌 ♨ 🅐 📺 🔌 🚪

LUDLOW, Shropshire   Map ref 4A3   SatNav SY8 1AA **H**

The Feathers Hotel

Bull Ring, Ludlow SY8 1AA **T:** (01584) 875261 **F:** (01584) 876030
E: enquiries@feathersatludlow.co.uk
W: feathersatludlow.co.uk **£ BOOK ONLINE**

B&B PER ROOM PER NIGHT
S: £85.00 - £95.00
D: £115.00 - £200.00
EVENING MEAL PER PERSON
£32.00 - £39.95

At the heart of the ancient market town of Ludlow with Jacobean architecture and a medieval heritage. Recently refurbished. Award winning restaurant. High standard of food and service. **Directions:** From A49 follow signs to Ludlow town centre. We are situated on the brow of the hill, near a pedestrian crossing. **Bedrooms:** 3 single, 23 dble, 12 twin, 2 family **Open:** All year

Site: ✿ **Payment:** 💷 **Leisure:** 👤 🎵 ► ♻ **Property:** 🍷 🐕 🖥 ◐ **Children:** 🧸 🍴 **Catering:** 🍷 🍴 **Room:** 🔌 ♨ 📞 🅐 📺 🚪

TELFORD, Shropshire   Map ref 4A3   SatNav TF1 2HA **B**

The Old Orleton Inn

378 Holyhead Road, Wellington, Shropshire TF1 2HA **T:** (01952) 255011
E: info@theoldorleton.com
W: www.theoldorleton.com **£ BOOK ONLINE**

B&B PER ROOM PER NIGHT
S: £65.00 - £125.00
D: £89.00 - £145.00
EVENING MEAL PER PERSON
£12.00 - £35.00

Contemporary Styled 17th Century Coaching Inn facing the famous Wrekin Hill. The Old Orleton Inn, Wellington, Shropshire is a charming retreat for both work and pleasure. **Directions:** 7 miles from Shrewsbury, 4 miles from Ironbridge, M54 (exit 7), 400yds on the left towards Wellington. **Bedrooms:** 1 single, 7 double, 2 twin **Open:** Closed for two weeks in January

Site: ✿ **P Payment:** 💷 **Leisure:** 👤 🎵 ► ♻ **Property:** ⊚ 🍷 🖥 🗄 🍷 **Catering:** ⟨✗ 🍷 🍴 **Room:** 🔌 ♨ 📞 🅐 📺 🚪

CHEADLE, *Staffordshire* *Map ref 4B2* SatNav ST10 1RA B

★★★★ FARMHOUSE

B&B PER ROOM PER NIGHT
S: £30.00
D: £55.00

Rakeway House Farm B&B

Rakeway Road, Cheadle, Alton Towers Area ST10 1RA **T:** (01538) 755295
E: rakewayhousefarm@btinternet.com
W: www.rakewayhousefarm.co.uk

Charming farmhouse and gardens. Fantastic views over Cheadle and surrounding countryside. Alton Towers 15 minutes drive. Good base for Peak District and Potteries. First-class accommodation, excellent menu, superb hospitality. **Bedrooms:** 1 double, 1 family
Open: All year

Site: ✿ P Leisure: 🚲 ♪ ⼘ ♺ Property: 🖵 Children: 🍼 Catering: 🍽 Room: 🥂 🖐 🕭 📺 ⛱ 🛏

LEEK, *Staffordshire* *Map ref 4B2* SatNav ST13 8TW H

★★★ HOTEL *Silver* AWARD

B&B PER ROOM PER NIGHT
S: £79.25 - £116.00
D: £88.50 - £162.00
HB PER PERSON PER NIGHT
£69.25 - £106.00

SPECIAL PROMOTIONS
See website for special promotions.

Three Horseshoes Inn & Country Hotel

Blackshaw Moor, Leek ST13 8TW **T:** (01538) 300296 **E:** enquiries@threeshoesinn.co.uk
W: www.3shoesinn.co.uk **£ BOOK ONLINE**

Family-run country hotel situated on the A53, two miles north of Leek on the edge of the Peak District National Park. 26 bedrooms ranging from boutique-style standard rooms to luxury rooms offering four-poster beds, whirlpool baths, large LCD TV. Traditional bar, carvery or 2AA Rosette brasserie.

Directions: 10 miles from Stoke-on-Trent on the A53 Leek-Buxton road.

Bedrooms: 21 dble, 3 twin, 2 family
Open: All year

Site: ✿ Payment: 💳 Leisure: 🚲 ♪ ⼘ ♺ Property: 🍴 🖵 Children: 🍼 🏊 🏃 Catering: 🍷 🍽
Room: 🥂 🖐 ☎ 🕭 📺 ⛱ 🛏 📶

LICHFIELD, *Staffordshire* *Map ref 4B3* SatNav WS14 0BG B

★★★★ GUEST HOUSE

B&B PER ROOM PER NIGHT
S: £35.00 - £42.00
D: £55.00 - £65.00

Copper's End Guest House

Walsall Road, Muckley Corner, Lichfield, Staffordshire WS14 0BG **T:** (01543) 372910
F: (01543) 360423 **E:** info@coppersendguesthouse.co.uk
W: www.coppersendguesthouse.co.uk **£ BOOK ONLINE**

Detached guesthouse, character and charm in own grounds. Wide screen TVs in all bedrooms. Conservatory dining room, large walled garden with patio, guests' lounge. Vegetarians catered for. 4 en suite rooms, 2 ground floor rooms, parking, Motorcyclist, cyclist & walker friendly. **Directions:** 100yds from Muckley Corner roundabout off the A5, 3 miles south of Lichfield, Walsall 5 miles. Ordnance Survey ref. SK083067. **Bedrooms:** 3 double, 3 twin
Open: All year except Christmas and New Year

Site: ✿ P Payment: 💳 Leisure: ⼘ Property: 🖵 Children: 🍼 🏊 Catering: 🍽 Room: 🥂 🖐 📺 ⛱

RUGELEY, Staffordshire Map ref 4B3 — SatNav WS15 3LL B

GUEST HOUSE / **Gold AWARD**

B&B PER ROOM PER NIGHT
S: £68.00 - £112.00
D: £91.00 - £200.00
EVENING MEAL PER PERSON
£10.00

Colton House
Bellamour Way, Colton, Rugeley, Staffs. WS15 3LL **T:** (01889) 578580 **F:** (01889) 578580
E: mail@coltonhouse.com
W: coltonhouse.com **£ BOOK ONLINE**

Colton House, highest rated guest accommodation in Staffordshire, with the facilities of a boutique country house hotel in 1.5 acre garden. Beautifully restored Grade II* property, in picturesque village of Colton on the edge of Cannock Chase. Wide variety of bedrooms available, all en suite and distinctively styled. Winner of 'Best Breakfast in Staffordshire' with eggs laid by village hens. **Directions:** M6 Toll Jct 7, A460 to Rugeley then B5013 towards Uttoxeter, after 2 miles, right into Colton. Colton House is 0.25 miles on the right. **Bedrooms:** 9 double, 1 twin **Open:** All year

Site: P Payment: Property: Catering: Room:

STAFFORD, Staffordshire Map ref 4B3 — SatNav call for directions B

FARMHOUSE

B&B PER ROOM PER NIGHT
S: £37.50
D: £60.00

Rooks Nest Farm
Weston Bank, Stafford, Staffordshire ST18 0BA **T:** (01889) 270624 **E:** info@rooksnest.co.uk
W: rooksnest.co.uk

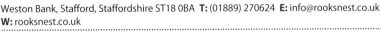

Modern farmhouse on working farm, with far-reaching views over the Trent valley. Close to Weston Hall, County Showground, Staffordshire University and Technology Park, with easy access to Staffordshires many attractions. **Directions:** Please refer to website. **Bedrooms:** 1 double, 1 twin **Open:** All year

Site: P Children: Catering: Room:

Visit our 2014 guide websites...

- Detailed information
- Up-to-date availability
- Book your accommodation online

Includes over 20,000 places to stay, all of them star rated.

Win amazing prizes, every month...

Enter our monthly competition at
www.visitor-guides.co.uk/prizes

STAFFORD, Staffordshire *Map ref 4B3* SatNav ST16 3LQ B

enjoyEngland.com ★★★ GUEST HOUSE

B&B PER ROOM PER NIGHT
S: £37.00 - £48.00
D: £58.00 - £70.00

EVENING MEAL PER PERSON
£7.00 - £20.00

SPECIAL PROMOTIONS
Offers are available, please ring 01785 223069 for more information.

Wyndale Guest House

199 Corporation Street, Stafford ST16 3LQ **T:** (01785) 223069 **E:** wyndale@aol.com
W: wyndaleguesthouse.co.uk

Wyndale is a comfortable Victorian house conveniently Situated 0.25 miles from town centre, with easy access to Stafford university, the M6, Stafford train station and Stafford record office. We are on route to county show ground, hospitals & business parks. Local attractions including Shugborough, Trentham Gardens & Amerton Farm. Enjoy home made preserves and locally sourced meat for breakfast.

Directions: Please go to our web site where we have full direction & maps. www.wyndaleguesthouse.co.uk.

Bedrooms: We offer 2 single, 2 double, 2 twin and 2 family rooms. Twin rooms have the capability of being used as double rooms. 5 en suite rooms.
Open: All year except Christmas

Site: P **Payment:** **Property:** **Children:** **Catering:** **Room:**

LEAMINGTON SPA, Warwickshire *Map ref 4B3* SatNav CV31 3PW B

enjoyEngland.com ★★★★ GUEST HOUSE

B&B PER ROOM PER NIGHT
S: £60.00
D: £70.00 - £80.00

Victoria Park Lodge

12 Adelaide Road, Royal Leamington Spa, Warwick CV31 3PW **T:** (01926) 424195
F: (01926) 421521 **E:** info@victoriaparkhotelleamingtonspa.co.uk
W: victoriaparkhotelleamingtonspa.co.uk **£ BOOK ONLINE**

29 en suite bedrooms and a spacious serviced apartment nearby for short/long stays. 4 mins walk from the town centre and 5 mins drive from Warwick Castle. **Bedrooms:** 8 single, 10 double, 2 twin, 9 family **Open:** All year except Christmas and New Year

Site: P **Payment:** **Leisure:** **Property:** **Children:** **Catering:** **Room:**

STRATFORD-UPON-AVON, Warwickshire *Map ref 2B1* SatNav CV37 6PB B

enjoyEngland.com ★★★★ GUEST HOUSE
enjoyEngland.com Silver AWARD

B&B PER ROOM PER NIGHT
S: £40.00 - £60.00
D: £75.00 - £95.00

Adelphi Guest House

39 Grove Road, Stratford-upon-Avon, Warwickshire CV37 6PB **T:** (01789) 204469
E: info@adelphi-guesthouse.com
W: http://adelphi-guesthouse.com

Breakfasts are popular, as are the home baked cakes. The rooms are decorated in period style. The bedding is pure cotton. The house over looks the Fir Gardens and is minutes from the train station, town centre, Shakespeare sites, and theatres. **Directions:** From the A3400 turn onto the A4390 which becomes Grove Road at the next crossroads. The Adelphi is approx 200m on the right as is a lane to parking. **Bedrooms:** Rooms have luxury toiletries and hospitality tray **Open:** All year

Site: P **Payment:** **Property:** **Catering:** **Room:**

For **key to symbols** see page 7

GUEST HOUSE

Avonlea

47 Shipston Road, Stratford-upon-Avon CV37 7LN **T:** (01789) 205940
E: enquiries@avonlea-stratford.co.uk
W: www.avonlea-stratford.co.uk

B&B PER ROOM PER NIGHT
S: £40.00 - £55.00
D: £65.00 - £80.00

SPECIAL PROMOTIONS
Discounts on stays of 4
or more nights. 50%
off Sunday when
booking 3 or more
nights, subject to T&C.

This is a stylish Victorian town house situated only five minutes walk from the theatre and Stratford town centre. All rooms are en suite and furnished to the highest quality with comfy beds. Guests are assured of a warm welcome and friendly atmosphere, with a fantastic breakfast the following morning.

Directions: A3400 Shipston Road, 100m from Clopton Bridge.

Bedrooms: 2 single, 2 double, 2 twin/superking, 2 family (1 Double 1 Single bed)
Open: All year except Christmas & January

Site: ✿ P Payment: 💷 Leisure: ♿ ♪ ▶ Property: 🖼 Children: 🛏 Catering: 🍴 Room: 🔌 👜 📺 ♨

GUEST HOUSE   Silver AWARD

Brook Lodge Guest House

192 Alcester Road, Stratford-upon-Avon CV37 9DR **T:** (01789) 295988
E: brooklodgeguesthouse@btinternet.com
W: brook-lodge.co.uk **£ BOOK ONLINE**

B&B PER ROOM PER NIGHT
S: £45.00 - £52.00
D: £66.00 - £72.00

Within an easy walk of all the town's major attractions, Brook Lodge offers first class accommodation and facilities with a personal touch. Your home away from home. **Bedrooms:** 3 double, 2 family, 1 suite **Open:** All year

Site: ✿ P Payment: 💷 Property: 🖼 🚭 ♨ Children: 🛏 🍴 🧍 Catering: 🍴 Room: 🔌 👜 📺

Need more information?

Visit our new 2014 guide websites for detailed information, up-to-date availability and to book your accommodation online. Includes over 20,000 places to stay, all of them star rated.

www.visitor-guides.co.uk

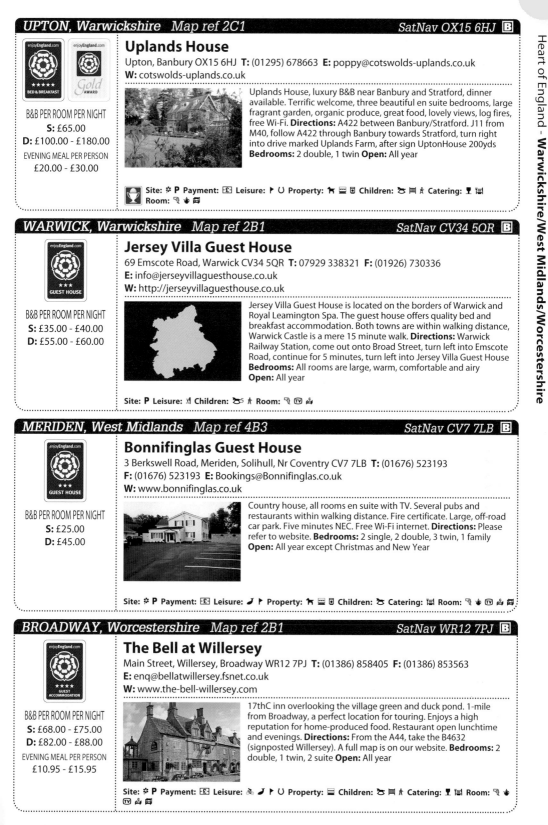

UPTON, Warwickshire   Map ref 2C1   SatNav OX15 6HJ B

★★★★★ BED & BREAKFAST — enjoyEngland.com
Gold AWARD — enjoyEngland.com

B&B PER ROOM PER NIGHT
S: £65.00
D: £100.00 - £180.00
EVENING MEAL PER PERSON
£20.00 - £30.00

Uplands House

Upton, Banbury OX15 6HJ **T:** (01295) 678663 **E:** poppy@cotswolds-uplands.co.uk
W: cotswolds-uplands.co.uk

Uplands House, luxury B&B near Banbury and Stratford, dinner available. Terrific welcome, three beautiful en suite bedrooms, large fragrant garden, organic produce, great food, lovely views, log fires, free Wi-Fi. **Directions:** A422 between Banbury/Stratford. J11 from M40, follow A422 through Banbury towards Stratford, turn right into drive marked Uplands Farm, after sign UptonHouse 200yds **Bedrooms:** 2 double, 1 twin **Open:** All year

Site: ✿ P Payment: 💷 Leisure: ▶ ∪ Property: ♉ 🖳 🗄 Children: 🛏 🏠 Catering: 🍷 🍴 Room: 🔌 🛁 🎧

WARWICK, Warwickshire   Map ref 2B1   SatNav CV34 5QR B

★★★ GUEST HOUSE — enjoyEngland.com

B&B PER ROOM PER NIGHT
S: £35.00 - £40.00
D: £55.00 - £60.00

Jersey Villa Guest House

69 Emscote Road, Warwick CV34 5QR **T:** 07929 338321 **F:** (01926) 730336
E: info@jerseyvillaguesthouse.co.uk
W: http://jerseyvillaguesthouse.co.uk

Jersey Villa Guest House is located on the borders of Warwick and Royal Leamington Spa. The guest house offers quality bed and breakfast accommodation. Both towns are within walking distance, Warwick Castle is a mere 15 minute walk. **Directions:** Warwick Railway Station, come out onto Broad Street, turn left into Emscote Road, continue for 5 minutes, turn left into Jersey Villa Guest House **Bedrooms:** All rooms are large, warm, comfortable and airy **Open:** All year

Site: P Leisure: ⚄ Children: 🛏5 🏠 Room: 🔌 📺 🛁

MERIDEN, West Midlands   Map ref 4B3   SatNav CV7 7LB B

★★★ GUEST HOUSE — enjoyEngland.com

B&B PER ROOM PER NIGHT
S: £25.00
D: £45.00

Bonnifinglas Guest House

3 Berkswell Road, Meriden, Solihull, Nr Coventry CV7 7LB **T:** (01676) 523193
F: (01676) 523193 **E:** Bookings@Bonnifinglas.co.uk
W: www.bonnifinglas.co.uk

Country house, all rooms en suite with TV. Several pubs and restaurants within walking distance. Fire certificate. Large, off-road car park. Five minutes NEC. Free Wi-Fi internet. **Directions:** Please refer to website. **Bedrooms:** 2 single, 2 double, 3 twin, 1 family **Open:** All year except Christmas and New Year

Site: ✿ P Payment: 💷 Leisure: ♪ ▶ Property: ♉ 🖳 🗄 Children: 🛏 Catering: 🍴 Room: 🔌 🛁 📺 🛁 🎧

BROADWAY, Worcestershire   Map ref 2B1   SatNav WR12 7PJ B

★★★★ GUEST ACCOMMODATION — enjoyEngland.com

B&B PER ROOM PER NIGHT
S: £68.00 - £75.00
D: £82.00 - £88.00
EVENING MEAL PER PERSON
£10.95 - £15.95

The Bell at Willersey

Main Street, Willersey, Broadway WR12 7PJ **T:** (01386) 858405 **F:** (01386) 853563
E: enq@bellatwillersey.fsnet.co.uk
W: www.the-bell-willersey.com

17thC inn overlooking the village green and duck pond. 1-mile from Broadway, a perfect location for touring. Enjoys a high reputation for home-produced food. Restaurant open lunchtime and evenings. **Directions:** From the A44, take the B4632 (signposted Willersey). A full map is on our website. **Bedrooms:** 2 double, 1 twin, 2 suite **Open:** All year

Site: ✿ P Payment: 💷 Leisure: ♿ ♪ ▶ ∪ Property: 🖳 Children: 🛏 🏠 Catering: 🍷 🍴 Room: 🔌 🛁 📺 🛁 🎧

BROADWAY, Worcestershire Map ref 2B1 SatNav WR12 7AA 🄷

The Broadway Hotel

The Green, Broadway WR12 7AA **T:** (01386) 852401 **F:** (01386) 853879
E: info@broadwayhotel.info
W: cotswold-inns-hotels.co.uk/broadway **£ BOOK ONLINE**

B&B PER ROOM PER NIGHT
S: £120.00 - £160.00
D: £160.00 - £220.00
HB PER PERSON PER NIGHT
£108.00 - £138.00

16th century Broadway Hotel in the Cotswold village of Broadway. Relax in the lounge and enjoy afternoon tea. Uniquely decorated bedrooms in warm and inviting colours creating perfect country-house style. **Directions:** M5 jct 6, A44 Continue for 18 miles. Turn right at roundabout onto Station Road. Hotel is off village green on the High Street. **Bedrooms:** 13 dble, 6 twin **Open:** All year

Site: ✿ P Payment: 💷 Leisure: 🚴 ↑ ∪ Property: 🐴 🖼 🗗 ♨ ⌀ Children: ⛁ 🛏 🛝 Catering: ♟ 🍴
Room: 🗣 ♨ 📞 📺 🎛

BROADWAY, Worcestershire Map ref 2B1 SatNav WR12 7LJ 🄱

Farncombe Estate

Farncombe Estate, Broadway, Worcestershire WR12 7LJ **T:** 0845 230 8580
F: (01386) 854350 **E:** enquiries@farncombeestate.co.uk
W: www.farncombeestate.co.uk

B&B PER ROOM PER NIGHT
S: £65.00 - £95.00
D: £70.00 - £100.00
EVENING MEAL PER PERSON
£18.00 - £25.00

A private 400-acre Estate in the heart of the Cotswolds. There are 89 en suite bedrooms, stunning long-distance views and lots of outdoor activities. Stratford and Cheltenham are nearby and lots of pretty villages and great gardens are on the doorstep. Groups also welcome. Free Wi-fi and good, locally sourced food. For the Farncombe programme of weekend leisure courses, visit www.farncombecourses.co.uk

Directions: Direct trains from London Paddington: 1.5hrs. Road access: via the A44 between Evesham and Moreton-in-Marsh.

Bedrooms: 89 en suite
Open: All year except Christmas and New Year

Site: ✿ P Payment: 💷 Leisure: ↑ 🎿 🎣 Property: ♟ 🐴 🖼 🍴 Catering: (✗ ♟ 🍴 Room: 🗣 ♨ 📞 📺

WORCESTER, Worcestershire Map ref 2B1 SatNav WR5 2JT 🄱

Holland House

210 London Road, Worcester WR5 2JT **T:** 01905 353939 **F:** 01905 353939
E: beds@holland-house.me.uk
W: www.holland-house.me.uk **£ BOOK ONLINE**

B&B PER ROOM PER NIGHT
S: £44.00
D: £54.00 - £58.00

A warm welcome awaits you at this Victorian mid-terrace house, situated within walking distance of the cathedral. It retains many original features and offers fully en suite rooms throughout. **Directions:** We are situated on A44 approximately half way between M5/J7 and the cathedral. **Bedrooms:** 2 double, 1 twin **Open:** All year

Payment: 💷 Property: 🖼 Children: ⛁ 🛏 Catering: 🍴 Room: 🗣 ♨ 📻 📺 📀

There are hundreds of "Green" places to stay and visit in England from small bed and breakfasts to large visitor attractions and activity holiday providers. Businesses displaying this logo have undergone a rigorous verification process to ensure that they are sustainable (green) and that a qualified assessor has visited the premises.

We have indicated the accommodation which has achieved a Green award... look out for the symbol in the entry.

Yorkshire

With the North York Moors, Yorkshire Dales and the Pennines within its borders, the largest county in the UK can also lay claim to being the greenest. There is a plethora of stunning locations and amazing sights to be found, and it's no wonder the area is popular with walkers, cyclists and tourists. Add cities like York, Leeds, Hull and Sheffield, and you have a region steeped in history. And if you enjoy breathtaking coastal views, then Yorkshire doesn't disappoint.

Leeds

Leeds offers everything you would expect from one of the UK's leading cities, from great shopping to listed buildings and green spaces.

North York Moors

The North York Moors National Park is a landscape of stunning moorland, spectacular coast, ancient woodland and historic sites. It also has one of the largest expanses of heather moorland in the UK.

Saltaire

Saltaire in West Yorkshire is a well-preserved industrial village of the second half of the 19th century, and the buildings offer a vivid impression of Victorian philanthropic paternalism.

Sheffield

Sheffield is also a city bursting with ideas and energy, having transformed the world with Stainless Steel production back in 1913.

Studley Royal Park

A striking landscape was created around the ruins of the Cistercian Fountains Abbey and Fountains Hall Castle in Yorkshire in the 18th and 19th centuries.

York

The city of York is renowned for its splendid cathedral, has been a meeting place throughout Roman, Viking and Medieval ages. Meanwhile, Harrogate and the surrounding district is one of the most spectacular areas in England.

Yorkshire coast

The coastline is spectacular, varied, and interesting. It can be rocky and wild in places but is enhanced by numerous fishing villages and resorts like Scarborough, Filey and Whitby.

Yorkshire Dales

The Yorkshire Dales is home to outstanding scenery, a rich cultural heritage and breathtakingly peaceful atmosphere.

Editor's Picks

Watch out for the whales

Whitby is the finest place for whale watching on the Yorkshire coast and early autumn evenings are the best time.

Learn about the railways

The National Railway Museum in York is the largest in the world, offering three giant halls packed full of incredible trains and interactive fun.

Enjoy the surroundings

Yorkshire's three National Parks offer more than 3,200 square kilometres of beautiful landscapes and seascapes – all just waiting to be explored.

Spot the gull

The cliffs of the coast are a haven for all manner of sealife and perfect for bird watching. RSPB Bempton Cliffs is a family favourite, and easily the best place in England to see, hear and smell seabirds.

Take in the sea air

From miles of award-winning sandy beaches to hidden coastal coves, the Yorkshire Coast has over 100 miles of stunning coastline.

Things to do

Entertainment & Culture

Clifton Park Museum
Rotherham, South Yorkshire S65 2AA
(01709) 336633
www.rotherham.gov.uk/graphics/Learning/Museums/
EDSCliftonParkMuseum.htm
*Local pottery, antiquities, natural and social history.
Restored period kitchen. Major collection of Rockingham
porcelain.*

East Riding Rural Life Museum
Beverley, Yorkshire HU16 5TF
(01482) 392777
www.eastriding.gov.uk
*Working early 19th century four-sailed windmill, plus
Museum of East Riding Rural Life.*

Eureka! The National Children's Museum
Halifax, West Yorkshire HX1 2NE
(01422) 330069
www.eureka.org.uk
*Eureka! The National Children's Museum is a magical
place where children play to learn and grown-ups learn
to play.*

Ferens Art Gallery
Hull, East Riding of Yorkshire HU1 3RA
(01482) 613902
www.hullcc.gov.uk/museums
*Combines internationally renowned permanent
collections with a thriving programme of temporary
exhibitions.*

National Coal Mining Museum for England
Wakefield, West Yorkshire WF4 4RH
(01924) 848806
www.ncm.org.uk
*The National Coal Mining Museum offers an exciting
and enjoyable insight into the working lives of miners
through the ages.*

National Media Museum
Bradford, West Yorkshire BD1 1NQ
0870 701 0200
www.nationalmediamuseum.org.uk
*The museum is open Tuesday to Sunday (along with
Bank and school holiday Mondays) from 10:00am until
6.00pm. Admission to the National Media Museum is free
(charges apply for cinemas/IMAX).*

National Railway Museum
York, North Yorkshire YO26 4XJ
0844 815 3139
www.nrm.org.uk
*Awesome trains, interactive fun – and the world's largest
railway museum is free.*

Royal Armouries Museum
Leeds, West Yorkshire LS10 1LT
0870 034 4344
www.royalarmouries.org
*Over 8,000 objects displayed in five galleries - War,
Tournament, Oriental, Self Defence and Hunting. Among
the treasures are Henry VIII's tournament armour and the
world record breaking elephant armour. Regular jousting
and horse shows.*

Sheffield: Millennium Gallery
South Yorkshire S1 2PP
(0114) 278 2600
www.museums-sheffield.org.uk
*The Millennium Gallery is one of modern Sheffield's landmark
public spaces. Whether you're in town or just passing
through, the Gallery always has something new to offer.*

Treasure House and Art Gallery
Beverley, East Riding of Yorkshire HU17 8HE
(01482) 392790
www.eastriding.gov.uk/treasurehouse
*Enthusiasts for East Riding history can access archive,
library, art gallery and museum material. Exhibitions.*

Xscape Castleford
Castleford, West Yorkshire WF10 4TA
(01977) 5230 2324
www.xscape.co.uk
*The ultimate family entertainment awaits! Dine, bowl,
snow, skate, climb, movies, shop, dance on ice.*

Yorkshire Air Museum
York, North Yorkshire YO41 4AU
(01904) 608595
www.yorkshireairmuseum.co.uk
*The Yorkshire Air Museum is based on a unique WWII
Bomber Command Station with fascinating exhibits
and attractive Memorial Gardens that have won 3
consecutive Yorkshire in Bloom awards.*

Family Fun

Flamingo Land Theme Park and Zoo
Malton, North Yorkshire YO17 6UX
0871 911 8000
www.flamingoland.co.uk
*One-price family funpark with over 100 attractions, 5
shows and Europe's largest privately-owned zoo.*

Magna Science Adventure Centre
Rotherham, South Yorkshire S60 1DX
(01709) 720002
www.visitmagna.co.uk
*Magna is the UK's 1st Science Adventure Centre set in
the vast Templeborough steelworks in Rotherham. Fun
is unavoidable here with giant interactives.*

Heritage

Beverley Guildhall

East Riding of Yorkshire HU17 9XX
(01482) 392783
www.eastriding.gov.uk
Beverley Guildhall is a Grade 1 listed building, originally late medieval, remodelled in 17th and 18th century.

Brodsworth Hall and Gardens
Doncaster, South Yorkshire DN5 7XJ
(01302) 722598
www.english-heritage.org.uk/daysout/properties/brodsworth-hall-and-gardens
One of England's most complete surviving Victorian houses. Inside many of the original fixtures & fittings are still in place, although faded with time. Outside the 15 acres of woodland & gardens have been restored to their 1860's heyday.

Castle Howard
Malton, North Yorkshire YO60 7DA
(01653) 648444
www.castlehoward.co.uk
Magnificent 18th century historic house and Stable Courtyard within 1,000 acres of breathtaking gardens.

Harewood House
Leeds West Yorkshire LS17 9LG
(0113) 218 1010
www.harewood.org
Harewood House, Bird Garden, Grounds and Adventure Playground - The Ideal day out for all the family.

JORVIK Viking Centre
York, North Yorkshire YO1 9WT
(01904) 615505
www.jorvik-viking-centre.co.uk
Travel back 1000 years on board your time machine through the backyards and houses to the bustling streets of Jorvik.

Lotherton Hall & Gardens
Leeds, West Yorkshire LS25 3EB
(0113) 264 5535
www.leeds.gov.uk/lothertonhall
Lotherton is an Edwardian country house set in beautiful grounds with a bird garden, red deer park and formal gardens.

Skipsea Castle
Hornsea, East Riding of Yorkshire
0870 333 1181
www.english-heritage.org.uk/daysout/properties/skipsea-castle/
The remaining earthworks of a motte-and-bailey castle dating from the Norman era.

Wilberforce House
Hull, East Riding of Yorkshire HU11NQ
(01482) 613902
www.hullcc.gov.uk/museums
Slavery exhibits, period rooms and furniture, Hull silver, costume, Wilberforce and abolition.

Yorkshire Sculpture Park
West Bretton, West Yorkshire WF4 4LG
(01924) 832631
www.ysp.co.uk
YSP is an extraordinary place that sets out to challenge, inspire, inform and delight.

Nature & Wildlife

RSPB Bempton Cliffs Reserve
Bridlington, East Riding of Yorkshire YO15 1JF
(01262) 851179
www.rspb.org.uk/reserves/guide/b/bemptoncliffs/index.aspx
Nature trail and spectacular cliff top walks.

RSPB Old Moor Nature Reserve
Barnsley, South Yorkshire S73 0YF
(01226) 751593
www.rspb.org.uk/reserves/guide/d/dearne-oldmoor/index.aspx
Whether you're feeling energetic or just fancy some time out visit Old Moor to get closer to the wildlife.

Sheffield Botanical Gardens
South Yorkshire S10 2LN
(0114) 267 1115
www.sbg.org.uk
Extensive gardens with over 5,500 species of plants, Grade II Listed garden pavillion.

The Deep
Hull, East Riding of Yorkshire HU1 4DP
(01482) 381000
www.thedeep.co.uk
Full with over 3500 fish and more than 40 sharks, it tells the story of the world's oceans using live animals and the latest hands on interactives.

The Walled Garden at Scampston
Malton, North Yorkshire YO17 8NG
(01944) 759111
www.scampston.co.uk
An exciting 4 acre contemporary garden, created by Piet Oudolf, with striking perennial meadow planting as well as traditional spring/autumn borders.

Wentworth Castle Gardens
Barnsley, South Yorkshire S75 3ET
(01226) 776040
www.wentworthcastle.org
This magnificent 600 acre Parkland estate features over 26 listed monuments as well as a 60-acre Garden.

Yorkshire Wildlife Park
Doncaster, South Yorkshire DN3 3NH
(01302) 535057
www.yorkshirewildlifepark.co.uk
A fabulous fun day and animal experience. Walk through 'Lemar Woods' and meet these mischievous primates, or come face to face with the wallabies in Wallaby Walk.

Outdoor Activities

York Boat Guided River Trips
North Yorkshire YO1 7DP
(01904) 628324
www.yorkboat.co.uk/buytickets-online.html
Sit back, relax and enjoy a drink from the bar as the sights of York city and country sail by onboard a 1 hour Guided River Trip with entertaining live commentary.

Diesel Gala Weekend
TBC, Haworth
Bringing together a collection of
vintage diesel locomotives.
www.kwvr.co.uk

Malton Food Lovers Festival
May 24-25, Malton
Chance to fill up on glorious
food and discover why Malton is
considered 'Yorkshire's Food Town'
with mountains of fresh produce.
www.maltonfoodfestival.co.uk

Swaledale Festival
May 24-June 7, Various locations
Varied programme of about 60 top-
quality events, individually ticketed,
realistically priced, and spread over
two glorious weeks.
www.swaledale-festival.org.uk

Beverley Festival
June 20-22, Beverley Racecourse
This will be the 30th anniversary of
this popular music festival.
www.beverleyfestival.com

Bradford Mela
June, Bradford
An annual celebration of the art,
craft, culture and community, of
Asian and global communities both
traditional and modern.
www.bradfordmela.org.uk

Filey Town Festival
June 28-July 6, Filey
Concerts, craft fairs and street
processions draw visitors to this
picturesque North Yorkshire town.
www.fileytownfestival.com

Grassington Festival
June 13-28, Grassington
15 days of music and arts in the
Yorkshire Dales.
www.grassington-festival.org.uk

Pontefract Liquorice Festival
July, Wakefield
The festival celebrates this unusual
plant, the many wonderful products
created from it and its historic
association with the town.
www.experiencewakefield.co.uk

Scarborough Seafest
July, Scarborough
Seafest celebrates Scarborough's maritime heritage and brings together seafood kitchen cooking demonstrations, exhibitor displays and musical performances.
www.seafest.org.uk

York Early Music Festival
July 10-19, York
The 2013 festival will will focus on Rome, with music created under the patronage of medieval Popes, the renaissance polyphony of Palestrina, and the exuberant baroque of Handel in Italy.
www.ncem.co.uk

Ilkley Summer Festival
August, Ilkley
A wide selection of activities and events in and around this idyllic town.
www.summerfestival.ilkley.org

Leeds Festival
August 22-24, Wetherby
Top performers, including world renowned acts like Eminem.
www.leedsfestival.com

Ripon International Festival
September 6-20, Ripon
A festival packed with music events, solo dramas, intriguing theatre, magic, fantastic puppetry, literary celebrities, historical walks - and more!
www.riponinternationalfestival.com

Scarborough Jazz Festival
September 26-28, Scarborough
The festival is now firmly on both the national and international stage. Audiences and performers have acknowledged the consistently high quality of the artists and find the variety and range of the programme refreshing.
www.scarboroughjazzfestival.co.uk

St Leger Festival
September 10-13, Doncaster
Four days of great horse racing, culminating in the final Classic of the year.
www.doncaster-racecourse.co.uk

Autumn Steam Gala
October, Haworth
Spectacular, action-packed three-day weekend of intensive steam action.
www.kwvr.co.uk

Tourist Information Centres

When you arrive at your destination, visit an Official Partner Tourist Information Centre for quality assured help with accommodation and information about local attractions and events, or email your request before you go. To find a Tourist Information Centre visit www.visitengland.com

Aysgarth Falls	Aysgarth Falls National Park Centre	01969 662910	aysgarth@yorkshiredales.org.uk
Beverley	34 Butcher Row	01482 391672	beverley.tic@eastriding.gov.uk
Bradford	Brittania House	01274 433678	bradford.vic@bradford.gov.uk
Bridlington	25 Prince Street	01262 673474	bridlington.tic@eastriding.gov.uk
Brigg	The Buttercross	01652 657053	brigg.tic@northlincs.gov.uk
Cleethorpes	Cleethorpes Library	01472 323111	cleetic@nelincs.gov.uk
Danby	National Park Centre, Danby Lodge	01439 772737	moorscentre@northyorkmoors.org.uk
Doncaster	Blue Building	01302 734309	tourist.information@doncaster.gov.uk
Filey	The Evron Centre	01723 383637	fileytic2@scarborough.gov.uk
Grassington	National Park Centre	01756 751690	grassington@yorkshiredales.gov.uk
Halifax	The Piece Hall	01422 368725	halifax@ytbtic.co.uk
Harrogate	Royal Baths	01423 537300	tic@harrogate.gov.uk
Hawes	Dales Countryside Museum	01969 666210	hawes@yorkshiredales.org.uk
Haworth	2/4 West Lane	01535 642329	haworth.vic@bradford.gov.uk
Hebden Bridge	Visitor Centre, New Road	01422 843831	hebdenbridge@ytbtic.co.uk
Helmsley	The Visitor Centre, Helmsley Castle	01439 770173	helmsley.tic@english-heritage.org.uk
Holmfirth	49-51 Huddersfield Road	01484 222444	holmfirth.tic@kirklees.gov.uk
Hornsea	Hornsea Museum	01964 536404	hornsea.tic@eastriding.gov.uk
Huddersfield	Huddersfield Library	01484 223200	huddersfield.information@kirklees.gov.uk
Hull	1 Paragon Street	01482 223559	tourist.information@hullcc.gov.uk
Humber Bridge	North Bank Viewing Area	01482 640852	humberbridge.tic@eastriding.gov.uk
Ilkley	Town Hall	01943 602319	ilkley.vic@bradford.gov.uk
Knaresborough	9 Castle Courtyard	01423 866886	kntic@harrogate.gov.uk
Leeds	The Arcade	0113 242 5242	tourinfo@leedsandpartners.com
Leeming Bar	The Yorkshire Maid	01677 424262	thelodgeatleemingbar@btconnect.com
Leyburn	The Dales Haven	01969 622317	

Malham	National Park Centre	01969 652380	malham@ytbtic.co.uk
Malton	Malton Library	01653 600048	maltontic@btconnect.com
Otley	Otley Library & Tourist Information	01943 462485	otleytic@leedslearning.net
Pateley Bridge	18 High Street	0845 389 0177	pbtic@harrogate.gov.uk
Pickering	Ropery House	01751 473791	pickeringtic@btconnect.com
Reeth	Hudson House, The Green	01748 884059	reeth@ytbtic.co.uk
Richmond	Friary Gardens	01748 828742	hilda@richmondtouristinformation.co.uk
Ripon	Minster Road	01765 604625	ripontic@harrogate.gov.uk
Rotherham	40 Bridgegate	01709 835904	tic@rotherham.gov.uk
Scarborough	Brunswick Shopping Centre	01723 383636	scarborough2@scarborough.gov.uk
Scarborough	Harbourside TIC	01723 383636	scarborough2@scarborough.gov.uk
Selby	Selby Library	0845 034 9540	selby@ytbtic.co.uk
Settle	Town Hall	01729 825192	settle@ytbtic.co.uk
Sheffield	Unit 1 Winter Gardens	0114 2211900	visitor@marketingsheffield.org
Skipton	Town Hall	01756 792809	skipton@ytbtic.co.uk
Sutton Bank	Sutton Bank Visitor Centre	01845 597426	suttonbank@northyorkmoors.org.uk
Todmorden	15 Burnley Road	01706 818181	todmorden@ytbtic.co.uk
Wakefield	9 The Bull Ring	0845 601 8353	tic@wakefield.gov.uk
Wetherby	Wetherby Library & Tourist Info. Centre	01937 582151	wetherbytic@leedslearning.net
Whitby	Langborne Road	01723 383637	whitbytic@scarborough.gov.uk
Withernsea	Withernsea Lighthouse Museum	01964 615683	withernsea.tic@eastriding.gov.uk
York	1 Museum Street	01904 550099	info@visityork.org

Regional Contacts and Information

For more information on accommodation, attractions, activities, events and holidays in Yorkshire, contact the regional tourism organisation. Their website has a wealth of information and produces many free publications to help you get the most out of your visit.

The following publication is available from the Yorkshire Tourist Board by logging on to www.yorkshire.com or calling Welcome to Yorkshire on 0113 322 3500.

This is Y Magazine

Yorkshire
Where to Stay

Entries appear alphabetically by town name in each county. A key to symbols appears on page 7

B&B PER ROOM PER NIGHT
S: £55.00 - £60.00
D: £65.00 - £70.00

Willow Tree Cottage

Boltby, Thirsk, North Yorkshire YO7 2DY **T:** (01845) 537406 **E:** townsend.sce@virgin.net
W: www.willowtreecottagebandb.co.uk

The B&B room is a large luxurious room with wonderful views with balcony, en suite bathroom and kitchenette. The Studio is a self-contained flat, separate entrance, well equipped kitchen, shower room and wood burner. Self-catering or B&B available. **Directions:** From Thirsk take the A170 Scarborough Road follow signs to Felixkirk and Boltby. In Boltby follow road up hill. At bend sign take LH U turn to Willow Tree Cottage. **Bedrooms:** 2: A Luxurious B&B and 1 self-contained studio. **Open:** All year

Site: ❀ P Leisure: ∪ Property: 🐾 🛏 🔲 ⌀ Children: 🍼 🎠 Catering: 🍴 Room: ⬚ ♨ 📺 📀

B&B PER ROOM PER NIGHT
S: £37.00 - £48.00
D: £74.00 - £128.00

EVENING MEAL PER PERSON
£15.00

Cober Hill

Newlands Road, Cloughton, Scarborough YO13 0AR **T:** (01723) 870310 **F:** (01723) 870271
E: enquiries@coberhill.co.uk
W: coberhill.co.uk

Impressive Edwardian building, with new annexes, set in a beautiful, peaceful and tranquil location between Scarborough and Whitby, in the North York Moors National Park and overlooking the Heritage Coast. Perfect for relaxation and inspiration, 6 acres of stunning grounds and superb sea views. Groups tariffs available. **Directions:** 6 miles north of Scarborough and 15 miles south of Whitby 100 yards off the A171 Scarborough to Whitby road. **Bedrooms:** 22 single, 6 double, 25 twin, 10 family **Open:** All year

Site: ❀ P Payment: 💳 Leisure: ♿ ♪ ⚑ ∪ ⚲ Property: 🐾 🛏 Children: 🍼 🎠 🧍 Catering: 🍴 Room: ♨ 📶

B&B PER ROOM PER NIGHT
S: £35.00 - £45.00
D: £70.00 - £90.00

EVENING MEAL PER PERSON
£12.00 - £20.00

SPECIAL PROMOTIONS
Reduced rates for children under 16 years. Discounts on stays of 3 nights or more.

South Moor Farm

South Moor Farm, Dalby Forest Drive, Langdale End, Scarborough YO13 0LW
T: (01751) 460285 **E:** gol@southmoorfarm.co.uk
W: southmoorfarm.co.uk **£ BOOK ONLINE**

Quiet rural location on Dalby Forest Drive between Pickering and Scarborough. An excellent base to explore Dalby Forest, North York moors, or coast on foot, bike or horse. A full English breakfast included. Packed lunches and evening meals by arrangement. Children's play area, orienteering courses, Go Ape, Ability Outdoors and astronomy in Dalby Forest.
Horse and Bike hire 5 miles away

Directions: GPS/SAT NAV not Reliable in Dalby Forest. Follow Dalby Forest Drive (look for brown tourism signs). We are 10 miles from Thornton-le-Dale, 3.5 miles from Langdale End. Grid Ref SE905905.

Bedrooms: 1 single, 1 double, 1 twin, 1 family **Open:** All year

Site: P Payment: 💳 Leisure: ♿ ∪ Property: 🐾 🛏 Children: 🍼 🎠 🧍 Catering: 《✗ 🍴 Room: ⬚ ♨ 📺 📀

DANBY, North Yorkshire Map ref 5C3 SatNav YO21 2LD B

★★★★ INN

B&B PER ROOM PER NIGHT
S: £56.00 - £72.00
D: £88.00

HB PER PERSON PER NIGHT
£68.00 - £80.00

Fox & Hounds Inn

45 Brook Lane, Ainthorpe, Danby, Whitby YO21 2LD **T:** (01287) 660218 **F:** (01287) 660030
E: info@foxandhounds-ainthorpe.com
W: www.foxandhounds-ainthorpe.com **£ BOOK ONLINE**

16th century former coaching inn, now a high-quality residential country pub and restaurant situated in the beautiful North York Moors National Park. Enjoy our freshly prepared dishes, cask ales and selected quality wines. **Directions:** Turn off A171 Guisborough to Whitby road. Follow signs to Castleton or Danby, then Ainthorpe. **Bedrooms:** 3 double, 3 twin, 1 family + cottage sleeps 7 **Open:** All year except Christmas Day

Site: ✿ P Payment: 💷 € Leisure: ♿ ♪ ▶ ∪ ♦ 🔲 ☜ Property: 🐾 🖭 🖉 Children: 🍼 🎮 🅰
Catering: 🍴 🍷 🍽 Room: 🗝 🌢 📺 ⊡

EGTON BRIDGE, North Yorkshire Map ref 5D3 SatNav YO21 1XD B

★★★★ GUEST HOUSE **Gold AWARD**

B&B PER ROOM PER NIGHT
S: £68.00
D: £90.00 - £140.00

EVENING MEAL PER PERSON
£19.95 - £25.00

Broom House and Whites Guest House & Restaurant

Broom House Lane, Egton Bridge, Whitby, North Yorkshire YO21 1XD **T:** (01947) 895279
F: (01947) 895657 **E:** mw@broom-house.co.uk
W: www.egton-bridge.co.uk **£ BOOK ONLINE**

Beautiful National Park Countryside, Moorland & the Whitby coastline, combine to offer the ultimate luxury hideaway. This delightful setting is an ideal base for relaxing, walking, bird watching etc. **Directions:** Please refer to website.
Bedrooms: 1 single, 4 double, 1 twin, 1 family, 2 suite
Open: February to November

WALKERS CYCLISTS Site: ✿ P Payment: 💷 € Leisure: ♿ ♪ ▶ ∪ Property: 🖭 ⓑ Children: 🍼
Catering: 🍷 🍽 Room: 🗝 🌢 ⓐ 📺 ⚏

FILEY, North Yorkshire Map ref 5D3 SatNav YO14 9JA B

★★★★ GUEST HOUSE **Silver AWARD**

B&B PER ROOM PER NIGHT
S: £50.00 - £90.00
D: £70.00 - £90.00

Abbot's Leigh Guest House

7 Rutland Street, Filey YO14 9JA **T:** (01723) 513334 **E:** booking@abbotsleighfiley.co.uk
W: www.fileybedandbreakfast.com **£ BOOK ONLINE**

Need a base to explore our stunning North Yorkshire coastline or just sit back and relax? Look no further than Abbot's Leigh. We are a short stroll fom Crescent Gardens, Beach, Glen Gardens, Town Centre and Bus & Rail Stations. **Bedrooms:** Doubles, superking, twin and ground floor room. **Open:** All year

Payment: 💷 Leisure: ▶ Property: 🐾 🖭 Catering: 🍽 Room: 🗝 🌢 📺 ⊡ ⚏

FILEY, North Yorkshire Map ref 5D3 SatNav YO14 9JA B

★★★★★ GUEST HOUSE

B&B PER ROOM PER NIGHT
S: £55.00 - £70.00
D: £75.00 - £110.00

All Seasons Guesthouse

11 Rutland Street, Filey YO14 9JA **T:** (01723) 515321 **E:** lesley@allseasonsfiley.co.uk
W: allseasonsfiley.co.uk **£ BOOK ONLINE**

All Seasons combines contemporary elegance and modern convenience with traditional warmth and hospitality. A five Star awarded guest house in Filey. **Directions:** From A165 follow signs for Filey at roundabout (bus station on right). Next right into West Avenue, Rutland Street is the 2nd left. **Bedrooms:** 3 double, 2 twin, 2 family, 1 suite **Open:** All year

Payment: 💷 Leisure: ♪ ▶ ∪ Property: 🖭 Children: 🍼¹⁰ Catering: 🍽 Room: 🗝 🌢 ⓐ 📺

FILEY, North Yorkshire   Map ref 5D3   SatNav YO14 9JX [H]

White Lodge Hotel

The Crescent, Filey YO14 9JX **T:** (01723) 514771 **E:** info@whitelodgehotelfiley.co.uk
W: whitelodgehotelfiley.co.uk

B&B PER ROOM PER NIGHT
S: £62.00 - £75.00
D: £114.00 - £179.00

SPECIAL PROMOTIONS
Special Weekend and Midweek Breaks frequently available please call for details.

The White Lodge Hotel occupies an unrivalled position on the cliff top, with panoramic views over Filey Bay, and is just a short stroll from the town centre. This privately owned hotel combines well appointed modern facilities with a traditional approach to personal service, to promote guest comfort and relaxation.

Directions: Once in Filey Town Center stay on the top of the cliff. The Hotel is at the southern end of the Crescent.

Bedrooms: 1 single, 9 dble, 9 twin, 1 family
Open: All year

Site: ❀ **Payment:** **Leisure:** **Property:** **Children:** **Catering:** **Room:**

GRASSINGTON, North Yorkshire   Map ref 5B3   SatNav BD23 5AQ [H]

Grassington House Hotel & Restaurant

5 The Square, Grassington, Skipton BD23 5AQ **T:** (01756) 752406 **F:** (01756) 752050
E: bookings@grassingtonhousehotel.co.uk
W: www.grassingtonhousehotel.co.uk

B&B PER ROOM PER NIGHT
S: £95.00
D: £110.00 - £130.00
HB PER PERSON PER NIGHT
£190.00 - £220.00

SPECIAL PROMOTIONS
Please check our website for Special Events each season.

The hotel combines Georgian architecture, chic decor and five star service to create an unparalleled experience for its guests. Guests are served food by award winning chef John Rudden.

Directions: Grassington is located approx 9 miles from Skipton; 20 miles from M65 Junc 13 and 20 miles from Leeds Bradford Airport.

Bedrooms: 5 Double, 1 twin, 2 family
Open: All year

Site: ❀ **Payment:** **Leisure:** **Property:** **Children:** **Catering:** **Room:**

Cairn Hotel

Ripon Road, Harrogate, North Yorkshire HG1 2JD **T:** (01423) 504005 **F:** (01423) 500056
E: salescairn@strathmorehotels.com
W: www.strathmorehotels.com **£ BOOK ONLINE**

enjoyEngland.com
★★★ HOTEL

B&B PER ROOM PER NIGHT
S: £50.00 - £130.00
D: £80.00 - £180.00
HB PER PERSON PER NIGHT
£60.00 - £150.00

SPECIAL PROMOTIONS
Free child places 0-4 years. Half-price 5-14 years. Christmas and New Year breaks available. Special last-minute breaks. See website.

Built during Harrogate's period as a spa town, stylish and comfortable decor goes hand in hand with gracious hospitality to offer a welcome that is second to none. This charming hotel is only five minutes walk from the town centre - ideal for leisure breaks, meetings/conferences and exhibitions.

Directions: By car: 7 miles off the north/south A1 and 17 miles from the M1/M62. By rail: Harrogate station. By air: Leeds/Bradford airport (12 miles).

Bedrooms: 13 single, 48 double, 65 twin, 8 family, 1 suite
Open: All year

Site: ✿ **Payment:** 💳 **Leisure:** 🕆 **Property:** 🍷 🖥 ● **Children:** 🛏 🏛 🏃 **Catering:** 🍴 🍽
Room: 🛁 📞 🍵 📺 🔌 📠 🔽

Cold Cotes Guest Accommodation, Gardens & Nursery

Cold Cotes Road, Felliscliffe, Harrogate HG3 2LW **T:** (01423) 770937
E: info@coldcotes.com
W: coldcotes.com

enjoyEngland.com
★★★★★ GUEST ACCOMMODATION
Gold AWARD

B&B PER ROOM PER NIGHT
S: £50.00 - £99.00
D: £50.00 - £99.00
EVENING MEAL PER PERSON
£7.50

On the edge of Nidderdale in the picturesque Yorkshire Dales. Guests say 'a special and relaxing place to stay, tranquil setting, beautiful and comfortable rooms, excellent food with an inspiring garden.' Convenient for RHS Harlow Carr. **Directions:** A59 west of Harrogate for 7 miles to Black Bull pub. Turn right after the pub onto Cold Cotes Road then third entrance on right. **Bedrooms:** All rooms have king or super king beds (+ 2 twins) **Open:** All year

Site: ✿ P **Payment:** 💳 **Leisure:** 🎵 ▶ ∪ **Property:** 🖥 **Children:** 🛏12 **Catering:** 🍴 🍽 **Room:** 🔌 🛁 🍵 📺 🔽

Coppice Guest House

9 Studley Road, Harrogate, Yorkshire, HG1 5JU HG1 5JU **T:** (01423) 569626
E: coppice@harrogate.com
W: www.guesthouseharrogate.com **£ BOOK ONLINE**

enjoyEngland.com
★★★★ GUEST HOUSE

B&B PER ROOM PER NIGHT
S: £40.00 - £50.00
D: £55.00 - £75.00
EVENING MEAL PER PERSON
£15.00 - £19.00

The Coppice Guest House B&B Harrogate. Quietly located on tree lined avenue 5 minutes walk from Harrogate town centre. Luxury en suite rooms. Free WiFi. Free parking. Full English or light breakfasts. A warm friendly welcome awaits you. **Directions:** Studley Road is off Kings Road close to The Conference Centre Kings Road is off the A59. The Coppice is close to the train and bus stations **Bedrooms:** 1 single, 2 double, 1 twin, 1 family **Open:** All year

Payment: 💳 € **Leisure:** ♿ 🎵 ▶ **Property:** 🖥 🗖 **Children:** 🛏 🏛 **Catering:** 🍽 **Room:** 🔽 🛁 🍵 📺

HARROGATE, North Yorkshire   Map ref 4B1   *SatNav HG3 1JH* H

★★★★ HOTEL

Gold AWARD

B&B PER ROOM PER NIGHT
S: £130.00 - £525.00
D: £151.00 - £555.00

Rudding Park

Follifoot, Harrogate, North Yorkshire HG3 1JH **T:** (01423) 871350 **F:** (01423) 872286
E: reservations@ruddingpark.com
W: ruddingpark.co.uk

The award winning hotel offers 90 bedrooms, contemporary Clocktower Restaurant, spa, gym, private cinema, two golf courses and extensive conference and banqueting facilities. **Directions:** Situated three miles south of Harrogate, Rudding Park lies just off the A658 linking the A61 from Leeds to the A59 York Road. **Bedrooms:** 90 Double/twin including 11 family and 8 suites
Open: All year

Site: ✿ **P Payment:** ⊡ € **Leisure:** ♪ ↱ ♈ 🎯 🏹 **Property:** ♟ 🖥 🗄 ☾ **Children:** 🛏 🎪 🧍
Catering: ♟ 🍴 **Room:** ☎ ♨ ☏ ⊙ TV 📺 ⚒ 🗄

HAWES, North Yorkshire   Map ref 5B3   *SatNav DL8 3PT* H

★★ HOTEL

Silver AWARD

B&B PER ROOM PER NIGHT
S: £60.00 - £190.00
D: £118.50 - £190.00
EVENING MEAL PER PERSON
£36.50

Stone House Hotel

Sedbusk, Hawes, Wensleydale DL8 3PT **T:** (01969) 667571 **F:** (01969) 667720
E: reception@stonehousehotel.co.uk
W: www.stonehousehotel.com **£ BOOK ONLINE**

A classic Edwardian Country House Hotel with delicious food, log fires and quality bedrooms. Discover the perfect setting for a revitalising short break in the Yorkshire Dales National Park. Secure storage available for mountain and motor bikes. **Directions:** Hotel is sign posted from Hawes (half mile) **Bedrooms:** 1 single, 11 dble, 5 twin, 1 family, 6 suite **Open:** Closed January

Site: ✿ **P Payment:** ⊡ **Leisure:** 🏊 ♪ ↱ ♈ 🐾 **Property:** 🐕 🖥 🗄 🎱 ⌀ **Children:** 🛏 🎪 🧍
Catering: (✗ ♟ 🍴 **Room:** ☎ ♨ ☏ ⊙ TV 📺 ⚒ 🗄

HUBY, North Yorkshire   Map ref 5C3   *SatNav YO61 1JB* H

★★★ HOTEL

B&B PER ROOM PER NIGHT
D: £50.00 - £120.00
HB PER PERSON PER NIGHT
£30.00 - £75.00

Tulip Inn York - Burn Hall Hotel

Tollerton Road, Huby, York YO61 1JB **T:** (01347) 825400 **F:** (01347) 838878
E: info@tulipinnyork.com
W: www.tulipinnyork.com **£ BOOK ONLINE**

Burn Hall is a perfect venue for weddings, events, business meetings and short breaks. You are invited to relax and unwind in the beautiful surroundings, enjoy the warm Yorkshire welcome from the experienced and friendly team and sample the delicious locally sourced produce in the restaurants.

Directions: Burn Hall is conveniently situated ¼ mile off the A19 heading north of York towards the market town of Easingwold.

Bedrooms: 84 double, 8 twin, 2 suite
Open: All year

Site: ✿ **Payment:** ⊡ **Leisure:** 🏊 ♪ ♈ 🎯 **Property:** ♟ 🐕 🖥 🗄 ☾ **Children:** 🛏 🎪 🧍 **Catering:** ♟ 🍴
Room: ☎ ♨ ☏ TV ⚒ 🗄

KIRKBY MALZEARD, North Yorkshire Map ref 5C3 SatNav HG4 3SR B

B&B PER ROOM PER NIGHT
S: £55.00 - £70.00
D: £80.00 - £95.00

Cowscot House

Back Lane, Kirkby Malzeard, Ripon, N. Yorkshire HG4 3SR **T:** (01765) 658181
E: liz@cowscothouse.co.uk
W: www.cowscothouse.co.uk **£ BOOK ONLINE**

Cowscot House offers a high standard of accommodation in a sympathetically converted stone barn and stables on the edge of a popular village. All the en suite bedrooms are on the ground floor and were refurbished in early 2009. **Directions:** From Ripon direction enter Kirkby Malzeard and continue down Main Street. Take right turn just after Highside Butchers turning immediately left into Back Lane. **Bedrooms:** 3 double, 1 twin **Open:** All year

Site: P **Payment:** **Leisure:** **Property:** **Children:** **Catering:** **Room:**

MALTON, North Yorkshire Map ref 5D3 SatNav YO60 6QD B

Gate Farm

Ganthorpe, Castle Howard, York, North Yorkshire YO60 6QD **T:** (01653) 648269
F: (01653) 648269 **E:** millgate001@msn.com
W: www.ganthorpegatefarm.co.uk

Working dairy farm, in quiet hamlet near to Castle Howard. Offering friendly, traditional Yorkshire hospitality. 5 star breakfasts, breakfast award. Convenient for the moors, East coast and York. Please contact us for prices. **Directions:** Close to Castle Howard, Yorkshire Lavender, Eden Camp, FlamingoLand, Coast and Moors, York. See map at www.ganthorpegatefarm.co.uk **Bedrooms:** 2 double, 2 twin, 1 family **Open:** All year

Site: P **Payment:** **Leisure:** **Property:** **Children:** **Catering:** **Room:**

MALTON, North Yorkshire Map ref 5D3 SatNav YO17 7EG B

B&B PER ROOM PER NIGHT
S: £85.00 - £96.00
D: £120.00 - £145.00

Old Lodge Malton

Old Maltongate, Malton YO17 7EG **T:** (01653) 690570 **F:** (01653) 690652
E: info@theoldlodgemalton.com
W: theoldlodgemalton.com **£ BOOK ONLINE**

Tudor mansion with luxurious four-poster bedrooms. Great restaurant serving freshly prepared, locally-sourced food. All-day Yorkshire Sunday lunch. All-day tea, coffee and clotted cream scones. Super gardens. **Directions:** Take the Malton exit from the A64. We are approx. 250 yards from the town centre, towards Old Malton. We're behind a big, old wall. **Bedrooms:** 20 double (onsite), 8 double (offsite) **Open:** All year

Site: P **Payment:** € **Leisure:** **Property:** **Children:** **Catering:** **Room:**

PICKERING, North Yorkshire Map ref 5D3 SatNav YO18 7JY B

B&B PER ROOM PER NIGHT
S: £45.00
D: £70.00

The Old Forge Bed & Breakfast

The Old Forge, Wilton, Pickering, North Yorkshire YO18 7JY **T:** (01751) 477399
E: theoldforge1@aol.com
W: forgecottages.co.uk

Dating from 1701. Comfortable, quality, relaxing, Bed and Breakfast. Private parking. Near Pickering Steam Railway, Dalby Forest, Yorkshire Moors, Eden Camp, fishing. Cyclists and walkers welcome. Close to Thornton-le-Dale. Excellent public transport. **Directions:** Follow the A170 Pickering Scarborough road. Turn left in Wilton, just after the bus stop. Park in courtyard behind The Old Forge. Sign on building **Bedrooms:** Comfortable, cosy and relaxing en suite rooms **Open:** All year. Ask about our special offers

Site: P **Leisure:** **Property:** **Children:** **Catering:** **Room:**

Yorkshire - North Yorkshire

BED & BREAKFAST

Frenchgate Guest House

66 Frenchgate, Richmond DL10 7AG **T:** 07889 768696 **E:** frenchgate66@icloud.com
W: www.66frenchgate.co.uk

B&B PER ROOM PER NIGHT
S: £55.00 - £70.00
D: £75.00 - £94.00

SPECIAL PROMOTIONS
Please see 'Special
Breaks' page on
website.

Award winning paradise, overlooking Richmond Countryside, the River Swale and Easby Abbey.
What a secret, a gem but found by the Lonely Planet Guide, The Rough Guide and the Virgin
magazine. Located near the centre of Richmond within level walking (200 metres) distance from the
town with great views and rooms with boutique style decor with king, queen, twin, comfy beds and
family en suite. Spacious bedrooms all provided with tea, coffee, biscuits, chocolates, fans, mini
fridges, hairdryer, mineral water and free Wi-Fi. Over breakfast enjoy the scrambled egg and salmon
or the full English Breakfast with a wide selection of fruit and juices and much more.

Directions: At the very top right of Frenchgate,   **Bedrooms:** 4 double, 2 twin, 2 family
from Market place, King Street, straight at rb,   **Open:** All year
right at rb, down 100metres, left into
Frenchgate, park on the top left.

Payment: 🔲 € **Leisure:** 🚴 ♪ ▸ ∪ **Property:** 🖥 🔲 🏛 **Children:** 🧒 **Catering:** 🍴
Room: 🔌 💧 📶 📺 🔌 📠

HOTEL

The Ripon Spa Hotel

Park Street, Ripon HG4 2BU **T:** (01765) 602172 **F:** (01765) 690770
E: sales@spahotelripon.co.uk
W: www.riponspa.com **£ BOOK ONLINE**

B&B PER ROOM PER NIGHT
S: £65.00 - £105.00
D: £69.00 - £145.00
EVENING MEAL PER PERSON
£12.95 - £22.95

Short walk from the centre of the ancient city of Ripon with its
magnificent Cathedral, the hotel stands in award-winning
landscaped gardens. You will discover traditional hospitality,
croquet lawns, free on-site parking & free Wi-Fi. Fountains Abbey
and Yorkshire Dales National Park nearby. **Directions:** Please see
website for directions **Bedrooms:** 4 single, 19 double, 15 twin & 2
family **Open:** All year

Site: ❀ **Payment:** 🔲 € **Property:** ♞ 🐾 🖥 🏛 ◐ ⌀ **Children:** 🧒 🏠 🎠
Catering: (✗ ▮ 🍴 **Room:** 🔌 💧 📶 📺 🔌 📠

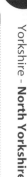

SALTBURN-BY-THE-SEA, North Yorkshire Map ref 5C3   SatNav TS12 2QX B

The Arches Country House

Manx Lodge, Low Farm, Ings Lane, Brotton, Salturn-By-The-Sea, North Yorkshire TS12 2QX
T: (01287) 677512 **F:** (01287) 677150 **E:** sales@gorallyschool.co.uk
W: www.thearcheshotel.co.uk **£ BOOK ONLINE**

B&B PER ROOM PER NIGHT
S: £45.00 - £60.00
D: £70.00 - £80.00

SPECIAL PROMOTIONS
Check website for
special offers.

The Arches Country House is an independent, family owned and run accommodation located not far from Saltburn in North Yorkshire. We pride ourselves on our relaxed, informal atmosphere. We offer bed and breakfast. We also offer functions and a conference facility. We are also licenced to hold a Civil Ceremony Weddings.

Directions: From North A1(M) Jnc60, A689 to A19 for Thirsk. From A19 to A174 toward Redcar, through Saltburn & Brotton. Stay on main road, 2nd left to St Margarets Way, past houses, past golf club, turn right

Bedrooms: All rooms en suite. Flat screen TV, tea & coffee making facilities. Four poster room, family, single, double, twin rooms and ground floor available
Open: All Year except Christmas and New Year

Site: ✿ P Payment: 💷 Leisure: ▶ Property: ⚡ 🐾 🖼 Children: 🌂 🛏 🚶 Catering: 🍽
Room: 📺 🖤 📺 🎿 📠

SCARBOROUGH, North Yorkshire Map ref 5D3   SatNav YO11 1XX B

Empire Guesthouse

39 Albemarle Crescent, Scarborough YO11 1XX **T:** (01723) 373564
E: gillian@empire1939.wanadoo.co.uk
W: empireguesthouse.co.uk

B&B PER ROOM PER NIGHT
S: £24.00 - £27.00
D: £54.00

The Empire overlooks pleasant gardens located in the centre of town, ideally situated for all Scarborough's many attractions and town centre amenities. Every effort made to make your visit enjoyable. Evening meals available from Easter until the end of September. **Directions:** The Empire is 5mins from bus & rail terminals. We extend a very warm welcome to all our guests **Bedrooms:** 2 single, 1 double, 1 twin, 1 family, 3 suite **Open:** All year except Christmas and New Year

Property: 🖼 📠 🏠 Children: 🌂 🛏 🚶 Catering: (X 🍽 🍴 Room: 📺 🖤 📺

SCARBOROUGH, North Yorkshire Map ref 5D3   SatNav YO12 7HU B

Howdale

121 Queen's Parade, Scarborough YO12 7HU **T:** (01723) 372696 **E:** mail@howdale.co.uk
W: howdale.co.uk

B&B PER ROOM PER NIGHT
S: £24.00 - £29.00
D: £54.00 - £72.00

Beautifully situated overlooking the North Bay and Scarborough Castle, yet close to town. We are renowned for our cleanliness and the friendly, efficient service we provide in a comfortable atmosphere. **Directions:** At traffic lights opposite railway station turn left. Next traffic lights turn right. At 1st roundabout turn left. Property is 0.5 miles on the right **Bedrooms:** 1 single, 11 double, 2 twin, 1 family **Open:** March to October

Site: ✿ P Payment: 💷 Property: 🐾 🖼 🏠 Children: 🌂 🛏 🚶 Room: 📺 🖤 📺

SCARBOROUGH, North Yorkshire   Map ref 5D3   SatNav YO11 3TP   B

Killerby Cottage Farm

Killerby Cottage Farm, Killerby Lane, Cayton, Scarborough YO11 3TP **T:** (01723) 581236
E: val@killerbycottagefarm.co.uk
W: www.killerbycottagefarm.co.uk **£ BOOK ONLINE**

B&B PER ROOM PER NIGHT
S: £45.00 - £50.00
D: £75.00 - £85.00
EVENING MEAL PER PERSON
£15.00 - £20.00

Situated between the seaside resorts of Scarborough and Filey, 1.5 miles from Cayton Bay next to the Stained Glass Centre. The farmhouse has been converted from 2 cottages and is tastefully decorated. Good food, lovely garden, warm welcome.
Directions: Situated just off the B1261 between Cayton and Lebberston **Bedrooms:** 2 double, 1 twin/double **Open:** All year except Christmas and New Year

Site: ❀ **P** **Payment:** 💷 € **Property:** ▭ **Catering:** ▦ **Room:** 🖐 🔌 📶 📺

SCARBOROUGH, North Yorkshire   Map ref 5D3   SatNav YO12 7HY   B

The Whiteley

99-101 Queens Parade, Scarborough YO12 7HY **T:** (01723) 373514 **F:** (01723) 373007
E: thewhiteley@gmail.com
W: yorkshirecoast.co.uk/whiteley

B&B PER ROOM PER NIGHT
S: £35.50 - £37.00
D: £58.00 - £70.00

SPECIAL PROMOTIONS
Oct-May inclusive (excl Bank Holidays): reduction of £1.50pppn when staying 2 nights or more.

Small, family-run, non-smoking, licensed guest accommodation located in an elevated position overlooking the North Bay, close to the town centre and ideally situated for all amenities. The bedrooms are well co-ordinated and equipped with useful extras, many with sea views. Good home cooking is served in the traditional dining room.

Directions: Left at traffic lights near railway station, right at next lights, Castle Road to roundabout. Left onto North Marine Road. 2nd right onto Queens Parade.

Bedrooms: 7 double, 3 family
Open: All year except Christmas and New Year

Site: ❀ **P** **Payment:** 💷 **Property:** ▭ ♨ **Children:** 🚼3 **Catering:** 🍴 ▦ **Room:** 🖐 🔌 📞 📺 🍳

Book your accommodation online

Visit our new 2014 guide websites for detailed information, up-to-date availability and to book your accommodation online. Includes over 20,000 places to stay, all of them star rated.
www.visitor-guides.co.uk

SINNINGTON, North Yorkshire   Map ref 5C3   SatNav YO62 6SQ **B**

B&B PER ROOM PER NIGHT
S: £59.00 - £84.00
D: £70.00 - £170.00

EVENING MEAL PER PERSON
£8.95 - £22.95

SPECIAL PROMOTIONS
2 and 3 night breaks
often available
throughout the year
for reduced rates.
Telephone or see
website for last-minute
offers.

Fox and Hounds

Main Street, Sinnington, Nr Pickering, North Yorkshire YO62 6SQ **T:** (01751) 431577
F: (01751) 432791 **E:** fox.houndsinn@btconnect.com
W: thefoxandhoundsinn.co.uk **£ BOOK ONLINE**

The Fox and Hounds Inn is an 18th century coaching inn which is located in the quiet village of
Sinnington, on the edge of the North York Moors National Park, just off the A170 Pickering to
Kirbymoorside road.

Directions: Between Pickering and
Kikbymoorisde on the A170.

Bedrooms: 8 double, 2 twin
Open: All year except Christmas

Site: **P** Payment: ⊞ Property: 🐾 🖼 Children: 🧸 🏚 🏃 Catering: 🍽 🍴 Room: 📶 🔌 📞 📺 🛁

SKIPTON, North Yorkshire   Map ref 4B1   SatNav BD23 4EA **H**

B&B PER ROOM PER NIGHT
S: £101.50 - £135.50
D: £116.00 - £150.00

EVENING MEAL PER PERSON
£10.00 - £32.00

Coniston Hotel and Country Estate

Coniston Cold, Skipton BD23 4EA **T:** (01756) 748080 **F:** (01756) 749487
E: reservations@theconistonhotel.com
W: www.theconistonhotel.com **£ BOOK ONLINE**

Set in 1,400 acre estate offering a warm friendly reception. Excellent
restaurant overlooking the lake. Onsite falconry centre, CPSA
Premier Plus clay pigeon shooting site, Land Rover experience,
archery, target golf, mountain bikes. **Directions:** On the A65
between Skipton (7 miles) and Settle (9 miles) at Coniston Cold. Just
8 miles from Malham **Bedrooms:** 65 double, 6 family.
Open: All year

 Site: ✿ **P** Payment: ⊞ € Leisure: 🚴 ⚓ 🏌 ⛵ 🎣 Property: ⊕ 🍽 🐾 🖼 🛏 🏵 ◐ 🕯 Children: 🧸 🏚
🏃 Catering: ⟨✗ 🍴 🍽 Room: 📶 🔌 📞 📺 📀 🛁

SKIPTON, North Yorkshire   Map ref 4B1   SatNav BD20 8LJ **B**

B&B PER ROOM PER NIGHT
S: £60.00 - £70.00
D: £70.00 - £90.00

Cononley Hall Bed & Breakfast

Main Street, Cononley, Skipton BD20 8LJ **T:** (01535) 633923
E: cononleyhall@madasafish.com
W: www.guesthouseskipton.co.uk **£ BOOK ONLINE**

Grade II Listed Georgian house in unspoilt village, near Skipton.
Cononley Hall is ideally located for those wishing to explore the
picturesque Yorkshire Dales or the Bronte countryside. All rooms en
suite with excellent facilities. **Directions:** A629, head for Cononley
station. Across level crossing, up Main Street. New Inn on right.
25yds up on left. **Bedrooms:** 1 Four-poster/family room. 1 Kingsize,
1 Twin **Open:** All year except Christmas & New Year

Site: ✿ **P** Payment: ⊞ Leisure: 🏌 Property: 🖼 Children: 🧸 🏚 🏃 Catering: 🍽 Room: 📶 🔌 📺 🛁

Poppy Cottage Guest House

Ivy Cottage Farm, Main Street, Carleton-in-Craven, Skipton, North Yorkshire BD23 3BY
T: (01756) 792874 **E:** sallystevehall@gmail.com
W: www.poppycottageguesthouse.co.uk **£ BOOK ONLINE**

B&B PER ROOM PER NIGHT
S: £45.00 - £55.00
D: £70.00 - £85.00

Idyllic 17C traditional 'Dales Longhouse' offering guests quality B&B accommodation in this 'lovingly restored' farmhouse. Just 2 miles and within comfortable walking distance of Skipton. In the lovely village setting of Carleton-in-Craven. **Bedrooms:** All rooms are en suite and have beautiful views. **Open:** All Year

Site: ✿ P Payment: 🖃 Leisure: ⚔ Property: 🖥 🗃 ⛏ ⌀ Children: 🍴 ⚲ Catering: 🍽 Room: 🛎 ♨ 📻 📺 📀

Tarn House Country Inn

Stirton, Nr Skipton BD23 3LQ **T:** (01756) 794891 **F:** (01756) 799040
E: reception@tarnhouse.net
W: partingtons.com **£ BOOK ONLINE**

B&B PER ROOM PER NIGHT
S: £65.00
D: £95.00

Conveniently located on the outskirts of Skipton, this Victorian country house is set in a 2 acre caravan park with superb gardens and magnificent views of the Yorkshire Dales. Recently refurbished bedrooms and public areas.

Directions: Please contact us for directions.

Bedrooms: 1 single, 4 double, 4 twin, 1 family
Open: February 14th - Mid December 2014

Site: ✿ P Payment: 🖃 Leisure: 🚴 🎵 ⛳ ⛷ Property: 🖥 🗃 Children: 🛝 ⚲ ⚲ Catering: 🍷 🍽 Room: 🛎 ♨ 📺 📀

Low Osgoodby Grange

Low Osgoodby Grange, Bagby, Thirsk, North Yorkshire YO7 2AL **T:** (01845) 597241
E: lowosgoodbygrange@googlemail.com
W: www.lowosgoodbygrange.com

B&B PER ROOM PER NIGHT
S: £55.00
D: £70.00 - £80.00

A warm welcome awaits at Georgian farm 4 star silver family run B&B situated below the Hambleton Hills. All en suite rooms, to high standard with breakfast using local produce. Ideal location for visiting attractions and local restaurants. **Directions:** Situated 5 miles out of Thirsk off the A170 between the villages of Bagby and Kilburn. **Bedrooms:** 1 double, 1 king size, 1 family double and single **Open:** All year except christmas

Site: ✿ P Leisure: 🎵 ⛳ ⛷ Property: 🖥 Children: 🛝 ⚲ ⚲ Catering: 🍽 Room: 🛎 ♨ 📻 📺 🍴

WEAVERTHORPE, North Yorkshire Map ref 5D3
SatNav YO17 8EX [H]

Blue Bell Inn

Main Street, Weaverthorpe, Malton YO17 8EX **T:** (01944) 738204 **F:** (01944) 738204
E: bluebellinn@hotmail.co.uk
W: bluebellweaverthorpe.com

Family owned country Inn, award winning restaurant and private dining rooms. Dinner B&B package available, ideally situated for east coast and Ganton Golf Club. Please contact for prices. **Directions:** Situated 4 Miles off the A64, six miles from Ganton Golf Course, 15 Mins From Bridlington, Scarborough and Filey. **Bedrooms:** 6 double, 4 twin, 2 suite **Open:** All year

Site: ✿ Payment: 🖃 Leisure: ♿ ♪ ▶ ♾ Property: 🍷 🖥 🗎 Children: 🍼 🏵 ⚐ Catering: 🍴 ▥ Room: 🔌 ☕ TV

WEST WITTON, North Yorkshire Map ref 5B3
SatNav DL8 4LU [B]

The Old Star

Main Street, West Witton, Leyburn, North Yorkshire DL8 4LU **T:** (01969) 622949
E: enquiries@theoldstar.com
W: www.theoldstar.com

B&B PER ROOM PER NIGHT
S: £28.00 - £40.00
D: £54.00 - £64.00

Former 18th century coaching inn set in the heart of Wensleydale with good views, oak beams, log fire, cottage gardens and a friendly atmosphere. Excellent centre for walking and exploring the Dales. Two nearby pubs serve good food and ale. **Directions:** West Witton is on the A684, 4 miles west of Leyburn. Northallerton is our nearest station, there is a bus from Northallerton to West Witton via Bedale **Bedrooms:** 4 double, 1 twin, 2 flexible/family **Open:** All year except Christmas

Site: ✿ P Payment: 🖃 € Leisure: ♪ Property: 🐾 🖥 ♫ ⌀ Children: 🍼 🏵 ⚐ Catering: ▥ Room: 🔌 ☕ TV ♨

WHITBY, North Yorkshire Map ref 5D3
SatNav YO21 1QL [H]

Bagdale Hall, No. 4 & Lodge

1 Bagdale, Whitby YO21 1QL **T:** (01947) 602958 **F:** (01947) 820714
E: bagdale@btconnect.com
W: www.bagdale.co.uk

B&B PER ROOM PER NIGHT
S: £70.00 - £130.00
D: £90.00 - £240.00
EVENING MEAL PER PERSON
£15.00 - £35.00

SPECIAL PROMOTIONS
3 nights for the price of 2.
2 nights for the price of 1.
Ring for details.

Whitby, Yorkshire. Bagdale Hall is an old Tudor Manor House dating back to 1516. No.4 Bagdale is a Georgian town house built around 1790. Bagdale Lodge is a large detached Georgian house circa 1770.

Directions: Bagdale Hall is located in the centre of town a 2 minute walk to Whitby Harbour.

Bedrooms: 21 dble, 2 twin, 4 suite
Open: All year

Site: P Payment: 🖃 Leisure: ♿ ♪ ▶ ♾ Property: 🍷 🖥 🗎 ♫ Children: 🍼 🏵 ⚐ Catering: (✗ 🍷 ▥ Room: 🔌 ☕ ☎ 🎥 TV ♨ 🖥

[f]

Need more information?

Visit our new 2014 guide websites for detailed information, up-to-date availability and to book your accommodation online. Includes over 20,000 places to stay, all of them star rated.

www.visitor-guides.co.uk

Dunsley Hall Country House Hotel

Dunsley, Whitby YO21 3TL **T:** (01947) 893437 **F:** (01947) 893505
E: reception@dunsleyhall.com
W: dunsleyhall.com **£ BOOK ONLINE**

B&B PER ROOM PER NIGHT
S: £105.00
D: £159.00

SPECIAL PROMOTIONS
Special break rates available, please see our website or call for details

A True Yorkshire welcome awaits you here at Dunsley Hall. Once a dream home tailor made for a Victorian shipping magnate, now a haven of tranquillity for visitors from all over the world. A true Victorian country house, Dunsley Hall offers traditional comfort and wonderful food against a backdrop of period elegance and modern charm. Locations such as Dunsley Hall are truly rare in these parts.

Directions: From the North: From A19 Middlesbrough follow the A174; then A171 Guisborough/Whitby. From the South: From the A64 East-bound take the A169 Pickering/Whitby.

Bedrooms: 2 single, 14 dble, 7 twin, 1 family, 2 suite
Open: All year

Site: ❀ Payment: £ € Leisure: ♒ ♪ ► ∪ ☍ Property: ♟ ▤ ▤ ◑ Children: ⛱ ⊞ ☂ Catering: ♟ ⛾ Room: ℞ ♨ ☏ ▦

The Middleham

3 Church Square, Whitby, North Yorkshire YO21 3EG **T:** (01947) 603423 **F:** (01947) 603423
E: themiddleham@btinternet.com
W: www.themiddleham.co.uk

B&B PER ROOM PER NIGHT
S: £35.00 - £68.00
D: £68.00 - £80.00

Family run guesthouse with stunning sea views. Situated on the magnificent West Cliff area of Whitby, close to the town centre and all other amenities. Also within a 5 minute walk of Whitby Pavilion. **Directions:** Please see website for details. **Bedrooms:** Single, Twin, Family and Double Four Poster room available. **Open:** All Year

Payment: £ Leisure: ♪ ► ☍ ◊ Property: ▤ ⅄ Children: ⛱ ⊞ ☂ Catering: ⛾ Room: ℞ ♨ ☏ ▦ ⌨

Sneaton Castle Centre

Castle Road, Whitby YO21 3QN **T:** (01947) 600051 **F:** (01947) 603490
E: reception@sneatoncastle.co.uk
W: www.sneatoncastle.co.uk

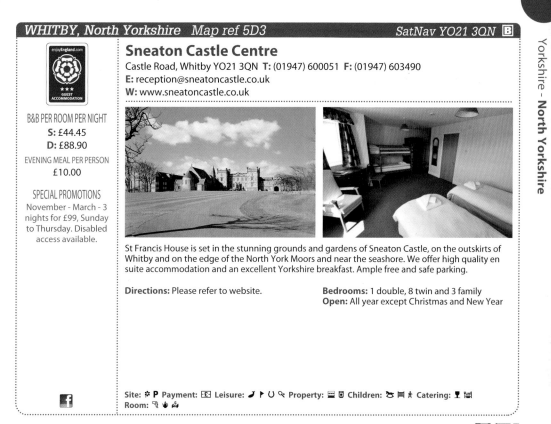

St Francis House is set in the stunning grounds and gardens of Sneaton Castle, on the outskirts of Whitby and on the edge of the North York Moors and near the seashore. We offer high quality en suite accommodation and an excellent Yorkshire breakfast. Ample free and safe parking.

Directions: Please refer to website.

Bedrooms: 1 double, 8 twin and 3 family
Open: All year except Christmas and New Year

B&B PER ROOM PER NIGHT
S: £44.45
D: £88.90

EVENING MEAL PER PERSON
£10.00

SPECIAL PROMOTIONS
November - March - 3 nights for £99, Sunday to Thursday. Disabled access available.

Site: ✿ **P** **Payment:** 💷 **Leisure:** ♪ ▶ ♿ ⚲ **Property:** 💻 🖥 **Children:** 🛏 🍴 **Catering:** 🍷 🍽 **Room:** 📺 ♨ 🍳

Looking for something else?

The official and most comprehensive guide to independently inspected, star rated accommodation.

B&Bs and Hotels - B&Bs, Hotels, farmhouses, inns, serviced apartments, campus and hostel accommodation in England.

Self Catering - Self-catering holiday homes, approved caravan holiday homes, boat accommodation and holiday cottage agencies in England.

Camping, Touring and Holiday Parks - Touring parks, camping holidays and holiday parks and villages in Britain.

Now available in all good bookshops and online at **www.hudsons.co.uk/shop**

OFFICIAL TOURIST BOARD GUIDE
New 39th edition

Self Catering
England's star-rated holiday h...
2014
www.visitor-guides.co.uk

OFFICIAL TOURIST BOARD GUIDE
New 39th edition

B&Bs and Hotels
England's star-rated guest accommodation
2014
www.visitor-guides.co.uk

OFFICIAL TOURIST...
New 39th edition

Camping, Touring & Holiday Parks
Britain's star-rated holiday parks
2014
www.visitor-guides.co.uk

Yorkshire - North Yorkshire

YORK, North Yorkshire *Map ref 4C1*   SatNav YO1 6JX **B**

Ace Hostel York

Micklegate House, 88-90 Micklegate, York YO1 6JX **T:** (01904) 627720 **F:** (01904) 651350
E: reception@acehostelyork.co.uk
W: www.acehostelyork.co.uk **£ BOOK ONLINE**

B&B PER ROOM PER NIGHT
S: £16.00 - £84.00
D: £80.00 - £84.00
BED ONLY PER NIGHT
£16.00 - £84.00

City centre 4 star hostel with en suite dorms and private rooms, 24 hour reception, free Wi-Fi, bar with snacks, guest kitchen, TV & games lounge, laundry facilities, courtyard & full air conditioning throughout. **Directions:** From train/bus station - turn right out of the station. Walk 300m the traffic lights. Turn left onto Micklegate and we are 200m on the left. **Bedrooms:** Rooms are en suite bar one. All privates have TV **Open:** 24 hours a day 365 days a year!

Payment: ... **Property:** ... **Catering:** ... **Bedroom:** ...

YORK, North Yorkshire *Map ref 4C1*   SatNav YO31 7YH **B**

Ascot House

80 East Parade, York YO31 7YH **T:** (01904) 426826 **F:** (01904) 431077
E: admin@ascothouseyork.com
W: ascothouseyork.com **£ BOOK ONLINE**

B&B PER ROOM PER NIGHT
S: £60.00 - £85.00
D: £75.00 - £110.00

A family-run Victorian guesthouse, built in 1869, with en suite rooms of character, some with four-poster or antique canopy beds. Award winning English, continental and vegetarian breakfasts. Fifteen minutes walk to historic walled city centre, castle museum or York Minster. Residential licence and residents lounge. Private enclosed car park. Free WiFi. All major credit cards accepted.

Directions: From M1 take A64 then A1036 from east into York. 100yds past 30mph signs, take 2nd exit off roundabout. Right at lights into East Parade.

Bedrooms: 7 double, 2 twin, 3 family all with en suite facilities. All rooms have flatscreen TV & complimentary tea and coffee making facilities. **Open:** All year except Christmas

Site: P **Payment:** ... **Property:** ... **Children:** ... **Catering:** ... **Room:** ...

YORK, North Yorkshire *Map ref 4C1*   SatNav YO23 1NX **B**

Avondale Guest House

61 Bishopthorpe Road, York, North Yorkshire YO23 1NX **T:** (01904) 633989 / 07958 021024
E: kaleda@avondaleguesthouse.co.uk
W: www.avondaleguesthouse.co.uk **£ BOOK ONLINE**

B&B PER ROOM PER NIGHT
S: £46.00
D: £68.00 - £84.00

Avondale, a lovely Victorian home, short walk to medieval walls, city, attractions, river walks, racecourse and station. Comfortable en suite rooms with award winning fresh breakfast menu, try our Whisky Porridge. **Directions:** Short walk from train/bus station. Drive from south A19, A1 or A64, from north A19 or A59. Find us easily from instructions on website. **Bedrooms:** 1 single, 3 double, 1 twin/king, 1 family **Open:** All year except Christmas

Site: P **Payment:** ... **Property:** ... **Children:** ... **Catering:** ... **Room:** ...

YORK, North Yorkshire   Map ref 4C1   SatNav YO30 7DH **H**

Hedley House Hotel & Apartments

3 Bootham Terrace, York YO30 7DH **T:** (01904) 637404 **F:** (01904) 639774
E: greg@hedleyhouse.com
W: www.hedleyhouse.com **£ BOOK ONLINE**

★★★ HOTEL *Silver* AWARD

B&B PER ROOM PER NIGHT
S: £70.00 - £110.00
D: £95.00 - £175.00

EVENING MEAL PER PERSON
£12.95 - £23.95

Award wining 3 star city centre hotel. In a quiet location, serving fabulous homemade food from local suppliers. Beautician (massage and nails etc), Gym, lounge bar, Jacuzzi and Sauna. Free wifi and off street parking. **Directions:** From south A1 A64 A1237 York North - A19 city centre under footbridge 2nd right. From North A1 A59 A1237 York North A19 as above **Bedrooms:** 2 single, 7 double, 6 twin, 11 family **Open:** All year except Christmas

Site: ✿ **P Payment:** ⊞ **Leisure:** 🎣 ♪ ▶ ♒ ⚲ **Property:** 🖥 🖳 ♨ ⌀ **Children:** 🛏 🏖 🅰 **Catering:** ⟨✗ 👤 🍴 **Room:** 🍵 🛁 📞 💿 📺 👚

YORK, North Yorkshire   Map ref 4C1   SatNav YO10 4HE **B**

Limes

135 Fulford Road, York YO10 4HE **T:** (01904) 624548 **F:** (01904) 624944
E: queries@limeshotel.co.uk
W: www.limeshotel.co.uk

★★★★ GUEST HOUSE *Silver* AWARD

B&B PER ROOM PER NIGHT
S: £55.00 - £99.00
D: £70.00 - £99.00

Friendly family guest house, near city, racecourse, university, golf course, designer outlet. Licensed, private car park, en suite rooms, welcome tray, colour TV, clock/radio alarm, ipod dock, hairdryer, toiletries. Award winning breakfast. **Directions:** From A1, take A64 to York. A64 becomes the outer ring road of York. Take slip road for York Centre, A19 (Selby). **Bedrooms:** 4 double, 3 twin, 1 family **Open:** All year except Christmas

Site: ✿ **P Payment:** ⊞ € **Property:** 🖥 **Children:** 🛏 🏖 🅰 **Catering:** 👤 🍴 **Room:** 🍵 🛁 💿 📺 👚

YORK, North Yorkshire   Map ref 4C1   SatNav YO1 6DH **H**

The Queens Hotel

Queens Staith Road, Skeldergate, York YO1 6DH **T:** (01904) 611321 **F:** (01904) 650690
E: sales@queenshotel-york.com
W: queenshotel-york.com

★★ HOTEL

B&B PER ROOM PER NIGHT
S: £70.00 - £99.00
D: £79.00 - £120.00

EVENING MEAL PER PERSON
£9.95 - £20.00

Ideally located on the banks of the river in the heart of the city of York, The Queens Hotel offers quality accommodation for leisure, families and groups. The restaurant is open daily and serves breakfast and dinner. A warm welcome awaits. **Bedrooms:** 30 dble, 25 twin, 23 family **Open:** All year

Payment: ⊞ **Property:** 🖥 **Children:** 🛏 🏖 🅰 **Catering:** 👤 🍴 **Room:** 🍵 🛁 📞 💿 📺 👚 🍽

For **key to symbols** see page 7

★★★★
GUEST
ACCOMMODATION

York House

62 Heworth Green, York YO31 7TQ **T:** (01904) 427070 **F:** (01904) 427070
E: info@yorkhouseyork.co.uk
W: yorkhouseyork.co.uk **£ BOOK ONLINE**

B&B PER ROOM PER NIGHT
S: £31.00 - £36.00
D: £70.00 - £95.00

SPECIAL PROMOTIONS
Early Bird Payment
discount scheme of
10% on double and
twin rooms on
bookings made and
paid 14 days prior to
date of arrival.

Located a short stroll from the heart of one of Europe's most historic cities, York House is the perfect base for a visit to York or the surrounding area. A Georgian house with later additions, rooms feature all the modern conveniences you could possibly need for a relaxing, enjoyable stay.

Directions: North east of York, A1036 signed City Centre. Straight over roundabouts and 2 sets traffic lights, next mini-roundabout 3rd exit. York House 300yds on left.

Bedrooms: 1 single, 6 double, 1 twin,
Open: All year except Christmas and New Year

Site: ✿ P Payment: 🔲 Property: 🛏 Children: 🚸 🍴 ♿ Catering: 🍽 Room: 🔌 ♨ 📺 ♨ 🧳

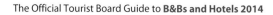

DONCASTER, South Yorkshire   Map ref 4C1   SatNav DN2 6AD   [H]

Earl of Doncaster Hotel

Bennetthorpe, Doncaster DN2 6AD **T:** (01302) 361371 **F:** (01302) 321858
E: reception@theearl.co.uk
W: www.theearl.co.uk

SPECIAL PROMOTIONS
Please contact us for prices.

The Earl of Doncaster Hotel is superbly located within 500 metres of Doncaster Racecourse and the town centre, offering free on site parking. This impressive Art Deco, 4 Star, Classic British Hotel, has beautifully designed executive bedrooms, a stylish restaurant and a magnificent Ballroom that epitomizes all the character and charm of the hotel. The Earl – one of Doncaster's best kept secrets.

Directions: Follow the signs for Doncaster Racecourse, at the roundabout take the A638 (Bennetthorpe) towards the Town Centre, the hotel is located on the left and car park is situated at the rear of the hotel.

Bedrooms: En suite, flat screen TVs, Wi-Fi, tea & coffee Facilities, 24 hour room service, climate control, iron & ironing boards
Open: All year

Site: P **Payment:** ▣ **Leisure:** ▶ ⚔ **Property:** ⊛ ♒ ♖ ⛁ ♨ ◑ **Children:** ➷ ⨶ ⚲ **Catering:** (✕ ♟ ⚏
Room: ⚲ ☕ ⚲ TV ♨ ▦

HEBDEN BRIDGE, West Yorkshire   Map ref 4B1   SatNav HX7 8PH   [B]

Mount Skip Bed & Breakfast

1 Mount Skip, Wadsworth, Hebden Bridge HX7 8PH **T:** (01422) 842903
E: mountskipbandb@hotmail.com
W: www.mountskipbandb.co.uk

B&B PER ROOM PER NIGHT
S: £40.00 - £45.00
D: £60.00 - £70.00

Mount Skip is a small family run B&B with a warm welcome. Set high on the Pennine hills we offer stunning views, a comfortable stay and an excellent hearty breakfast. **Directions:** Approaching Hebden Bridge from Halifax pass the railway station, fork right onto Commercial Street, then right Birchcliffe Road. Keep going!! House in front T junction **Bedrooms:** 1 double, 1 twin, 1 family **Open:** All year

Site: ✿ P **Payment:** € **Leisure:** ▶ ♒ **Property:** ▣ ♨ **Children:** ➷ ⚲ **Catering:** ⚏ **Room:** ⚲

WAKEFIELD, West Yorkshire   Map ref 4B1   SatNav WF1 1EH   [B]

The Bank House Hotel

11 Bank Street, Westgate, Wakefield WF1 1EH **T:** (01924) 368248 **F:** (01924) 363724
E: manager@thebankhousehotelandrestaurant.com

B&B PER ROOM PER NIGHT
S: £40.00
D: £50.00
EVENING MEAL PER PERSON
£5.00 - £10.00

City-centre licensed hotel run by professional staff. All rooms have en suite facilities, digital television, telephones, tea/coffee facilities, restaurant facilities and room service. All party bookings welcome. **Directions:** City central, 2 minutes walk away from Westgate's railway station and main bus depot. Close to all the main shops, restaurants, bars and the theatre. **Bedrooms:** 3 single, 6 double, 3 twin, 1 family **Open:** All year

Site: P **Payment:** ▣ **Leisure:** ♿ ♪ ▶ **Property:** ▦ ▣ **Children:** ➷ **Catering:** ♟ ⚏ **Room:** ⚲ ☕ ④ TV ♨ ▦

North West

The North West is a region of contrast, from the cosmopolitan style and contemporary built environment of Manchester to the cultural credentials and architectural grandeur of Liverpool, from the Roman and medieval heritage of Chester to the rolling hills of Lancashire and the stunning scenery around the Lake District. Whether you are looking for urban or rural scenery, a relaxed or an energetic atmosphere, this region will not disappoint.

Highlights

Blackpool

Blackpool is Britain's most popular holiday destination, which comes as no surprise when you think about the resort's range of year-round attractions. But Blackpool is changing. There's a breathtaking new seafront plus world class events and spectacular lighting shows.

Chester

Visit Chester and Cheshire and you'll find a region bursting with character and variation. Quaint market towns and villages can be found dotted throughout the largely unspoilt rural landscape, while Chester provides top-class shopping, entertainment and dining opportunities.

Lake District

The largest of the UK's National Parks, this area contains 16 lakes, more than 150 high peaks, with four over 3000 feet, including England's highest mountain, Scafell Pike (3206 ft).

Liverpool

Liverpool was one of the largest ports in the world during the 18th and 19th centuries, and was a major port involved in the slave trade until its abolition in 1807.

Manchester

The city has over 90 museums and galleries, and its theatres offer a variety of performances from classic plays to spectacular musicals. Manchester is also a haven for shopping.

Scafell Pike

Scafell Pike is the highest mountain in England at 978 metres, and is located in the Lake District National Park. It is sometimes confused with the neighbouring Sca Fell, to which it is connected by the col of Mickledore.

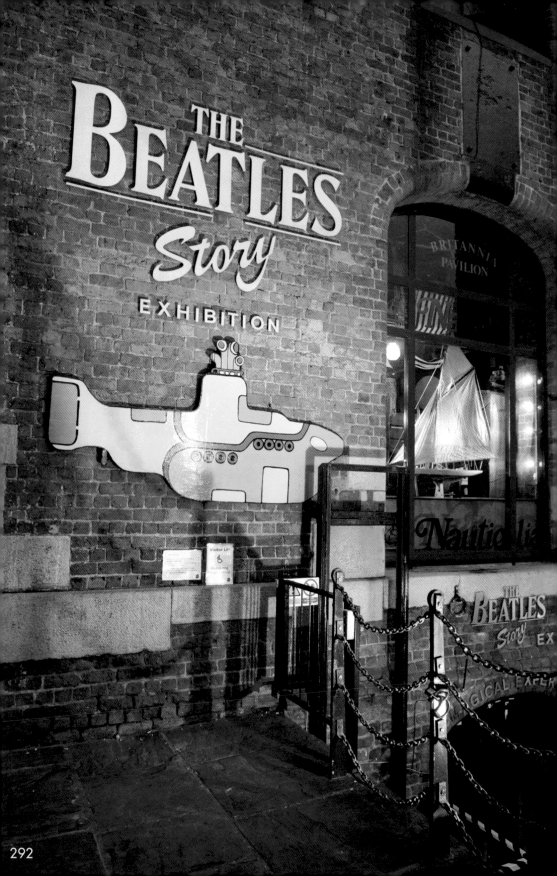

Editor's Picks

Visit a sporting venue

The North West has a great sporting tradition with football, cricket, golf and horse racing, and a trip to one of the area's main stadiums is a must for fans.

Cruise the Mersey

Mersey Ferries offer a 50-minute River Explorer cruise with commentary. Stop at Spaceport and experience the space themed attraction.

Don't get lost

The Lake District National Park runs map-reading skills days to improve visitors' navigation skills and organises hunting for treasure sessions for children.

Take to the water

With over 16 lakes and numerous tarns in the Lake District plus a stretch of coastline there's plenty of opportunity to go rowing, sailing, windsurfing, kayaking, fishing or simply splash about on the shore.

Discover the Beatles Story

Be transported on an incredible journey and see how four young lads from Liverpool were propelled to the dizzy heights of fame and fortune from their humble childhood beginnings.

Things to do

Entertainment & Culture

Beatles Story
Liverpool, Merseyside L3 4AD
(0151) 709 1963
www.beatlesstory.com
Located within Liverpool's historic Albert Dock, the Beatles Story is a unique visitor attraction that transports you on an enlightening and atmospheric journey into the life, times, culture and music of the Beatles.

Imperial War Museum North
Greater Manchester M17 1TZ
(0161) 836 4000
www.iwm.org.uk/north
Located at The Quays and offers dynamic display techniques to reflect on how people's lives are shaped by war. Free Admission.

Liverpool Football Club
Merseyside L4 0TH
(0151) 260 6677
www.liverpoolfc.tv
Meet an LFC Legend; get your photograph with one of our many trophies or indulge yourself in one of our award winning Experience Days.

Lowry
Salford, Greater Manchester M50 3AZ
08432 086000
www.thelowry.com
Salford's answer to the Sydney Opera House and the Guggenheim rolled into one. See LS Lowry's works and other outstanding exhibitions or take in a performance.

Manchester Art Gallery
Greater Manchester M2 3JL
(0161) 235 8888
www.manchestergalleries.org
Houses one of the country's finest art collections in spectacular Victorian and Contemporary surroundings. Also changing exhibitions and a programme of events and a host of free family friendly resources.

Manchester Museum
Greater Manchester M13 9PL
(0161) 275 2648
www.manchester.ac.uk/museum
Found on Oxford Road, on The University of Manchester campus (in a very impressive gothic-style building), highlights include Stan the T.rex, mummies, live animals such as frogs and snakes, object handling and a varied programme of events.

Manchester United Museum & Tour Centre
Greater Manchester M16 0RA
(0161) 868 8000
www.manutd.com
*The official museum and tour offers every football fan a
unique insight into Manchester United Football Club and a
fantastic day out.*

Museum of Lakeland Life
Kendal, Cumbria LA9 5AL
(015397) 22464
www.lakelandmuseum.org.uk
*This award-winning museum takes you and your family
back through time to tell the story of the Lake District and
its inhabitants.*

National Waterways Museum
Ellesmere Port, Cheshire CH65 4FW
(0151) 335 5017
www.nwm.org.uk/ellesmere
Unlock the wonders of our waterways.

People's History Museum
Greater Manchester M3 3ER
(0161) 838 9190
www.phm.org.uk
The new People's History Museum is now open

Ribchester Roman Museum
Preston, Lancashire PR3 3XS
(01254) 878261
www.ribchesterromanmuseum.org
*Lancashire's only specialist Roman museum, located on the
North bank of the beautiful River Ribble.*

Tate Liverpool
Merseyside L3 4BB
(0151) 702 7400
www.tate.org.uk/liverpool
*Tate Liverpool presents displays and international
exhibitions of modern and contemporary art in beautiful
light filled galleries.*

The Gallery Liverpool
Merseyside L8 5RE
(0151) 709 2442
www.thegalleryliverpool.co.uk
*Set in the heart of Liverpool's Independent Cultural District,
the gallery occupies the entire upper floor of the industrial
premises of John O'Keeffe and Son Ltd*

The World of Beatrix Potter
Bowness, Cumbria LA23 3BX
(015394) 88444
www.hop-skip-jump.com
*A magical indoor attraction that brings to life all 23 Beatrix
Potter's Peter Rabbit tales*

Walker Art Gallery
Liverpool, Merseyside L3 8EL
(0151) 478 4199
www.walkerartgallery.org.uk
*Home to outstanding works by Rubens, Rembrandt,
Poussin, Gainsborough and Hogarth, the Walker Art Gallery
is one of the finest art galleries in Europe.*

Whitworth Art Gallery
Manchester M15 6ER
(0161) 275 7450
www.whitworth.manchester.ac.uk
*The Whitworth Art Gallery is home
to an internationally-famous collection of British
watercolours, textiles and wallpapers.*

World Museum Liverpool
Merseyside L3 8EN
(0151) 478 4393
www.liverpoolmuseums.org.uk/wml
*One of Britain's finest museums, with extensive collections
from the Amazonian Rain Forest to the mysteries of outer
space.*

Family Fun

Catalyst Science Discovery Centre
Widnes, Cheshire WA8 0DF
(0151) 420 1121
www.catalyst.org.uk
Interactive science centre whose aim is to make science exciting and accessible to people of all ages and abilities.

Go Ape! Hire Wire Forest Adventure - Delamere
Northwich, Cheshire CW8 2JD
0845 643 9215
www.goape.co.uk
"Take to the trees and experience an exhilarating course of rope bridges, tarzan swings and zip slides...all set high above the forest floor."

Grizedale Forest Visitor Centre
Hawkshead, Cumbria LA22 0QJ
(01229) 860010
www.forestry.gov.uk/northwestengland
Grizedale Forest offers a range of activities for all ages through the year, from mountain biking to relaxing walks, Go-Ape to the sculpture trails.

Sandcastle Waterpark
Blackpool, Lancashire FY4 1BB
(01253) 343602
www.sandcastle-waterpark.co.uk
The UK's Largest Indoor Waterpark and with 18 slides and attractions.

Museum of Wigan Life
Greater Manchester WN1 1NU
(01942) 828128
www.wlct.org/culture/heritage/historyshop.htm
A magnificent Grade II listed building, designed by Alfred Waterhouse in 1878 as a public library for Wigan, and is now the hub of Wigan Heritage Services.

Heritage

Arley Hall & Gardens
Northwich, Cheshire CW9 6NA
(01565) 777353
www.arleyhallandgardens.com
Arley Hall's gardens are a wonderful example of the idea that the best gardens are living works of art.

Chester Cathedral
Cheshire CH1 2HU
(01244) 324756
www.chestercathedral.com
A must see for Chester, a beautiful cathedral with a fascinating history.

Croxteth Hall & Country Park
Liverpool, Merseyside L12 0HB
(0151) 233 6910
www.croxteth.co.uk
Stately home with 500 acres estate including visitor farm, Victorian walled garden and seasonal events.

East Lancashire Railway
Bury, Greater Manchester BL9 0EY
(0161) 764 7790
www.east-lancs-rly.co.uk
The beautifully restored East Lancashire Railway takes you on a captivating journey to discover the region's rich transport heritage.

Holker Hall & Gardens
Grange-over-Sands, Cumbria LA11 7PL
(015395) 58328
www.holker.co.uk
Home to Lord and Lady Cavendish, Victorian wing, glorious gardens, parkland and woodlands.

Jodrell Bank Discovery Centre
Macclesfield, Cheshire SK11 9DL
(01477) 571339
www.jodrellbank.manchester.ac.uk/visitorcentre
Come and take a trip to Mars...

Levens Hall & Gardens
Kendal, Cumbria LA8 0PD
(015395) 60321
www.levenshall.co.uk
*Elizabethan mansion and world famous topiary gardens
designed by M Beaumont in 1694, fountain garden and
buttery, licenced restaurant and gift shop.*

Mendips & 20 Forthlin Road [Beatles]
Liverpool, Merseyside
(0151) 427 7231
www.nationaltrust.org.uk/beatles
*Take a tour inside the childhood homes of John Lennon
and Paul McCartney, and the places where many of the
earliest Beatles songs were composed and rehearsed.*

Penrith Castle
Cumbria CA11 7HX
(01912) 691200
www.english-heritage.org.uk/daysout/properties/
penrith-castle/
*The mainly 15th Century remains of a castle begun by
Bishop Strickland of Carlisle and developed by the Nevilles
and Richard III.*

Ravenglass & Eskdale Railway
Cumbria CA18 1SW
(01229) 717171
www.ravenglass-railway.co.uk
*Heritage steam engines haul open-top and cosy covered
carriages from the Lake District coastal village of
Ravenglass to the foot of England's highest mountains.*

Speke Hall, Gardens & Estate
Liverpool, Merseyside L24 1XD
(0151) 427 7231
www.nationaltrust.org.uk/main/w-spekehall
*One of the most famous half timbered houses in Britain,
dating from the 15th century.*

Nature & Wildlife

Chester Zoo
Cheshire CH2 1EU
(01244) 380280
www.chesterzoo.org
*With over 7,000 animals, including some of the most exotic
and endangered species on the planet.*

Farmer Ted's Farm Park
Ormskirk, Lancashire L39 7HW
(0151) 526 0002
www.farmerteds.com
*A safe environment for families with children 0-12 yrs, with
older children also welcome.*

Hare Hill Gardens
Macclesfield, Cheshire SK10 4QB
(01625) 584412
www.nationaltrust.org.uk/main/w-harehill
A small but perfectly formed wooded and walled garden.

Knowsley Safari Park
Merseyside L34 4AN
(0151) 430 9009
www.knowsley.com/safari
Enjoy a 5 mile safari through 450 acres of historic parkland.

Old Holly Farm
Garstang, Lancashire PR3 1AA
(01524) 791200
www.oldhollyfarm.com
Appeals to visitors of all ages.

South Lakes Wild Animal Park
Dalton-in-Furness, Cumbria LA15 8JR
(01229) 466086
www.wildanimalpark.co.uk
*The ultimate interactive animal experience. Get close to
wildlife at Cumbria's top tourist attraction.*

Wyre Estuary Country Park
Thornton Lancashire FY5 5LR
(01253) 857890
www.wyrebc.gov.uk/tourismplacestovisit.htm
*Located in a Green Flag area and the centre catering for all
ages with the ability to cater for all persons with a wide range
of foods and drink.*

Outdoor Activities

Ullswater Steamers
Cumbria CA11 0US
(01768) 482229
*The 'Steamers' create the perfect opportunity to combine a
cruise with some of the most famous and spectacular walks
in the lake District.*

Windermere Lake Cruises, Lakeside
Newby Bridge, Cumbria LA12 8AS
(015394) 43360
www.windermere-lakecruises.co.uk
*Steamers and launches sail daily between Ambleside,
Bowness and Lakeside. Additional summer routes.
Timetabled services.*

Manchester Histories Festival
March 21-30,
Various city centre locations
The ten-day MHF celebrates the heritage and history of Manchester across numerous city centre venues. The festival offers a fantastic opportunity to explore and learn this great city and is a great event for old and young alike.
www.manchesterhistoriesfestival.org.uk

FutureEverything
March,
Various city centre locations
FutureEverything is a collaborative festival which draws all kinds of artists together to present their visions of 'the future' to audiences. The festival uses art, digital culture, music and performance together to create something truly unique.
www.futureeverything.org

Global Village Market
Date TBC, Bolton
Bolton will be hosting two international food, gifts and crafts markets as Market Place (Europe) Limited, one of the UK's leading special event market companies, brings their Global Village Market to Bolton town centre for the third year running.
www.marketplaceeurope.co.uk

Wigan Food and Drink Festival
Date TBC, Wigan
Now in its sixth year, the Wigan Food and Drink Festival has evolved into one of the region's premier foodie feasts. Celebrating taste and tradition, the festival includes the CAMRA Wigan Beer Fest, Kitchen Theatre and over 20 food and drink events in local restaurants including celebrity chef events.
www.wlct.org./foodanddrink

Ramsbottom Chocolate Festival
April 12-13, Ramsbottom
Ramsbottom Chocolate Festival is the most talked about event in the North West. Alongside the two-day chocolate market showcasing high quality cocoa from award winning chocolatiers, expect interactive workshops and activities for adults/children, alfresco dining, chocolate rail ale tour, music, competitions, Giant Easter Egg display, our loveable mascot Charlie Chick and much more.
www. ramsbottomchocolatefestival.com

John Smith's Grand National
April 3-5, Aintree
The most famous horse race over jumps takes place over the challenging Aintree fences.
www.aintree.co.uk

Greater Manchester Marathon in Trafford
April 6, Trafford, Manchester
The second Greater Manchester Marathon has a new race village at Manchester United Football Club where the course also finishes. The improved course, entirely on main roads, is even flatter with only 55m of elevation gain. This is a great race for a first marathon, or if you're looking to set a new personal best time.
www.greatermanchestermarathon.com

Liverpool Sound City
May 1-3, Liverpool
Liverpool Sound City is the largest international music, digital and film festival and conference in the UK, welcoming over 360 artists, in over 25 venues in Liverpool's city centre.
www.liverpoolsoundcity.co.uk

Garstang Walking Festival
May, Garstang
A celebration of springtime in the stunning countryside of Garstang and the surrounding area. Guided walks and activities for all the family.
www.visitlancashire.com

Saddleworth and District Whit Friday Brass Band Contest
June 13, Oldham
Last year well over a hundred brass bands participated in some 20 different contests at venues scattered around the moorland villages and towns on the western edge of the Pennines. All of the contests are open-air, many in delightful surroundings. whitfriday.brassbands.saddleworth.org

Electric Garden Progressive Rock Festival
May, Blackpool
The North West's newest progressive rock music festival is now in its second year.
www.electricgardenfestival.com

Blackpool Dance Festival
May 22-30, Blackpool
The world's first and foremost festival of dancing.
www.blackpooldancefestival.com

Wirral Folk on the Coast Festival
June 5-8, Wirral
All-on-one-site friendly festival at Whitby Sports & Social Club, with fine music real ale and good food being served plus many more visitor attractions.
www.wirralfolkonthecoast.com

Great North Swim
TBC, Windermere
Europe's biggest open water swim series comes to the Lake District.
www.greatswim.org

Horwich Festival of Racing
June 15, Bolton
Since it began in 2002, Horwich Festival of Racing has grown to become one of the most popular sporting events in the North West. The 2013 event features British standard cycling, running and road walking championships, a young person's swim and run plus street orienteering.
www.horwichfestivalofracing.co.uk

Cheshire County Show
June 17-18, Knutsford
Agricultural event at Tabley Showground, near Knutsford, with many new attractions and thousands of animals, including livestock, horses, dogs and pigs.
www.cheshirecountyshow.org.uk

Manchester International Festival
July, Various venues
Manchester International Festival, the world's first festival of original, new work and special events.
www.mif.co.uk

RHS Flower Show Tatton Park
July 23-27, Tatton Park, Knutsford
A fantastic display of flora and fauna and all things garden related in stunning Cheshire countryside.
www.rhs.org.uk

Audlem Festival of Transport
July, Audlem
This is a festival of transport and gathering of historic boats.
www.audlem-aset.org

Coniston Water Festival
July, Coniston Water, Lake District
Features fun activities and events focused on the Coniston lake and the unique aspects of water-related culture and sport.
www.conistonwaterfestival.org.uk

Grosvenor Park Open Air Theatre
July-August, Grosvenor Park, Chester
The greatest open air theatre outside of London returns for a summer of exciting performances.
www.grosvenorparkopenairtheatre.co.uk

Lytham Proms Festival
August 1-3, Lytham & St Annes
Summer proms spectacular including performances from Russell Watson.
www.visitlancashire.com

Clitheroe Food Festival
August, Clitheroe
Celebrating the very finest Lancashire food and drink produces. Includes chef demos, tastings and cookery workshops.
www.visitlancashire.com

Birkenhead Festival of Transport
September, Birkenhead
Featuring classic cars, steam engines and other modes of vintage transport.
www.bheadtransportfest.com

Blackpool Illuminations
Sept-Nov, Blackpool
This world famous display lights up Blackpool's promenade with over 1 million glittering lights.
www.visitlancashire.com

Tourist Information Centres

When you arrive at your destination, visit an Official Partner Tourist Information Centre for quality assured help with accommodation and information about local attractions and events, or email your request before you go. To find a Tourist Information Centre visit www.visitengland.com

Accrington	Town Hall	01254 380293	information@leisureinhyndburn.co.uk
Altrincham	20 Stamford New Road	0161 912 5931	tourist.information@trafford.gov.uk
Ambleside	Central Buildings	015394 32582	tic@thehubofambleside.com
Barnoldswick	Post Office Buildings	01282 666704	tourist.info@pendle.gov.uk
Barrow-in-Furness	Forum 28	01229 876543	touristinfo@barrowbc.gov.uk
Blackburn	Blackburn Market	01254 688040	visit@blackburn.gov.uk
Bolton	Central Library Foyer	01204 334321	tourist.info@bolton.gov.uk
Bowness	Glebe Road	015394 42895	bownesstic@lake-district.gov.uk
Burnley	Parker Lane	01282 447210	tic@burnley.gov.uk
Bury	The Fusilier Museum	0161 253 5111	touristinformation@bury.gov.uk
Carlisle	Old Town Hall	01228 625600	tourism@carlisle.gov.uk
Chester	Town Hall	0845 647 7868	welcome@chestervic.co.uk
Cleveleys	Victoria Square	01253 853378	cleveleystic@wyrebc.gov.uk
Clitheroe	Platform Gallery, Station Road	01200 425566	tourism@ribblevalley.gov.uk
Congleton	Town Hall	01260 271095	congletontic@cheshireeast.gov.uk
Coniston	Ruskin Avenue	015394 41533	mail@conistontic.org

Discover Pendle Centre	Boundary Mill Stores	01282 856186	discoverpendle@pendle.gov.uk
Ellesmere Port	McArthur Glen Outlet Village	0151 356 5562	enquiries@cheshiredesigneroutlet.com
Garstang	1 Cherestanc Square	01995 602125	garstangtic@wyrebc.gov.uk
Kendal	25 Stramongate	01539 735891	info@kendaltic.co.uk
Keswick	Moot Hall	017687 72645	keswicktic@lakedistrict.gov.uk
Lancaster	The Storey	01524 582394	lancastervic@lancaster.gov.uk
Liverpool Albert Dock	Anchor Courtyard	0151 233 2008	jackie.crawford@liverpool.gov.uk
Liverpool John Lennon Airport	Arrivals Hall	0151 907 1058	information@liverpoolairport.com
Lytham St Annes	Town Hall	01253 725610	touristinformation@fylde.gov.uk
Macclesfield	Town Hall	01625 378123	karen.connon@cheshireeast.gov.uk
Manchester	45-50 Piccadilly Plaza	0871 222 8223	touristinformation@visit-manchester.com
Morecambe	Old Station Buildings	01524 582808	morecambevic@lancaster.gov.uk
Nantwich	Civic Hall	01270 537359	nantwichtic@cheshireeast.gov.uk
Northwich	1, The Arcade	01606 288828	infocentrenorthwich@cheshirewestandchester.gov.uk
Oldham	Oldham Library	0161 770 3064	tourist@oldham.gov.uk
Pendle Heritage Centre	Park Hill	01282 677150	pendleheritagecentre@htnw.co.uk
Penrith	Middlegate	01768 867466	pen.tic@eden.gov.uk
Preston	The Guildhall	01772 253731	tourism@preston.gov.uk
Rheged	Redhills	01768 860015	tic@rheged.com
Rochdale	Touchstones	01706 924928	tic@link4life.org
Saddleworth	Saddleworth Museum	01457 870336	saddleworthtic@oldham.gov.uk
Salford	The Lowry, Pier 8	0161 848 8601	tic@salford.gov.uk
Southport	112 Lord Street	01704 533333	info@visitsouthport.com
Stockport	Staircase House	0161 474 4444	tourist.information@stockport.gov.uk
Ulverston	Coronation Hall	01229 587120	ulverstontic@southlakeland.gov.uk
Windermere	Victoria Street	015394 46499	info@ticwindermere.co.uk

Regional Contacts and Information

There are various publications and guides about England's North West available from the following Tourist Boards or by logging on to www.visitenglandsnorthwest.com or calling 0845 600 6040:

Visit Chester and Cheshire
Chester Railway Station, 1st Floor, West Wing Offices, Station Road, Chester, CH1 3NT
Tel: (01244) 405600
Tel: 0844 647 7868 (accommodation booking)
Email: info@visitchesterandcheshire.co.uk
Web: www.visitchester.com

Cumbria Tourism
Windermere Road, Staveley, Kendal, LA8 9PL
Tel: (015398) 22222
Email: info@cumbriatourism.org
Web: www.golakes.co.uk

The Lancashire and Blackpool Tourist Board
St. George's House, St. George's Street,
Chorley, PR7 2AA
Tel: (01257) 226600 (Brochure request)
Email: info@visitlancashire.com
Web: www.visitlancashire.com

Visit Manchester – The Tourist Board
For Greater Manchester
Manchester Vic
Piccadilly Plaza, Portland Street
Manchester
M1 4BT
Tel: 0871 222 8223
Email: touristinformation@visitmanchester.com
Web: www.visitmanchester.com

The Mersey Partnership – The Tourist Board
for Liverpool City Region
12 Princes Parade, Liverpool, L3 1BG
Tel: (0151) 233 2008 (information enquiries)
Tel: 0844 870 0123 (accommodation booking)
Email: info@visitliverpool.com
(accommodation enquiries)
Email: liverpoolvisitorcentre@liverpool.gov.uk
(information enquiries)
Web: www.visitliverpool.com

North West
Where to Stay

Entries appear alphabetically by town name in each county. A key to symbols appears on page 7

North West - Cheshire

CHESTER, Cheshire   Map ref 4A2

SatNav CH2 2AP **H**

B&B PER ROOM PER NIGHT
S: £50.00 - £65.00
D: £70.00 - £99.00
EVENING MEAL PER PERSON
£18.95

SPECIAL PROMOTIONS
Weekend breaks: Stay
Friday and Saturday
and have Sunday at
half price. Please
enquire for special
offers and promotions.

Brookside Hotel

Brook Lane, Chester CH2 2AP **T:** (01244) 381943 **F:** (01244) 651910 **E:** info@brookside-hotel.co.uk
W: brookside-hotel.co.uk **£ BOOK ONLINE**

Brookside Hotel is affordable luxury. All rooms individually decorated, en suite with flat screen TV, DVD player, toiletries & attended daily by our professional H/K team. A family run Hotel with free on site car parking and wi-fi, Bar & Restaurant. Quiet & cosy just 10 minute walk from the city centre.

Directions: Please visit our website or call the hotel for directions.

Bedrooms: 4 single, 10 double, 7 twin, 7 family
Open: All year except Christmas and New Year

Payment: Leisure: Property: Children: Catering: Room:

CHESTER, Cheshire   Map ref 4A2

SatNav CH4 9DG **H**

B&B PER ROOM PER NIGHT
S: £130.00 - £200.00
D: £140.00 - £210.00
HB PER PERSON PER NIGHT
£90.00 - £105.00

Grosvenor Pulford Hotel & Spa

Wrexham Road, Pulford, Chester, Cheshire CH4 9DG **T:** (01244) 570560 **F:** (01244) 570809
E: enquiries@grosvenorpulfordhotel.co.uk
W: grosvenorpulfordhotel.co.uk **£ BOOK ONLINE**

Set in the breathtaking Cheshire countryside, this luxury, privately owned hotel boasts 73 en suite bedrooms, a Mediterranean themed restaurant, a stylish gastro bar and luxurious spa facilities. **Directions:** Exit A55 jct36 (A483 Chester, Wrexham & N Wales). Left onto B5445 (Eccleston & Pulford); hotel 2 miles on rhs. **Bedrooms:** 1 single, 50 dble, 13 twin, 8 family, 1 suite **Open:** All year

Site: **P** Payment: Leisure: Property: Children: Catering: Room:

CHESTER, Cheshire   Map ref 4A2

SatNav CH4 8JQ **B**

B&B PER ROOM PER NIGHT
S: £40.00 - £50.00
D: £68.00 - £98.00

Mitchell's of Chester Guest House

28 Hough Green, Chester CH4 8JQ **T:** (01244) 679004
E: welcome@mitchellsofchester.com
W: mitchellsofchester.com **£ BOOK ONLINE**

Highly recommended by good guides. Relax in this tastefully restored Victorian residence with rooms having hospitality tray, clock/radio, TV, free Wi Fi, hairdryer and many other comforts. Easy walking to city. **Directions:** Leave south side of Chester on A483, turning right to A5104 (Saltney). This is Hough Green . We are 300m along on the right. **Bedrooms:** 1 single, 4 double, 1 twin, 1 family
Open: All year except Christmas

Site: **P** Payment: Leisure: Property: Catering: Room:

The Official Tourist Board Guide to **B&Bs and Hotels 2014**

NORTHWICH, Cheshire   Map ref 4A2   SatNav CW8 3QE B

GUEST ACCOMMODATION ★★★★★

B&B PER ROOM PER NIGHT
S: £58.00
D: £75.00 - £85.00

Wall Hill Farm Guest House
Acton Lane, Acton Bridge, Northwich, Cheshire CW8 3QE **T:** (01606) 852654
E: info@wallhillfarmguesthouse.co.uk
W: wallhillfarmguesthouse.co.uk **£ BOOK ONLINE**

7 bed guesthouse offering luxury accommodation. Super beds & great showers. Award winning full English breakfast cooked to order. 24hr check in. 2 restaurants & 3 Inns within walking distance, all serving real ale and good food. **Directions:** M56 junction 10. A49 Whitchurch. 4 miles right Acton Lane. 400 yards Guest House on the right hand side top of the hill. **Bedrooms:** 3 double and 4 twin bedrooms all en suite **Open:** All year

Site: ✿ P Payment: 🔢 Leisure: ♪ ▶ ∪ Property: 🛏 Children: 🚼 Catering: 🍴 Room: ✆ ⬤ 📺

AMBLESIDE, Cumbria   Map ref 5A3   SatNav LA22 9BA B

GUEST ACCOMMODATION ★★★

B&B PER ROOM PER NIGHT
S: £30.00 - £50.00
D: £60.00 - £120.00

Meadowbank
Rydal Road, Ambleside LA22 9BA **T:** (01539) 432710 **F:** (01539) 432710
E: enquiries@meadowbank.org.uk
W: www.meadowbank.org.uk

Country house in private grounds with ample parking. Overlooking meadowland and fells with an easy walk into Ambleside. Good walking and cycling base. **Directions:** On the A591 (main road through) on the Northern edge of town. **Bedrooms:** 1 single, 3 double, 2 twin, 1 family **Open:** All year except Christmas

Site: ✿ P Payment: 🔢 Leisure: ♿ ♪ ▶ ∪ Property: 🛏 🏊 Children: 🚼 Catering: 🍴 Room: ✆ ⬤ 📺

AMBLESIDE, Cumbria   Map ref 5A3   SatNav LA22 0EP B

INN ★★★★

B&B PER ROOM PER NIGHT
S: £40.00 - £65.00
D: £79.00 - £124.00
EVENING MEAL PER PERSON
£11.00 - £25.00

Wateredge Inn
Waterhead Bay, Ambleside, Cumbria LA22 0EP **T:** (015394) 32332 **F:** (015394) 31878
E: stay@wateredgeinn.co.uk
W: www.wateredgeinn.co.uk **£ BOOK ONLINE**

Delightfully situated family-run inn on the shores of Windermere at Waterhead Bay. Enjoy country inn style dining, freshly prepared bar meals, real ales and fine wines all served overlooking the lake. **Directions:** From M6 jct 36 follow A591 through to Ambleside. At Waterhead bear left at traffic lights, Wateredge is on left at end of promenade. **Bedrooms:** Lake & Fell Views, Superfast Wi-Fi, TV, tea & coffee making facilities, en suite available **Open:** All year except 25th & 26th Dec

Site: ✿ P Payment: 🔢 Leisure: ♿ ♪ ▶ ∪ Property: 🛏 🏊 Children: 🚼 Catering: 🍴 Room: ✆ ⬤ 📺

ASPATRIA, Cumbria   Map ref 5A2   SatNav CA7 2JU B

BED & BREAKFAST ★★★★

Castlemont
Aspatria, Wigton, Cumbria CA7 2JU **T:** (016973) 20205 **F:** (016973) 20205
E: castlemont@tesco.net
W: britainsfinest.co.uk

Castlemont is a large Victorian residence, set in two acres of gardens, giving unrestricted views of lakes, sea and mountains. Extensive breakfast menu. Spacious, warm, comfortable, relaxing. Please contact for prices. **Directions:** A596, through Aspatria (west) towards Maryport. Brown and white tourist board signs, (Castlemont B&B). Large house on right amongst trees, large offroad parking space. **Bedrooms:** 1 single, 1 double, 1 twin, 1 family **Open:** All year

Site: ✿ P Payment: € Leisure: ♪ ▶ ∪ Property: 🛏 Children: 🚼 Catering: 🍴 Room: ✆ ⬤ 📺

BASSENTHWAITE, Cumbria Map ref 5A2 — SatNav CA12 4QG [H]

Ravenstone Lodge
Bassenthwaite, Keswick CA12 4QG T: (01768) 776629
E: enquiries@ravenstonelodge.co.uk
W: ravenstonelodge.co.uk £ BOOK ONLINE

B&B PER ROOM PER NIGHT
D: £60.00 - £150.00
HB PER PERSON PER NIGHT
£114.00 - £189.00

A small privately owned hotel set in 5 acres of grounds between Skiddaw & Bassenthwaite Lake with a unique atmosphere and well known for its superb locally sourced food. **Directions:** 5 miles north of Keswick on the A591. **Bedrooms:** 1 luxury super king, 5 dble, 2 twin, 1 family **Open:** All year except Christmas

Site: ✿ Payment: 💳 € Leisure: 🚶 🎣 ▶ U Property: 🖼 Children: 🍼 🛏 ★ Catering: 🍷 🍴 Room: 📺 🔌 🧺

BOWNESS-ON-WINDERMERE, Cumbria Map ref 5A3 — SatNav LA23 3EW [B]

May Cottage B&B
Kendal Road, Bowness-on-Windermere, Cumbria, England LA23 3EW
T: (01539) 446478 / 07793 056322 E: bnb@maycottagebowness.co.uk
W: www.maycottagebowness.co.uk £ BOOK ONLINE

B&B PER ROOM PER NIGHT
S: £45.00 - £65.00
D: £65.00 - £95.00

Quiet Bowness location, close to Lake Windermere, restaurants, shops. Healthy breakfast; Comfortable, light rooms; High spec en suites & cleanliness. Free parking, Wi-Fi, leisure facilities, dry/bike room. Help with walks, drives & activities. We care; come, relax and enjoy! **Directions:** North: M6/J39/A6 Shap Rd. East: A65. South: M6/J36/A590/A591. Trains: Oxenholme to Windermere. Please see website for more details. **Bedrooms:** 1 single, 3 double, 2 twin, 1 family **Open:** All year through

Site: P Payment: 💳 € Leisure: 🚶 🎣 ▶ U 🎾 🏊 Property: 🖼 Children: 🍼10 Catering: 🍴 Room: 📺 🔌 📺

CARLISLE, Cumbria Map ref 5A2 — SatNav CA1 1HR [B]

Langleigh House
6 Howard Place, Carlisle CA1 1HR T: (01228) 530440 E: langleighhouse@aol.com
W: langleighhouse.co.uk

B&B PER ROOM PER NIGHT
S: £30.00 - £40.00
D: £70.00 - £77.00
EVENING MEAL PER PERSON
£5.00 - £25.00

Highly recommended. Victorian house, comfortably furnished situated in a quiet conservation area with Private car park, just five minutes walk from the city centre. **Directions:** Junction 43 off the M6. Drive along Warwick Road and we are the third turning on the right after St. Aidans church. **Open:** All year

Site: ✿ P Payment: 💳 Leisure: 🚶 Property: 🖼 Children: 🍼 🛏 ★ Catering: 🍴 Room: 📺 🔌 📺

Book your accommodation online

Visit our new 2014 guide websites for detailed information, up-to-date availability and to book your accommodation online. Includes over 20,000 places to stay, all of them star rated.

www.visitor-guides.co.uk

CARLISLE, Cumbria   Map ref 5A2

University of Cumbria - Carlisle
Fusehill Street, Carlisle, Cumbria CA1 2HH **T:** (01228) 616317 **F:** (01228) 616235
E: conferences.carlisle@cumbria.ac.uk
W: www.cumbria.ac.uk

B&B PER ROOM PER NIGHT
S: £22.10 - £38.16
D: £56.16
BED ONLY PER NIGHT
£17.60 - £48.00

Comfortable, modern, en suite rooms (summer only) in which to relax and unwind at the end of a busy day. Each flat has internet access and a fully equipped kitchen, plus laundry and drying facilities and a gym on site. The campus is situated just a short walk from the city centre. Within easy reach of the motorway, Hadrian's Wall and the Lake District. Ideally placed for cycling & walking routes.

Directions: Head into Carlisle along Warwick Road (A69), from J43 of the M6. Turn left at the third set of traffic lights into Greystone Rd then turn right into Fusehill St.

Bedrooms: 85 single en suite bedrooms, arranged in 13 flats of between 5 and 9 bedrooms. Two rooms can be twinned. Ground floor accessible rooms available.

Site: ✿ Payment: 🖼 Leisure: 🕸 Property: ♟ 🖥 🖸 Children: 🛏 🕺 Catering: 🍴 🍽 🍷 Bedroom: 👆 🐾 💻

CLIFTON, Cumbria   Map ref 5B2

George and Dragon
Clifton, Penrith, Cumbria CA10 2ER **T:** (01768) 865381
E: enquiries@georgeanddragonclifton.co.uk
W: www.georgeanddragonclifton.co.uk

B&B PER ROOM PER NIGHT
S: £79.00 - £120.00
D: £95.00 - £155.00
EVENING MEAL PER PERSON
£11.95 - £22.50

The George and Dragon is a stylish and welcoming country inn with a lovely restaurant, cosy bar and 12 elegant yet comfortable en suite bedrooms. A great foodie destination where the menu changes seasonally and the specials daily. The owners grow and rear much of their own produce at their nearby sister establishment Askham Hall. **Directions:** Just a few miles from Penrith and junction 40 of the M6 in Clifton village. By direct train, Penrith is just three hours from London. **Open:** All year (closed on Boxing Day)

Site: P Payment: 🖼 Leisure: 🎣 Property: 🐾 🖥 🏫 Children: 🛏 🕺 Catering: 🍷 🍽 Room: 🐾 📶 📺 📀

CONISTON, Cumbria   Map ref 5A3

The Sun, Coniston
The Sun, Coniston LA21 8HQ **T:** (01539) 441248 **F:** (01539) 441219
E: info@thesunconiston.com
W: thesunconiston.com

B&B PER ROOM PER NIGHT
S: £35.00 - £50.00
D: £60.00 - £90.00
EVENING MEAL PER PERSON
£20.00

Classic Lakeland bar, diner & 4 star Inn. 8 hand-pulls from mostly local micro-breweries. Food, cooked to order using locally sourced ingredients. 8 en suite bedrooms enjoy superb panoramic views. **Directions:** M6 Junction 36, follow signs for Barrow A590. Turn off at Greenodd. Follow signs for Coniston. On entering the village, turn left (signposted) before bridge. **Bedrooms:** 4 double, 2 twin, 1 family, 1 single **Open:** All year except Christmas

Site: ✿ P Payment: 🖼 Leisure: ⛳ 🎣 ♨ Property: 🐾 🖥 Children: 🛏 🛏 🕺 Catering: 🍷 🍽 Room: 🐾 👆 📞 📀 📺

DUFTON, Cumbria   Map ref 5B3
SatNav CA16 6DF   **B**

FARMHOUSE ★★★★

Brow Farm Bed & Breakfast
Dufton, Appleby-in-Westmorland, Cumbria CA16 6DF **T:** (01768) 352865
E: stay@browfarm.com
W: www.browfarm.com

B&B PER ROOM PER NIGHT
S: £35.00 - £37.00
D: £70.00 - £74.00

Situated on the edge of the Pennines, with superb views from every room. Tasteful barn conversion offers rest and relaxation. Also self-catering cottages - see website for details www.browfarm.com.
Directions: From Appleby take Dufton road for 3 miles. Farm is on right. From Penrith (A66) take Dufton road. Travel through village. Farm on left. **Bedrooms:** 2 double, 1 twin
Open: All year except Christmas

Site: **P** Payment: 💷 Children: 🐾 🛏 🏃 Room: 🍵 🖙 📺 🎱

GILSLAND, Cumbria   Map ref 5B2
SatNav CA8 7AF   **B**

GUEST HOUSE ★★★★

Bush Nook Guest House
Upper Denton, Gilsland, Brampton CA8 7AF **T:** (01697) 747194 **E:** info@bushnook.co.uk
W: bushnook.co.uk **£ BOOK ONLINE**

B&B PER ROOM PER NIGHT
S: £35.00 - £45.00
D: £80.00 - £90.00
EVENING MEAL PER PERSON
£12.00 - £20.00

Bush Nook is a traditional farm house tastefully converted to a comfortable country guest house. Situated in open country, approximately 1 mile from Gilsland on Hadrian's Wall, with expansive views to the Scottish Lowlands, Keilder Forest and Northumberland. Evening meals for groups of 6 or more only, pre-ordered. **Directions:** Travelling from Newcastle or Carlisle follow the A69 turning of at the RAF Spadeadam/Gilsland junction. Bush Nook is approximately 800 yards on the right. **Bedrooms:** 1 single, 4 double, 2 twin **Open:** All year except Christmas

Site: ⚡ **P** Payment: 💷 € Leisure: 🚴 ♪ ▶ ∪ Property: 🐕 🖙 🗄 Children: 🐾 🛏 🏃 Catering: (✗ 🍽 🍴
Room: 🍵 🖙 📺 🎱 ▣

GILSLAND, Cumbria   Map ref 5B2
SatNav CA8 7DA   **B**

GUEST ACCOMMODATION ★★★★★   Gold AWARD

The Hill on the Wall
Gilsland, Brampton, Cumbria CA8 7DA **T:** (016977) 47214 **E:** info@hillonthewall.co.uk
W: www.hillonthewall.co.uk **£ BOOK ONLINE**

B&B PER ROOM PER NIGHT
S: £62.50
D: £37.50 - £42.50

The Hill on the Wall is a fascinating grade 2 listed, 16th Century fortified farmhouse. It is located within half a mile of Hadrian's Wall and with views over the beautiful Irthing Valley. It has a 5 star gold award from Enjoy England. **Directions:** Located 0.5 miles out of Gilsland on the road to Birdoswald Roman Fort. **Open:** 1st March - 30th November

WALKERS / CYCLISTS Site: ⚡ **P** Payment: 💷 Property: 🖙 🚲 ⌀ Room: 🖙 📺 🎱

Need more information?

Visit our new 2014 guide websites for detailed information, up-to-date availability and to book your accommodation online. Includes over 20,000 places to stay, all of them star rated.

www.visitor-guides.co.uk

Clare House

Park Road, Grange-over-Sands, Cumbria LA11 7HQ **T:** (01539) 533026
E: info@clarehousehotel.co.uk
W: www.clarehousehotel.co.uk

HB PER PERSON PER NIGHT
£90.00 – £97.00

SPECIAL PROMOTIONS
Early-season terms in
April, mid-summer and
autumn. Special 4-day
breaks available all
season.

Charming hotel in its own grounds, with well-appointed bedrooms, pleasant lounges and superb bay views, offering peaceful holidays to those who wish to relax and be looked after. Delightful meals, prepared with care and pride from fresh local produce, will add greatly to the enjoyment of your stay.

Directions: From M6 jct 36 follow A590 through Grange, keep alongside sea. Clare House is on Park Road next to bandstand, between sea and road.

Bedrooms: 4 single, 2 double, 12 twin
Open: Mid March to mid December

Site: ❀ P Payment: 💷 Property: 🖥 🛎 ⌖ Children: 👶³ Catering: ✗ 🍷 🍽 Room: 📶 🧴 ☎ 📺 🔌

Cumbria Grand Hotel

Lindale Road, Grange-over-Sands, Cumbria LA11 6EN **T:** (01539) 532331
F: (01539) 534534 **E:** salescumbria@strathmorehotels.com
W: www.strathmorehotels.com **£ BOOK ONLINE**

B&B PER ROOM PER NIGHT
S: £40.00 – £100.00
D: £60.00 – £150.00
HB PER PERSON PER NIGHT
£50.00 – £120.00

SPECIAL PROMOTIONS
Free child places 0-4
years. Half-price 5-14
years. Murder Mystery
and themed
weekends. Christmas
and New Year breaks.

Set in 20 acres of private gardens and woodlands, and overlooking the stunning Morecambe Bay, you will receive a warm and friendly welcome at this charming Victorian hotel. Only a short drive from Lake Windermere, there is much to see and do in the beautiful surrounding area.

Directions: By car: 15 minutes from the M6. By train: connections to Grange-over-Sands station from London, Birmingham, Leeds, Glasgow and Edinburgh.

Bedrooms: 14 single, 31 dble, 66 twin, 10 family, 3 suite
Open: All year

Site: ❀ Payment: 💷 Leisure: 🎵 ♪ ∪ ✎ Property: 🐾 🐕 🖥 🌙 Children: 👶 🍽 ♿ Catering: 🍷 🍽
Room: 🧴 ☎ 📷 📺 🔌 📠

North West - Cumbria

GRANGE-OVER-SANDS, Cumbria   Map ref 5A3   SatNav LA11 6ET [H]

Netherwood Hotel

Lindale Road, Grange-over-Sands LA11 6ET **T:** (015395) 32552 **F:** (015395) 34121
E: enquiries@netherwood-hotel.co.uk
W: www.netherwood-hotel.co.uk

B&B PER ROOM PER NIGHT
S: £65.00 - £90.00
D: £120.00 - £160.00
HB PER PERSON PER NIGHT
£95.00 - £130.00

SPECIAL PROMOTIONS
Special midweek short breaks available. Specialised bridge holidays. Visit our website for latest special offers and late availability rates.

Built in 1893, a building of architectural and historical interest set amid 17 acres of gardens and woodland overlooking Morecambe Bay. Original oak panelled public rooms with log fires. Elevated restaurant with dramatic views. Swimming pool, spa, steam room and beauty salon. Morning coffees, lunches, bar snacks and dinners available.

Directions: Take the M6, exit 36 then the A590 towards Barrow-in-Furness, then the B5277 into Grange-over-Sands. The hotel is on the right before the town.

Bedrooms: 1 single, 20 dble, 7 twin, 6 family
Open: All year

Site: ❀ **Payment:** 💷 **Leisure:** 🏊 ♪ ▸ ♃ ☆ ☄ ☌ **Property:** 🍴 🐾 📺 ◑ **Children:** 🌣 🛏 🏃
Catering: 🍷 🍴 **Room:** 🍵 💧 📞 📶 📺 🧺 🌡

GRASMERE, Cumbria   Map ref 5A3   SatNav LA22 9SW [H]

Dale Lodge Hotel & Tweedies Bar

Red Bank Road, Grasmere LA22 9SW **T:** (01539) 435300 **F:** (01539) 435570
E: enquiries@dalelodgehotel.co.uk
W: www.dalelodgehotel.co.uk £ **BOOK ONLINE**

B&B PER ROOM PER NIGHT
S: £60.00 - £170.00
D: £90.00 - £180.00

Situated in the centre of Grasmere in three acres of gardens, refurbished in a classic yet contemporary style, the choice of two restaurants serving modern cuisine. Tweedies Bar, serving guest ales, world wines plus live music every weekend. **Directions:** From Windermere take A591 towards Grasmere entering Grasmere at mini roundabout 1st exit, follow 400yds, 1st left after church. Dale Lodge on right. **Bedrooms:** 9 double, 1 twin, 2 family rooms, 4 suites **Open:** Every day except Christmas Day

Site: ❀ **Payment:** 💷 **Leisure:** ♪ ▸ ♃ **Property:** 🍴 🐾 📺 🏛 🐕 **Children:** 🌣 🛏 🏃 **Catering:** 🍴 🍷 🍴 **Room:** 🍵 💧 📞 📺 🧺

GRASMERE, Cumbria   Map ref 5A3   SatNav LA22 9QW [B]

Thorney How Independent Hostel

Grasmere, Cumbria LA22 9QW **T:** (01539) 435597 **F:** (01539) 435339
E: enquiries@thorneyhow.co.uk
W: www.thorneyhow.co.uk £ **BOOK ONLINE**

B&B PER ROOM PER NIGHT
D: £52.80 - £68.40
BED ONLY PER NIGHT
£16.50 - £24.00

A family run hostel, offering simple B&B licensed accommodation, bunkhouse and camping barn. The tranquil location provides a perfect place from which to explore everything Lakeland has to offer. **Directions:** Located under Helm Crag via Easedale Road and Helm Close, just over half a mile north of the village of Grasmere. **Bedrooms:** Bunk bed style accommodation, comfortable & warm. **Open:** All year

Site: ❀ P **Payment:** 💷 **Leisure:** 🏊 **Property:** 🐕 📺 🐕 **Children:** 🌣 🛏 🏃
Catering: 🍴 🍴 🍷 **Bedroom:** 🍵 🍵

HAWKSHEAD, Cumbria   Map ref 5A3   SatNav LA12 8JU B

★★★★
FARMHOUSE

B&B PER ROOM PER NIGHT
S: £50.00 - £55.00
D: £72.00 - £84.00
EVENING MEAL PER PERSON
£19.00

Crosslands Farm

Rusland, Nr Hawkshead, Ulverston, Cumbria LA12 8JU **T:** (01229) 860242
E: enquiries@crosslandsfarm.co.uk
W: crosslandsfarm.co.uk

Crosslands Farm is a early 17th century Lakeland Farmhouse set in the beautiful Rusland Valley 5 miles south of Hawkshead & near Grizedale Forest. It has delightful bedrooms, lovely bathrooms and a cosy lounge with log fire. Breakfast is served in the dining room converted from the old dairy with original slate flag floors and beams. It is an ideal base for walking and biking. Private parking.

Directions: Take the M6 at J36 follow the A590 until Newby Bridge past The Steam Railway turn right & follow the signs for Grizedale. At 4 miles turn right at y junction. Go up the little hill to the Farmhouse.

Bedrooms: 3 rooms, 1 double with en suite shower room and window seat, twin room with private bathroom & underfloor heating, 1 double room and en suite bathroom
Open: All year except Christmas. Restrictions at New Year

Site: ✿ P Payment: £ Leisure: 🏊 🎣 ∪ Property: 🐾 🖿 🚲 ⌀ Children: 🧸 🛏 👶 Catering: 🍴 🍳
Room: 🕯 ♨ 📶 📺

HAWKSHEAD HILL, Cumbria   Map ref 5A3   SatNav LA22 0PR B

★★★★★
GUEST
ACCOMMODATION

Silver
AWARD

B&B PER ROOM PER NIGHT
S: £60.00 - £75.00
D: £98.00 - £130.00

SPECIAL PROMOTIONS
3 night mid Week break that includes 2x3 course dinners at our award winning restaurants in Ambleside £335.00 per couple.

Yewfield Vegetarian Guest House

Hawkshead Hill, Hawkshead, Ambleside LA22 0PR **T:** (01539) 436765
E: derek.yewfield@btinternet.com
W: yewfield.co.uk

Yewfield is an impressive country house set in over 80 acres of private grounds, a peaceful and quiet retreat with lovely walks straight from the grounds. Following recent refurbishments, Yewfield was awarded a 5 stars silver VisitBritain award. We also host classical concert evenings.

Directions: One mile from Hawkshead, 4 miles from Ambleside, 2 miles past The Drunken Duck. See website for map.

Bedrooms: 8 double, 4 twin, 3 suite & 3 Apartments
Open: Closed December and January

Site: ✿ P Payment: £ Leisure: ∪ Property: 🖿 Children: 🧸 Catering: 🍳 Room: 🕯 ♨ 📶 📺 🛁 🍴

HEADS NOOK, Cumbria *Map ref 5B2* — *SatNav CA8 9EG* B

B&B PER ROOM PER NIGHT
S: £45.00 - £55.00
D: £60.00 - £100.00
EVENING MEAL PER PERSON
£7.95 - £15.95

String of Horses Inn

Faugh, Heads Nook, Brampton, Carlisle CA8 9EG **T:** (01228) 670297
E: info@stringofhorses.com
W: www.stringofhorses.com **£ BOOK ONLINE**

Dating from 1659, this traditional coaching inn is set in quiet country village only 10 minutes from Carlisle and Junction 43 of the M6 motorway. Near Hadrian's Wall and The Lake District. With great food, oak beams and panelling, real ales, log fires, free Wi-Fi and all rooms en suite.

Directions: A69 from J43 M6-Newcastle. 5 miles turn right at Lights Corby Hill/Warwick Bridge at BP Station. 1 mile through Heads Nook, turn left into Faugh.

Bedrooms: 9 double, 1 twin, 1 family
Open: All year

Site: P **Payment:** **Leisure:** **Property:** **Children:** **Catering:** **Room:**

KENDAL, Cumbria *Map ref 5B3* — *SatNav LA9 4JW* B

B&B PER ROOM PER NIGHT
S: £35.00 - £45.00
D: £72.00 - £85.00

Hillside Bed & Breakfast

4 Beast Banks, Kendal, Cumbria LA9 4JW **T:** (01539) 722836 **E:** info@hillside-kendal.co.uk
W: www.hillside-kendal.co.uk **£ BOOK ONLINE**

A warm welcome awaits you at this 4 Star B&B, just 2 mins walk to town centre. Located in a quiet conservation area, close to golf course, Brewery Arts Centre, museums, restaurants and shops. Ideally placed for exploring the Lakes and Dales. **Directions:** 10 mins drive from M6 motorway, within easy walking distance to Kendal train and bus stations **Bedrooms:** En suite, LCD TV, free Wi-Fi and hospitality tray. **Open:** All Year

Site: P **Payment:** **Leisure:** **Property:** **Catering:** **Room:**

KESWICK, Cumbria *Map ref 5A3* — *SatNav CA12 4LJ* B

B&B PER ROOM PER NIGHT
D: £50.00 - £80.00

Ash Tree House

Penrith Road, Keswick CA12 4LJ **T:** (01768) 772203 **E:** peterredfearn@aol.com
W: www.ashtreehouse.co.uk

Family run Bed and Breakfast in a former farm house built in 1841 with large garden. Comfortable en suite rooms and full English breakfast. Plenty of off road parking. **Directions:** 15 minute walk from town centre and a good base for all Lake District attractions. Detailed directions on our web site www.ashtreehouse.co.uk. **Bedrooms:** 1 double, 1 twin **Open:** All year except Christmas

Site: P **Leisure:** **Property:** **Children:** **Catering:** **Room:**

Burleigh Mead

The Heads, Keswick CA12 5ER **T:** (01768) 775935 **E:** info@burleighmead.co.uk
W: burleighmead.co.uk

enjoyEngland.com — GUEST HOUSE ★★★★
enjoyEngland.com — Silver AWARD

B&B PER ROOM PER NIGHT
D: £80.00 - £106.00

Conveniently situated between town centre and Derwentwater, our charming Victorian house offers excellent accommodation with outstanding views of surrounding fells. **Directions:** Once in Keswick follow signs for Lake and Borrowdale. The Heads is across from Central Car Park, we are 100 yards up road on right. **Bedrooms:** All en suite with fantastic views, tv, all mod cons **Open:** February to December

Site: ✿ P Leisure: ♪ ▶ ♅ Property: 🖥 ⵘ Children: ⛟⁸ Catering: 🍽 Room: ☖ ♨ 📺

Charnwood Guest House

6 Eskin Street, Keswick CA12 4DH **T:** (01768) 774111 **E:** sue.banister@gmail.com
W: www.charnwoodkeswick.co.uk

enjoyEngland.com — GUEST HOUSE ★★★★

B&B PER ROOM PER NIGHT
S: £45.00
D: £35.00 - £40.00

Elegant listed building. Close to lake and fells and in a quiet street. A warm welcome and really good food can be found at Charnwood. We cater for vegetarians. **Directions:** From A66 join the A591 to town centre and before the traffic lights turn left into Greta Street which leads to Eskin Street. **Bedrooms:** 2 double, 3 family **Open:** All year except Christmas

Payment: 💷 Property: 🖥 Children: ⛟⁵ Catering: 🍽 Room: ☖ ♨ 🔲 📺 🛏 🧺 ⤵

Rooms36

36 Lake Road, Keswick CA12 5ES **T:** 0800 056 6401 / 07721 957899 **F:** (01768) 772764
E: andy@rooms36.co.uk
W: www.rooms36.co.uk **£ BOOK ONLINE**

enjoyEngland.com — GUEST HOUSE ★★★★
enjoyEngland.com — Silver AWARD

B&B PER ROOM PER NIGHT
S: £60.00 - £95.00
D: £110.00 - £275.00

Rooms36 is set midway between Derwentwater & Keswick town centre. A short flat walk to the theatre by the lake with Views over Hope Park towards Borrowdale - Cat Bells & kiddaw. Awarded AA 4 Star Gold and Visit Britain 4 Star Silver. High standards of quality, from the fresh local ingredients selected for breakfast, to the sheets on your bed and the Herdwick carpet from our local sheep.

Directions: Follow the sign to Borrowdale and the Lake take the Heads Road on your right Rooms36 (seymour-house) is the last property on your left.

Bedrooms: 2 double, 4 family
Open: All year

Site: P Payment: 💷 € Leisure: 🚲 ♪ ▶ ♅ Property: 🐾 🖥 ⵘ Children: ⛟¹ 🎯 Catering: 🍽
Room: ☖ ♨ 🔲 📺

KESWICK, Cumbria Map ref 5A3   SatNav CA12 4EG B

Sandon Guest House

Southey Street, Keswick CA12 4EG **T:** (01768) 773648
E: enquiries@sandonguesthouse.com
W: sandonguesthouse.com

B&B PER ROOM PER NIGHT
S: £36.00 - £40.00
D: £72.00 - £80.00

Charming Lakeland-stone Victorian guest house, conveniently situated for town, theatre or lake. Friendly, comfortable accommodation. Ideal base for walking or cycling holidays, storage for up to 10 bicycles. Superb English breakfast. **Directions:** 3 minutes from town centre **Bedrooms:** 2 Super King, 2 Single, 4 Double, 2 Twin **Open:** All year except Christmas

Site: ✿ Payment: 💷 Leisure: 🦢 🎣 ⚑ ᴗ Property: 🖥 Children: 🚼4 Catering: 🍴
Room: 🔔 ☕ TV

KIRKBY LONSDALE, Cumbria Map ref 5B3   SatNav LA6 2AU B

Copper Kettle Restaurant & Guest House

3-5 Market Street, Kirkby Lonsdale LA6 2AU **T:** (015242) 71714 **F:** (015242) 71714
E: gamble_p@btconnect.com

B&B PER ROOM PER NIGHT
S: £35.00
D: £49.00 - £59.00
EVENING MEAL PER PERSON
£9.00 - £12.00

Building was built in 1610-1640. Lovely restaurant on site. In town there is Ruskin's View with the river and Devil's Bridge. Lots of good walking and plenty of shops and pubs in the nearby town. **Directions:** M6, exit 36, follow road for 5 miles. Turn into Kirkby Lonsdale on Market Street. **Bedrooms:** 2 single, 3 double, 3 twin, 2 family **Open:** All year

Site: **P** Payment: 💷 € Leisure: 🎣 ⚑ Property: 🐾 Children: 🚼 🛏 🎋 Catering: 🍷 🍴 Room: 🔔
📻 TV

KIRKBY LONSDALE, Cumbria Map ref 5B3   SatNav LA6 2LZ B

Ullathorns Farm

Middleton, Kirkby Lonsdale, Cumbria LA6 2LZ **T:** (01524) 276214 / 07800 990689
E: pauline@ullathorns.co.uk
W: ullathorns.co.uk

B&B PER ROOM PER NIGHT
S: £30.00 - £35.00
D: £54.00 - £60.00

A warm welcome awaits you at Ullathorns. Ideal touring base for lakes and dales. Good overnight stopping-off point, situated between junctions of M6. Refreshments served upon arrival. Individual breakfast tables. **Directions:** Ullathorns is set midway between Sedbergh and Kirkby Lonsdale just off the A683. **Bedrooms:** 1 double, 1 family **Open:** March to end of October

Site: ✿ **P** Payment: € Leisure: 🎣 ⚑ ᴗ Property: 🐾 🖥 Children: 🚼 🛏 🎋 Catering: 🍴 Room: 🔔 ☕ TV

MUNCASTER, Cumbria Map ref 5A3   SatNav CA18 1RQ B

Muncaster Coachmans Quarters

Muncaster Castle, Muncaster, Ravenglass CA18 1RQ **T:** (01229) 717614 **F:** (01229) 717010
E: info@muncaster.co.uk
W: muncaster.co.uk **£ BOOK ONLINE**

Within the magnificent Muncaster Gardens. One room has facilities for people with disabilities. Tariff includes admission to the Gardens, World Owl Centre, Meadow Vole Maze, Darkest Muncaster when operational, reduced entry to the Castle. Please contact us for prices. **Directions:** 1 mile south Ravenglass on A595. Jct 36 of M6 follow Brown Western Lake District signs. From north: from Carlisle follow A595 Cockermouth, Whitehaven, Ravenglass. **Bedrooms:** 4 double, 4 twin, 2 family **Open:** All year

Site: ✿ **P** Payment: 💷 Leisure: ⚑ ᴗ Property: 🖥 🎏 Children: 🚼 🛏 🎋 Room: 🔔 ☕ TV

NEWBY BRIDGE, Cumbria   Map ref 5A3   SatNav LA12 8NQ B

GUEST HOUSE ★★★★
Silver AWARD

B&B PER ROOM PER NIGHT
S: £42.50 - £50.00
D: £68.00 - £80.00

Old Barn Farm, Luxury Lakeland Guesthouse & Cottages

Fiddler Hall, Newby Bridge, Nr Windermere, Cumbria LA12 8NQ **T:** (01539) 531842
E: bookings@oldbarnholidays.com
W: www.oldbarnholidays.com / www.oldbarncottages.com **£ BOOK ONLINE**

Built in the 17thC Old Barn Farm is a charming Lakeland guest house set in beautiful open countryside at the head of the Cartmel valley 1 mile from Lake Windermere. This picturesque and tranquil location offers the ideal base for a holiday. **Directions:** Leave M6 at J36 and follow A590 for 14 miles. By-pass High Newton, turn left for Cartmel, we are a further 300 metres on the left. **Bedrooms:** En suite with toiletries, tv, beverages & biscuits. **Open:** All year. Special deals available.

Site: ✿ P Payment: 💷 Property: 🖥 ⛺ ⌀ Catering: 🍽 Room: 🍵 ♨ 📺

PORTINSCALE, Cumbria   Map ref 5A3   SatNav CA12 5RW B

GUEST HOUSE ★★★★
Gold AWARD

B&B PER ROOM PER NIGHT
S: £37.00 - £50.00
D: £74.00 - £84.00

Powe House

Portinscale, Keswick CA12 5RW **T:** (01768) 773611 **E:** andrewandhelen@powehouse.com
W: powehouse.com **£ BOOK ONLINE**

A Grade II Listed property in an ideal location for exploration of the northern and western lakes. Rooms are clean and bright, and it has a large car park. **Bedrooms:** 1 single, 4 double, 1 twin
Open: February - mid-December

Site: P Payment: 💷 Property: 🖥 Room: 🍵 ♨ 📶 📺

ROSTHWAITE, Cumbria   Map ref 5A3   SatNav CA12 5XB H

HOTEL ★★★
Gold AWARD

B&B PER ROOM PER NIGHT
S: £50.00 - £85.00
D: £100.00 - £170.00

EVENING MEAL PER PERSON
£15.95 - £39.45

SPECIAL PROMOTIONS
Spring, summer, autumn and winter breaks available throughout the year. Please call or check the website for details.

Scafell Hotel

Rosthwaite, Borrowdale, Keswick CA12 5XB **T:** (01768) 777208 **F:** (01768) 777280
E: info@scafell.co.uk
W: scafell.co.uk

The Scafell Hotel is in the heart of Borrowdale Valley, considered by many to be England's finest valley. Situated almost at the foot of Great Gable and Scafell Massif, the hotel is an excellent centre for walking. Recently refurbished, the Scafell boasts great food, great service and a great atmosphere.

Directions: From jct 40 (Penrith) of the M6 follow A46 to Keswick. From Keswick follow the B5298 for Borrowdale. Travel 6.5 miles to Rosthwaite.

Bedrooms: 3 single, 9 dble, 8 twin, 2 family, 1 suite
Open: All year

Site: ✿ Payment: 💷 € Leisure: 🚴 ⛳ Property: 🐾 ⌂ Children: ⛺ 🛏 🚼 Catering: 🍷 🍽 Room: 🍵 ♨ 📞 📶 📺 🧺

Buckle Yeat Guest House

Nr Sawrey, Hawkshead, Ambleside, Cumbria LA22 0LF **T:** (01539) 436446 / 07703 654219
E: info@buckle-yeat.co.uk
W: www.buckle-yeat.co.uk **£ BOOK ONLINE**

B&B PER ROOM PER NIGHT
S: £40.00 - £45.00
D: £80.00 - £90.00

SPECIAL PROMOTIONS
Weekly rates available

Buckle Yeat Guest House is situated in the Miss Potter village of Near Sawrey, an ideal location for touring the English Lake District. Hill Top Farm, former home of writer and artist, Beatrix Potter is situated almost next door. A traditional 17th Century Lakeland cottage with six en suite bedrooms, which are tastefully decorated and furnished with your comfort in mind.

Directions: Situated on the western side of Windermere on the road between Hawkshead and the ferry.

Bedrooms: 1 single, 4 double, 2 twin
Open: All year

Site: ✿ **P** Payment: ⊞ Leisure: 🛆 ♪ ↾ ↻ Property: 🚃 🏠 🐾 Children: 🧸 🛏 🏃 Catering: 🍴
Room: 🥃 🖐 📺 🍴

Holmeshead Farm

Skelwith Fold, Ambleside LA22 0HU **T:** (015394) 33048 **F:** (015394) 31337
E: info@holmesheadfarm.co.uk
W: holmesheadfarm.co.uk

B&B PER ROOM PER NIGHT
S: £54.00
D: £40.00 - £45.00

Holmeshead is a spacious 17thC farmhouse which has been updated while still retaining its character. All rooms have a peaceful atmosphere. Single room rate is offered with a supplement.
Bedrooms: 1 double, 1 twin, 1 family **Open:** All year

Site: **P** Leisure: 🛆 ♪ ↻ Property: ↾ Children: 🧸 🛏 🏃 Catering: 🍴 Room: 🥃 🖐 📺 🍴 🛏 🔱

Troutbeck Inn

Troutbeck, Penrith CA11 0SJ **T:** (01768) 483635 **F:** (01768) 483639
E: info@troutbeckinn.co.uk
W: www.thetroutbeckinn.co.uk **£ BOOK ONLINE**

B&B PER ROOM PER NIGHT
S: £45.00 - £55.00
D: £70.00 - £80.00
EVENING MEAL PER PERSON
£14.50 - £35.00

Country hotel/inn with open fire, bar, lounge, restaurant. Quality food, wines & real ales. Dogs welcome in our bedrooms & cottages. Close to Penrith, Keswick & Ullswater. **Directions:** From J40 on M6 travel west towards Keswick. After 8 miles exit onto the A5091 to Ullswater. Troutbeck Inn is on the left. **Bedrooms:** 1 single, 4 double, 1 twin, 1 family **Open:** All year

WALKERS CYCLISTS PETS
WALKERS CYCLISTS PETS
Site: ✿ **P** Payment: ⊞ Leisure: ↻ Property: ↾ 🚃 🖥 Children: 🧸 Catering: ❢ 🍴
Room: 🥃 🖐 📶 📺

Knotts Mill Country Lodge

Watermillock, Ullswater, Penrith CA11 0JN **T:** (01768) 486699 **E:** relax@knottsmill.com
W: www.knottsmill.com **£ BOOK ONLINE**

GUEST HOUSE

B&B PER ROOM PER NIGHT
S: £45.00 - £65.00
D: £80.00 - £90.00

SPECIAL PROMOTIONS
2 Nights minimum stay
at weekends during
school holidays.

A country lodge offering quality, serviced accommodation and big breakfasts. Knotts Mill is set in its own grounds in the Lake District National Park close to lake Ullswater with stunning views of the surrounding hills. Nine comfortable en suite bedrooms some on the ground floor, ample parking. Ideal location for touring, walking, sailing, cycling, a short break or longer stay. Peaceful setting only 10min from M6 exit 40 on the A592 lakeside road in Watermillock. Pets by arrangement only.

Bedrooms: 4 double, 2 twin, 3 family
Open: All year except Christmas

Site: ❖ P Payment: £ € Leisure: 🚲 ♪ ▶ ♻ Property: 🐾 🛏 ⛺ Children: 🛝 🎠 Catering: 🍽 🍴
Room: 🍵 👜 📶 📺 🎮 🛁

St Marys Mount

Belmont, Ulverston LA12 7HD **T:** (01229) 583372 **E:** gerry.bobbett@virgin.net
W: www.stmarysmount.co.uk

GUEST ACCOMMODATION

B&B PER ROOM PER NIGHT
S: £45.00
D: £75.00 - £80.00
EVENING MEAL PER PERSON
£20.00 - £25.00

Guest house overlooking Morecambe Bay in own grounds. 5 minutes walk to Ulverston town centre at the foot of the Hoad Monument. Peaceful surroundings and guests can enjoy homecooked food. **Directions:** Follow the A590 into Ulverston, pass Booths. At next major roundabout take the 3rd exit onto Fountain Street. At mini roundabout take a sharp right. **Bedrooms:** 4 double, 2 twin **Open:** All year

Site: ❖ P Payment: £ Leisure: 🚲 ♪ ▶ ♻ Property: 🛏 Children: 🛝 🍽 Catering: 🍴 Room: 🍵 👜 📺 🛁 🍴

Mellfell House Farm

Watermillock, Penrith, Ullswater CA11 0LS **T:** (01768) 486295 **E:** ben@mellfell.co.uk
W: www.mellfell.co.uk **£ BOOK ONLINE**

B&B PER ROOM PER NIGHT
D: £70.00

SPECIAL PROMOTIONS
For seven nights or more, £60 per double room per night .Sorry, no children in b and b.

Lovely 17th century farmhouse, full of character, with a wealth of traditional features, in a beautiful setting high above Ullswater in the Lake District National Park. Enjoy a hearty breakfast with a fire burning in the range, guest lounge with tv & log fire, free wifi, central heating, en suite rooms, use of kitchen facilities, laundry & drying room. An excellent base for walking and exploring.

Directions: Please obtain directions from our website at www.mellfell.co.uk

Bedrooms: We have three double en suite rooms, one of which can be turned into a twin. Each room has a powerful shower over a bath, digital tv and scenic views
Open: March to November. Minimum stay two nights

Site: ✿ P Property: ▦ ▤ ♨ ∅ Catering: ▦ Room: ◳ ✦ TV DVD ♨ ▦

Bowfell Cottage

Middle Entrance Drive, Storrs Park, Bowness-on-Windermere LA23 3JY **T:** (01539) 444835
E: annetomlinson45@btinternet.com
W: bowfell-cottage.co.uk

B&B PER ROOM PER NIGHT
S: £32.00 - £35.00
D: £58.00 - £70.00
EVENING MEAL PER PERSON
£14.50

Cottage in a delightful setting, about 1mile south of Bowness off A5074, offering traditional Lakeland hospitality with comfortable accommodation and good home-cooking. Secluded parking in own grounds surrounding the property. **Directions:** From Bowness opposite church, take A5074 Kendal Rd for 1.2 miles. Turn right into Middle Entrance Drive, entrance 100 yards down Lane on left. **Bedrooms:** 1 double, 1 twin, 1 family **Open:** All year

Site: ✿ P Leisure: ♨ ♪ ⌁ ∪ Property: ⌁ ▦ ▤ Children: ⌁ Catering: ⟨✗ ▦ Room: ◳ ✦ ☎ TV

Cragwood Country House Hotel

Windermere LA23 1LQ **T:** (01539) 488177 **E:** info@cragwoodhotel.co.uk
W: www.cragwoodhotel.co.uk **£ BOOK ONLINE**

Set in 20 acres of gardens, meadows and woodland with our own lake frontage. Panoramic views of Lake Windermere and the surrounding fells. Recommended for food. Licensed gazebo for civil weddings. Log fires. Please contact us for prices. **Directions:** Exit M6 at Junction 36. Take the A591 towards Windermere. Cragwood is located between Windermere and Ambleside, next to the Brockhole Visitor Centre. **Bedrooms:** 19 double, 3 family, 1 single, disabled access **Open:** All year

Site: ✿ P Payment: ⊞ Leisure: ♪ ⌁ Property: ⌁ ⌁ ▦ ▤ ♨ ∅ Children: ⌁ ▦ ♿ Catering: ⟨✗ ▮ ▦ Room: ◳ ✦ ☎ ◱ TV ♨ ▦

WINDERMERE, Cumbria Map ref 5A3   SatNav LA23 3JB **B**

Fair Rigg

Ferry View, Bowness-on-Windermere, Windermere LA23 3JB **T:** (01539) 443941
E: stay@fairrigg.co.uk
W: fairrigg.co.uk **£ BOOK ONLINE**

B&B PER ROOM PER NIGHT
S: £40.00 - £55.00
D: £64.00 - £90.00

Fine Victorian house with superb views, in rural setting on edge of Bowness. Lovely rooms, plenty of space to relax and unwind. High standards assured. **Directions:** M6 jct 36, A590/591 Windermere, Kendal/South Lakes. At roundabout north of Kendal left B5284, Hawkshead via the ferry. 10 minutes T-junction, Fair Rigg on left. **Bedrooms:** 5 double, 1 twin **Open:** All year except Christmas

Site: P Payment: Leisure: Property: Children: 14 Catering: Room:

WINDERMERE, Cumbria Map ref 5A3   SatNav LA23 3NE **H**

Gilpin Hotel & Lake House

(formerly Gilpin Lodge Country House Hotel), Crook Road, Nr Windermere, Lake District LA23 3NE **T:** (015394) 88818 **F:** (015394) 88058 **E:** hotel@thegilpin.co.uk
W: www.thegilpin.co.uk **£ BOOK ONLINE**

B&B PER ROOM PER NIGHT
S: £185.00 - £515.00
D: £215.00 - £515.00

EVENING MEAL PER PERSON
£58.00

SPECIAL PROMOTIONS
Year round 3 to 10 night breaks from £97.50pppn DBB. Pony trekking, tours, fishing, golf, biking and spa treatments.

This family owned and run Lake District Relais & Chateaux hotel is dedicated to nourishment, recuperation and relaxation. Gilpin Hotel has twenty luxurious rooms and suites, most leading onto the gardens, six with private hot tubs. Gilpin Lake House is a sanctuary with exquisite service, where just 6 suites enjoy 100 acres of private grounds, lake, swimming pool & the 'Jetty' spa.

Directions: Leave M6 at jct 36. Take A590/A591 to roundabout north of Kendal, then take first exit B5284 (signposted Crook, Hawkshead via ferry) for 5 miles.

Bedrooms: 7 dble, 7 twin, 12 suite
Open: All year

Site: P Payment: Leisure: Property: Children: 7 Catering: Room:

Book your accommodation online

Visit our new 2014 guide websites for detailed information, up-to-date availability and to book your accommodation online. Includes over 20,000 places to stay, all of them star rated.
www.visitor-guides.co.uk

Kenilworth Guest House

Holly Road, Windermere LA23 2AF **T:** (015394) 44004 **E:** busby@kenilworth-lake-district.co.uk
W: http://kenilworth-lake-district.co.uk **£ BOOK ONLINE**

B&B PER ROOM PER NIGHT
S: £40.00 - £42.00
D: £68.00 - £84.00

Grand 4-star Victorian Guest House, offering warm and welcoming accommodation, centrally located in the town of Windermere. Hearty breakfasts include locally made Cumberland sausage, with vegetarian or lighter alternatives. Non-smoking throughout. Parking.

Directions: Leave A591 and drive through one-way system. After last shop, take 2nd left then 1st left - we are next to last on the right hand side.

Bedrooms: All en suite - 1 king-size double, 2 doubles, 1 twin, 1 single, 1 family (for 3 people)
Open: All year except Christmas.

Site: ❀ P **Payment:** 💷 **Leisure:** 🎣 🚶 ► **Property:** ♨ **Children:** 🧒4 **Catering:** 🍴 **Room:** 🍵 💧 📺

St John's Lodge

Lake Road, Windermere LA23 2EQ **T:** (01539) 443078 **F:** (01539) 488054
E: mail@st-johns-lodge.co.uk
W: st-johns-lodge.co.uk **£ BOOK ONLINE**

B&B PER ROOM PER NIGHT
D: £70.00 - £140.00

Ideal location between Windermere and Lake and close to all amenities. Serving award winning breakfasts including traditional English, veggie/vegan and gluten-free. Free Wi-Fi. Please contact us for prices. **Directions:** A591 to Windermere Village, follow signs Bowness and lake. Leave Windermere on New Road which becomes Lake Road. Destination 100m after Catholic Church on left. **Bedrooms:** 9 double **Open:** All year except Christmas

Payment: 💷 **Leisure:** 🎣 🚶 ► ◡ **Property:** 🛏 **Children:** 🧒10 **Catering:** 🍴 **Room:** 🍵 💧 📺

Stockghyll Cottage

Rayrigg Road, Bowness-on-Windermere, Bowness LA23 1BN **T:** (015394) 43246
E: welcome@stockghyllcottage.co.uk
W: stockghyllcottage.co.uk **£ BOOK ONLINE**

B&B PER ROOM PER NIGHT
S: £37.50 - £70.00
D: £60.00 - £80.00

Lovely Lakeland stone cottage & gardens surrounded by woodland, with its own waterfall & stream. Situated within a 5 min walk of Bowness village & Lakeside attractions. **Directions:** Travelling North M6 Junction 36 follow signs to Windermere. Travelling South Juntion 40 follow signs to Windermere. We are located opposite the Steam Boat Museum. **Bedrooms:** 2 double, 1 King **Open:** All year

Site: ❀ P **Payment:** 💷 € **Leisure:** 🎣 🚶 ► ◡ **Property:** 🛏 **Children:** 🧒10 **Catering:** 🍴 **Room:** 🍵 💧 ④ 📺

SALE, Greater Manchester   Map ref 4A2   SatNav M33 2AE B

Belforte House

7-9 Broad Road, Sale, Manchester M33 2AE **T:** (0161) 973 8779 **F:** (0161) 973 8779
E: belfortehousehotel@aol.co.uk
W: belfortehousehotel.co.uk

B&B PER ROOM PER NIGHT
S: £34.00 - £49.95
D: £55.00 - £59.95

EVENING MEAL PER PERSON
£4.95 - £12.95

Privately owned hotel with a personal, friendly approach. Ideally located for Manchester Airport, the Metrolink and the city centre. Situated directly opposite Sale Leisure Centre. **Directions:** 1 mile from Junction 6 M60. 200 metres from Tram Station. **Bedrooms:** 14 single, 4 double, 2 twin, 3 family **Open:** All year except Christmas and New Year

Site: ❀ **P Payment:** 💳 **Leisure:** ♪ ♨ **Property:** 🛏 🖫 🖻 **Children:** 🛌 🛏 🏃 **Catering:** 🍴 🍽 **Room:** 📶 ♨ 📞 📶 TV 🛏

BLACKBURN, Lancashire   Map ref 4A1   SatNav BB6 8BE H

Northcote

Northcote Road, Langho, Blackburn BB6 8BE **T:** (01254) 240555 **F:** (01254) 246568
E: reception@northcote.com
W: northcote.com **£ BOOK ONLINE**

B&B PER ROOM PER NIGHT
S: £240.00 - £265.00
D: £275.00 - £300.00

Northcote is an award-winning restaurant with individual rooms offering total luxury and comfort. Adding to the atmosphere is a new stylish and tastefully enlarged lounge with sumptuous sofas and an impressive cocktail bar. Enjoy the gardens and grounds, with breath taking views of the Ribble Valley.
Directions: Visit the website for detailed directions.
Bedrooms: 10 double, 4 twin. **Open:** All year

Site: ❀ **P Payment:** 💳 **Leisure:** ♪ ▶ **Property:** 🍴 🖫 🖻 🛌 🌙 ∅ **Children:** 🛌 🛏 🏃 **Catering:** (✗ 🍴 🍽 **Room:** 📶 ♨ 📞 📶 TV DVD 🛏

BLACKBURN, Lancashire   Map ref 4A1   SatNav BB2 7NP H

Stanley House Hotel & Spa

Further Lane, Mellor, Blackburn BB2 7NP **T:** (01254) 769200 **F:** (01254) 769206
E: info@stanleyhouse.co.uk
W: www.stanleyhouse.co.uk **£ BOOK ONLINE**

B&B PER ROOM PER NIGHT
S: £155.00 - £205.00
D: £185.00 - £285.00

HB PER PERSON PER NIGHT
£135.00 - £150.00

Stanley House is an award-winning hotel, with 30 first-class bedrooms, unrivalled wedding and conference facilities, the stylish Grill on the Hill restaurant, the hugely popular Mr Fred's and a world-class spa, truly a hotel like no other **Directions:** Located on the A677, 4 miles from the M6/M65. Preston station 6 miles. Blackpool International Airport 25 miles. Manchester International Airport 40 miles. **Open:** All year

Site: ❀ **P Payment:** 💳 **Leisure:** ♪ ▶ 🎿 ☠ 🎱 **Property:** ⊛ 🍴 🖫 🖻 🛌 🌙 **Children:** 🛌 🛏 🏃 **Catering:** (✗ 🍴 🍽 **Room:** 📶 ♨ 📞 📶 TV 🛏 🖾

BLACKPOOL, Lancashire   Map ref 4A1   SatNav FY1 4PR B

The Allendale

104 Albert Road, Blackpool FY1 4PR **T:** (01253) 623268 **F:** (01253) 317833
E: the-allendale@btconnect.com
W: allendalehotelblackpool.co.uk

B&B PER ROOM PER NIGHT
S: £20.00 - £30.00
D: £40.00 - £60.00

EVENING MEAL PER PERSON
£9.00

We are situated in the heart of Blackpool, very close to the Winter Gardens and the famous Blackpool Tower, The Allendale offers guests the very best in a family run guest accommodation, where your comfort and pleasure is our prime concern. **Directions:** Exit M55, Yeadon Way towards Blackpool central, Central Drive stay right lane then in the left hand lane after you pass McDonalds, then straight. **Bedrooms:** 9 double, 3 twin, 3 family **Open:** All year except Christmas and New Year

Site: ❀ **P Payment:** 💳 **Property:** 🖫 **Children:** 🛌 🛏 🏃 **Catering:** 🍴 🍽 **Room:** 📶 ♨ 📞 TV 🛏 🖾 🖳

For **key to symbols** see page 7

BLACKPOOL, Lancashire   Map ref 4A1
SatNav FY1 4PR **B**

★★★★
GUEST HOUSE

Arabella

102 Albert Road, Blackpool FY1 4PR **T:** (01253) 623189 **E:** graham.waters3@virgin.net
W: thearabella.co.uk

We provide clean and comfortable accommodation within a family friendly atmosphere. Home cooking, dietary needs catered for, rooms are serviced daily, 5 minutes walk from the winter gardens, 10 minutes from the Tower and sea front. We do not take stag or hen parties. Specials available Mon - Fri. Prices on application. **Directions:** Contact our website for google map directions.
Bedrooms: 1 single, 2 double, 2 twin, 9 family. **Open:** All year

Site: ✿ **P** **Payment:** 🔢 **Property:** ▭ **Children:** 👶 🛏 🎿 **Catering:** 🍷 🍽 **Room:** 📶 ♨ 🔌 📺

BLACKPOOL, Lancashire   Map ref 4A1
SatNav FY1 4JG **B**

★★★
GUEST HOUSE

B&B PER ROOM PER NIGHT
S: £27.00 - £29.00
D: £54.00 - £68.00

Ash Lodge

131 Hornby Road, Blackpool FY1 4JG **T:** (01253) 627637
E: admin@ashlodgeguesthouse.co.uk
W: ashlodgeguesthouse.co.uk **£ BOOK ONLINE**

Ash Lodge central Blackpool is situated in quiet residential area. It is a late Victorian house with many original features but with modern facilities and onsite car park. **Directions:** M55 jct4. Take 3rd left onto A583. Travel approx 3 miles. At 10th set of lights turn right onto Hornby Road. Hotel on right.
Bedrooms: 3 single, 2 double, 2 twin, 1 family
Open: All year except Christmas

Site: **P** **Payment:** 🔢 **Leisure:** ⛳ ▸ **Property:** ▭ **Children:** 👶 🛏 🎿 **Catering:** 🍽 **Room:** 📶 ♨ 📺

BLACKPOOL, Lancashire   Map ref 4A1
SatNav FY2 9TA **B**

★★★★
GUEST
ACCOMMODATION

B&B PER ROOM PER NIGHT
S: £28.00 - £35.00
D: £56.00 - £70.00
EVENING MEAL PER PERSON
£10.00

SPECIAL PROMOTIONS
Monday - Friday 4 night breaks March and April £115.00 with free evening meal. Over 60s special rates. (excl Bank Holidays). Discount for longer stays.

The Berwick

23 King Edward Avenue, North Shore, Blackpool, Lancashire FY2 9TA **T:** (01253) 351496
F: (01253) 351496 **E:** enquiries@theberwickhotel.co.uk
W: www.theberwickhotel.co.uk

Receive a warm and friendly welcome in comfortable surroundings, enjoy a relaxing break while experiencing award winning customer service at its best. Extensive choice of home made meals. BB & BBEM available. Located in North Shore area, close to Gynn gardens & spectacular cliff walks. Convenient for Blackpool attractions, Cleveleys & Fleetwood. Discounts for over 60's & extended stays. Car park.

Directions: M55 jct 4. A583 North Shore. Right at lights, Whitegate Drive to North Shore. Left at island to promenade. 3rd right. Hotel 100m on right.

Bedrooms: 5 double, 2 twin, 1 superior twin. Beautifully decorated en suite rooms with flat screen TV with Freeview. Well stocked hospitality tray & hairdryer.
Open: All year except new year

Site: ✿ **P** **Payment:** 🔢 **Leisure:** ⛳ 🎵 ▸ **Property:** ▭ **Children:** 👶2 🎿 **Catering:** ❨✗ 🍷 🍽 **Room:** 📶 ♨ 🔌 📺

The Official Tourist Board Guide to **B&Bs and Hotels 2014**

BLACKPOOL, Lancashire   Map ref 4A1   SatNav FY4 1ND [H]

enjoyEngland.com
★★★★ HOTEL

Big Blue Hotel

1 Clifton Drive, Ocean Boulevard, Blackpool Pleasure Beach, Blackpool, Lancashire
FY4 1ND **T:** 0871 222 4000 **F:** (01253) 400046 **E:** reservations@bigbluehotel.com
W: bigbluehotel.com **£ BOOK ONLINE**

The Big Blue offers contemporary accommodation right next to
Blackpool Pleasure Beach and is within easy reach of all of
Blackpool's main attractions. Visit website for best available rate,
special offers and packages throughout the year. **Directions:** M6 jct
32, onto M55. Follow signs to Pleasure Beach south shore. Hotel is
on the right next to the Big One rollercoaster. **Bedrooms:** 59
double, 10 twin, 84 family, 4 suite **Open:** All year except Christmas

B&B PER ROOM PER NIGHT
S: £57.00 - £137.00
D: £57.00 - £147.00
EVENING MEAL PER PERSON
£22.95

Site: P **Payment:** ⊞ **Leisure:** ✗ **Property:** ⊛ ☕ ☒ ➊ **Children:** ⅌ ⩫ **Catering:** ✗ ☕ 🍽 **Room:** ☖ ⬥ ☏ 📺 🔤 🛗

BLACKPOOL, Lancashire   Map ref 4A1   SatNav FY1 4TA [B]

enjoyEngland.com
★★★ GUEST ACCOMMODATION

Chaplins

15 Albert Road, Blackpool FY1 4TA **T:** (01253) 294440 **F:** 0872 115 2944
E: chaplinshotel@live.com
W: www.chaplinshotelblackpool.com **£ BOOK ONLINE**

Chaplins guest accommodation offers bed and breakfast in the
heart of central Blackpool on the very popular Albert Road. Close to
the Tower and Winter Gardens our accommodation has 13 en suite
bedrooms ranging from single to family rooms. **Directions:** From
the National Express coach station and Central Car Parks, head
towards Coral Island , turn right and we are on the right hand side.
Bedrooms: All en suite with flat screen tv & tea & coffee. **Open:** All
year except Christmas & New Year

B&B PER ROOM PER NIGHT
S: £25.00 - £30.00
D: £50.00 - £60.00
EVENING MEAL PER PERSON
£9.00

Payment: ⊞ **Property:** ☒ **Children:** ⅌ ⩫ **Catering:** ✗ ☕ 🍽 **Room:** ☖ ⬥ 📺

BLACKPOOL, Lancashire   Map ref 4A1   SatNav FY2 9RP [H]

enjoyEngland.com
★★ HOTEL

Doric Hotel

48-52 Queens Promenade, Blackpool FY2 9RP **T:** (01253) 352640 **F:** (01253) 596842
E: info@dorichotel.co.uk
W: www.dorichotel.co.uk

Situated on Queens Promenade with breathtaking views over the
Irish Sea. The Doric has become popular offering a wide range of
facilities and good-value holidays for all. **Directions:** Exit M55
signposted Fleetwood A585 onto Promenade B5265 approximately
0.5miles on the right hand side. **Bedrooms:** 10 single, 20 double, 13
twin, 47 family, 13 suite **Open:** All year

B&B PER ROOM PER NIGHT
S: £32.00 - £55.00
D: £64.00 - £125.00
HB PER PERSON PER NIGHT
£34.00 - £60.00

Site: ✿ **Payment:** ⊞ € **Leisure:** ↖ ↗ **Property:** ☕ ☒ ➊ **Children:** ⅌ ⩫ **Catering:** ☕ 🍽 **Room:** ☖ ⬥ ☏ 📺 🛗

BLACKPOOL, Lancashire   Map ref 4A1   SatNav FY2 9RW [H]

enjoyEngland.com
★★ HOTEL

Elgin Hotel

36-42 Queens Promenade, Blackpool FY2 9RW **T:** (01253) 353535 **F:** (01253) 351109
E: info@elginhotel.com
W: www.elginhotel.com **£ BOOK ONLINE**

The Elgin is a family run hotel situated near to the Cliffs overlooking
the Blackpool sands. This 89 bedroom Hotel offers 5 room types,
Lift to all floors, exciting entertainment and car parking. 2012
Winners of Trip Advisor's Family Hotel **Directions:** Situated one
mile north of Blackpool Tower on the promenade facing sea. Easy
access by tram/bus (5 mins) to Town Centre. Walking (20 mins).
Bedrooms: 2 single, 24 dble, 25 twin, 38 family **Open:** All year

B&B PER ROOM PER NIGHT
S: £50.00 - £66.00
D: £70.00 - £100.00
EVENING MEAL PER PERSON
£11.95 - £15.00

Site: ✿ **Payment:** ⊞ **Leisure:** ♿ ♪ ▶ ∪ **Property:** ☕ ✟ ☒ ➊ **Children:** ⅌ ⩫ **Catering:** ☕ 🍽 **Room:** ☖ ⬥ ⬤ 📺 🛗

For **key to symbols** see page 7

BLACKPOOL, Lancashire   Map ref 4A1   SatNav FY1 4PF B

Helmshore

24 28 Charnley Road, Central, Blackpool, Lancs FY1 4PF **T:** (01253) 623075
F: (01253) 625468 **E:** helmshorehotel@googlemail.com
W: helmshoreblackpool.com

B&B PER ROOM PER NIGHT
S: £35.00 - £45.00
D: £50.00 - £70.00
EVENING MEAL PER PERSON
£8.00 - £10.00

A friendly family hotel, the Helmshore is under the personal supervision of the owners Terry and Jenny Bailey. **Directions:** The Helmshore is ideally situated in the town centre approximately three minutes walk from the beach, Tower, Winter Gardens, shopping centre and car parks. **Bedrooms:** 5 single, 6 double, 8 twin, 16 family **Open:** March to End of November and New Year

Site: **P** Payment: Leisure: Property: Children: Catering: Room:

BLACKPOOL, Lancashire   Map ref 4A1   SatNav FY1 6AN H

Lyndene Hotel

305-315 Promenade, Blackpool FY1 6AN **T:** (01253) 346779 **F:** (01253) 346466
E: enquiries@lyndenehotel.com
W: lyndenehotel.com **£ BOOK ONLINE**

B&B PER ROOM PER NIGHT
S: £24.00 - £122.00
D: £38.00 - £126.00
HB PER PERSON PER NIGHT
£38.00 - £63.00

SPECIAL PROMOTIONS
Big Reductions Early Season

Situated between Tower/Pleasure Beach, the Lyndene is an ideal location from which to enjoy all the resort has to offer. 140 comfortable bedrooms makes us the right choice for your stay in Blackpool. Three lifts access all floors inc ground floor rooms. Three bars, two air conditioned sea-view Cabaret lounges (entertainment nightly). Two restaurants with choice of cuisine. Bar snacks served daily.

Directions: See web page for directions

Bedrooms: 1 single, 52 dble, 21 twin, 66 family
Open: All year round

Site: Payment: Property: Children: Catering: Room:

Need more information?

Visit our new 2014 guide websites for detailed information, up-to-date availability and to book your accommodation online. Includes over 20,000 places to stay, all of them star rated.

www.visitor-guides.co.uk

BLACKPOOL, Lancashire   Map ref 4A1   SatNav FY1 4HT B

The Marston Guest House

22 Park Road, Blackpool, England, United Kingdom FY1 4HT **T:** (01253) 627760
E: brianjl@hotmail.co.uk
W: www.marstonhotel.net

B&B PER ROOM PER NIGHT
S: £20.00 - £35.00
D: £40.00 - £50.00

EVENING MEAL PER PERSON
£8.00 - £12.00

SPECIAL PROMOTIONS
Tarriff and Quality
Guaranteed all seasons

A warm welcome guaranteed at 'The Marston Guest House' a mid- victorian (1878) Semi-detached property sympathetically restored for your comfort. En suite rooms, comfy beds & good grub. (Most diets are catered for). Quiet location close to the town centre and main attractions but far enough away to feel like a home from home. We appreciate everyone's needs differ, we will strive to meet yours.

Directions: M55 leave at Junction 4 R/H Lane follow onto A583 Blackpool North. Straight on to B5390 (Park Road) for Town Centre approx.1.5 miles to Marston House on the right after St. John Ambulance

Bedrooms: En Suite Rooms D/G, C/H, Quality carpets. Comfy beds with quality mattresses and bedding & Feather quilts (Or alternative). Towels, soaps, tea & coffee provided.
Open: All Year

Site: P Payment: ⊞ **Leisure:** & ♪ ▶ **Property:** ▤ ♨ **Children:** ☒ ♨ ♣ **Catering:** ⛺ **Room:** ♦ 📺 📀

BLACKPOOL, Lancashire   Map ref 4A1   SatNav FY4 2EL B

Number One St Luke's

1 St Lukes Road, Blackpool FY4 2EL **T:** (01253) 343901 **E:** info@numberoneblackpool.com
W: www.numberoneblackpool.com

B&B PER ROOM PER NIGHT
S: £70.00 - £100.00
D: £100.00 - £140.00

SPECIAL PROMOTIONS
Stay 2 nights 3rd night
half price midweek

Car park, gardens including hot tub, putting green & designer rooms with king-size beds, 42" TV, CD, DVD, PS2, Free Wi-fi, remote lighting, refreshment tray, usual bits'n pieces & full bathroom en suite with Whirlpool bath, SplashTV, power shower & music system. A short walk from the Promenade & Pleasure Beach or a tram ride to Blackpool Tower & other amazing attractions. The ultimate boutique B&B experience!

Directions: M6, M55 to end & turn left following signs to Bpl Airport. At traffic lights outside airport turn right on to Lytham Rd. Follow road to traffic lights, go straight ahead & St Luke's is 3rd on right.

Bedrooms: Individual rooms with a king-size bed, (one a four poster), 42" TV, CD, DVD, PS2, Wi-fi, remote lighting, refreshment tray, usual bits and pieces & full bathroom en suite including a Whirlpool bath, SplashTV, power shower and music system.
Open: All Year

Site: ⚶ **P Payment:** ⊞ € **Leisure:** & ♪ ▶ ∪ **Property:** ▤ ▣ ♨ **Children:** ☒5 **Catering:** ⛺
Room: ⌐ ♦ ▣ 📺 📀 🛏

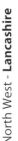

North West - Lancashire

★★★
HOTEL

B&B PER ROOM PER NIGHT
S: £32.00 - £55.00
D: £64.00 - £120.00
EVENING MEAL PER PERSON
£12.95

Park House Hotel

308 North Promenade, Blackpool FY1 2HA **T:** (01253) 620081 **F:** (01253) 290181
E: enquiries@blackpoolparkhousehotel.com
W: blackpoolparkhousehotel.com **£ BOOK ONLINE**

Ideally situated on north promenade within walking distance of town centre and all major attractions. Fabulous cuisine. Entertainment seven nights a week in our ballroom or bar lounge. **Directions:** End of M55 along Yeadon Way onto Promenade from A584 heading north approximately 1 mile. **Bedrooms:** 12 single, 34 double, 33 twin, 20 family, 4 suites **Open:** All year

Site: ✿ **Payment:** 🖃 **Property:** ⵛ 🖴 ◗ **Children:** 🛏 🏠 ♿ **Catering:** ⵢ 🍽 **Room:** 🖩 ⬇ ☎ 📺 ⌁

★★★★
GUEST
ACCOMMODATION

B&B PER ROOM PER NIGHT
S: £36.00 - £39.00
D: £72.00 - £78.00
EVENING MEAL PER PERSON
£9.95 - £14.95

SPECIAL PROMOTIONS
3 nights for the price of 2, Mon-Fri (excl Bank Holidays), Jan-Aug.

The Raffles Guest Accommodation

73-77 Hornby Road, Blackpool FY1 4QJ **T:** (01253) 294713 **F:** (01253) 294240
E: enquiries@raffleshotelblackpool.fsworld.co.uk
W: raffleshotelblackpool.co.uk **£ BOOK ONLINE**

Excellent central location for promenade, shopping centre, Winter Gardens, theatres. All rooms en suite. Licensed bar, English tea rooms, parking and daily housekeeping. Imaginative choice of menus. Listed in the Good Hotel Guide and the Which? Guide to Good Hotels. Four new luxury apartments each sleeping up to four people.

Directions: Follow signs for central car park. Exit onto Central Drive, left then right onto Hornby Road. Through 1st set of lights, on the right.

Bedrooms: 2 single, 12 double, 3 twin, , 4 suite
Open: All year

Site: **P** **Payment:** 🖃 **Leisure:** ⚗ **Property:** 🐾 🖴 **Children:** 🛏 🏠 ♿ **Catering:** ⵢ 🍽 **Room:** 🖩 ⬇ ☎ 📺 ⌁

★★★
GUEST
ACCOMMODATION

Roselea

67 Albert Road, Blackpool FY1 4PW **T:** (01253) 622032 **E:** info@roseleahotel.com
W: roseleahotel.com

The Roselea is a friendly, family-run hotel with an enviable reputation for its quality accommodation, good food and efficient cheerful service, where you can relax and enjoy your holiday. Please contact us for prices. **Directions:** M6 Motorway to M55 Blackpool straight through car park, onto one-way system. Leads to Albert Road. We are half way up on the right. **Bedrooms:** 2 single, 6 double, 7 twin, 3 family **Open:** All year

Site: ✿ **Payment:** 🖃 **Leisure:** ⚗ ⌖ ∪ **Property:** 🖴 🏚 **Children:** 🛏 🏠 ♿ **Catering:** (✕ ⵢ 🍽 **Room:** 🖩 ⬇ ☎ 📺 ✉ ⌁

BLACKPOOL, Lancashire Map ref 4A1   SatNav FY1 4PW H

Ruskin Hotel

55-61 Albert Road, Blackpool FY1 4PW **T:** (01253) 624063 **F:** (01253) 623571
E: reception@ruskinhotel.com
W: ruskinhotel.com

★★ HOTEL

B&B PER ROOM PER NIGHT
S: £35.00 - £77.00
D: £60.00 - £71.00
HB PER PERSON PER NIGHT
£30.00 - £71.00

Centrally located. Conference facilities, fabulous food and nightly entertainment (in season). Four bars, three dance floors, public bar and bistro. Cabaret weekends available. **Bedrooms:** 5 single, 29 dble, 24 twin, 13 family **Open:** All year

Site: ✿ Payment: ⊡ Leisure: ⚓ ♪ ▸ Property: ♟ 🐾 ▭ ⊟ ◖ Children: ⛲ ▥ ♣ Catering: ♟ ⚏
Room: ⚲ ⚮ ☎ 📺 ⛴

CHORLEY, Lancashire Map ref 4A1   SatNav PR7 5SL B

Parr Hall Farm

Parr Lane, Eccleston, Chorley, Lancashire PR7 5SL **T:** (01257) 451917
E: enquiries@parrhallfarm.com
W: www.parrhallfarm.com **£ BOOK ONLINE**

★★★★ GUEST ACCOMMODATION

B&B PER ROOM PER NIGHT
S: £45.00 - £50.00
D: £70.00 - £80.00

18thC farmhouse tastefully restored with oak beams and open views. Village location with good pubs and restaurants nearby. Prices are based on 2 people sharing. Single occupancy rates are available at £45 per room. **Directions:** M6 J27 B5250 north for 5 miles. Parr lane on right. M61 J8 A581 Left turn to Eccleston, Parr Lane on left, after the Original Farmers Arms. **Bedrooms:** Free Wi-Fi, TV, Tea and Coffee making facilities, Off Road Parking. **Open:** All Year

Site: ✿ P Payment: ⊡ € Leisure: ♪ ▸ ∪ Property: ▭ ⊟ ∅ Children: ⛲ ▥ ♣ Room: ⚲ ⚮ 📺 📀 ⛴

North West - Lancashire

CLITHEROE, Lancashire Map ref 4A1 SatNav BB7 1QB B

Angram Green Farmhouse B&B

Angram Green, Worston, Clitheroe, Lancashire BB7 1QB **T:** (01200) 441441
E: angela@angramgreenfarm.co.uk
W: www.angramgreenfarm.co.uk

B&B PER ROOM PER NIGHT
S: £42.00 - £48.00
D: £65.00 - £75.00

A warm welcome awaits you at our award winning farmhouse B&B. Nestled at the foot of Pendle Hill with outstanding views of the surrounding countryside. Ideal for walkers, cyclists, tourists and buisness. **Directions:** Turn off the A59 signposted Worston continue on the village road for approx ¾ mile. Turn right over cattle grid keeping to the right on Farm Road. **Bedrooms:** Well appointed double & single rooms all en suite. **Open:** All year

Site: ❀ P Leisure: 🚲 ♪ ► Property: 🏠 Children: 👶8 Catering: 🍴 Room: 🍵 👣 📺

CLITHEROE, Lancashire Map ref 4A1 SatNav BB6 8AB 🐾 H

Best Western Mytton Fold Hotel & Golf Complex

Whalley Road, Langho, Nr Blackburn BB6 8AB **T:** (01254) 240662
F: (01254) 248119 **E:** reception@myttonfold.co.uk
W: www.bw-myttonfoldhotel.co.uk **£ BOOK ONLINE**

B&B PER ROOM PER NIGHT
S: £59.00 - £69.00
D: £82.50 - £114.50
EVENING MEAL PER PERSON
£17.95 - £22.00

Mytton Fold, a tranquil, friendly oasis. Lovingly created colourful gardens. Private 18-hole golf course. Fifteen minutes M6, M65. All en suite rooms. Free golf for residents after 16:00. **Directions:** Junction 31 M6 follow A59 signposted Clitheroe until you reach large roundabout. Follow Whalley signpost hotel is 200 yrd on the right. **Bedrooms:** 17 double, 14 twin, 12 family **Open:** All year

Site: ❀ P Payment: 💳 Leisure: 🚲 ♪ ► ♨ Property: 🏠 🐕 📶 🍴 🌙 ∅ Children: 🐾 🏠 🚼 Catering: 🍴 Room: 🍵 👣 📞 📺 📻

CLITHEROE, Lancashire Map ref 4A1 SatNav BB7 2HE B

Rowan Tree

10 Railway View Road, Clitheroe BB7 2HE **T:** (01200) 427115
E: query@the-rowan-tree.org.uk
W: the-rowan-tree.org.uk

B&B PER ROOM PER NIGHT
S: £45.00
D: £70.00
EVENING MEAL PER PERSON
£10.00 - £15.00

Luxurious en suite double/twin/family room, in a welcoming, well-appointed Victorian home. Ideally situated for town and country pursuits. Evening meal by arrangement. **Directions:** Close to bus and rail interchange. Five minute walk from town centre. **Bedrooms:** 1 double **Open:** All year

Property: 📶 📶 Children: 🐾1 Catering: 🍴 Room: 🍵 👣 📺 📻

LANCASTER, Lancashire Map ref 5A3 SatNav LA1 1RD B

Wagon and Horses

27 St Georges Quay, Lancaster, Lancashire LA1 1RD **T:** (01524) 846094
E: carolesquires@ymail.com
W: www.wagonandhorseslancaster.co.uk **£ BOOK ONLINE**

B&B PER ROOM PER NIGHT
S: £75.00
D: £75.00

Grade II listed building with delightful riverside location offering excellent accommodation, all with tea and coffee making facilities, flat screen TV, free wi-fi. We serve cask conditioned ales and offer a wide range of freshly cooked food. **Open:** All Year

Site: ❀ Payment: 💳 Leisure: ♪ ► ♨ Property: 📶 ∅ Children: 🚼 Catering: (✗ 🍷 🍴 Room: 🍵 👣 📺

The Chadwick Hotel

113 - 115 South Promenade, St. Annes on Sea, Lytham St Annes, Lancashire FY8 1NP
T: (01253) 720061 **F:** (01253) 714455 **E:** Sales@thechadwickhotel.com
W: thechadwickhotel.com **£ BOOK ONLINE**

B&B PER ROOM PER NIGHT
S: £55.00 - £70.00
D: £90.00 - £113.00

EVENING MEAL PER PERSON
£23.50 - £34.95

SPECIAL PROMOTIONS
Special 5-day breaks from: DB&B £265.00-£315.00 per person (sharing a double room or twin). Theme-weekend breaks from £150.00. For special offers see website.

Modern family run, seventy three bedroomed hotel, commanding a beautiful seafront position. Just Yards from the sandy beach. The bright and comfortable lounges have panoramic views, the Bugatti bar is cosy and relaxed while the Four Seasons restaurant offers classically elegant atmosphere in which to enjoy the quality food and service. All bedrooms are en suite. Pool, Jacuzzi, Sauna and Turkish bath.

Directions: M55 onto A5230, left to B5261. At 2nd roundabout right onto dual carriageway, Progress Way 2.5 miles, left Clifton Drive, 2.5 miles, right Lightburne Avenue.

Bedrooms: 3 single, 13 dble, 24 twin, 33 family.
Open: All year

Site: ✿ **Payment:** 💷 € **Leisure:** 🏊 ♪ ► ◉ ✕ ♫ ⚘ **Property:** ◉ ⚓ 🖥 📺 👪 ◐ **Children:** 🛏 🍴 ♿ **Catering:** ⟨✕ ♟ ♥ 🍴 **Room:** 🔌 🔥 ◉ 📞 📺 🛏

Dam Head Accommodation Roughlee

Dam Head Barn, Studio and Cottage, Dam Head Farm, Pendle, Lancashire BB9 6NX
T: (01282) 617190 / 07769 680473 **E:** info@damheadbarn.com
W: www.damheadbarn.com

B&B PER ROOM PER NIGHT
S: £40.00 - £50.00
D: £60.00 - £90.00

SPECIAL PROMOTIONS
Cottage from £100 per night (sleeps 4-6) or from £550.00 per week.

We offer boutique Bed & Breakfast in Dam Head Barn and the Garden Studio, self catering in Blacksmith's Cottage. Set in the Forest of Bowland (AONB) within the village of Roughlee, Pendle. We cater for individuals or groups seeking quality accommodation in a rural setting.

Prices are based on room only, breakfast can be included at an additional cost.

Directions: M65 J13, through Barrowford to White Bear, turn up Pasture Lane, turn left at bridge, drive to School, properties are next drive after the school.

Bedrooms: 2 double, 2 twin, 1 family
Open: All year

Site: ✿ P **Leisure:** 🏊 ♪ ► ∪ **Property:** 🐕 🖥 🖥 **Children:** 🛏 🍴 ♿ **Catering:** 🍴 **Room:** 🔌 🔥 ◉ 📺 🛏 📻

Briardene Hotel

56 Kelso Avenue, Cleveleys FY5 3JG **T:** (01253) 338300 **F:** (01253) 338301
E: briardenehotel@yahoo.co.uk
W: briardenehotel.co.uk

B&B PER ROOM PER NIGHT
S: £46.00 - £53.00
D: £66.00 - £106.00
HB PER PERSON PER NIGHT
£59.95 - £71.75

SPECIAL PROMOTIONS
Special promotions
available enquire with
our reception.
Promotions changing
on a weekly/monthly
basis.

Briardene Hotel is located in the centre of the Fylde Coast giving the perfect location from which to experience the unique environment that our area has to offer. The hotel has a 3 star rating, and has also just been awarded a 5 star food quality award in Restaurant and Breakfasts.

Directions: M55 exit Junction 3, follow A585 Cleveleys, at third roundabout take first turning past Morrisons, second set of lights turn left 200 yrds on left.

Bedrooms: 2 single, 7 double, 3 twin, 2 family, 2 suite
Open: All year

Site: ✿ Payment: 💷 Leisure: 🏊 ♪ ► Property: ♟ 🐕 🖥 🅱 ◐ Children: 🛏 🛏 🎋 Catering: 🍽 🍴
Room: 🔌 ⬇ 🕯 🛏 📺 🛁 🖥

Looking for something else?

The official and most comprehensive guide to independently inspected, star rated accommodation.

B&Bs and Hotels - B&Bs, Hotels, farmhouses, inns, serviced apartments, campus and hostel accommodation in England.

Self Catering - Self-catering holiday homes, approved caravan holiday homes, boat accommodation and holiday cottage agencies in England.

Camping, Touring and Holiday Parks - Touring parks, camping holidays and holiday parks and villages in Britain.

Now available in all good bookshops and online at **www.hudsons.co.uk/shop**

LIVERPOOL, Merseyside Map ref 4A2   SatNav L1 9DA H

Hope Street Hotel
40 Hope Street, Liverpool, Merseyside L1 9DA **T:** (0151) 7093000 **F:** (0151) 7092454
E: sleep@hopestreethotel.co.uk
W: www.hopestreethotel.co.uk **£ BOOK ONLINE**

B&B PER ROOM PER NIGHT
S: £86.00 - £690.00
D: £96.00 - £700.00
EVENING MEAL PER PERSON
£22.50 - £58.50

SPECIAL PROMOTIONS
Lazy Sunday Package - from £121 for two. Stay Sunday, enjoy a two course dinner in The London Carriage Works followed by a full Liverpool breakfast and a late check out of 12 noon on the Monday.

Liverpool's original boutique hotel, built around 1860 in the style of a Venetian palazzo. Reinvented & renovated in 2003 and extended in 2009 into 89 simple, stylish, contemporary and comfortable hotel rooms with a great 2 AA Rosettes restaurant - The London Carriage Works. Privately owned and independently run.

Directions: From M62, continue to end of motorway, follow signs for cathedrals (approx 3 miles). Hope Street links the two cathedrals and Hope Street Hotel is in the middle opposite the Philharmonic Hall.

Bedrooms: Oversized beds with white Egyptian cotton, solid birch and oak floors, bespoke furniture, original beams and brickwork, REN toiletries and free Wi-Fi.
Open: All Year

Payment: **Leisure:** **Property:** **Children:** **Catering:**
Room:

LIVERPOOL, Merseyside Map ref 4A2   SatNav L1 9JG B

International Inn
4 South Hunter Street, Liverpool L1 9JG **T:** (0151) 709 8135 **F:** (0151) 709 8135
E: info@internationalinn.co.uk
W: www.internationalinn.co.uk **£ BOOK ONLINE**

BED ONLY PER NIGHT
£17.00

Tourist hostel, located in the heart of the city centre, near to theatres, cathedrals and nightlife. With a variety of dormitory sizes, Free tea/coffee, toast. No curfew, bedding provided. Free Wi-Fi.
Directions: Check out our web site for full directions. We have great connections from all transport links. **Bedrooms:** 3 double, 4 twin **Open:** All year except Christmas

Payment: **Leisure:** **Property:** **Children:** **Room:** **Bedroom:**

LIVERPOOL, Merseyside Map ref 4A2   SatNav L1 9JG B

International Inn Cocoon
4 South Hunter Street, Off Hardman Street, Liverpool, Merseyside L1 9JG
T: (0151) 709 8135 **F:** (0151) 709 8135 **E:** info@internationalinn.co.uk
W: www.cocoonliverpool.co.uk

BED ONLY PER NIGHT
£45.00 - £62.00

Conceptual, innovative, stylish, budget boutique pod hotel rooms in the heart of Liverpool's city centre. **Directions:** Check out our website for full directions. We have great connections from all transport links. **Bedrooms:** 32 en suite boutique pods located in the basement. **Open:** All Year except 24th-26th December.

Payment: **Leisure:** **Property:** **Children:** **Bedroom:**

North East

Historic houses, breathtaking coastline, stunning countryside and vibrant cities make a visit to the North East a truly memorable experience. The region may only consist of County Durham, Northumberland, Tees Valley and Tyne & Wear, but it is packed with diverse visitor attractions, such as the World Heritage Sites, Durham Cathedral and Hadrian's Wall. This is a magical place filled with ancient castles, golden sand beaches and rolling hills.

County Durham

From ancient relics to railways, and from priceless art to archaeological finds, Durham's cultural treasures are waiting to be discovered.

Durham Castle and Cathedral

Built to house the relics of St Cuthbert and the Venerable Bede, Durham Cathedral is the largest example of Norman architecture in England. The castle housed the Durham prince-bishops.

Frontiers of the Roman Empire

Hadrian's Wall was built in 122 AD to defend the Roman Empire from 'barbarians'. The World Heritage Site was expanded to include all the frontiers of the Roman Empire, ranging from Antonine's Wall in the north to Trajan's Wall in eastern Europe.

Newcastle/Gateshead

Newcastle/Gateshead is a destination of icons – from the seven spectacular bridges crossing the River Tyne to Antony Gormley's contemporary sculpture Angel of the North. In the heart of Newcastle city centre the Castle Keep hints at the region's thousands of years of heritage.

Northumberland

Northumberland National Park is the northernmost National Park in England, and is a magical place filled with ancient castles, rolling hills and rugged moorland.

Tees Valley

People tend to think of the Tees Valley as an urbanised region consisting of towns like Darlington, Hartlepool, Middlesbrough, Redcar and Stockton-on-Tees, but it also contains miles of stunning coastline, countryside and ancient woodland.

Editor's Picks

Marvel at Bamburgh Castle

Try standing on Bamburgh beach one sunny morning or sunset and view the site of the fortress towering over the dunes looking out defiantly towards the North Sea.

Step back in time

Discover Durham's fascinating history and heritage at award-winning attractions like the Beamish Museum.

Follow the code

Hadrian's Wall is a fragile environment and the archaeology is easily damaged, so the World Heritage Site urges visitors to follow its country code called 'Every Footstep Counts'.

Time to discover

At Discovery Museum find out about life in Newcastle and Tyneside, from the area's renowned maritime history to world-changing science and technology.

Things to do

Attractions with this sign participate in the Places of Interest Quality Assurance Scheme.

Attractions with this sign participate in the Visitor Attraction Quality Assurance Scheme.

Both schemes recognise high standards in all aspects of the visitor experience (see page 7)

Entertainment & Culture

Bailiffgate Museum
Alnwick, Northumberland NE66 1LX
(01665) 605847
www.bailiffgatemuseum.co.uk
Bailiffgate Museum brings to life the people and places of North Northumberland in exciting interactive style.

BALTIC Centre for Contemporary Art
Gateshead, Tyne and Wear NE8 3BA
(01914) 781810
www.balticmill.com
BALTIC is the biggest gallery of its kind in the world - presenting a dynamic, diverse and international programme of contemporary visual art.

Beamish Museum
County Durham DH9 0RG
(01913) 704000
www.beamish.org.uk
Beamish - The Living Museum of the North, is an open air museum vividly recreating life in the North East in the early 1800's and 1900's.

Discovery Museum
Newcastle-upon-Tyne,Tyne and Wear NE1 4JA
(01912) 326789
www.twmuseums.org.uk/discovery
Discovery Museum offers a wide variety of experiences for all the family to enjoy.

DLI Museum and Durham Art Gallery
Durham, County Durham DH1 5TU
(01913) 842214
www.durham.gov.uk/dli
Museum tells the 200-year story of Durham's famous regiment. Art Gallery has changing exhibition programme.

Great North Museum: Hancock
Newcastle-upon-Tyne,
Tyne and Wear NE2 4PT
(01912) 226765
www.greatnorthmuseum.org
See major new displays showing the wonder of the animal and plant kingdoms, spectacular objects from the Ancient Greeks and a planetarium and a life-size T-Rex.

Hartlepool Art Gallery

Hartlepool, Tees Valley TS24 7EQ
(01429) 869706
www.hartlepool.gov.uk/info/100009/leisure_and_
culture/1506/hartlepool_art_gallery/1/3
*Former church building also includes the TIC and a bell
tower viewing platform looking over Hartlepool.*

Hartlepool's Maritime Experience

Tees Valley TS24 0XZ
(01429) 860077
www.hartlepoolsmaritimeexperience.com
An authentic reconstruction of an 18th century seaport.

Hatton Gallery

Newcastle-upon-Tyne, Tyne and Wear NE1 7RU
(01912) 226059
www.twmuseums.org.uk/hatton
*Temporary exhibitions of contemporary and historical art.
Permanent display of Kurt Schwitters' Merzbarn.*

Head of Steam Darlington Railway Museum
Tees Valley DL3 6ST
(01325) 460532
www.darlington.gov.uk/Culture/headofsteam/welcome.
htm
*Restored 1842 station housing a collection of exhibits
relating to railways in the North East of England, including
Stephenson's Locomotion, call for details of events.*

Hexham Old Gaol

Northumberland NE46 3NH
(01434) 652349
www.tynedaleheritage.org
*Tour the Old Gaol, 1330AD, by glass lift. Meet the gaoler,
see a Reiver raid and try on costumes.*

Killhope, The North of England
Lead Mining Museum
Bishop Auckland, County Durham DL13 1AR
(01388) 537505
www.killhope.org.uk
*The North East's Small Visitor Attraction of the Year and the
most complete lead mining site in Great Britain.*

Laing Art Gallery

Newcastle-upon-Tyne, Tyne and Wear NE1 8AG
(01912) 327734
www.twmuseums.org.uk/laing
*The Laing Art Gallery is home to an important collection of
18th and 19th century painting, which is shown alongside
temporary exhibitions of historic and contemporary art.*

Locomotion: The National Railway
Museum at Shildon
Shildon, County Durham DL4 1PQ
(01388) 777999
www.nrm.org.uk/locomotion
*The first National Museum in the North East. Free
admission. View over 60 vehicles, children's play area and
interactive displays.*

mima
Middlesbrough, Tees Valley TS1 2AZ
(01642) 726720
www.visitmima.com
*mima, Middlesbrough Institute of Modern Art, is a £14.2m
landmark new gallery in the heart of Middlesbrough. mima
showcases an international programme of fine art and
applied art from the 1900s to the present day.*

Museum of Hartlepool
Hartlepool, Tees Valley TS24 0XZ
(01429) 860077
www.hartlepoolsmaritimeexperience.com
*Hartlepool Museum, situated beside Hartlepool Historic
Quay, includes local historical exhibits, PSS Wingfield Castle,
exhibitions and the original lighthouse light.*

Preston Hall Museum and Park
Stockton-on-Tees, Tees Valley TS18 3RH
(01642) 527375
www.stockton.gov.uk/museums
*A Georgian country house set in beautiful parkland
overlooking the River Tees. A Museum of social history with
a recreated Victorian street and working craftsmen.*

RNLI Grace Darling Museum
Bamburgh, Northumberland NE69 7AE
(01668) 214910
www.rnli.org.uk/gracedarling
*A museum dedicated to Grace Darling and her family, as
well as all those who Save Lives at Sea.*

Segedunum Roman Fort, Baths and Museum
Wallsend, Tyne and Wear NE28 6HR
(01912) 369347
www.twmuseums.org.uk/segedunum
*Segedunum Roman Fort is the gateway to Hadrian's Wall.
Explore the excavated fort site, visit reconstructions of a
Roman bath house, learn about the history of the area in
the museum and enjoy the view from the 35 metre viewing
tower.*

The Bowes Museum
Barnard Castle, County Durham DL12 8NP
(01833) 690606
www.thebowesmuseum.org.uk
*The Bowes Museum houses a collection of outstanding
European fine and decorative arts and offers an acclaimed
exhibition programme, alongside special events and
children's activities.*

Vindolanda (Chesterholm) Hadrian's Wall
Bardon Mill, Northumberland NE47 7JN
(01434) 344277
www.vindolanda.com
*Visitors may inspect the remains of the Roman fort and
settlement, see its extraordinary finds in the superb
museum. Full-scale replicas of Roman buildings. Please ring
to check winter opening times.*

Family Fun

Centre for Life
Newcastle-upon-Tyne, Tyne and Wear NE1 4EP
(01912) 438210
www.life.org.uk
The Centre for Life is an award-winning science centre where imaginative exhibitions, interactive displays and special events promote greater understanding of science and provoke curiosity in the world around us.

Nature's World

Middlesbrough, Tees Valley TS5 7YN
(01642) 594895
www.naturesworld.org.uk
Nature's World now has a new Adventure Arena with assault course, climbing walls, pedal go-karts and tractors.

Heritage

Arbeia Roman Fort and Museum
South Shields, Tyne and Wear NE33 2BB
(01914) 561369
www.twmuseums.org.uk/arbeia
Arbeia is the best reconstruction of a Roman fort in Britain and offers visitors a unique insight into the every day life of the Roman army, from the soldier in his barrack room to the commander in his luxurious house.

Bamburgh Castle
Northumberland NE69 7DF
(01668) 214515
www.bamburghcastle.com
A spectacular castle with fantastic coastal views. The stunning Kings Hall and Keep house collections of armour, artwork, porcelain and furniture.

Belsay Hall, Castle and Gardens
Northumberland NE20 0DX
(01661) 881636
www.english-heritage.org.uk/belsay
With so much to see and do, a trip to Belsay is one of the best value family days out in North East England. Stunning gardens, beautiful acrrchitecture and magnificent views all in one place.

Durham Castle
County Durham DH1 3RW
(01913) 343800
www.durhamcastle.com
Durham Castle is part of the Durham City World Heritage Site. Entrance by guided tour only. Opening can vary - please telephone 0191 334 3800 to check days open and guided tour times.

HMS Trincomalee
Hartlepool, Tees Valley TS24 0XZ
(01429) 223193
www.hms-trincomalee.co.uk
HMS Trincomalee, built in 1817, is one of the oldest ship afloat in Europe. Come aboard for a unique experience of Navy life two centuries ago.

Housesteads Roman Fort
Haydon Bridge, Northumberland NE47 6NN
(01434) 344363
www.english-heritage.org.uk/daysout/properties/ housesteads-roman-fort-hadrians-wall
The most complete example of a British Roman fort, Housesteads features magnificent ruins and stunning views of the countryside surrounding Hadrian's Wall.

Kielder Castle Forest Park Centre
Northumberland NE48 1ER
(01434) 250209
www.forestry.gov.uk/northeastengland
Features include forest shop, information centre, tearoom and exhibitions. Bike hire available.

Lindisfarne Priory
Holy Island, Northumberland TD15 2RX
(01289) 389200
www.english-heritage.org.uk/lindisfarnepriory
Take in panoramic views of the Northumbrian coast, unpack a picnic in the priory grounds, and take a break from the hustle and bustle of life.

National Glass Centre
Sunderland, Tyne and Wear SR6 0GL
(01915) 155555
www.nationalglasscentre.com
Enjoy an ever-changing programme of exhibitions, live glass blowing, and banqueting and a stunning restaurant overlooking the River Wear.

Raby Castle

Staindrop, County Durham DL2 3AH
(01833) 660202
www.rabycastle.com
Home of Lord Barnard's family since 1626, includes a 200 acre deer park, gardens, carriage collection, adventure playground, shop and tearoom.

Saltburn Smugglers Heritage Centre
Saltburn-by-the-Sea, Tees Valley TS12 1HF
(01287) 625252
www.redcar-cleveland.gov.uk/museums
Step back into Saltburn's past and experience the authentic sights, sounds and smells.

Warkworth Castle

Warkworth, Northumberland NE65 0UJ
(01665) 711423
www.english-heritage.org.uk/warkworthcastle
Set in a quaint Northumberland town, this hill-top fortress and hermitage offers a fantastic family day out.

Nature & Wildlife

Adventure Valley

Durham, County Durham DH1 5SG
(01913) 868291
www.adventurevalley.co.uk
Adventure Valley is Durham's newest day out! Split into six Play Zones (with three under cover), you'll find the very best in family fun come rain or shine.

Hall Hill Farm

Durham, County Durham DH7 0TA
(01388) 731333
www.hallhillfarm.co.uk
Award-winning farm attraction set in attractive countryside, see and touch the animals at close quarters.

High Force Waterfall

Middleton-in-Teesdale, County Durham DL12 0XH
(01833) 640209
www.rabycastle.com/high_force.htm
The most majestic of the waterfalls on the River Tees.

Hamsterley Forest

Bishop Auckland, County Durham DL13 3NL
(01388) 488312
www.forestry.gov.uk/northeastengland
A 5,000 acre mixed woodland open to the public all year.

Saltholme Wildlife Reserve and Discovery Park

Middlesbrough, Tees Valley TS2 1TU
(01642) 546625
www.rspb.org.uk/reserves/guide/s/saltholme
Saltholme is an amazing wildlife experience in the Tees Valley.

WWT Washington Wetland Centre

Washington, Tyne and Wear NE38 8LE
(01914) 165454
www.wwt.org.uk/visit/washington
45 hectares of wetland, woodland and wildlife reserve. Home to wildfowl, insects and flora with lake-side hides, wild bird feeding station, waterside cafe, picnic areas, sustainable garden, playground and events calendar.

Events 2014

Bishop Auckland Food Festival

April, Bishop Auckland

Be inspired by cookery demonstrations and entertained by performers.
www.bishopaucklandfoodfestival.co.uk

Evolution Festival

May, Newcastle

The North East's premier music event, taking place over a Bank Holiday.
www.evolutionfestival.co.uk

Haydon Bridge Beer Festival

July, Haydon Bridge

A celebration of the finest real ales and wines.
www.haydonbeerfestival.co.uk

Eat! Newcastle-Gateshead

July, Newcastle

For three days, the heart of Newcastle-Gateshead is turned into a taste bud-tempting array of foodie events. From cooking demos to cookery workshops, choice foods to chilli bonanzas, fish barbecues to street food festival.
www.newcastlegateshead.com/eat-home

Durham Folk Party

July, Durham

It is a celebration of folk song, music and dance which began in 1990 after the demise of the excellent Durham City Folk Festival and has developed into an important part of the music year of the city.
www.communigate.co.uk/ne/durhamfolkparty

Gateshead Summer Flower Show

July, Gateshead

The Gateshead Summer Flower Show is an annual horticultural event and competition.
www.gateshead.gov.uk

Billingham International Folklore Festival

August, Billingham

A festival of traditional and contemporary world dance, music and arts.
www.billinghamfestival.co.uk

Alnwick Beer Festival

September, Alnwick

If you enjoy real ale, or simply want to enjoy a fantastic social event, then make sure you pay this festival a visit.
www.alnwickbeerfestival.co.uk

Hexham Abbey Festival

September-October, Hexham

An exciting array of events to capture the imagination, bringing the very best world-class musicians and artists to Hexham.
www.hexhamabbey.org.uk

Wunderbar Festival

October-November, Newcastle

A week of activity, spontaneity, interaction, dialogue and play.
www.wunderbarfestival.co.uk

Tourist Information Centres

When you arrive at your destination, visit an Official Partner Tourist Information Centre for quality assured help with accommodation and information about local attractions and events, or email your request before you go. To find a Tourist Information Centre visit www.visitengland.com

Alnwick	2 The Shambles	01670 622152	alnwick.tic@northumberland.gov.uk
Amble	Queen Street Car Park	01665 712313	amble.tic@northumberland.gov.uk
Bellingham	Station Yard	01434 220616	bellinghamtic@btconnect.com
Berwick-upon-Tweed	106 Marygate	01670 622155	berwick.tic@northumberland.gov.uk
Bishop Auckland	Town Hall Ground Floor	03000 269524	bishopauckland.touristinfo@durham.gov.uk
Corbridge	Hill Street	01434 632815	corbridge.tic@northumberland.gov.uk
Craster	Craster Car Park	01665 576007	craster.tic@northumberland.gov.uk
Darlington	Central Library	01325 462034	crown.street.library@darlington.gov.uk
Durham	3 Millennium Place	03000 262626	visitor@thisisdurham.com
Gateshead	Central Library	0191 433 8420	libraries@gateshead.gov.uk
Guisborough	Priory Grounds	01287 633801	guisborough_tic@redcar-cleveland.gov.uk
Haltwhistle	Westgate	01434 322002	haltwhistle.tic@northumberland.gov.uk
Hartlepool	Hartlepool Art Gallery	01429 869706	hpooltic@hartlepool.gov.uk
Hexham	Wentworth Car Park	01434 652220	hexham.tic@northumberland.gov.uk
Middlesbrough	Albert Road	01642 729700	tic@middlesbrough.gov.uk
Morpeth	The Chantry	01670 623455	morpeth.tic@northumberland.gov.uk
Newcastle-upon-Tyne	8-9 Central Arcade	0191 277 8000	visitorinfo@ngi.org.uk
North Shields	Unit 18	0191 2005895	ticns@northtyneside.gov.uk
Once Brewed	Northumberland National Park Centre	01434 344396	tic.oncebrewed@nnpa.org.uk
Redcar	24 High Street	01642 471921	redcar_tic@redcar-cleveland.gov.uk
Saltburn by Sea	Saltburn Library	01287 622422	saltburn_library@redcar-cleveland.gov.uk
Seahouses	Seafield Car Park	01665 720884	seahouses.tic@northumberland.gov.uk
South Shields	South Shields Museum & Gallery	0191 454 6612	museum.tic@southtyneside.gov.uk
South Shields	(Amphiltheatre) Sea Road	0191 455 7411	foreshore.tic@southtyneside.gov.uk
Stockton-on-Tees	High Street	01642 528130	visitorinformation@stockton.gov.uk
Whitley Bay	York Road	0191 6435395	susan.clark@northtyneside.gov.uk
Wooler	Wooler TIC, The Cheviot Centre	01668 282123	wooler.tic@northumberland.gov.uk

Regional Contacts and Information

Log on to the North East England website at www.visitnortheastengland.com for further information on accommodation, attractions, events and special offers throughout the region. A range of free information is available to download from the website.

Where to Stay

Entries appear alphabetically by town name in each county. A key to symbols appears on page 7

DURHAM, Co Durham Map ref 5C2
SatNav DH1 4PS **B**

Castle View Guest House

4 Crossgate, Durham DH1 4PS **T:** (0191) 3868852 **E:** castle_view@hotmail.com
W: www.castle-view.co.uk

GUEST ACCOMMODATION ★★★★

B&B PER ROOM PER NIGHT
D: £100.00 - £130.00

Two hundred and fifty year old listed building in the heart of the old city, with woodland and riverside walks and magnificent views of the cathedral and castle. Complimentary parking. **Directions:** From A1(M) take junction 62, follow signs A690 Crook until river crossing. At traffic lights turn left into Crossgate, next to St Margarets Church. **Bedrooms:** 3 double, 2 twin **Open:** All year except Christmas and New Year

Site: ❀ Payment: 🖃 Property: 🛏 Children: 🐴2 Catering: 🍴 Room: 📺

DURHAM, Co Durham Map ref 5C2
SatNav DH1 3RH **B**

St Chad's College

18 North Bailey, Durham DH1 3RH **T:** (0191) 334 3358 **F:** (0191) 334 3371
E: chads@durham.ac.uk
W: www.dur.ac.uk/chads/

GUEST ACCOMMODATION ★★★

B&B PER ROOM PER NIGHT
S: £30.00 - £38.00
D: £55.00 - £72.00

EVENING MEAL PER PERSON
£15.00 - £35.00

In the heart of historic Durham, adjacent to the World Heritage Site and next to the Cathedral, St Chad's provides comfortable modern accommodation, supported by friendly service, in its range of listed buildings - a spectacular location. Group Bookings Welcome. **Directions:** Follow the A1(M) until the A690, direct to Durham, towards Cathedral. The college lies opposite of Durham Cathedral. **Bedrooms:** Over 150 en suite and standard bedrooms. Evening Meals Pre Book Only. **Open:** Easter/Summer student vacations.

Site: ❀ Payment: 🖃 Leisure: 🎵 ↑ Property: ▣ Children: 🐴 🍴 Catering: 🍷 🍴 Room: 🛁

DURHAM, Co Durham Map ref 5C2
SatNav DH1 3RJ **B**

St John's College

3 South Bailey, Durham DH1 3RJ **T:** (0191) 3343877 **E:** s.l.hobson@durham.ac.uk
W: durham.ac.uk/st-johns.college

GUEST ACCOMMODATION ★★★

B&B PER ROOM PER NIGHT
S: £33.00
D: £60.00

Located in the heart of Durham City alongside the cathedral, St John's offers accommodation in distinctive, historic buildings with riverside gardens. **Directions:** Take A1(M) motorway junction 62, dual carriageway A690 Gilesgate roundabout. Take third exit, second left exit, then left to Market Square, 200 yards to College. **Bedrooms:** 66 single, 15 double, 2 twin **Open:** Easter and summer vacations only

Site: ❀ Payment: 🖃 Property: 🛏 ▣ Children: 🐴 ↑ Catering: 🍴 Room: 🛁

Book your accommodation online

Visit our new 2014 guide websites for detailed information, up-to-date availability and to book your accommodation online. Includes over 20,000 places to stay, all of them star rated.

www.visitor-guides.co.uk

The Official Tourist Board Guide to **B&Bs and Hotels 2014**

DURHAM, Co Durham   Map ref 5C2   SatNav DH1 4RW B

★★★★ GUEST ACCOMMODATION

Gold AWARD

B&B PER ROOM PER NIGHT
S: £60.00 - £70.00
D: £85.00 - £95.00

The Victorian Town House

2 Victoria Terrace, Durham City DH1 4RW T: (0191) 3709963
E: stay@durhambedandbreakfast.com
W: durhambedandbreakfast.com

Victorian terraced family home. Three en suite rooms. City centre, train, bus all five minutes walk. Private and nearby parking. **Directions:** 5 minute walk from train station. Turn right at bottom of station approach road. Pass hospital and left onto Western Hill. Turn first right. **Bedrooms:** 1 double, 1 twin, 1 family **Open:** All year except Christmas

Site: ✿ P Leisure: 🏊 ♪ Property: ⬚ Children: 🏇5 Catering: 🍴 Room: 📶 🕯 🄰 📺 🍽

SPENNYMOOR, Co Durham   Map ref 5C2   SatNav DL16 7JT B

★★★★ GUEST HOUSE

B&B PER ROOM PER NIGHT
S: £47.00
D: £67.00

Highview Country House

Kirk Merrington, Spennymoor DL16 7JT T: (01388) 811006 F: (01388) 811006
E: jayne@highviewcountryhouse.co.uk
W: highviewcountryhouse.co.uk £ BOOK ONLINE

Country house in one acre of gardens surrounded by countryside. Peaceful. Safe parking. Situated on the edge of delightful village. Good pubs, newly refurbished rooms. Ten minutes from motorway/Durham. Please contact us for prices. **Bedrooms:** 1 single, 4 double, 1 twin, 1 family **Open:** All year

Site: ✿ P Payment: 💷 Leisure: ♪ Property: ⬚ Children: 🏇 🍽 🖐 Room: 📶 🕯 📺 🍽

ALNWICK, Northumberland   Map ref 5C1   SatNav NE66 2HJ B

★★★ GUEST ACCOMMODATION

B&B PER ROOM PER NIGHT
S: £40.00 - £49.00
D: £55.00 - £120.00

EVENING MEAL PER PERSON
£15.00 - £30.00

SPECIAL PROMOTIONS
Stay Mon-Thu get Thursday Half Price. Stay Fri & Sat get Sunday Half Price, Ex Bk Hols. Adaptable family rooms.

Alnwick Lodge

West Cawledge Park, Alnwick NE66 2HJ
T: (01665) 604363 / (01665) 603377 / 07881 696769 E: bookings@alnwicklodge.com
W: alnwicklodge.com £ BOOK ONLINE

Lonely Planet recommended and Trip Advisor 4* rated accommodation in beautiful Northumberland. A unique creation AD1650-2012. Alnwick Lodge at West Cawledge Park is a combination of history and rural charm with an air of sophistication, whilst linked to technology. Fascinating, incomparable accommodation for business, pleasure, conferences, functions and parties. Antique galleries and log fires.

Directions: 1.75 miles south of Alnwick. Direct access from A1 (trunk road) highway signposted to West Cawledge Park (chair on the roof).

Bedrooms: 4 single, 4 double, 3 twin and 4 family. Assorted Forester's Huts & Gypsy Caravans available.
Open: All year

Site: ✿ P Payment: 💷 Leisure: 🏊 ♪ ♭ ♃ Property: 🐾 ⬚ Children: 🏇 🍽 🖐 Catering: 🍴
Room: 📶 🕯 📺 🍽 🛏 🖊

ALNWICK, Northumberland Map ref 5C1 SatNav NE66 1XU B

Greycroft
Tom & Audrey Bowes, Croft Place, Alnwick, Northumberland NE66 1XU T: (01665) 602127
E: greycroftalnwick@aol.com
W: greycroftalnwick.co.uk £ BOOK ONLINE

B&B PER ROOM PER NIGHT
S: £60.00 - £68.00
D: £90.00 - £130.00

A warm welcome awaits you at Greycroft, a delightful 6 bedroom Victorian guesthouse offering quality guest accommodation. Tastefully furnished. Large walled garden. Guest parking in private road. Conservation area. Two minute walk to Alnwick town centre and a short stroll to Alnwick Castle, The Garden and local amenities.

Directions: Opposite the Police Station (very reassuring) off Prudhoe Street.

Bedrooms: 1 single, 4 double, 1 twin
Open: All year except Christmas

Site: P Payment: Leisure: Property: Catering: Room:

AMBLE, Northumberland Map ref 5C1 SatNav NE65 0AL B

Amble Guesthouse
16 Leazes Street, Amble NE65 0AL T: (01665) 714661 E: stephmclaughlin@aol.com
W: ambleguesthouse.co.uk

A family run 4 bedroom guest house. All rooms en suite. In picturesque fishing port of Amble. Ten+ golf courses within twelve mile radius. Please contact us for prices. **Directions:** From main A1 follow signposts to Amble. Will supply more concise details on request by e-mail or phone. **Bedrooms:** 1 single, 1 double, 1 twin, 1 family **Open:** All year except Christmas and New Year

Payment: Leisure: Property: Children: Room:

BAMBURGH, Northumberland Map ref 5C1 SatNav NE70 7EE H

Waren House Hotel
Waren Mill, Belford NE70 7EE T: (01668) 214581 F: (01668) 214484
E: enquiries@warenhousehotel.co.uk
W: www.warenhousehotel.co.uk £ BOOK ONLINE

B&B PER ROOM PER NIGHT
S: £105.00 - £125.00
D: £130.00 - £190.00
HB PER PERSON PER NIGHT
£85.00 - £120.00

Traditional, award-winning country-house hotel in 6 acres of grounds and walled garden overlooking Holy Island. Superb accommodation, excellent food, wines. Attractions nearby. Children 14+ welcome. Ground-floor suite with wheelchair access. **Directions:** Midway between Belford and Bamburgh on B1342 and 2 miles from the A1 on which we have a sign from both north and south. **Bedrooms:** 8 double, 4 twin, 3 suite **Open:** All year

Site: P Payment: Leisure: Property: Children: Catering: Room:

BEADNELL, Northumberland Map ref 5C1
SatNav NE67 5AY **B**

GUEST ACCOMMODATION ★★★★

B&B PER ROOM PER NIGHT
S: £46.00 - £74.00
D: £76.00 - £104.00

SPECIAL PROMOTIONS
1st Oct 2013 - 30th Mar 2014: Stay 3 nights for 2 or stay 4 nights for 3. Dinner, B&B for £48.50 pppn, price based on 2 people sharing inc 2 course meal (Min 2 Nights). Excluding Christmas & New Year. Please contact for further details.

Beadnell Towers
The Wynding, Beadnell, Chathill, Northumberland NE67 5AY **T:** (01665) 721211
E: info@beadnelltowers.co.uk
W: www.beadnelltowers.co.uk **£ BOOK ONLINE**

The Hotel is situated in the heart of the delightful village of Beadnell on the Northumberland coast and is only a short walk from some of Britain's most beautiful, unspoilt beaches. A very warm welcome awaits you from Michael, Allyson and all of the team.

Directions: From A1 take B1304 signposted Christon Bank/Seahouses. Follow signs for Beadnell. Turn right off B1304 to Beadnell village.

Bedrooms: 1 single, 5 double, 1 twin, 3 family
Open: All year except Christmas

Site: ✿ P Payment: 💳 Leisure: ♿ ♪ ▶ Property: 🖥 Children: ⛟ 🛏 ☂ Catering: (✗ ♟ 🍴
Room: 🍵 ♨ ☎ 📺 🔌 🧺

BEAL, Northumberland Map ref 5B1
SatNav TD15 2PB **B**

GUEST ACCOMMODATION ★★★★

B&B PER ROOM PER NIGHT
S: £35.00 - £50.00
D: £65.00 - £80.00

Brock Mill Farmhouse
Brock Mill, Beal, Berwick-upon-Tweed TD15 2PB **T:** (01289) 381283 **F:** (01289) 381283
E: brockmillfarmhouse@btinternet.com
W: holyislandaccommodation.com **£ BOOK ONLINE**

Working farm. Peaceful surroundings. Ideal for touring North Northumberland and Scottish Borders. Quality accommodation with en suite/suite and private bathrooms new for 2010. Superb English breakfasts or tasty vegetarian alternatives.
Directions: About 1.5 miles from A1 at Beal on the Holy Island road.
Bedrooms: 1 single, 1 double, 1 twin, 1 family **Open:** All year except Christmas

WALKERS / CYCLISTS Site: ✿ P Payment: 💳 € Leisure: ♿ ♪ ▶ ♺ Property: 🐾 🖥 🖳 Children: ⛟ 🛏 ☂
Catering: 🍴 Room: 🍵 ♨ 📻 📺 🔌 🧺

BERWICK-UPON-TWEED, Northumberland Map ref 5B1
SatNav TD15 1DU **B**

BED & BREAKFAST ★★★★
Silver AWARD

B&B PER ROOM PER NIGHT
S: £45.00 - £60.00
D: £70.00 - £80.00

Alannah House
84 Church Street, Berwick upon Tweed, Northumberland TD15 1DU **T:** (01289) 307252
E: info@alannahhouse.com
W: alannahhouse.com

Georgian town house, situated in town centre within the famous Elizabethan town walls. We have a well maintained walled garden and patio area for guests' use. Parking permits available. All rooms en suite and have digital TV. **Directions:** Enter Berwick town centre, head for town hall turn immediately left behind the hall, 400yds on the right past the police station. **Bedrooms:** 1 double, 1 triple, 1 family. **Open:** All year

WALKERS / CYCLISTS Site: ✿ Leisure: ♿ ♪ Property: 🖥 🖳 Children: ⛟ 🛏 ☂ Catering: 🍴 Room: 🍵 ♨ 📻 📺

BERWICK-UPON-TWEED, Northumberland *Map ref 5B1*   SatNav TD15 2PL **B**

Fenham Farm Coastal Bed & Breakfast
Beal, Berwick-upon-Tweed TD15 2PL T: (01289) 381245 E: stay@fenhamfarm.co.uk
W: fenhamfarm.co.uk **£ BOOK ONLINE**

B&B PER ROOM PER NIGHT
S: £55.00 - £70.00
D: £80.00 - £95.00

Quality Bed & Breakfast accommodation in converted farm outbuildings on a beautiful coastal spot overlooking the Holy Island of Lindisfarne. 5 warm & comfortable en suite bedrooms. Delicious breakfasts served in the farmhouse. **Directions:** Fenham Farm is on the coast approximately 1.5 miles off the A1, 10 miles south of Berwick upon Tweed and 6 miles north of Belford. **Bedrooms:** 4 double/ twin, 1 family **Open:** March until December

Site: P Payment: Leisure: Property: Children: Catering: Room:

BERWICK-UPON-TWEED, Northumberland *Map ref 5B1*   SatNav TD15 2RW **B**

Ladythorne House
Cheswick, Berwick upon Tweed, Northumberland TD15 2RW T: (01289) 387382
E: ladythornehouse@gmail.com
W: www.ladythornehouse.co.uk

B&B PER ROOM PER NIGHT
S: £35.00 - £60.00
D: £64.00 - £75.00

Family run, historical (1721) Georgian country house in beautiful rural location, nr beach. Between Berwick and Holy Island. Traditionaly decorated with en suite/private facilities, televsion rooms. Luxury breakfasts, friendly hosts. **Directions:** One mile from A1, signposted Cheswick. 10 mins drive South Berwick-upon-Tweed. **Bedrooms:** 2 double, 1 twin, 2 family **Open:** All year

Site: P Payment: Leisure: Property: Children: Catering: Room:

BERWICK-UPON-TWEED, Northumberland *Map ref 5B1*   SatNav TD151HB **B**

The Walls
8 Quay Walls, Berwick-upon-Tweed TD15 1HB T: (01289) 330233
E: info@thewallsberwick.com
W: http://thewallsberwick.com

B&B PER ROOM PER NIGHT
S: £70.00 - £75.00
D: £80.00 - £135.00

We established 'The Walls' in March 2007 using a simple premise: to provide our guests with an elegant, welcoming and stylish haven in one of the most beautiful regions of the British Isles. **Directions:** When you arrive at the Town Hall, take a right onto Hide Hill then right again into Bridge St. Park in Bridge St carpark. Proceed up the steps. **Bedrooms:** Large en suite rooms **Open:** All year

Site: P Property: Room:

CORBRIDGE, Northumberland *Map ref 5B2*   SatNav NE45 5LW **B**

2 The Crofts
Newcastle Road, Corbridge NE45 5LW T: (01434) 633046 E: welcome@2thecrofts.co.uk
W: www.2thecrofts.co.uk

B&B PER ROOM PER NIGHT
D: £65.00 - £80.00

Traditional large Victorian terrace on edge of Corbridge in quiet location with friendly attention and Aga-cooked breakfast. Two guest rooms one double, one twin, both with en suite shower rooms. We are on the Hadrian's Cycleway route 72. Recommended in Lonely Planet England. **Directions:** Please contact us for directions **Bedrooms:** 2 King sized bedrooms and 1 Twin Bedroom **Open:** All Year

Site: P Payment: Leisure: Property: Children: Catering: Room:

CORBRIDGE, Northumberland Map ref 5B2
SatNav NE45 5LP **B**

The Hayes (Bed & Breakfast)

Newcastle Road, Corbridge NE45 5LP **T:** (01434) 632010 **E:** camon@onebillinternet.co.uk
W: hayes-corbridge.co.uk

GUEST ACCOMMODATION

B&B PER ROOM PER NIGHT
S: £35.00 - £48.00
D: £73.00 - £76.00

Fine country house in lovely setting in historic Corbridge providing family-run well-appointed accommodation. Easy access to Hadrian's Wall, A68 and A69 and Northumbria countryside. **Directions:** From East: leave A69 at Styford roundabout follow road into Corbridge for 2 mls. From West: pass petrol station, then up hill 0.25mls. **Bedrooms:** 1 single, 3 family **Open:** All year except Christmas and New Year

Site: ✿ **P** **Payment:** 💷 € **Leisure:** 🏌 🗡 ▸ ∪ **Property:** 🖼 **Children:** 🐾 🎠 ✶ **Catering:** 🍴 **Room:** 🌡 👆 📷 📺

CORNHILL-ON-TWEED, Northumberland Map ref 5B1
SatNav TD12 4UH **H**

Collingwood Arms Hotel

Main Street, Cornhill-on-Tweed TD12 4UH **T:** (01890) 882424 **F:** (01890) 883098
E: enquiries@collingwoodarms.com
W: www.collingwoodarms.com **£ BOOK ONLINE**

HOTEL — **Silver AWARD**

B&B PER ROOM PER NIGHT
D: £130.00 - £190.00

HB PER PERSON PER NIGHT
£165.00 - £215.00

The Collingwood Arms has an enviable reputation for its Food, Service and Accommodation. Refurbished and maintained to a very high standard, a warm welcome awaits you. **Directions:** The Hotel is located on the A697 in the village of Cornhill On Tweed, about a mile South of the Scottish border. **Bedrooms:** 9 double, 3 twin, 1 family, 2 suite **Open:** All year

Site: ✿ **Payment:** 💷 € **Leisure:** 🏌 🗡 ▸ **Property:** 🐕 🖼 📷 **Children:** 🐾 🎠 ✶ **Catering:** 🍷 🍴 **Room:** 🌡 👆 ☎ 📷 📺 ♨ 🎛

GREAT TOSSON, Northumberland Map ref 5B1
SatNav NE65 7NW **B**

Tosson Tower Farm B&B

Rothbury, Morpeth, Northumberland NE65 7NW **T:** (01669) 620228 **F:** (01669) 620228
E: stay@tossontowerfarm.com
W: tossontowerfarm.com

FARMHOUSE — **Gold AWARD**

B&B PER ROOM PER NIGHT
D: £85.00 - £95.00

Excellent luxury accommodation in perfect location with fantastic views. Rooms tastefully furnished. Delicious breakfasts. The perfect place for a truly relaxing holiday. Recommended by The Guardian Travel. Private fishing available. **Directions:** A1 North to Morpeth then A697 then B344 (Rothbury). A1 south to Alnwick. Take B6341 to Rothbury. **Bedrooms:** 6 double, 1 twin **Open:** All year except Christmas and New Year

Site: ✿ **P** **Payment:** 💷 **Leisure:** 🏌 🗡 ▸ ∪ **Property:** 🖼 📷 **Catering:** 🍴 **Room:** 🌡 👆 📷 📺 ♨

GREENHEAD, Northumberland Map ref 5B2
SatNav CA8 7HE **B**

Holmhead Guest House

Holmhead, Hadrian's Wall, Greenhead, Northumberland CA8 7HY **T:** (016977) 47402
E: holmhead@forestbarn.com
W: bandbhadrianswall.com **£ BOOK ONLINE**

GUEST ACCOMMODATION

B&B PER ROOM PER NIGHT
S: £50.00
D: £65.00 - £78.00

Built 1800 with Hadrian's Wall stone. Quiet location next to river with beautiful views. Directly on Hadrian's Wall path and Pennine Way. Self catering and camping barn facilities also available. **Directions:** Greenhead is off the A69, 3 miles west of Haltwhistle. Take lane by tearoom, after 100m turn right and cross bridge. Holmhead is about 1km. **Bedrooms:** 2 double, 2 twin **Open:** All year except Christmas and New Year

Site: **P** **Payment:** 💷 € **Leisure:** ▸ ∪ **Property:** 🖼 🍴 **Children:** 🐾 🎠 ✶ **Room:** 🌡 👆

Houghton North Farm Visitor Accommodation

Houghton North Farm, Heddon-on-the-Wall, Northumberland NE15 0EZ
T: (01661) 854364 F: (01661) 854364 E: wjlaws@btconnect.com
W: hadrianswallaccommodation.com

B&B PER ROOM PER NIGHT
S: £35.00 - £40.00
D: £64.00 - £70.00

Comfortable, attractive, luxurious and spacious accommodation in converted barn setting. Bunk-style rooms, some en suite. Self catering kitchen, luxurious lounge, courtyard. Internet, laundry, parking. Ideally situated on Hadrian's Wall. Bedrooms: 1 double en suite, 1 twin, 1 triple, 3 bunkrooms Open: All year except Christmas and New Year

Site: ✿ P Payment: 💷 Leisure: 🚴 ⚓ ► ひ Property: 🍴 🖥 🔲 Children: 🪑4 Catering: 🔲 🍴
Room: 🛏

Langley Castle Hotel

Langley-on-Tyne, Hexham NE47 5LU T: (01434) 688888 F: (01434) 684019
E: manager@langleycastle.com
W: langleycastle.com £ BOOK ONLINE

B&B PER ROOM PER NIGHT
S: £119.50 - £209.50
D: £155.00 - £279.00

HB PER PERSON PER NIGHT
£159.00 - £299.00

SPECIAL PROMOTIONS
Reserve a castle-view room and we will upgrade to a 'castle' room (if available at check-in), at no extra charge.

A genuine 14th Century Castle set in woodland estate. All rooms with facilities, some with window seats set into seven foot thick walls. Sauna, four poster beds. The magnificent drawing room, with blazing log fire, complements intimate Josephine Restaurant. Perfect to explore Hadrians Wall, Northumberland, Bamburgh Castle, Holy Island and Borders.

Directions: Half an hour drive from Newcastle airport. From A69 take A686 for 2 miles.

Bedrooms: 27 rooms in total
Open: All year

Site: ✿ P Payment: 💷 Leisure: 🚴 ⚓ ひ Property: 🔲 🍴 🐾 🖥 🔲 🔴 🎣 Children: 🐎 🛏 🚶
Catering: (✕ 🍷 🍴 Room: 🍵 🛁 📞 📺 🛏

Loughbrow House

Dipton Mill Road NE46 1RS T: (01434) 603351 E: patriciaclark351@btinternet.com
W: loughbrow.fsnet.co.uk

B&B PER ROOM PER NIGHT
S: £50.00 - £55.00
D: £110.00 - £120.00

HB PER PERSON PER NIGHT
£80.00 - £100.00

A mansion house built in 1780 set in 9 acres of garden, surrounded by own farm land looking up the North Tyne valley. Situated 1 mile from Hexham. Ample parking. Directions: From Hexham take B6306. After 0.25 miles take right-hand fork, Dipton Mill Road, for further 0.25 miles. Turn into drive gates, house is 0.5 miles. Bedrooms: 2 single, 1 double, 2 twin Open: All year except Christmas and New Year

Site: ✿ P Leisure: ► Property: 🔲 Children: 🐎5 Catering: 🍴 Room: 🍵 🛁 📺

Longhirst Hall

Longhirst, Morpeth NE61 3LL   T: (01670) 795000   F: (01670) 791385
E: enquiries@longhirst.co.uk
W: longhirst.co.uk   £ BOOK ONLINE

B&B PER ROOM PER NIGHT
S: £70.00 - £105.00
D: £75.00 - £125.00

SPECIAL PROMOTIONS
Weekend breaks from
£70 per person, 2
nights minimum stay.

An iconic Georgian building nestled in 75 acres of woodland and landscaped gardens in rural Northumberland. An inspiring location for lovers of local and organic produce looking for a real taste of Northumberland; an exciting getaway for golfing breaks; the ideal base to explore Northumbria's castles and coastlines.

Directions: Located just off the A1. Take turning marked Hebron, follow road, turn left at T-junction. Longhirst 1 mile along the B1337.

Bedrooms: 52 dble, 24 twin
Open: All year

Site: ❀ **Payment:** 💳 **Leisure:** ⚙ 🎣 ▶ ∪ 🎯 ⚲ **Property:** 🍴 🐕 🖥 🗄 ◗ **Children:** 🐾 🎮 🏃
Catering: 🍽 🍴 **Room:** 🍵 🛏 📞 📀 📺

Tomlinson's Cafe and Bunkhouse

Bridge Street, Rothbury, Morpeth NE65 7SF   T: (01669) 621979
E: info@tomlinsonsrothbury.co.uk
W: www.tomlinsonsrothbury.co.uk

Tomlinsons Cafe and Bunkhouse provides low cost accommodation overlooking the River Coquet in a newly renovated Grade 2 listed former schoolhouse. Family, Walker and Cyclist Friendly. We are the perfect base to explore Northumberland's great outdoors whether you are a cyclist, walker, climber or just want to enjoy the spectacular scenery. Tomlinson's café serves wholesome, hearty breakfasts, lunches and light evening meals. Tomlinson's now has an alcohol licence so if you fancy a glass of wine or even a bottle, that isn't a problem as we are fully stocked with red, white, rose and sparkling wines and also a choice of ciders and largers. Please contact us for prices.

Directions: Rothbury is 40 minutes by road from Newcastle upon Tyne and Newcastle International Airport. There are main line rail stations at Alnmouth and Morpeth.

Bedrooms: Our five dormitory-style bedrooms sleep a total of 27. Most rooms have an en suite shower room. You can choose from a family room or opt for double, single or bunk beds.
Open: All year except Christmas Day

Payment: 💳 € **Leisure:** ⚙ 🎣 ▶ ∪ **Property:** 🐕 🖥 📺 📀 🗄 **Catering:** ⟨✗ 🍴 **Bedroom:** 🖥

POWBURN, Northumberland   Map ref 5B1   SatNav NE66 4JD   [B]

B&B PER ROOM PER NIGHT
S: £50.00
D: £80.00

Low Hedgeley Farm
Powburn, Alnwick NE66 4JD **T:** (01665) 578815 **E:** dianavickers@hotmail.com
W: lowhedgeleyfarm.co.uk

Grade II Listed farmhouse with extensive grounds. Situated in the Breamish Valley at the foot of the Cheviot Hills. Ideal base for visiting Cragside, and Alnwick Castle and Garden.
Directions: Low Hedgeley is located one mile north of Powburn close to the A697 road. **Bedrooms:** 1 double, 1 twin **Open:** All year except Christmas and New Year

Site: ❀ P Leisure: ∪ Property: ▭ ▣ Catering: 🍴 Room: 🔌 📺

ROTHBURY, Northumberland   Map ref 5B1   SatNav NE65 7TQ   [B]

Katerina's Guest House
Katerina's Guest House, Sun Buildings, High Street, Rothbury, Northumberland NE65 7TQ
T: (01669) 620691 **E:** cath@katerinasguesthouse.co.uk
W: www.katerinasguesthouse.co.uk **£ BOOK ONLINE**

B&B PER ROOM PER NIGHT
S: £50.00 - £60.00
D: £68.00 - £80.00
EVENING MEAL PER PERSON
£18.75

SPECIAL PROMOTIONS
Reduced rates for longer stays up to 6 nights all year round. Bookings for less than three nights and some special offers are only available via direct telephone or e-mail contact with the owners.

Lovely country village situation. Three beautiful en suite four poster bedrooms, two with original fireplaces/beamed ceilings. All have fridge, TV, Wi-Fi, superbly stocked tea tray, tea-time treats and other little perks to enjoy. Award winning breakfasts. Central for Cragside, National Park and hills, Alnwick Castle/Gardens, Coast, Hadrian's Wall and Scottish Borders.

Directions: Located in quiet position on Rothbury High Street, c.100 metres west of main shopping area.

Bedrooms: 3 double en suite 4 poster bedded rooms with well stocked tea tray, mini-fridge, hairdryer, ample drawer/wardrobe space, TV and teatime treats!
Open: Open 12 months except for holidays and refurbishment.

Payment: 💳 € Leisure: 🚴 ♪ ▶ ∪ Property: ▭ Children: 🚼 🅰 Catering: 🍴 Room: 🔌 🖤 📺 🖥

SEAHOUSES, Northumberland   Map ref 5C1   SatNav NE68 7YB   [B]

B&B PER ROOM PER NIGHT
S: £45.00
D: £65.00 - £75.00

Holly Trees
4 James Street, Seahouses NE68 7YB **T:** (01665) 721942
E: margaret.tucker4@btinternet.com
W: www.holly-trees.com

Margaret has been providing a warm welcome to her guests for the past eight years and she serves delicious breakfasts with her freshly baked homemade bread. **Directions:** See website for directions
Bedrooms: 3 doubles and 1 single, all en suite. Can offer 2 twins.
Open: All year except Christmas and New Year

Site: ❀ Leisure: ♪ ▶ ∪ Property: 🐾 ▭ ⊘ Children: 🚼¹² Catering: 🍴 Room: 🔌 🖤 🅰 📺 🖥

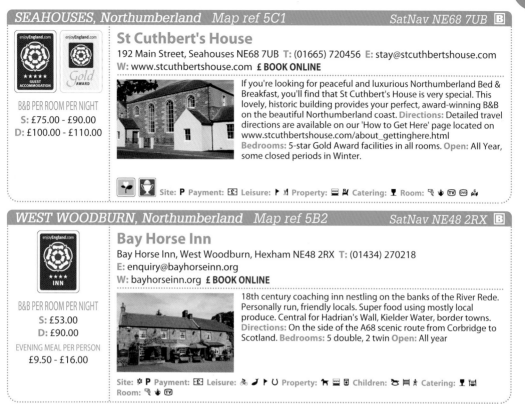

SEAHOUSES, Northumberland   Map ref 5C1   SatNav NE68 7UB B

St Cuthbert's House

192 Main Street, Seahouses NE68 7UB **T:** (01665) 720456 **E:** stay@stcuthbertshouse.com
W: www.stcuthbertshouse.com **£ BOOK ONLINE**

B&B PER ROOM PER NIGHT
S: £75.00 - £90.00
D: £100.00 - £110.00

If you're looking for peaceful and luxurious Northumberland Bed & Breakfast, you'll find that St Cuthbert's House is very special. This lovely, historic building provides your perfect, award-winning B&B on the beautiful Northumberland coast. **Directions:** Detailed travel directions are available on our 'How to Get Here' page located on www.stcuthbertshouse.com/about_gettinghere.html
Bedrooms: 5-star Gold Award facilities in all rooms. **Open:** All Year, some closed periods in Winter.

Site: **P** Payment: Leisure: Property: Catering: Room:

WEST WOODBURN, Northumberland   Map ref 5B2   SatNav NE48 2RX B

Bay Horse Inn

Bay Horse Inn, West Woodburn, Hexham NE48 2RX **T:** (01434) 270218
E: enquiry@bayhorseinn.org
W: bayhorseinn.org **£ BOOK ONLINE**

B&B PER ROOM PER NIGHT
S: £53.00
D: £90.00
EVENING MEAL PER PERSON
£9.50 - £16.00

18th century coaching inn nestling on the banks of the River Rede. Personally run, friendly locals. Super food using mostly local produce. Central for Hadrian's Wall, Kielder Water, border towns. **Directions:** On the side of the A68 scenic route from Corbridge to Scotland. **Bedrooms:** 5 double, 2 twin **Open:** All year

Site: **P** Payment: Leisure: Property: Children: Catering: Room:

Looking for something else?

The official and most comprehensive guide to independently inspected, star rated accommodation.

B&Bs and Hotels - B&Bs, Hotels, farmhouses, inns, serviced apartments, campus and hostel accommodation in England.

Self Catering - Self-catering holiday homes, approved caravan holiday homes, boat accommodation and holiday cottage agencies in England.

Camping, Touring and Holiday Parks - Touring parks, camping holidays and holiday parks and villages in Britain.

Now available in all good bookshops and online at **www.hudsons.co.uk/shop**

NEWCASTLE-UPON-TYNE, Tyne and Wear   Map ref 5C2   SatNav NE1 5JE   B

Albatross, Backpackers In!

51 Grainger Street, Newcastle-upon-Tyne NE1 5JE T: (01912) 331330 F: (01912) 603389
E: info@albatrossnewcastle.co.uk
W: albatrossnewcastle.com £ BOOK ONLINE

B&B PER ROOM PER NIGHT
D: £17.00 - £23.00

City centre, shopping, bars, galleries and leisure facilities all within 5 minute walking distance. 24 hour reception, free Wi-Fi, free complimentary snack, linen inclusive, free lockers. **Directions:** From Central Station main entrance, head to your right, first street on your left (Grainger St), you'll find us on your left 200m uphill.
Bedrooms: 2 twin, 24 family **Open:** All year

Site: ✿ Payment: 💷 Leisure: ♿ Property: 💻 📱 Children: ⛄ Room: ♨ 🛏 🔔

NEWCASTLE-UPON-TYNE, Tyne And Wear   Map ref 5C2   SatNav NE27 0BY   H

De Vere VILLAGE Urban Resort Newcastle

Cobalt Business Park, West Allotment, Newcastle upon Tyne, Tyne and Wear NE27 0BY
T: (0871) 222 4600 F: (0191) 270 1515 E: village.newcastle@village-hotels.com
W: www.villageurbanresorts.co.uk £ BOOK ONLINE

B&B PER ROOM PER NIGHT
S: £69.00 - £169.00
D: £79.00 - £179.00
EVENING MEAL PER PERSON
£8.95 - £40.00

Village Urban Resort Newcastle is conveniently located just 6 miles from Newcastle city centre, close to the A1(M) & A19, making it a perfect location to sample one of the country's liveliest cities, for business or for pleasure. **Directions:** Car - From A19 follow the A191 to Cobalt Business Park. Rail - Newcastle Central Station - 6 miles. Air - Newcastle International Airport - 12 miles
Bedrooms: Modern en suite bedrooms - Standard & Upperdeck
Open: All year

Site: P Payment: 💷 Leisure: ✗ 🏋 🎱 ? Property: ® 🐾 🚭 🍴 ◐ Children: ⛄ ♜ 🎯 Catering: (✗ 🍷 🍴 Room: 🔌 ♨ 📞 🗄 📺

NEWCASTLE-UPON-TYNE, Tyne and Wear   Map ref 5C2   SatNav NE2 2PR   B

Jesmond Park

74-76 Queens Road, Jesmond, Newcastle-upon-Tyne NE2 2PR T: (01912) 812821
F: (01912) 810515 E: vh@jespark.fsnet.co.uk
W: www.jesmond-park.co.uk

B&B PER ROOM PER NIGHT
S: £35.00
D: £72.50

Enjoy the comfort of the relaxed atmosphere in this privately run hotel. Conveniently situated for all of Newcastle's attractions, including the Metro Centre, Newcastle Metro Radio Arena, Hadrian's Wall and Northumberland's stunning coast and countryside. **Directions:** Please contact us for directions.
Bedrooms: Single, double, twin and family rooms are available.
Open: All year

Site: P Payment: 💷 Property: 💻 Catering: 🍷 Room: 🔌 🗄 📺

Win amazing prizes, every month...

Visit our new 2014 guide websites for detailed information, up-to-date availability and to book your accommodation online. Includes over 20,000 places to stay, all of them star rated.

Enter our monthly competition at www.visitor-guides.co.uk/prizes

So much to see, so little time – how do you choose?

Make the most of your leisure time; look for attractions with the Quality Marque.

VisitEngland operates the Visitor Attraction Quality Assurance Scheme.

Annual assessments by trained impartial assessors test all aspects of the customer experience so you can visit with confidence.

For ideas and inspiration go to www.visitengland.com

Map 1

Location
Maps

Every place name featured in the regional accommodation sections of this guide has a map reference to help you locate it on the maps which follow. For example, to find Colchester, Essex, which has 'Map ref 3B2', turn to Map 3 and refer to grid square B2.

All place names appearing in the regional sections are shown with orange circles on the maps. This enables you to find other places in your chosen area which may have suitable accommodation – the place index (at the back of this guide) gives page numbers.

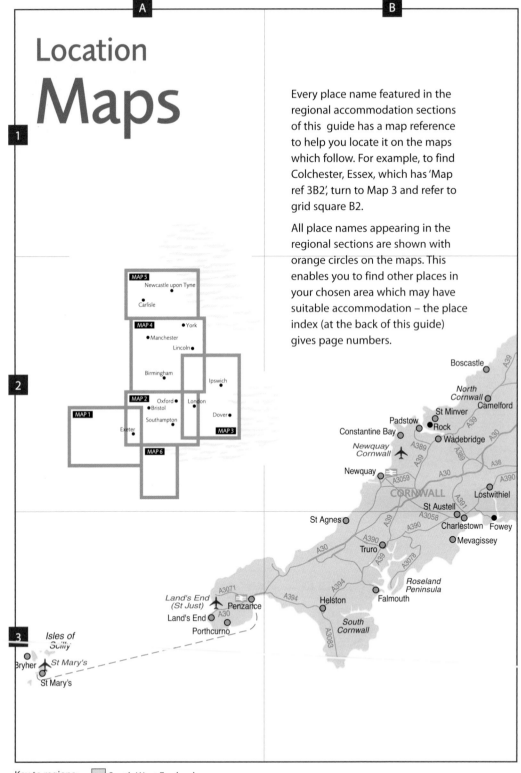

Key to regions: ▢ South West England

Map 1

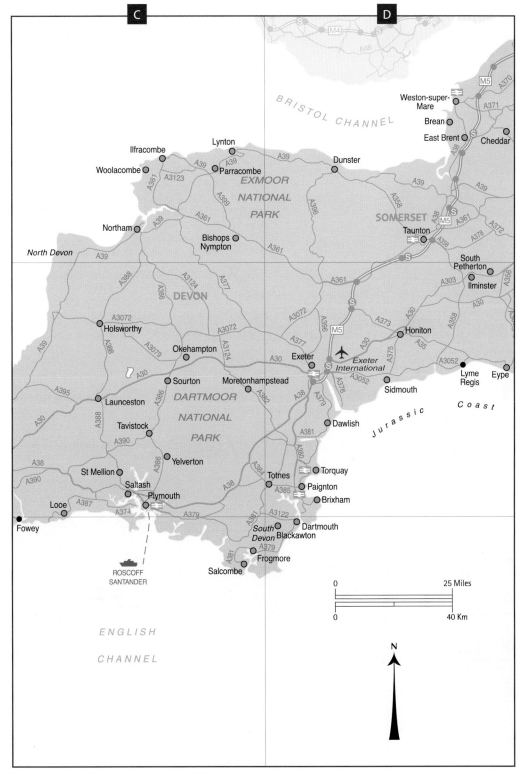

Orange circles indicate accommodation within the regional sections of this guide

Map 2

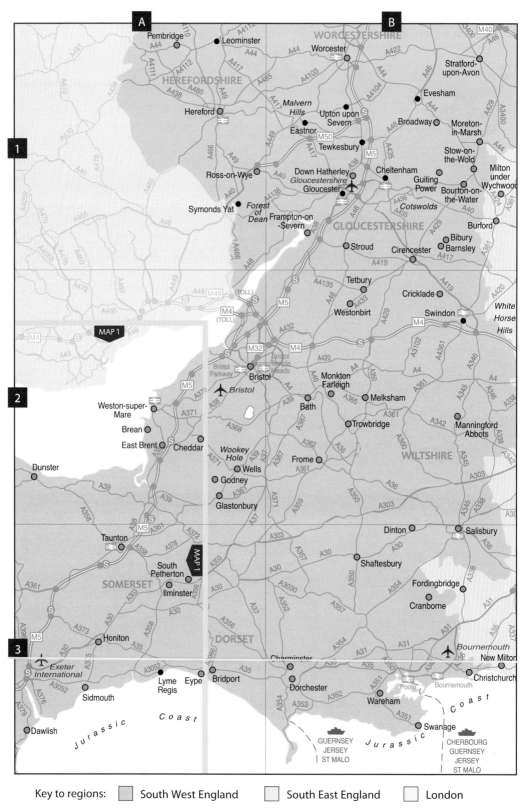

Key to regions: ◼ South West England ◻ South East England ◻ London

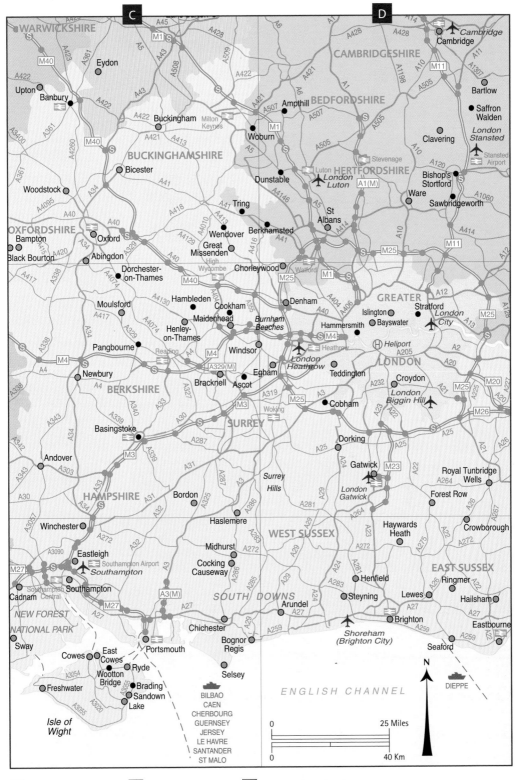

Map 2

East of England   East Midlands   Heart of England
Orange circles indicate accommodation within the regional sections of this guide

Map 3

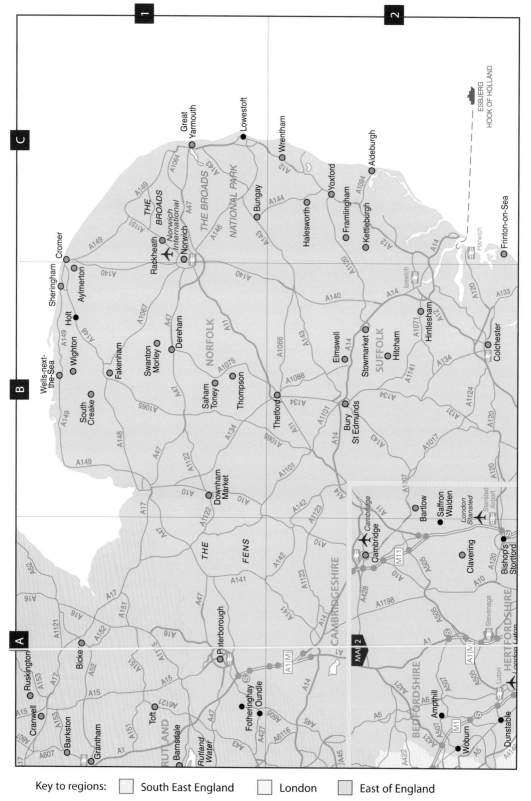

Key to regions: ☐ South East England ☐ London ☐ East of England

362

Map 3

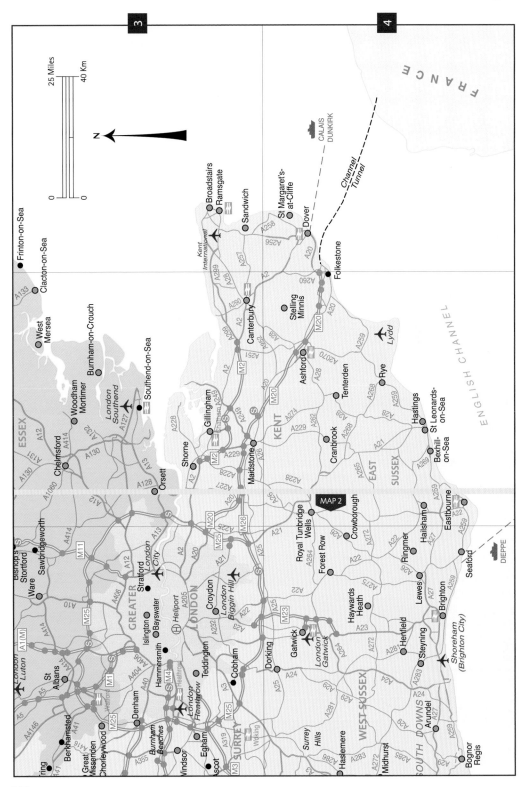

East Midlands

Orange circles indicate accommodation within the regional sections of this guide

Map 4

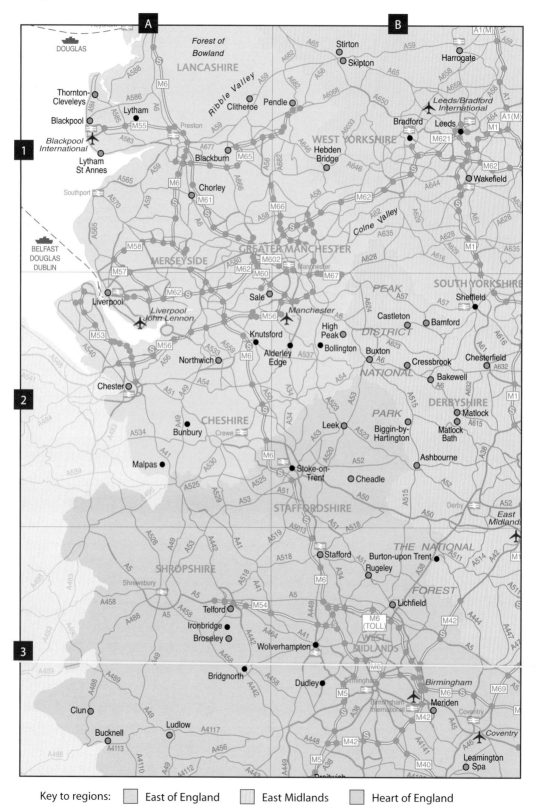

Key to regions: ▢ East of England ▢ East Midlands ▢ Heart of England

Map 4

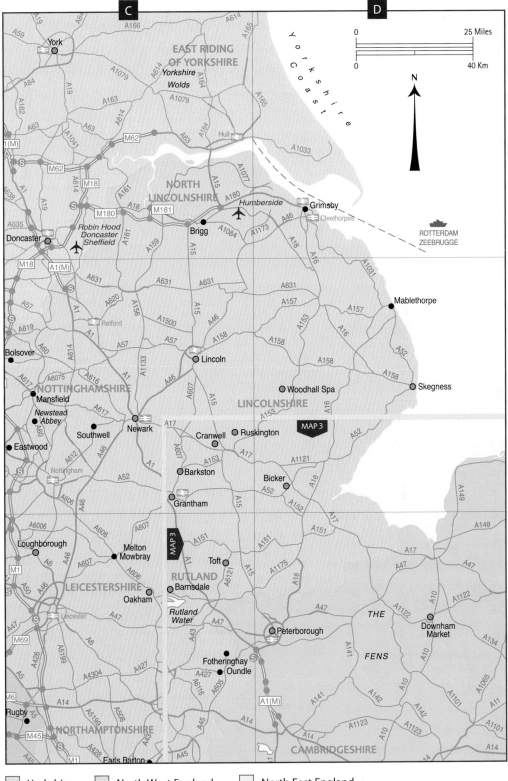

Yorkshire   North West England   North East England
Orange circles indicate accommodation within the regional sections of this guide

Map 5

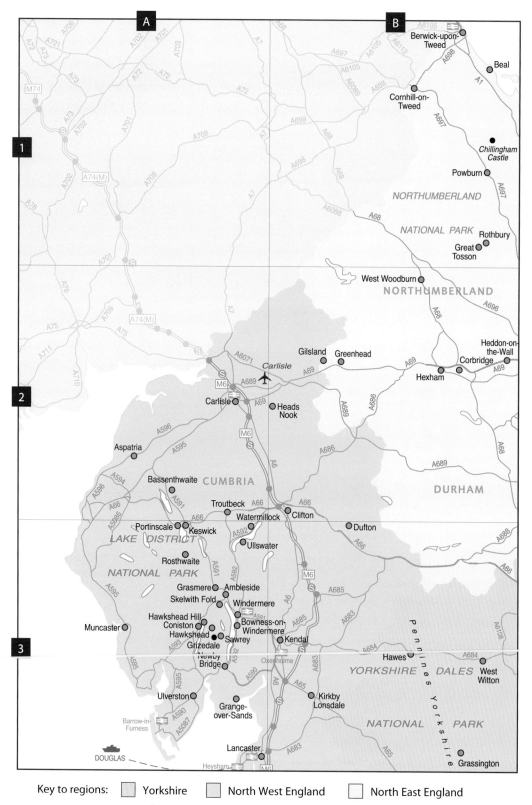

Key to regions: Yorkshire   North West England   North East England

Map 5

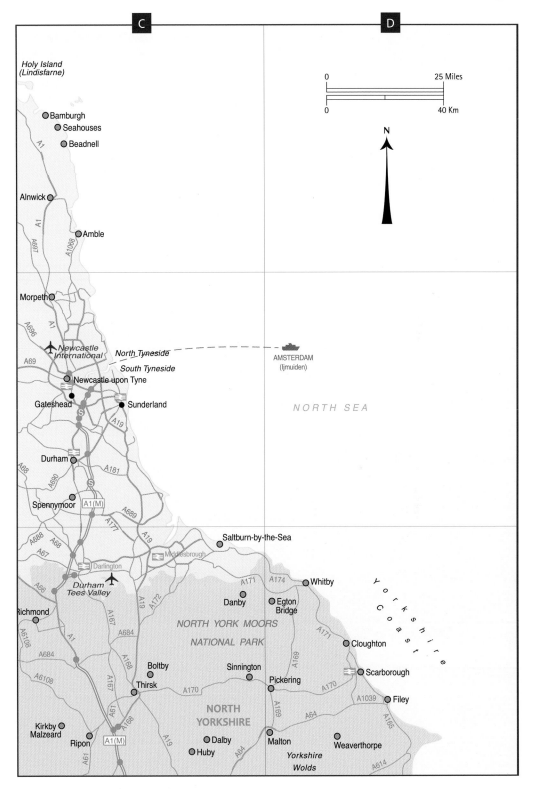

C

D

0 _____ 25 Miles

0 _____ 40 Km

N

*Holy Island
(Lindisfarne)*

Bamburgh
Seahouses
Beadnell

A1

A697

A1068

Alnwick

Amble

Morpeth

A696

A1

Newcastle
International

A69

North Tyneside

South Tyneside

Newcastle upon Tyne

AMSTERDAM
(Ijmuiden)

Gateshead

Sunderland

NORTH SEA

A19

Durham

A181

A68

A690

Spennymoor

A1(M)

A689

A688

A68

A67

A177

A19

Saltburn-by-the-Sea

A66

Darlington

Middlesbrough

Durham
Tees Valley

A171

A174

Whitby

Richmond

A167

A172

A19

Danby

Egton
Bridge

Y
o
r
k
s
h
i
r
e

C
o
a
s
t

A6108

A1

A684

NORTH YORK MOORS

A169

A171

Cloughton

A684

A168

NATIONAL PARK

A6108

Boltby

Sinnington

Pickering

Scarborough

A170

Thirsk

A170

Kirkby
Malzeard

A168

A167

A169

A64

A1039

Filey

NORTH
YORKSHIRE

A19

Dalby

Malton

A165

Ripon

A1(M)

Huby

A64

Weaverthorpe

A61

*Yorkshire
Wolds*

A614

Orange circles indicate accommodation within the regional sections of this guide

Map 6

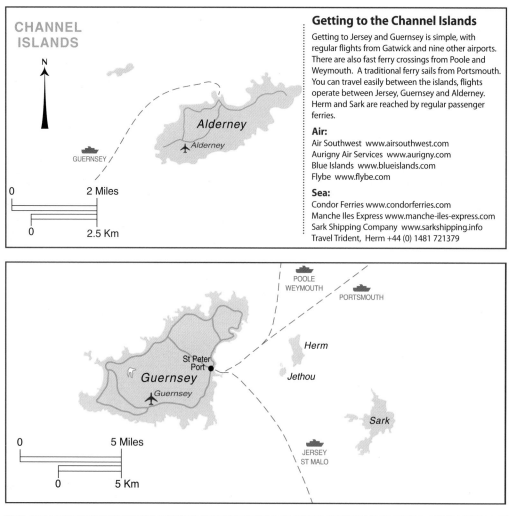

CHANNEL ISLANDS

N

Alderney

Alderney ✈

GUERNSEY 🚢

0 — 2 Miles

0 — 2.5 Km

Getting to the Channel Islands

Getting to Jersey and Guernsey is simple, with regular flights from Gatwick and nine other airports. There are also fast ferry crossings from Poole and Weymouth. A traditional ferry sails from Portsmouth. You can travel easily between the islands, flights operate between Jersey, Guernsey and Alderney. Herm and Sark are reached by regular passenger ferries.

Air:
Air Southwest www.airsouthwest.com
Aurigny Air Services www.aurigny.com
Blue Islands www.blueislands.com
Flybe www.flybe.com

Sea:
Condor Ferries www.condorferries.com
Manche Iles Express www.manche-iles-express.com
Sark Shipping Company www.sarkshipping.info
Travel Trident, Herm +44 (0) 1481 721379

POOLE 🚢
WEYMOUTH
PORTSMOUTH 🚢

Herm

St Peter Port ●
Guernsey
Guernsey ✈

Jethou

Sark

JERSEY 🚢
ST MALO

0 — 5 Miles

0 — 5 Km

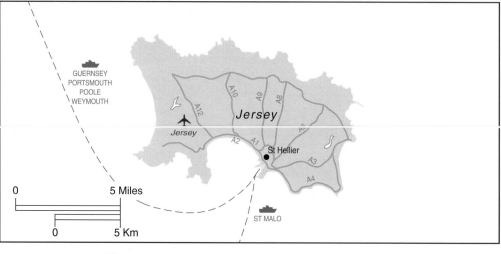

GUERNSEY 🚢
PORTSMOUTH
POOLE
WEYMOUTH

Jersey ✈
A12
A10
A9
A8
Jersey
Jersey
A2 A1
St Hellier ●
A3
A4

0 — 5 Miles

0 — 5 Km

ST MALO 🚢

Key to regions: ▢ Channel Islands

Orange circles indicate accommodation within the regional sections of this guide

Map 7
London

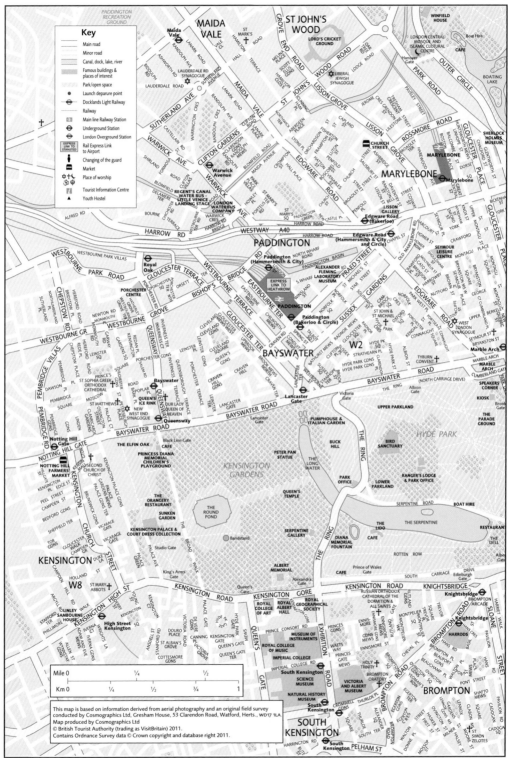

Map 8
London

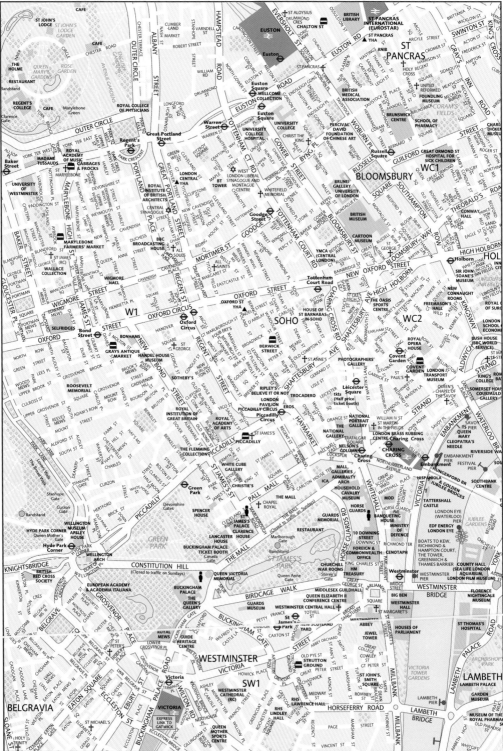

Map 8
London

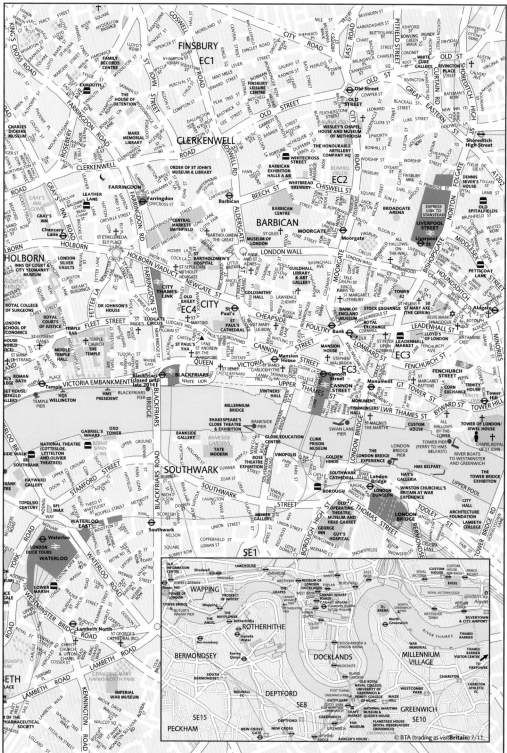

Motorway Service Area Assessment Scheme

Something we all use and take for granted but how good are they?

The star ratings cover over 250 different aspects of each operation, including cleanliness, the quality and range of catering and also the quality of the physical aspects, as well as the service. It does not cover prices or value for money.

OPERATOR: EXTRA

Baldock	★★★★
Beaconsfield	★★★★
Blackburn	★★★★
Cambridge	★★★
Cullompton	★★★
Peterborough	★★★★

OPERATOR: MOTO

Birch E	★★★
Birch W	★★★
Bridgwater	★★★
Burton in Kendal	★★★
Cherwell Valley	★★★★★
Chieveley	★★★
Doncaster N	★★★★
Donington Park	★★★★
Exeter	★★★
Ferrybridge	★★★
Frankley N	★★★
Frankley S	★★★
Heston E	★★★
Heston W	★★★
Hilton Park N	★★★
Hilton Park S	★★★
Knutsford N	★★★
Knutsford S	★★★
Lancaster N	★★★
Lancaster S	★★
Leigh Delamere E	★★★★
Leigh Delamere W	★★★★
Medway	★★★
Pease Pottage	★★★
Reading E	★★★★
Reading W	★★★
Severn View	★★
Southwaite N	★★★
Southwaite S	★★★

Stafford N	★★★★
Tamworth	★★★
Thurrock	★★★★
Toddington N	★★★★
Toddington S	★★★
Trowell N	★★★
Trowell S	★★★
Washington N	★★★
Washington S	★★★★
Wetherby	★★★★
Winchester N	★★★★
Winchester S	★★★
Woolley Edge N	★★★★
Woolley Edge S	★★★★

OPERATOR: ROADCHEF

Chester	★★
Clacket Lane E	★★★
Clacket Lane W	★★
Durham	★★★
Killington Lake	★★★
Maidstone	★★★
Northampton N	★★★
Northampton S	★★★
Norton Canes	★★★★
Rownhams N	★★
Rownhams S	★★★
Sandbach N	★★
Sandbach S	★★★
Sedgemoor S	★★
Stafford S	★★★
Strensham N	★★★★
Strensham S	★★★
Taunton Deane N	★★
Taunton Deane S	★★★
Tibshelf N	★★★
Tibshelf S	★★★
Watford Gap N	★★★
Watford Gap S	★★

OPERATOR: WELCOME BREAK

Birchanger Green	★★★★
Burtonwood	★★★
Charnock Richard W	★★★
Charnock Richard E	★★★
Corley E	★★★
Corley W	★★★
Fleet N	★★★★
Fleet S	★★★
Gordano	★★★★
Hartshead Moor E	★★★
Hartshead Moor W	★★★
Hopwood Park	★★★★
Keele N	★★★
Keele S	★★★
Leicester Forest East N	★★★
Leicester Forest East S	★★★
London Gateway	★★★★
Membury E	★★★
Membury W	★★★★
Michaelwood N	★★★
Michaelwood S	★★★
Newport Pagnell S	★★★
Newport Pagnell N	★★★
Oxford	★★★★
Sedgemoor N	★★★
South Mimms	★★★★
Telford	★★★
Warwick N	★★★
Warwick S	★★★★
Woodall N	★★
Woodall S	★★★

WESTMORLAND

Tebay N	★★★★
Tebay S	★★★★★

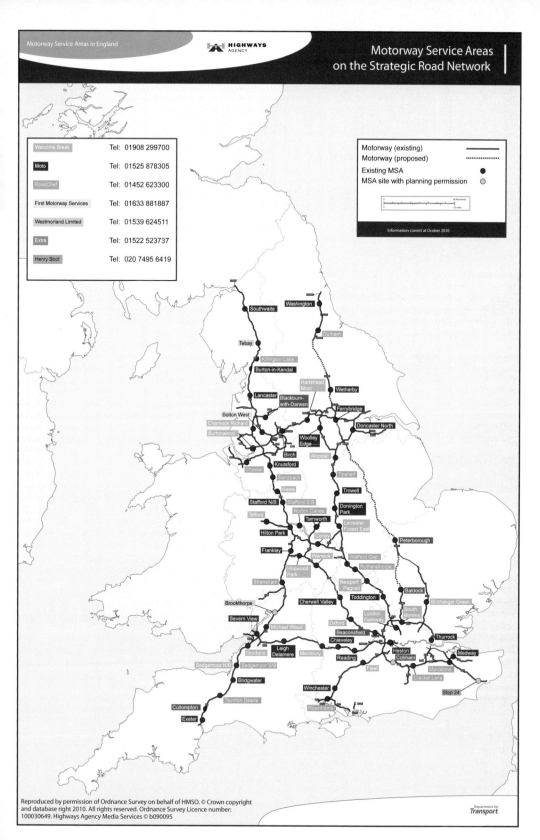

Welcome Break	Tel: 01908 299700
Moto	Tel: 01525 878305
RoadChef	Tel: 01452 623300
First Motorway Services	Tel: 01633 881887
Westmorland Limited	Tel: 01539 624511
Extra	Tel: 01522 523737
Henry Boot	Tel: 020 7495 6419

Motorway (existing)
Motorway (proposed)
Existing MSA
MSA site with planning permission

Information correct at October 2010

Southwaite
Washington
Durham
Tebay
Killington Lake
Burton-in-Kendal
Hartshead Moor
Wetherby
Lancaster
Blackburn-with-Darwen
Ferrybridge
Bolton West
Charnock Richard
Doncaster North
Burtonwood
Woolley Edge
Birch
Woodall
Chester
Knutsford
Tibshelf
Sandbach
Keele
Trowell
Stafford N/B
Stafford S/B
Donington Park
Telford
Norton Canes
Tamworth
Leicester Forest East
Hilton Park
Corley
Peterborough
Frankley
Warwick
Watford Gap
Hopwood Park
Rothersthorpe
Strensham
Newport Pagnell
Baldock
Brookthorpe
Cherwell Valley
Toddington
Birchanger Green
Severn View
South Mimms
Michael Wood
Oxford
London Gateway
Beaconsfield
Thurrock
Gordano
Leigh Delamere
Chieveley
Heston
Medway
Sedgemoor N/B
Membury
Reading
Cobham
Maidstone
Sedgemoor S/B
Fleet
Clacket Lane
Bridgwater
Winchester
Stop 24
Cullompton
Taunton Deane
Rownhams
Exeter

Department for
Transport

sustrans

JOIN THE MOVEMENT

Here are just some of the most popular long distance routes on the 12,000 mile Sustrans National Cycle Network. To see the Network in it's entirety and to find routes near you, **visit www.sustrans.org.uk**

Sustrans is the UK's leading sustainable transport charity working on practical projects to enable people to choose to travel in ways which benefit their health and the environment.

68 National Cycle Network Route Number
Long Distance Routes
① Coast & Castles Cycle Route
② Pennine Cycleway - North Pennines
③ Hadrian's Cycleway
④ Sea to Sea
⑤ Pennine Cycleway - South Pennines & the Dales
⑥ Derby to York
⑦ Hull to Fakenham
⑧ East of England
⑨ South Midlands Cycle Route
⑩ Thames Valley Cycle Route
⑪ Garden of England
⑫ Downs & Weald Cycle Route
⑬ Devon Coast to Coast
⑭ The Cornish Way
⑮ The West Country Way
⑯ The Severn & Thames

Map reproduced from Ordnance Survey material with the permission of Ordnance Survey on behalf of the Controller of Her Majesty's Stationery Office © Crown copyright. Unauthorised reproduction infringes Crown copyright and may lead to prosecution or civil proceedings.
Licence number 100020852 (2009)

Further Information

Advice and information

Making a booking

When enquiring about accommodation, make sure you check prices, the quality rating and other important details. You will also need to state your requirements clearly and precisely, for example:

- Arrival and departure dates, with acceptable alternatives if appropriate
- The type of accommodation you need – for example, a room with twin beds or an en suite bathroom
- The terms you want – for example, bed and breakfast only; dinner and breakfast (where provided)
- The age of any children with you, whether you want them to share your room or be next door, and any other special requirements, such as a cot
- Any particular requirements you may have, such as a special diet or a ground-floor room.

Booking by letter or email

Misunderstandings can easily happen over the telephone, so do request a written confirmation, together with details of any terms and conditions that apply to your booking.

Deposits

If you make your reservation weeks or months in advance, you will probably be asked for a deposit, which will then be deducted from the final bill when you leave. The amount will vary from establishment to establishment and could be payment in full at peak times.

Payment on arrival

Some establishments ask you to pay for your room on arrival if you have not booked it in advance. This is especially likely to happen if you arrive late and have little or no luggage. If you are asked to pay on arrival, it is a good idea to see your room first, to make sure it meets your requirements.

Cancellations

Legal contract

When you accept accommodation that is offered to you, by telephone or in writing, you enter into a legally binding contract with the proprietor. This means that if you cancel your booking, fail to take up the accommodation or leave early, you will probably forfeit your deposit and may expect to be charged the balance at the end of the period booked if the place cannot be re-let. You should be advised at the time of the booking of what charges would be made in the event of cancelling the accommodation or leaving early, which is usually written into the properties terms and conditions. If this is not mentioned you should ask the proprietor for any cancellation terms that apply before booking your accommodation to ensure any disputes are avoided. Where you have already paid the full amount before cancelling, the proprietor is likely to retain the money. However if the accommodation is re-let, the proprietor will make a refund to you which normally excludes the amount of the deposit.

Remember, if you book by telephone and are asked for your credit card number, you should check whether the proprietor intends to charge your credit card account should you later cancel your reservation. A proprietor should not be able to charge your credit card account with a cancellation fee without your consent unless you agreed to this at the time of your booking. However, to avoid later disputes, we suggest you check whether this is the intention before providing your details.

Telephone charges

Establishments can set their own charges for telephone calls made through their switchboard or from direct-dial telephones in bedrooms. These charges are often much higher than telephone companies' standard charges (to defray the cost of providing the service).

Comparing costs

It is a condition of the quality assessment schemes that an establishment's unit charges are on display by the telephones or with the room information. It is not always easy to compare these charges with standard rates, so before using a telephone for long-distance calls, you may decide to ask how the charges compare.

Security of valuables

You can deposit your valuables with the proprietor or manager during your stay, and we recommend you do this as a sensible precaution. Make sure you obtain a receipt for them. Some places do not accept articles for safe custody, and in that case it is wisest to keep your valuables with you.

Disclaimer

Some proprietors put up a notice that disclaims liability for property brought on to their premises by a guest. In fact, they can only restrict their liability. By law, a proprietor is liable for the value of the loss or damage to any property (except a car or its contents) of a guest who has engaged overnight accommodation, but if the proprietor has the notice on display, liability is limited to £50 for one article and a total of £100 for any one guest. The notice must be prominently displayed in the reception area or main entrance. These limits do not apply to valuables you have deposited with the proprietor for safekeeping, or to property lost through the default, neglect or wilful act of the proprietor or his staff.

Insurance

There are so many reasons why you might have to cancel your holiday, which is why we strongly advise people to take out a cancellation insurance policy. In fact, many self-catering agencies now advise their customers to take out a policy when they book their holiday.

Arrival time

If you know you will be arriving late in the evening, it is a good idea to say so when you book. If you are delayed on your way, a telephone call to say that you will be late is often appreciated.

It is particularly important to liaise with the proprietor about key collection as he or she may not be on site.

Service charges and tipping

These days many places levy service charges automatically. If they do, they must clearly say so in their offer of accommodation, at the time of booking. The service charge then becomes part of the legal contract when you accept the offer of accommodation.

If a service charge is levied automatically, there is no need to tip the staff, unless they provide some exceptional service. The usual tip for meals is 10% of the total bill.

Travelling with pets

Dogs, cats, ferrets and some other pets can be brought into the UK from certain countries, provided they meet the requirements of the Pet Travel Scheme (PETS) they may not have to undertake six months' quarantine on arrival.

For full details, visit the PETS website at
w www.gov.uk/take-pet-abroad
or contact the PETS Helpline
t +44 (0)870 241 1710
e pettravel@ahvla.gsi.gov.uk
Ask for fact sheets which cover dogs and cats, ferrets or domestic rabbits and rodents.

There are no requirements for pets travelling directly between the UK and the Channel Islands. Pets entering Jersey or Guernsey from other countries need to be Pet Travel Scheme compliant and have a valid EU Pet Passport. For more information see www.jersey.com or www.visitguernsey.com.

What to expect

The proprietor/management is required to undertake the following:

Prior to booking
- To describe accurately in any advertisement, brochure, or other printed or electronic media, the facilities and services provided;
- To make clear to guests in print, electronic media and on the telephone exactly what is included in all prices quoted for accommodation, including taxes and any other surcharges. Details of charges for additional services/facilities should also be made clear, for example breakfast, leisure etc;
- To provide information on the suitability of the premises for guests of various ages, particularly for the elderly and the very young;
- To allow guests to view the accommodation prior to booking if requested.

At the time of booking
- To clearly describe the cancellation policy to guests i.e. by telephone, fax, internet/email as well as in any printed information given to guests;
- To adhere to and not to exceed prices quoted at the time of booking for accommodation and other services;
- To make clear to guests if the accommodation offered is in an unconnected annexe or similar, and to indicate the location of such accommodation and any difference in comfort and/or amenities from accommodation at the property.

On arrival
- To welcome all guests courteously and without discrimination in relation to gender, sexual orientation, disability, race, religion or belief.

During the stay
- To maintain standards of guest care, cleanliness, and service appropriate to the type of establishment;
- To deal promptly and courteously with all enquiries, requests, bookings and correspondence from guests;
- To ensure complaints received are investigated promptly and courteously to an outcome that is communicated to the guest.

On departure
- To give each guest, on request, details of payments due and a receipt, if required/requested.

General
- To give due consideration to the requirements of guests with special needs, and make suitable provision where applicable;
- To ensure the accommodation, when advertised as open, is prepared for the arrival of guests at all times;
- To advise guests, at any time prior to their stay, of any changes made to their booking;
- To have a complaints handling procedure in place to deal promptly and fairly with all guest complaints;
- To hold current public liability insurance and to comply with all relevant statuory obligations including legislation applicable to fire, health and safety, planning and food safety;
- To allow, on request, VisitEngland representatives reasonable access to the establishment, to confirm that the Code of Conduct is being observed or in order to investigate any complaint of a serious nature;

Comments and complaints

Information

Other than rating information the proprietors themselves supply descriptions of their properties and other information for in this book. They have all signed a declaration to confirm that their information accurately describes their accommodation business. The publishers cannot guarantee the accuracy of information in this guide, and accept no responsibility for any error or misrepresentation. All liability for loss, disappointment, negligence or other damage caused by reliance on the information contained in this guide, or in the event of bankruptcy or liquidation or cessation of trade of any company, individual or firm mentioned, is hereby excluded. We strongly recommend that you carefully check prices and other details before you book your accommodation.

Quality signage

All establishments displaying a quality sign have to hold current membership of VisitEngland's Quality Assessment Scheme.

When an establishment is sold, the new owner has to re-apply and be re-assessed. In certain circumstances the rating may be carried forward before the property is re-assessed.

Problems

Of course, we hope you will not have cause for complaint, but problems do occur from time to time. If you are dissatisfied with anything, make your complaint to the management immediately. Then the management can take action by investigating the matter in attempts to put things right. The longer you leave a complaint, the harder it is to deal with it effectively.

In certain circumstances, the national tourist board may look into your complaint. However, they have no statutory control over establishments or their methods of operating and cannot become involved in legal or contractual matters such as financial compensation.

If you do have problems that have not been resolved by the proprietor and which you would like to bring to their attention, please write to:
Quality in Tourism, Security House, Alexandra Way, Ashchurch, Tewkesbury, Gloucestershire GL20 8NB

About the accommodation entries

Entries

All accommodation featured in this guide has been assessed or has applied for assessment under a quality assessment scheme.

Start your search for a place to stay by looking in the 'Where to Stay' sections of this guide where proprietors have paid to have their establishment featured in either a standard entry (includes photograph, description, facilities and prices) or an enhanced entry (photograph(s) and extended details).

Locations

Places to stay are listed by town, city or village, if a property is located in a small village, you may find it listed under a nearby town (providing it is within a seven-mile radius).

Within each region, counties run in alphabetical order. Place names are listed alphabetically within each county, and include interesting county information and a map reference.

Map references

These refer to the colour location maps at the back of the guide. The first figure shown is the map number, the following letter and figure indicate the grid reference on the map. Only place names that have a standard or enhanced VisitEngland entry feature appear on the maps. Some standard or enhanced entries were included in the scheme after the guide went to press, therefore they do not appear on the maps.

Telephone numbers

Booking telephone numbers are listed below the contact address for each entry. Area codes are shown in brackets.

Evening meal: the prices shown are per person per night. Some places only provide a continental breakfast in the set price, and you may have to pay extra if you want a full English breakfast.

Half board: the prices shown are per person per night for room, evening meal and breakfast. These prices are usually based on two people sharing a room.

Checking prices
According to UK law, establishments with at least four bedrooms or eight beds must display their charges in the reception area or entrance. There is no legal requirement for establishments in the Channel Islands to display their prices but they should make them clear at the time of booking.

In your own interests, do make sure you check prices and what they include.

Children's rates
You will find that many places charge a reduced rate for children, especially if they share a room with their parents. Some places charge the full rate, however, when a child occupies a room which might otherwise have been let to an adult. The upper age limit for reductions for children varies from one accommodation to another, so check this when you book.

Seasonal packages and special promotions
Prices often vary through the year and may be significantly lower outside peak holiday weeks. Many places offer special package rates – fully inclusive weekend breaks, for example – in the autumn, winter and spring. A number of establishments taking an enhanced entry have included any special offers, themed breaks, etc. that are available.

You can get details of other bargain packages that may be available from the establishments themselves, regional tourism organisations or your local Tourist Information Centre (TIC). Your local travel agent may also have information and can help you make reservations.

Prices

The prices printed are to be used as a guide only; they were supplied to us by proprietors in summer 2013.

Remember, changes may occur after the guide goes to press, therefore we strongly advise you to check prices before booking book your accommodation.

Prices are shown in pounds sterling, including VAT where applicable. There are many different ways of quoting prices for accommodation. We use a standardised method in the guide to allow you to compare prices. For example, when we show:

Bed and breakfast: the prices shown are per room for overnight accommodation with breakfast. The double room price is for two people. (If a double room is occupied by one person, there is sometimes a reduction in price.)

Bathrooms

En suite bathroom means the bath or shower and wc are contained behind the main door of the bedroom. Private bathroom means a bath or shower and wc solely for the occupants of one bedroom, on the same floor, reasonably close and with a key provided. If the availability of a bath, rather than a shower, is important to you, remember to check when you book.

Meals

It is advisable to check the availability of meals and set times when making your reservation. Some smaller places may ask you at breakfast whether you want an evening meal. The prices shown in each entry are for bed and breakfast or half board, but many places also offer lunch.

Opening period

If an entry does not indicate an opening period, please check directly with the establishment.

Symbols

The at-a-glance symbols included at the end of each entry show many of the services and facilities available at each establishment. You will find the key to these symbols on page 7.

Smoking

In the UK and the Channel Islands, it is illegal to smoke in enclosed public spaces and places of work. Some establishments may choose to provide designated smoking bedrooms, and may allow smoking in private areas that are not used by any staff. If you wish to smoke, it is advisable to check whether it is allowed when you book.

Alcoholic drinks

Many places listed in the guide are licensed to serve alcohol. The licence may be restricted – to diners only, for example – so you may want to check this when you book. If they have a bar this is shown by the ▼ symbol

Pets

Many places accept guests with dogs, but we advise that you check this with the proprietor before booking, remember ask if there are any extra charges or rules about exactly where your pet is allowed. The acceptance of dogs is not always extended to cats and it is strongly advised that cat owners contact the property well in advance of your stay.

Some establishments do not accept pets at all. Pets are welcome by arrangement where you see this symbol 🐾. The quarantine laws have changed and now dogs, cats and ferrets are able to come into Britain and the Channel Islands from over 50 countries. For details of the Pet Travel Scheme (PETS) please turn to page 377.

Payment accepted

The types of payment accepted by an establishment are listed in the payment accepted section. If you plan to pay by card, check that the establishment will accept the particular type of card you own before booking. Some proprietors will charge you a higher rate if you pay by credit card rather than cash or cheque. The difference is to cover the charges paid by the proprietor to the credit card company.

When you book by telephone, you may be asked for your credit card number as confirmation. Remember, the proprietor may then charge your credit card account if you cancel your booking. See details of this under Cancellations on page 376.

Conferences and groups

Places which cater for conferences and meetings are marked with the symbol ▼. Rates are often negotiable, depending on the time of year, number of people involved and any special requirements you may have.

Awaiting confirmation of rating

At the time of going to press some properties featured in this guide had not yet been assessed therefore their rating for this year could not be included. The term 'Rating Applied For' indicates this throughout your guide.

Property names

Under the Common Standards for assessment, guest accommodation may not include the word 'hotel' in its name. The majority of accommodation in this guide complies with this rule and the national assessing bodies, including VisitEngland, are working towards bringing all guest accommodation in line with this.

Looking for something else?

The official and most comprehensive guide to independently inspected, star rated accommodation.

B&Bs and Hotels - B&Bs, Hotels, farmhouses, inns, serviced apartments, campus and hostel accommodation in England.

Self Catering - Self-catering holiday homes, approved caravan holiday homes, boat accommodation and holiday cottage agencies in England.

Camping, Touring and Holiday Parks - Touring parks, camping holidays and holiday parks and villages in Britain.

Now available in all good bookshops and online at **www.hudsons.co.uk/shop**

Getting around

Travelling in London

London transport

London Underground has 12 lines, each with its own unique colour, so you can easily follow them on the Underground map. Most lines run through central London, and many serve parts of Greater London. Buses are a quick, convenient way to travel around London, providing plenty of sightseeing opportunities along the way. There are over 6,500 buses in London operating 700 routes every day. You will need to buy a ticket before you board the bus – available from machines at the bus stop.

London's National Rail system stretches all over London. Many lines start at the main London railway stations (Paddington, Victoria, Waterloo, Kings Cross) with links to the tube. Trains mainly serve areas outside central London, and travel overground.

Children usually travel free, or at reduced fare, on all public transport in London.

Oyster cards

Oyster cards can be used to pay fares on all London Underground, buses, Docklands Light Railway and trams, however are generally not valid for National Rail services in London.

Oyster cards are very easy to use, you just touch the card on sensors at stations or on buses and you are charged the lowest fare available for your journey. You buy credit for your journey and when it runs out you simply top up with more.

Oyster cards are available to adults only. Children below the age of 11 can accompany adults free of charge. Children between the ages of 11 and 15 should use the standard child travel card. You can purchase an Oyster card for a fee of £5, which is refundable on its return, at any underground station, one of 3,000 Oyster points around London displaying the London Underground sign (usually shops), or from www.visitbritainshop.com, or www.oyster.tfl.gov.uk/oyster

London congestion charge

The congestion charge is £10 daily charge to drive in central London at certain times. Check if the congestion charge is included in the cost of your car before booking. If your car's pick up point is in the congestion-charging zone, the company may pay the charge for the first day of your hire.

Low Emission Zone

The Low Emission Zone is an area covering most of Greater London, within which the most polluting diesel-engine vehicles are required to meet specific emissions standards. If your vehicle does not, you will be required to pay a daily charge.

Vehicles affected by the Low Emission Zone are older diesel-engine lorries, buses, coaches, large vans, minibuses and other heavy vehicles such as motor caravans and motorised horse boxes. This also includes vehicles registered outside of Great Britain. Cars and motorcycles are not affected by this scheme. For more information visit www.tfl.gov.uk

Rail and train travel

Britain's rail network covers all main cities and smaller regional towns. Trains on the network are operated by a few large companies running routes from London to stations all over Britain. Therefore smaller companies that run routes in regional areas. You can find up-to-the-minute information about routes, fares and train times on the National Rail Enquiries website (www.nationalrail.co.uk). For detailed information about routes and services, refer to the train operators' websites (see page 389).

Railway passes

BritRail offer a wide selection of passes and tickets giving you the freedom to travel on all National Rail services. Passes can also include sleeper services, city and attraction passes and boat tours. Passes can usually be purchased from travel agents outside Britain or by visiting the BritRail website (www.britrail.com).

Bus and coach travel

Public buses

Every city and town in Britain has a local bus service. These services are privatised and managed by separate companies. The largest bus companies in Britain are First (www.firstgroup.com/ukbus), Stagecoach (www.stagecoachbus.com) and Arriva (www.arrivabus.co.uk), and run buses in most UK towns. Outside London, buses usually travel to and from the town centre or to the busiest part of town. Most towns have a bus station, where you'll be able to find maps and information about routes. Bus route information may also be posted at bus stops.

Tickets and fares

The cost of a bus ticket normally depends on how far you're travelling. Return fares may be available on some buses, but you would usually need to buy a 'single' ticket for each individual journey.

You can also buy your ticket when boarding a bus by telling the driver where you are going. One-day and weekly travel cards are available in some towns, and these can be purchased from either the driver or from an information centre at the bus station. Tickets are valid for each separate journey rather than for a period of time, so if you get off the bus you'll need to buy a new ticket when getting on another.

Domestic flights

Flying is a time-saving alternative to road or rail when it comes to travelling around Britain. Domestic flights are fast and frequent and there are 33 airports across Britain that operate domestic routes.

Domestic flight advice

Photo ID is required to travel on domestic flights. However it is advisable to bring your passport as not all airlines will accept other forms of photo identification. Please be aware of the high security measures at all airports in Britain which include include restrictions on items that may be carried in hand luggage. It is important that you check the restrictions in place with your airline prior to travel, as these can vary over time and don't forget to allow adequate time for check-in and boarding on arrival.

Cycling

Cycling is a great way to see some of England's iconic scenery and there are many networks of cycling routes available across England. The National Cycle Network offers over 10,000 miles of walking and cycling routes details for connecting towns and villages, countryside and coast across England. For more information and view these routes see page 374 or visit Sustrans at www.sustrans.co.uk.

Think green

If you'd rather leave your car behind and travel by 'green transport' to some of the attractions highlighted in this guide you'll be helping to reduce congestion and pollution as well as supporting conservation charities in their commitment to green travel.

The National Trust encourages visits made by non-car travellers and it offers admission discounts or a voucher for the tea room at a selection of its properties if you arrive on foot, cycle or public transport (you may need to produce a valid bus or train ticket if travelling by public transport.).

More information about The National Trust's work to encourage car-free days out can be found at www.nationaltrust.org.uk. (Refer to the section entitled 'Information for Visitors').

Book your accommodation online

Visit our new 2014 guide websites for detailed information, up-to-date availability and to book your accommodation online. Includes over 20,000 places to stay, all of them star rated.
www.visitor-guides.co.uk

By car and by train

Distance chart

The distances between towns on the chart below are given to the nearest mile, and are measured along routes based on the quickest travelling time, making maximum use of motorways or dual-carriageway roads. The chart is based upon information supplied by the Automobile Association.

To calculate the distance in kilometres multiply the mileage by 1.6

For example: Brighton to Dover
82 miles x 1.6 =131.2 kilometres

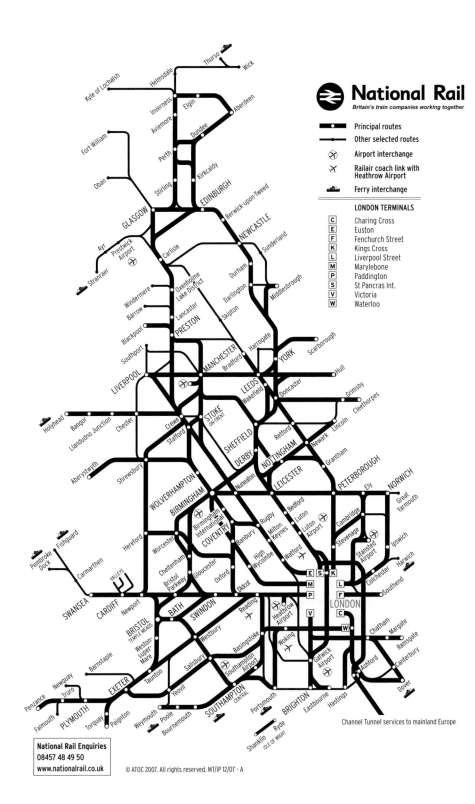

Travel information

General travel information

Streetmap	www.streetmap.co.uk	
Transport Direct	www.transportdirect.info	
Transport for London	www.tfl.gov.uk	0843 222 1234
Travel Services	www.departures-arrivals.com	
Traveline	www.traveline.info	0871 200 2233

Bus & coach

Megabus	www.megabus.com	0900 160 0900
National Express	www.nationalexpress.com	08717 818 178
WA Shearings	www.shearings.com	0844 824 6351

Car & car hire

AA	www.theaa.com	0800 085 2721
Green Flag	www.greenflag.co.uk	0845 246 1557
RAC	www.rac.co.uk	0844 308 9177
Alamo	www.alamo.co.uk	0871 384 1086*
Avis	www.avis.co.uk	0844 581 0147*
Budget	www.budget.co.uk	0844 544 3407*
Easycar	www.easycar.com	
Enterprise	www.enterprise.com	0800 800 227*
Hertz	www.hertz.co.uk	0870 844 8844*
Holiday Autos	www.holidayautos.co.uk	0871 472 5229
National	www.nationalcar.co.uk	0871 384 1140
Thrifty	www.thrifty.co.uk	01494 751500

Air

Air Southwest	www.airsouthwest.com	0870 043 4553
Blue Islands (Channel Islands)	www.blueislands.com	08456 20 2122
BMI	www.flybmi.com	0844 848 4888
BMI Baby	www.bmibaby.com	0905 828 2828*
British Airways	www.ba.com	0844 493 0787
British International (Isles of Scilly to Penzance)	www.islesofscillyhelicopter.com	01736 363871*
CityJet	www.cityjet.com	0871 663 3777
Eastern Airways	www.easternairways.com	08703 669100
Easyjet	www.easyjet.com	0843 104 5000
Flybe	www.flybe.com	0871 700 2000*
Jet2.com	www.jet2.com	0871 226 1737*
Manx2	www.manx2.com	0871 200 0440*
Ryanair	www.ryanair.com	0871 246 0000
Skybus (Isles of Scilly)	www.islesofscilly-travel.co.uk	0845 710 5555
Thomsonfly	www.thomsonfly.com	0871 231 4787

Train

National Rail Enquiries	www.nationalrail.co.uk	0845 748 4950
The Trainline	www.trainline.co.uk	0871 244 1545
UK train operating companies	www.rail.co.uk	
Arriva Trains	www.arriva.co.uk	0191 520 4000
c2c	www.c2c-online.co.uk	0845 601 4873
Chiltern Railways	www.chilternrailways.co.uk	0845 600 5165
CrossCountry	www.crosscountrytrains.co.uk	0844 811 0124
East Midlands Trains	www.eastmidlandstrains.co.uk	0845 712 5678
Eurostar	www.eurostar.com	08432 186 186*
First Capital Connect	www.firstcapitalconnect.co.uk	0845 026 4700
First Great Western	www.firstgreatwestern.co.uk	0845 700 0125
Gatwick Express	www.gatwickexpress.com	0845 850 1530
Heathrow Connect	www.heathrowconnect.com	0845 678 6975
Heathrow Express	www.heathrowexpress.com	0845 600 1515
Hull Trains	www.hulltrains.co.uk	0845 071 0222
Island Line	www.islandlinetrains.co.uk	0845 600 0650
London Midlands	www.londonmidland.com	0121 634 2040
Merseyrail	www.merseyrail.org	0151 702 2071
National Express East Anglia	www.nationalexpresseastanglia.com	0845 600 7245
National Express East Coast	www.nationalexpresseastcoast.com	0845 722 5333
Northern Rail	www.northernrail.org	0845 000 0125
ScotRail	www.scotrail.co.uk	0845 601 5929
South Eastern Trains	www.southeasternrailway.co.uk	0845 000 2222
South West Trains	www.southwesttrains.co.uk	0845 600 0650
Southern	www.southernrailway.com	0845 127 2920
Stansted Express	www.stanstedexpress.com	0845 600 7245
Translink	www.translink.co.uk	(028) 9066 6630
Transpennine Express	www.tpexpress.co.uk	0845 600 1671
Virgin Trains	www.virgintrains.co.uk	08450 008 000*

Ferry

Ferry Information	www.discoverferries.com	0207 436 2449
Condor Ferries	www.condorferries.co.uk	0845 609 1024*
Steam Packet Company	www.steam-packet.com	08722 992 992*
Isles of Scilly Travel	www.islesofscilly-travel.co.uk	0845 710 5555
Red Funnel	www.redfunnel.co.uk	0844 844 9988
Wight Link	www.wightlink.co.uk	0871 376 1000

Phone numbers listed are for general enquiries unless otherwise stated.
* Booking line only

National Accessible Scheme index

Establishments with a detailed entry in this guide who participate in the National Accessible Scheme are listed below. At the front of the guide you can find information about the scheme. Establishments are listed alphabetically by place name.

Mobility level 1

Abingdon-on-Thames South East	**Abbey Guest House** ★★★★ GOLD	127
Aldeburgh East of England	**Brudenell Hotel** ★★★★ GOLD	193
Ashbourne East Midlands	**Peak District Spa** ★★★★ SILVER	214
Berwick-upon-Tweed North East	**Fenham Farm Coastal Bed & Breakfast** ★★★ SILVER	350
Bicker East Midlands	**Supreme Inns** ★★★	221
Blackpool North West	**Big Blue Hotel** ★★★★	323
Chester North West	**Brookside Hotel** ★★★	304
Chichester South East	**George Bell House** ★★★★	138
Cornhill-on-Tweed North East	**Collingwood Arms Hotel** ★★★ SILVER	351
Godney South West	**Double-Gate Farm** ★★★★ GOLD	79
Grange-over-Sands North West	**Netherwood Hotel** ★★★ SILVER	310
Hastings South East	**Seaspray Bed and Breakfast** ★★★★ SILVER	142
Ilfracombe South West	**Mullacott Farm** ★★★★	52
Loughborough East Midlands	**Burleigh Court Conference Centre & Hotel** ★★★★ SILVER	220
Lytham St Annes North West	**The Chadwick Hotel** ★★★	329
Penzance South West	**Hotel Penzance** ★★★★	44
St. Mary's South West	**Isles of Scilly Country Guest House** ★★★	48
Woodhall Spa East Midlands	**Petwood Hotel** ★★★	225
Woodhall Spa East Midlands	**Village Limits Country Pub, Restaurant & Motel** ★★★★ SILVER	225

Mobility level 2

Abingdon-on-Thames South East	**Abbey Guest House** ★★★★ GOLD	127
Ashbourne East Midlands	**Peak District Spa** ★★★★ SILVER	214
Aylmerton East of England	**Roman Camp Inn** ★★★★	186
Chester North West	**Grosvenor Pulford Hotel & Spa** ★★★★	304
Clitheroe North West	**Best Western Mytton Fold Hotel & Golf Complex** ★★★	328
Dorchester South West	**Aquila Heights Guest House** ★★★★ SILVER	65
Northwich North West	**Wall Hill Farm Guest House** ★★★★★	305

Hearing impairment level 1

Abingdon-on-Thames South East	**Abbey Guest House** ★★★★ GOLD	127
Bamford East Midlands	**Yorkshire Bridge Inn** ★★★★ SILVER	215
Chester North West	**Grosvenor Pulford Hotel & Spa** ★★★★	304
Hastings South East	**Seaspray Bed and Breakfast** ★★★★ SILVER	142
Loughborough East Midlands	**Burleigh Court Conference Centre & Hotel** ★★★★ SILVER	220

Visual impairment level 1

Abingdon-on-Thames South East	**Abbey Guest House** ★★★★ GOLD	127
Bamford East Midlands	**Yorkshire Bridge Inn** ★★★★ SILVER	215
Chester North West	**Grosvenor Pulford Hotel & Spa** ★★★★	304
Hastings South East	**Seaspray Bed and Breakfast** ★★★★ SILVER	142
Loughborough East Midlands	**Burleigh Court Conference Centre & Hotel** ★★★★ SILVER	220

If you have
access needs...

Guests with hearing, visual or mobility needs can feel confident about booking accommodation that participates in the National Accessible Scheme (NAS).

Look out for the NAS symbols which are included throughout the accommodation directory. Using the NAS could help make the difference between a good holiday and a perfect one!

For more information on the NAS and tips & ideas on holiday travel in England, go to: www.visitengland.com/accessforall

Gold and Silver Award winners

Establishments with a detailed entry in this guide that have achieved recognition of exceptional quality are listed below. Establishment are listed alphabetically by place name.

South West

GOLD AWARD

Barnsley **Barnsley House** ★★★★	68
Bath **Marlborough House Guest House** ★★★★	76
Bath (6 miles) **Lucknam Park Hotel and Spa** ★★★★★	76
Bibury **Swan Hotel** ★★★★	68
Bishops Nympton **Kerscott Farm** ★★★★★	48
Camelford **Pendragon Country House** ★★★★★	39
Christchurch **Druid House** ★★★★★	64
East Brent **Burton Row Farmhouse** ★★★★★	78
Godney **Double-Gate Farm** ★★★★	79
Honiton **Combe House Devon** ★★★★	52
Launceston **Primrose Cottage** ★★★★★	41
Lostwithiel **Hazelmere House** ★★★★	42
Lynton **Highcliffe House** ★★★★★	52
Moreton-in-Marsh **Manor House Hotel** ★★★★	71
Parracombe **Higher Bodley Farm** ★★★★	55
Salcombe **Tides Reach Hotel** ★★★	56
Saltash **Lantallack Getaways** ★★★★★	45
Sidmouth **The Barn & Pinn Cottage Guest House** ★★★★	56
Sidmouth **Hotel Riviera** ★★★★	57
St. Mellion **Pentillie Castle & Estate** ★★★★★	46
Stroud 1 **Woodchester Lodge** ★★★★	72
Stroud **The Bear of Rodborough Hotel** ★★★	72
Stroud **The Old Coach House** ★★★★	73
Tavistock **Tor Cottage** ★★★★★	58
Tetbury **Calcot Manor Hotel & Spa** ★★★★	74
Torquay **The Somerville** ★★★★★	60
Wareham **Bradle Farmhouse** ★★★★	68

SILVER AWARD

Bath **Apple Tree Guest House** ★★★★	74
Bryher **Hell Bay Hotel** ★★★★	47
Constantine **Bay Treglos Hotel** ★★★★	39
Dartmouth **Royal Castle Hotel** ★★★	49
Dorchester **Aquila Heights Guest House** ★★★★	65
Falmouth **The Beach House** ★★★★	40
Falmouth **Budock Vean Hotel on the River** ★★★★	40
Glastonbury **Tordown B & B and Healing Centre** ★★★★	79
Guiting Power **Guiting Guest House** ★★★★	71
Helston **Tregathenan House** ★★★★	40
Holsworthy **Leworthy Farmhouse B&B** ★★★★	51
Lands End **Bosavern House** ★★★★	41
Looe **Barclay House** ★★★★	41
Monkton **Farleigh Muddy Duck** ★★★★	84
Salisbury **Lodge Farmhouse Bed & Breakfast** ★★★★	86
Shaftesbury **The Retreat** ★★★★	66
Sidmouth **Royal York & Faulkner Hotel** ★★	57
Sourton **Collaven Manor Hotel** ★★	57
St. Austell **The Chapel Guest House** ★★★★	45
Stroud **Pretoria Villa** ★★★★	73
Torquay **The Downs, Babbacombe** ★★★★	59
Totnes **Royal Seven Stars Hotel** ★★★★	61
Truro **Townhouse Rooms** ★★★★	46
Wadebridge **St Enodoc Hotel Rock** ★★★★	47
Westonbirt **Hare & Hounds Hotel** ★★★★	74

South East

GOLD AWARD

Abingdon-on-Thames **Abbey Guest House** ★ ★ ★ ★	127
Arundel **The Barn at Penfolds** ★ ★ ★ ★	136
Bampton **Manor Farm Barn B&B** ★ ★ ★ ★	128
Burford **Bay Tree Hotel** ★ ★ ★ ★	129
Burford **The Lamb Inn** ★ ★ ★	129
Canterbury **Magnolia House** ★ ★ ★ ★ ★	119
Chichester **Millstream Hotel** ★ ★ ★ ★	139
Cranbrook **Beacon Hall House** ★ ★ ★ ★ ★	120
Dover **Hubert House Guesthouse and Bistro** ★ ★ ★ ★	122
Haslemere **Colliers Farm** ★ ★ ★ ★ ★	135
Maidstone **Ash Cottage** ★ ★ ★ ★ ★	123
New Milton, New Forest **Chewton Glen** ★ ★ ★ ★ ★	111
Rye **Rye Lodge Hotel** ★ ★ ★	109
Rye **Jeake's House** ★ ★ ★ ★ ★	144
Sandwich **White Rose Lodge** ★ ★ ★ ★ ★	126

SILVER AWARD

Andover **May Cottage** ★ ★ ★ ★	109
Ashford **Downsview Guest House** ★ ★ ★ ★	117
Cadnam **Twin Oaks Guest House** ★ ★ ★ ★	110
Cowes **Endeavour House** ★ ★ ★ ★	113
Cranbrook **1 Maytham Cottages** ★ ★ ★ ★	120
Dorking **Stylehurst Farm** ★ ★ ★ ★	135
Egham **the runnymede-on-thames** ★ ★ ★ ★	135
Fordingbridge **The Three Lions** ★ ★ ★ ★	111
Gatwick **Southbourne Guest House Gatwick** ★ ★ ★ ★	141
Hastings **Seaspray Bed and Breakfast** ★ ★ ★ ★	142
Henley-on-Thames **The Baskerville** ★ ★ ★ ★	130
Lewes **The Blacksmiths Arms** ★ ★ ★ ★	143
Maidenhead **The Black Boys Inn** ★ ★ ★ ★	106
Maidstone **The Limes** ★ ★	124
Newbury **Thatched House B&B** ★ ★ ★ ★	106
Oxford **Cotswold Lodge Hotel** ★ ★ ★ ★	132
Ramsgate **Glendevon Guest House** ★ ★ ★ ★	125
Ringmer **Bryn Clai** ★ ★ ★ ★	143
Royal Tunbridge Wells **Manor Court Farm Bed & Breakfast** ★ ★ ★	125
Sandown **The Belmore** ★ ★ ★ ★	116
Seaford **The Silverdale** ★ ★ ★ ★	144
St. Leonards-on-Sea **Sea Spirit Guest House** ★ ★ ★ ★	145
Sway **The Mill At Gordleton** ★ ★ ★ ★ ★	113
Windsor **Bluebell House** ★ ★ ★ ★	107
Woodstock **The Blenheim Buttery** ★ ★ ★ ★	133

London

SILVER AWARD

London W2 **The Caesar Hotel** ★ ★ ★ ★	161

East of England

GOLD AWARD

Aldeburgh **Brudenell Hotel** ★ ★ ★ ★	193
Chorleywood **Ashburton Country House** ★ ★ ★ ★ ★	185
Swanton Morley **Carricks at Castle Farm** ★ ★ ★ ★ ★	191
Ware **Hanbury Manor, A Marriott Hotel & Country Club** ★ ★ ★ ★ ★	185
Wells-Next-The-Sea **Machrimore** ★ ★ ★ ★	192
Wighton **Meadow View Guest House** ★ ★ ★ ★ ★	192

SILVER AWARD

Bungay **Rose Cottage Bed and Breakfast** ★ ★ ★ ★	193
Bury St. Edmunds **St Edmunds Guesthouse** ★ ★ ★ ★	193
Cambridge **Tudor Cottage** ★ ★ ★ ★	181
Cambridge **Worth House** ★ ★ ★ ★	181
Clacton-on-Sea **Chudleigh** ★ ★ ★ ★	182
Clavering **The Cricketers** ★ ★ ★ ★	183
Cromer **Northrepps Cottage Country Hotel** ★ ★ ★	186
Elmswell **Kiln Farm Guest House** ★ ★ ★ ★	195
Hintlesham **College Farm Bed & Breakfast** ★ ★ ★ ★	196
Norwich **Marsham Arms Coaching Inn** ★ ★ ★ ★	188
South Creake **Valentine Studio** ★ ★ ★ ★	190
St. Albans **St Michael's Manor** ★ ★ ★ ★	185
Yoxford **Sans Souci B&B** ★ ★ ★ ★	197

East Midlands

GOLD AWARD

Grantham **Glebe House Muston** ★ ★ ★ ★	222

SILVER AWARD

Ashbourne **Peak District Spa** ★ ★ ★ ★	214
Bakewell **Chy-an-Dour** ★ ★ ★ ★	214
Bamford **Yorkshire Bridge Inn** ★ ★ ★ ★	215
Buxton **Grosvenor House** ★ ★ ★ ★	216
Buxton **Kingscroft Guest House** ★ ★ ★ ★	216
Cranwell **Byards Leap Lodge and Country Kitchen** ★ ★ ★ ★	221
Loughborough **Burleigh Court Conference Centre & Hotel** ★ ★ ★ ★	220
Newark **The Grange Hotel** ★ ★ ★	226
Oakham **Barnsdale Lodge Hotel** ★ ★ ★	227
Woodhall Spa **Village Limits Country Pub, Restaurant & Motel** ★ ★ ★ ★	225

Heart of England

GOLD AWARD

Broadway **The Broadway Hotel** ★ ★ ★	252
Pembridge **Lowe Farm B&B** ★ ★ ★ ★	244
Rugeley **Colton House** ★ ★ ★ ★ ★	248
Upton **Uplands House** ★ ★ ★ ★ ★	251

There are hundreds of "Green" places to stay and visit in England from small bed and breakfasts to large visitor attractions and activity holiday providers. Businesses displaying this logo have undergone a rigorous verification process to ensure that they are sustainable (green) and that a qualified assessor has visited the premises.

We have indicated the accommodation which has achieved a Green award... look out for the 🌱 symbol in the entry.

Walkers Welcome & Cyclists Welcome

Establishments participating in the Walkers Welcome and Cyclists Welcome schemes provide special facilities and actively encourage these recreations. Accommodation with a detailed entry in this guide is listed below. Place names are listed alphabetically.

Walkers Welcome & Cyclists Welcome

Godney South West	**Double-Gate Farm ★ ★ ★ ★** GOLD	79
Grasmere North West	**Thorney How Independent Hostel ★ ★ ★**	310
Heddon-on-the-Wall North East	**Houghton North Farm Visitor Accommodation ★ ★ ★ ★**	352
Hexham North East	**Langley Castle Hotel ★ ★ ★ ★** GOLD	352
Hitcham East of England	**Stanstead Hall ★ ★ ★ ★**	196
Honiton South West	**Combe House Devon ★ ★ ★ ★** GOLD	52
Ilfracombe South West	**Mullacott Farm ★ ★ ★ ★**	52
Keswick North West	**Rooms36 ★ ★ ★ ★** SILVER	313
Keswick North West	**Sandon Guest House ★ ★ ★ ★**	314
Looe South West	**Barclay House ★ ★ ★ ★** SILVER	41
Maidstone South East	**Ash Cottage ★ ★ ★ ★ ★** GOLD	123
Morpeth North East	**Tomlinson's Cafe and Bunkhouse**	353
Norwich East of England	**Becklands ★ ★ ★ ★**	188
Norwich East of England	**Marsham Arms Coaching Inn ★ ★ ★ ★** SILVER	188
Norwich East of England	**Old Rectory Hotel ★ ★ ★**	189
Parracombe South West	**Higher Bodley Farm ★ ★ ★ ★** GOLD	55
Pembridge Heart of England	**Lowe Farm B&B ★ ★ ★ ★** GOLD	244
Plymouth South West	**Caraneal ★ ★ ★ ★**	55
Rackheath East of England	**Barn Court ★ ★ ★ ★**	189
Ramsgate South East	**Glendevon Guest House ★ ★ ★ ★** SILVER	125
Richmond Yorkshire	**Frenchgate Guest House ★ ★ ★ ★**	276
Ripon Yorkshire	**The Ripon Spa Hotel ★ ★ ★**	276
Rosthwaite North West	**Scafell Hotel ★ ★ ★** GOLD	315
Saltburn-by-the-Sea Yorkshire	**The Arches Country House ★ ★ ★ ★**	277
Sandown South East	**The Sandhill ★ ★ ★**	116
Stroud South West	**The Amberley Inn ★ ★ ★ ★**	72
Swanage South West	**Corner Meadow ★ ★ ★ ★**	67
Sway South East	**The Mill At Gordleton ★ ★ ★ ★ ★** SILVER	113
Troutbeck North West	**Troutbeck Inn ★ ★ ★ ★**	316
Yelverton South West	**Barnabas House B&B ★ ★ ★ ★**	61
Yelverton South West	**Overcombe House ★ ★ ★ ★**	62
York Yorkshire	**Ace Hostel York ★ ★ ★ ★**	284

Walkers Welcome

Ashbourne East Midlands	**Peak District Spa ★ ★ ★ ★** SILVER	214
Barkston East Midlands	**Kelling House ★ ★ ★ ★**	220
Penzance South West	**Cornerways Guest House ★ ★ ★**	43
Penzance South West	**Hotel Penzance ★ ★ ★ ★**	44
St. Mary's South West	**Isles of Scilly Country Guest House ★ ★ ★**	48
St-Margarets-At-Cliffe South East	**The White Cliffs Hotel ★ ★ ★**	127

Cyclists Welcome

Southampton South East	**Eversley Guest House ★ ★ ★ ★**	112

Walkers and cyclists welcome

Look out for quality-assessed accommodation displaying the Walkers Welcome and Cyclists Welcome signs.

Participants in these schemes actively encourage and support walking and cycling. In addition to special meal arrangements and helpful information, they'll provide a water supply to wash off the mud, an area for drying wet clothing and footwear, maps and books to look up cycling and walking routes and even an emergency puncture-repair kit! Bikes can also be locked up securely undercover.

The standards for these schemes have been developed in partnership with the tourist boards in Northern Ireland, Scotland and Wales, so wherever you're travelling in the UK you'll receive the same welcome.

Families and Pets Welcome

Establishments participating in the Families Welcome or Welcome Pets! schemes provide special facilities and actively encourage families or guests with pets. Accommodation with a detailed entry in this guide is listed below. Place names are listed alphabetically.

🏠 🐾 Families and Pets Welcome

Clifton North West	**George and Dragon** ★★★★	307
Cornhill-on-Tweed North East	**Collingwood Arms Hotel** ★★★ SILVER	351
Dalby Yorkshire	**South Moor Farm** ★★★★	270
Dover South East	**Castle House Guest House** ★★★★	121
Keswick North West	**Rooms36** ★★★★ SILVER	313
Norwich East of England	**Old Rectory Hotel** ★★★	189
Rackheath East of England	**Barn Court** ★★★★	189
Ripon Yorkshire	**The Ripon Spa Hotel** ★★★	276
York Yorkshire	**Ace Hostel York** ★★★★	284

🏠 Families Welcome

Abingdon-on-Thames South East	**Abbey Guest House** ★★★★ GOLD	127
Barnsdale East Midlands	**Barnsdale Hall Hotel** ★★★	226
Bicker East Midlands	**Supreme Inns** ★★★	221
Black Bourton South East	**The Vines** ★★★★	128
Bury St. Edmunds East of England	**St Edmunds Guesthouse** ★★★★ SILVER	193
Chester North West	**Brookside Hotel** ★★★	304
Grasmere North West	**Thorney How Independent Hostel** ★★★	310
Ilfracombe South West	**Mullacott Farm** ★★★★	52
Looe South West	**Barclay House** ★★★★ SILVER	41
Morpeth North East	**Tomlinson's Cafe and Bunkhouse**	353
Norwich East of England	**Marsham Arms Coaching Inn** ★★★★ SILVER	188
South Creake East of England	**Valentine Studio** ★★★★ SILVER	190
St-Margarets-At-Cliffe South East	**The White Cliffs Hotel** ★★★	127
Sway South East	**The Mill At Gordleton** ★★★★★ SILVER	113

🐾 Pets Welcome

Dunster South West	**Yarn Market Hotel** ★★★	77
Eastbourne South East	**Best Western Lansdowne Hotel** ★★★	140
Filey Yorkshire	**White Lodge Hotel** ★★★	272
Kirkby Lonsdale North West	**Copper Kettle Restaurant & Guest House** ★★	314
Oakham East Midlands	**Barnsdale Lodge Hotel** ★★★ SILVER	227
Seaford South East	**The Silverdale** ★★★★ SILVER	144
Sinnington Yorkshire	**Fox and Hounds** ★★★★ SILVER	279
St. Agnes South West	**Little Trevellas Farm** ★★★	45
St. Mary's South West	**Isles of Scilly Country Guest House** ★★★	48
Troutbeck North West	**Troutbeck Inn** ★★★★	316

Welcome Pets!

Want to travel with your faithful companion? Look out for accommodation displaying the **Welcome Pets!** sign. Participants in this scheme go out of their way to meet the needs of guests bringing dogs, cats and/or small birds. In addition to providing water and food bowls, torches or nightlights, spare leads and pet washing facilities, they'll buy in food on request, and offer toys, treats and bedding. They'll also have information on pet-friendly attractions, pubs, restaurants and recreation. Of course, not everyone is able to offer suitable facilities for every pet, so do check if there are any restrictions on type, size and number of animals when you book.

Look out for the following symbol in the entry.

Swimming Pools index

If you're looking for accommodation with swimming facilities use this index to see at a glance detailed accommodation entries that match your requirement. Establishments are listed alphabetically by place name.

🏊 Indoor pool

Bath (6 miles) South West	**Lucknam Park Hotel and Spa ★ ★ ★ ★ ★** GOLD	76
Bicester South East	**Bicester Hotel Golf and Spa ★ ★ ★ ★**	128
Blackpool North West	**Doric Hotel ★ ★**	323
Bognor Regis South East	**Best Western Beachcroft Hotel ★ ★ ★**	137
Bowness-on-Windermere North West	**May Cottage B&B ★ ★ ★** SILVER	306
Brixham South West	**Berry Head Hotel ★ ★ ★**	49
Cadnam South East	**Twin Oaks Guest House ★ ★ ★ ★** SILVER	110
Chester North West	**Grosvenor Pulford Hotel & Spa ★ ★ ★ ★**	304
Chesterfield East Midlands	**Abigails Guest House ★ ★ ★**	217
Colchester East of England	**Stoke by Nayland Hotel, Golf and Spa ★ ★ ★**	183
Constantine Bay South West	**Treglos Hotel ★ ★ ★ ★** SILVER	39
Dawlish South West	**Langstone Cliff Hotel ★ ★ ★**	50
Egham South East	**the runnymede-on-thames ★ ★ ★ ★** SILVER	135
Falmouth South West	**Budock Vean Hotel on the River ★ ★ ★ ★** SILVER	40
Freshwater South East	**The Orchards ★ ★ ★ ★**	114
Frome South West	**The Lighthouse ★ ★ ★ ★**	78
Grange-over-Sands North West	**Netherwood Hotel ★ ★ ★** SILVER	310
Great Yarmouth East of England	**Burlington Palm Hotel ★ ★ ★**	188

Lands End South West	**Bosavern House ★ ★ ★ ★** SILVER	41
Looe South West	**Hannafore Point Hotel and Spa ★ ★ ★**	42
Loughborough East Midlands	**Burleigh Court Conference Centre & Hotel ★ ★ ★ ★** SILVER	220
Lytham St Annes North West	**The Chadwick Hotel ★ ★ ★**	329
Maidstone South East	**The Limes ★ ★** SILVER	124
New Milton, New Forest South East	**Chewton Glen ★ ★ ★ ★ ★** GOLD	111
Newcastle-upon-Tyne North East	**De Vere VILLAGE Urban Resort Newcastle**	356
Portsmouth South East	**Royal Maritime Club ★ ★**	112
Rye South East	**Rye Lodge Hotel ★ ★ ★** GOLD	109
Rye South East	**Old Borough Arms ★ ★ ★ ★**	144
Saham Toney East of England	**Broom Hall Country Hotel ★ ★ ★**	190
Salcombe South West	**Tides Reach Hotel ★ ★ ★** GOLD	56
Sidmouth South West	**Royal York & Faulkner Hotel ★ ★** SILVER	57
Skegness East Midlands	**Southview Park Hotel ★ ★ ★**	224
St. Minver South West	**Tredower Barton ★ ★ ★**	46
Teddington London	**Lensbury ★ ★ ★ ★**	163
Tetbury South West	**Calcot Manor Hotel & Spa ★ ★ ★ ★** GOLD	74
Torquay South West	**The Osborne Hotel ★ ★ ★ ★**	60
Ware East of England	**Hanbury Manor,**	
	A Marriott Hotel & Country Club ★ ★ ★ ★ ★ GOLD	185
Weston-super-Mare South West	**Beachlands Hotel ★ ★ ★**	81
Woolacombe South West	**Trimstone Manor Country House Hotel ★ ★ ★**	61

🏊 Outdoor pool

Bath South West	**Church Farm Monkton Farleigh ★ ★ ★**	75
Blackpool North West	**Doric Hotel ★ ★**	323
Bryher South West	**Hell Bay Hotel ★ ★ ★ ★** SILVER	47
Dawlish South West	**Langstone Cliff Hotel ★ ★ ★**	50
Egham South East	**the runnymede-on-thames ★ ★ ★ ★** SILVER	135
Looe South West	**Barclay House ★ ★ ★ ★** SILVER	41
Manningford Abbots South West	**Huntly's Farmhouse ★ ★ ★ ★**	83
New Milton, New Forest South East	**Chewton Glen ★ ★ ★ ★ ★** GOLD	111
Northam South West	**Durrant House Hotel ★ ★ ★**	53
Norwich East of England	**Old Rectory Hotel ★ ★ ★**	189
Penzance South West	**Hotel Penzance ★ ★ ★ ★**	44
Saltash South West	**Lantallack Getaways ★ ★ ★ ★ ★** GOLD	45
St. Mellion South West	**Pentillie Castle & Estate ★ ★ ★ ★ ★** GOLD	4
Steyning South East	**Springwells ★ ★ ★**	145
Tavistock South West	**Tor Cottage ★ ★ ★ ★ ★** GOLD	58
Tetbury South West	**Calcot Manor Hotel & Spa ★ ★ ★ ★** GOLD	74
Torquay South West	**Corbyn Head Hotel ★ ★ ★**	59
Torquay South West	**Livermead House Hotel ★ ★ ★**	59
Torquay South West	**The Osborne Hotel ★ ★ ★ ★**	60
Wadebridge South West	**St Enodoc Hotel Rock ★ ★ ★ ★** SILVER	47

Budget accommodation

If you are travelling on a budget, the following establishments offer accommodation at £25 per single room per night or less, or £50 per double room per night or less. These prices are only an indication - please check carefully before confirming a reservation. Establishments are listed alphabetically by place name.

South West

Bath **Bath YMCA** ★ ★ ★	75
Falmouth **The Beach House** ★ ★ ★ ★ SILVER	40
Newquay **Harrington Guest House** ★ ★ ★	43
Paignton **Rowcroft Lodge** ★ ★ ★	54
Paignton **Redcliffe Lodge Hotel** ★ ★	54
Plymouth **Athenaeum Lodge Guest House** ★ ★ ★ ★	55
Plymouth **Gabber Farm** ★ ★ ★	55
Salisbury **Evening Hill** ★ ★ ★	85
St. Agnes **Little Trevellas Farm** ★ ★ ★	45
St. Agnes **Penkerris** ★ ★	45
Torquay **Acorn Lodge** ★ ★ ★	58
Torquay **Whitburn Guest House** ★ ★ ★	61

South East

Bordon **Spring Cottage** ★ ★	109
Canterbury **Kipps Independent Hostel** ★ ★ ★	118
Cocking **Causeway Sunnyside** ★ ★ ★	139
Dover **Longfield Guest House** ★ ★ ★	122
Hailsham **Bader International Study Centre** ★ ★ - ★ ★ ★ ★	142
Ramsgate **Comfort Inn Ramsgate** ★ ★ ★	124
Royal Tunbridge Wells **Badgers End Bed & Breakfast** ★ ★	125
Woodstock **Shepherds Hall** ★ ★ ★	134

East of England

Aylmerton **Roman Camp Inn** ★ ★ ★ ★	186
Cambridge **Southampton Guest House** ★ ★ ★	180
Cromer **Cliff Cottage** ★ ★ ★ ★	186
Dereham **Hunters Hall** ★ ★ ★ ★	187
Downham **Market Chestnut Villa** ★ ★ ★	187
Great Yarmouth **Burlington Palm Hotel** ★ ★ ★	188
Orsett **Jays Lodge** ★ ★ ★ ★	184
South Creake **Valentine Studio** ★ ★ ★ ★ SILVER	190
Wells-Next-The-Sea **Machrimore** ★ ★ ★ ★ GOLD	192

East Midlands

Skegness **Southview Park Hotel** ★ ★ ★	224
Skegness **Stepping Stones** ★ ★ ★	224

Heart of England

Meriden **Bonnifinglas Guest House** ★ ★ ★	251

Yorkshire

Harrogate **Cold Cotes Guest Accommodation, Gardens & Nursery** ★ ★ ★ ★ ★ GOLD	273
Huby **Tulip Inn York - Burn Hall Hotel** ★ ★ ★	274
Scarborough **Empire Guesthouse** ★ ★ ★	277
Scarborough **Howdale** ★ ★ ★ ★	277
Wakefield **The Bank House Hotel** ★	287
York **Ace Hostel York** ★ ★ ★ ★	284

North West

Blackpool **The Allendale** ★ ★ ★	321
Blackpool **Chaplins** ★ ★ ★	323
Blackpool **Helmshore** ★ ★ ★	324
Blackpool **Lyndene Hotel** ★ ★	324
Blackpool **The Marston Guest House** ★ ★ ★	325
Carlisle **University of Cumbria - Carlisle** ★ ★ ★ ★	307
Gilsland **The Hill on the Wall** ★ ★ ★ ★ ★ GOLD	308
Keswick **Ash Tree House** ★ ★ ★ ★	312
Keswick **Charnwood Guest House** ★ ★ ★ ★	313
Kirkby Lonsdale **Copper Kettle Restaurant & Guest House** ★ ★	314
Skelwith Fold **Holmeshead Farm** ★ ★ ★ ★	316

North East

Newcastle-upon-Tyne **Albatross, Backpackers In!** ★ ★ ★	356

Hostel and campus accommodation

The following establishments all have a detailed entry in this guide.

Hostels

Campus accommodation

Index by property name

Accommodation with a detailed entry in this guide is listed below.

Index by place name

The following places all have detailed accommodation entries in this guide. If the place where you wish to stay is not shown the location maps (starting on page 358) will help you to find somewhere to stay in the area.

Index by place name

National Accessible Scheme

Finding suitable accommodation is not always easy, especially if you have to seek out rooms with level entry or large print menus. Use the National Accessible Scheme to help you make your choice.

Proprietors of accommodation taking part in the National Accessible Scheme have gone out of their way to ensure a comfortable stay for guests with special hearing, visual or mobility needs. These exceptional places are full of extra touches to make everyone's visit trouble-free, from handrails, ramps and step-free entrances (ideal for buggies too) to level-access showers and colour contrast in the bathrooms. Members of staff may have attended a disability awareness course and will know what assistance will really be appreciated.

Appropriate National Accessible Scheme symbols are included in the guide entries (shown opposite). If you have additional needs or special requirements, we strongly recommend that you

make sure these can be met by your chosen establishment before you confirm your reservation. The index at the back of the guide gives a list of accommodation that has received a National Accessible Scheme rating.

'Holiday in the British Isles' is an annual guidebook produced by Disability Rights UK. It lists NAS rated accommodation and offers extensive practical advice to help you plan your trip.

£12.99 (inc. P&P), www.disabilityrights.org

England

Mobility Impairment Symbols

Older and less mobile guests
Typically suitable for a person with sufficient mobility to climb a flight of steps but who would benefit from fixtures and fittings to aid balance.

Part-time wheelchair users
Typically suitable for a person with restricted walking ability and for those who may need to use a wheelchair some of the time and can negotiate a maximum of three steps.

Independent wheelchair users
Typically suitable for a person who depends on the use of a wheelchair and transfers unaided to and from the wheelchair in a seated position. This person may be an independent traveller.

Assisted wheelchair users
Typically suitable for a person who depends on the use of a wheelchair and needs assistance when transferring to and from the wheelchair in a seated position.

Access Exceptional is awarded to establishments that meet the requirements of independent wheelchair users or assisted wheelchair users shown above and also fulfil more demanding requirements with reference to the British Standards BS8300.

The criteria VisitEngland has adopted does not necessarily conform to British Standards or to Building Regulations. They reflect what the organisation understands to be acceptable to meet the practical needs of guests with mobility or sensory impairments and encourage the industry to increase access to all.

Visual Impairment Symbols

Typically provides key additional services and facilities to meet the needs of visually impaired guests.

Typically provides a higher level of additional services and facilities to meet the needs of visually impaired guests.

Hearing Loss Symbols

Typically provides key additional services and facilities to meet the needs of guests with hearing loss.

Typically provides a higher level of additional services and facilities to meet the needs of guests with hearing loss.

For more information on the NAS and tips and ideas on holiday travel in England go to:
www.visitengland.com/accessforall

Additional help and guidance on accessible tourism can be obtained from the national charity Tourism for All:

Tourism for All

Tourism for All UK
7A Pixel Mill
44 Appleby Road
Kendal
Cumbria LA9 6ES

Information helpline 0845 124 9971
(lines open 9-5 Mon-Fri)
E info@tourismforall.org.uk
W www.tourismforall.org.uk
    www.openbritain.net

HUDSONS MEDIA LIMITED

Published by: Hudson's Media Ltd
35 Thorpe Road, Peterborough, PE3 6AG
Tel: 01733 296910 Fax: 01733 209292

On behalf of: VisitBritain, Sanctuary Buildings, 20 Great Smith Street, London SW1P 3BT

Publisher: Lisa Barreno
Editorial: Neil Pope
Production team: Deborah Coulter, Rebecca Owen-Fisher, Rhiannon McCluskey,
Sarah Phillips & Gemma Wall

Creative team: Jamieson Eley & Nicola Bennett
Advertising team: Ben Piper, Matthew Pinfold, Sumita Ghosh & Claire Hotson
Email: VEguides@hudsons-media.co.uk Tel: 01733 296913
Production: NVG – leaders in Tourism Technology. www.nvg.net
Printer: Stephens & George, Merthyr Tydfil
Retail Sales: Compass – Tel: 020 8996 5764

© British Tourist Authority (trading as VisitBritain) 2014
ISBN 978-0-85101-525-5
A VisitBritain guide